MARKETING

MARKE

Concepts, Strategies, and Decisions

TING

David J. Reibstein
Wharton School of Business, University of Pennsylvania

PRENTICE-HALL, INC.

ENGLEWOOD CLIFFS, NEW JERSEY

Library of Congress Cataloging in Publication Data

Reibstein, David J.
  Marketing, concepts, strategies, and decisions.

  Includes index.
  1. Marketing. I. Title.
HF5415.R365   1985   658.8   84–18206
ISBN 0-13-556861-7

© 1985 by Prentice-Hall Inc., Englewood Cliffs, NJ 07632

All rights reserved. No part of this book may be reproduced in any form or by any means without permission in writing from the publisher.

Printed in the United States of America

10 9 8 7 6 5 4 3 2 1

Prentice-Hall International, Inc., *London*
Prentice-Hall of Australia, Pty. Ltd., *Sydney*
Editora Prentice-Hall do Brasil Ltda., *Rio de Janeiro*
Prentice-Hall Canada Inc., *Toronto*
Prentice-Hall of India Private Limited, *New Delhi*
Prentice-Hall of Japan, Inc., *Tokyo*
Prentice-Hall of Southeast Asia Pte. Ltd., *Singapore*
Whitehall Books Limited, *Wellington, New Zealand*
Prentice-Hall Hispanoamericana, S.A., *Mexico*

Art Director: Florence Dara Silverman
Development Editor: Deirdre Silberstein
Production Editor: Eleanor Perz
Book Designer: Diana Hrisinko
Cover Designer: Jules Perlmutter
Cover Photo: The Image Bank/Gabe Palmer
Line Art: Creative Group, Inc.
Photo Researcher: Eleanor Perz
Manufacturing Buyer: Ray Keating

Table of contents and chapter opener photo credits: Chap. 1—courtesy of Fisher Corporation; chap. 2—courtesy of Procter & Gamble; chap. 3—courtesy of AT&T Bell Laboratories; chap. 4—courtesy of Manhattan Cable TV; chap. 5—Laimute E. Druskis; chap. 6—courtesy of General Electric; chap. 7—Anita Duncan; chap. 8—courtesy of Polaroid Corporation; chap. 9—courtesy of American Motors Corporation; chap. 10—courtesy of Apple Computer, Inc.; chap. 11—Laimute E. Druskis; chap. 12—courtesy of Inter-Continental Hotels; chap. 13—courtesy of Computerland; chap. 14—courtesy of Eastman Kodak Company; chap. 15—Anita Duncan; chap. 16—courtesy of American Cyanamid Company; chap. 17—Laimute E. Druskis; chap. 18—Ken Karp (table of contents photo by Laimute E. Druskis); chap. 19—Anita Duncan; chap. 20—Ira Kirchenbaum, Stock/Boston; chap. 21—Ken Karp; chap. 22—courtesy of NCR Corporation.

ISBN 0-13-556861-7

CONTENTS

PART I The Role of Marketing

Chapter 1 Marketing and Its Role in Business   1

The Nature of Marketing   2
The Growth of the Marketing Concept   6   •   Marketing Defined   8

Decisions about the Elements of Marketing   9
Target Marketing   10   •   The Marketing Mix   13   •   Marketing Strategy   18   •   Facets of Marketing   19

Criticisms of Marketing   19
Criticism: Marketing Tries to Create Rather than Satisfy Needs   20   •   Criticism: Marketing Creates Low-Quality Products   21   •   Criticism: Marketing Makes Products Overpriced   21   •   Criticism: Advertising Is Deceptive   22

Summary   22   •   Questions for Discussion   24

Chapter 2

Marketing within the Organization   27

The Growth of the Marketing Department   29
From a Production Orientation to a Marketing Orientation   29

Organizing the Marketing Department   31
Functional Organization   31   •   Product or Brand Management   32
Focus 2–1: Product Management at General Mills   36
Market Management   37   •   Matrix Management   39

The Role of the Marketing Department   41
The Marketing Department as Communicator   41   •   The Marketing Department as the Coordinator of Activities   45   •   The Marketing Department as Filter and Analyzer of Environmental Factors   47

The Marketing Department and Marketing Strategy   48

Summary   49   •   Questions for Discussion   50

Chapter 3

The Marketing Environment   53

An Analytical Perspective   55

The Economic Environment   56
The World Economic Environment   56   •   The National Economic Environment   57   •   The Regional and Local Environments   58

The Competitive Environment   60
External Competition   60   •   Internal Competition   61

Marketing and Public Policy   63
Focus 3–1: How Deregulation Affects Marketing Practices   64
Types of Public Policy in Marketing   64   •   Antitrust Legislation and Marketing   67   •   Consumer Protection   70

The Technological Environment   72

Cultural and Social Environments   74
Some Cultural and Social Factors   74
Focus 3–2: How Social Changes Affect Companies' Plans   75

Summary   77   •   Questions for Discussion   78

Case 1   Tylenol   80
Case 2   General Motors and the Small-Car Market   83

PART II   Target Marketing

Chapter 4

Defining the Business   87

The Business Definition   90

Identifying Needs to Be Satisfied   90   •   *Identifying Competitors*   90   •   *Identifying Strengths and Weaknesses*   91   •   *How a Business Definition Works*   91   •   *Company Mission and Objectives*   94

Paradigms of Business Definition   96

Derek Abell's Three Dimensions   96   •   *Bruce Henderson's Identification of an SBU*   98   •   *William Rothschild's Identification of an SBU*   99   •   *Arthur D. Little's Characteristics of an SBU*   99

Should We Be in This Business?   100

Forecasting Demand   101

Questions to Ask   101   •   *Methods to Answer Each Question*   103

An Overview of Marketing Strategy   105

Summary   106   •   *Questions for Discussion*   107

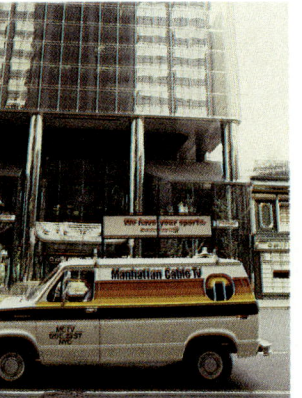

Chapter 5

Marketing Research and Marketing Information Systems   109

The Role of Marketing Research   111

When to Use Marketing Research   113

The Marketing Research Process   114

Defining the Problem   114   •   *Designing the Research*   115   •   *Collecting the Data*   119
Focus 5–1: National Purchase Diary Collects Data on Eating Habits   124
Analyzing the Data   130   •   *Making Recommendations*   130
Focus 5–2: The New York City Opera Studies Its Audience   131

Summary   135   •   *Questions for Discussion*   136

Chapter 6

Buyer Behavior 139

Types of Buyers 142
Three Types of Decision-Making Units 142 • Roles of Buyers 143

The Buyer Decision Process 144
Problem Recognition 146 • Information Search 148
Focus 6–1: Influentials 150
Evaluation of Alternatives 153 • Purchase Decision 155 • Postpurchase Evaluation 155

Types of Buying Situations 156
Focus 6–2: General Foods Goes Shopping 157
Automatic Response Buying 158 • Limited Problem Solving 159 • Extensive Problem Solving 159

Summary 159 • Questions for Discussion 160

Chapter 7

Consumer Buying Behavior 163

Factors that Influence Consumer Behavior 165

The Internal Factors: Psychological Influences on Consumer Behavior 166
Needs and Motives 166 • Personality 167 • Perception 170 • Learning 173 • Attitudes 174 • Involvement 176

The External Factors: Sociocultural Factors 178
Values 178 • Economic Factors 179 • Media 180 • Reference Groups 181

The External Factors: Demographic Characteristics 184
Age 184 • Gender 185 • Income 186
Focus 7–1: How the Dual-Income Family Shops 187
Educational Level 189 • Occupation 189 • Social Class 190 • Ethnic Group 191 • Place of Residence 192

Factors that Influence Household Buyer Behavior 193
Composition of the Households 193 • Stages in the Family Life Cycle 195 • Changing Family Lifestyles 195 • Changing Family Roles and Behaviors 197

Summary 198 • Questions for Discussion 199

Chapter 8

Organizational Buying Behavior 203

Influences on Organizational Buying Behavior 205

The Marketing Environment 206
Focus 8–1: Selling Airplanes to Government-Owned Thai Airways International 208
The Nature of the Organization 209 • The Nature and Structure of the Buying Center 213 • The Similarities and Differences in Individual Participants in the Buying Process 217
Focus 8–2: How B. F. Goodrich Buys 222

Steps in the Organizational Buying Process 222

Identification of Needs 223 • Establishment of Objectives and Specifications 224 • Identification of Suppliers and Obtaining Bids 224 • Evaluation of Alternative Suppliers 227 • Evaluation of the Supplier 228

A Model of Organizational Buying Behavior 228

Similarities between Organizational and Household Buying Decision Processes 230

Summary 231 • Questions for Discussion 232

Chapter 9

Segmentation and Positioning 235

Segmentation 236

How Segmentation Works 237 • Advantages of Segmentation 239 • Criteria for Segmentation 240 • Bases for Segmentation 242 • Attributes Used to Select Target Segments 248

Positioning 251

What Is Positioning? 251 • Ways to Position a Product 253

Summary 255 • Questions for Discussion 256

Case 3   Pepsi-Cola's "New Generation" Campaign 259
Case 4   Schlitz Beer 261
Case 5   American Express and the Women's Market 263
Case 6   IBM PC and PCjr 265

PART III The Marketing Mix

Chapter 10 Products and Their Characteristics 269

What Is a Product 271

Classification of Products 272
Consumer Products 272 • Industrial Products 274

Product Mix and Product Line 275
Modifications and Extensions of the Product Line 277

Branding 279
The Importance of a Brand 280 • Family Branding vs. Individual Branding 281
Focus 10–1: Generic Products 282
Brand Loyalty 284 • Trademarks 286
Focus 10–2: Why Campbell's Is Changing Its Soup Package 288

Packaging 289

Services 291
Focus 10–3: Why Companies Provide Services 292

Summary 293 • Questions for Discussion 294

Chapter 11 Product Development and the Product Life Cycle 297

Product Development 299
Why Develop New Products? 299 • Step 1: Idea Generation 300
Focus 11–1: Meeting Needs for Special Clothing 301
Step 2: Idea Screening 302 • Step 3: Idea Testing 303 • Step 4: Business Analysis 304 • Step 5: Product Development 305
Focus 11–2: Carnation Tests Its Cat Foods 306
Step 6: Market Testing 307 • Step 7: Commercialization 308
Focus 11–3: The Development of New Tires 310
Interaction between Marketing and Research and Development 312

The Product Life Cycle 313
Stage 1: Introduction 314 • Stage 2: Growth 314 • Stage 3: Maturity 316 • Stage 4: Decline 317 • Variations in the Product Life Cycle 317 • Marketing Strategy in the Product Life Cycle 318

Summary 319 • Questions for Discussion 320

Chapter 12

Pricing Objectives and Methods 323

Definition and Nature of Price 325

Pricing Objectives 326

Profit 327 • Profit Maximization 327 • Market Share 327 • Sales Growth 328 • Return on Investment (ROI) 329 • Status Quo 330 • Product Quality 330

Methods of Setting Prices 330

Cost-Oriented Method 330 • Competition-Oriented Method 334 • Demand-Oriented Method 338 • Customer-Oriented Method 340 • Bidding and Negotiated Pricing 344
Focus 12–1: Flexible Pricing 345

Summary 346 • **Questions for Discussion** 347

Chapter 13

Pricing Modifications, Policies, and Considerations 351

Various Pricing Modifications 353

Discounts 353
Focus 13–1: Discount Medicine 355
Geographic Pricing 356 • Psychological Pricing 357

Skimming and Penetration Pricing 358

Product Line Pricing 360

Pricing and the Product Life Cycle 362

Price Discrimination 363

Motivations to Modify Prices 364

Responses to Actions by Competitors 364 • Excess Production Capacity 365 • Falling Market Share 365 • When Demand Exceeds Production Capacity 365 • Increasing Costs 366 • Inflation 366

The Relation of Pricing to the Marketing Mix 367

Legal Issues in Pricing 369

The Robinson-Patman Act 369 • Price-Fixing 369 • Unfair Trade Practices 370

Summary 370 • **Questions for Discussion** 371

Chapter 14   Communication and the Promotional Mix   375

An Overview of Marketing Communication   378

The Recipients of the Information   378   •   The Nature of the Message   378   •   The Form of the Communication   379   •   Communication Objectives   379

Models of Communication   380

A Basic Model of Communication   380   •   A Marketing Communication System   381

The Nature of the Communication Message   383

The Hierarchy of Effects   383   •   The DAGMAR Model   387   •   The Low-Involvement Hierarchy   388

The Forms of Marketing Communication   389

Advertising   390   •   Sales Promotion   390   •   Publicity   390   •   Personal Selling   391

Creating the Promotional Mix   392

The Type of Product   392   •   The Stage of the Product Life Cycle   392
Focus 14–1: Promoting Cameras and Film   393
The Consumer's Stage in the Buying Process   394   •   Interrelationships among the Forms of Communication   394

Summary   395   •   **Questions for Discussion**   396

Chapter 15   Advertising, Sales Promotion, and Publicity   399

Advertising   401

Advertising Objectives   401   •   Advertising Decisions   403   •   Decisions about the Media   406   •   Measuring Advertising Effectiveness   416
Focus 15–1: Can Advertising Effectiveness Be Measured through Psychological Research?   418

Sales Promotion   418

Sales Promotion Objectives   420   •   Decisions about Sales Promotion   422
Focus 15–2: Sales Promotions   426
Measuring Sales Promotion Effectiveness   427

Publicity   428

Measuring Publicity Effectiveness 430

Summary 432 • **Questions for Discussion** 433

Chapter 16

Personal Selling 437

The Roles of the Salesperson 438

Personal Selling Communication 440

Sales Strategy 443

Prospecting 443 • *Approach* 444 • *Sales Presentation* 444 • *Handling Objections* 444 • *Closing* 445 • *Follow-up* 446

Types of Sales Representatives 446

Order Getters 446 • *Order Takers* 446
Focus 16–1: Electronic Selling 448
Missionary and Technical Salespeople 448 • *Support Salespeople* 449

Sales Force Management 449

Recruitment 450 • *Training* 452 • *Motivation* 452 • *Compensation* 452 • *Evaluation* 454 • *Types of Sales Force Structures* 454
Focus 16–2: Team Xerox 456

Summary 457 • **Questions for Discussion** 458

Chapter 17

Channels of Distribution and Physical Distribution 461

Channels of Distribution 463

Types and Functions of Intermediaries 464 • *Types of Market Coverage* 468 • *Types of Channels* 469
Focus 17–1: Cooperation in a VMS 472
Managing a Channel of Distribution 473 • *Determining the Structure of Marketing Channels* 476

Physical Distribution 478

Functions of Physical Distribution 479 • *Transportation* 480 • *Inventory Management* 483
Focus 17–2: The Growth of Intermodal Transportation 484
Order Processing 486 • *Supporting Activities* 487 • *Customer Service* 488 • *Basic Concepts in Physical Distribution* 488

Summary 489 • **Questions for Discussion** 491

Chapter 18 — Retailing and Wholesaling 493

Retailing 494

Retailing Decisions and the Retailing Mix 496 • Classifications of Retailers 501 • Retailers Classified by Retailing Mixes 501
Focus 18–1: Different Retailing Mixes for Hardware Stores 503
Focus 18–2: Off-Price Retailing 510
Retailers Classified by Ownership 512 • Retailers Classified by Store Location 514 • Future of Retailing 516

Wholesaling 517

Wholesaling Functions 517 • Types of Wholesalers 519
Focus 18–3: Industrial Wholesalers 520
Future of Wholesaling 524

Summary 525 • Questions for Discussion 527

Case 7   Polaroid and Polavision   528
Case 8   Lotus 1-2-3 and Symphony   529
Case 9   Texas Instruments and the Home-Computer Market   531
Case 10   The Miller Brewing Company and Meister Brau   533
Case 11   Miller Lite   534
Case 12   Comparative Advertising in the Fast-Food Industry   535
Case 13   Levi Strauss   536
Case 14   Pricing in the Videocassette Market   538
Case 15   R. H. Macy & Company   539

PART IV   Marketing Strategy and Planning

Chapter 19 — Marketing Strategy 543

Introduction to Marketing Strategy 545

Establishing a Competitive Advantage 545

Lower Costs 546 • Control over Distribution 547 • Product Differentiation 547

The Growth Matrix 547

Deeper Penetration in the Same Market with the Same Products 548 • Offering

New Products to the Same Market   548   •   Offering the Same Products to New Markets   549   •   Diversification: Offering New Products in New Markets   550

Factors in Creating a Marketing Strategy   550

Focus 19–1: Growth Strategies   551
Gaining Market Share   552   •   Market Growth   553   •   Portfolio Analysis   554   •   The Boston Consulting Group (BCG) Matrix   555   •   The General Electric (GE) Business Screen   557   •   To Pioneer or to Follow   558   •   Barriers to Entry   560   •   Competition   561   •   Buyers and Suppliers   562   •   The Marketing Plan   562

Budgeting   563

Marketing Control   564

Summary   568   •   Questions for Discussion   568

Case 16   RCA Videodiscs   571
Case 17   Dana Corporation   573

PART V   Facets of Marketing

Chapter 20   International Marketing   577

The International Marketing Environment   579

Choosing International Markets   580

The Role of Marketing Research in Identifying and Segmenting International Markets   580
Focus 20–1: Countertrade   581
Factors to Consider in Choosing International Markets   582

Ways to Enter International Markets   590

Exporting   590   •   Contract Manufacturing   591   •   Licensing   591   •   Joint Ventures   592   •   Wholly Owned Subsidiaries   592

The International Marketing Mix   593

Product Decisions   593
Focus 20–2: How Beecham Entered the United States   594
Promotion Decisions   595   •   Pricing Decisions   597   •   Physical Distribution Decisions   598

Summary   600   •   Questions for Discussion   602

Chapter 21 Services and Nonprofit Marketing   605

The Marketing of Services   606

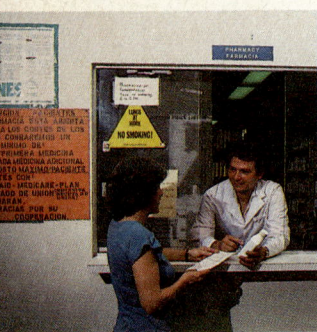

What Is a Service?   607   •   Key Characteristics of Services   608   •   Special Problems and Strategies in the Services Marketing Mix   610   •   Marketing in Service Firms   616

Nonprofit Marketing   616

What Is Nonprofit Marketing?   617   •   How Is Nonprofit Marketing Different?   618   •   Problems and Strategies in Nonprofit Marketing   619
Focus 21–1: The Advertising Council   620
Marketing in Nonprofit Organizations   624

Summary   624   •   **Questions for Discussion**   625

Chapter 22 Marketing's Future   629

Trends in the Marketing Environment   631

Computers   631   •   Trends in the Market   632

Trends in the Marketing Mix   634

Product   634   •   Place   635   •   Price   637   •   Promotion   637

Trends in Marketing Management   637

Summary   639   •   **Questions for Discussion**   639
Case 18   Nestlé: The Infant Formula Decision   641
Case 19   Midway Airlines   643
Case 20   Videotex   645

Appendix A Careers in Marketing   641

Appendix B Marketing Arithmetic   660

Glossary   668

Index   676

PREFACE

The function of marketing within an organization is to identify prospective customers and determine which products to offer to satisfy the customers while promoting the organization's goals. In the past, when the number of suppliers was low and demand exceeded supply, the marketing function consisted primarily of production and distribution. If an organization could manufacture and deliver a product more efficiently than its competitors, the organization was more successful in the marketplace.

More recently, environmental changes, such as increased competition and slackening economic growth, have affected the function of marketing. As national markets shrink, organizations seek growth from existing competitors' shares of the domestic market and from international markets. Organizations have become more precise in defining their businesses, choosing their customers, and developing need-satisfying products in order to gain market shares. Many giants of American industry recognize that what leads to success today does not guarantee success tomorrow. Customers' needs and buying processes are continually changing, and new competitors continually enter the markets. Adjustments in strategy are required to meet the challenges of the future.

The purpose of this textbook is to present the basic marketing concepts in relation to their applications. Many of the chapters include an *extended example*, which will help students see how the marketing concepts they are studying can apply to real decision-making processes within an organization. It is my hope that this feature will make the conceptual material more relevant and will foster good decision-making skills.

Pedagogical Aids

To help students learn the marketing concepts and material presented in the text, this book includes a number of pedagogical aids. **Chapter objectives** introduce students to the material in the chapter. **Extended examples** show students how the marketing concepts are applied in actual decision making. **Focus boxes** give examples of actual marketing strategies, decisions, and practices. **Figures, photographs, and tables** illustrate and further explain the marketing concepts. A **chapter summary** reviews the marketing concepts and material presented in each chapter. **Review questions** help students review and work with the material in the chapter. **Case studies** at the end of each part present actual situations in which marketing decisions are being made and require students to apply the marketing concepts. A study of questions accompanies each case study. Two **appendixes,** one on Marketing Arithmetic and the other on Careers in Marketing, review areas of practical concern to students. A **glossary** defines the key terms presented throughout the book. The **index** assists in finding the concepts, examples, and authors presented in the text.

Supplements

The following supplements are available to accompany the text. For instructors:

1. The **Instructor's Manual** contains a summary and outline for each chapter, answers to discussion questions, case analyses, and suggested class exercises.
2. The **Test Item File** is a bank of approximately 2,000 objective test questions. Tests may be prepared (a) from the bank itself; (b) through Prentice-Hall's Computerized Testing Service; or (c) from floppy disks compatible with Apple computers or the IBM PC.
3. A set of approximately 60 **Color Acetates** to be used on an overhead projector feature illustrations and advertisements not contained in the text.

For students there are the following supplements:

1. The **Study Guide** features objectives, key terms and concepts, completion questions, and multiple-choice tests for each chapter. It also contains questions relating to the extended example and additional short cases, which may be assigned by the instructor for quizzes and/or homework.
2. **Software,** developed by an expert in computer-assisted instruction and keyed specifically to the text, uses presentation frames on major concepts, mini-case problems, and aided/unaided recall questions to help students "unpack" and organize important material covered in the text. Software is available free to adopters and is compatible with the IBM PC.

Acknowledgments

In the multidimensional field of marketing, it is nearly impossible to be an expert in all areas. I am grateful to several colleagues who greatly enhanced this text by making a substantial contribution to the preparation of the following chapters and cases: Dr. Sandra Huszagh of the University of Georgia, International Marketing; Dr. George Jackson of Oklahoma State University, Marketing Channels and Distribution, and Retailing and Wholesaling; Dr. Mary Lou Roberts of Boston University, Consumer and Organizational Behavior; Dr. Ronald Savitt of Michigan State University, the Marketing Environment; Dr. Margery Steinberg of the University of Hartford, Personal Selling; Dr. Valarie Zeithaml of Texas A&M University, Services and Nonprofit Marketing; and Dr. Edward T. Popper of Northeastern University for his critique and editing of the case material.

The following professors should be noted for their insightful comments and suggestions that were invaluable in the development of this text: Louis R. Bravman, University of Delaware; Gerald O. Cavallo, Fairfield University; Nancy J. Church, SUNY, Plattsburgh; James E. Cox, Jr., Illinois State University; Rohit Deshpande, University of Texas at Austin; Charles W. Ford, Arkansas State University; John M. Gwin, University of Virginia; Ronald H. Hobson, SUNY, Plattsburgh; Sandra L. Lueder, Southern Connecticut State University; D. Terry Paul, University of Houston at Clear Lake City; Paul Prabhacker, SUNY, Buffalo; and Kaylene Williams, University of Delaware.

Many people have played a significant role in preparing me for the task of writing this book. Dean John Tollefson at the University of Kansas initially excited me about marketing and inspired me to pursue marketing as a career. Professor Frank Bass was my principal educator in the theory and methodologies of marketing. My colleagues at Harvard and now at Wharton have provided me with immeasurable insights and role models that have been instrumental in my understanding of the field. Over the past five years, those colleagues at Wharton who have been influential are Professors Erin Anderson, Scott Armstrong, Neil Beckwith, Ray Burke, Stewart DeBruicker, Jehoshua Eliashberg, Ron Frank, Hubert Gatignon, Charles Goodman, Paul Green, Leonard Lodish, Tom Robertson, David Schmittlein, Scott Ward, Barton Weitz, Jerry Wind, and Joan Zielinski. In writing this book I also received tremendous research support from my research assistants: Melissa Bernhardt, William Boulding, Rhonda Novick, and Lisa Samet.

The staff at Prentice-Hall has provided invaluable assistance, support, and editorial guidance. Without Elizabeth Classon I never would have contracted or completed this book. She has continually provided me with the nudge and guidance to produce a book that would appeal to students. Deirdre Silberstein's editing and sound judgment helped to shape a cohesive textbook. Eleanor Perz, my production editor and photo researcher, supervised the manuscript through copyediting, galleys, and page proofs. Florence Dara Silverman supervised the design of the text and the cover. Linda Pieper, Sara Lewis, and Elisa Turner assisted in the preparation of manuscript. Emily Baker has been helpful in exposing the book to more than my immediate family. Ray Keating was the manufacturing buyer for this book.

I would be terribly remiss (and in deep trouble) if I did not extend my deep appreciation and love to my wife, Karen, and children, Sasha and Seth, who allowed me the time and support to write this book.

D.R.

PART I
The Role of Marketing

OBJECTIVES

1. To define and describe marketing.

2. To explain the role of marketing in business.

3. To discuss the different stages of growth of the marketing concept.

4. To list the different decision elements involved in marketing.

5. To identify some of the leading criticisms made against marketing.

1

Marketing and Its Role in Business

Manufacturers of video equipment are introducing a spate of new products. Digital television sets, which join computer and broadcast technologies, receive sounds and pictures as a digital code rather than as the standard wave-like signals. This new technology is expected to speed the growth of home communications centers, allowing for telemarketing, personal computing, and information gathering through the television set. The main producer of the digital television sets and the computer chips they are based on is ITT's Standard Electrik Lorenz unit, based in West Germany, although Sony, Matsushita, Blaupunkt, and other electronic companies have started to produce their own models. Most of these competitors, however, are purchasing ITT's chips to use in their own sets. Digital television sets sell for approximately $1,000.

Stereo television sets, for viewers interested in enhanced sound, are also being offered. As with stereo components, the quality of the sound varies with the features and price of the stereo television sets. Consumers with "stereo-ready" sets can purchase the extra equipment for $100 to $200; a completely new set can cost $1,000 and up.

For half the price of a digital or stereo television set, consumers can buy a pocket-size—it has a 2-inch screen—color television set from Seiko. Smaller, cheaper videocassette recorders (VCRs), some available in stereo, are also becoming widely available. Sales of VCRs are soaring as consumers are discovering their convenience and as companies are using them to demonstrate, display, or sell products. The camera companies—Eastman Kodak, Polaroid, and Konica—are offering 8-millimeter camcorders that combine cameras and recorders with television sets that can play back the images. Camcorders cost approximately $2,000. Consumers who own home computers can purchase digital record-

ing systems for approximately $1,200 that will allow them to record music on their computer floppy discs. A compact disc player featuring better sound reproduction than tape players is available for as little as $400.

All of these products drew great attention and consumer interest when they were exhibited at the International Audio & Video Fair in West Berlin and at the International Summer Consumer Electronics Show in Chicago.[1]

Will these products succeed? Who will buy them? Are the prices too high? Are too many companies producing too many of these products? How can these products be promoted and distributed? Marketing is concerned with asking all of these questions and with making decisions based on the answers. In this chapter, we will look at marketing and the role that it plays in business. This involves exploring the nature of marketing, considering the range of decisions made by marketers as they apply marketing principles in business, and presenting an overview of the elements in the field of marketing.

The Nature of Marketing

What is marketing? Perhaps the best way to understand the multifaceted and wide-ranging field of marketing is to look at its various aspects.

Figure 1–1
Videodisc players were technical triumphs, but videocassette recorders, such as Panasonic's PV-1730, were more successful at meeting consumers' needs and wants.

Photo courtesy of Panasonic

The first aspect is: *Marketing requires an understanding of consumers' needs and wants.* To understand this aspect, consider the following examples. It is sometimes hard to predict whether or not a new product will succeed. There are products that have great potential and quality and still do not sell. In the 1970s, Zenith and RCA introduced the videodisk player, a technical triumph that enhanced the quality of video pictures on the home screen. But videodisk players that could not record had to compete directly with another new product, videocassette recorders (VCRs), which could not only play videocassettes purchased or rented from stores but could also record television programs as they were broadcast so that the VCR owners could watch them at a later time. This feature was important to buyers of video equipment; they bought videocassette recorders rather than videodisk players. While the VCR thrived, the videodisk player failed to find a market.

AT&T developed the technology for a picture telephone that enabled callers to see on an attached screen the person at the other end. It was a "great" idea and a technically viable product. The problem was that no one bought it. After introducing the picture telephone, AT&T discovered that some telephone customers did not want to have to be concerned about their appearance as they spoke on the telephone. Some considered it an invasion of privacy; almost everyone considered it too expensive. The picture phone for personal use did not succeed.

These are two illustrations of what can happen when a firm does not understand customer needs and wants. A company not geared toward analyzing and identifying these is likely to come up with the wrong product.

A second aspect is: *Understanding consumers' needs and wants requires a constant analysis and knowledge of the market.* Many products with great potential succeed for a time but fail as the market shifts away from the product. The Robert Hall retail clothing chain made good, functional clothing, easily available at low prices, and, for a time, succeeded by providing what customers wanted. But more customers became more fashion-oriented, and style became as important as durability and low price. Stores such as Bloomingdale's offered the style customers desired, and Robert Hall's sales declined.

A third aspect is: *Marketing involves matching a product to a specific market.* An understanding of what consumers need is useless unless it is connected to what the company provides. A company may try to serve too diverse a market with a product and find that it winds up not really satisfying anyone. The more specifically a given product matches the needs of its intended market, the more likely it is to succeed. Coors was a very popular western beer that sold well in the 1960s, but the company didn't respond in the 1970s to a changing and segmenting market. There was no longer a single type of beer that suited all beer drinkers. Some preferred the slightly different taste and fewer calories of light beer; others liked the image and the perceived taste of a premium beer and were willing to pay a higher price for it; and still others continued to buy regular beer. Brewing companies began to appeal more specifically to the various market segments. For example, Philip Morris's Miller Brewing Company began to produce Lowenbrau, appealing to the premium beer drinkers; Miller, for regular beer drinkers; and Lite, for those who wanted a light beer. Coors missed the market evolution, and its sales fell. The company is now producing a light beer to appeal to the changing market.

A company cannot afford to misjudge the needs of the market at which it is aiming. When a company has competitors, its customers have a choice about which product to buy; when those customers think they have some knowledge about the choices offered to them, understanding what consumers need is especially crucial. Failing to provide what consumers want leads to problems.

In 1909 the Ford Motor Company began to sell the first mass-produced automobiles. Henry Ford believed that one model and one color, black, would suit all customers. He saw no need to diversify the line. Since Ford was creating the automobile market, this strategy worked as long as there was no competition. But in 1926 General Motors introduced the Chevrolet, which was available in different colors. Once customers were offered this choice of color by General Motors, Ford's sales plummeted. Ford closed its doors for over a year to retool its factory, enabling it to offer more choices to customers, but Ford's sales never again caught up with its competition.

There are also those products with potential that simply seem to fall into the cracks. With regular colas and diet colas appealing to specific parts of the market, Pepsi Light, in its original formulation as a semidietetic soft drink with 55 calories per 12 ounces, never found a successful niche. It has been more successful in its revised formulation as a diet drink with only one calorie per 12 ounces. These examples indicate that the uniqueness and superior quality of a product can contribute greatly toward its success, but having a great technology or product is not enough to guarantee success. Knowledge of the market and skillful marketing efforts are critical. The commercial viability of a product is determined by its ability to attract customers. A company must understand who those customers are and what their wants and needs are, and then it can develop a product based on the technology to meet those needs. By presenting the solution to customer needs, a company can find a niche in the market.

Food companies, for example, recognized the growing market of young, health-conscious, sophisticated, two-income families that wanted convenient, but high-quality, food. Their solution has been the premium frozen meal; more than $750 million was spent in 1983 on Stouffer's Lean Cuisine, Swanson Foods' Le Menu, Armour Food's Dinner Classic, and other similar brands.[2]

A fourth aspect is: *Marketers must understand what customers are buying.* A company must consider how its product appears from the customer's point of view rather than from the company's own perspective. A student who goes to a bookstore to purchase a dictionary is not buying the book, per se, but is seeking to spell more accurately and thus write better papers.

Companies in the computer industry have demonstrated an understanding of their product from a customer's point of view. IBM, for example, has enjoyed immense success as a supplier of data processing hardware and software for business. IBM found out what companies needed to process information more efficiently and then developed mainframe computers to match those needs. Moreover, it effectively communicated to businesses how IBM products could help solve their information processing problems. More importantly, IBM recognized that businesses were entrusting their important financial and accounting data to a new process and needed "hand-holding," security, and service. IBM provided this.

Later, Digital Equipment Company (DEC) recognized that there were a significant number of small companies that couldn't afford and didn't need the capacity or power of a mainframe, and yet had applications in which computing power could provide a tremendous help. Seeing this need in the market, DEC developed and successfully sold the minicomputer.

A fifth aspect is: *Marketers must be aware of how well the needs of customers are or can be satisfied by the competition.* No company operates alone in a given market; competitors are trying to develop solutions to the same consumer problems. Marketers, then, must constantly analyze how well competitors' products and capabilities are solving consumer problems in relation to the success of their own products and capabilities.

A sixth aspect is: *Marketing recognizes the overall objectives of the firm and develops strategies that meet those objectives within the capabilities of the firm.* As an example, consider ITT's entry into the digital television market. Before entering this market, the company determined that it was technically capable of providing the computer chips and that it had the resources to compete against Sony and Mitsubishi. It also recognized that a company objective was to be involved in high-growth, high-technology industries. The digital television market fit in with both the company's capabilities and objectives. Entry into the market may not provide profits for ITT right away, but it does provide involvement, within the objectives of the firm.

The six aspects named above may seem straightforward, but the functions they describe have not always been a normal part of doing business. As the next section shows, companies have not always emphasized marketing.

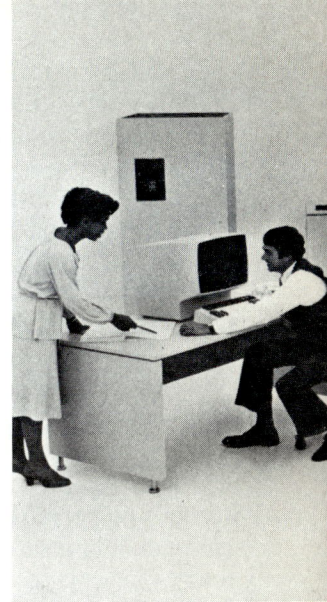

**Figure 1–2
Successful computer manufacturers recognize that the solution to information-processing problems includes not only the hardware but also "hand-holding" and service.**

Photo courtesy of International Business Machines Corporation

Before the Industrial Revolution, families made products to meet their own needs.[3] As some families became more proficient than others at producing particular items, they traded the excess of what they produced for the excess of different products made by other families. In this environment, sellers knew their markets well. Transportation and communication were limited, and only small amounts were traded.

During the Industrial Revolution, factories developed, making possible the large-volume production of goods. These business organizations had a **production orientation** and were primarily identified by their output, or by what they produced. That is, a company might be a steel mill, a railroad, or a furniture maker, and it was organized to focus on production. Managers hoped to dispose of their output but had no systematic plan for doing so.

Gradually there developed specialists who concentrated on selling the companies' output. They realized that in order to be economically viable, mass production required mass distribution. Distribution networks grew in response to this need, and most companies had primarily a **sales orientation.** Generally, the company would make a product and simply instruct the sales department to "sell it." This orientation implies a single-directional flow of information: the product to the customers.

In the last 40 years, the sales orientation has evolved to a **marketing orientation.** (The growth of the marketing orientation is shown in fig. 1–3.) Marketing used to be synonymous with sales in the minds of many, but marketing is more than sales. As demonstrated by the examples already discussed in this chapter,

The Growth of the Marketing Concept

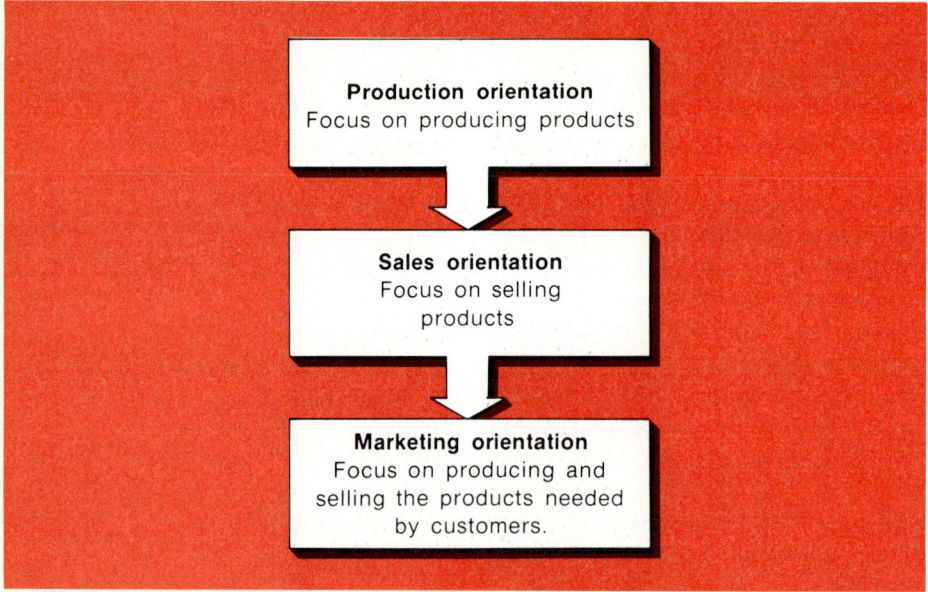

Figure 1–3 Growth of the marketing orientation

Figure 1–4 Sales and marketing concerns contrasted

Sales Concerns	Marketing Concerns
1. Short-term sales volumes	1. Long-term corporate growth
2. Individual customers and accounts	2. Market segments
3. Field selling	3. Overall integrated strategies for satisfying consumers' needs and company growth
4. Executives evaluated in terms of sales revenue	4. Executives evaluated in terms of the company's profitability

marketing requires two-way communication between a company and the market it is trying to serve. Moreover, companies must sell the products that consumers want, and their marketing efforts must communicate the benefits of the products to customers. Marketing requires an understanding of markets and of customers and their needs and wants; then products are developed to meet those needs. There is truth in the saying that selling is getting rid of what you have, but marketing is having what you can get rid of.

A marketing orientation can be described further by reviewing some of the differences between sales and marketing concerns.[4] Sales executives tend to focus their attention on short-term sales volumes, individual customers and accounts, and the actual selling in the field as opposed to overall sales plans and strategies. They are generally evaluated in terms of sales revenue. In contrast, marketing executives think about balancing products, customers, and all the marketing elements to achieve profitable production and sales volumes. They are generally evaluated in terms of the company's profitability.

Marketing executives concentrate on translating long-term trends and opportunities into new products, markets, and strategies to achieve long-term corporate growth. They also think of groups, or segments, of customers and how to offer the best value to the most profitable segments of customers. Moreover, marketing executives also think about systems for market analysis, planning, and control and about the financial implications of various options. Beyond merely current sales, then, marketing involves analyzing environmental changes, new consumer needs, competitive challenges, and new strategies for company growth. These differences are summarized in figure 1–4.

The marketing orientation has not been universally adopted. Even in the 1980s, some companies put all of their resources into developing superb technologies, with the notion that any brainstorm turned into a product will sell. This has not been the case.

Marketing Defined

The American Marketing Association (AMA) defines **marketing** as "the performance of business activities that direct the flow of goods and services from producer to consumer or user."[5] These activities include the decisions and actions of buyers and sellers in a **market,** or situation in which there is a transfer of goods and services. In a broader sense, marketing relates to business activities through which human needs and wants are satisfied.

In this text we will look beyond the definition of marketing as the exchange of goods and services between buyers and sellers. We will examine the underlying impetus for that transfer—that is, for a company to meet customer wants and needs while simultaneously achieving its own objectives. The **marketing concept** is considered the satisfaction of customers' needs while meeting the objectives of the organization.

Marketing involves gathering information from customers and potential customers to identify the wants and needs of specific groups of customers, then developing products to satisfy those needs. It involves pricing those products and services at a level to compensate the company for providing them, thus helping to meet company objectives. Other crucial aspects of marketing are creating a distribution system that effectively gets the company's products to its customers and developing

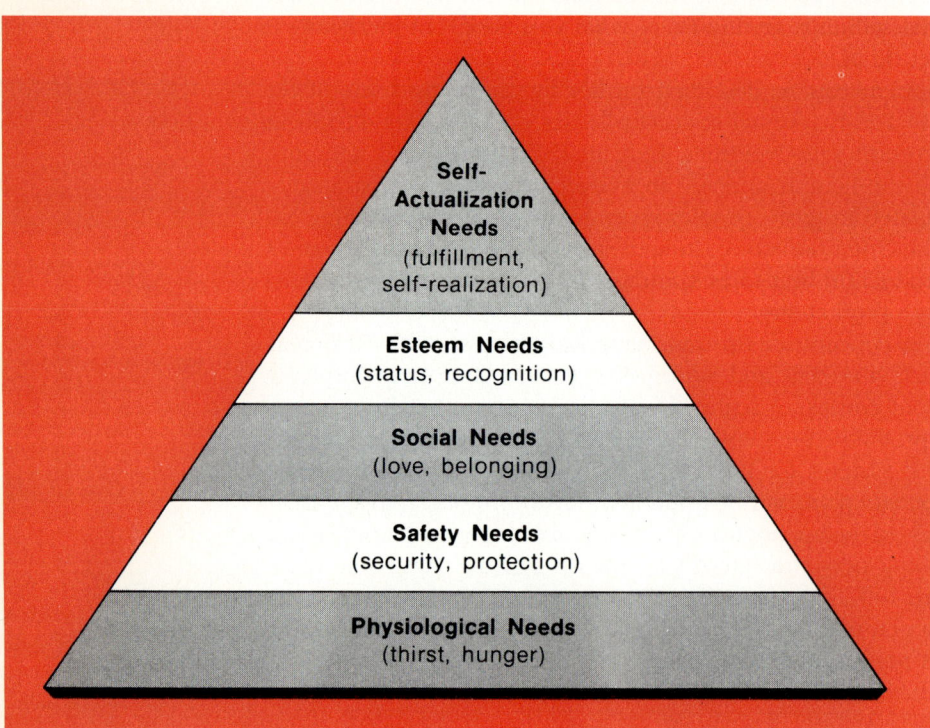

Figure 1–5
Maslow's hierarchy of human needs

Chapter 1 / Marketing and Its Role in Business

strategies for communicating information to customers about what the company offers. We will examine all of these marketing elements in great detail.

It cannot be overemphasized that marketing is the interaction between a company and its customers, and that its aim is to satisfy customer **needs,** or the current lack of useful or required items, and **wants,** or desire for items. The distinction between needs and wants continues to be a subject of debate among philosophers, social scientists, and others.

Consider, for example, the hierarchy of human needs formulated by the psychologist Abraham Maslow (see fig. 1–5). Maslow suggested that the most basic needs are the physiological needs, such as hunger, and that human needs form a progression upward to succeeding levels—to the need for safety; the need for belongingness and love; the need for esteem; and finally the need for self-actualization and pursuit of various aesthetic goals.

According to Maslow's hypothesis, as the lower-level needs are satisfied, the individual becomes concerned with the next higher level of needs. Some people need to have prestige in the eyes of their friends. Others need to go on a certain trip. Are these actually needs, or are they wants? The difference is not always clear and, from a marketing viewpoint, not always important. Marketing might be involved with any problem about which customers care strongly enough to seek a solution. It is the goal of marketing to solve a problem by providing the solutions that meet consumers' needs and wants.

Decisions about the Elements of Marketing

How is the marketing concept applied in business? The customer is at the crux of all marketing decisions. The objective is to understand what the customer needs and then prepare an offering of the right combination of product, price, distribution, and communications to help satisfy those needs. Companies carry out their marketing activities according to decisions they make about the various elements of marketing. In this section we review the elements and present some of the decisions to be made. Subsequent chapters explore the considerations on which the decisions are based.

One of the projected uses of digital television is home banking, or the conducting of certain financial transactions from the home. Before they develop a home-banking capability for their sets, manufacturers, such as ITT, Sony, Mitsubishi, must make decisions about a number of elements in marketing. We look at these decisions as we consider each element.

For all decisions, marketers must consider the overall environment in which their business organization operates. Important factors include not only the legal, cultural, political, and economic environments of the overall society but also the company's corporate environment and the financial constraints in which it operates. The marketing environment is discussed in chapter 3.

Target Marketing

As customers are the crux of marketing, key decisions are made about which customers to serve, based on knowledge about the customers. Marketers ask the following:

—Which set of customers should we try to satisfy?
—What do these customers need and want?
—How do these customers currently try to satisfy their needs?
—Can our company serve these customers?
—Should we select a small set of customers not served by any competitors, or a large set that may already be served by competitors?
—What sort of target market do we want—one with a few, large-volume buyers or one with a large number of different buyers?

The answers to these questions and decisions about target marketing come from the areas discussed below.

Defining the business. Marketers must define the company's business: what general type of product or service it is offering; which markets (or sets of customers) it is trying to serve; who the competitors are that are trying to serve the same market. An accurate business definition will help the company identify and select which markets to serve. In setting goals for the company, marketers must examine the company's resources as well as the weaknesses it must overcome to achieve those objectives. Competition will affect marketing activities, and marketers must define the company's business broadly so that less obvious competitors may be considered. There may be competitors that do not provide precisely the same product or service, but that offer a commodity that can substitute for what the company is selling. For example, a trucking company is in the freight business and must consider not only other trucking companies but also air freight companies as its competitors.

ITT has to make a number of decisions at this point. It must first decide whether offering home banking is consistent with its objectives. Then it must identify which and how many customers are interested in home banking and decide which market it is going to pursue. Finally, it must identify the competitors in the home-banking field; these include not only other manufacturers of digital television sets, such as Sony and Mitsubishi, but also other providers of financial services, such as the post office, pay-by-telephone services, and banks' automatic teller machines.

Before launching a new product, a company must predict as closely as possible the demand for that product, identifying not only the need for the product but also the intensity of that need and how the new product will satisfy it. Marketers estimate the number of potential customers for a product, how often they are likely to buy, and how much they are likely to buy. They also consider what competitors are offering. Chapter 4 covers defining the business and forecasting demand.

Marketing research. How is marketing information obtained? Marketing research is the phase of marketing concerned with obtaining usable information. **Marketing research** is defined by the American Marketing Association as "the systematic gathering, recording, and analyzing of data about problems relating to the marketing of goods and services." The process is designed to help make better decisions about various aspects of marketing. For example, before ITT decides to invest heavily in producing a digital television set with a home-banking capability, it must find out whether consumers are interested in home banking and which particular features—transferring funds, finding out about account balances, and so on—they want.

In order for marketing research to be effective, it is necessary to define carefully what information is required to make a better decision. After defining the problem, the marketers specify the source of the information to be collected and the procedures that will be used. Then the data are collected and analyzed. Recommendations are made on the basis of the research so that information is applied specifically to the problem that it was intended to help solve.

In many companies a data base of relevant information, a **marketing information system,** is continually and systematically collected so that it can be used on an ongoing basis for problem solving and decision making. Marketing research and the marketing information system are discussed in chapter 5.

Buyer behavior. Questions about the potential demand for a product fall under the category of market analysis, which involves studying the size, location, nature, and characteristics of specific markets.

Consumer research, another important aspect of marketing research, concentrates on buyer behavior. Marketers study buying patterns in an attempt to discover how consumers behave, why customers buy, what factors influence what they buy, and how they make up their minds about products. The focus is to understand better what is important to customers and to predict how they will respond to various offerings.

Customers are often individual consumers, in which case researchers study the buying habits of consumers, attempting to ascertain patterns among them. In other situations customers are organizations, such as businesses or government entities. If the customer is an organization, then it is important for the marketer to understand organizational buyer behavior—that is, how buying decisions are made within the organization.

As ITT serves both the consumer and organizational markets, it must understand what both types of buyers need and how they behave. For the consumer market, it must know which individuals or households are interested in home banking and why; in other words, it must recognize what needs would be satisfied by the purchase of home banking and how to present a specific product to appeal to this need. For the industrial market, it must understand how companies purchase technical products such as computer chips, what functional capabilities the companies are looking for, and what other possible suppliers can provide. Buyer

Photos by Laimute E. Druskis

Figure 1–6 Both individual consumers and organizations, such as retailers and wholesalers, purchase fruit, but their buying behavior differs. Producers must understand what is important to each and how each responds to various offerings.

behavior, consumer buying behavior, and organizational buying behavior are discussed in chapters 6, 7, and 8.

Segmentation. The customers who need products within any given product category are diverse; not everybody will want the same thing from the product category, will want to buy it in the same place, is interested in the same kinds of information about the product, or is looking for the same combination of product features or services. On the other hand, it is not realistic to offer a unique product for each customer. There are groups of customers with similar sets of needs, and the market can be divided into such groups. This concept is known as **market segmentation.**

To segment a market successfully, there must exist differences in what customers seek from the product category, and there must be commonalities among what groups of people want. A group, known as a **market segment,** or **target market,** must have enough customers to make it viable from a marketing point of view. Moreover, the customers who fit in a given segment and what will satisfy them must be clearly identifiable. Segmentation is discussed in chapter 9.

The Marketing Mix

Once the needs of the market are understood, the marketer considers the details of what the company might offer. The company must try to develop a product that will satisfy the needs of the customers in the market segment that has been identified and selected; provide the product at a price customers are willing to pay; create a distribution system that makes the product available to the customer in the place where it can be purchased; and communicate the appropriate information to promote the product, making customers aware of and interested in the product, helping them understand what the product offers, and reminding them that the product is available.

These four elements—**product, price, promotion** (communication about the product), and **place** (the distribution network)—constitute the **marketing mix** (see fig. 1–7). They are sometimes referred to as the "four P's of marketing." The appropriate marketing mix varies with the market targeted.

After market segments have been identified, the elements of the marketing mix are used to position the product. **Positioning** is the activity of trying to get customers to perceive a company's product differently from the way they perceive what competitors are offering. The customer viewpoint is the crucial aspect of product positioning. The marketer's objective is to position the company's product closer to what customers want than any other alternative available to them. All types of products, and companies too, are positioned. If a company wishes to change the way it is perceived, it can change the elements in the marketing mix and thus reposition itself in customers' minds.

This text will discuss the four elements of the marketing mix in great detail. As we outline them briefly here, it is well to keep in mind that a decision about

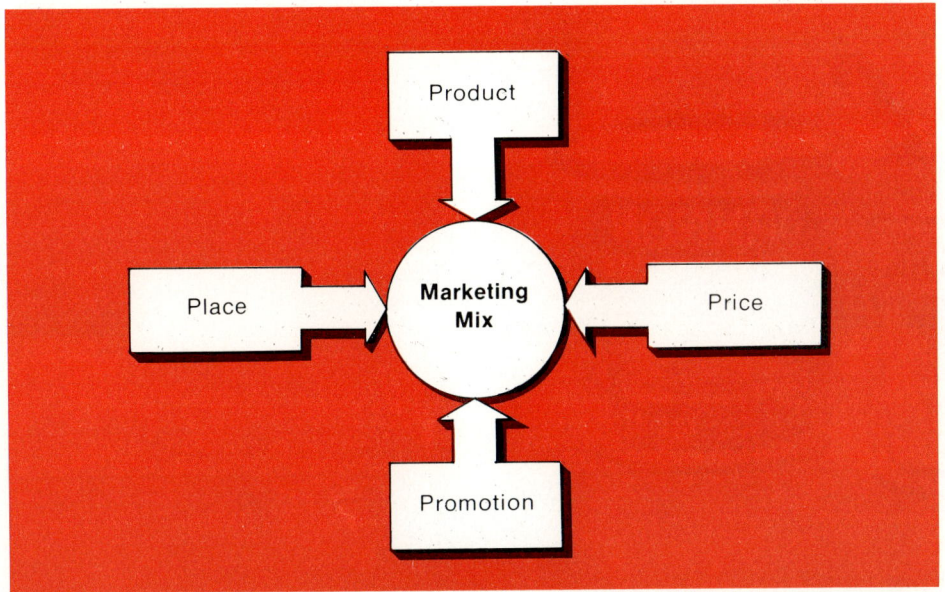

Figure 1–7 The marketing mix

Chapter 1 / Marketing and Its Role in Business

any one of the elements of a marketing program cannot be made without regard to its effect on the others.

Product. A product is a potential satisfier of a need or want. Whether it is a tangible good, a service, or an idea, the product is that for which the customer makes a transaction. The questions and decisions marketers consider about products include:

—What image should be created for the product?
—What product features should be included? Which should be stressed?
—How many varieties should be offered?
—What kind of package is best? In what sizes?
—Are auxiliary services necessary? Which ones?
—How should the product be named?
—When should a new product be developed?
—When should a product be dropped from the product line?

From this list, you can see that the product is more than a commodity that is transferred to the customer. The product satisfies a specific need for the customer, which gives it added value. For example, a customer who goes to the hardware store to buy a ¼-inch drill bit has a problem that can be solved by drilling a ¼-inch hole. From the customer's viewpoint, it is the ¼-inch hole, rather than the drill bit, that is being purchased.[6] For the merchant, selling something that makes

Figure 1–8 This product is more than 8 ounces of yogurt. The total product includes consumers' image of yogurt as a healthful food, the Dannon name, and the handy, one-serving-size container.

Courtesy of R.C. Auletta & Company, Inc.

Chapter 1 / Marketing and Its Role in Business

a ¼-inch hole is far more important than selling a drill bit. Thus, the product should be defined, not from the supplier's point of view, but from that of the buyer.

Charles Revson, founder of the Revlon cosmetics company, contended that he was not selling cosmetics, but hope. This reflects an understanding that a product is a combination of physical components and psychological features that satisfies a customer's needs.

A digital television set providing a home-banking service is a good example of this concept. ITT must understand exactly what it is producing. Is it a status-laden way for the elite to conduct financial transactions from their homes, or is it a functional way for busy working people to quickly do their banking? The choice of auxiliary services, support systems, features, and specific capabilities depends on the exact nature of the product. For example, a customer seeking status may want to be able to call a service representative to discuss transactions, while a busy customer may be far more interested in being able to carry out a wide range of transactions.

The total product, then, includes the package in which the physical product is contained, the name under which it is sold, its image and need-satisfying qualities, and the warranty or guarantee it carries. In the purchase of some products, services, such as installation or maintenance centers, are included. The product may, from the customer's perspective, include such intangible components as the ease of use, or fashionability. Chapters 10 and 11 discuss the marketing of all kinds of consumer as well as industrial products.

Price. Price defines the value of a product or service to the customer. How much the customer is willing to give in order to have a particular item indicates how much that item is worth to the customer. Again, it must be remembered that the value is defined from the customer's perspective, and that price means different things to different customers.

For the marketer, formulating a price strategy requires studying the interrelationships between cost, demand, and profit.[7] Price is the element of the marketing mix through which a company tries to recover all the costs of its marketing efforts, including the costs of the product itself.

The questions and decisions marketers consider about price include:

—What do we want to achieve through our pricing?
—How are we going to set a price?
—What general price level should we choose?
—Do we want to make a profit now or later?
—Should the same price be charged to all customers?
—What shall we charge our distributors?
—Should we use discounts? Rebates? Psychological pricing?
—How will our competitors react to our prices?

The answers depend in part on the pricing objectives of the firm. These can include making a profit, profit maximization, obtaining market share, sales growth, maximizing return on investment, and maintaining the status quo.

Pricing strategy is also tied to product quality. The prices of a product reflect the quality that the marketer wishes to portray. Moreover, in some cases, the price of a product serves as an indicator in the mind of the customer as to the quality of that product or service.

When ITT is developing its pricing policies for both the home-banking service and the computer chips, it must make some basic decisions. What are its pricing objectives? Should these objectives and the pricing policies be the same in both the consumer and organizational markets? Should ITT set high prices to recover the high costs of developing these products? If it wants to attract the market segment of busy working customers, can it set a high price? Will these customers be more apt to buy a lower-priced product. Will status-conscious customers shun a lower-priced product. These decisions are all interrelated, and they must be made in relation to the decisions already made about the product and about general marketing strategy.

Chapters 12 and 13 examine pricing objectives, methods of setting prices, and some specific pricing strategies.

Promotion. The purpose of promotion is to communicate a message to the customer about a product a firm is offering. The specific purposes of messages may vary, perhaps to make customers aware of a product, of a brand name, or of some of the product's characteristics. Generally, the messages are geared toward convincing customers to purchase the product.

In planning a company's communication, marketers make decisions about the following:

—What needs to be communicated?

—To whom is the communication directed?

—What is the best form of communication for our product—advertising, sales promotion, publicity, personal selling?

—If advertising, which media should we use?

—How much should be spent on each form of communication?

—How shall we measure the effectiveness of our communication?

For ITT, these questions become: Must we explain how this technology works? How can we explain the benefits of home banking? If we're going after status-conscious consumers, which forms of communication and media should we use? Can the same forms of communication and media be used for the busy working-consumer market segment? How much of our budget should be allotted for each form?

The answers are based on an understanding of the various forms of communication. **Advertising** is a product message directly sponsored by a company and being communicated to a large number of people simultaneously, often through the mass media.

Sales promotion is a combination of price and advertising. Customers are offered a special price on a product for a limited time through coupons, premiums, free samples, or other incentives. For the trade it might include trade allowances, volume discounts, or trade shows.

Publicity is a form of communication not directly sponsored by the company and not directly geared toward stimulating sales. It is generally aimed at creating a favorable image and reputation for the company.

Personal selling is a two-way communication between a company's salesperson and the customer. The message is tailored to a specific customer and is usually an oral presentation to that customer about the product.

In chapters 14, 15, and 16 we explore the importance and purpose of communication in marketing and how a company decides which forms of communication to employ in the marketing mix for a product.

Place. The fourth element of the marketing mix discussed in the text is place, or **physical distribution:** getting the product physically from the manufacturer to the place where consumers can buy it.

The members of the **distribution channel** are the people and businesses involved in moving the product from the point of production to the point of use. The distribution channel commonly includes the **wholesaler,** which is a business that buys and resells merchandise to retailers and/or to industrial, institutional, and commercial users. Wholesalers, as we will discuss, render a wide variety of services to their customers. Another member of the distribution channel is the **retailer,** a merchant who sells the product directly to the ultimate consumer.

These members of the distribution channel are sometimes referred to as marketing intermediaries. Marketers weigh many factors in deciding which distribution channel to employ for a product.

—Should the product be sold directly to the customers or through distributors?
—How shall we structure the channel of distribution?
—Who shall handle the distribution functions?
—What forms of distribution are best for our product?
—How many distributors should carry the product?
—Shall all of our products be carried by the same distributors?
—How should the products be physically distributed?

How can ITT distribute its digital television sets? It could choose to open its own stores to distribute the sets and teach people how to use the home-banking

Photo courtesy of United Airlines

Figure 1–9
Decisions about modes of distribution are based on a knowledge of buyer behavior and the other elements in the marketing mix.

service. It could choose to distribute the sets through video stores or department stores. If it wanted to distribute the sets as widely as possible, it could choose to use mass merchandisers as well as all other types of stores. For ITT, as well as for other companies, the nature of the product and the priorities of its customers are major determinants. Where and how the product is distributed influence customers' perception of it. Chapters 17 and 18 explore these decisions further.

Marketing Strategy

All four elements of the marketing mix are closely interrelated in formulating a marketing strategy.

Marketing planning involves establishing objectives for marketing activity, determining and scheduling the steps necessary to achieve the objectives, and then allocating the necessary resources. The **marketing plan** includes the business definition discussed previously and requires adequate, up-to-date information gathered through marketing research. The marketing plan sets forth specifically the activities that will enable the company to fulfill the strategy it has outlined. It is important that there be a clearly defined system for developing, evaluating, testing, and launching new products and for pricing them, distributing them, and promoting them. Beyond a clear, innovative, data-based central strategy, the marketing plan should include contingency plans related to possible new developments. ITT, for example, would constantly monitor the various aspects of its marketing plan and make adjustments as necessary. If sales of digital television sets were lower than expected, the company would try to determine the reason. If ITT found that an insufficient number of retailers carried the digital television sets, they may make the adjustment of lowering their prices. If the targeted market segment remains unaware of the sets, ITT may decide to increase its communication budget. If a sufficient number of retailers carry the product and the targeted market segment is aware of the sets, ITT may have to redesign the product. Another alternative, if all adjustments of the marketing plan fail to increase sales, is to withdraw from the market.

Marketing strategy includes the activities of finding a competitive advantage, planning for the company's growth, analyzing the company's portfolio (or array of businesses), and allocating the company's resources.

The most effective marketing decisions are initiated at a high level of the company and are effectively communicated throughout the company. A comprehensive marketing strategy helps coordinate marketing efforts with managers in such areas as research and development, manufacturing, purchasing, physical distribution, and finance.

Marketing control involves a careful monitoring of the results of the marketing plan to ensure that the plan is achieving the objectives that were set and that it is cost-effective. Chapter 19 discusses marketing planning, strategy, and control.

Facets of Marketing

There are diverse facets of marketing, but the tasks of marketing remain the same: to understand the customer, know who's involved in making the purchase decision, and then develop a marketing mix—product, price, distribution system, and communication—that will satisfy those customers. This process is important in the marketing of both consumer and industrial products; both services are a combination of people characteristics and physical goods. Moreover, the marketing principles discussed in this text apply to both domestic and international markets and to marketing in both profit and nonprofit environments. We will examine these facets of marketing in chapters 20 and 21.

Criticisms of Marketing

Marketing is invaluable in the production and distribution of goods and services. Nonetheless, in an era of antibusiness movements, or for those people who are highly critical of business, marketing has been a target for some negative criticisms. This is often because marketing serves as the mediator between the business organization and the consumer. In this section we will address some of those criticisms.

Figure 1–10 The American Association of Advertising Agencies responds to criticisms about marketing.

THIS AD IS FULL OF LIES.

LIE #1: ADVERTISING MAKES YOU BUY THINGS YOU DON'T WANT. Advertising is often accused of inducing people to buy things against their will. But when was the last time you returned home from the local shopping mall with a bag full of things you had absolutely no use for? The truth is, nothing short of a pointed gun can get *anybody* to spend money on something he or she doesn't want.

No matter how effective an ad is, you and millions of other American consumers make your own decisions. If you don't believe it, ask someone who knows firsthand about the limits of advertising. Like your local Edsel dealer.

LIE #2: ADVERTISING MAKES THINGS COST MORE. Since advertising costs money, it's natural to assume it costs *you* money. But the truth is that advertising often brings prices down.

Consider the electronic calculator, for example. In the late 1960s, advertising created a mass market for calculators. That meant more of them needed to be produced, which brought the price of producing each calculator down. Competition spurred by advertising brought the price down still further.

As a result, the same product that used to cost hundreds of dollars now costs as little as five dollars.

LIE #3: ADVERTISING HELPS BAD PRODUCTS SELL. Some people worry that good advertising sometimes covers up for bad products.

But nothing can make you like a bad product. So, while advertising can help convince you to try something once, it can't make you buy it twice. If you don't like what you've bought, you won't buy it again. And if enough people feel the same way, the product dies on the shelf.

In other words, the only thing advertising can do for a bad product is help you find out it's a bad product. And you take it from there.

LIE #4: ADVERTISING IS A WASTE OF MONEY. Some people wonder why we don't just put all the money spent on advertising directly into our national economy.

The answer is, we already do.

Advertising helps products sell, which holds down prices, which helps sales even more. It creates jobs. It informs you about all the products available and helps you compare them. And it stimulates the competition that produces new and better products at reasonable prices.

If all that doesn't convince you that advertising is important to our economy, you might as well stop reading.

Because on top of everything else, advertising has paid for a large part of the magazine you're now holding.

And that's the truth.

ADVERTISING.
ANOTHER WORD FOR FREEDOM OF CHOICE.
American Association of Advertising Agencies

Criticism: Marketing Tries to Create Rather than Satisfy Needs

It has been charged by some that through marketing companies try to create needs rather than satisfy existing needs. Although undeniably some companies do attempt to create needs, it is a cumbersome task and probably not a sensible business strategy.

There are some needs that might not be completely clear in the minds of consumers until they see a product that solves a given problem; perhaps a latent need or desire existed that customers didn't previously think of satisfying. People did not know, for example, that they could have an oven that allowed them to cook a variety of foods in a brief period of time. But now, knowing microwave ovens are available, they enjoy the opportunity to use them. Did marketing create the need to cook quickly? Obviously not.

Creating a need involves extra effort by the company to persuade the customer of a need for the product before the company can communicate to those customers how the product satisfies the need. It is much easier to satisfy existing needs than to persuade people to want something they don't already want.

Criticism: Marketing Creates Low-Quality Products

A second criticism of marketing is that it creates an environment in which low-quality products, and products that do not contribute positively to society, are produced and sold. There is no question that such products are sold. But are they the result of marketing? Or are they the result of consumer interests and preferences?

Let's look at some examples. As a whole, we use more disposable products than ever before. The short-term use of such items as disposable lighters is not a positive contribution to society. But consumers tend to choose them over permanent lighters. They are cheaper to own and create less of a problem if they are lost. Are disposable lighters good products? That depends on from whose point of view the question is considered.

Several years ago almost all telephones were standard black, extremely durable models. Today many phones on the market are more fashionable in appearance but less durable. Is this planned obsolescence? No, it is simply the result of companies' responding to what customers want and will buy by making lower-quality phones. Whether or not the telephones are good products depends, once again, on the viewpoint. Many consumers prefer more fashionable-looking phones and are not bothered by, and may even prefer, the idea of replacing them more often.

We cannot criticize the desires and preferences of consumers or the companies that provide products to satisfy those desires. If customers want and need change, then it would be wise business practice to offer new products to satisfy the new set of needs. Is it the role of business to direct customer needs and wants so that they become of a higher quality? By assuming this role, businesses would open themselves to the criticism discussed earlier—creating needs rather than filling existing needs.

Criticism: Marketing Makes Products Overpriced

Marketing is sometimes accused of causing products to be overpriced. This criticism results partly from the added features and functions that have evolved through the marketing process. The marketing of cheese can serve as an example. Cheese used to be sold only in wheels. Later, when it was discovered that some customers prefer buying cheese in smaller packages, these were produced. Some cheese-producing companies have now gone a step further. In response to customer desires, they

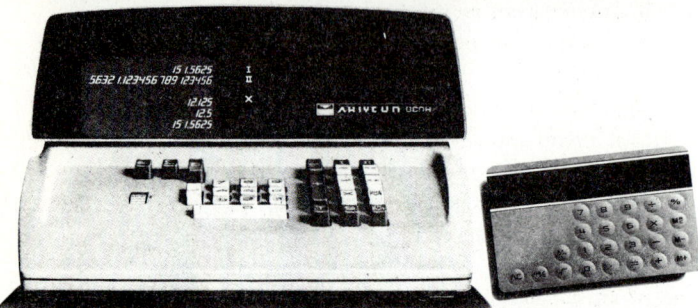

Figure 1–11 A response to the criticism that marketing makes products overpriced.

package cheese with individually wrapped slices. The cost of providing cheese in this form is much higher for the company, but the value is much greater to consumers who buy it. Added handling, packaging, and features add value to customers; consequently, they pay more for the same amount of cheese. Customers are given a choice among different forms of packaging. If there is a form that customers do not want, and therefore do not buy, the company should stop offering it.

Are products overpriced? How do we define overpriced? Price translates into the value that customers are willing to pay for a product and in return for which the company is willing to offer a product. It is logical that if no customers are willing to pay a certain price for a product, then the product will no longer be offered at that price.

It appears that most products, if one adjusts for inflation, are introduced at a relatively high price, which is reduced over time. There are several explanations for this. First, as time goes on, everyone willing to pay the higher price for a new product already has the product; the company then reduces the price in order to attract customers willing to pay a lower price. Moreover, as the company becomes more and more efficient at producing the product, it can provide it for a lower cost and can thus make a profit even by charging a lower price. Another factor that tends to lower prices is the result of competitive pressures. Pricing of products is discussed in more detail in chapters 12 and 13.

Criticism: Advertising Is Deceptive

A fourth criticism leveled at business, and particularly at the marketing function, is that companies provide advertisements that are deceptive. While this practice may sometimes occur, a company that engages in such activity will not be successful over the long run. As ads become more deceptive, their credibility decreases and they become less effective. As a result the company has less means of providing information for the customers.

Overall, it is wise business practice for a company to try to provide products that satisfy customers' needs; price them at a level consistent with what customers are willing to pay and that provides a reasonable compensation for the firm; distribute them efficiently; and communicate truthful information about the products. Firms that adopt these practices are likely to be the most successful over the long run.

Summary

The commercial viability of a product is determined by its potential customers, and a company must understand who those customers are and what their wants and needs are. The company must also determine how the customer views its product.

The current view of the marketing concept is that a marketing specialist must be a systems manager who develops profitable marketing strategies that balance the other business functions, such as production and finance, as well as integrating these strategies with the roles of customers, distributors, and suppliers. An increasing number of companies are adopting the view that the most profitable way to operate is to select the markets they can serve best and aim at offering the most attractive products to those customers.

In addition to advertising and sales, marketing involves analyzing environmental changes, new consumer needs, competitive challenges, and new strategies for growth. The AMA defines marketing as "the performance of business activities that direct the flow of goods and services from producer to consumer or user." Legally, marketing is concerned with the decisions and activities of buyers and sellers that result in the transfer of the possession of goods and services. From an economic viewpoint, marketing relates the business activity through which human wants are satisfied by the exchange of goods and services for some form of compensation.

The difference between wants and needs may not be clear or important to marketers, who are interested only in any concern about which customers care enough to seek a solution.

Both the formal structure of a business and the corporate culture affect marketing activities. In setting objectives, marketers must examine the company's resources as well as its weaknesses. Before launching a new product, marketers must also investigate the competition and, through market research, the demand for the product.

Market research involves defining the problem for study, collecting and analyzing data, and making recommendations on the basis of findings. The purpose of consumer research is to predict how customers will respond to various combinations of product, price, distribution, and communication.

Market segmentation is the process of dividing consumers into groups identified by specific sets of needs.

The marketing mix is composed of four elements: product, price, distribution network, and communication about the product. Positioning is the process of creating a perception of the product that distinguishes it from the competition.

A product is a potential satisfier of a need or want and can be a tangible good, a service, or an idea for which the consumer makes a transaction. When marketers define products in terms of the buyer's need, they include the package, name, warranty or guarantee, and possible maintenance service.

Price defines the value of the product or service to the customer. For the marketer, formulating a pricing strategy involves studying the interrelationships between cost, demand, and profit. Organizational objectives involved in pricing include profit maximization, obtaining a market share, sales growth, maximizing return on investment, and maintaining the status quo.

The purpose of promotion is to communicate information to customers about a product in order to convince them to buy it. Means of promotion include advertising, sales promotion, personal selling, and publicity.

The distribution channel is composed of the people and businesses involved in moving the product from the point of production to the point of use, commonly including wholesalers and retailers.

One criticism of marketing is the argument that businesses try to create needs rather than satisfying existing ones. Another criticism is that marketing creates an environment in which low-quality products are sold. Critics also say that marketing causes overpricing. Finally, marketers are accused of deceptive advertising. Firms that adopt any of these practices are likely to be unsuccessful in the long run, however.

Questions for Discussion

1. In what different ways can marketing help business managers?
2. Differentiate between the sales orientation and marketing orientation stages of growth of the marketing concept.
3. How would you define marketing?
4. Why should we study marketing as a field of discipline?
5. Identify and explain the different components involved in target marketing.
6. Critically examine the role of marketing control in making marketing strategy decisions.
7. Do you agree with any of the criticisms made against marketing? Explain with examples.
8. In what manner is your understanding of marketing different from your understanding before you read chapter 1? Explain your answer.

References

1. Based on Mary Galligan, "Video Explosion on the Way for Buyers," *U.S. News & World Report,* June 18, 1984, p. 56; and " 'Smart' Digital TV Sets May Replace the Boob Tube," *Business Week,* September 26, 1983, pp. 160, 163.
2. "TV Dinners Seek Gourmet Market," *New York Times,* February 10, 1984, pp. D1, D13.
3. This section is based on Samuel V. Smith, "Managerial Aspects of Marketing," in *Managerial Marketing Policies and Decisions,* ed. Taylor Meloan, Samuel V. Smith, and John J. Wheatley (Boston: Houghton Mifflin, 1970).
4. This section is based on Philip Kotler, "From Sales Obsession to Marketing Effectiveness," *Harvard Business Review,* November–December 1977, pp. 67–75.
5. The definitions in this chapter are based on *Marketing Definitions: A Glossary of Marketing Terms* (Chicago: American Marketing Association, 1960).
6. Theodore Levitt, "Marketing Myopia," *Harvard Business Review,* July–August 1960, pp. 45–56.
7. Smith, p. 13.

OBJECTIVES

1. To recognize the need for an efficient marketing organization structure.

2. To describe the various ways in which marketing departments are organized.

3. To discuss the roles of the marketing department as communicator, coordinator, and processor of environmental information.

4. To explain how conflicts develop between different departments and how they are handled.

5. To identify the role played by marketing organization in overall corporate planning and strategy.

2
Marketing within the Organization

Procter & Gamble (P&G) markets more than 90 consumer, industrial, and pharmaceutical products in the United States. Its top products include Pampers, Tide and Cheer detergents, Charmin and Bounty paper products, Folger's and High Point coffee, Crisco, Crest toothpaste, Ivory soap, Sure deodorant, Head and Shoulders shampoo, and Scope mouthwash. In 1983, the company had sales of $12.452 billion.

Procter & Gamble's success is attributed to its thorough involvement in marketing. The company actively identifies consumer needs and wants, develops high-quality products to meet those needs, informs consumers about the products, and makes the products available to consumers. Several departments within the company—including marketing research, research and development, advertising, and sales—work together on these marketing activities.

The work for each brand is coordinated by a brand manager, who has a thorough knowledge of the product, the market, and the customers. Based on this knowledge, the brand manager plans and carries out the marketing strategy for the brand, drawing on the resources available throughout the company.

Procter & Gamble developed and introduced the brand manager system as a way of making sure each brand receives the attention and push it needs to succeed. The company recognizes that an appropriate organizational structure is needed to carry out marketing strategies and to plan for future growth. As one executive vice-president said (at a Procter & Gamble general meeting in 1955):

"The main thing to understand about this thinking is that the Company's organization structure is geared to its plans for the *future* of the business—not for just today, not for just tomorrow, but for a number of years to come. The Company makes plans for its fu-

ture growth before making any adjustments in its organization structure. It obviously can't carry out its plans for the future unless it has the organization which is needed to handle them.

"The Company makes fairly specific plans for at least 5 or 6 years ahead covering such things as personnel needs, housing needs (in the form of office and laboratory space), manufacturing capacity needs, money needs, and sales, advertising and buying requirements. It also makes plans for the organization structure which is required to put these plans into effect."[1]

The implementation of the marketing concept described in chapter 1 requires a company-wide orientation toward marketing, as reflected in the company's organizational structure and the role of marketing within the company. An **organizational structure** shows how a company arranges and allocates work among its employees. Like Procter & Gamble, most companies develop an organizational structure that reflects their goals and philosophy and helps them carry out their plans. In this chapter we are going to look at the various ways in which companies can organize themselves to carry out marketing functions and at the role given to the marketing department in a marketing-oriented company.

Chapter 2 / Marketing within the Organization

28

The Growth of the Marketing Department

In chapter 1, we traced the emergence of the marketing concept and its effect on companies. Most companies have come to recognize that marketing is a distinct and important business function that involves far more than merely producing or selling products. However, this was not always the case. Before the marketing concept became widely accepted, most companies relied on either a production orientation ("We make products") or a sales orientation ("We sell products"). For those companies, selling and advertising were often the only marketing tasks carried out. Figure 2–1 shows a typical organizational structure of a production- or sales-oriented company with separate departments to carry out sales and advertising tasks.

With the spread of the marketing concept over the past few decades, many companies have developed a marketing orientation ("We make and sell products that satisfy the needs of our customers"). In addition to sales and advertising, marketing tasks now include setting product and brand policies, pricing, packaging, distribution, marketing research, advertising, and personal selling. The marketing

From a Production Orientation to a Marketing Orientation

Figure 2–1 Outdated organization chart with a narrow interpretation of selling

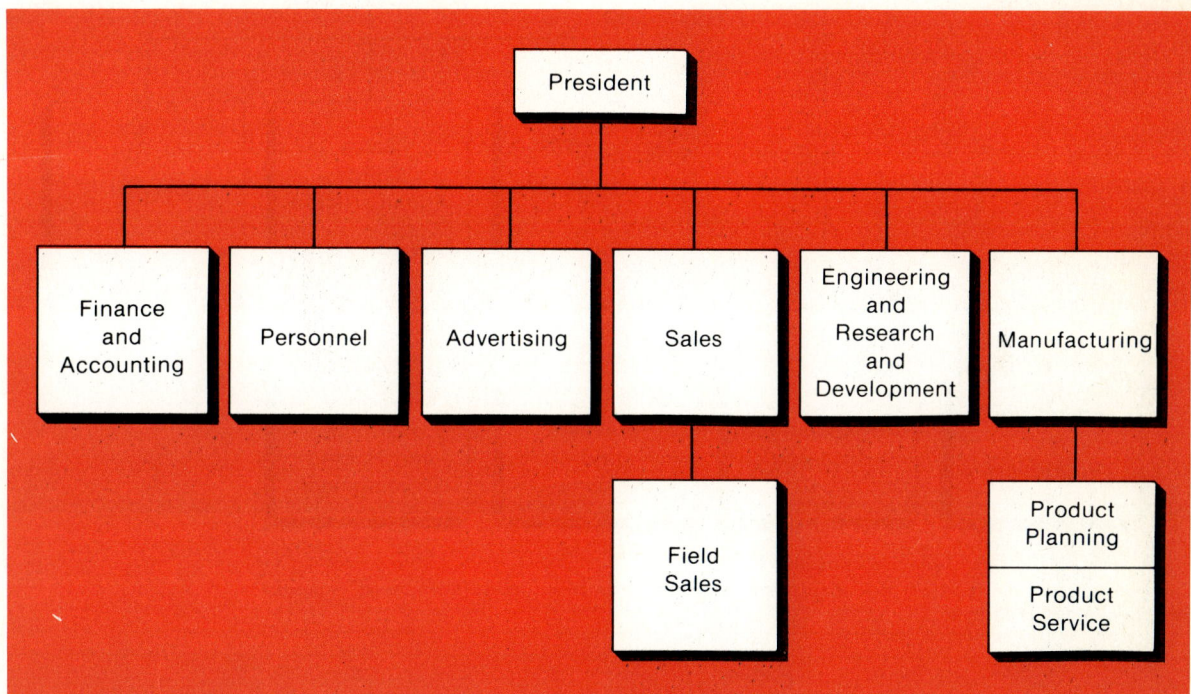

Source: Adapted from George F. Mackenzie, "How to Make the Marketing Concept Make Sense," *Industrial Marketing*, March 1960, p. 58.

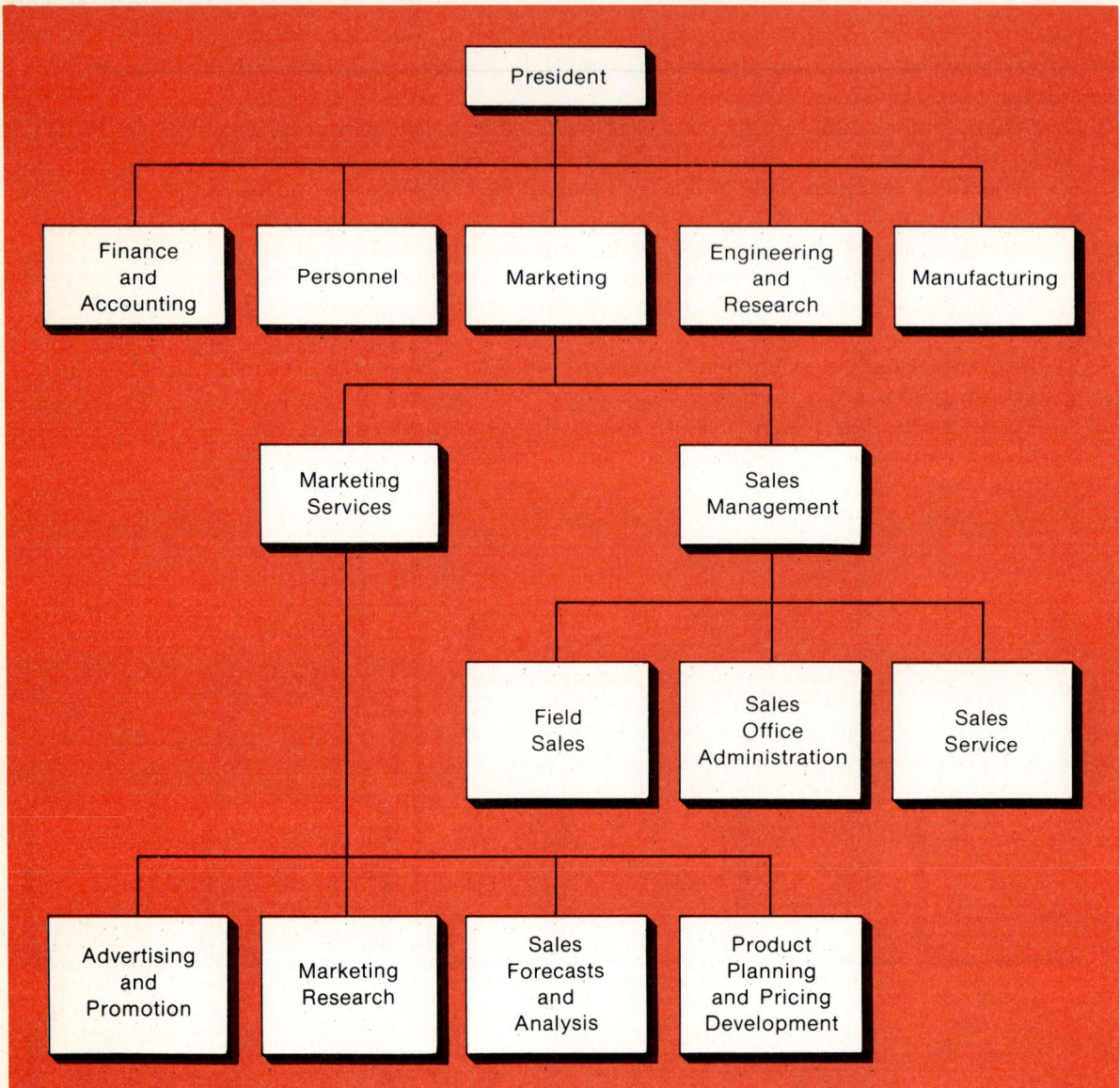

Source: Adapted from George F. Mackenzie, "How to Make the Marketing Concept Make Sense," *Industrial Marketing*, March 1960, p. 58.

Figure 2–2 Modern organization for a marketing-oriented company

concept requires the careful and effective *integration* of all of these tasks with a consistent focus on profitably satisfying consumer needs. Many companies, therefore, established a marketing department to supervise and coordinate all of these tasks. Figure 2–2 shows a typical organizational structure for a marketing-oriented company. In many companies the new marketing department did not replace the sales department, but was created to handle the nonsales marketing tasks.

Organizing the Marketing Department

How should a company organize its marketing department? This is a critical question, as even the most astute marketing plan will be ineffective if the firm cannot carry it out. Therefore, the organizational structure must be carefully designed to provide the most suitable and supportive framework for the company's particular marketing strategy.[2]

In this section, we will examine four types of organizational structures: functional organization, product or brand management, market management, and matrix management. No one of these structures is best for all companies in all situations. Rather, the structure that will be most effective is the one that best helps a company perform its marketing tasks in its environment and market conditions.[3] Such factors as the number of products offered by the firm and the diversity of its markets will help to determine the most appropriate organizational structure.

Under **functional organization,** specific units are established within the marketing department to handle basic marketing functions, such as sales, advertising, marketing research, promotion, and customer service (see fig. 2–3). The work of these units is coordinated by the marketing manager. Functional organization is most effective when a firm offers one product and serves one market. Each unit can concentrate on becoming highly efficient and capable at its job and can focus

Functional Organization

Figure 2–3 Functional organization

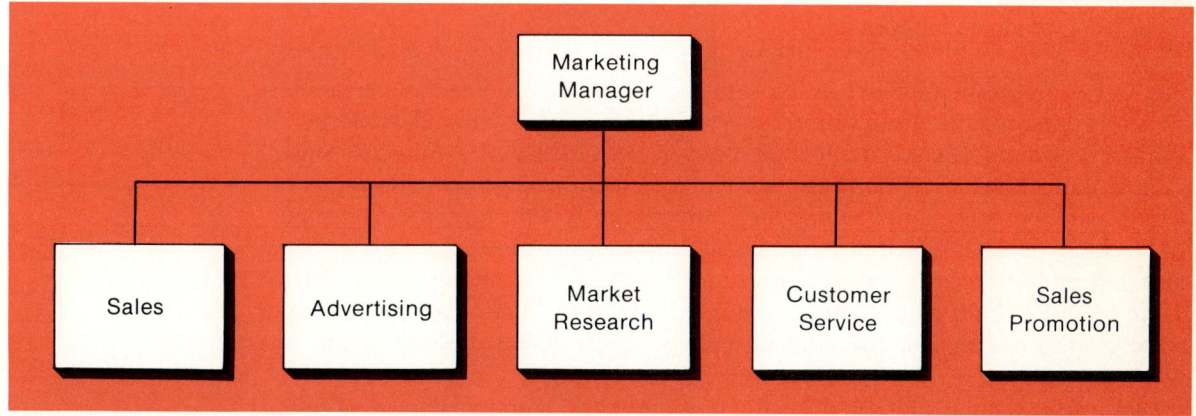

Source: Barton Weitz and Erin Anderson, "Organizing the Marketing Function," University of California, Los Angeles, Working Paper Series, Center for Marketing Studies, Paper No. 105, April 1981.

its efforts on the particular market. The various units work independently but are united in working toward the same marketing goals.

Functional organization is less effective in a more complex business environment. If a firm makes many products for diverse markets, functional organization may not contribute to an integrated marketing effort. Each unit tends to focus on its own needs, plans, responsibilities, and interests rather than on broad marketing objectives. Similarly, having different units specializing in their own tasks makes it difficult for the firm to react in a coordinated manner to changes in its markets or the business environment. The marketing manager, who is responsible for planning and coordinating the marketing activities of the various units and the company as a whole, may not have the information or the support staff to study and develop new courses of action. Levi Strauss & Company changed from its functional organization. The company is now divided into three operating units—Levi Strauss USA, Levi Strauss International, and Battery Street Enterprises—and each unit is further broken down into divisions. Levi Strauss USA, for example, contains Jeans wear, Activewear, Menswear, Accessories, Womenswear, and Youthwear Divisions. The reasons given for the new structure were to emphasize innovation, productivity enhancement, and marketing programs and to be able to respond to changes in the marketing environment.[4]

Product or Brand Management

In the 1980s, few companies produce only one product aimed at one market. Thus, companies with more than one product may find that functional organization does not allow them to carry out their marketing plans. They may then shift to **product management**—an organizational structure in which each product category is assigned to a manager who plans and coordinates all marketing activity for that product. For example, a food manufacturer may have one division that markets all its breakfast cereals, another that markets all its frozen foods, another that markets beverages, and so forth. Figure 2–4 shows the organization of a marketing department using product management.

Brand management is similar to product management, but allows for further division of responsibilities in terms of specific brands. A breakfast cereal division of a food manufacturing firm, for example, may have a brand manager for Cranberry Walnut Flakes, another for Bran 'n' Bananas, and a third for Sugar-Coated Barley Squares. A company may utilize brand management when it is offering many products aimed at one large, diverse market (in this case, consumers of breakfast cereals). (Since the concepts of product management and brand management are interrelated, we will use the term "product manager" in a general sense to refer to both product and brand managers. We will also describe generally what product management is, although each company adapts the structure to suit its own needs.)

Procter & Gamble pioneered the use of product and brand management in the late 1920s. This form of organization caught on slowly, but became much more popular during the 1950s and 1960s. A study published in 1974 by the Association

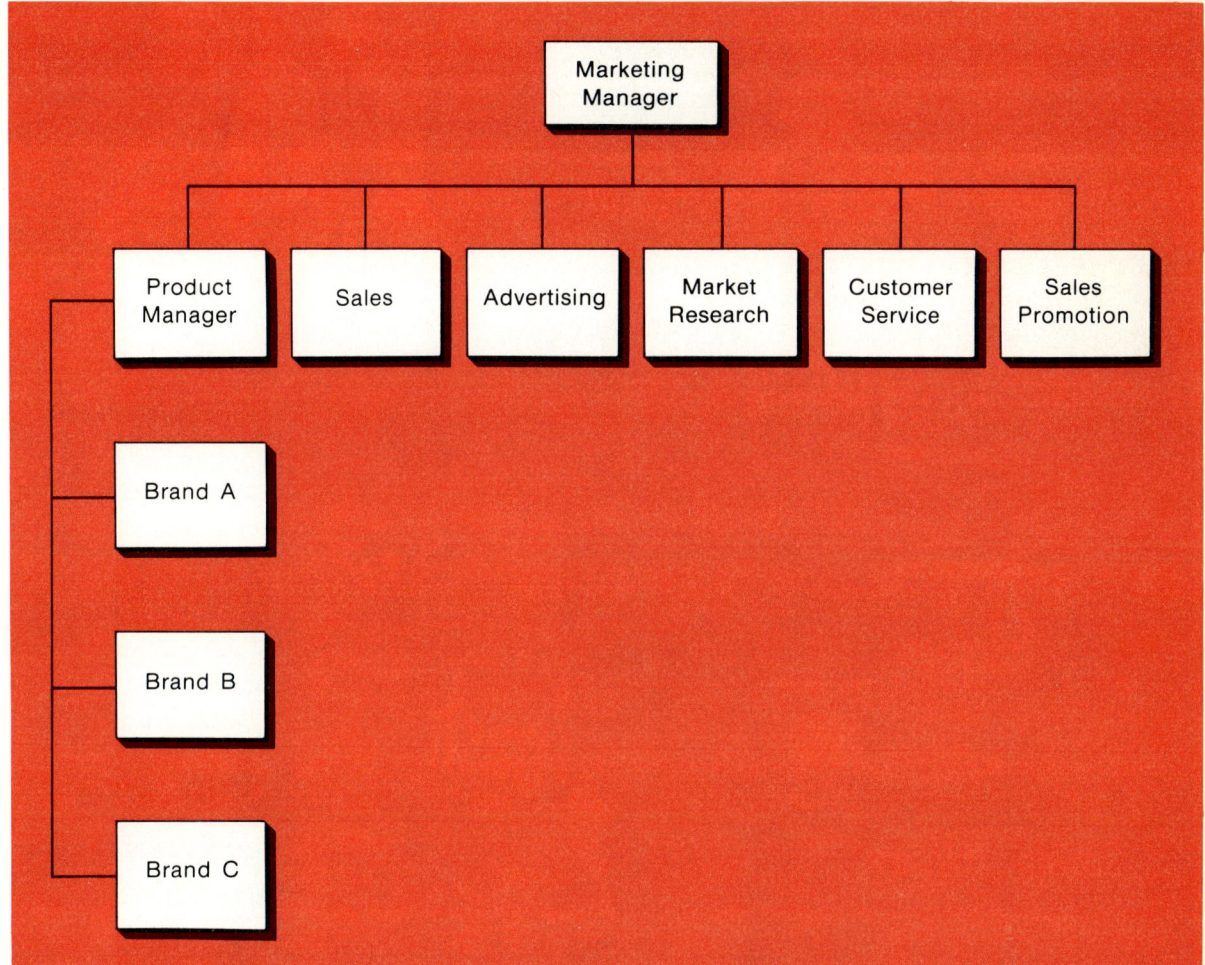

Source: Barton Weitz and Erin Anderson, "Organizing the Marketing Function," University of California, Los Angeles, Working Paper Series, Center for Marketing Studies, Paper No. 105, April 1981.

Figure 2—4 Brand management organization

of National Advertisers revealed that product management was used by 85 percent of packaged goods manufacturers, 34 percent of other consumer goods firms, and 55 percent of industrial goods manufacturers.[5] A 1980 survey of more than 470 firms found that roughly 58 percent of them employed product management.[6] Without question, product management has become the predominant form of organization.

Responsibilities of the product manager. The product manager was originally envisioned as a kind of entrepreneur within a company. Under this view,

Courtesy of The Procter & Gamble Company

the manager for Procter & Gamble's Ivory Snow would function, in effect, as the head of a firm whose sole purpose is to sell Ivory Snow—even though he or she is actually responsible to higher executives within a large and diverse manufacturing firm.

While product managers are rarely considered entrepreneurs today, they generally retain overall responsibility for developing and implementing specialized marketing plans for a product and accountability for the profitability of the product. They are "the firm's main intelligence center for its product lines, . . . an action center at which all strategy and plans for his [or her] product lines converge, . . .

Figure 2–5 The brand manager for each of these Procter & Gamble products is responsible for developing, coordinating, and monitoring its marketing strategy.

Chapter 2 / Marketing within the Organization

34

and gatekeeper . . . at the spot where market needs and opportunities meet the firm's capabilities, objectives, and strategies."[7]

Product managers are generally responsible for the following tasks:[8]

—Establishing marketing objectives for the product.
—Creating a marketing plan and outlining marketing activities to achieve the marketing objectives.
—Determining the budget for each marketing activity and the overall budget.
—Scheduling the marketing activities.
—Establishing measurements and control procedures.
—Communicating the marketing plan to other executives and personnel.
—Creating and maintaining enthusiasm for the plan.
—Monitoring progress and the effectiveness of the plan.
—Revising the marketing plan, as needed.
—Preparing and presenting an end-of-year report to higher management.
—Guiding an evaluation of the marketing plan to learn from achievements and failures.

The greatest areas of responsibility involve creating and implementing the marketing plan. Product managers must promote understanding of and enthusiasm for the plan within their department as well as in other areas of the company.[9] They serve as the main advocates and champions for their products within the company. They interact with other departments to create interest in their products and to coordinate marketing activities. They try to persuade the sales force that the product is worth selling and provide the sales force with information. They try to get the financial resources to advertise and promote their product as they would like. They try to get the manufacturing and distribution departments to treat their product as they would like it to be treated.

This is not always easy. Companies have several product managers, and often they must compete against each other for the same financial resources and interest. For example, Procter & Gamble produces several kinds of laundry detergent, including Ivory Snow, Tide, Cheer, and Bold. Each of these products has its own product manager, who is trying to get a certain advertising budget, sales promotion, or quick distribution system for the product. Similarly, product managers do not have the authority over the sales force or other departments and can only try to influence them to follow their marketing recommendations. Product managers are often most successful when they can establish good working relationships with others within the company.

In addition to Procter & Gamble, a number of other companies use product management. In 1979, Pabst Brewing Company switched to a brand management system to give brands individual attention and to coordinate their separate marketing mixes. A reason given was to facilitate increased advertising and promotion for each brand of Pabst beer.[10]

2–1 Focus on a Marketing Practice
PRODUCT MANAGEMENT AT GENERAL MILLS

General Mills adopted a product management system more than 20 years ago. Some of the company's first product managers had been trained at Procter & Gamble, the company that introduced the system in the 1920s. Product managers are assigned to one General Mills brand for which they oversee everything from the brand's ingredients to the amount of shelf space allotted to it.

Product managers at General Mills sometimes feel as though they're running their own one-product companies. In 1965, when then product manager Robert W. Hatch was assigned to General Mills' Bisquick, the product was more than 35 years old and not selling very well. Some people might have considered this the end of the product's life cycle. "But that was my brand," says Hatch. "I wasn't going to caretake my brand into oblivion." Hatch decided to take an aggressive approach. Researching competing brands showed him that one area of the country preferred another brand over his own. So Hatch had General Mills analyze the competitor's ingredients and make Bisquick more like that product. As a result of the changes in its recipe, the aging Bisquick made a healthy comeback and is still doing well. The product managers at General Mills are responsible for just about everything that concerns their product; they feel almost as if they're in charge of a company. Actually, though, the product manager is only one position in the very complex General Mills corporate hierarchy.

Each year General Mills recruits about 30 MBAs from top schools for its product management training program. These recruits begin as marketing assistants, working under product managers' supervision. It takes the trainees about three years to become product managers themselves. Above the product managers are marketing directors, who re-

---

Ocean Spray strengthened its product management system in 1981 by reorganizing and giving product managers profit responsibility along with the new title of business unit managers. The marketing department has become the department of business operations. The reorganization was made to improve cooperation between the marketing and finance departments.[11]

As another example, the General Mills system of brand management is described in focus 2–1.

Criticisms of product management. Some companies have dropped product management and have turned to other forms of organization. For them, product management did not work, for several reasons: too little authority, too many trivial tasks, too much interaction with other departments for product managers, and a confusing chain of command.[12]

port to a division general manager. While the product manager is responsible for one particular brand, marketing directors and division general managers are concerned with a larger view of the corporation's activity. At this level, directors and managers make sure that the product manager's plans for a brand conform to General Mills' goals. Recently three former product managers (who were hired soon after General Mills adopted this system) have been promoted to chief executive and chairman at the highest level of the hierarchy.

A major responsibility for product managers at General Mills is to develop a three-part annual plan for their brands. The first part is identification of key issues that will affect the product during the coming year. Advertising strategy would be a concern here as would an increasingly successful competing brand. Next the product manager conducts a business review, or a detailed survey of all recent data on the brand and its competitors. Based on these first two steps, the product manager develops "the plan," a budget for the product. This plan is subject to the marketing director's approval. Marketing directors stress long-term goals for General Mills products, some of which are more than 50 years old. For example, a marketing director might discourage a product manager's plans to cut back on advertising because, despite short-term savings, such a strategy might damage the product's future.

Ultimately, General Mills' product managers are responsible for their brand's profits. If a brand is failing or a competitor is gaining ground, the product manager's concern is anything that might stand in the way of the brand's success. By placing one person in charge of a brand, General Mills ensures that the business of that product—from its ingredients to the picture on its package—will be run as if it were a small company rather than part of a major corporation.

Source: Based on Ann M. Morrison, "The General Mills Brand of Managers," *Fortune*, January 12, 1981, pp. 99–107.

Perhaps the underlying problem of product or brand management is its basic orientation to the product rather than to the consumer. This approach strays too far from a marketing orientation. Although product managers are expected to be sensitive to the needs of current and potential customers, they can easily fall back into a sales orientation: "We've got the product; now how do we best advertise and promote it?" As the deficiencies of product management became more apparent, some companies have shifted back to functional organization, while others have shifted to a different form of organization: market management.

Market Management

Under **market management,** the organization of the marketing department is determined by the markets the company serves rather than by its products. Thus, in a bank one manager may focus on the residential market, another on the small business market, and still another on major businesses and industries. (Figure 2–6 shows a market management organizational structure.)

Market management differs from product management in that the same product can be handled by several managers when it is aimed at different markets. In a company that manufactures office machines, one product manager may handle the entire line of typewriters. He or she has the general responsibility for selling all brands of typewriters to all customers. By contrast, if the firm switches to market management, one market manager will focus on sales of typewriters and other office machines to retail stores; a second marketing manager will concentrate on sales to schools and colleges, and a third will aim at sales to business and industry.

There are many examples of market management. After it decided to replace its product management system in 1965, Eastman Kodak established separate Kodak divisions for consumer markets; professional, commercial, and industrial markets; motion picture and educational markets; and radiography markets.[13] When Heinz Ketchup began to lose its market share, the company established separate divisions for grocery sales and institutional sales—and sales increased dramatically.[14]

Market management offers three major advantages. It allows a company to market the same product to different types of customers, using a marketing strategy developed specifically for each type. Moreover, market management helps a firm develop a deep understanding of its markets. Managers become specialists in the specific needs of their customers and can represent those needs in organizational planning sessions. A further advantage of market management is that it is decentralized. Each market-oriented division contains all of the functional resources needed to fulfill its responsibilities. Decisions can be made with relative speed, and competition for shared resources among product managers is eliminated.[15]

This very decentralization, however, has its own drawbacks. There will at least be some duplication of services if, for example, one marketing division is drawing up a promotional brochure to sell its office machines to retail establishments while another division prepares a brochure aimed at schools and colleges. A specialist in

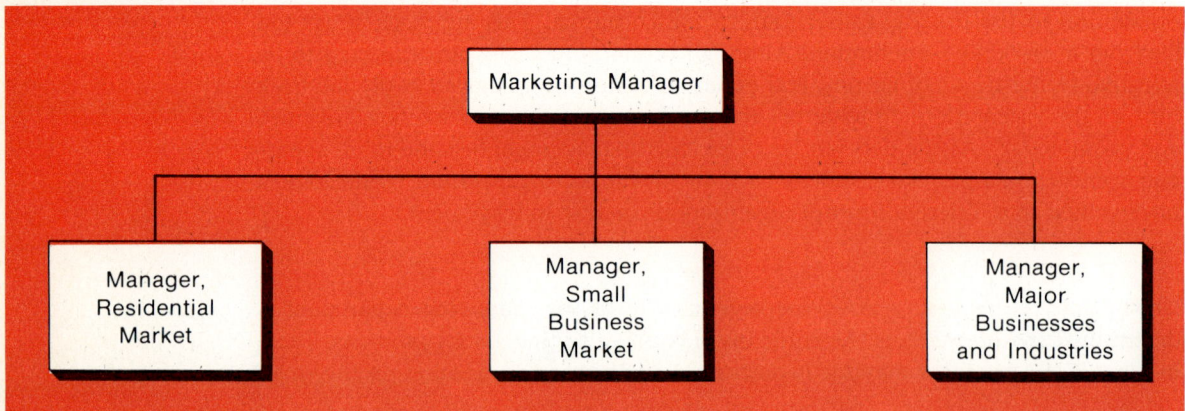

Figure 2–6 Market management organization

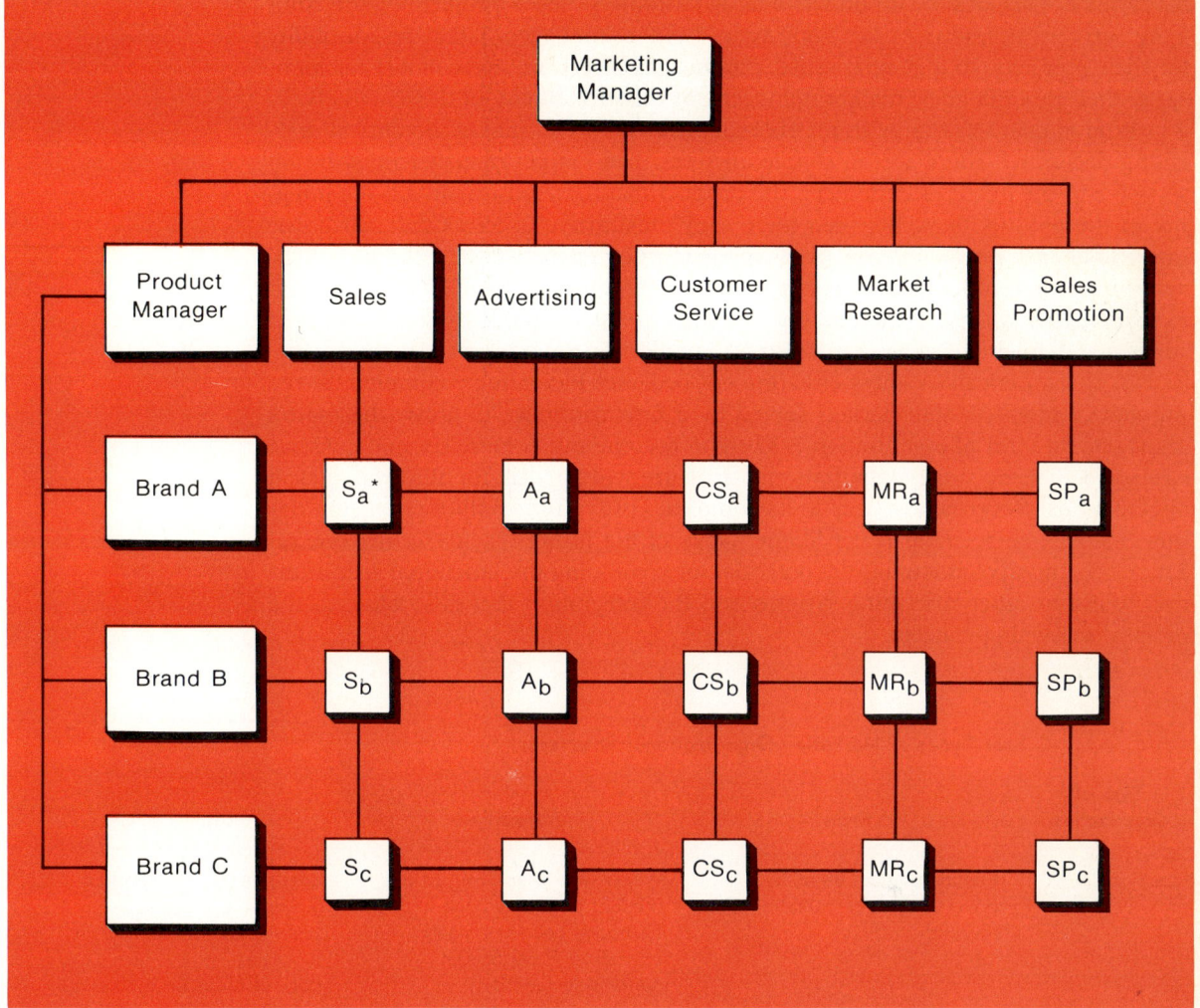

*Position reports to two supervisors.

Source: B.A. Weitz and Erin Anderson, "Organizing the Marketing Function," in Enis, Bernard, Roering, and Kenneth (eds.), *1981 Annual Review of Marketing* (Chicago, American Marketing Association, 1981). Used with permission.

Figure 2–7 Matrix management organization

one market management division may be overworked, whereas a similar specialist in another division is underutilized.

Matrix Management

Should a firm use product managers or market managers? While both forms of organization can be used successfully in some situations, neither may be workable when a company is offering many products in many markets. One solution is to use **matrix management** (see fig. 2–7). Under this form of organization, market managers are responsible for understanding customers' needs and helping the company serve its markets. At the same time, product managers retain responsibility for their products. In a general sense, product managers are accountable for managing their product lines, market managers for the profitability of their markets.[16]

Who is really in charge in matrix management? Who makes the critical marketing decisions? There are no simple answers. The market manager must be responsive to the needs of customers; the product manager must maintain the integrity of the product lines. Between them they must arrive at terms that satisfy the interests of each party, without sacrificing marketing effectiveness. If the two managers maintain a cooperative and constructive spirit, they can develop creative ways to market the product. If they do not cooperate, conflict could easily develop, and support staff might soon feel caught in the middle of an unnecessary battle.

As the American business environment becomes increasingly complex, as the number of products and markets served by a firm continues to grow, the matrix management form of organization is likely to become much more common. As we stressed earlier, no single organizational structure will be ideal for all companies in all situations. Nevertheless, despite its complex, costly, and conflict-producing nature, matrix management is the likely "wave of the future" in marketing organization. The matrix system has the potential for combining the functional specialization found in other marketing systems and the integration that is so basic to the modern marketing concept.

TABLE 2–1 Four Types of Marketing Organizational Structures

Type of Organization	Focus	Advantages	Disadvantages
Functional	Functions, such as sales, advertising, and marketing research	Works well when firm has one product and serves one market Company becomes highly efficient and capable at performing functions	Less effective in complex business environment Lack of coordination of functions Lack of focus on marketing objectives
Product or Brand	Products or brands	Coordination of all marketing activities for product Attention given to each product	Orientation toward product, not toward consumer Confusing chain of command Too little authority for product manager
Market	Markets served by company	Individual strategy for each target market Managers understand needs of their consumers Decentralized organization	Duplication of efforts due to decentralization
Matrix	Both products and markets	Needs of both products and markets are met	No single authority Possibility of conflict

Figure 2–8 The marketing department as communicator

The characteristics of the four types of marketing organizational structures are shown in table 2–1.

The Role of the Marketing Department

Regardless of the type of organizational structure, the marketing department in a marketing-oriented company carries out three roles:

1. The marketing department is a communicator.
2. The marketing department is the coordinator of the company's activities.
3. The marketing department is the filter and analyzer of environmental factors.

Each of these roles contributes to the implementation of a company-wide marketing orientation as the roles provide the information and direction the company requires to serve its customers. We will look at each of these roles.

Figure 2–8 shows the marketing department as the communicating link between the company and its customers. Note that the arrows in the figure run in both directions. Marketing not only transmits, but it also receives.

The Marketing Department as Communicator

Marketing transmissions. When communicating with customers (arrow 1 in fig. 2–8), the marketing department transmits both information and products. The information is delivered through the promotional tools of advertising, sales

Chapter 2 / Marketing within the Organization

41

Figure 2-9 An advertisement is one tool used by a marketing department to communicate information about a product's marketing mix to customers.

Courtesy of Sporting Edge, A Division of Aqua Bug International

promotion, publicity, and the sales force; it includes information about the product in terms of the elements of its marketing mix. Figure 2–9, for example, shows a typical advertisement for a product. The advertisement describes the product and the features that should make customers want to try the product. The product is a "tough, gutsy" outboard motor with the feature of Aquamatic Drive that keeps the motor running at very low speeds (as opposed to the competitions' products, which sputter and stall at very low speeds).

Various product features are mentioned: the two-year parts and service warranty, the light weight, the versatility. Other motors produced by the company are also mentioned, along with their features. The product itself is shown, so customers know what they are purchasing. The price is given and compared with competitors' prices ("Costs the least"). A special promotional deal is offered—if the motor is ordered by a certain time, the company will include a free fuel tank outfit and a tool case.

Finally, customers are given information about physical distribution; they are given both a toll-free number and a form to order the product. Through its physical distribution functions, the marketing department will also deliver the product to customers. Once the company receives the order from a customer, the order will be processed, the motor delivered, and the customer services provided.

When communicating with the company (arrow 2 in fig. 2–8), the marketing department transmits information on three topics. The first topic is forecasts of demand. Marketing will analyze the market and customer needs and create a forecast of demand for a particular product. This forecast is used by the manufacturing department to estimate how many products to produce; by the research and development department in deciding what products to be developed and how customers are reacting to existing products; and by the finance department to allocate money for the development and promotion of the products and to anticipate the revenues that will be received by the company through the sales of the products.

The second topic is the needs and wants of customers. This information is used in the development of specific products and in the creation of corporate strategy. Marketing will also determine whether the company's product ideas fit the needs and wants of customers. The company may decide that it wants to produce a better mousetrap. It is marketing that must determine whether customers have mice, whether or not they are happy with their present mousetrap, and whether they are willing to purchase a better mousetrap.

The third topic is resource requirements. Based on the forecast of demand, the company has to allocate both financial and personnel resources. The finance department has to know the size of the budget needed to support the product. The personnel department wants to know what human resources are needed in terms of sales personnel, researchers, advertising personnel, order processors, and production workers to handle the work required by the production of the product.

Marketing receptions. Marketing receives two things from customers (arrow 3 in fig. 2–8). As we have seen, marketing communicates the needs and wants

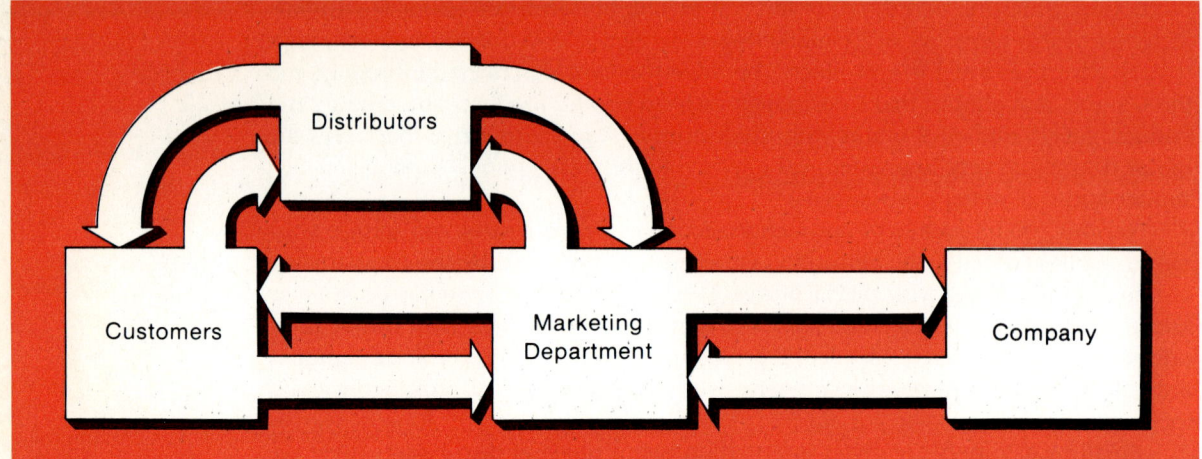

Figure 2–10 The marketing department communicates with distributors

of consumers to the company, so it must receive information from customers about their needs, wants, and sensitivities (or their degree of need). The second reception from customers is the revenue from the sales of the product. By carrying out its activities, marketing provides the actual funds that are needed by the company for survival and that are used by the company for growth and for carrying out its strategies.

Marketing receives two things from the company (arrow 4 in fig. 2–8). The various departments tell marketing what can be provided: Research and development provides new product concepts; finance provides information on the resources that can be allocated to a product; manufacturing provides information on the costs of production, the capability of the company to produce the product, and the anticipated delivery time. The second reception is the actual product, which marketing will then distribute.

Communication with distributors. Figure 2–10 shows another version of the marketing communication model shown in figure 2–8. Marketing also communicates with a third group—the distributors of the products. Marketing's transmissions will be the same information and physical products as it communicates to its customers. The receptions from distributors include information about the needs, wants, and sensitivities of customers. They also include information about the needs and wants of the distributors. Distributors, for example, may tell Procter & Gamble that a particular product is selling very well and that the distributor needs more of that product to satisfy customers. The company will then know that it has to produce more of that product and allocate more resources to it. Distributors also serve as the channels through which the marketing department receives the sales revenues that are then passed along to the company.

The Marketing Department as the Coordinator of Activities

As we've just seen, the marketing department serves as the link and means of communication between the company and its customers. It is the marketing department that looks at the market, analyzes it, and identifies new opportunities for the company. It is the marketing department that communicates to the customers the need-satisfying attributes of the company's products. The marketing department, through its contact with customers, provides the information about the drives of the marketplace that creates a company-wide marketing orientation. The more transmission along arrow 2 in figure 2–8, the stronger the marketing orientation.

Other departments within the company are not in the position to communicate with the market. The manufacturing department, for example, operates within the company itself. When it does go outside the company to buy supplies and raw materials, it does not interact with customers. The products made by the manufacturing department are sold to the customers through the efforts of the marketing department.

The research and development department (R&D) is similarly isolated from customers. The engineers, technicians, and researchers in it can discover and implement new technologies and products, but it is the marketing department that tells R&D whether customers are interested in them or what products customers are interested in.

The financial department is certainly concerned with the internal workings of the company. Yet the financial resources for new product development and for promotional budgets are set by the financial department. As it does not have direct contact with the market and consumers, it needs the information from the marketing department in order to make decisions.

The marketing department, then, interacts with factors outside the company to help the company direct its plans and meet its goals. At the same time, the marketing department communicates with other departments within the company concerning the company's goals and marketing plans in order to get the support and resources it needs to carry out its plans. With the appropriate funding, technology, and production, the marketing department—and the company—can succeed. Without them, it may fail.

The interaction between marketing and other departments. Ideally, all departments will be guided by the marketing concept as they carry out their work. This is true some, but not all, of the time. The marketing department and the marketing orientation may be seen as threats to the responsibilities, privileges, and power of other departments. Efforts to promote a marketing orientation may be met with skepticism and resistance. The interests of the marketing department and other departments often coincide, but they can also clash.

Marketing and Research and Development. Under a production orientation, a firm's research and development department proposes and creates new products.

When a new product is developed, it is manufactured, and the sales staff is told: "Here's a new product; get out there and sell it!" If the company shifts to a marketing orientation, the role of R&D is substantially redefined.

One of the roles of the marketing department is to identify needs that exist in the marketplace and identify types of new products that can satisfy these needs. This information is communicated to R&D. At the same time, R&D is identifying new technologies and communicating to marketing the types of new products that can be developed for the market. Before these products are developed, though, marketing analyzes whether there is an unfilled need for the product in the marketplace and whether there is demand for the proposed product. Marketing and R&D must work hand in hand, even though they are different departments. As R&D is expected to respond to instructions and suggestions from the marketing department, it may be limited in the types of products it can develop under a marketing orientation.

Marketing and Finance. When a new market opportunity is identified, a new product is developed, or a promotional campaign for an existing product has to be altered because of actions of competitors, financial resources must be requested to support production and marketing programs. The marketing department must be able to justify the expenditure of those resources and communicate the need for the funds to the finance department. Part of this involves making forecasts about demand for the product and about the company's ability to produce the product. Based on this information, the financial department can prepare budgets and allocate the resources necessary to carry out marketing activities.

Marketing and the Sales and Advertising Departments. Often, a company establishes separate sales, advertising, and marketing departments to carry out marketing functions. The sales and advertising departments take over the functions of communicating the company and the products to customers. The marketing department still must communicate with both about the market and customers, and both pass information back to the company through the marketing department.

Marketing tells sales about new products and about various promotional campaigns. Sales, in return, tells marketing about the reactions of customers to new products, about consumer needs that are not currently being met by any products on the market, and about the actions and products of competitors.

Marketing tells advertising who the customers are and what message should be conveyed to customers. Advertising then fashions the nature of the message and tailors it for the customers specifically targeted by marketing.

Sales and advertising departments that carry out marketing functions can be part of the company or they can be external. For example, a company may not feel that it is large enough to support its own sales force, so it uses a sales force that already exists in the marketplace. Or a company may hire an outside advertising agency to handle the advertising functions. If these departments are external, the role of the marketing department in communicating the company's products and plans to them becomes even more critical.

Marketing and Manufacturing. The manufacturing department is in charge of producing the products. It often finds itself in direct conflict with marketing. Marketing wants to appeal to as many potential customers as possible and therefore wants many different products in different sizes and colors. Manufacturing, however, wants to simplify operations and limit costs by becoming more efficient at producing a narrow range of products. Marketing may want quick production and delivery to satisfy customers; manufacturing may say it needs more time. Marketing thinks in terms of producing new products that will produce greater benefits for customers and allow the firm to move into new, untapped markets. When manufacturing contemplates new products, it thinks in terms of new technology needed, employee retraining, and trial-and-error operations to perfect new manufacturing processes. While acknowledging the concerns and viewpoints of manufacturing, marketing must communicate its knowledge of the marketplace and of the company's goal to gain manufacturing's cooperation in producing need-satisfying and market-oriented products.

In its concern to satisfy the needs of customers, marketing may want the company to have large inventories of its products and rapid delivery procedures. Marketing may forecast high sales to have a sizable inventory that will help them fill orders quickly; similarly, an unexpected "rush" order from a steady and valued customer can be processed and filled almost immediately. Manufacturing, however, is concerned with the high costs and storage problems involved with carrying a large inventory.

The Marketing Department as Filter and Analyzer of Environmental Factors

As we will see in chapter 3, both consumers and the company act in an environment and react to various factors and changes in the environment. It is marketing's role to gather information about these factors, look at their effects and potential effects on the company's activities, and communicate the effects to the company. Figure 2–11 shows some of the environmental factors; a different set of factors influences the customer and the company. Marketing looks at both sets and communicates to both groups what the other is doing in terms of these factors.

For example, if the marketing department tells R&D that it should develop a particular type of product, it is basing its recommendation on its knowledge of what consumers want, what the competition is doing, what social trends call for the development of a new product, and so on. The impetus can also come from the other direction. R&D can tell marketing that it has developed a new technology that will allow the company to create a new type of product. Marketing can analyze this technology in terms of the economy, the competition, company resources, and consumers, and decide whether R&D should proceed with the development of the product.

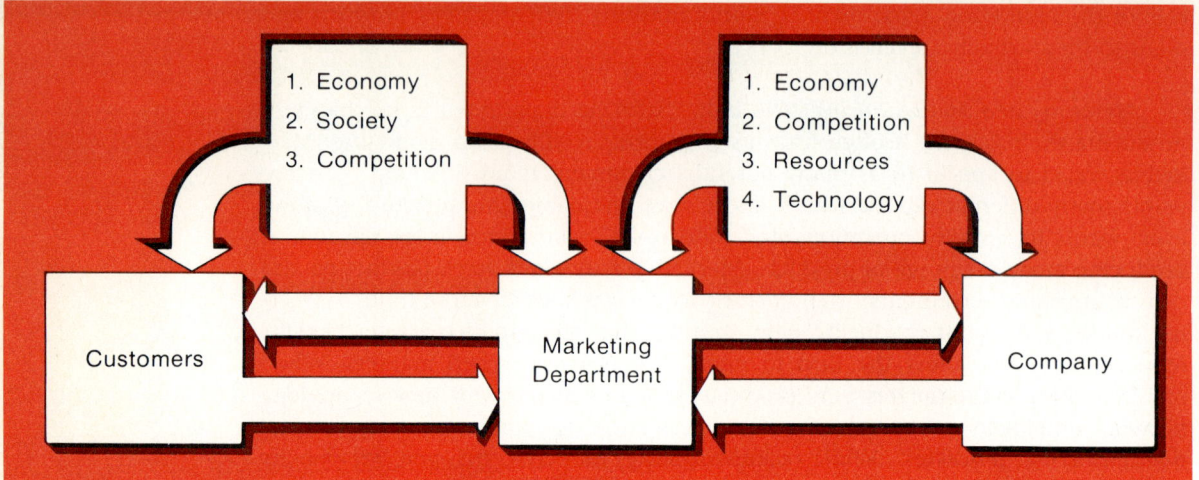

Figure 2–11 The marketing department as filter and analyzer of environmental factors

The Marketing Department and Marketing Strategy

The roles of the marketing department put it in the position of influencing and developing strategy. There are two types of strategy: The first is the strategy that controls the marketing mix for each product. The marketing department has the knowledge about the consumers and the market to make the decisions about the nature of the product, the price level and pricing method, the types of promotion that will reach the targeted customers, and the methods of distribution that will get the products to the right distribution outlets.

The second type of strategy is the broader corporate strategy that determines the activities carried out by the company. When devising this strategy, a company has to decide which businesses it wants to be in, and it has to analyze whether its resources and knowledge allow it to be in these businesses. The marketing department looks at two fits:

1. The company/product fit. Does the company want to produce this product? Does it have the resources—in terms of finances, personnel, and knowledge—to produce and promote this product?
2. The company/market fit. Can the company reach the target market? Can it operate successfully in this market?

Generally, the answers to all of these questions must be positive before a company can decide to be in a certain business. The marketing department will assess the factors that influence these questions; the actual decision to be in a business or not comes from a strategic planning group.

We will look at how the marketing department makes its assessments in chapters 4 and 19.

Summary

An organizational structure shows how a company arranges and allocates work among its employees and reflects the company's goals and philosophy. Many companies have a marketing department to integrate marketing tasks.

The functional organizational method of structuring a marketing department relies on establishing specific units to handle basic marketing functions, such as sales, advertising, marketing research, promotion, and customer service, all coordinated by a marketing manager. This method is most effective when a firm offers one product and serves one market.

In a product management system, each product category is assigned to a manager who plans and coordinates all marketing activity for that product. Brand management allows for futher division of responsibilities in terms of specific brands. Product managers generally have overall responsibility for developing and implementing specialized marketing plans for a product and accountability for the product's profitability.

Under market management, the organization of the marketing department is determined by the markets the company serves rather than by its products. The same product may be handled by different managers if it is aimed at different markets. This system offers three advantages. It allows the company to market the same product to different types of customers, it helps a firm develop a deep understanding of its customers, and it is decentralized.

Under matrix management, market managers are responsible for understanding customers' needs and helping the company serve its markets, while product managers retain responsibility for their products.

As communicator, the marketing department transmits information through the promotional tools of advertising, sales promotion, publicity, and the sales force. Through distribution functions, the marketing department will also deliver the product to customers. The marketing department transmits information on forecasts of demand, the needs and wants of customers, and resource requirements. Another communicator role for the marketing department is to receive information from customers about their needs, wants, and sensitivities. The marketing department also receives information from the company on new product concepts from research and development; on resources that can be allocated; and on costs of production, the capability of the company to produce the product, and the anticipated delivery time. Marketing also communicates with the distributors of the product.

The marketing department is also a coordinator of activities of other departments, such as manufacturing, research and development, and finance. These departments would otherwise be isolated from one another. Conflicts between these departments can occur when their various goals and capabilities are not thoroughly communicated to one another.

Questions for Discussion

1. "The implementation of the marketing concept presupposes an organizational orientation to marketing." Explain.
2. What factors would you consider in choosing the type of organizational structure for a company?
3. What are the advantages and disadvantages of the functional type of organization?
4. Examine the role of the product manager in the product management type of organization.
5. Identify the reasons why some companies have given up product management and turned to other organizational types.
6. Distinguish clearly between the product management and market management types of organization.
7. Explain the advantages and disadvantages of the market management type of organization.
8. Compare the focuses of the marketing and manufacturing departments in an organization.
9. "The marketing department is in a position to influence and develop marketing strategy." Explain.

References

1. Based on "Answers About Marketing," "Procter & Gamble Brand Management," and "Organizational Planning for the Future," publications produced by Procter & Gamble, Cincinnati, Ohio.
2. Barton Weitz and Erin Anderson, "Organizing the Marketing Function," University of California, Los Angeles, Working Paper Series, Center for Marketing Studies, Paper No. 105, April 1981, p. 1.
3. Ibid., p. 2
4. Annual report of Levi Strauss & Company, 1983.
5. *Current Advertising Practices: Opinions as to Future Trends* (New York: Association of National Advertisers, 1974), cited in Victor P. Buell, "The Changing Role of the Product Manager in Consumer Goods Companies," *Journal of Marketing,* July 1975, p. 4.
6. Carl McDaniel and David A. Gray, "The Product Manager," *California Management Review,* Fall 1980, p. 90.
7. David J. Luck, "Interfaces of a Product Manager," *Journal of Marketing,* October 1969, pp. 34–35.

8. Richard M. Clewett and Stanley F. Stasch, "Shifting Role of the Product Manager," *Harvard Business Review,* January–February 1975, p. 71.
9. McDaniel and Gray, p. 88.
10. *Advertising Age,* April 16, 1979, p. 3.
11. *Advertising Age,* April 6, 1981, p. 4.
12. Richard T. Hise and J. Patrick Kelly, "Product Management on Trial," *Journal of Marketing,* October 1978, pp. 28–33, cited in Weitz and Anderson, p. 3.
13. "The Brand Manager: No Longer King," *Business Week,* June 9, 1973, pp. 61–62.
14. "H. J. Heinz Pours It On in Products and Profits," *Business Week,* November 11, 1967, p. 148.
15. Weitz and Anderson, p. 15.
16. B. Charles Ames, "Dilemma of Product/Market Management," *Harvard Business Review,* March–April 1971, pp. 66–68.

OBJECTIVES

1. To highlight the environmental factors that directly or indirectly affect marketing decisions.

2. To explain how business decisions are shaped by economic forces.

3. To discuss how marketing decisions shape and are shaped by the competitive environment.

4. To illustrate the wide variety of public policy issues that affect the marketing system.

5. To highlight the effects of technological advances on product competition in the marketplace.

6. To provide an insight into how cultural and social forces shape the needs and behaviors of consumers.

3
The Marketing Environment

Based on new technologies, such as fiber optics, communications satellites, and telephone/computer links, the telecommunications industry is giving countries, companies, and individual consumers the ability to communicate with anyone anywhere and to send and receive information quickly and accurately. "Telecommunications," said a senior vice-president at the First National Bank of Boston, "is beginning to be the thread that enables us to pull everything together and to reach out for new markets."

In 1983, almost $60 billion was spent on communications equipment; the figure is expected to reach almost $90 billion a year by 1988. In addition, almost $50 billion a year is spent on fees for communication services and software. The United States, France, and Japan, for example, spend as much as 9 percent of their gross domestic product on telecommunications. These expenditures are expected to grow by 15 percent annually.

The explosive growth of the telecommunications industry has been aided by a number of factors. One of the main ones is the growth of other new technologies. Another is the series of decisions that has largely deregulated the industry in the United States. The most publicized move was the breakup of the old AT&T company into the new AT&T and independent local telephone companies. Similarly, deregulation has allowed many competitors, both American and foreign, to sell telecommunications equipment and services in this country. At present, the United States is the most deregulated country. Other countries still tend to protect their own government-owned telecommunications company (and at the same time protect local manufacturers of telecommunications equipment) and discourage foreign competition.

The competition among the various telecommunications companies is fierce, and of-

ten it focuses on services offered, price structure, and marketing strategy. The competition can also come from other sources; cable television networks are also starting to offer communications services. Some competitors with different capabilities, such as IBM and Rolm, have formed joint ventures to make the most of each company's technological know-how.

One of the uncertainties in the growth of the telecommunications industry is acceptance of the new technology by companies and individuals. Much of the equipment is expensive, and not all consumers can or are willing to purchase it. Similarly, some consumers are displaying reluctance to purchase some services, such as video conferencing. Others are confused by the proliferation of services and equipment.

The possibilities for increased business efficiency and ease in communication, though, make telecommunications one of the fastest growing and most lucrative industries worldwide.[1]

The story of the telecommunications industry shows how companies are affected by factors in their environment. The major factors are the economy, competition, public policy, technology, and the country's culture and society (see fig. 3–1). In this chapter we will examine each of these factors and show their effect on how companies make decisions and plan their marketing strategy.

Each factor in its own way influences marketing decisions. Sometimes, the effects of other factors, such as culture and social values, are more subtle. It is not always easy to measure the importance of these factors or to forecast with any certainty their impact on any marketing decision. Furthermore, they are in constant flux, and what may seem important and relevant in one decision or in one place

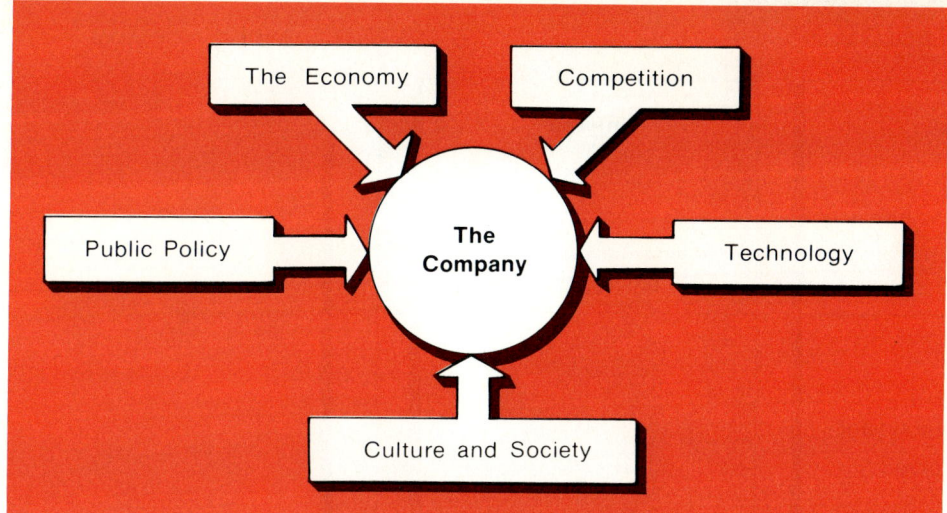

Figure 3–1
Environmental factors that affect companies and marketing decisions

or at one time may not be important in another decision or in another place or at another time.

An Analytical Perspective

Before describing each of these environmental factors and how they affect marketing decisions, we will put them into an analytical perspective. This approach provides a way to classify the factors and understand their relationship to the marketing decision-making process. We consider environmental factors, first, in terms of their location to the firm: Are they internal or are they external to the firm? Then we consider the amount of control the firm has over these factors and how they affect the decision-making process.

These two dimensions are illustrated in figure 3–2. The matrix is labeled across the top external and internal and from top to bottom controllable and uncontrollable. Note that no event is completely controllable or uncontrollable; there is actually a scale running from 100 percent controllable to completely uncontrollable. The matrix describes the location of the environmental factor to the marketing decision and the degree to which that factor will affect the decision.

For example, a marketer may have the authority to create an advertising budget; this is internal and controllable and would be found in the upper right-hand quadrant of the figure. An external and uncontrollable factor might be a union contract that sets forth the exact duties of the sales force. Another external and uncontrollable factor is the political policies of a country; for example, the advertising of alcoholic beverages is prohibited in some countries. Another external factor that a firm will have to deal with is the actions and the reactions of compet-

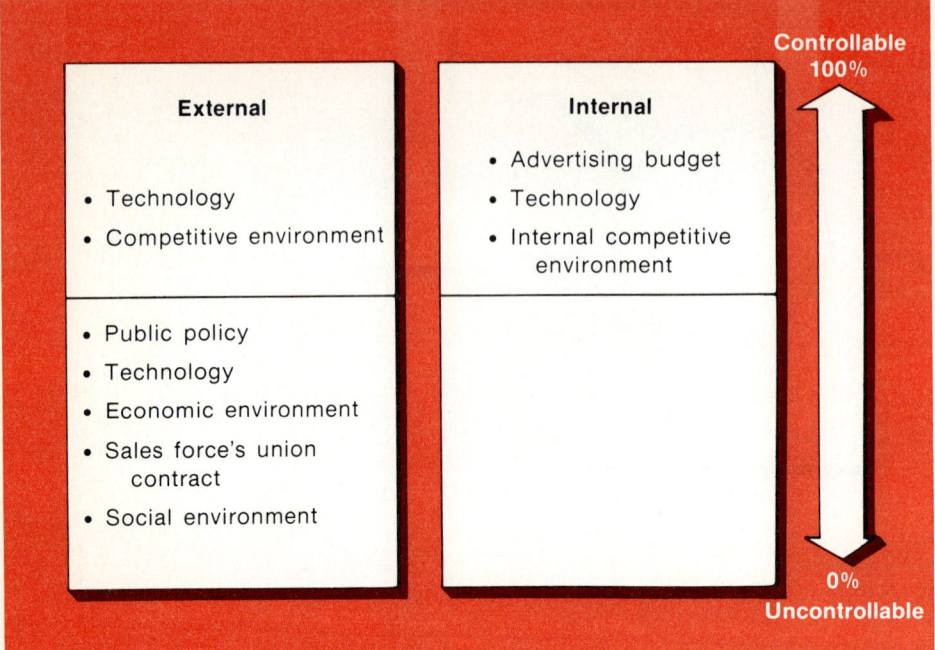

Figure 3–2 An analytical perspective

Source: Adapted from S. A. Brown, M. M. Dunn, and R. Savitt, eds., *Analysis for Marketing Strategies: A Canadian Perspective* (Edmonton: University of Alberta, 1976), p. 70.

itors. These are clearly external but may be controllable; running a price promotion *may* lead direct competitors to do the same.

Now we will look at each of the major environmental factors.

The Economic Environment

The **economic environment** consists of the factors that affect the ability of suppliers to provide goods and services and the ability of buyers to purchase those goods and services. These factors differ from locality to locality and increase in complexity at the national and world levels. While many firms act only in the local or national economic environment, they are all part of a worldwide economic environment. Even the smallest firm whose management claims that it is really only serving local demand is affected by changes in an entire set of economic environments that surrounds it.

The World Economic Environment

The international or world economic environment is the combination of all the national, regional, and local environments. Each of the local economic environments reflects the desires of the various societies that comprise them. Each society has its own ways of deciding what should be produced, how production should take place, and how the rewards of the economy should be distributed to the members of society. Within that complex framework there is no single best way to organize the economy, though Western nations tend to believe in free markets as the best solution. Most economies are a blend of free markets, which are influenced by market forces; of regulated markets, where the behavior of participants is controlled; and of government-dominated markets, where the operation of markets lies within the direct control of the government.

The economic environment for each society or country varies dramatically, since the "bounty of nature"—physical and human resources—is not evenly distributed throughout the world. A number of factors, such as inflation, interest rates, real income, productivity, labor policies, distribution of income, and balance of payments, affect how a country establishes its economy and pursues economic development. In the modern world, however, each country is highly and inextricably intertwined with every other country, and its economic policies are affected by those of other countries.

Just as a major multinational corporation like Texaco is affected by the world economy, so is the local gas station. The supply of gasoline for Texaco, the price at which it is sold to Texaco, and the costs of Texaco's operations are a result of what takes place in the world economy. The same is true through all levels of the marketing process. The availability of gasoline to the local gas station and the price it charges may be drastically affected by economic and political conditions in another country as well as conditions at home. When an oil-producing country changes the level of its output, certain products may not be available or available only at exceedingly high prices.

While the state of the international economy is extremely important, and most important for firms that either purchase goods from abroad or that market abroad, most firms will be most affected by the national-level economic environment. It is to that factor that we now turn.

The National Economic Environment

The policies a nation pursues in regard to the availability of money, interest rates, and credit have great impact on marketing decisions. In 1983, the United States was coming out of a period of double-digit inflation. To reduce inflation, the government had to pursue policies that created high interest rates and high unemployment. The net result of these policies was to limit the financial resources consumers had for making purchases; as consumers had less purchasing power they were unable to buy the same range of goods and in many cases had to cut back on both quantity and quality of the items of merchandise. Such times created difficulties for marketers across the board. Clothing sales plummeted. Few houses were sold, and few new houses were built. High gasoline prices, high interest rates, and lower incomes forced American automobile manufacturers to cut back on the number and size of the automobiles that they were producing.

Much of the economic recovery in 1983 and 1984 was based on placing more money in the hands of consumers through tax reductions. The last of the three tax reductions took place on January 1, 1984. To be certain, with the reduction of inflation, the increase in disposable income, and the increase in consumer confidence, business picked up.

How do marketers adjust to variations in the national economic environment? Some only have to make marginal changes, since their products, such as food, are essential; these changes include promoting lower-priced store brands (Ann Page, Foodtown) or selling generic products. Whether these store brands and generic products will still be as popular once the economy has improved is an interesting issue for marketers to be concerned with. Other adjustments to changes in the economic environment include expanding distribution of products, searching for other sources for costly supplies, and emphasizing selling in overseas markets.

The Regional and Local Environments

Firms operate in a variety of regions and local areas where the economic conditions may differ greatly from the nationwide ones. While a state's unemployment rate may be well over 10 percent, any region or local community may have greater or lesser unemployment. Pursuing the same policies throughout the nation may be unsound; while one area may require the closing of an underutilized supermarket, another area may well call for the expansion of stores.

Let's look at a situation in which the world, national, and local economic environments interacted. The Napa Valley, north of San Francisco, is one of the prime wine-producing areas in the country. A favorable climate led to the establishment of many wineries in the valley in the nineteenth century; a rise in wine consumption in the United States led to a proliferation of wineries in the late 1970s. But the Napa Valley wine industry went into a slump in the early 1980s as a result of its economic environments.

The amount of wine produced depends on the size of the harvest; in 1982, a bumper crop of grapes led to a tremendous surplus of wine. Many of the wineries had to cut prices and increase promotion in order to sell their wine and thus survive. Some wineries went bankrupt. This is the local economic environment. At the same time, a nationwide recession contributed to a decline in the consumption of domestic wine. This is the national economic level. Consumption of imported wine was rising, though. Foreign wine industries are subsidized by their governments through strong advertising and promotion campaigns. And the strength of the dollar in relation to the French franc allowed even some well-known French wines to be sold more cheaply than Napa Valley ones. Different approaches by governments toward supporting their industries and foreign exchange rates are part of the world economic environment.[2]

Let's look at another example. By its nature, the telecommunications industry crosses local, regional, and national borders and functions at all three levels of economic environments. At the same time, different countries support and demand services from their own telecommunications companies in different ways. Each country has traditionally had its own major communications company. In the United States, the domination of the almost-official communications company, AT&T, was diminished by judicial decisions that encouraged competition. A num-

Figure 3–3 The Prestel viewdata service is one part of the British telecommunications system. The operator is entering an updated weather forecast. Subscribers to the service can dial into the service's computers by telephone and receive on their television screens this weather forecast, stock exchange reports, travel information, and so on.

Crown copyright reserved. Issued for British Information Services by Photographs Division, Central Office of Information, London.

ber of companies now offer long-distance telephone service. Local telephone service is usually provided by regional companies spun off from AT&T.

In most Western European countries, there is still an official communications company. In Great Britain, there is British Telecom; in France, the Direction Générale des Télécommunications; and in West Germany, the Deutsche Bundespost. The governments of these companies are keeping the dominant status of these companies because they seem to work as efficiently as needed and because the government monopolies can protect and support domestic suppliers of telecommunications equipment. Moreover, when a foreign telecommunications company wants to transmit into one of the protected countries, it must hook up with that country's equipment. The governments of these countries are starting to modernize their equipment and are paying for it by charging customers higher rates.

One of the strongest arguments European governments give for maintaining government monopolies on telecommunications is to protect service in local areas; they feel that small, especially rural markets, which might not be considered lucrative in a competitive environment, might be overlooked. Communication, they feel, is a public service that should be operated for the general good.

The economic environment is probably the easiest for marketers to understand in theory since it is directly related to the issues of the supply and demand for products. It is easy to construct decision models that allow the economists' measures to be entered into the decision-making process. For example, a jewelry manufacturer will most likely increase production and marketing efforts when income levels, and consequently demand, increase. Similarly, the jewelry manufacturer will attempt to stock up on gold when its price is low. Economic patterns are well established. In general, there are definite relationships between drops in interest rates and the increase in demand for capital goods by industrial firms and in the decline in mortgage rates and the increase for new housing.

The most frustrating part about the marketer's position in the economic environment is the lack of ability to control major elements. In the analytical perspective in figure 3–2, the economic environment falls into the lower left-hand quadrant. Since the economic environment is really the sum of all the economic activities at any level of aggregation, the individual firm will have few opportunities to control it. One possible way of controlling it is to form trade associations that lobby to change government policies toward a given industry. Steel companies, for example, have banded together to support government limits on the amount of foreign-made steel let into this country. But, generally, companies attempt to adapt to the economic conditions instead of controlling them.

The Competitive Environment

The **competitive environment** is the marketplace in which firms compete among themselves for business and resources. Of all of the economic environments in which the firm finds itself, this is the one over which it has some influence and control. The competitive environment affects a company at both ends: Marketing decisions must be made concerning the purchase of supplies that will be turned into the products that, in turn, are marketed to customers. In this context, the marketplace is dynamic, and a firm has the opportunity to affect the behavior of other firms by the actions that it takes; it is also affected by the actions of other firms.

How far a firm can affect competitive behavior is a function of several things. First, a firm has limited internal resources—human, physical, and monetary—and can only undertake certain competitive activities. Second, management can be active or reactive in relation to competitors. Third, the firm's physical resources, including its finances, production capacity, and technological ability, affect how it competes.

External Competition

Marketers want to sell a product to a selected group of consumers. In order to attract customers, they must provide a product that customers want and that is different from all others with similar uses and characteristics. This differentiation is created by differences in the product itself, in the prices charged, in the promotion and advertising campaigns, and in the places in which the product is offered for sale. Marketers will create the combination of those characteristics that best allow their products to compete. At the same time, firms in certain types of market situations will respond in kind to other firms that engage in competitive behavior; for example, price reductions lead to competitors' price reductions.

Marketing competition, however, is more complex. Some firms are known to be aggressive in the use of advertising, others are known for price reductions, while still others are known for intense personal selling. Marketers study the behavior of competitors in order to understand what their response should be to the change in the competitive actions of another. Many years ago, in the soft-drink industry, the traditional response of the smaller and lesser-known producers to the extensive advertising campaigns of Coca-Cola was a sharp reduction in prices in selected markets. In part this was dictated by their lack of resources to match Coca-Cola's advertising and their knowledge that in the short run the only feasible response was in the form of a lower price.

The competitive process will create winners and losers just as in any type of sporting event. There will be changes as new competitors enter the arena, and there will be firms that fall by the wayside. The recent period of change in the airline industry is an excellent example of the competitive process. Many airlines expanded routes, others lowered prices, others changed services, and still others did a little bit of each. Some of the firms were successful because they understood their environments and limitations. Others, such as Braniff, threw anything and everything they had into competitive activity and ended up going out of business. The competitive environment is dynamic because of the coming and going of market participants.

Internal Competition

The previous discussion has focused on the competition among various firms. Many firms in the United States are large and extensive, though, and within them there is also a competitive environment for scarce resources. Some of this competition within the firm is the rivalry for internal resources between products. Should soap powders receive more marketing support than liquid detergents, not to mention the resources devoted to toothpaste? Obviously, if one product receives more of the company's resources, the other may be at a disadvantage in competing in its own market. One of the critical tasks of the marketing manager is to develop plans that spread resources as widely as possible.

Many large companies produce and market several products that are in direct competition with one another. Procter & Gamble, for example, produces both Tide and Bold. It is argued that internal competition is an important stimulus for the overall productivity of the firm. As a management issue it is one that must be examined. What happens when the Tide product group is more successful in getting resources than the Bold product group?

In the United States, the opening up of the telecommunications industry has spurred competition in a number of ways. First, many service-providing companies are entering the industry and are fighting for customers. In addition to domestic companies competing to provide communications services, foreign companies are allowed to join the competition. (We have already seen that American telecommunications companies cannot compete in many countries overseas.) A large number of equipment manufacturers have created an overabundance of equipment and intense competition to sell it. At the present time, there are only a limited number of communications systems to be installed, and customers can shop around for the best deals. Much available equipment is underutilized. In 1983, for example, only 54 percent of the capacity of communications satellites was being used, due to an oversupply of satellites and transmission capacity.[3] In contrast, there are too few digital switches, and many companies can survive or even thrive in this competitive environment.

Most of the major companies can provide the same basic services, so the companies are competing largely on the basis of price and the range of value-added services they offer. As can be seen in figure 3–4, the major companies are stressing their low costs. Some of the value-added services offered include range of coverage, expertise, customized equipment, and optional links like teleconferencing and WATS lines (see fig. 3–5).

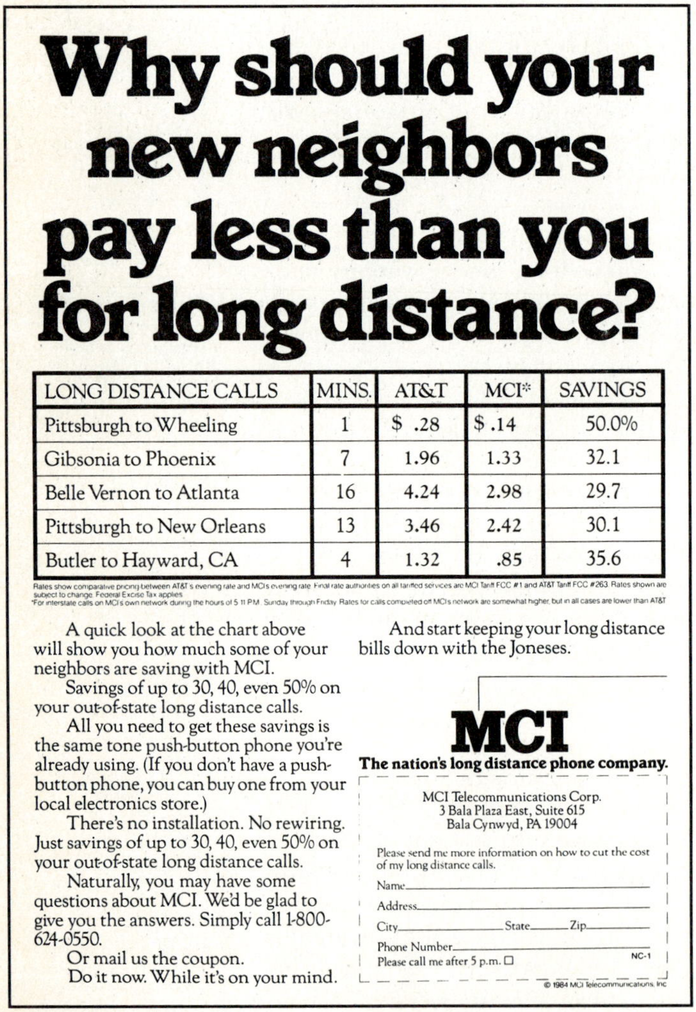

Figure 3–4 In the United States, telecommunications companies are competing on two bases. The first basis is price.
Courtesy of MCI Telecommunications Corp.

Why should your new neighbors pay less than you for long distance?

LONG DISTANCE CALLS	MINS.	AT&T	MCI*	SAVINGS
Pittsburgh to Wheeling	1	$ .28	$ .14	50.0%
Gibsonia to Phoenix	7	1.96	1.33	32.1
Belle Vernon to Atlanta	16	4.24	2.98	29.7
Pittsburgh to New Orleans	13	3.46	2.42	30.1
Butler to Hayward, CA	4	1.32	.85	35.6

A quick look at the chart above will show you how much some of your neighbors are saving with MCI.

Savings of up to 30, 40, even 50% on your out-of-state long distance calls.

All you need to get these savings is the same tone push-button phone you're already using. (If you don't have a push-button phone, you can buy one from your local electronics store.)

There's no installation. No rewiring. Just savings of up to 30, 40, even 50% on your out-of-state long distance calls.

Naturally, you may have some questions about MCI. We'd be glad to give you the answers. Simply call 1-800-624-0550.

Or mail us the coupon. Do it now. While it's on your mind.

And start keeping your long distance bills down with the Joneses.

MCI
The nation's long distance phone company.

MCI Telecommunications Corp.
3 Bala Plaza East, Suite 615
Bala Cynwyd, PA 19004

Chapter 3 / The Marketing Environment

But competition does not only come from other telecommunications companies. In New York City, for example, cable television networks are being used as a private communications system. Furthermore, competition can result from joint ventures. There is a trend for companies to link their areas of expertise to provide complete services. IBM, for example, is linking its computer knowledge with Rolm's communications expertise. On an international level, AT&T, with its Western Electric equipment, and Netherlands-based Philips Telecommunications, with its distribution channels and worldwide presence, have formed a joint venture to sell equipment throughout the world.

Figure 3–5 The second basis of competition for telecommunications companies is value-added services.
Courtesy of AT&T Information Systems

Marketing and Public Policy

Public policy includes those actions taken by governments that affect the operations of the marketing system. Public policy in marketing is defined as any government policy at the federal, state, or local level that in any way affects the supply of or demand for goods and services. Included in this definition is a wide range of government policies that affect firms and consumers in their search for satisfaction of their wants in the marketplace.

Chapter 3 / The Marketing Environment 63

3-1 Focus on an Issue
HOW DEREGULATION AFFECTS MARKETING PRACTICES

Regulated industries are those whose policies are set by government agencies, such as the Civil Aeronautics Board or the Interstate Commerce Commission. In many respects, the marketing practices of regulated businesses differ dramatically from those of nonregulated businesses. Probably the most important difference is the fact that regulated businesses tend to focus their marketing efforts on meeting the demands of the regulatory agency, while nonregulated businesses focus on the needs and wants of consumers.

Characteristic of nonregulated companies is the fact that businesses within an industry usually act as rivals, competing with one another for territories, sales, and customer loyalty. In contrast, companies within a regulated industry do not compete as intensely. Respect for other firms' territories is common among regulated businesses.

Price as a competitive factor is also absent from regulated companies' operations because the regulatory agency standardizes the amounts firms are allowed to charge for their products. Prices charged to consumers are often based on companies' operating costs, so that these businesses are not nearly as motivated to reduce expenses as nonregulated businesses. Often the price for a given product does not truly reflect its cost but the company's overall expenses. For instance, under regulation, an airline might set flight fares on the basis of an average cost for many different flights. Some fares would be lower than the actual cost of the flight, while others would cost more.

For some regulated companies, growth is not a goal because with standardized prices, growth of the business does not necessarily mean increased profits. In fact, expansion of operations may lead to more problems than opportunities, as the regulatory agency evaluates each new move by the company. The evaluation process can be quite a bit slower than in a nonregulated business, and, meantime, opportunities may be lost. Because of this continuous observation, regulated businesses are often more concerned with their operations than they are with the results of their actions in the marketplace. Nonregulated companies tend to downplay their means of operation and emphasize results.

The differences between regulated and nonregulated businesses are particularly apparent when we look at what happens when an industry that has been regulated is de-

Types of Public Policy in Marketing

Based on the above definition, the following types of policies can be described as public policy in marketing: economic regulation, direct and indirect subsidies, trade policies, fiscal and monetary policies, government procurement policies, antitrust regulation, and consumer protection laws.[4]

Economic regulation. *Economic regulation* is the specific government control over the activities of firms, as is seen in radio and television broadcasting, public utilities, commercial banking, and insurance. Under regulation, specific lim-

Chapter 3 / The Marketing Environment

64

regulated. In 1978, the commercial airlines industry was deregulated, creating new opportunities as well as some major problems for established airlines. The benefits of deregulation included generally lower fares, particularly for people who travel the major flight routes. Most of the problems stemmed from the established airlines' inability to make a rapid transition to the market orientation. Under deregulation, airlines failed to protect their established territories while expanding with new routes. For example, one airline, Braniff, went bankrupt because it expanded into many new routes (several of which were not heavily traveled) while not focusing enough of its efforts on its own established market in Texas. (In the spring of 1984, Braniff started to operate again in a greatly restructured form.)

Another problem area has been airline costs and fare pricing. The established airlines failed to cut costs sufficiently, while the new, smaller airlines found ways to operate much more cheaply. In addition, the larger airlines maintained the practice of setting fares at a level that covered overall costs for the airline, not on the basis of the cost of specific flights. Longer, more frequently traveled routes still helped to pay for shorter, less popular flights. The result was that the established airlines lost a great deal of business on their most profitable routes to the new companies that offered lower fares.

The trucking industry is another area that is changing as a result of its recent deregulation. Some of the results have been the same as they were for the airlines industry. Here, also, territory restraints have been lifted, setting up tough competition for prime regions. Smaller, new businesses (with lower operating costs) have snatched away some of the larger trucking companies' business. Deregulation has also brought about some new trends in the trucking industry. Under government regulations, trucking companies were allowed to handle the internal shipping of no more than eight businesses. Now, without that restriction, companies compete for contracts to handle internal shipping for as many businesses as possible, often using such strategies as discounting. Growth for the deregulated companies has become a goal because it means increased profits.

Sources: Thomas S. Robertson, Scott Ward, and William M. Caldwell IV, "Deregulation: Surviving the Transition," *Harvard Business Review*, July–August 1982, pp. 20–25; Thomas S. Robertson and Scott Ward, "Management Lessons from Airline Deregulation," *Harvard Business Review*, January–February 1983, pp. 2–4; and John Mutter, "The Open Road Gets Bumpy," *Sales & Marketing Management*, July 6, 1981, pp. 31–34.

its are placed on marketing activities, such as price-setting and choice of products offered, through the actions of regulatory bodies. The general idea behind regulation is that, by the very nature of certain industries, rivalry and extensive competition are not possible. While this idea may hold true for public utilities, it has recently been dropped in the airline, the long-distance telephone, and the motor carrier transportation industries. The **deregulation** of these industries has led to the development of new marketing practices and management actions, as can be seen in focus 3–1.

Many of the conditions in the economic and competitive environments for the telecommunications industry have been brought about through deregulation. Consider the effects of three actions:

—In 1968, the FCC allowed non-AT&T equipment to be hooked up to the telephone system. This decision led to the production of a variety of equipment by many domestic and foreign manufacturers.

—In 1981, Congress and the FCC increased the amount of competition in the industry by allowing more companies to send messages within the United States and by allowing domestic message carriers to compete internationally.

—In 1982, the breakup of the AT&T Bell System was ordered, with three main effects. First, regional telephone companies were created to provide local telephone service. Second, competition to provide long-distance telephone service was increased. Third, AT&T was allowed to send data in addition to voice transmissions through its system, thus allowing AT&T to compete with other companies in the computer and telecommunications fields.

The government actions were intended to increase the operations of a free market. The results, as we have seen, include a proliferation of equipment and value-added services, potentially lower costs, a range of options in communications systems and methods, and greater competition among a greater number of companies.

Subsidies. Direct and indirect *subsidies* are public policies that affect marketing by supporting industries or encouraging them to engage in certain activities. In the nineteenth century, the railroads were given a variety of incentives, including gifts of vast amounts of land, to expand their operations across the country. In the last several decades the federal government, through the National Aeronautics and Space Agency (NASA), has given similar types of incentives to firms to develop space-oriented products. Types of subsidies vary throughout the world as individual governments decide which industries they want to support to further their economic goals.

Trade policies. International and interregional *trade policies* represent another category of public policies that affect marketing. Some of these have attempted to protect American firms in the domestic markets by placing high tariffs on certain imported goods. Trade policies and international trade are discussed further in chapter 20.

Fiscal and monetary policies. *Fiscal and monetary policies* affect marketing through changes in the amount of money that customers have to spend. High interest rates, for example, limit consumer purchases of large expensive items, such as houses and automobiles.

Government procurement policies. Although not traditionally viewed as public policy, *government procurement policies* clearly affect business and marketing decisions. The policies set the procedures and priorities followed by governments in the purchase of goods and services, as well as in the letting of contracts for research and development. The policies cover the assortment of goods and services purchased and will thus influence competition in certain industries. The choice of suppliers is also affected through affirmative action policies.

Government procurement policies, though, change from administration to administration due to different priorities and philosophies. Under the Reagan administration, spending on defense is a priority, and companies selling defense-related products are doing very well. State Machine Products of Dry Ridge, Kentucky, sells lanterns, mess kits, and field stoves to the government. In 1979, the company had sales of about $500,000; in 1983, sales rose to $5.5 million. The company's tremendous growth spurt can be directly traced to the high levels of defense-related purchases. The company recognizes, though, that the defense budget could drop at some time. It has thus made the intelligent marketing decision of expanding into commercial markets to ensure that sales remain high.[5]

Other government activities and policies affect marketing activities, even though this is not their main intention. Among these are postage rates, farm subsidies, municipal building codes, and zoning regulations, as well as many others. While it is not correct to suggest that all public policy is marketing-oriented, a substantial amount is. Given the general increasing levels of complexity in the modern world, even more public policies will arise that marketers must consider when making decisions.

Antitrust Legislation and Marketing

Antitrust legislation is the attempt to maintain competition among business firms by the diffusion of economic power so that market forces will be maximized. The underlying assumption is that firms *independently* pursuing their self-interest will generate economies in production, use resources in the optimum fashion, and will improve consumer welfare. In this regard, antitrust legislation supports the free market economy and serves as an important alternative to direct government regulation of business or to state ownership of business institutions.

Antitrust statutes and the case law that was developed over the years appear to place substantial constraints on marketing decision making. These constraints are real insofar as they affect directly what marketing managers can and cannot do, but as suggested previously, they are aimed at making the entire economic system work in the optimum way. This difference between the broad view and the view of the individual marketing manager will always be present, and any attempt to reconcile them will be difficult. Simply, what may be best for the economy as a whole may not necessarily be best for any given marketer.

Antitrust legislation in the United States has been passed to minimize unfair methods of competition, unfair exercise of market power, and monopolistic practices and mergers. The basic antitrust law is the Sherman Act of 1890; its provisions are listed in figure 3–6. In both its application and interpretation by the judicial

Sherman Act of 1890

The *Sherman Act of 1890* contains two main prohibitions:

Section 1: "Every contract, combination in the form of trust or otherwise, or conspiracy, in restraint of trade or commerce among the several States, or with foreign nations, is hereby declared to be illegal. . . ."

Section 2: "Every person who shall monopolize, or attempt to monopolize, or combine or conspire with any other person or persons, to monopolize any part of the trade or commerce among the several States, or with foreign nations, shall be deemed guilty of a misdemeanor."

Clayton Act of 1914

The *Clayton Act of 1914* declared illegal four types of restrictive or monopolistic practices:

Section 2: "That it shall be unlawful for any person engaged in commerce, in the course of such commerce, either directly or indirectly to discriminate in price between different purchasers of commodities . . . where the effect of such discrimination may be to substantially lessen competition or tend to create a monopoly in any line of commerce." The act made "only due allowance for difference in the cost of selling or transportation, or discrimination in price in the same or different communities made in good faith." (See Robinson-Patman Act of 1936.)

Section 3: Forbids leasing or making "a sale or contract for sale of goods, wares, merchandise, machinery, supplies or other commodities whether patented or unpatented . . . on the condition, agreement or understanding that the lessee or purchaser shall not use or deal in the goods, wares . . . of a competitor or competitors of the lessor or seller. . . ." Extends only to those situations where the effect may be to "substantially lessen competition or tend to create a monopoly. . . ." This section basically prohibits the use of tying agreements between sellers and resellers.

Section 7: "That no corporation engaged in commerce shall acquire, directly or indirectly, the whole or any part of the stock or other share capital of another corporation engaged also in commerce, where the effect of such acquisition may be to substantially lessen competition between the corporation whose stock is so acquired and the corporation making the acquisition, or to restrain such commerce in any section or community, or tend to create a monopoly in any line of commerce." (See Celler-Kefauver Act of 1950.)

Section 8: ". . . no person at the same time shall be a director in any two or more corporations, any one of which has capital, surplus, and undivided profits aggregating more than $1 million . . . if such corporations are or shall have been theretofore by virtue of their business or location or operation competitors, so that the elimination of competition by agreement between them would constitute a violation of any provisions of the antitrust laws."

Federal Trade Commission Act of 1914

The *Federal Trade Commission Act of 1914* created the Federal Trade Commission to enforce the provisions of the Clayton Act.

Section 5: "Unfair methods of competition and unfair or deceptive acts or practices in commerce are hereby declared illegal." (See Wheeler-Lea act of 1938.)

Robinson-Patman Act of 1936

The *Robinson-Patman Act of 1936* was passed to replace Section 2 of the Clayton Act with a very elaborate set of provisions designed to prevent the powerful buyer from obtaining undue favors from its suppliers. Under the terms of the act, a seller in interstate trade may not discriminate in price between buyers under the following circumstances:

1. Buyers purchase goods of the same grade and quality.
2. The difference in price substantially lessens competition, tends to create a monopoly, and destroys, or presents competition with vendor or buyer, or customers of either.
3. The price difference does not merely reflect cost savings that result from the way or the quantity the favored purchaser buys or the price difference is not offered in good faith to meet the equally low price of one of the seller's competitors.

The act also deals with other practices:

4. "Dummy brokerage" allowances given by a seller to a buyer or a brokerage firm owned by the buyer are illegal.
5. Supplementary allowances, such as for advertising and promotion and services, must be made to all purchasers on a proportionately equal basis.
6. Buyers are prohibited from knowingly inducing discriminatory prices from sellers.

Wheeler-Lea Act of 1938

The *Wheeler-Lea Act of 1938* amended the Federal Trade Commission Act, sections as noted earlier. It also prohibited other practices that might injure the public without affecting competition. It also provides the FTC with jurisdiction over false advertising of food, drugs, cosmetics, and therapeutic devices.

Celler-Kefauver Act of 1950

The *Celler-Kefauver Act of 1950* revised the main provision of Section 7.1 of the Clayton Act. The purpose of the revision was to check mergers of all types. The new section reads as follows:

> "No corporation engaged in commerce shall acquire, directly or indirectly, the whole or any part of the stock or other share capital and no corporation subject to the jurisdiction of the Federal Trade Commission shall acquire the whole or any part of the assets of another corporation engaged also in commerce, where in any line of commerce in any section of the country, the effect of such acquisition may be substantially to lessen competition, or tend to create a monopoly."

Source: A. D. Neale and D. G. Goyder, *The Antitrust Laws of the U.S.A.: A Study of Competition Enforced by Law*, 3rd ed. (Cambridge: Cambridge University Press, 1980).

Figure 3–6 Summary of elements of major antitrust acts

system, there has been recognition that it is not complete. Since 1890 several major statutes have been implemented to amend the Sherman Act and to regulate marketing practices. Some aspects of inappropriate marketing behavior, such as conspiring to fix prices, are clearly described in the acts. Other aspects come from more general statements that are open for definition by the enforcement agencies. For example, the Federal Trade Commission (FTC) is given the authority to define and then declare unfair methods of competition. Figure 3–6 presents the major acts and their relevant sections.

The antitrust statutes require that every part of the marketing program be tested in terms of the possibility of being uncompetitive and unfair.[6] While price-fixing activities among competitors is clearly spelled out and per se illegal, whether any of the other activities is illegal may not be as clear. For example, a firm might want to develop a product strategy that includes several products that it does not currently produce. Because of time demands, it might be more appropriate to merge with a competitor. This, though, may lead to an antitrust suit for monopolization under Section 7 of the Clayton Act, as amended. Other areas to watch are the establishment of discount schedules and promotion allowances for purchasers and resellers; the marketer must be keenly aware of the requirements of the Robinson-Patman Act.

From time to time there are differences in philosophy in the application of the laws by the government. In the Reagan administration there has been a reluctance to actively invoke the antitrust laws in all cases. In 1983, though, the single largest antitrust case in American history was brought to a settlement with the breakup of the American Telephone and Telegraph Company.

The government is not the only enforcer of antitrust legislation. One firm can bring an antitrust suit against another firm. Instead of being simply a constraint on marketing behavior, then, the antitrust laws can be used as a competitive weapon. Late in 1983 the Federal Trade Commission approved the joint production arrangement between General Motors and Toyota to build a small car in the United States. The approval was sought by these firms to see if the joint venture would be attacked by the FTC as being unfair or harmful to competition. Other automobile companies, though, protested the product development arrangement between General Motors and Toyota.

Consumer Protection

The protection of consumer interests is included in the basic antitrust statutes. The assumption was that if firms engaged in great competition, the consumer was bound to benefit, since firms would pay close attention to consumer wants. While the assumption has merit, the antitrust statutes were not sufficiently strong enough to deal with the issues of the market as they evolved over the course of the present century. The vast changes in technology and the products and services made competition by itself unable to protect consumers and provide what they needed, and a new body of laws arose.

TABLE 3–1 Selected Consumer Protection Legislation

Year	Act	Features
1906	Pure Food and Drug Act	Prohibits adulterated food and drugs in interstate commerce.
1938	Federal Food, Drug and Cosmetic Act	Extended 1906 act to cosmetics and required premarketing clearance on drugs in matters of safety; also required clear product identification.
1939	Wool Products Labeling Act	Required correct labels for type and percentage of wool.
1953	Flammable Fabrics Act	Prohibited in interstate commerce any clothing or material that could easily ignite.
1962	Kefauver-Harris Drug Amendments	Required pretesting of drugs for safety and efficacy; labeling of drugs generically.
1966	Child Safety Act	Prevented the marketing of potentially harmful products; permitted Food and Drug Administration to remove potentially hazardous products.
1967	Wholesale Meat Act	Required state inspection standards to meet federal standards; ordered meat plants to be cleaned up.
1968	Consumer Credit Protection Act	Truth-in-lending required full disclosure of annual interest rates and other charges.
1969	Child Protection and Toy Safety Act	Ensured protection of children from toys and other products and substances intended for them.
1971	Fair Credit Reporting Act	Regulated the reporting and use of credit data.
1972	Consumer Product Safety Act	Created a Consumer Product Safety Commission that identifies and warns consumers of unsafe products.
1975	Magnuson-Moss Warranty/FTC Improvement Act	Made warranty language easy to understand; limited warranty provisions.
1976	Energy Policy and Conservation Act	Required disclosure of energy-efficient ratings for appliances.
1980	Fair Debt Collection Act	Protected debtors from abuse and harassment; prohibited use of unfair methods of debt collection.

Specific consumer protection legislation was developed in the first decade of this century as a result of the efforts of the so-called "muckrakers." The first piece of legislation was the Pure Food and Drug Act of 1906, which prohibited the adulteration and misbranding of foods and drugs sold in interstate commerce. Subsequent legislation covered many products and almost every part of the purchase decision process, including consumer credit, consumer product safety, environmental protection, freedom of information, and fair debt collection. A selected list of these acts is found in table 3–1.

The combination of consumer protection legislation and increasing levels of awareness and knowledge has created an important market segment composed of individuals who are actively concerned about the goods and services they consume. Some of their actions are supported by independent agencies such as Consumers Union, publishers of *Consumer Reports,* as well as by individual marketers who want consumers to know that they care about what they produce and market. Consumer protection is here to stay and will become more important as the complexity of what we consume becomes greater.

The wise marketer will recognize that fact and will attempt to develop programs that allow the firm to take advantages of the ideas behind the concept; instead of viewing these programs as constraints on the freedom to market, it is possible to look at them as elements to include in marketing programs. For example, in 1978, the Food and Drug Administration told manufacturers of suntan lotions to number their products on a scale of 1 to 15 according to how effectively the sunscreens blocked the rays of the sun. The reason was a growing concern by consumers about the possibilities of skin damage or even skin cancer from too much exposure to the sun and too little sunscreen. As part of this system, the manufacturers are allowed to state on the package that the use of a sunscreen can help prevent skin cancer. This idea has become a very effective promotional tool and the center of many advertising campaigns.[7]

The protection of consumer interests can be seen in recent legislation concerning allowable amounts of the pesticide and suspected carcinogen ethyl dibromide (EDB) in agricultural products. A number of packaged products, such as cake mixes and cereals, were found to contain high levels of EDB. Many of these products were ordered off the shelves of food stores, and both the federal government and various state governments set stringent standards for acceptable levels. Marketers were faced with the problem of reacting in a responsible manner, convincing consumers of their concern and goodwill in arranging recall programs, and revising marketing strategies for the affected products.[8]

The Technological Environment

Inventions and changes in technology have created a constant stream of new products, improvements in old products, and increased capacity for established industries. The search for better calculating machines led to the beginnings of the computer industry. The development and improvement of engines led to the growth of transportation industries. Improved fertilizers and agricultural methods have improved the quality and quantity of farm produce. Discoveries by medical researchers have led to the production and distribution of new drugs and treatments by pharmaceutical companies. One of the latest advances in this area is recombinant-DNA technology. One company, for example, developed a hormone that speeds up the growth of chickens by 15 percent, an advance that could allow poultry growers to get their chickens to market sooner.[9] Inventions, developments, and advances all form the **technological environment.**

Figure 3–7 The development of new technologies, such as glass optical fibers, has led to the tremendous growth of the telecommunications industry.

Courtesy of AT&T Bell Laboratories

The use of a technological advance affects a company in several ways. The effects largely depend on whether the company itself or a competitor introduces the advance. If one poultry grower started to use the growth hormone, for example, that company would have a competitive advantage until other companies also started to use it. Companies that did not use the growth hormone might be left behind. (These companies might be able to cater to a market segment that wanted "naturally grown" chickens, though, if such a segment existed.)

Another possible effect may be to make a company or its products obsolete. The standard example is the buggy-whip factory after the growth of the automobile industry. Electric and electronic typewriters and word processors have made manual typewriters obsolete. Color television sets have almost made black-and-white television sets obsolete. And so on.

In terms of the analytical perspective in figure 3–2, the technological environment can fall into three quadrants. A company's internal research and development department can come up with advances and refinements of present products. This is internal and controllable. The advances can come from another company or inventor; these are external. They can be controlled to some extent if a company can match the advances. They are uncontrollable if the company does not have the ability to match the advances.

The telecommunications industry provides a strong example of the effects of the technological environment. It has largely been created by the development of new technologies. Moreover, the rapid development of even newer technologies makes some of the new equipment obsolete almost as soon as it is installed. Let's look at a few of these advances.

— The development of glass optical fibers that carry pulses of light rather than electrical signals has vastly increased the speed and capacity of transmission cables.
— The development of cellular radio, with its computer-controlled use of radio frequencies, will allow telephones in all cars and vehicles.
— The use of communications satellites will allow wider communication, even in areas where there are no telephone lines.
— A new integrated-services digital network turns standard electrical waves into a digital code understood by computers, allowing the transmission of data as well as voices along telephone and computer links.

The development of new technologies and the ability to translate these technologies into forms usable by and desirable to consumers would give a company in this field an advantage over its competitors. Moreover, companies in the field must continue to keep up with the others in terms of technology if they are to continue to be viable competitors.

Cultural and Social Environments

The **cultural and social environments** consist of a set of factors, attitudes and beliefs, held by a society that give overall direction to behavior in economic, political, and social affairs. Cultural and social factors are the most difficult for marketers to control and predict, as they are the most complex. More likely, marketers must understand and respond to these factors. Unlike public policy issues, where one can expect more consumer protection legislation under a Democratic president and less under a Republican one, cultural and social forces seem to change on their own. While it is true that marketing can affect the social and cultural forces to some degree, it is not fully clear that marketers attempt to do so. It is certainly a question open to great debate as to whether *Playboy* magazine originally attempted to affect sexuality or whether Hugh Heffner simply perceived change and catered to it.

Some Cultural and Social Factors

Some of the cultural and social factors that are directly important to marketing include marriage, the family and family formation, the work ethic, religion, morality and honesty, individuality, respect for the law, appreciation for people who are different, and self-reliance. The list could obviously be extended to include other items. As these factors change, they affect how people behave in the marketplace. The details of these factors and their effects on marketers will be discussed in chapter 7. (Focus 3–2 provides a preview.)

3–2 Focus on Marketing Strategy
HOW SOCIAL CHANGES AFFECT COMPANIES' PLANS

The demographic characteristics of the United States are changing. Most obvious of these changes is the aging of the population, due to increased longevity and declining birth rates. For the first time, people over 65 outnumber teenagers, and this disparity is expected to increase in the future. The baby boomers are now in their late twenties and thirties. Many of them are now setting up traditional (that is, husband and wife) households. Women are working and having fewer children, so that family income is rising and family size decreasing.

These changes have far-reaching implications for all marketers, because they mean that the market is changing. Sales of record albums and movie tickets, normally bought heavily by young people, have started to decline, while the fitness, health care, and financial services desired by those of middle age are expanding. In the relatively near future we can expect the following: a decline in the number of households with members under 25 years of age (which will spell potential trouble for home builders, realtors, building materials industries, and construction workers); more two-career families with high incomes (over $50,000 per year) who will need new investment services and convenience foods; and a shortage of young, cheap labor, which could eat into the profits of firms (such as restaurants) that rely on that resource. A little further down the road, when the second baby boom hits, we can expect a shortage of public schools (many of which are now closing due to dropping enrollment) and an increased demand for private-school tuition tax breaks.

When the market changes, marketers must follow suit, and many already have. Consumer goods are no longer so heavily geared to large families. Sears, Roebuck carries a greater range of appliances, including many smaller-sized models. Supermarket operators, finding that the average number of items bought is decreasing along with the portion sizes chosen, respond by doubling the number of express lanes and stocking shelves with smaller cans. Levi Strauss manufactures more jeans in larger waist sizes for older, heavier purchasers, and retail clothing stores are shifting the focus of their women's clothing from juniors to larger sizes. Insurance companies and financial institutions are developing an array of programs, from IRAs and direct banking to supplemental insurance policies, aimed at a population thinking more and more about financial security and retirement. And travel companies offer special senior citizen packages (fly wherever you want in the United States all year long for only $1,200, for example).

Nor are the changes confined to products. Products must be promoted and therefore advertised, and this advertising must reach the groups likely to make purchases. So McDonald's, traditionally a youth-oriented company, has expanded its adult target market to include people as old as 50 (whereas 34 had been the previous limit), and major advertisers are including many more older people in their commercials, thereby producing a mini-boom for silver-haired models and actors.

More changes will certainly occur, and smart marketers will watch them closely and adjust their production, distribution, and marketing strategies accordingly—or they will lose out to their competitors.

Sources: Ewart Rouse, "The Graying of America—and Its Retailing," *The Philadelphia Inquirer*, March 27, 1983, p. 1D; and Charles Koshetz, "Couples Marrying More, Spending More," *USA Today*, November 11, 1983, p. 1A.

Also important to the marketer is the concept that not all individuals in a society share all of the factors in the same way; there are subcultures within any society. It is often difficult to define in specific terms what each of the subcultures looks like. More importantly, it is very difficult to make quantitative estimates about the number of people who belong to any subculture, that is, share a common set of these values.

One way of understanding change in these factors is to attempt to define the "traditional" values and then contrast them with what might be termed the "contemporary" values. Of course, what may be contemporary today may well become the traditional value of a future time; and in some cases values that once were traditional may become contemporary ones, much like items of clothing that may be in or out of vogue across several fashion cycles.

At one time, for example, American values were based on a rural existence. Advertisements stressed the simple values of families together; Norman Rockwell, the artist, documented so much of this type of life on the covers of the *Saturday Evening Post.* This rural (traditional) value has given way to cosmopolitan values; many advertisements stress the large city; New York is the "Big Apple." Yet, at the same time, there has been a recent movement back to the country, albeit with all the trappings of the cosmopolitan setting.

Let us look at one particular factor—the change of the role and status of women in the American work force—and see how it affects marketing decisions. Over the past years the numbers and percentage of women in the American workplace have increased significantly. In 1970, 38.1 percent of the work force over 16 years of age was female; by June 1982, that had increased to 43.4 percent. At the same time, the number of female workers had increased from 31.3 million to 47.8 million.[10] This increase in women's participation in the labor force came about as the result of several factors: an increased need for financial stability by families through a second income; a change in social values leading to the acceptance of women as professional workers and managers; and the effects of federal legislation promoting affirmative action and equal opportunities for women. The results are worth looking at.[11]

An overall result has been an increase in family and individual incomes and in purchasing power. Another result has been a change in the structure of the family and a postponement of parenthood. This led to a reevaluation of the baby food and baby products markets; for example, Gerber's went from proclaiming that "babies are our only business" to "babies are our business"—not simply a minor sleight of hand as the firm attempted to develop other product lines that were not dependent on babies. Offsetting the decrease in demand for these products was the new, increased demand for child care. Firms such as Kindercare developed in response to the need of working mothers for competent daytime care for their children.

The effects on retailing were also noticeable. Dual-career families required nontraditional shopping times, beyond the traditional 9–6. At the same time, the fact that women were not home during the day led door-to-door merchants to

Chapter 3 / The Marketing Environment

readjust their marketing activities to include evening sales. They also had to be ready to offer products to men who were at home during the day. Also, fewer shopping hours gave mail-order firms an important opportunity to redevelop markets, since their catalogs could be examined at any time of the day or night. Mail-order companies were greatly aided by the new technologies in communications, such as the 800 numbers, which allow shoppers to place orders anytime, day or night.

There are many other changes due to the increase of women in the work force. What is important to recognize is that a social factor can affect the marketing program of a firm at all levels.

While it is easy to describe a cultural or social change once it has taken place, it is more difficult to trace fully all of the causes and effects. It is even more difficult to know how to react to each of the possible outcomes. It is most difficult to predict when such a change will take place and plan for it. Marketers can be aware, though, that social and economic factors affect marketing, that they do change over time, and that they should be monitored if they touch any particular business.

Summary

Environmental factors affecting marketing decisions are either internal or external to the firm and fall somewhere on the scale of 100 percent controllable to completely uncontrollable.

The economic environment consists of the factors that affect the ability of suppliers to provide goods and services and the ability of buyers to purchase those goods and services. The world economic environment is the combination of all national, regional, and local environments reflecting the desires of the various societies that comprise them. Although the economic environment for each society varies, each is intertwined with that of every other country. The national economic environment includes conditions within a country that affect demand, such as the availability of money, interest rates, and credit. Regional and local economic environments may differ greatly from nationwide ones.

The competitive environment is the marketplace in which firms compete among themselves for business and resources. A firm's control over the competitive environment is affected by its resources and whether management is active or reactive in its policies.

Marketers study the behavior of competitors in order to decide what their response should be to the changes in the competitive actions of another. Competition also occurs within large companies when the marketers of the company's numerous products vie for resources.

Public policy includes any federal, state, or local government actions that affect the operation of the marketing system. Economic regulation is the specific government control over the activities of firms. Subsidies are public policies that affect marketing by supporting industries or encouraging them to engage in certain activities. Fiscal and monetary policies affect marketing through changes in the amount of money that consumers have to spend. Government procurement policies set the procedures and priorities followed by governments in the purchase of goods and services and the contracting of research and development.

Antitrust legislation is the attempt to maintain competition among business firms by the diffusion of economic power so that market forces will be maximized. Antitrust statutes are designed to protect consumers by promoting competition among firms.

A technological advance can affect a company in different ways, depending on whether the company itself developed the advance or a competitor did. Another effect of a technological advance may be that it renders a company or product obsolete.

The cultural and social environments consist of the attitudes and beliefs held by a society that give overall direction to behavior in economic, political, and social affairs. Not all individuals in a society share all of these beliefs in the same way, however.

Questions for Discussion

1. "Economic environment affects the large firms rather than the small firms." Comment.
2. Are U.S. firms necessarily affected more by the state of the international economy than that of the domestic national economy? Explain.
3. Discuss in what different ways marketing decisions can govern the major elements of the economic environment.
4. Distinguish clearly between internal and external competition and the corresponding marketing implications.
5. Explain the goal of antitrust legislation and the role such legislation plays in marketing decisions.
6. Examine the role of consumer protection in marketing.
7. Compare the "traditional" and "contemporary" cultural values in terms of their impact on major marketing decisions of companies.
8. In what specific ways have marketing programs of industries been reshaped by deregulation?
9. Evaluate the impact of technological change on marketing decisions.

References

1. The discussions of the telecommunications industry here and throughout the chapter are based on "Telecommunications: The Global Battle," *Business Week,* October 24, 1983, pp. 126–48; "Telecommunications," *Business Week,* October 11, 1982, pp. 60–66; "A World of Communications Wonders," *U.S. News & World Report,* April 9, 1984, pp. 59–63; and "The Long-Distance Runners," *Time,* June 11, 1984, pp. 46–47.

2. "Why Wine Makers Aren't Breaking Out the Bubbly," *Business Week*, October 24, 1983, pp. 36B–36F.
3. "Satellites Outpace Customers," *New York Times*, April 10, 1984, p. D1.
4. This section is based on John C. Narver and Ronald Savitt, *The Marketing Economy; An Analytical Approach* (New York: Holt, Rinehart and Winston, 1971), chap. 14, especially pp. 345–49.
5. "State Machine Products, Inc.," *Inc.*, December 1983, p. 107.
6. G. David Hughes, "Antitrust Caveats for the Marketing Planner," *Harvard Business Review*, March–April 1978, p. 40.
7. Barbara Rudolph, "Don't Let the Sunshine In," *Forbes*, June 21, 1982, pp. 80–81.
8. "Food Having EDB Found on Shelves," *New York Times*, February 2, 1984, p. D22.
9. "Biotechnology Struts into the Hen House," *Business Week*, April 11, 1983, p. 36.
10. "Employment Status of the Noninstitutional Population 16 Years Old and Over: 1947 to 1982," *Statistical Abstracts of the United States, 1982–83*, 103rd ed. (Washington, D.C.: U.S. Bureau of the Census, 1982), p. 375.
11. This section based on: Delbert J. Duncan, Stanley C. Hollander, and Ronald Savitt, *Modern Retailing Management; Basic Concepts and Practices*, 10th ed. (Homewood, Ill.: Irwin, 1983), pp. 19–20.

CASES FOR PART I

1 Tylenol

At the beginning of 1983, executives at Johnson & Johnson were facing an unprecedented crisis. One of their leading brands, Tylenol, had been linked to the deaths of seven people, and the sales of the product had plummeted. Now the marketing executives had to find a marketing strategy to bring back the lost sales, if, indeed, the brand could be saved at all.

In 1982, Tylenol was a highly successful internal analgesic (painkiller), which was available without prescription in both tablet and capsule form. The previous year, Tylenol generated sales of $400 million and profits of around $70 million. Although initially marketed only as a prescription drug, Tylenol gained over-the-counter (OTC) status in 1975 and quickly gained 37 percent of the nonprescription painkiller market. In the process of gaining this dominant market share, Tylenol had become the nation's best-selling OTC drug.

A key component of Tylenol's marketing strategy was product differentiation. In a market where most of the leading products contained essentially the same ingredient (aspirin) and worked in the same way, it was crucial for Tylenol to show that its product was different—that Tylenol contained a different ingredient (acetaminophen) and that it worked in a different way. Between 1977 and 1982, Johnson & Johnson spent more than $85 million to advertise Tylenol. A key message of this advertising was to stress that not only was Tylenol different than aspirin-based products, it was also safer in that people who used it had fewer stomach problems and that there was no risk of Reyes syndrome developing in children.

In October 1982, Johnson & Johnson executives were shocked to hear that seven people in the Chicago area died after taking Extra-Strength Tylenol capsules. The police quickly determined that the capsules had been laced with cyanide; it seemed that an unknown perpetrator had tampered with the capsules before they reached consumers. Sales of all Tylenol products plummeted as fearful consumers responded to the widely publicized poisonings. Industry analysts predicted severe problems for Johnson & Johnson, believing that the adverse publicity would taint the name of the manufacturer and might affect the sales of other Johnson & Johnson products.

Tylenol's market share quickly fell from 35 percent to 7 percent as consumers avoided both Tylenol capsules and tablets. As surveys indicated that a majority of Tylenol users would probably not purchase Tylenol again, Madison Avenue executives agreed that the brand name would never recover.

The situation demanded quick action, but what action? Many factors had to be considered. Officials in a number of cities, including Chicago, ordered the product taken off the shelves. Numerous other sources advised Johnson & Johnson against a massive recall of the capsules. The Food and Drug Administration (FDA) for one feared that a recall might trigger panic; the FBI suggested that recalling the medication might encourage both the unknown assailant and others with criminal intentions.

Planning its actions carefully, Johnson & Johnson swiftly withdrew and destroyed 31 million bottles of Tylenol capsules nationwide and then offered a $100,000 reward for information leading to the arrest of those responsible for the poisonings. The company also left Tylenol tablets (the most widely purchased form of the product, prior to the tragedy) on the market.

Instead of being defensive about the deaths, Johnson & Johnson opened its doors, cooperating actively in the investigation and facing the issue publicly. Johnson & Johnson chairman James Burke appeared on the *Phil Donahue Show* and *60 Minutes* talking about the trust that the company and the brand name had created over the years and emphasizing the company's willingness and efforts to rebuild that trust. He urged customers to buy Tylenol tablets until the capsules were introduced with new tamperproof packaging. Other actions included suspending regular brand advertising for Tylenol and, instead, running public-service messages that discussed tamperproof packaging and the goodwill between the company and the public.

At the same time, Johnson & Johnson started to develop new and safer packaging. The company's executives contacted their suppliers and began meeting with the companies that would be involved in redesigning the Tylenol package. The new packaging that was developed included gluing the ends of the boxes, a plastic band around the bottle that had to be broken before the bottle could be opened, and an aluminum seal across the bottle opening. Just ten weeks after the product had been withdrawn, the company was ready to reissue the capsules in their new, triple-sealed packages. The question facing Johnson & Johnson remained, however. The package was ready, but was the market ready for Tylenol?

Although the FDA had formally notified Johnson & Johnson that the tampering did not occur at the plant and had, most likely, happened at the retail level, the company faced an arduous and expensive battle. The mystery surrounding the poisonings and the fears of consumers posed challenges to the company. Given the uncertainties in the marketplace and the enormous costs involved, reissuing the capsules involved tremendous risks.

To help reduce the uncertainties, Johnson & Johnson conducted marketing research to learn more about consumer attitudes. This research indicated that many people did not realize that only Tylenol capsules, and not tablets, were involved in the tampering. Moreover, many did not realize that all of the authorities (both the police and the FDA) had exonerated the company and that the deaths were confined to the Chicago area. The research also showed that consumers wanted to hear something from the company. Even those who knew, intellectually, that the product did not pose danger couldn't, emotionally, overcome the fear of returning to it. The research showed that 80 percent of all Tylenol users had first used the product at the suggestion of their doctors, dentists, or druggists, but most of them no longer planned to use it. With this information, the marketing managers prepared to make their decision.

Sources: Based on Dennis Kneale, "Tylenol, the Painkiller, Gives Rivals Headache in Stores and in Court," *Wall Street Journal,* September 2, 1982, p. 1; Michael Waldholz and Dennis Kneale, "Tylenol's Maker Tries to Regain Good Image in Wake of Tragedy," *Wall Street Journal,* October 8, 1982, p. 1; Pamela G. Hollie, "Drug Rules Met on Time," *New York Times,* February 7, 1983, p. D1; and Michael Waldholz, "Tylenol Maker Mounting Campaign to Restore Trust of Doctors, Buyers," *Wall Street Journal,* October 29, 1982, p. 33.

Questions

1. Should Johnson & Johnson withdraw all Tylenol products from the market and reintroduce acetaminophen (the chemical name of Tylenol) under a new, untainted brand name? Why?
2. If Tylenol products are left on the market, should Johnson & Johnson reintroduce the capsules?
3. What three steps would you recommend to Johnson & Johnson for the reintroduction of the Tylenol capsules?
4. What role can advertising play in overcoming a negative brand image?
5. Would your decisions about this case have been different if the product had a low-market share, such as the analgesic Datril, instead of leading the market? Why?
6. One of the Johnson & Johnson responses to the Tylenol tragedy was to introduce safer packaging. Other firms quickly adopted the same strategy for their OTC products. Should this kind of packaging have been used before the tragedies? Why, or why not? Who should be responsible for the safety of packages?

2 General Motors and the Small-Car Market

Late in 1983, senior management at the General Motors Corporation (GM), was wrestling with a major problem. The corporation had experienced a series of declines in market share and a reduction in overall sales. While the economic recovery had improved the company's performance in 1983, General Motors was still reeling from the $763 million dollar loss reported for 1980—the first losing year the company had experienced since the Depression.

Particularly troubling to management was the performance of GM's small cars. General Motors sold proportionally fewer small cars than any other major automobile manufacturer. Yet the small-car market continued to be one of the healthiest segments of the automotive industry with demand for small cars growing steadily. Unfortunately for GM, Japanese car manufacturers were becoming increasingly competitive and their share of the small-car market was increasing. The problem facing GM management was how to rekindle their small-car business.

Under the stewardship of Alfred E. Sloan, GM's first chairman, the corporation had been divided into five divisions: Chevrolet, Pontiac, Oldsmobile, Buick, and Cadillac. The overall product line that resulted included a product in each market segment, with no duplication (either between or within divisions) in any of the automobile market's price and size segments.

The company's traditional marketing strategy involved selling Chevrolets and Pontiacs to younger buyers and trading those buyers up to larger (and more expensive) Oldsmobiles, Buicks, and, eventually, Cadillacs as the buyers grew older and more affluent. The goal of this strategy was to keep customers in the General Motors family throughout their lives. Obviously, the key to this strategy was getting the first-time car buyers to purchase a GM car. This task was the principal function of the Chevrolet and Pontiac lines. Now the ability of these divisions to succeed in that crucial task was coming into question.

Chevrolet, which had a 20.8 percent share of the total U.S. car market in 1978, had dropped to a market share of only 14.8 percent by 1983. Pontiac, which had a 7.9 percent market share in 1978, had dropped to a 6 percent share in 1983. The two divisions that had the responsibility for drawing new customers into the General Motors family had lost nearly a quarter of their combined market share in just five years. Part of the reason for this precipitous decline was that the purchasing behavior for first-time car buyers had changed.

Traditionally, the way first-time consumers entered the car market was to focus their shopping on the less expensive lines of cars from a given manufacturer, in GM's case the Chevrolet and Pontiac lines. Most of the cars in those lines were low-priced and generally similar in size—the principal intraline differentiation were in features and options. But those market conditions were changing. Where as recently as 1950 GM sold only its five initial lines, by 1983 (the 1984 model year) GM offered 34 different lines. There were lower-priced cars in each line, and the distinctions between lines became blurred. It was no longer clear what was a Chevy and what was an Olds—except that the Olds cost more. This left many consumers confused.

At the very low end of the market, the small Chevrolets (such as the Chevette) offered little luxury, particularly when compared with Japanese cars that included far more features as standard equipment. Thus, to the consumer who wanted to spend the least possible money for a new car, the Japanese models seemed a good value. At the same time, many of the consumers who bought that first car from GM bought the small car that was most comparable to the Japanese in terms of features—the small cars in the lines that had once been the GM top end—Olds and Buick. This meant that the traditional trade-up strategy might not work when these consumers returned to the market for their next cars. They might want something more "elegant" than the line of their first car.

The problems of brand identity were made worse by the GM organizational structure. After the 1973 oil embargo, GM had scaled down the size of all cars and set up "project centers" without clearly defined responsibilities. To cut costs, GM allowed more and more car divisions to share nearly identical body styles. Designers were given only vague direction and responsibility. Engineering was spread among the corporation's five car divisions, the Fisher Body Division, and the GM Assembly Division. For example, Buick specialized in brakes, Pontiac in rear suspensions, and the Fisher Body Division in car bodies and body panels. Under this structure, middle management mushroomed. Too little cost accountability and diffused responsibility for decisions regarding each model posed an increasing problem.

In early 1984, GM announced its most extensive reorganization ever. Gone were the five basic car divisions and Fisher Body. In their place were two new units. One unit was for small cars (which would be engineered and built by Chevrolet, Pontiac, and GM Canada). The other unit was for large and middle-sized cars, engineered and built by Buick, Oldsmobile, and Cadillac.

Top management expected that the reorganization would help their marketing problems. The unresolved question was exactly what steps should be taken in the marketplace.

Sources: Based on John Holusha, "G.M.'s Overhaul: A Return to Basics," *New York Times*, January 15, 1984, p. F1; "Can GM Solve Its Identity Crisis?" *Business Week*, January 23, 1984, pp. 16–17; and John Koten, "GM Seeks to Solve Corporate Ills That Persist Despite Rebound in Finances," *Wall Street Journal*, January 12, 1984, p. 8.

Questions

1. Evaluate what had happened to the GM segmentation and differentiation strategies before the reorganization.
2. Is reorganization a marketing action?
3. Should GM cut back from the 34 lines of cars they have? If yes, how far should they cut back? (Conceptually, the reorganization could result in only two lines!)

4. If GM cuts back on some of its existing lines, how should they expect the marketplace to react?
5. How would you expect GM's dealers to react to this reorganization? Will the reorganization affect the dealers? Should it matter to GM?
6. Will consumers, in general, be aware of the new GM organization? How will it affect them?

PART II
Target Marketing

OBJECTIVES

1. To highlight the importance of formulating a business definition before determining the corporate mission and objectives.

2. To identify the components involved in the formulation of a business definition and the determination of the company's mission and objectives.

3. To describe the different approaches for developing a business definition and breaking a company into manageable strategic business units.

4. To identify the components of and the methods employed in forecasting market demand.

5. To provide a general overview of the role of marketing strategy in the development of a company's marketing plan.

4

Defining the Business

CBS Cable Television provided a glittering array of classy entertainment, from the ballet *Swan Lake* to performances by the jazz musician Count Basie. Its lavish programming included Royal Shakespeare Company productions, opera, dance, and made-for-television dramas with top actors. The cable company created 60 percent of its own programming, although similar cable channels aired less than half that amount of original programs. Critics raved about CBS Cable and heralded it as a highbrow oasis among the wasteland of mass-market series on broadcast television.

After just a few years in operation, however, CBS Cable and its television theater went dark. The channel had lost more than $30 million in 1982 alone. Also severely debt-ridden were its smaller cable competitors, ARTS network of ABC and another channel, BRAVO, both offering distinguished cultural fare.

In order to survive, CBS Cable needed to decide how or if it was going to make money. It had four potential sources of revenue: (1) cable operators, who would subscribe to the service and, in turn, offer it to private residences as part of their basic service; (2) a pay service, which could be connected directly to private residences; (3) advertisers, who would pay for air time to reach the CBS Cable viewer; and (4) other networks, who would pay to use the original programs developed by CBS Cable. Each of these sources of revenue focused on different customers and had a different set of competitors; pursuing each required CBS Cable to formulate a unique business definition. Since trying to push equally on all four fronts would have diluted marketing efforts and potential success, CBS Cable, to focus its efforts, needed to define what its primary business was. With a clear business definition, CBS Cable could have assessed what it would have taken to increase customer demand, based on its understanding of the

customers and its determination of how to provide a competitively superior product.

Once the business was clearly defined, at least internally, the company had to ask whether the business was attractive enough to warrant more investment or whether the losses were insurmountable and likely to continue, thus demanding a withdrawal from the market.

Should CBS Cable and other similar cable channels have ever entered this business? Probably not. Cable television executives overestimated their potential audience and failed to attract their predicted number of viewers. Similarly, they failed to attract other sources of revenue. In trying to lure both viewers and advertisers, the cable channels inaccurately predicted the demand for cultural entertainment and access to viewers interested in the arts.[1]

Let's examine how those predictions, also called forecasts, went wrong. In some instances, CBS Cable attempted to satisfy a demand that didn't exist. For example, CBS Cable had planned to finance expensive programming by selling rights to foreign markets, especially to the European television market. Yet the company failed to recognize a lack of demand, as European governments restrict imported programs, and the programs that are bought are popular ones like "Dallas" and "Charlie's Angels."[2]

Another problem was faulty forecasting caused by the cable channels' skewed perception of their customers'—both viewers and advertisers—needs. CBS Cable and ARTS, for example, aimed for college-educated viewers between 25 and 45 years of age, with annual incomes of at least $25,000.[3] Cable television executives reasoned that this audience was worthwhile because broadcast television did not satisfy these viewers' entertainment needs. They also believed that advertisers would welcome the opportunity to reach an affluent, educated audience. Both assumptions proved to be wrong.

The targeted pay service viewers rarely looked to television for entertainment. When a new production of *Hamlet* was aired on public television, for example, only 4.7 percent of the viewing audience switched on the channel.[4] Combined cable programming from CBS Cable and ARTS reached only a small audience, and, additionally, this small audience was sliced up by several competitors. "It's questionable," according to one Wall Street analyst before CBS Cable collapsed, "whether there is a big enough pie to support one cultural service, much less five."[5]

Advertisers were not drawn to the cable television channels. One reason was that the number of viewers was too small to be measured by the Nielsen rating system. Advertisers depend on the Nielsen ratings to decide whether to purchase commercial time on broadcast networks, and without such information from cable channels they were unwilling to buy access to a cable audience. Nor could companies like CBS Cable provide the demographic data about their viewers that advertisers use in planning their campaigns.[6]

Finally, CBS Cable could not attract cable operators. These potential customers might have been interested in adding CBS Cable to the program mix they offered subscribers if they felt it would increase the number of subscribers. Unfortunately, not enough operators believed that a cultural channel would be a major lure.

The cable channels' difficulties in satisfying customer needs and in forecasting the demand for their product reflect changing customer needs, competitors, and goals. The variety of programming available on cable television, for example, ranges from 24-hour news and sports shows to presentations like "The Haunted Mouth" from the American Dental Association.[7] Given this vast range of possibilities, many cable channels are defining their business in new ways.

Moving away from entertainment, some cable companies, including Warner Amex Communications and American Television Communications, have defined their business as business communication, serving corporate clients. Rather than offer programming in order to sell commercial time to advertisers, these companies plan to provide a range of communication services, including transmitting voices, pictures, and computer data. Their capabilities should meet the needs of corporations that are always looking for more economical ways to transmit data and to link headquarters with branch offices.

In defining business communication, cable companies have not only analyzed their customers' needs but have also forecasted a heavy demand. Industry analysts agree that cable companies could grab an $11 billion share of the business telecommunications market by 1990. Furthermore, companies like Warner Amex have also identified as their competition companies like AT&T, MCI, and Western Union—all new and unfamiliar competitors to television companies.[8] In response to the most basic question that a company can ask, "Should we be in this business?" the answer seems to be "yes" for these cable companies.

The Business Definition

All of these various cable companies have gone through the process of defining the nature of their business. Some have been more successful than others in understanding the basic characteristics of their operations. But how does a company actually go about defining its business?

To formulate a **business definition,** a company must specify (1) the market it plans to serve and (2) the general type of product or service it will promote to the specific market. This involves identifying the customer needs to be satisfied, the company's competitors, and the company's strengths and weaknesses (see fig. 4–1).

Identifying Needs to Be Satisfied

As discussed in chapter 1, the marketing concept involves satisfying customers' needs. With a set of potential customers in mind, a company can identify the needs that it must satisfy. Companies cannot please every customer; rather, they must choose the sets of customers, or market segments, whose needs they are best equipped to satisfy. In chapter 9, we will discuss the concepts and methods of segmentation. For the present, it is important to remember that to define its business, a company must identify exactly which customers and which customer needs it plans to satisfy.

Identifying Competitors

Another component of defining a business is identifying a firm's appropriate competitors. Once customers have been chosen and their needs identified, companies can see which other businesses are seeking a share of the same market. Given the range of competitors, marketers can sometimes make mistakes in identifying competitors. Some competitors are obvious, but others may be missed because they supply the same product or service in an unusual way. With a clear business definition, companies are more likely to recognize all their competitors. In the case of cable television companies' expanding into business communications, for instance, we saw that companies like Warner Amex have identified competitors outside the field of television.

- Identification of customer needs to be satisfied
- Identification of the company's competitors
- Identification of the company's strengths and weaknesses

Figure 4–1 The components of a business definition

TABLE 4–1 Alternative Business Definitions in the Television Industry

Business Definition	Product	Customers	Needs Satisfied	Competitors	Strengths (and Weaknesses)
1. Entertainment	Programming	Viewers	Entertainment	Other television networks	Popular programs (Unpopular programs)
2. Advertising	Access to viewers	Advertisers	Access to targeted customers	All media	Ability to compete against other media; ability to attract viewers (Inability to compete or to attract viewers)

Identifying Strengths and Weaknesses

The third component of a sound business definition is the identification of the company's strengths and weaknesses within a given market. That is, firms need to decide whether their overall capabilities, in addition to the product, will fit the demands of the targeted market. A firm's strengths can include advantages in technological expertise, distribution channels, and cost. For instance, when the makers of Campbell's Soup decided to enter the frozen foods market, they could count on their strength in distribution; from marketing Campbell's Soup to grocers, the soup makers had already developed the appropriate distribution channels for their new product. Such advantages not only indicate that a company will fit its market, but they can also give a product a distinctive edge over the competition.

How a Business Definition Works

To show how an organization might go about defining its business, we will look at organizations in television, education, and the hotel industries.

Defining the business of the television industry. In our earlier discussion of cable networks, we found that several cable companies counted heavily on attracting advertising revenue to finance lavish programming. Yet they suffered huge losses when only a few advertisers actually bought time. As these difficulties suggest, television may be defined more broadly as an advertising, rather than an entertainment, business. To look at this notion in more detail, let's compare two business definitions of a national network like the American Broadcasting Company (ABC) (see table 4–1).

It's easy, at first glance, to say that ABC is in the entertainment business. In formulating this business definition, ABC is identifying its product as programming and its goal as satisfying the needs of viewers, the customers, by airing programs that appeal to the tastes of the viewing audience. The customers, however, pay nothing for the product. Competitors of ABC, from this perspective, are other networks: CBS, NBC, and, to a certain extent, public and cable television. ABC's major strengths and weaknesses are determined by the programs that viewers watch and those that make people switch to another channel. With such a definition, ABC finds itself in a secure position. On the average, it should capture about 30 percent of the market, or perhaps 20 percent in a particular time slot if a program fails to appeal to the customers.

From another point of view, television is in the advertising business. By formulating this alternate business definition, ABC identifies its product as access to a viewing audience and its customers as the advertising market. Advertisers, rather than viewers, are the true customers of television and the true source of revenue, since advertisers actually pay for services that the network provides. In fact, advertising dollars support the network.

Adopting this second business definition, ABC must now consider all media, not just other television networks, as its competition. In this case, ABC's potential market share drops substantially. Competition can become fierce if magazines, for example, start to offer lower rates to advertisers, prompting a decline in the demand for commercial time on networks.

The distinction, for television, between the entertainment and advertising business grows sharper if we consider the price of the product sold by each business. For example, the price for programs sold by the entertainment business is hard to determine. We could argue that the price is zero, as viewers do not directly pay for any program on broadcast television and, thus, do not provide revenue. On the other hand, television as an advertising business can charge a great deal for its product, depending on the type of audience it delivers.

Although successful programming will draw millions of viewers to the television set, programming itself is not a product if we adhere to the second business definition for ABC. Instead, programming is a part of the manufacturing process that allows the network to produce a certain type and size of viewing audience, such as the audience for daytime soap operas. ABC can then sell access to this audience to companies like Procter & Gamble. In persuading Procter & Gamble to purchase a 30-second commercial spot on a top-rated soap opera, for example, ABC must demonstrate that the viewers of this program share the income, family size, tastes, and other characteristics that Procter & Gamble deems most appropriate for the product it is promoting. That is, ABC must ascertain that its product answers the needs of its customers, the advertisers.

To continue with the guidelines for defining a business, we find that ABC can look at its strengths and weaknesses in a different light. These qualities involve its ability to compete for the kind of viewers valuable to advertisers, those interested in the advertisers' products.

Defining the business of a university's MBA program. What is the business of a university offering an MBA program? The university can formulate the business definition of education. In that case, the school is selling the product of an education to students, who are the customers. To meet the needs of its customers for the education leading to an MBA degree, the university can offer a solid range of classes taught by a superlative faculty, excellent research facilities, and an up-to-date, outstanding library. The creation of such faculty and academic resources then becomes an element in the manufacturing process. The university can identify competitors as other institutions offering an MBA program of the same caliber. To measure its strengths and weaknesses, it can also examine the number of scholarly honors won by the faculty, the quality of research conducted by the faculty, and the strengths of the curriculum.

In taking another point of view, the university can formulate the business definition as providing opportunities to expand careers. Its product becomes job opportunities, and its customers, although still students, have somewhat different needs from those seeking the best education. The university must take different steps to meet these needs. Rather than invest its resources in a first-class library and faculty, the school will devote its energies to establishing an active and effective placement office that attracts on-campus recruiters from many of the best corporations. From the perspective of this second business definition, we can consider the placement office as a part of the manufacturing process. It creates the job opportunities that the school is selling.

In our alternate definition, competitors again include schools offering an MBA program on the same level. But this definition requires the university to consider a broader range of competitors, including placement services and employment agencies that offer aspiring professionals a step up on the career ladder. To define its business further, the university considers its strengths and weaknesses in terms of job opportunities created. For example, career-minded students will decide if a school offers a superior MBA program by looking at the average starting salary of the program's graduates, the number of interviews conducted on campus, the types of jobs that graduates have held, and the number of alumni who have become chief executive officers. The university will want to make sure that it is strong in these areas.

From contrasting these two business definitions for a university offering an MBA program (see table 4–2), you can see that different business definitions lead to different allocations of resources and to different messages to customers regarding the school's best features. As in any industry, the university must have a firm

TABLE 4–2   Alternative Business Definitions for a University

Business Definition	Product	Customers	Needs Satisfied	Competitors	Strengths (and Weaknesses)
1. Education	Education, including classes, faculty, and facilities	Students	Education leading to MBA degree	Other universities offering MBA program	Quality of curriculum; quality of faculty
2. Providing opportunities to expand careers	Job opportunities	Students	Preparation for jobs; access to employers	Other universities offering MBA program; placement services; employment agencies	Success of past students; number of opportunities created by placement center

TABLE 4–3 Alternative Business Definitions in the Hotel Industry

Business Definition	Product	Customers	Needs Satisfied	Competitors	Strengths (and Weaknesses)
1. Hotel business	Lodging	Travelers	Lodging	Other hotels	Ability to attract travelers
2. Business communications business	Lodging; meeting place; business facilities	Business travelers	Access to high-quality service and business facilities	Premier hotels; business communications centers	Business facilities offered

sense of its business, including its customers' needs, competitors, and strengths and weaknesses within the targeted market. It would be in a shaky position if it viewed its business as offering education, for instance, while its customers were seeking another product, like job opportunities.

Defining the business in the hotel industry. To explore a third example, let's take the case of Inter-Continental Hotels, a worldwide chain with several prestigious hotels in the United States and abroad (see table 4–3). For years, Inter-Continental viewed itself as a company in the hotel business. It then redefined itself as involved in the business hotel business, since it had always catered to executives on the road. Such a definition indicated that Inter-Continental was competing with premier inns, not with chains that had been price promoters or spartan in decor. Furthermore, this definition allowed the company to be more precise in defining and satisfying its customers' needs. Inter-Continental's hotels offer, for example, higher quality service, numerous meeting rooms to accommodate conventions, and other features that appeal to business people. Targeting this market also allowed the chain to charge higher prices for these services.

As the market has moved in new directions, Inter-Continental has refined its business definition. Now it regards itself as involved in the business communication business, as it recognizes that business travelers rely on hotels during trips and meetings to facilitate business communication. Under this definition, a hotel can offer many more services than simply setting up meeting rooms. Taking advantage of recent strides in telecommunication, Inter-Continental now provides teleconferencing capabilities in some of its hotels, allowing people at one location to talk to other people at another location, with full audio and visual transmission. Saving companies time and money in international travel, Inter-Continental can now set up a teleconference between executives in, for instance, its London and New York hotels.

Company Mission and Objectives

By identifying customer needs, competitors, and strengths and weaknesses, a company can spell out its mission and objectives. Like the business definition, a **company mission** identifies the company's product or service and the needs that this item must satisfy. The mission also sets forth the technologies that the company

Chapter 4 / Defining the Business

Figure 4–2 As a business communication company, Inter-Continental offers the Intelmet Videoconference Service, which allows executives in Inter-Continental's New York and London hotels to communicate directly with each other.

Courtesy of Inter-Continental Hotels

will use in its production process or delivery of a given service. Essentially, it is "a broadly defined but enduring statement of purpose that distinguishes a business from other firms of its type."[9]

Executives who articulate the company's mission and objectives are charting long-term goals concerning survival, growth, and profitability. With these long-term goals clearly in mind, a company may turn down opportunities that promise only a "quick fix" or a hot bargain. Such short-term opportunities could run counter to the mission that points the way to lasting prosperity.

Company mission and objectives also deal with a company's self-image and its public image. A firm, for instance, may view itself, and be viewed, as a responsible member of society but also as an aggressive seeker of new markets. These images can help determine which opportunities will attract the company and which ventures to pursue. The manufacturer of Cross Pens, for example, conveys prestige through its product. It would have little interest in marketing a 49-cent disposable pen under the Cross trademark, because such a flimsy product could damage its reputation for quality.

Paradigms of Business Definition

In most cases, a company is involved in many businesses. ABC, for example, is involved with both television and radio broadcasting, and it has recently purchased the ESPN cable television channel. CBS is also involved with television and radio broadcasting, and it has divisions for record production and book publishing. When a company defines each of these businesses, it will find that the components of each business definition are different. In order to manage its various units, then, the company will divide itself into separate manageable businesses called **strategic business units (SBUs).** Each SBU within a company has its own markets, sets of customers, competitors, and technologies and, thus, needs to be handled differently from other SBUs.

As an example, Parker Bros. was recently reorganized to include two SBUs. To meet the changing needs within the quick-paced toy industry, Parker now operates two marketing groups, one for electronic products and one for traditional products. The electronic group has launched a direct hit at the video game cartridge market, scoring high points with Frogger and The Empire Strikes Back. The traditional group is moving into juvenile book publishing, with a series of books about stuffed animals called the Care Bears.[10] Because the groups are markedly different in customers, customer needs, and technologies, they are treated as two distinct SBUs.

In this section, we are going to take a look at four alternative paradigms of business definition developed by Derek Abell, Bruce Henderson, William Rothschild, and the Arthur D. Little Company. These paradigms serve as ways to break up a company into SBUs and then as ways to manage each SBU.

Derek Abell's Three Dimensions

A well-known marketing strategist, Derek Abell argues that an SBU can be defined along any one of three separate dimensions.[11] The first dimension is the group of customers that are being served and whose needs are being met by the SBU's product or service. The second dimension is the customer functions or needs that the company is serving. Keep in mind that the group of customers is a dimension quite distinct from customer needs. Although a company may be serving one set of customers, there can exist different needs within that set. In such a case, the company may be involved in two or more distinct businesses, each serving a particular need.

The third dimension in Abell's paradigm involves the specific technologies used to make the product or service. From this perspective, the technologies show how the customers' needs are being satisfied. By analyzing its operations along the dimensions of customer groups, customer needs, and technologies, a firm can identify its separate SBUs. These three dimensions and SBUs defined along each are shown in figure 4–3.

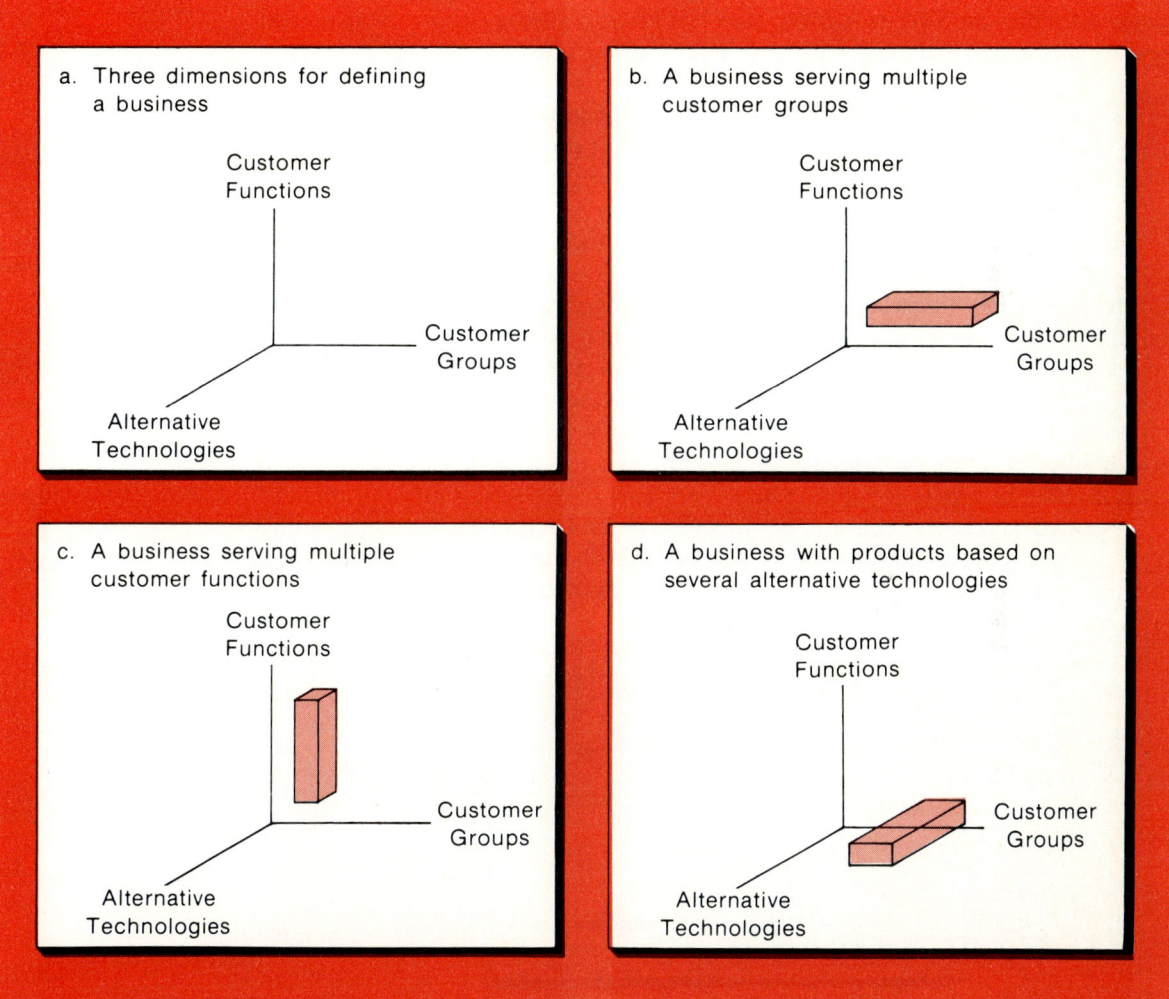

Figure 4–3 Abell's three dimensions

Source: Derek F. Abell, *Defining the Business: The Starting Point of Strategic Planning* (Englewood Cliffs, N.J.: Prentice-Hall, 1980), pp. 30–31. Adapted from the cases PCM (A), 9-576-211, and PCM (B), 9-577-104, prepared by Joseph R. D'Cruz under the direction of Derek F. Abell. Copyright © 1976 and 1977 by the President and Fellows of Harvard College. Used with permission of the Harvard Business School.

Consider the alternate technologies at Gould, Inc. Gould makes brush instruments that are used in instrument plotting. The company uses another technology to make electrostatic printers for computer plotting. Even though these two instruments serve the same function, plotting, they are intended to serve different customers with different technologies. As a result, the two functions are treated as separate SBUs at Gould, and each is managed according to strategies designed for its individual market.

Bruce Henderson's Identification of an SBU

Bruce Henderson, a consulting strategist and founder of the Boston Consulting Group, identifies an SBU as a group that has its own strategy and a clear market focus.[12] Like Abell, Henderson believes that an SBU must aim for its own set of customers. Henderson goes beyond Abell, however, by adding that an SBU must also be characterized by an identifiable set of competitors. This last requirement is based on the fact that most SBUs market a range of products. For these products to belong to a single SBU, they should compete against the same rivals.

Turning to how to manage an SBU, Henderson recommends that a company form a matrix organization of program units and functional departments. In his view, program units are marketing programs, each devoted to a single product line. On the other hand, functional departments, like advertising divisions, handle several product lines. For example, a food company may sell an instant coffee and a ground coffee, devising a separate marketing strategy for each product to reach different consumers with different needs. Yet, according to Henderson's recommendation, both products would be handled by the same advertising department, even though separate campaigns would be created. According to this paradigm, both types of coffee belong to the same SBU.

Finally, Henderson believes that an SBU can be of any magnitude. In other words, there are no established ranges for the size of an SBU; it can handle from one up to any number of products, as long as all of the products correspond with the characteristics of the SBU.

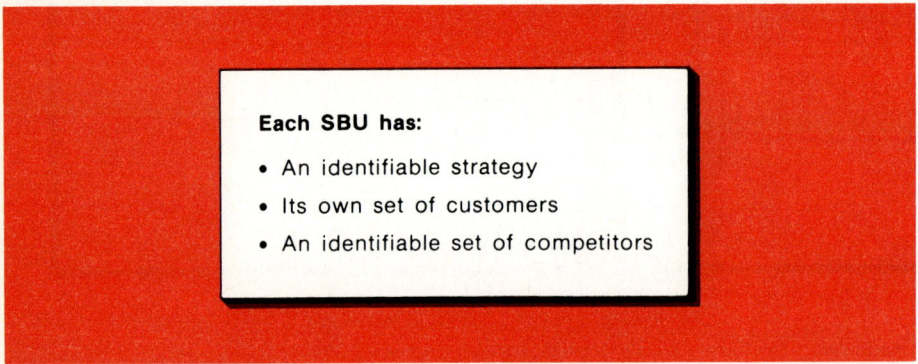

Figure 4–4
Henderson's characteristics of an SBU

Figure 4–5 Rothschild's definition of an SBU

Each SBU must control:
- The choice of products
- The choice of distribution channels
- The choice of timing decisions
- The choice of sources of supply

In addition, each SBU must be able to meet two of the following requirements:
- Ability to define external markets
- Ability to identify competitors
- Ability to measure profitability

William Rothschild's Identification of an SBU

Adopting a slightly different perspective is William Rothschild, who has developed strategic planning for General Electric and written several texts on business strategy.[13] Rothschild forms his definition by showing how an SBU can exert control over its course within the marketplace. Recognizing that no organization is a pure SBU, he does assert that any unit must control the following areas: (1) choice of products, (2) choice of distribution channels through which products will be made available, (3) choice of timing decisions, and (4) choice of suppliers. To operate an SBU, managers must exercise control over these choices.

Additionally, an SBU must meet at least two of the following requirements: Its management must be able to define external markets, identify a clear set of competitors, and apply a method to measure the profitability of the organization. If an SBU does not meet at least two of these requirements, it is not an SBU, but rather a cost center, or an aggregation of businesses or products.

Arthur D. Little's Characteristics of an SBU

Arthur D. Little, the consulting firm, has formulated its own characteristics of SBUs.[14] The firm requires a single set of identifiable customers and competitors. This paradigm, however, introduces the additional notion of product substitutability, that products are potential substitutes for each other within an SBU. Returning to the food company example, we can point out that the instant coffee could serve as a substitute for the ground coffee.

Another characteristic is that products in the SBU must exhibit high price cross-elasticity. Similarly, the products must exhibit quality and feature cross-elasticity. For example, within the food company's coffee SBU, if the price on a second instant coffee goes down, it will probably take sales away from the first instant coffee. The two coffees are purchased by the same customers for the same purpose, so customers are willing to exchange one for the other. The two instant coffees, then, belong in the same SBU. On the other hand, if the price for the food company's line of flavored coffees drops, sales of the instant coffee are probably not affected, as the two types of coffee are bought for different purposes, perhaps by different customers.

Finally, if the SBU were sold, major changes in strategy would be necessary for the remaining operations.

What is the purpose of these paradigms? To a large extent, they lead to similar creations of business definitions of SBUs. As we have seen, though, a complete business definition—including an identification of the needs to be satisfied, the competition, and the company's strengths and weaknesses—leads a company to develop an appropriate total product and marketing strategy for that product. The four paradigms make companies think about themselves, their marketing environment, and their products and thus formulate complete business definitions and strategies for each of their SBUs. The purpose of the paradigms, therefore, is to give companies ways to break themselves into manageable SBUs and then implement the marketing strategies appropriate for each SBU.

Should We Be in This Business?

We've just looked at how a company can define its business and determine whether it is, in fact, operating more than one SBU. It's now time to address a question of basic concern to companies and marketing managers: "Should we be in this business?"

Top executives at Mattel, Inc., the toy maker renowned for Barbie Dolls, recently posed that very question in order to evaluate the company's entry into the video game and home computer business. Stunned by heavy losses after an initial success with video games, Mattel has decided that it doesn't belong in the electronics business. Its home computer, Aquarius, was abandoned as "too little, too late," after being test-marketed with a price tag of $50 more than the prices of competing computers. Although Mattel's video game Intellivision initially was a best-seller, the company let this position slip when it failed to secure licenses to produce video arcade games for the home market. The chief problem, according to a former manager at Mattel, was that the company lacked the resources and expertise to keep pace with the swift-moving electronics industry.[15]

When companies are seeking to answer this basic question about their business, they should evaluate how well their resources and expertise in terms of

Figure 4–6 Arthur D. Little's characteristics of an SBU

Each SBU has:

- A set of identifiable customers
- A set of identifiable competitors
- Product substitutability
- High price cross-elasticity
- High feature and quality cross-elasticity
- Strategic importance (if the SBU were sold, the company would have to make major strategy changes for its other operations)

strengths and weaknesses fit the demands of the market. In addition, there are several specific methods for determining whether a company should be in a particular business. We will look at these methods in detail in chapter 19, Marketing Strategy.

For the moment, keep in mind that when managers evaluate a company's fit in a certain business, they must consider the size of the market and its attractiveness to the company. That is, the market should reflect a substantial demand for the company's product, and the market should be large enough to make the venture worthwhile.

All these considerations lead to the necessity of forecasting demand for a particular product.

Forecasting Demand

To predict the demand for a specific product or service, companies ask a number of questions about the targeted market. They also draw upon a variety of methods to find answers to these questions. Both the questions and answers are listed and discussed below.

When preparing forecasts, managers need to ask probing questions regarding the size of the market, trends within the market, and changing components of the market (see fig. 4–7).

Questions to Ask

**Figure 4–7
Questions to ask in forecasting demand**

1. What is the size of the current market?
    a. How many customers are there?
    b. How often do they buy?
    c. How much do they buy?
2. What are the trends in the market?
3. What are the changing components in the market?
    a. Are consumer demographics shifting?
    b. What are our competitors doing?

What is the size of the current market? In seeking to determine the size of a market, companies want to know whether a market is large enough to warrant their pursuing it. To answer this question, managers can take a hard look at (1) the number of customers in that market, (2) how often they buy, and (3) how much they buy. These factors can be measured in general terms, although the number of customers, as well as the frequency and volume of their purchases, can change over time.

What are the trends in the market? When new approaches and conditions sweep the market, they often stretch and pull the three factors of market size into a new shape. Being able to spot these future trends helps a company to gear up for changing demands.

For instance, say that you are a marketer for a relatively new airline like People Express. Your job is to determine the size of the market and how certain trends affect the volume of air travel. You might first consider what conditions influence the rise or fall in the number of business travelers. As an example, when the number of white-collar workers and of companies with various branches rises, the volume and frequency of business travel are likely to increase as well. Additionally, the health of the economy and other indicators produce trends that can swell or diminish the ranks of business travelers. When the economy is in a period of stagnation, the number of businesses and, therefore, of business travelers is also stagnant.

On the other hand, you would find that the number of personal travelers is likely to be most affected by the cost of airline tickets in comparison with the cost of car rentals or other means of transportation. Still other trends affect the volume of travelers by air. When air fares were very high, reflecting soaring oil prices and federal regulations, the overall number of travelers shrank. With deregulation and a stronger economy, the airlines became fiercely competitive and slashed fares, leading to an increase in the number of passengers. As this example illustrates, a variety of trends can signal changes in the size of a particular market.

Take the case of the movie industry. New technologies in the distribution of movies, from cable television to videocassette recorders, are cutting into movie theater attendance. As a result, analysts expect that theater attendance could plummet more than 50 percent by 1990. In the past, movie executives counted on box-office sales to generate 80 percent of a film's revenue. Since ticket sales are likely to continue their decrease, filmmakers will need to increase their sales to television, cassettes, and other nontheater markets—sales that could bring in up to half of a movie company's revenues.[16] This recent trend, as it gains strength, is transforming the size and shape of the market for films. Marketers are now forecasting a demand among filmgoers for greater control over what movies they see and when they see the movies.

What are the changing components in the market? The variety of components that determine market size are often in a state of flux. One component is demographics. For example, shifting demographics have prompted marketers to forecast an increased demand for pharmaceutical products. Not only are people experiencing greater longevity and thus a greater need for medicine, but the number of older people will increase as the baby boomers move past middle age. Similar demographics have influenced Kellogg to lessen its dependence on breakfast cereals. Most of the customers for cereals—usually promoted by characters such as Tony the Tiger and the Froot Loop gang—are under 20 years of age, a group that is shrinking in size. To appeal to the larger market of adults who like food with a pure, healthful image, the company has introduced Whitney's Yogurt. It is a creamy, custard-like concoction, designed as the "ice cream" of yogurts. Kellogg believes it has targeted a winning combination, since 88 percent of the population eats ice cream.[17] Demographics will be discussed in detail in chapter 7.

Geographic shifts are another changing component that can help marketers forecast growth in the size of a market. For instance, the steady exodus from the Northeast to the Sunbelt states promises a surge in the demand for recreational products and apparel made for a warm, sunny climate.

Another component studied when forecasting demand is the number of competitors and how they are positioned in the market. As we saw in the movie industry, new technologies have created many competitors whose products are designed to offer customers greater convenience and control over the movies they see. After analyzing this particular component, filmmakers have predicted a decline in their traditional market.

We've just taken a look at the questions that a marketer can ask when forecasting the demand for a particular product or service. Once companies have asked the right questions, how do they find the right answers? A number of methods can be used to prepare forecasts.

Methods to Answer Each Question

One technique is to examine economic indicators, which measure the health of various areas of the economy. For instance, new housing starts are fairly accurate indicators of an upcoming demand for household appliances. Another approach to forecasting demand for a product is to gather opinions from experts, including the company's sales force, about the growth rate of particular markets.

Forecasting the demand for a new product is an especially challenging task. Difficulties increase when the product is not simply new to the company but is also new to the market. As with any product, however, marketers must determine whether customers place a high value on having particular needs satisfied by the product, and, if so, who the customers are, the number of customers, and how the given product or service is used. Additionally, by looking at the new product as a replacement for a successful, competing one, companies gain a sense of the upper limit of the market size.

Once market size has been determined, companies can measure how well the new product suits customers' needs in comparison with the degree to which existing products satisfy those same needs. Another step is to take a survey of buyers' intentions. Using this approach, marketers explain the new product to potential customers and then ask them to rate their willingness to buy it. These answers may not be accurate, and such surveys may, in fact, overstate the level of demand.

There are several ways to compensate for this inaccuracy. Results from a survey can be scaled down to reflect the actual sales of a similar product for which a similar survey was conducted. As an example, let's say a recent market study showed that 40 percent of the people surveyed were willing to buy call-forwarding service if it were available for their phone. But in surveys regarding similar products already on the market, marketers observed that the results were overstated by 50 percent. If this were a persistent overstatement, marketers would be prudent to expect only 20 percent of the customers to purchase the call-forwarding service.

Another way to compensate for overstated results is to describe various products to customers and ask them how likely they are to buy each product. For example, in choosing among automobiles A, B, and C, a group of customers might reveal that 30 percent are likely to buy A, 20 percent to buy B, and 10 percent to buy C. The actual percentages are not reliable figures, but the overall trend, that more customers are likely to drive home automobile A than B or C, is most likely valid. Applying the results of this survey, a company would be wise to introduce automobile A (if all other factors, such as expected profit margin, are equal).

A third approach is to survey different segments of the population. Marketers can ask customers in each segment how likely they are to purchase automobile A, and then target the product to the segment that was most likely to purchase it.

The above has been a general description of the factors considered in forecasting demand. There are a number of sophisticated econometric models that marketers use when surveying the market.[18]

An Overview of Marketing Strategy

In this chapter, we have looked at how companies define their business and divide themselves into separate, manageable strategic business units, what companies consider when they decide whether to engage in a business, and how companies forecast demand. These topics are the first ones considered when a company develops its marketing strategy. Creating the actual marketing strategy depends on a knowledge of buyer behavior and of the elements in the marketing mix. For this reason, the development of marketing strategy is discussed after these topics are presented. Here, however, is an overview of the discussion of marketing strategy in chapter 19.

A purpose of marketing strategy is to ensure a company's survival and success. One way to do this is to create a *competitive advantage*. The elements of the marketing mix can be adjusted to create the advantage. Some possible actions are to operate with lower costs, control the distribution channels, and differentiate products from competitors' products.

Another purpose of marketing strategy is to determine the nature and direction of the company's *growth*. There are a number of strategies companies can use to pursue growth. The strategies include development of new products or markets or acquiring new businesses through diversification.

A number of factors influence the creation of marketing strategy. *Gaining market share* and *market growth* are two major objectives of companies, which are constantly looking for ways to meet these objectives. The search for growth leads companies to conduct *portfolio analysis,* or an analysis of the characteristics and potential of their strategic business units, divisions, and products. The analysis helps companies plan strategy for each; another option for the company is to drop or divest itself of unprofitable units.

Another factor to consider is whether the company should be the first to introduce a product or enter a market (*pioneering*) or wait for competitors to take actions (*following*). Companies must also be aware of various *barriers* that may keep them from entering a market. The barriers are often related to the resources of the company. A final factor is the *actions of competitors, buyers, and suppliers* that affect what a company can and cannot do.

The formulation of marketing strategy leads to the development of the *marketing plan.* The plan identifies the company's businesses, markets, and customers, names the company's goals, and sets forth the strategies that the company follows.

Marketing strategy also involves *budget planning,* or the process the company uses to allocate resources. Finally, a company develops a system of *marketing control,* or a system for evaluating the marketing plan and revising the marketing strategy, if necessary.

These topics are discussed in detail in chapter 19. For the present, it is enough to remember that companies consider these factors and take these actions as they develop their overall marketing strategy.

Summary

To formulate a business definition, a company must specify the market it plans to serve and the general type of product or service it will promote to the specific market; identify the needs that it plans to satisfy; identify its competitors; and recognize its strengths and weaknesses within a given market.

A company mission is "a broadly defined but enduring statement of purpose that distinguishes a business from other firms of its type." A company mission is made up of its long-term goals as defined by top executives.

A standard business unit (SBU) is one area of business that may be among several within a company. An SBU includes a set of customers, customer needs, and technology unique to this segment of the organization. Abell argues that an SBU can be defined along three dimensions: the customer group that the product is serving, the customer needs the company is serving, and the technologies used to make the product or service.

Henderson asserts that every SBU should have its own strategy and clear market focus and that the SBU should also be characterized by a distinct set of competitors. He also recommends that a company, in defining an SBU, form a matrix of program units, or marketing programs for individual product lines, and functional departments. He believes an SBU can be of any magnitude.

Rothschild's perspective is that an SBU can control its course in the marketplace by choosing its products, distribution channels, timing decisions, and suppliers. In this view, an SBU must be able to define external markets and a set of competitors and to apply a method to measure the profitability of the organization.

Consulting firm Arthur D. Little requires SBUs to have a single set of identifiable customers and competitors. This paradigm introduces the characteristic that products can be substitutes for each other within an SBU. Also, within an SBU, products must exhibit high price cross-elasticity. There must also be quality and feature cross-elasticity. Finally, if the SBU were sold major changes in strategy would be necessary for the remaining operations.

When managers evaluate a company's fit to a certain business, they must consider the size of the market and its attractiveness to the company. The company must define the size of the market, determining the number of customers, how often they buy, and how much they buy. Spotting future trends helps a company to gear up for changing demands. Market components that are often in a state of flux include demographics, geographic shifts, and the number of competitors and their positions in the market.

To prepare forecasts of the demand for a particular product, a company can examine economic indicators and survey buyers' intentions.

Questions for Discussion

1. Discuss the importance of formulating a business definition before deciding on the corporate mission and objectives.
2. Identify and explain the components involved in the determination of a company's mission.

3. In what ways are the four paradigms of business definition different? Explain.
4. In what ways are the four paradigms of business definition similar? Explain.
5. Discuss the kinds of information needed in forecasting demand for the following products/services: (a) videocassette recorder; (b) drive-in grocery store; and (c) satellite antenna.
6. Explain why we should employ a paradigm of business definition.
7. Identify what methods you would employ in forecasting demand for a new neighborhood gas station.
8. What purposes does a company's marketing strategy serve?
9. What factors are generally considered in the development of a company's marketing strategy?

References

1. John Gruen, "Dancevision," *Dance Magazine,* December 1982, p. 91; and "Culture Shock on Cable," *Newsweek,* March 15, 1982, p. 85.
2. "Sifting Through the Fallout of CBS Cable, Disney," *Broadcasting,* September 20, 1982, pp. 28–30.
3. Peter W. Bernstein, "The Race to Feed Cable TV's Maw," *Fortune,* May 1, 1981, pp. 308–18.
4. Ibid.
5. "Culture Shock on Cable."
6. "The Rush into Cable TV Is Now Turning into a Retreat," *Business Week,* October 17, 1983, pp. 135, 139, 142.
7. Bernstein, "The Race to Feed Cable TV's Maw."
8. "Cable Gets Ready for Business," *Business Week,* November 22, 1982, pp. 119–21.
9. John A. Pearce III, "The Company Mission as a Strategic Tool," *Sloan Management Review,* Spring 1982, pp. 15–24.
10. "The New Kid in Children's Books," *Business Week,* February 28, 1983, p. 98.
11. Derek F. Abell, *Defining the Business: The Starting Point of Strategic Planning* (Englewood Cliffs, N.J.: Prentice-Hall, 1980).
12. Bruce D. Henderson, *Henderson on Corporate Strategy* (Cambridge, Mass.: Abt Books, 1979).
13. William E. Rothschild, *Putting It All Together: A Guide to Strategic Thinking* (New York: American Management Assoc., 1976).
14. Arthur D. Little, Inc., *Impact Series* (Cambridge, Mass.: Decision Resources).
15. "Mattel: Back to Barbie Dolls after Getting Zapped in Electronics," *Business Week,* February 20, 1984, pp. 84A–B.
16. "How TV Is Revolutionizing Hollywood," *Business Week,* February 21, 1983, pp. 78–89.
17. "Kellogg Looks Beyond Breakfast," *Business Week,* December 6, 1982, pp. 66–69.
18. Steven C. Wheelwright, Spyros Makridakis, and Victor E. McGee, *Forecasting: Methods and Applications,* 2nd ed. (New York: Wiley, 1983).

OBJECTIVES

1. To highlight the importance of marketing research to a firm and the role played by marketing research in making effective marketing decisions.

2. To describe the different steps involved in undertaking marketing research.

3. To identify the different sources of marketing information—their advantages, disadvantages, and applications.

4. To identify the role and components of marketing information systems in marketing decision making.

5. To illustrate the manner in which formal research studies are actually done.

5

Marketing Research and Marketing Information Systems

Sara Lee, a longtime leader in frozen, ready-made desserts and baked goods, has come up against some sales obstacles in recent years. Supermarket bakery departments and companies like Entenmann's, makers of fresh baked goods, have begun to take a larger piece of the pie. In addition, many people are cutting back on sweets as a part of a growing concern for health and fitness. While Sara Lee maintained a leading edge in the dessert market, the company's sales began to slip.

In order to boost sales and regain momentum in the market, the company tried to determine what consumers wanted. This process involved putting a number of new products on the market over the past 15 years—usually in just a small region of the country—and evaluating consumers' responses to them. Early marketing research studies showed that one alternative would be to develop fresh baked goods to compete in that part of the dessert market. A study of consumer trends showed a growing number of smaller households. For this group, the company developed a line of smaller desserts, Cakes for Two. Sara Lee hoped that people who wouldn't ordinarily buy a frozen dessert because of its large size would buy the smaller cakes. Sara Lee also noticed the growing number of diet-conscious consumers and introduced a line of low-calorie desserts called Light 'n Luscious. To take advantage of its expertise in frozen foods, Sara Lee developed and introduced frozen entrees.

Sara Lee continued to study consumers' tastes in its development of new products. The company's studies showed that a major portion of its consumers live in or near major cities and tend to be affluent. They are also the same group who are concerned about health and fitness. Sara Lee also wanted its new products to be part of an expanding market.

With its knowledge of its consumers and this goal in mind, Sara Lee introduced another product: frozen croissants. Six different recipes were developed and tested. Based on these tests, the company decided to introduce three flavors: Wheat 'n Honey, Cheese, and All Butter. Other flavors added to the line include Apple, Strawberry, and Chocolate. The company was attracted to the croissant market because a similar product, Sara Lee's Crescent Dinner Roll, had been gaining 10 to 15 percent in sales annually without any promotion from the company. In addition, research showed that diet-conscious Sara Lee consumers consider croissants more nutritious than more heavily sugared breakfast baked goods.[1]

T he people at Sara Lee are using the process known as **marketing research** to solve their marketing problems. The American Marketing Association defines marketing research as "the systematic gathering, recording, and analyzing of data about problems relating to the marketing of goods and services."[2]

The first step in marketing research is to define the problem, or to identify precisely which portions of the marketing mix will need adjustment. Then, using techniques similar to those used in scientific research, a company designs the research project and collects data about that area of its operations. The analysis of the data, the company hopes, should provide a basis for making recommendations about how to resolve the problem. A necessary feature of marketing research is for

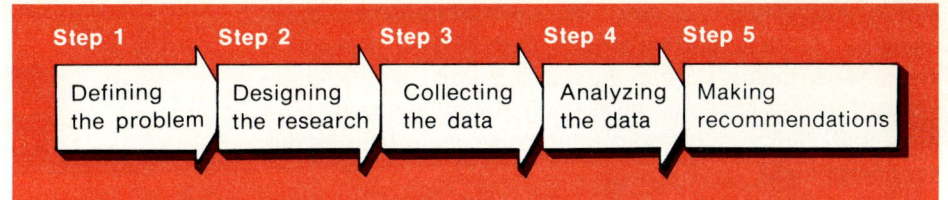

Figure 5–1 Steps in the marketing research process

it to be both objective and systematic. The researchers clearly outline the procedure to be followed before the project begins, including specific precautions to account for biases in data collection and analysis. The steps in the marketing research process are shown in figure 5–1.

For Sara Lee, the company's goals were to increase sales and regain market leadership. Marketing research revealed several alternatives: to develop fresh baked goods and enter a new market, to develop frozen entrees and expand Sara Lee's involvement in the frozen foods market, or to develop a new product aimed at a specific group of consumers. From this set of choices, Sara Lee was able to develop a solution to its problem.

It used to be that most retailers, and even manufacturers, came into direct contact with their customers. If a product was unsatisfactory, business people heard about it directly from the customer; if the company wasn't providing an item that its customers wanted, it would probably hear about that, too. Today many business people never meet their customers. Sara Lee's vice-president in charge of marketing will probably never know that 41-year-old Mona Vernon of Anytown, New York, now eats Sara Lee croissants every day. Only through marketing research can Sara Lee's marketers find out what Mona Vernon (and others with similar needs and wants) likes to eat for breakfast, develop a product to match her wants, promote it so that she becomes aware of the product's availability, and boost Sara Lee's sales as a result. Marketing research serves as an increasingly vital link between the business and the consumer.

The Role of Marketing Research

An important role of marketing research is to help companies predict their consumers' behavior—not a simple task. Without objective, thorough research and analysis, marketing managers would have to rely on only their experience and their intuition to make decisions about marketing issues. Of course, no method can provide completely accurate information about which soft drink will catch on next, whether consumer spending will be up or down in the next few years, or which movies will draw best at the box office. The role of marketing research is to reduce uncertainty about marketing issues by providing specific, verifiable, hard data about the market, the company's competition, consumers and their perceptions, and the ways consumers respond to the marketing mix.

In relation to consumers, marketing researchers measure attitudes and opinions, awareness and knowledge, motives, and intentions. Each of these concepts is related to buying behavior. What makes people choose one product rather than another, and how can marketers influence that decision? Using scientifically conducted marketing research, marketers can measure these concepts to help predict and influence the choices people make.

Attitudes or opinions are people's positive or negative beliefs about an object, event, situation, or idea, and these beliefs are thought to influence their behavior toward the object or event. If researchers at Sara Lee found that a majority of consumers questioned about a proposed frozen pastry thought that the product sounded tasty and a lot more convenient than making it themselves, the researchers would probably recommend the product's introduction. If, on the other hand, a majority of consumers expressed the attitude that eating this kind of pastry increases the risk of heart disease, that the product probably wouldn't taste good, or that frozen desserts are a product used by lazy people who do not care enough about their families to do their own baking, then the researchers would probably recommend one of two alternatives. They could propose dropping plans to introduce the product or developing marketing strategies to change these negative views.

Marketers also study people's awareness and knowledge of a product, often in relation to advertisements in newspapers and magazines. Questionnaires are used to determine whether consumers have noticed an advertisement and the amount of information they have absorbed from it. Measuring people's awareness of a product helps marketers set their advertising budgets. If most people are not aware of a product, marketers may want to spend heavily on advertising. Furthermore, measuring people's knowledge about a product tells marketers something about the effectiveness of their advertising.

A motive is a set of internal thoughts and feelings that direct people to behave in a particular way. Motives are the "why" behind behavior; investigation of motives for past behavior helps researchers make predictions about future behavior.

The study of people's intentions is important to researchers who need to predict people's future behavior, particularly whether or not they will purchase a certain product. An intention to buy is far from being a completely reliable predictor of actual buying, though. In many cases, the intention may be relative. If people are shown two products, they are most likely to buy the one they say they will. For example, if 70 percent of the people asked say they would buy frozen croissants and 30 percent say they would buy frozen eclairs, the Sara Lee researchers can count on close to a 2–1 split in consumer preferences.

Measuring intangible concepts is difficult and tricky. Yet consumer perceptions, actions, and responses are so intrinsic to marketing that companies need to be able to study them. Marketing research provides the framework and the means to gather and analyze this needed information. (These concepts, their effects on consumer behavior, and the interaction of consumer behavior with marketing are discussed in detail in chapter 7.)

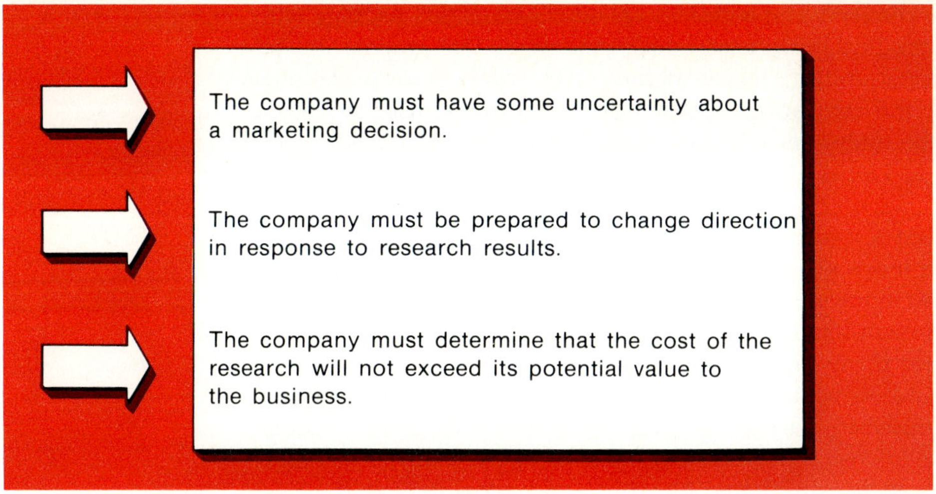

Figure 5–2 The three criteria for using marketing research

→ The company must have some uncertainty about a marketing decision.

→ The company must be prepared to change direction in response to research results.

→ The company must determine that the cost of the research will not exceed its potential value to the business.

When to Use Marketing Research

The decision about whether or not to use marketing research depends on three criteria (see fig. 5–2). First, the company must have some uncertainty about a marketing decision. For example, Sara Lee was uncertain about whether or not to enter the fresh baked goods market, to develop a new frozen dessert, or to develop a new frozen food in a different category. If the company had been certain that its frozen croissants would have been the most successful of its options, marketing research would not have been necessary or worthwhile. Second, the company must be prepared to change direction in response to research results. If after finding that its customers were looking for less fattening foods, Sara Lee had decided to ignore this and continue all its old lines and philosophies, then researching consumer attitudes about frozen baked goods would have been wasted. At the same time, the company did not have to change radically and instead develop a line of frozen vegetables, for example. The company must be willing to modify its strategy to some extent in order for the research to be valuable. Third, before beginning such a venture, the company must determine that the cost of the research will not exceed its potential value to the business.

Let's look at two situations in which companies decided to use marketing research. Mirro, a producer of housewares, had developed a line of microwave oven cookware that was selling poorly. The company's sales force claimed that the problem was the cocoa brown color of the cookware; most competitors' cookware was beige. Mirro's top management was not sure that the color was the problem, and they were not willing to change it unless they could determine that it was. The company, therefore, conducted an extensive marketing research study. The study showed that the main problem was the Mirro name, which was associated with aluminum, which can't be used in microwave ovens; the company responded by changing the product's name to Koolware. The study also indicated that the package was confusing; the company responded by creating a simplified package with a photo showing the product being used and a microwave-like graphic design. Consumers took the opportunity to tell researchers about other microwave oven products they wanted; the company responded by producing a casserole and a coffee maker. Finally, the study showed that consumers like the cocoa brown color because it resists stains and looks expensive. The company did *not* change the products' color.[3]

Jovan had developed a suntan lotion, Dial-a-Tan, which came in a tube that could dispense different levels of sunscreen. The company was not certain how to tell consumers about this innovation and how to make its product stand out among all the many kinds of suntan lotions. Jovan conducted a marketing research study and, as a result, changed many aspects of its proposed marketing mix. The study led the company to change its white package to brown-tan-gold to convey the idea of the three levels of sunscreen. Each of the three sunscreens was given a distinct name to emphasize the difference between them. The study showed that the most effective advertisements were educational ones that told people about the new technology; thus, Jovan's new ad stood out among the standard beach-scene, bikinied-volleyball player ads for other suntan lotions. Finally, the study showed that price was important to consumers in choosing a suntan lotion; Jovan decided to encourage stores to cut the retail price of Dial-a-Tan.[4]

In both these cases, the companies were uncertain as to what to do and were willing to take action based on survey results. The marketing research process worked effectively, and profitably, for both. We are now going to look at the marketing research process itself.

The Marketing Research Process

The marketing research process consists of five steps: defining the problem; designing the research; collecting the data; analyzing the data; and making recommendations.

The first, and probably the most essential, step in the marketing research process is **defining the problem.** This step involves specifying the problem that needs solving, as well as stating the decision to be made about it. The decision makers within a company must outline their goals for the project to those who are conducting the research to make sure the project addresses the correct issues. In the problem-definition step, researchers also need to determine what kind of information will be necessary to help reach a decision. This enables researchers to choose an appropriate set of procedures to supply the needed information. Without a clear definition of the problem, research is of little or no value. Researchers may also find that a clear, accurate definition of the problem details the decisions to the point where

Defining the Problem

the problem is actually solved; in that case, the marketing research process is completed.

Since each study can answer only one question, it is important to determine how many issues the project will cover. In the Sara Lee project, the company used its Cakes for Two to find out if smaller households were the reason for lower sales; Light 'n Luscious products showed whether high calories were to blame. If the company had introduced the low-calorie and smaller-size features in one product, then neither question would have been answered clearly. Some research projects require many studies, each answering one question, before the whole problem can be solved. While few studies can answer all the questions, several studies can be carried out simultaneously.

In the problem-definition step, researchers and decision makers also need to try to identify any possible causes of the problem. Causal factors can include features of the product, competitors in the market, and virtually any possible influence on consumers' response to the product.

Designing the Research

Designing the research is the specification of procedures for data collection and analysis. Researchers sometimes think of research design as the "road map" or "blueprint" for all subsequent steps. The research can be designed as one of three general types: **exploratory, descriptive,** or **causal.** There is some overlap in these classifications, however, so sometimes a study that seems to belong to one category may also serve the purposes of one or both of the others.

Exploratory research. Exploratory research is concerned with gathering general information about the nature of the problem. In this type of research, there is no fixed plan or set of hypotheses. Researchers usually use **secondary data,** or information that has been gathered for some other purpose, to gain a fuller understanding of the problem, especially important when the issue is new to them. Exploratory research also allows researchers to develop clear hypotheses and more concrete plans for further investigation of the problem. Researchers often think of exploratory studies as a preliminary step in the research process.

There are several types of exploratory studies. An obvious one is known as the *literature search,* in which researchers examine all the published data that are relevant to the problem. Such a search can include the marketing trade publications as well as the literature of other areas. The psychological literature, for example, might provide information on a number of marketing-related topics, such as environmental factors found to make people more likely to buy frozen instead of fresh baked goods or sources of job satisfaction for salespeople.

An *experience survey* uses the knowledge of individuals involved in various aspects of the marketing process under study. Researchers at Sara Lee could have interviewed the executives of the company, its research and development staff, its salespeople, several grocery store managers, and some consumers to gain insight into how to improve sales.

A third type of exploratory research is known as *analysis of case histories*. Here researchers use others' findings about similar situations to suggest ways of approaching the problem. But before they can reach any conclusions about these issues, researchers need to develop more concrete evidence about their own situation. Case histories help researchers to develop an approach designed specifically for a particular problem, but they do not provide information from which researchers can make recommendations for solving the present problem.

In the process of conducting exploratory studies, researchers often change focus and direction as they become more knowledgeable on the topic. No definite research plan is set until after the researchers feel they have developed a firm grasp of the issues.

Descriptive research. The purpose of descriptive research is to outline the characteristics of certain groups, to determine the proportion of a population that engages in some activity, or to make predictions. By the time researchers begin a descriptive study, they have done a good deal of exploratory work. Specific research questions have been developed beforehand. The researchers state exactly what the study will measure and precisely how that will be accomplished. Included in the design are a list of sources to be consulted for information. A descriptive study also includes one or more hypotheses formulated as the guiding purpose behind the study. All the details about how the research is to be conducted must be worked out in advance because after the data are collected, it will be too late to make changes.

One type of descriptive study is the *consumer profile study,* which outlines the demographic characteristics of consumers of a product, including their age, sex, income, rural or urban area residence, and their education level. Sara Lee used this approach to determine where many of its customers live, their average income, and dietary issues that concern them. A consumer profile study is an effort to get a detailed view of customers in order to tailor the marketing approach to attract them.

The *longitudinal study* is one that questions the same subjects repeatedly over a period of time. An example of this type of investigation would be if Sara Lee selected a group of families who had purchased the company's products within the last six months. The company could ask these people to record their frozen foods purchases for an extended period, say, one year. Each month the families could mail in a list of their frozen foods purchases. Sara Lee could use the information to find out the influence of its own promotional efforts, as well as the competition's activities. The information might be useful for studying what factors lead to product purchases.

Causal research. Even after gathering a good deal of detailed information on a particular problem and putting together a description of the variables involved, the researchers still may not know the cause of customer behavior. Causal research looks at just this issue. There are two kinds of causal studies: the **natural experiment** and the **controlled experiment.** The former is unstructured in design, while the latter uses a highly structured one. Hypotheses are stated in advance, as are methods of data collection and analysis.

In a natural experiment researchers measure variables just as they occur in the environment without changing the behaviors or situation they are investigating. An example of a natural experiment might be Sara Lee's observation that one of its products was selling better in the North than in the South. The variables in this example might be climate, regional preference, number of competitors, and so on.

A controlled experiment involves intervention by the researcher. If Sara Lee experimenters wanted to compare the effectiveness of two different magazine advertisements, they could show the ads to members of a community matched by demographic characteristics—age, sex, income level, and so on. The study would follow whether, how much, and how long each ad influenced the purchase of Sara Lee products for the people in each of the two groups and then compare them.

The above is an example of a field-controlled experiment, conducted out in a natural setting. Sara Lee experimenters could also have conducted a laboratory-controlled experiment by bringing people into a theater, showing them the two different advertisements, and then asking them about their attitudes and purchase intentions. As there is less clutter and interference in the theater, the researchers are better able to see the effects of the different advertisements. The field-controlled experiment is more valid, though, because it shows consumers' actual behavior.

Researchers say there is a causal relationship between variables if that relationship meets one or more of three criteria. The first is an *associative variation,* meaning that when changes in one variable occur, changes occur in the other(s) also. For instance, Sara Lee researchers might find that the introduction of a new magazine advertisement for a Sara Lee cake in an area is associated with an increase in sales for that cake. Another criterion hinges on the *sequence of events,* or the idea that for an event to be considered a cause, it must occur before its result. If cake sales increased before the advertisement was printed, then the ad could not be considered a causal factor. A third criterion is the *absence of other causal factors.* If the researchers could not identify any other reason why consumers might suddenly start to buy more Sara Lee cakes, then they can be reasonably sure that their advertisement produced the increase. However, Sara Lee researchers might find that the only similar cake had gone off the market just before the advertisements began. At the same time, in the town where the study took place, the ad campaign could have coincided with the winter holiday season, when people tend to buy more frozen desserts. In this case, researchers would not be so sure about the cause of the increase in Sara Lee cake sales.

Even if all three criteria are met, researchers can never be absolutely sure they've identified a causal relationship. Of course, the more evidence accumulated in favor of a causal relationship, the more confident researchers will be that they are correct.

Error in research design. Any research design contains potential error. Marketing researchers try to design projects that will minimize the possibility of error. The following are possible errors researchers must watch for.[5]

One type of error is known as *concomitant variation,* which occurs when information researchers collect is not related to solving the problem. If Sara Lee researchers wanted to know how consumers select their dessert purchases, they might ask them to list a number of desserts in order of their taste preferences and the products' convenience. However, these two factors might not be the ones that determine which desserts consumers actually purchase. Perhaps some feel that Sara Lee cakes taste best and are most convenient, but instead they buy dessert mixes to save money. Others might perceive a particular brand as most wholesome and choose that one, regardless of the fact that they perceive a different brand to be more convenient, cheaper, and tastier. Measuring taste preference and consumers' perception of convenience does not give researchers direct information on how consumers select their dessert purchases in this case.

Population specification error occurs when researchers choose the wrong group of people from whom to gather data. For example, researchers might ask consumers of Sara Lee's frozen desserts why they eat the products, but the consumers might not be the people who actually buy the products.

Frame error occurs when the list of possible subjects for a study is inaccurate or incomplete. One example of frame error is using the telephone directory to choose subjects when the study calls for subjects from the entire population. Many people have unlisted numbers, so the sample would exclude that group of people. If the Sara Lee researchers used the telephone directory as a sample frame for a study of consumers' dessert preferences, they might be leaving out many of the people they particularly wanted to study. For example, it may be that more affluent consumers, those most likely to use Sara Lee products, are those most likely to have a voluntarily unlisted phone number.

Sampling error happens when researchers have drawn incorrect conclusions because the number of people they studied was too small. Sara Lee researchers would have to get answers from enough people if their answers are to be accurate.

Some other kinds of research error include *selection error,* or choosing an incorrect group of people to study; *measurement error,* or the presence of a gap between the needed information and the data provided by the study; and *nonresponse error,* when those who actually participate in the study differ from those who were selected to participate, but for some reason did not. These errors often occur in sampling and in the use of questionnaires. In experiments, there can be *history effect,* as when, for example, researchers work with cities that have different histories that can influence results; and *maturation effect,* or the influence of the mere passage of time on the problem being studied.

Researchers cannot be sure that they have completely excluded these sources of error from their studies, but they can minimize their effects. Statisticians have determined confidence levels with which to view research results. Confidence levels, because they are always less than 100 percent, are experimenters' way of recognizing that the possibility of some amount of error is always present in research. Another way to minimize error is to compare the results against those gotten from studying a control group. If the study has been affected by maturation effect on other variables, for example, it should up in a comparison of the two sets of results.

Collecting the Data

After the research has been designed, the researchers will move to the third step, **collecting the data.** The data can be either secondary or primary.

Secondary data. Researchers have many sources of information at their disposal. One category of data is secondary data. As we mentioned earlier in the chapter, secondary data are bits of information that have been collected for some reason other than the current problem under study. Three important advantages of using secondary data are savings in time, savings in money, and the reduction of duplication of effort. Gathering even a large amount of published material on a given topic is far less expensive than conducting a field study and can be accomplished in a matter of days. There is also the possibility that analyzing secondary data may solve the problem.

There are disadvantages and problems with using secondary data. The data may not apply precisely to the study or they may not be current enough. Another problem is availability. There may be no information that is relevant to the current investigation.

Judging the accuracy of data is always a problem. The accuracy depends on the original source and the motivation behind the publication. Some data are provided by bureaus of the federal government that exist solely to provide facts and figures. Other kinds of publications are designed to promote industries, products, political causes, and so on. Promotional publications may tend to slant the evidence to support a particular viewpoint. The accuracy of these data, though they may be useful for many purposes, is less reliable than that of sources not designed to advance a particular view.

Secondary data may also itself be based on secondary data. For instance, an article on washing machine purchases in Wisconsin might include statistics on family income in the area. If the researchers intend to use those data, they must be traced to their original source to make sure all the relevant information has been included. Figures on income may have been rounded off for the convenience of the washing machine study, while the precise figures might be essential to the present research.

Another problem is comparability of units. If researchers need data on potential markets expressed in terms of individual income, figures on family income probably will not suffice; if researchers need information on the record-purchasing behavior of 11- to 15-year-olds, data on 13- to 19-year-olds probably will not serve very well.

Sources of Secondary Data. There are two sources for secondary data: *internal*

TABLE 5–1 Sources of Secondary Data

Source	Examples
Internal Sources	
Sales department	Sales records; quarterly sales reports
Accounting department	Financial data
External Sources	
Government agencies	Bureau of the Census; National Center for Health Statistics; Departments of Agriculture, Commerce, Labor, and Transportation
Associations	Chambers of commerce; Association of American Railroads; AFL-CIO
Syndicated sources	Selling Areas-Marketing, Inc. (SAMI); A. C. Nielsen Company; National Purchase Diary (NPD)
Miscellaneous publications	Dun & Bradstreet; general business magazines—*Fortune, Business Week*; newspapers—*Wall Street Journal*; specialized business magazines—*Merchandising Week, Automotive News*

sources and *external sources*. These sources are described below and listed in table 5–1. Internal secondary data are generated from within the company conducting the research. Sales invoices, quarterly sales reports, accounting records, and other records of the company's activities are all sources of internal data. This information is the least expensive type to acquire. Researchers use these data for a variety of purposes, including identifying profitable products and sales methods, monitoring changes in purchasing trends, evaluating promotional campaigns, and pinpointing sources of marketing problems. Internal secondary data can serve as a good starting point for marketing research: They provide a wealth of specific information that can be applied to the immediate problem, they are inexpensive, and they are easily accessible.

The amount of external data is even more vast. The major sources include government agencies, associations, and syndicated services.

Government agencies that provide statistical information include the Bureau of the Census, the Department of Agriculture, and the National Center for Health Statistics. The Bureau of the Census is responsible for a large number of publications that provide information on topics ranging from the income of individuals and families, to retail trade reports, to crime studies, to county business patterns. Businesses rely on these publications for accurate, regularly published statistical data covering a broad range of topics. Sara Lee, for example, could turn to the Bureau of the Census for demographic data about its consumers.

Associations are another rich secondary information source. Most libraries have bibliographies that list the publications of special-interest groups. Researchers can locate trade associations and other groups in almost any topic area. These groups are often the authors of their own marketing-related studies. Supermarket associations could give Sara Lee data on sales and shelf space for frozen baked goods; various food manufacturers' associations could provide information on competitors' products.

Syndicated information sources are in the business of providing data by subscription to other businesses. Companies can subscribe to a service like Selling Areas-Marketing Inc. (SAMI) or Simmons Market Research Bureau to find out the amounts of food products shipped from warehouses to grocery stores. SAMI provides information on wholesale activity during four-week periods and covers most grocery product categories throughout the United States. Subscribers to this service receive the information about three weeks after the reporting interval. From these reports, subscribers can follow changes in their own and competitors' volume sales as well as market share.

Simmons provides data on demographic characteristics and media habits of consumers for all types of products. Figure 5–3 shows part of the information collected by Simmons for frozen baked goods, such as Sara Lee croissants.

Section A shows that 46.2 percent of the female homemakers questioned used frozen baked goods. When asked which brands they used, 19.6 percent said they used Sara Lee cakes, 9.3 percent said they used Sara Lee pastries, and 6.6 percent said they used Sara Lee pies. Sara Lee can compare these figures against the figures for competing brands.

Section B shows some of the demographic data Simmons collects. The data for Sara Lee cakes is on the right. For example, 47.2 percent of users of Sara Lee cakes live in metro suburban areas; 22.1 percent of the metro suburbanites use Sara Lee cakes. The index figure of 113 shows that this distribution is 13 percent above the average. The income breakdown indicates that users of Sara Lee cakes tend to be affluent.

Section C shows part of Simmons's analysis of Sara Lee cake users according to their media habits. The high index figure for *Travel & Leisure* magazine suggests that it might be a good magazine for Sara Lee to advertise in. The index figure for *Weight Watchers* magazine suggests that it might not be.

A store audit collects information on sales at the retail level. One firm that provides this kind of service is A. C. Nielsen Company. Nielsen sends auditors to retail stores throughout the country to record sales for certain products during a two-week period. In addition to information on sales, the auditors provide data on local advertising and promotion, prices, and other facts relevant to the marketing mix. Nielsen also compiles a television index. Participants' television sets are equipped with an electronic device called an audimeter that records when the set is turned on and to which channel the set is tuned. With this information, Nielsen estimates the number of households watching a particular program. Nielsen publishes reports of these data every two weeks for most clients and more often for those that need more frequent updates.

Another type of service focuses specifically on consumer behavior. The National Purchase Diary (NPD) gathers data from 13,000 families on their purchasing

A

1A. DO YOU OR OTHER MEMBERS OF YOUR HOUSEHOLD USE THEM?		ALL		SOLE		PRIMARY		SECONDARY		
	YES	34622	46.2	3636						
	NO	40353	53.8	3883						
		'000	%	'000	%	'000	%	'000	%	UNWEIGHTED

IF YES

1B. WHICH BRANDS ARE USED BY YOUR HOUSEHOLD?

Brand	'000	%	'000	%	'000	%	'000	%	UNWEIGHTED
BURNY BROS. (CAKES)	560	.7	71	.1	417	.6	72	.1	71
BURNY BROS. (PASTRIES)	319	.4			224	.3	95	.1	33
CHEF PIERRE (PASTRIES)	1261	1.7	117	.2	786	1.0	358	.5	164
DRESSEL'S (CAKES)	908	1.2	45	.1	550	.7	313	.4	115
DRESSEL'S (PASTRIES)	435	.6	34	*	197	.3	204	.3	49
JOHNSTON'S (PIES)	3398	4.5	308	.4	2371	3.2	719	1.0	327
LLOYD HARRIS (PIES)	2615	3.5	363	.5	1586	2.1	667	.9	305
MORTON (CAKES)	2649	3.5	176	.2	1976	2.6	498	.7	255
MORTON (PASTRIES)	2632	3.5	213	.3	1790	2.4	629	.8	259
MORTON (PIES)	6674	8.9	944	1.3	4369	5.8	1361	1.8	632
MRS. SMITH (CAKES)	1829	2.4	93	.1	1300	1.7	436	.6	174
MRS. SMITH (PASTRIES)	1393	1.9	111	.1	1122	1.5	160	.2	153
MRS. SMITH (PIES)	11782	15.7	1848	2.5	8199	10.9	1735	2.3	1268
OLE SOUTH (PASTRIES)	1242	1.7	186	.2	644	.9	412	.5	105
PEPPERIDGE FARM (CAKES)	11490	15.3	1096	1.5	7517	10.0	2877	3.8	1268
PEPPERIDGE FARM (PASTRIES)	5385	7.2	409	.5	3211	4.3	1766	2.4	620
PILLSBURY STRUDEL	1006	1.3	84	.1	612	.8	310	.4	108
PET RITZ (PASTRIES)	3181	4.2	375	.5	1984	2.6	822	1.1	316
RICH'S (PASTRIES)	946	1.3	54	.1	537	.7	355	.5	87
SARA LEE (CAKES)	14678	19.6	1945	2.6	9658	12.9	3075	4.1	1657
SARA LEE (PASTRIES)	6973	9.3	599	.8	4560	6.1	1815	2.4	830
SARA LEE (PIES)	4975	6.6	478	.6	3168	4.2	1329	1.8	559
SMUCKER (CAKES)	475	.6	9	*	296	.4	170	.2	36
STOUFFER (CAKES)	1588	2.1	96	.1	887	1.2	606	.8	170
STOUFFER (PASTRIES)	1127	1.5	22	*	706	.9	399	.5	132
OTHERS	1564	2.1	413	.5	935	1.2	258	.3	170
DO NOT KNOW	293	.4							27

B

	TOTAL U.S. '000	PEPPERIDGE FARM (CAKES)				PEPPERIDGE FARM (PASTRIES)				PET RITZ (PASTRIES)				SARA LEE (CAKES)			
		A '000	B % DOWN	C % ACROSS	D INDX	A '000	B % DOWN	C % ACROSS	D INDX	A '000	B % DOWN	C % ACROSS	D INDX	A '000	B % DOWN	C % ACROSS	D INDX
METRO CENTRAL CITY	23082	3363	29.3	14.6	95	1515	28.1	6.6	91	939	29.5	4.1	96	4583	31.2	19.9	101
METRO SUBURBAN	31254	5210	45.3	16.7	109	2688	49.9	8.6	120	1016	31.9	3.3	77	6921	47.2	22.1	113
NON METRO	20639	2917	25.4	14.1	92	1183	22.0	5.7	80	1226	38.5	5.9	140	3174	21.6	15.4	79
HSHLD INC $35,000 OR MORE	8229	1767	15.4	21.5	140	958	17.8	11.6	162	*431	13.5	5.2	123	2451	16.7	29.8	152
$25,000 OR MORE	19918	4147	36.1	20.8	136	2094	38.9	10.5	146	1114	35.0	5.6	132	5440	37.1	27.3	140
$20,000 - $24,999	9366	1536	13.4	16.4	107	668	12.4	7.1	99	*450	14.1	4.8	113	1826	12.4	19.5	100
$15,000 - $19,999	10045	1719	15.0	17.1	112	790	14.7	7.9	109	*380	11.9	3.8	89	1968	13.4	19.6	100
$10,000 - $14,999	15094	2077	18.1	13.8	90	1050	19.5	7.0	97	*572	18.0	3.8	89	2715	18.5	18.0	92
$ 5,000 - $ 9,999	11542	1087	9.5	9.4	61	*450	8.4	3.9	54	*380	11.9	3.3	78	1507	10.3	13.1	67
UNDER $5,000	9010	924	8.0	10.3	67	**334	6.2	3.7	52	**285	9.0	3.2	75	1222	8.3	13.6	69

C

	TOTAL U.S. '000	PEPPERIDGE FARM (CAKES)				PEPPERIDGE FARM (PASTRIES)				PET RITZ (PASTRIES)				SARA LEE (CAKES)			
		A '000	B % DOWN	C % ACROSS	D INDX	A '000	B % DOWN	C % ACROSS	D INDX	A '000	B % DOWN	C % ACROSS	D INDX	A '000	B % DOWN	C % ACROSS	D INDX
TRAVEL & LEISURE	1055	*247	2.1	23.4	153	*126	2.3	11.9	166	**27	.8	2.6	60	318	2.2	30.1	154
TRAVEL/HOLIDAY	489	*128	1.1	26.2	171	**38	.7	7.8	108	**26	.8	5.3	125	*158	1.1	32.3	165
TRUE STORY	3604	561	4.9	15.6	102	*152	2.8	4.2	59	*203	6.4	5.6	133	622	4.2	17.3	88
TV GUIDE	20850	3592	31.3	17.2	112	1797	33.4	8.6	120	936	29.4	4.5	106	4425	30.1	21.2	108
US	1700	287	2.5	16.9	110	**169	3.1	9.9	138	**87	2.7	5.1	121	388	2.6	22.8	117
U.S. NEWS & WORLD REPORT	2542	485	4.2	19.1	124	277	5.1	10.9	152	**133	4.2	5.2	123	583	4.0	22.9	117
VOGUE	4145	759	6.6	18.3	119	407	7.6	9.8	137	**141	4.4	3.4	80	1005	6.8	24.2	124
WALL STREET JOURNAL	1160	251	2.2	21.6	141	*139	2.6	12.0	167	**62	1.9	5.3	126	295	2.0	25.4	130
WEIGHT WATCHERS MAGAZINE	2273	285	2.5	12.5	82	*105	1.9	4.6	64	**103	3.2	4.5	107	371	2.5	16.3	83
WOMAN'S DAY	14912	2564	22.3	17.2	112	1406	26.1	9.4	131	805	25.3	5.4	127	3314	22.6	22.2	114

Figure 5–3 Samples of the information collected by Simmons for frozen baked goods, including Sara Lee
Simmons Market Research Bureau: 1980 Study of Media and Markets. Used with permission.

habits over month-long intervals. Each participating family receives a printed diary to record their purchases in 50 product categories. Selection of families for participation in NPD is based on family size, income level, and several other variables. The sample is designed to represent purchasing patterns for consumers across the country. This service could identify sales data and market shares for all Sara Lee products. Sara Lee researchers could also see the number of two-person families, potential customers for Cakes for Two, or the amount of fresh baked goods bought. (See focus 5–1 for an example of an NPD survey.)

Primary data. Secondary data very often serve as a starting point for marketing research but do not usually provide enough specific information on which to base a decision about the marketing problem at hand. When this is the case, researchers must work with **primary data,** or information gathered specifically for the purpose of addressing the present problem. In marketing research a major portion of primary data comes from communication with consumers or others important to the marketing process. Analysts gather a good deal of marketing information through the use of focus groups, observation, interviews, surveys, and experimentation. In this section we will look at these methods for collecting primary data.

Sampling. From where are primary data collected? In most research situations, it is not possible or even desirable to study each member of the **population,** or the total number of cases that possess some set of qualifications of interest to researchers. For example, the researchers at Sara Lee would not even consider talking to each potential frozen foods buyer. Rather, researchers will study a **sample,** a relatively few representative members of the larger population from which researchers draw conclusions about the group as a whole. **Sampling** is the process of selecting those individual members from the population to make up a representative group. For this process, researchers use a **sample frame,** or a list of possible members. The method of sampling will have been specified in the research design. The biggest problem in sampling is the selection of a group that truly represents all the critical characteristics of the population under study. The types of samples are shown in figure 5–4 and are discussed below.

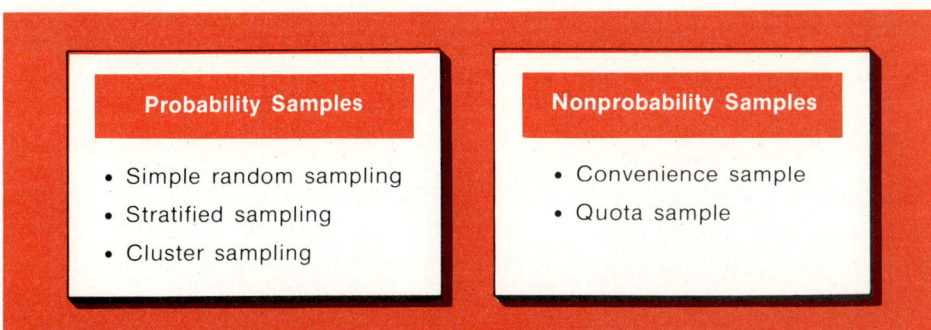

Figure 5–4 Types of samples

Chapter 5 / Marketing Research and Marketing Information Systems

5–1 Focus on a Marketing Research Study
NATIONAL PURCHASE DIARY COLLECTS DATA ON EATING HABITS

When you tiptoe to the refrigerator for that midnight snack, what do you eat: A crunchy stalk of celery, an apple, or a piece of chocolate cake made with refined sugar and flour? Companies that manufacture and distribute food products would like to know and are willing to pay a great deal of money to find out. They have good reasons, for each year some 500 new food products enter the marketplace. Some, like granola bars, with sales of $350 million in 1983, are enormously successful, but many are not. In 1983, for instance, food companies developed and promoted dozens of low-salt food products, believing that nutrition-minded consumers would buy them. After all, the marketing research conducted had shown that 60 percent of the people in the country expressed concern about salt in their diet.

Sales for these products, however, were almost uniformly disappointing. People had said they wanted less salt, but they did not actually buy what they said they wanted. Something had gone wrong. The research had been carried out by the traditional method of interviewing. Selected (and presumably representative) individuals and families were asked about their food preferences and concerns, and the results were tabulated. This method has an unfortunate limitation. People didn't *really* want what they *said* they did. How, then, could the food companies obtain the information they needed to make correct marketing and product development decisions?

A New York-based market research concern, National Purchase Diary (NPD), came up with an innovative solution. NPD distributed more than 1,000 questionnaires to chosen households, asking about their attitudes toward food and nutrition. It also asked each

---

There are two general types of samples. In **probability samples,** members are selected by an objective process. Each member of the population has a known statistical probability of being included in the sample. The advantage of this method is that it enables researchers to estimate the amount and the influence of sampling error. In **nonprobability samples,** sample selection is not based on any statistical method. Because the selection method is not objective, it is impossible to measure the amount of error and the effects of any error on the collection of data or on the research results.

Probability Samples. Probability samples include **simple random sampling,** a selection process in which each element of the population has the same chance of inclusion in the sample. In **stratified sampling,** the population is divided into subsets from which a simple random sample is drawn. Each member can belong

household to record in a diary every snack or meal consumed during a two-week period in each of the two years covered by the survey. So far, NPD was using traditional market research methods. What it did that was new was to correlate the data from *both* sources, thus providing information on broader eating trends and practices.

Subjects were divided into five groups, called, respectively, Meat and Potatoes, Families with Children, Dieters, Naturalists (natural-food eaters), and Sophisticates (primarily urban dwellers with above-average incomes). NPD concentrated on the last three groups since they were the ones that most interested food companies. The companies were interested primarily in these groups because sales to them were increasing much more than food sales in general. The data correlation produced some surprising (and valuable) results.

Only 8 percent of the subjects, it turned out, were strict natural-food eaters, and an equal number chose their food primarily for flavor and sweetness. As expected, Naturalists liked fresh fruit, rice, bran bread, natural cereal, wheat germ, yogurt, and granola bars, but they also ate a lot of French toast with syrup, chocolate chips, pretzels, and gelatin desserts. Sophisticates, who were expected to like wine, beer, mixed drinks, Swiss cheese, and bagels, also ate cream cheese, doughnuts, frozen dinners, prepackaged cakes, and olives. Dieters liked sugar-free and dietetic products, but also drank coffee and ate zucchini and squash.

Possible applications for NPD's results are many. Companies that buy the data, as some major corporations did even before the study was completed, expect to have a more accurate picture of what consumers actually prefer and thus target their advertising and new product lines accordingly. Cream cheese products might be advertised in a way designed to appeal to the Sophisticates, coffee makers might direct their advertising toward Dieters, and pancake flour might be promoted as healthful food.

Source: Betsy Morris, "Study to Detect True Eating Habits Finds Junk-Food Fans in the Health-Food Ranks," *Wall Street Journal*, February 3, 1984, p. 33.

---

to only one subset, or stratum. This procedure ensures that all strata will be represented in the sample. In a simple random sample it is possible to under- or overrepresent some portion of the population; this is not likely to be significant, though, if the sample is large. Stratified sampling involves identifying and choosing strata within the population that are relevant to the purposes of the study and including a random sample of their members.

Cluster sampling is another kind of probability sample that involves subsets. In this case, though, each subset has the same characteristics as the population as a whole. The sample is chosen either by using all the members of one subset or by selecting subset members at random. For part of its marketing research study, Mirro used a cluster sample of registered owners of its cookware. Members of this cluster sample were then called at random and asked about the color, name, and packaging of the cookware.

Nonprobability Samples. An example of a nonprobability sample is the **convenience sample.** Participants in the sample are chosen on the basis of their availability to the person making the selection. Jovan, for example, could have questioned anyone purchasing sunscreen in a particular store, and Mirro could have questioned people it found in a department store's housewares area. The problem with this type of selection process is that the researchers have no way to determine whether or not the sample represents the population.

Another form of nonprobability sample is the **quota sample.** Here researchers have estimated the frequency with which a certain characteristic occurs in the population. The sample is picked so that the characteristic of interest occurs in the same ratio as it does in the population. For example, a group of physicians might want to test the appeal and effectiveness of a new weight-loss program before publishing a book for overweight people. The doctors might find that one-third of overweight people are under age 40 and two-thirds are over age 40. The doctors would then select a sample proportionate to the age distribution.

A group of businesses can also constitute the population under study. If the population is numerous, as with food stores, researchers will choose and work with a sample. If it is small, as with makers of aircraft engines, researchers may want to talk with all members of the population.

Methods of collecting primary data. Once researchers have a sample, the next step is to actually gather the data. The specific methods are described below and summarized in table 5–2. Methods of data collection, of course, vary, depending on the goals of the investigation. The particular methods to be used will have been specified in the research design.

TABLE 5–2 Types of Data Collection Methods

Method	Features
Focus group	Part of exploratory stage; allows researchers to identify issues, consumers' complaints, and consumers' terminology.
Observation	Allows researchers to observe actual behavior; can be conducted electronically (as with optical scanners) or personally.
Interview	
Personal	Face-to-face contact between interviewer and respondent; flexible; high degree of respondent cooperation; possible interviewer bias.
Telephone	Respondents more open to sensitive questions; quick method; difficult to ask complex questions.
Mail survey	Most common method; researchers can ask many, sometimes complex questions.
Experimentation	
Natural	Reflects what is actually happening in real life; no researcher intervention.
Controlled	Researcher sets up experiment, either in field or in laboratory; good way to study actual behavior.

Leo Rutigliano, Decisions Center, Inc.

Figure 5–5
Researchers use focus groups to gain insights into people's views and to identify people's interests in and terminology used about a product.

Focus Groups. A **focus group** consists of a small number of people who meet to discuss a marketing issue. The leader of the group is a moderator who guides the discussion so that it meets the researchers' goals. Focus groups work best as part of the exploratory stage of research. The group can give researchers background information on which to base hypotheses for additional research. Figure 5–5 shows a focus group at work. By listening to people's views on a particular topic, researchers can also gain insights into a problem area. Focus groups can serve as an early step in developing a questionnaire by identifying issues of interest to consumers and the terminology they use, particularly when the company is unsure about how to approach the problem. This method is viewed as an early step in the data collection process. It would be inappropriate to draw final conclusions from the information gathered in a focus group; not only is the focus group too small to serve as a reliable sample, but also researchers are still formulating their hypotheses and the research design.

Observation. Another method of data collection is **observation.** Researchers might want to learn what portion of shoppers in a certain store notice an advertising display. To find out, an observer could be positioned nearby to record such data as the number of shoppers who stopped to read the display's ad copy, the number who just looked at the display, and the number who walked by without even glancing at it.

People-watching is not the only means of observation, though. Some more complex methods are among the data collection methods we discussed earlier in the chapter. Nielsen's recording of the size of television audiences is one example.

Figure 5–6 A bank of telephone interviewers. The telephone interview is a quick way to get information, although it is difficult to ask complex questions.

Leo Rutigliano, Decisions Center, Inc.

Another is the recently developed electronic optical scanner that gathers a large amount of data from the Universal Product Code (UPC), the 11-digit numbers that appear on most supermarket items. Use of the scanner is a more sophisticated method of recording some of the same information that, until now, has come from consumer diaries, such as the National Product Diary.

Interview. One of the most frequently used methods of data collection is the **interview.** Companies often find out what consumers think about a product or an issue by sending trained interviewers out into the field to ask questions. One company that relies on this method is Airwick Industries, Inc., makers of air-freshening products. A few years ago, stiff competition threatened the company's lead in this market. Airwick's research and development department went to work on developing a new product. They came up with a carpet cleaner/room deodorizer in one product. Instead of putting the product directly into stores, though, Airwick selected a few locations in which to test the product. By using television commercials and samples of the product, Airwick was able to test consumers' responses. After extensive interviews, the company found that some modifications were necessary. Consumers thought the product was too grainy and said they would be afraid to use it on rugs because it might get caught under furniture. The company made changes in the product so that it had a more powdery consistency. With two new products, Carpet Fresh and Plush, Airwick enjoyed renewed success in the market. Executives at the firm credit these results to the use of early interviews to measure consumer response.[6]

Chapter 5 / Marketing Research and Marketing Information Systems

There are several types of interviews. A *personal interview* involves face-to-face dialogue between interviewer and respondent. Interviews often take place in the respondent's home, or place of business, or a shopping mall. Usually the interviewer records the respondent's answers during the interview. In a personal interview, the interviewer is more likely to get cooperation from the respondent. The interviewer also has the flexibility to explore answers if something is unclear. A disadvantage is that any bias on the part of the interviewer can creep in, bias in terms of interpretation of answers or visual cues or word emphasis that influences the answers the respondent provides.

The *telephone interview* is a variation on this procedure. Some researchers believe that because the telephone interview involves less personal contact, respondents are more likely to answer questions honestly, leaving less room for biased results.[7] Respondents are thought to reply more openly to potentially embarrassing questions and to those concerning their social status, for example. The main advantage of telephone interviewing is that it is a quick way of getting information. On the other hand, it is difficult to ask complex questions over the telephone.

Mail Surveys. **Mail surveys** are the most common approach to data collection. They are not simple to design, though. The terminology used may not be familiar to respondents or may seem ambiguous. Pretesting the surveys with typical respondents is a way to ensure that the researchers and respondents are talking the same language. In this procedure, respondents receive questionnaires through the mail, answer them, and mail them back to the company. In many cases the warranty card that comes with many products serves as a form of written questionnaire. The card often contains a number of questions about where and for what purpose the item was purchased. Mail surveys allow researchers to ask a large number of questions, some of them complex and some showing photographs. A problem with mail surveys is low response rate and, thus, the possibility of nonresponse error.

Experimentation. **Experimentation** is most often used to study causal relationships between variables. The main advantage of experimentation is that researchers have more control over the situation they are studying. They can also observe actual behavior better than with any other data collection method. Greater control gives them more confidence in their findings. In an experiment, the researcher manipulates an independent variable to measure changes in the dependent variable. As described earlier, experimentation can take place either in a laboratory, where researchers have a maximum degree of control, or in a natural setting, where researchers have greater certainty that what they are measuring reflects real life.

Recent use of electronic optical scanners in grocery stores has provided researchers with laboratory control in a natural setting. One company, Information Resources, Inc., has enlisted 2,000 families in each of two test markets, Pittsfield, Massachusetts, and Marion, Indiana.[8] Because local supermarkets had been slow to install the scanning systems, Information Resources purchased the equipment and gave it to the stores. The purchases of each participating family are computer-recorded using the UPC bar codes and sent to Information Resources, whose subscriber companies benefit from information about consumers' buying behavior.

The company also studies how promotions like coupons, displays, and TV and newspaper ads influence consumers' purchases. With the cooperation of cable television systems, the company can control the TV commercials that come into each household. This enables Information Resources to compare responses to different commercials. Ocean Spray recently used the scanners when it introduced juice in its paper bottle.[9] Data from the scanners showed that after consumers learned about the product from TV commercials, sales increased almost 300 percent. Information from the scanners also showed where Ocean Spray should display the product: Sales were greater when the juice in paper bottles was in stores' single-service area than when it was shelved with other Ocean Spray products.

Analyzing the Data

After all the data have been collected, researchers move to the next step, **analyzing the data.** The researchers tabulate the data to find frequencies, means, correlations between variables, and other statistical data that will be useful in making decisions about the problem that is being investigated. The choice of a method for analyzing the data depends on the objectives of the study and the method of data collection. When the study was originally designed the objectives suggested the type of analysis needed. This, in turn, led to the types of data collected. For the analysis to be as accurate as possible, then, the entire study must be thought through at the beginning.

Making Recommendations

The final step for researchers is **making recommendations,** or presenting their findings and analysis to marketing managers. The research must answer the question for which it was designed. The best way to do this is to provide only information that relates specifically to the problem. Presentation of irrelevant information may be confusing and a waste of time. The recommendations should be feasible and appropriate for the company and the product. For example, the studies conducted by Mirro and Jovan both suggested specific, practical actions, such as changing a product's name or redesigning a package.

Focus 5–2 presents the methods, findings, and analysis in a marketing research study conducted by the New York City Opera.

Marketing Information Systems (MIS)

A recent development in marketing research is the **marketing information system (MIS),** or the set of all information and procedures that can be used in the study and solution of marketing problems. Such a system is occasionally referred to as a Marketing Research Information System (MRIS) or Marketing Management Information System (MMIS).

5–2 Focus on a Marketing Research Study
THE NEW YORK CITY OPERA STUDIES ITS AUDIENCE

In 1982, the New York City Opera (NYCO) was considering changing its performing season. It had been doing two ten-week seasons, one in the fall and one in the spring, and wanted to shift to one 20-week season running from summer through late fall. This move would help help reduce the cost of promoting two separate seasons and would take advantage of an open summer market. The idea of doing summer opera was new, and NYCO wanted to find out how its current and potential audience would respond. NYCO also wanted to gather information about its audience's cultural habits and ticket-buying patterns in order to make intelligent choices about the season and to find the best way of mounting its subscription drive. Did people want to hear international stars in familiar operas? New operas? English-language operas? American musicals? What potential audience, in fact, existed for opera in New York, and specifically for summer opera? Would enough people subscribe? If not, why not? To answer these and other questions, NYCO, in conjunction with professional market research firms, developed a three-stage program of marketing research.

In Stage One, four separate groups (current subscribers, former subscribers, new subscribers, and single-ticket buyers) were recruited to form focus groups. In order to minimize any possible bias, the participants were not told that NYCO was sponsoring the survey, but only that they were being asked to participate in a national survey on the arts. Separate panel discussions were held with those who responded favorably to the recruitment. Professional market researchers led the participants in discussions on a series of questions designed to find out what factors were important in determining whether or not people subscribed to a given opera company or season. In addition, participants were asked to detail their cultural habits and ticket-buying patterns and their perceptions both of NYCO and of its major rival, the Metropolitan Opera Company (the Met). Were NYCO and the Met seen as competitors? If so, what should NYCO do to distinguish itself from the Met? How important was NYCO's location (in Lincoln Center)? Was it crucial to attendance, or could NYCO have a season in another location? What ancillary educational processes could NYCO provide for its audience? And so on.

When the results of these discussions had been tabulated and synthesized, NYCO made a number of preliminary findings. They found that the participants felt NYCO was an excellent company for introducing a person to opera, was distinguished by a strong ensemble spirit, and was "more comfortable" and "less intimidating" than the Met. They found that people were initially reluctant to subscribe (but not necessarily reluctant to attend) in the summer because they feared scheduling conflicts with vacations, trips, and free time. They also found some areas of concern, most notably the high degree of crossover that existed between audiences of the Met and of NYCO. This suggested that the opera audience in New York might be static, and that it would be necessary to change the general perception or nature of opera to draw new customers.

Using the information gathered in Stage One, NYCO developed a ten-minute telephone interview that focused on attendance patterns, the new season's structure, and the choice of operas heard. Over three-hundred interviews were completed, which gave more quantitative answers to these key questions—necessary to create a marketing plan for the new season.

(continued)

The survey results of Stage Two confirmed the findings from Stage One. They showed that a potential audience did exist for opera performed in the summer, that resistance to the idea was based on its novelty rather than on concrete reasons, and that people's reluctance to subscribe was primarily due to fear of conflicts in scheduling. Acting on these findings, NYCO developed a season and marketing approach that built on the company's apparent strengths (operas in English, ensemble playing, a friendly atmosphere) and minimized their weaknesses (opera itself being perceived as inaccessible and elite, and apprehension about scheduling conflicts).

A direct mail and promotional campaign was designed with a friendly, accessible tone, using illustrations rather than photographs, and printed in warm, friendly colors. In an innovative move, simultaneous translations, or "subtitles," were added so that foreign opera would be more understandable. A "Bring-A-Friend" voucher, entitling a subscriber to purchase two additional tickets for the price of one, was added to each subscription. A variety of activities, including a Puccini opera festival and an outdoor café serving light suppers and drinks, were developed to show that opera could be done in the summer in New York and that it could be enjoyable. To deal with reluctance about subscribing, NYCO introduced an exchange policy whereby subscribers could keep their regular good seats to performances (which has been perceived as a principal benefit of subscribing), but could exchange any tickets to any performances, in person or even by mail, if a scheduling conflict were to crop up.

In Stage Three of the marketing research, NYCO (which had decided to run a summer and fall season of 20 weeks) wanted to find the best way to promote subscription sales for this new season. Three actual brochures were prepared, presenting three different subscription offers. One offered a subscription covering the entire 20-week season, the second the summer portion of the season only, and the third offered the fall portion of the season with the option of adding the summer. NYCO wanted to find out which approach would be most successful in terms of number of seats sold, total ticket income, and number of additional tickets purchased. The offers were mailed to three groups of randomly selected individuals: current subscribers, former subscribers, and single-ticket buyers. (These "test" offers were genuine, in that those who subscribed did receive exactly what they had ordered.)

The individuals selected were instructed to complete the order form but not to mail it in. Instead, they were to wait until called. A professional organization was hired to make the follow-up calls, take the orders, and conduct short interviews. More than 1,200 people were thus interviewed, and the results showed that the brochure offering the fall portion of the season with the option to add the summer was the most successful. Two months later, the brochure was mailed to more than 300,000 homes. Response greatly exceeded NYCO's expectations, and more than 150,000 tickets, worth nearly $2.5 million, were sold before the season opened.

Alas, even the best-laid plans of mice and men (and market researchers) often go astray. On the opening night of the newly developed summer season, the musicians' union went on strike against NYCO, a strike that lasted part way into the fall. The result was that the summer season, produced with such careful attention to the wishes of the audience, never happened.

Note: Information about NYCO's approach to its new season was provided by Alan Toman, president of The Marketing Department, formerly Director of Marketing for NYCO.

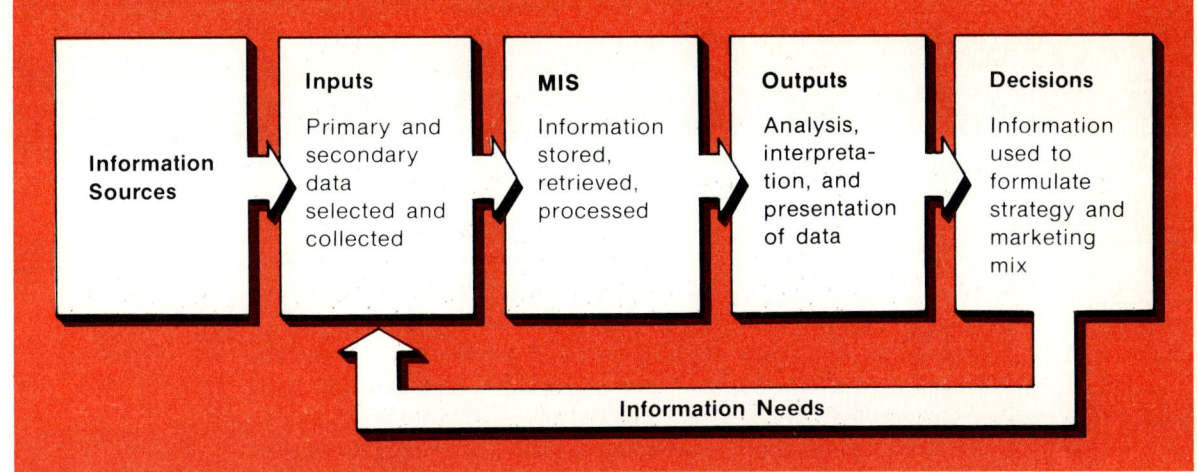

Figure 5–7 An example of an MIS

Every business has some form of MIS. In a small retail store, the MIS might consist of the proprietor's knowledge about what items have sold well in the past, hunches about new and rising consumer demand for a certain product, records of purchases and sales, and perhaps ideas about effective window displays from a member of the sales staff. In more complex businesses the MIS might include computers and a data processing staff working in conjunction with both marketing researchers and salespeople in retail outlets in territories across the country. Figure 5–7 shows a typical MIS for a complex business.

In many cases, it is not practical to launch a special project for each marketing problem that arises. Nor is there time to gather needed information for new or sudden problems. Development of an MIS enables marketers to use marketing research resources on a continuous basis. Part of the purpose of an MIS is to monitor constantly the marketing situation so that when problems arise there is already a good deal of detailed background information. The data that go into the MIS can come from a variety of sources: internal data, including sales records, reports from the company's sales force, and past marketing research reports; and external data, from articles from trade publications as well as newspapers and magazines, information on the activities of competitors, and marketing information from syndicated data services.

An example of a typical use for an MIS would be a company's monitoring of its market share of a particular brand. The MIS would store all information relevant to this question: the price of the brand, price changes and their effect on sales, competitors' prices, and market share at the end of previous quarters. Each new piece of information on this issue would be added to the MIS as the company learns of it. Whenever the question of the brand's market share comes up, the MIS can provide the most current information.

How could Sara Lee use an MIS? On a continual basis, Sara Lee marketing researchers could track and record sales figures and market share percentages for all Sara Lee products. They could gather information about competitors' products, prices, and distribution patterns. The researchers could develop demographic profiles of their consumers and analyses of the consumers' tastes. As changes in food consumption habits affect purchases of Sara Lee products, the researchers could monitor social trends and pertinent scientific research. All of this information, constantly updated, would provide a data bank managers could use in making decisions. When Sara Lee conducts individual studies, as in testing consumer reactions to new products, the data and analyses from these, too, could be added to the information system.

Sears has been a leader in developing and using an MIS. One use has been to keep track of purchases of appliances and their service and maintenance requirements. When it is time for the buyer of a washing machine, for example, to renew a maintenance contract, Sears automatically sends a reminder. This program has helped to create a more efficient and welcome service program. Another use has been the analysis of its information about its 40 million customers. Sears can target purchasers and likely purchasers of certain types of products and can pass information and names of sales prospects along to its various subsidiaries, such as Allstate Insurance.

For many companies, an integral component of the MIS is a computer system. Using the computer enables marketers to integrate information from a variety of sources and access that data rapidly. The computer also enables users to have immediate access to current data. Information on price changes, unit sales, or warehouse shipments, for example, can be entered as soon as they are known and be immediately available to all users. As changes in the marketing environment occur with greater frequency, having up-to-date data becomes more and more vital to marketing researchers.

One concern to developers of an MIS is the level of detail that the computer should store. The needs of the individual company are the best guide here. Sales data, for example, can be stored in a number of ways. The salesperson responsible for the sale might be an important source of information, as might the price of the item sold, the name and location of the retail store, product and model numbers, reason for purchase, and a number of other details. For other companies, much of this information will be unnecessary. In developing an MIS, an important issue is how much detail is necessary for the company's use and what items can be omitted to enhance efficiency. The concept of the level of information detail included in an MIS is known as *information aggregation*. MISs will also differ in the level of complexity of their analytical functions. Here again the company's needs will determine the appropriate level.

How did Sara Lee's marketing research and product development turn out? Not all of Sara Lee's attempts to develop strong new products were well received. The line of fresh baked goods failed, as did many of the lines of frozen foods. The plan behind Cakes for Two backfired. People who usually bought the large cakes switched to the smaller, lower-priced product, and the smaller cakes didn't seem to attract a significant number of new buyers. Light 'n Luscious desserts also failed.

The experimental procedure, fortunately, kept many of these tested products from being developed or marketed further.

Frozen croissants, on the other hand, are a tremendous success. Due to this success, Sara Lee is concentrating on developing additional frozen baked goods. In the fall of 1983, for example, Sara Lee planned to start testing Creative Cake Layers—baked cakes that consumers could frost and decorate themselves. Most important, Sara Lee is continuing with its development and testing of new products, based on its analysis of markets and food trends.

Summary

Marketing research is "the systematic gathering, recording, and analyzing of data about problems relating to the marketing of goods or services." Its role is to reduce uncertainty about marketing issues by providing specific, verifiable, hard data about the market, the company's competition, and consumers and their perceptions.

The decision about whether or not to use marketing research should be based on three criteria: There must be uncertainty about a marketing decision, the company must be prepared to make changes in response to research results, and the cost of the research must not exceed its potential value.

The first and most important step in marketing research is to define the problem.

The second step is designing the research. A research design is the specification of procedures for data collection and analysis. Exploratory research is concerned with gathering general information about the nature of the problem and relies heavily on secondary data. Three types of exploratory studies are the literature search, the experience survey, and the analysis of case histories. Descriptive research is characterized by the use of detailed planning and the statement of guiding hypotheses. The consumer profile study and the longitudinal study are both examples of descriptive studies. Causal research is conducted either in a natural setting or in a controlled setting (laboratory).

Some of the types of error that can occur in marketing research include surrogate information error, in which researchers choose the wrong people from whom to gather data; frame error, in which the list of possible subjects is inaccurate or incomplete; and sampling error, in which researchers have used random sampling procedures but have generated a nonrepresentative sample.

The third step is collecting the data, both secondary and primary. Secondary data are information that has been gathered for some reason other than for the problem at hand. Researchers using secondary data look for potential problems in currency, availability, accuracy, and comparability of units. Internal sources of secondary data are generated from within the company conducting the research. External sources include government agencies, associations, and syndicated data services. Primary data are information gathered specifically to help resolve the present problem.

A sample is a group of a relatively few representative members of the larger population from which researchers draw conclusions about the population as a whole; sampling is the process of selecting the representative group; the sample frame is the list of possible elements in the sample. In probability samples, elements are selected by an objective process so that each element has a known probability for inclusion. Examples include simple random samples, stratified samples, and cluster samples. Nonprobability samples are selected on the basis of personal judgment. Examples include convenience samples and quota samples.

A focus group, used primarily in exploratory research, is a small number of people who meet to discuss their views on a particular issue. Observation methods consist of recording behavior or events either by watching them or by using some mechanical method. Other means of gathering primary data include personal interviews, telephone interviews, mail surveys, and experimentation.

When all the data have been collected, researchers use mathematical procedures to analyze and interpret them. These are the fourth and fifth steps in the marketing research process. Finally, they present their findings to marketing managers. The specific methods used in both these steps depend on the objectives of the research.

The marketing information system (MIS) is the set of all information and procedures that can be used in the study and solution of marketing problems. Today computers play an integral role in the MIS. The purpose of an MIS is to provide current data to managers on a continuous basis.

Questions for Discussion

1. Explain in what way marketing research is scientific in nature.
2. Can a marketing manager rely completely on marketing research data before making his or her decision?
3. "The first and probably most essential step in the marketing research process is to define the problem." Explain.
4. How would a marketing researcher conclude that there is indeed a causal relationship between variables?
5. What are the advantages and disadvantages of using secondary data in marketing research?
6. Examine the important role played by syndicated information services in marketing research.
7. Distinguish between probability and nonprobability sampling.
8. Examine the role of focus groups in collecting marketing research data.
9. Discuss the role of marketing information systems (MISs) in making marketing decisions.

References

1. Janet Neiman, "Sara Lee Reacts, Tries Basketful of New Sweets," *Advertising Age*, December 27, 1982, p. 4.; "A Leaner Consolidated Foods Rediscovers Marketing,"

Business Week, August 29, 1983, pp 58–59; and "Sara Lee President Says 'Convenience' Still Sells," *Advertising Age*, August 21, 1976, pp. 69–70.

2. *Marketing Definitions: A Glossary of Marketing Terms* (Chicago, American Marketing Association, 1960), p. 16.
3. "Mirro Changes the Recipe," *Sales & Marketing Management*, February 8, 1982.
4. "Jovan Offers a Hi-Tech Tan," *Sales & Marketing Management*, June 7, 1982.
5. Gilbert A. Churchill, *Marketing Research: Methodological Foundations* (New York: Dryden Press, 1983), p. 399ff.
6. "Airwick's Discovery of New Market Pays Off," *Business Week*, June 16, 1980, pp. 139–40.
7. Donald S. Tull and Del I. Hawkins, *Marketing Research: Measurement and Method*, 2nd ed. (New York: Macmillan, 1980), p. 116.
8. "Market Research by Scanner," *Business Week*, May 5, 1980, pp. 113, 116.
9. "Scanners Juice Up Ocean Spray's Test," *Sales & Marketing Management*, March 13, 1982.
10. "Business Is Turning Data into a Potent Strategic Weapon," *Business Week*, August 22, 1983, pp. 92–94.

OBJECTIVES

1. To discuss the importance of understanding customer needs and wants in the overall success of the marketing program.

2. To identify and explain the differences between three types of buyer decision-making units.

3. To discuss the roles played by different members in group decision making.

4. To explain the steps involved in the buyer decision process.

5. To highlight the goal orientation and evaluative character of buyer decisions.

6. To describe three types of buying situations.

6

Buyer Behavior

The implementation of the marketing concept requires that companies find out what customers need and want and then develop products to meet those needs. It also requires that companies find out about the factors and processes that affect customers' decisions to buy. A number of companies have done this successfully.

General Electric has long been responsive to and researched the needs of its customers. Engineers in GE's Video Products Division visit customers and dealers and ask questions about what they like and need. The engineers use this feedback directly to develop new products and product features. For example, because homes are getting smaller, customers have identified lack of space as a problem. General Electric responded by producing a microwave oven that can hang from below kitchen cabinets, freeing counter space. In another program, GE set up an Answer Center; both industrial and individual customers can dial a toll-free number and get information, assistance, or just reassurance about the products they have bought.

Campbell has also surveyed its markets and is creating products to suit developing needs. Recognizing that a growing number of affluent customers want tasty and convenient frozen foods, Campbell created its successful Le Menu line of dinners. Campbell has also recognized that consumers are not all alike, and it has developed products and advertising campaigns to appeal to specific groups within the population. For example, Campbell sells its spicy Ranchero Beans only in the South and Southwest.

The Safeway supermarket chain recognized that the nature of food shoppers had changed. No longer is food shopping done by a housewife for the standard "family of four." Instead, many shoppers are male or single or working women or are shopping for smaller families. Thus the chain decided to change its

policies to meet the needs of these new types of shoppers. Stores are open longer. The number and types of products carried have been increased to make shopping more convenient for time-pressed shoppers. New departments within the stores, such as bakeries and delis, appeal to more affluent customers. Safeway also conducts marketing research surveys to find out what other policies could be adopted to meet the needs of customers.[1]

Marketing managers have to consider many things when making decisions about marketing strategy. Such factors as costs, production abilities and constraints, the organization's goals, and the coordination of the marketing mix must be considered. No matter how carefully these factors are handled, however, the marketing program will not be successful unless it meets one key criterion: It must be based on a sound knowledge of the needs and wants of target customers. Knowledge of customer attitudes, preferences, and behavior is the keystone on which successful marketing programs are formulated.

This chapter looks at the basic concepts that marketers use to understand buyer behavior, including identification of buyers and analyses of the buyer decision process and types of buying decisions. Chapter 7 looks at the consumer market and factors that affect consumer buying behavior. Chapter 8 looks at organizations and their buying behavior.

The concepts presented in this chapter are based on research in psychology and sociology. Understanding the concepts, however, does not give marketers the ability to predict buyer behavior accurately in relation to any one product or brand in any one situation. Understanding these concepts, however, *will* help marketers ask the right questions about buyer behavior.

Organizations search for information about current and prospective buyers in many ways. The most formal, organized, and reliable way to search for information on buyer behavior is to conduct marketing research. It is very unusual for even the most seasoned marketing executive not to find that the research uncovered several totally unexpected issues or that buyers felt quite differently about products or marketing strategy than had been expected.

Such a situation occurred not long ago with a group of marketing executives from a regional chain of discount stores that specialize in household products, such as sheets and towels. These stores positioned themselves against traditional department stores, which they perceived to be their major competition, by showing comparative prices on all merchandise tags—"Compare at $15. Our price $11.99," for example. The stores also featured frequent sales.

Management began to wonder whether the frequency of the sales was diluting the customer's image of the stores' everyday low prices. Thus it was decided to conduct marketing research—specifically, to assemble focus groups composed of customers—to help the regional chain understand how customers viewed this issue. As the researchers questioned the first focus group, quite a different picture from what management had envisioned began to emerge. First, these customers simply did not believe the comparison prices on the tags. Second, it quickly became apparent that these customers saw the stores as being more like other discount stores than like the traditional department stores against which management believed it was competing.

Some of the younger marketing managers became quite agitated. "How could these people be so misinformed? We know our price comparisons are accurate; both company policy and governmental regulations require that they be verified frequently. And our quality—we buy merchandise under our own brand from the same mills that produce for major names and the major department stores!" The marketing vice-president, a seasoned pro who had heard these arguments many times before, listened for a few minutes and then cut the discussion short.

"Remember what we are here to find out," he said. "It doesn't matter that *we know* that our price comparisons are accurate and that our merchandise quality is high. What matters is what customers *believe* is true, because that is what governs their actions. If further research confirms what we've heard today, we have work to do, but we can only do it effectively if we base our strategies on how customers think and act, not what *we* think they should or do feel."[2]

Chapter 6 / Buyer Behavior

Types of Buyers

Buyer behavior is a complex topic precisely because it deals with people. People are complex, unpredictable, and, at times, even irrational. They are also unique. No two buying situations are exactly alike because the buyers are not exactly alike. Yet all buyer behavior is goal-oriented; people are trying to satisfy particular needs when they purchase and consume products and services. It is the marketer's task to recognize the needs of the particular buyer and attempt to satisfy them.

In every buying situation, the actual decision to buy is made by a **decision-making unit (DMU).** There are three basic types of DMUs: individual consumers, households, and organizations. When developing marketing strategy, marketers must identify the type of DMU and understand the process each type uses to make buying decisions.

Three Types of Decision-Making Units

Individual consumers.   Many buying decisions are made, and many products are consumed by, an **individual consumer.** The decision to buy is made by the individual, and the purchase is used to satisfy a personal need. When a hungry individual runs into a fast-food restaurant to grab a quick lunch, he or she is acting as an individual consumer. (Individual consumers are discussed in chapter 7.)

Households.   Many times, a product is used by, and perhaps purchased by, a group of consumers who form a **household.** A family meal is an example of this type of buyer behavior. A group of people consumed the meal together. One or more people prepared the meal. One or more people shopped for the food. Each of these activities could be carried out in a different way, because a group of people instead of just a single individual was involved in making the buying decisions and performing the activities. (As households have characteristics of both individual consumers and organizations, they will be discussed in chapters 7 and 8.)

Organizations.   The third type of DMU is the **organization.** Businesses, governments, and nonprofit organizations are all formal organizations. DMUs in organizations are composed of a number of members with different roles to play. The buying decision itself is highly institutionalized, with many formal procedures to follow. (Organizations are discussed in chapter 8.)

This classification of DMUs is based on the *process* of buyer behavior, not on the *products* consumed. Individuals and households do consume similar products, while the products consumed by businesses and governments are often quite different. It is not the nature of the product that is difficult to understand and predict. Rather, it is the nature of the process by which buyers decide to buy a product that is often not clearly understood. Yet it is the ability to inform or influence that process which is crucial to successful marketing strategy.

Let's look at two examples. The 3M Company developed a product called Embark, a spray that makes grass grow slower. The intended customers were businesses—cemeteries, golf courses, and so on—which could use it to save money on mowing costs. These customers, however, are slow to purchase Embark, because they are reluctant to change their business practices. Individual consumers, especially suburbanites, are interested in purchasing Embark, but 3M is reluctant to sell to them, as it is easy to misuse the product. The same product fits into both the organizational and consumer markets, but the buyer decision processes are obviously different for both types of DMUs.[3]

Matsushita sells videocassette recorders and other electronic products. Its traditional market of consumers, however, is rapidly becoming saturated with similar products; at the same time, consumers may not be interested in some of the novelty electronics products the company is producing. Organizational consumers, however, are interested in some of the novelty products, such as big television screens. Again, the products are the same, but different DMUs are making different buying decisions about the products.[4]

Roles of Buyers

While individual consumers make buying decisions for themselves, the purchases of households and organizations are the results of group decision-making processes by a DMU. The processes can be quite formal, as when a committee is appointed in a business firm to consider the purchase of a personal computer for each member of a large department. It can be quite informal, as with a shopper standing in front of the cereal display in the supermarket trying to decide which cereal will come closest to pleasing the entire household. Whether the DMU is a formal or an informal one, various members play various roles. Rarely is a group organized around these roles, however. Instead, the roles exist because of the relationship of the group members to one another and to the product category.

The first role is that of **initiator.** The initiator recognizes the need for a purchase and puts the rest of the buying process in motion. Another role is that of **purchaser.** Someone must actually perform the activities of purchasing the product. However, a question often asked is "Is the purchaser also the **decision maker**?" Often they are not the same. In the case of the firm that was considering purchasing personal computers, the entire DMU may join in making the decision, while the purchasing agent merely makes out the order forms. Similarly, the purchaser of the cereal may have been requested by another household member to purchase a particular brand and may be merely executing that request.

On the other hand, a shopper at the cereal counter may or may not comply with the request of a small child for a highly sugared brand of cereal. The shopper retains the role of final decision maker. However, the child has attempted to act as an **influencer** in the choice of cereal brand. The child thinks he or she has a right to influence the decision—after all, he or she has the role of **user** of the product.

Another role is possible, that of **gatekeeper.** A gatekeeper is a person who controls a flow of information, thereby controlling whether or not a potential cus-

Bob Rashio, Click/Chicago

Figure 6–1 Buyers can play a number of roles. One of these consumers, for example, may be the purchaser, decision maker, and user, while the other may serve as influencer.

tomer hears about a product. This role can be especially critical in the organizational setting. Often a salesperson is prevented from seeing the actual decision maker, whether it be a technical expert such as an engineer or the president of the corporation. Only the purchasing agent receives sales calls. All information is funneled through him or her. If the purchasing agent does not think highly of the brand—or perhaps of the salesperson—the information simply is not passed on. The brand, then, has no opportunity to become part of a set of alternatives to be evaluated. Even if the gatekeeper does not make a final positive decision, he or she may make preliminary negative decisions that greatly influence the nature of the final decision.

In our discussion of the buyer decision process below, we will show how buyers assume these various roles and how marketers appeal to buyers in each of these roles.

The Buyer Decision Process

Since understanding buyer behavior is the keystone to developing successful marketing strategies, marketing managers must have a clear understanding of the process by which buying decisions are made, whether by individual consumers, by households, or by organizations. Yet, for a variety of reasons, they sometimes do not.

Changes in the marketing environment can put managers into situations where buyer behavior is relatively unknown. For example, not too long ago a number of drugs were reclassified by the Food and Drug Administration (FDA).

Chapter 6 / Buyer Behavior

144

These drugs had previously been available only by prescription, but the FDA's ruling meant that consumers could buy these drugs over the counter without even the advice of a physician. Confronted by knowledge of this impending change, marketing managers for a pharmaceutical firm that sold an analgesic cream recognized that they needed a great deal of information about the consumer decision process. As long as consumers had to use what their physicians prescribed, this information was not critical. When consumers could choose for themselves, understanding the steps they go through in making a purchasing decision suddenly assumed great importance.

Figure 6–2 shows the steps in the buyer decision process: **problem recognition, information search, evaluation of alternatives, purchase decision,** and **postpurchase evaluation.** Buyer behavior may occur in this neat sequence, but at other times, the buyer may terminate the process, go back to an earlier stage, or skip one or more stages.

As the marketing managers for the analgesic cream sat down to face the new situation they realized that a number of important questions about the buyer decision process had to be answered if they were to create appropriate strategies for

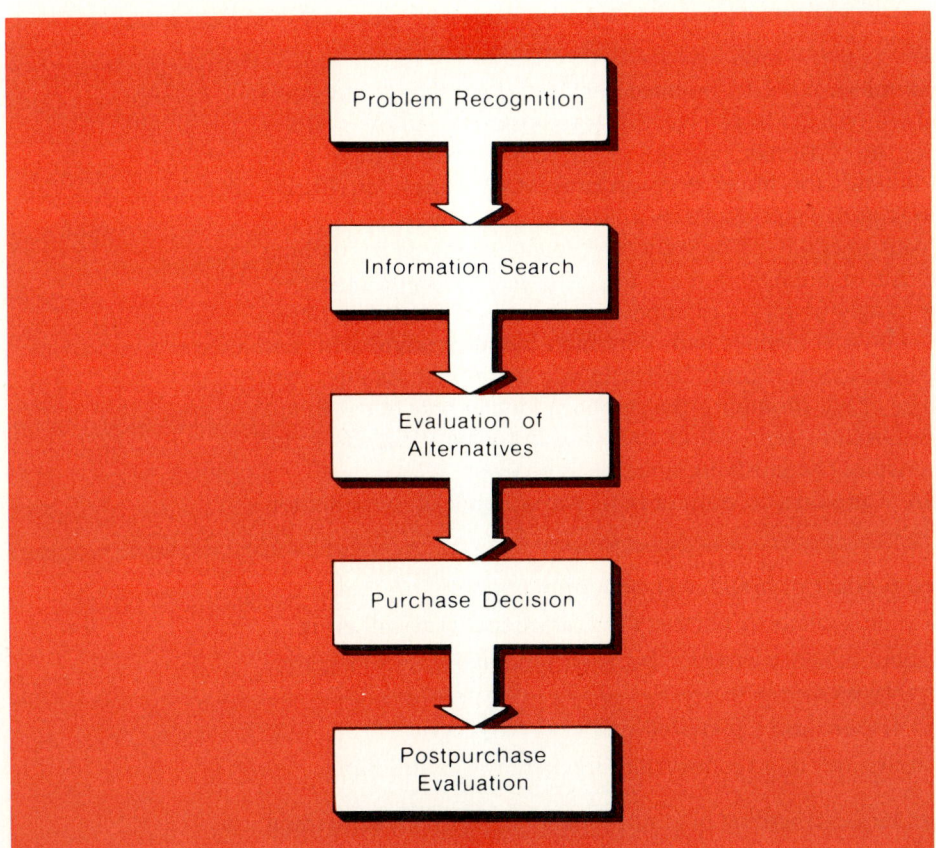

Figure 6–2 The steps in the buyer decision process

selling their product directly to the individual consumer. Some of the major questions they listed were:

1. What will cause consumers to decide that an analgesic cream is what they need for a particular health problem?
2. In what kinds of stores will they expect to purchase this type of product?
3. Will they want the advice of a medical professional before purchasing this product? If they do, will they be comfortable asking the pharmacist or will they want a physician's advice?
4. What can we tell them that will cause them to purchase our brand instead of a competing brand?
5. What benefits do they expect to experience as a result of using this product?

The managers realized that there was much other information that would be useful to them, but they felt that these questions were basic to an understanding of their consumer. Answering these questions required looking at the steps in the buyer decision process.

Problem Recognition

Buyer behavior is rarely aimless. It is goal-oriented behavior, even though the goals may not be explicit to the buyer. Its basic objective is to contribute to the maintenance or improvement of the consumer's quality of life. Consequently, there must be some stimulus that initiates the buyer decision process. The most productive way for a marketer to look at this stimulus is as a "consumer problem."

A "problem" is a consumer's need or want. In broader terms, it is anything that makes it more difficult or impossible for a buyer to achieve some objective. The problem may be seemingly trivial—a toothpaste that leaves a funny aftertaste. It may be potentially lethal—a consumer with very high blood pressure who has difficulty finding low-sodium foods. It could be something trivial that assumes particular importance because of the situation—the stubborn lock of hair that will not behave just before an important event. All of these are "problems" in the sense that they frustrate the consumer in satisfying some need or want.

Consumers recognize a problem in a number of ways. Some of the common ways are:

1. A currently used product or brand isn't performing properly.
2. A buyer wants to do something but can't find a product that will do it.
3. A buyer hears about or sees a product that seems to have features superior to the one currently used.
4. It is hard to find or purchase a preferred product.
5. The buyer is running out of a product that is generally kept on hand.

In general, the buyer lacks something or is not totally pleased with something that he or she currently has.

It is important to look at consumer problems from the standpoint of the marketer. Can the company make a product that will solve this problem for a sizable segment of consumers? Even if there is no perceived need for a new product, can it produce one that solves the problem better? In other words, the consumer's problem represents an *opportunity* for the marketer—a toothpaste with a pleasant aftertaste, sodium-free processed foods, a product that controls unruly hair.

By recognizing and taking advantage of the opportunities, marketers can affect the problem recognition process in two ways. First, they can help define problems—such as cleaner teeth, a whiter wash, or a user-friendly computer. Second, they can present solutions to known problems, such as a toothpaste with brightener, a detergent with bleach, or a computer with a built-in set of user instructions. Figure 6–3 shows how one manufacturer defines and solves a problem.

Figure 6-3 The problem is defined: Reheated coffee does not taste good. The solution? This manufacturer suggests the Coffee Butler, which solves the problem by keeping coffee hot and fresh for hours.

Reprinted courtesy of Thermos

The specific problems or desired objectives that initiate the buyer's decision process can be determined by marketing research. Let us assume that our pharmaceutical marketers have done some initial research. They found that the ways consumers approached a large number of individual problems fell into three broad categories.

One group of consumers said, "I have a skin problem—itching, rash, minor injury. I need to get something to put on it." The second group approached the same problem differently: "I have some kind of skin discomfort. I'd better go to the doctor and find out what to do about it." The last group said, "I have a minor skin problem. If I ignore it, it will probably go away." Consumers in the first and last groups also tended to voice a common problem. "It's a real hassle to have to go to the doctor just to get a prescription to clear up a minor skin problem." The marketers were pleased. It had been obvious that a skin problem was the stimulus that caused the consumer to consider using an analgesic cream, but now they knew that not all consumers reacted to the stimulus in the same way. Not only that, they could see that the consumers in the first group could be reached and influenced directly, those in the second group could be reached through physicians, and those in the third group were going to be very difficult to reach at all. The marketers were progressing, but they still had far to go to understand thoroughly the buyer decision process.

Information Search

If the problem is a stimulus that leads the buyer to engage in the decision process, the next step the buyer is likely to take is to begin to search for and accumulate information.

It is easy for marketers to assume that consumers want to acquire a great deal of information. After all, marketers reason, consumers will make better decisions if they have all relevant information. In fact, buyers may not make better decisions when they have large amounts of information.[5] Instead, they may become confused and make suboptimal decisions. Usually, however, consumers do not seem to acquire enough information to cause confusion. In some cases, little or no information search took place even though the purchase seemed "important"—it was being purchased for the first time, it was expensive, or a lot of choices were available.[6] These characteristics suggest when the purchase is somewhat risky, information is obtained to reduce the risk. When little risk is present, it is not surprising that buyers do not spend large amounts of time acquiring product-related information. Other factors that affect the amount of information search include the availability of information and such variables as experience, time and financial resources available, education, occupation, age, and beliefs about the marketplace.[7]

Sources of information. There are two major sources of information available to buyers—the mass media and personal sources. The mass media provide the greater *quantity* of information, but personal sources generally provide the higher *quality*, or more credible, information.

The mass media are all around us—from billboards to magazines to radio and television—and all carry advertising. The "average" American has the opportunity to be exposed to hundreds, if not thousands, of ads on any given day.[8] The sheer volume of mass media advertising has produced "clutter," or the existence of large numbers of commercial messages, which makes it difficult for any one communication to receive significant attention that would lead consumers to recall it and take the intended action.

One recent study suggests that the problem may be even more acute than advertisers have yet realized. The study dealt with cynicism, or suspicion of the motives of others, and with alienation, or the degree to which individuals feel connected to the larger society. In a large sample of women from four representative U.S. cities, fully half of the women displayed cynicism and alienation. Adding to the potential woes of advertisers, more than 65 percent of the women displayed independence of thought, indicating (in the terms of the study) an unwillingness to accept advertising claims without personal evaluation.

A pilot study had previously demonstrated the degree to which cynicism could affect receptivity to advertising appeals. Celebrity spokespeople and product demonstrations are frequently used in advertisements to attract attention and increase credibility. In the pilot study, a group of subjects was shown ads with Lee Iacocca speaking for Chrysler, F. Lee Bailey as spokesperson for Smirnoff, a demonstration of a Schlitz beer taste test, and Tom Watson representing E. F. Hutton. High cynics, as opposed to those who scored medium or low on the cynicism scale, rejected both the message and the spokesperson in all except the Tom Watson/E. F. Hutton ad. Drawing on the experiences of advertisers in Europe, the researchers recommended that advertisers take a less intense approach to advertising style and content. Low-keyed, mildly humorous advertising that suggests the advertised brand "may not be for everyone and should be personally checked out" should be more credible to a cynical populace.[9]

On the other hand, buyers perceive information from personal sources as being credible. Persons whose opinions are highly valued and frequently sought out are called **opinion leaders** or **influentials.** They tend to be outgoing individuals who are knowledgeable about the product and who like to try new things. Opinion leaders are *not* higher in social status than the people they influence; they are members of the same face-to-face social groups. Also, opinion leadership is often specific to one or more closely related product categories; a person knowledgeable about video products, for example, may know nothing about automobiles. Some opinion leaders, however, may know about a range of products. Opinion leaders obtain information from the mass media or from user experience with the product and transmit it to the opinion seekers. Focus 6–1 describes further how influentials contribute to the information search.

Methods of information search. Buyers have a variety of ways in which they can go about acquiring information. The search can be internal versus external or active versus passive.

6-1 Focus on Consumer Behavior
INFLUENTIALS

We all know an influential or two. The influential, or product recommender, may be a friend in school, who will give you advice when you have saved enough money to purchase a new stereo, or your cousin, who will tell you where to get a good buy on a winter coat. Your mother might have gone to an influential she knows at the office when the family car finally gave out and it was time to buy a new one. The influentials we all know are those people who can give advice on a number of types of major purchases—from which home computer is compatible with which software programs to which refrigerator has the best service record. Most often, influentials learn about products by reading consumer magazines on a regular basis and by noting what people they know say about their purchases.

An influential often has had a good deal of experience in giving consumer advice. As a youngster this person may have studied the available alternatives for the purchase of his or her own bicycle or radio. Weeks or months of study paid off in the form of a satisfactory purchase and earned this person a reputation for being knowledgeable about certain types of products. Perhaps as the reputation grew, so did the range of knowledge. The influential may have begun to look for information about many types of products in order to help

Internal versus External Search. **Internal search** involves retrieving information from the individual's own memory. This is obviously a quick and easy way to search for information and is usually the first kind of search. If it is satisfactory, the search may stop there. The less the buyer knows about the product, the more he or she may use **external search.** The external search covers the mass media or personal sources discussed above.

Active versus Passive Search. **Active search** is undertaken when the buyer has inadequate or conflicting information or when the buyer is nearing a decision and wishes to confirm the correctness of the decision.[10] The extent to which the buyer actively searches for information will be determined by trading off the cost in both time and money of searching for information against the value of the information in terms of reducing the risk inherent in the purchase.

Exposure to information not actively sought is **passive search.** Most mass media advertising fits into this category. The issue for marketers is how to make passively received information, such as television commercials, compelling enough to the passive recipient, such as the television viewer, that he or she will remember the information. The likelihood of the information being remembered may be related to how well the information is presented; usually it is more strongly related

others decide what to buy. This individual enjoys talking with friends and co-workers and helping them make important purchasing decisions.

A product recommender may be responsible for thousands of dollars worth of purchases. Understandably, many companies would like a list of influentials so that they could ply them with information about their own products. According to some estimates, word-of-mouth advertising sells as many products as paid advertisements. But influentials are hard to find. One attempt to reach them was the Chrysler Corporation's campaign to spread information on its 1963 Plymouth by word of mouth. Chrysler paid taxi drivers to talk to passengers about the car. One reason this strategy has been abandoned may be that influentials themselves respond more strongly to published information than to word-of-mouth advertising.

There are two main reasons that we go to influentials for product information. One is convenience. It is easier to ask someone to tell you about a product's reputation than to do the research yourself. Another reason is that people trust an impartial influential's opinion more than they do advertising that has been paid for by the manufacturer. Research has shown that the more expensive the product, the more likely consumers are to seek the advice of an influential.

Source: Stephen P. Morin, "'Influentials' Advising Their Friends Sell Lots of High-Tech Gadgetry," *Wall Street Journal*, February 28, 1983, p. 23.

---

to the degree to which the buyer perceives the information to have current or future relevance to his or her personal situation.

Marketers can assist in an active, external information search by providing information about their products, as in figure 6–4.

In considering how consumers might search for information about medications that would relieve skin discomfort, the marketing managers identified three basic sources for information about their product:

1. Medical professionals, which includes both physicians and pharmacists
2. Media advertising, which should create brand awareness, preference, and knowledge about where to find the brand
3. Personal sources, who could be influenced to some degree by media advertising but are basically outside their control

They recognized that medical professionals and the general public were unlikely to respond to the same information. They also recognized that medical professionals could be reached by advertisements in medical and pharmaceutical

Figure 6–4 Lennox is assisting in the information search not only by describing the benefits of its product in this advertisement, but also by providing a toll-free number that consumers can call for even more information.
Courtesy of Lennox Industries Inc.

journals or through salespeople. The general public could be reached by in-store information as well as by media advertising. Once a consumer was in the store, however, would he or she be content to obtain information from the product package, or would the consumer wish to seek the advice of a pharmacist? This final question had important implications for their distribution channels policy. If most consumers wanted professional advice, the marketers could rely on drugstores as their primary distribution outlet. If consumers were content to rely on mass media advertising, the product could be sold in supermarkets and even discount houses, in addition to drugstores.

Chapter 6 / Buyer Behavior

152

Evaluation of Alternatives

Once the buyer feels that adequate information has been obtained, he or she can begin the process of choosing which product or service to purchase. This choice process takes place on two levels—the product category level and the brand choice level.

Several types of products may appear to have the potential to solve the buyer's problem when it is first recognized. The buyer who wishes to cure a minor rash may consider, besides an analgesic cream, a calamine lotion product, a general-purpose spray product, vigorous applications of soap and water, or even the time-honored remedy of witch hazel and baking soda. Once the product category is chosen, the buyer evaluates the brands within the category and chooses a specific one to buy.

It is difficult to find out how buyers make the choice between product categories, as questions often do not get at the criteria buyers use to choose among such a diverse set of alternatives. As a result, we have little concrete information about how buyers make the category-level choices. One study did find that consumer values affect this process. The researchers looked at two types of values—terminal, or states of being, and instrumental, or doing—in relation to appliance purchases. **Terminal values** included "Being the kind of person who wishes to have a beautiful home; being the kind of person who wishes to have a high level of physical comfort at home." **Instrumental values** included appearances and usability. The researchers concluded that terminal values are more strongly related to product-category choice and instrumental values to brand choice.[11]

Relating this finding to buyers wanting to cure rashes, marketers can assume that the terminal values of a buyer choosing an analgesic cream and a buyer choosing to use soap and water are quite different. Marketers selling the analgesic cream will try to show the characteristics of their product that meet the instrumental values of the buyer.

Whether the choice be product category or brand level, buyers do not ordinarily consider all available alternatives. They seriously evaluate only a subset of available alternatives. Called the **evoked set,** this group of alternatives is made up of those of which the buyer is aware and has sufficient positive information to be willing and able to evaluate. One of the marketer's first tasks, then, is to ensure that the product becomes known, so it has an opportunity to be in the evoked set.

The multiattribute model. Buyers have *choice rules:* "I will consider all brands below a certain price." "The suit must be conservative in style, made of high-quality materials, and a good value for the money." Choice rules establish the criteria by which the buyer will make the choice. The criteria are applied to the various attributes of each product under consideration. Buyers also apply weights to each of the attributes, based on the importance of the attribute to the buyer. The weight given to each attribute varies from buyer to buyer, based on the needs of the particular buyer. The result is to develop an overall preference for one of the brands in the evoked set. Buyers go through the process of weighting attributes in every buying situation, but the intensity of the process varies. In routine purchases,

Figure 6–5 A multiattribute model

	Location				
Job A	1	2	3	4	5
Job B	1	2	3	4	5
Job C	1	2	3	4	5
	Salary				
Job A	1	2	3	4	5
Job B	1	2	3	4	5
Job C	1	2	3	4	5
	Size of Company				
Job A	1	2	3	4	5
Job B	1	2	3	4	5
Job C	1	2	3	4	5
	Reputation of Company				
Job A	1	2	3	4	5
Job B	1	2	3	4	5
Job C	1	2	3	4	5
	Importance (Weight of Attribute)				
Location	1	2	3	4	5
Salary	1	2	3	4	5
Size	1	2	3	4	5
Reputation	1	2	3	4	5

1 = low; 5 = high.

the process is almost subconscious. The riskier and more unfamiliar the buying situation, the more important and deliberate the process becomes.[12]

The attributes considered can be either tangible or intangible. One tangible attribute of the suit mentioned above is that it is made of 100 percent wool; another is that the manufacturer is well known. An intangible asset is that the suit does not wrinkle easily. The buyer could weight these three attributes equally, or the buyer could weight the prestige of the manufacturer so heavily that the other attributes become unimportant.

Figure 6–5 shows a **multiattribute model** for a graduating senior deciding which job offer to accept based on the four attributes of location, salary, size of company, and reputation of company. Each job offer is rated on a scale according to the buyer's (the graduating senior's) beliefs about each job offer. When making the decision, a weight is applied to each of the attributes. For this buyer, salary is most important, followed by reputation of company, size of company, and location. This weighting makes it likely that the senior will accept job offer B. If location and size of company were more important, the senior might accept job offer A.

Purchase Decision

The purchase decision is not a simple yes or no decision. Even if the buyer has decided to make a purchase, there are a number of subdecisions that must be made before the product is actually bought. These include the following:

1. Timing. A purchase can be made immediately or it can be deferred until some future time. The buyer may think, "I'll pick up a tube of toothpaste the next time I'm in a store."
2. Situation. Some purchases are affected by the situation that exists when the purchase is made. The buyer may say, "I never order beer on a date."
3. Place of purchase. The choice may be between a department store or a discount outlet; in the suburbs or in the city; in a store with a prestige image or one with low prices. The buyer may consider, "Where can I find the type of suit I want at a reasonable price?" Or perhaps, "Where can I find good advice about the quality and fit of a suit?"

The marketer has two jobs in this step: presenting the buyer with the type of information that is most relevant and presenting the information in such a way that the buyer positively evaluates the brand (or the store or the manufacturer). The pharmaceutical manufacturer, for example, may find that medical professionals want technical information that explains *how* the analgesic cream works and *why* it has no side effects. They want to see the information in professional journals or hear an endorsement by a respected medical practitioner.

Consumers, on the other hand, want to know the need-satisfying attributes of the product, that it works, that it is easy to use, and that it has no unpleasant side effects. They are not interested in the technical details of how and why it works. When looking for an appealing way to present information to consumers, the pharmaceutical firm used a well-known football player as a spokesperson. The firm knew that burns from the Astroturf on playing fields are similar in nature to household burns and other minor skin irritations. To their surprise, the information presented by the football player was rejected because his problems were seen as "different" by the average consumer. Consumers, however, responded well to information presented by a medical expert. The most powerful information was that until recently the product had been available only by prescription. Consumers interpreted this to mean that the cream was "strong medicine." In addition, relatively few consumers felt it necessary to consult a pharmacist prior to purchase, implying that heavy mass media advertising coupled with intensive distribution would provide the necessary information plus easy availability.

Postpurchase Evaluation

The marketer's interest in the product and the buyer does not end with the purchase of the product. The marketer must determine whether the buyer was satisfied with the product. Buyer satisfaction increases the probability of a repeat purchase and affects the amount and type of information the buyer informally passes along to others about the product. The product's performance is an important component of the buyer's satisfaction, but it is not the only component. The buyer's expectations about the product are equally important.

TABLE 6–1	Buyer Reactions Based on Expectation and Product Performance	
Product Performance	Expectation	
	High	Low
Satisfactory Performance	It's ok. It's a good product.	This is really a super product!
Unsatisfactory Performance	This product is the pits!	It's not great, but what did you expect?

Table 6–1 suggests hypothetical buyer reactions based on both level of performance and level of expectations. If the buyer's expectations are confirmed—high expectations/satisfactory performance *or* low expectations/unsatisfactory performance—existing beliefs are reinforced, and the buyer's overall reaction is not strong. When expectations are *dis*confirmed, however, buyers do tend to react strongly. The high expectations/unsatisfactory performance situation results in an evaluation of the product ("It's the pits!") that is even worse than the product deserves based on "objective" criteria. The low expectations/satisfactory performance situation leads to an evaluation that may be even better than the product warrants. *Only* the high expectations/unsatisfactory performance situation creates genuine buyer dissatisfaction.

The dissatisfaction can be explained by the presence of **cognitive dissonance.** Cognitive dissonance happens "when two cognitions or beliefs do not fit together, and the result is a state of psychological discomfort."[13] In this case the two conflicting cognitions are the high expectation and the unsatisfactory product performance. The result is a deeply unsatisfied buyer who will probably never buy that product again.

The moral of this story for marketers is clear. They must not create expectations that the product cannot meet. They should encourage the formation of expectations that are slightly lower than subsequent performance can match. They must not tell consumers that their skin problems will magically vanish after a single application of the analgesic cream unless this is true. Even then, consumers may not believe it.

Our discussion of the buyer decision process has focused on the buying behavior of an individual consumer. Households and organizations also follow the steps in the buyer decision process, with the modifications discussed in chapter 8. Focus 6–2 presents an example of how a company goes through the steps in the buyer decision process.

Types of Buying Situations

While the steps in the buyer decision process give us a way of thinking about any buying situation, it is clear that actual buying situations can vary widely. The decision can be a difficult and complex one—the purchase of a multimillion-dollar

6–2 Focus on Organizational Buying Behavior
GENERAL FOODS GOES SHOPPING

When the buyers at General Foods shop, they do it in a big way. General Foods' buyers are responsible for purchasing all the ingredients that go into the company's products, as well as all packaging materials and just about anything else the company might need to get its products onto store shelves. Each year, General Foods spends between $800 million and $1 billion on coffee, for example. In a recent year, one buyer was responsible for purchasing $170 million worth of sugar, $18 million worth of raisins, $8 million worth of plastic bottles, and $23 million worth of rice. The buying decisions involved in organizational purchasing of this kind involve all the same stages as consumer purchasing, even though quantities may be almost unimaginably large.

The first step in the buying decision process is to examine each General Foods division's marketing plan at the start of the year to determine the company's needs. The plan shows how much of its products each division expects to sell. In addition, buyers must examine environmental factors that will influence their purchases. These include the economy, anticipated crop prices, and so on. Based on a detailed information search, the buyers make a prediction of the cost of each needed item.

The next step is to find suppliers, evaluate the alternative suppliers, and choose among them. The buyers for General Foods try to have at least two—and preferably several—suppliers to choose from for each needed item. If only one potential supplier exists, buyers try to determine what will happen if that supplier goes out of business or if there is a strike. Buyers evaluate alternative suppliers based on the services they offer, price, and quality of their products.

Once the buyer has identified the most satisfactory supplier, the next step is to place an order, or to make the purchase. While the buyers for General Foods do test products before purchasing them, mistakes sometimes occur. One General Foods' buyer recalls dog food bags that fell apart when filled with food, Jell-O packages that didn't carry the product's name, and a salad dressing bottle that instructed consumers to fill it with an incorrect amount of vinegar. When an error does occur, General Foods analyzes the cause of it in attempting to correct it. When bottles break during the manufacturing process, for instance, General Foods' employees attempt to put them back together to find out why.

Buyers also look for ways to save the company money. The buyer's role is crucial when small adjustments in ingredients and packaging can lead to tremendous cost reductions. Changing from metal bottle caps to plastic caps for barbecue sauce and syrup saved General Foods $1 million.

Source: N. R. Kleinfeld, "How a Company Does Its Shopping," *New York Times*, January 17, 1982, pp. F1, F27.

TABLE 6–2   Three Basic Types of Buying Situations

Automatic Response Behavior	Limited Problem Solving	Extensive Problem Solving
Problem Recognition	Problem Recognition	Problem Recognition
Information Search (limited internal)	Information Search (internal; limited external)	Information Search (internal; external)
	Evaluation of Alternatives (limited)	Evaluation of Alternatives (extensive)
Purchase Decision	Purchase Decision	Purchase Decision
Postpurchase Evaluation (very limited)	Postpurchase Evaluation (limited)	Postpurchase Evaluation (extensive)

Source: Adapted from Del I. Hawkins, Roger J. Best, and Kenneth A. Coney, *Consumer Behavior: Implications for Marketing Strategy* (Plano, Tex.: Business Publications, 1983), p. 449.

generator for a power plant, for example—or so routine it can hardly be described as a decision—picking up a tube of toothpaste because your current one is almost empty. In between there is a whole spectrum of decisions that require more or less of the buyer's attention.

Three basic types of buying situations have been identified: **automatic response buying, limited problem solving,** and **extensive problem solving.** In organizational buying, these types of buying situations are sometimes referred to as a **straight rebuy situation,** a **modified rebuy situation,** and a **new task.** Each type involves a different level of involvement with the various steps in the buyer decision process, as can be seen in table 6–2.

Automatic Response Buying

Automatic response buying (ARB) may be triggered by a type of problem recognition that is so specific that little room is left for decision making. If, standing in front of your medicine chest in the morning, you think, "I'd better get some Crest; I'm about out," there is little left to decide. Information search, if any, has involved only recalling from your memory the name of the brand usually purchased. You are planning to stick with that brand, so there is no reason to evaluate alternatives.

The major decision may be where and when to purchase: "Do I make a special trip to the drugstore for it, or can I just pick up a tube the next time I'm in a store that sells it?" As the toothpaste has been purchased and used satisfactorily before, postpurchase evaluation is likely to be almost nonexistent, unless something happens to change the level of satisfaction. Possible changes are the brand switching to a flavor that you don't really like, an advertisement that persuasively states that a new toothpaste has far superior benefits, or an occurrence that causes a level of cognitive dissonance that would reinstitute conscious decision making for toothpaste.

Limited Problem Solving

The existence of a state of limited problem solving (LPS) also implies previous satisfactory use of a product. The amount of conscious decision making is greater than in ARB, however. Suppose that a purchasing agent recognized that the firm's inventory of typing paper has reached the reorder point just as its contract with its stationery supplier is about to expire. Even if it is not a requirement, the purchasing agent may choose to check a few alternative suppliers to ensure that the firm cannot get a better deal. The longer standing the relationship and the higher the level of satisfaction with the current stationer, the less aggressive the purchasing agent is likely to be in searching out and thoroughly evaluating the offerings of alternative suppliers.

Similarly, unless something happens to destabilize the relationship, postpurchase evaluation is unlikely to be very thorough. The marketer who wishes to appeal to the buyer who is in a state of ARB or LPS will have to take some action that will cause the buyer to consciously consider the marketer's alternative product. The more deeply ingrained the habitual behavior and the lower the importance of the product or brand choice to the buyer, the more difficult it will be to cause him or her to deviate from the habitual behavior.

Extensive Problem Solving

Extensive problem solving (EPS) implies carrying out each stage of the purchase decision process in considerable detail. This is most likely to occur when the decision is new, is infrequently made, or is of great importance to the potential buyer. An individual who is suffering from a severe poison ivy rash for the first time probably lacks information about helpful products but has a strong desire to find a product that will relieve the problem quickly without side effects. The marketer's task then includes having both information and product available when the prospective buyer begins to search for them.

Summary

The keystone around which successful marketing programs are formulated is knowledge of customer attitudes, preferences, and behavior.

There are three types of decision-making units (DMUs). An individual consumer makes the decision to buy in order to satisfy a personal need. A household is a group of consumers living under one roof who make the decision to buy in order to satisfy the personal needs of the group. An organization's buying decision is characterized by highly institutionalized formal procedures. The classification of DMUs is based on the process of buyer behavior, not on the products consumed.

The group purchasing decision is based on several buyer roles. The initiator recognizes the need for a purchase and puts the rest of the buying process in motion. The decision maker reaches a conclusion about what product to purchase. The purchaser actually makes the transaction. An influencer affects the ultimate choice. The gatekeeper controls the flow of information to the group. The user is the actual consumer of the product.

The buyer decision process has five stages. In the problem recognition stage, marketers can either help identify problems that consumers face or present solutions to known problems.

In the second stage, consumers conduct an information search to reduce the risk involved in making purchases. Two major information sources are the mass media and personal sources. The high volume of advertising to which most consumers are exposed daily makes them suspicious of commercial messages. Persons whose opinions are highly valued and frequently sought out are called opinion leaders or influentials.

In the third stage of the buyer decision, consumers begin the evaluation of alternatives on both the product category and brand choice levels. Consumers usually consider only the evoked set of alternatives, or the subset of alternatives of which the consumer is aware and has sufficient positive information to be willing to evaluate.

The purchase decision involves either a decision to buy, a decision not to buy, or a decision to defer the purchase until another time, situation, or place.

The postpurchase evaluation stage involves an estimation of satisfaction with the product. Important factors include product performance and the buyer's level of expectations for the product.

One type of buying situation is automatic response buying (ARB), which is triggered by a type of problem recognition that is so specific that little room is left for decision making. The buyer is satisfied with the product purchased on an earlier occasion. A limited problem solving (LPS) situation involves a slightly higher level of conscious decision making, though the buyer is satisfied with a previous purchase. Extensive problem solving (EPS) involves carrying out each stage of the purchase decision in considerable detail.

Questions for Discussion

1. Explain in what ways knowledge of customer needs and wants can enable a dentist to develop a better marketing program for his or her services.
2. What are the most important differences between the three types of decision-making units—individual consumers, households, and organizations?
3. Discuss the roles played by different members of your family (including yourself) in your seeking a college degree.
4. "Buyer behavior is not aimless but goal-oriented." Explain this statement with particular reference to any two purchases you made today.
5. Identify and distinguish between the different sources of information available to buyers.
6. How would you generally describe the salient characteristics of opinion leaders?
7. Illustrate how an understanding of the two types of consumer values—terminal values and instrumental values—can help Apple promote a new line of home computers.

8. Based on your knowledge of postpurchase evaluation, how would you go about promoting a cure for baldness?
9. Distinguish between three types of buying situations—automatic response buying, limited problem solving, and extensive problem solving—in terms of the level of involvement shown by the buyer.

References

1. Based on "To Market, to Market," *Newsweek,* January 9, 1984, pp. 70–72; "Marketing: The New Priority," *Business Week,* November 21, 1983, pp. 96–106; and "Listening to the Voice of the Marketplace," *Business Week,* February 21, 1983, pp. 90–95.
2. Example from Danny N. Bellenger, Kenneth L. Bernhardt, and Jac L. Goldstucker, *Qualitative Research in Marketing* (Chicago: American Marketing Association, 1976), p. 7.
3. Lee Smith, "The Lures and Limits of Innovation," *Fortune,* October 20, 1980, p. 85.
4. Lee Smith, "Matsushita Looks Beyond Consumer Electronics," *Fortune,* October 31, 1983, p. 99.
5. Jacob Jacoby, Donald E. Speller, and Carol Kohn Berning, "Brand Choice Behavior as a Function of Information Load: Replication and Extension," *Journal of Consumer Research,* June 1974, pp. 33–42.
6. Joseph W. Newman and Richard Staelin, "Prepurchase Information Seeking for New Cars and Major Household Appliances," *Journal of Marketing Research,* August 1972, pp. 249–57.
7. Calvin P. Duncan and Richard W. Olshavsky, "External Search: The Role of Consumer Beliefs, *Journal of Marketing Research,* February 1982, pp. 32–33.
8. William M. Weilbacher, *Advertising in Business and Society* (New York: Macmillan, 1979), p. 546.
9. Donald L. Kanter and Lawrence Wortzel, "Cynicism and Alienation as Marketing Considerations: Some New Ways to Approach The Female Consumer," *Journal of Consumer Marketing* (article to be published in 1985).
10. Henry Assael, *Consumer Behavior and Marketing Action* (Boston: Kent Publishing, 1981), p. 34.
11. Dorothy Cohen, *Consumer Behavior* (New York: Random House, 1981). p. 376.
12. Martin Fishbein, "A Behavior Theory Approach to the Relations between Beliefs about an Object and the Attitude toward the Object," in M. Fishbein, ed., *Readings in Attitude Theory and Measurement* (New York: Wiley, 1967).
13. James F. Engel and Roger D. Blackwell, *Consumer Behavior,* 4th ed. (Chicago: Dryden Press, 1982), p. 505.

OBJECTIVES

1. To provide an overview of the diversity and complexity of factors influencing consumer behavior.

2. To discuss the role of needs and motives underlying consumer behavior.

3. To explain how a customer's behavior is modified by his or her perceptions.

4. To explore learning as an important phenomenon in consumer behavior.

5. To discuss the effect of buying behavior on a number of other specific psychological influences, such as personality, attitude, involvement, values, and so on.

6. To understand the marketing implications of demographic trends in regard to age, income, and education.

7
Consumer Buying Behavior

In the United States, 47 million people need vision correction, but only one-fourth of them wear contact lenses. An additional 48 million people wear bifocals, and, as the population in the United States ages, the number of bifocal wearers is expected to increase. These numbers are appealing to the makers of contact lenses, who see tremendous potential for growth and product development in this market.

In the early 1970s, Bausch & Lomb dominated the soft contact lens market, but its market share leadership was being threatened by a growing number of competitors entering the market. The company took a number of steps to reestablish its position. One step was to develop a new, thinner lens that, as it was half as thick as the original soft lens, became the easiest fitting lens on the market. To promote this lens, Bausch & Lomb took a second step—it launched a massive advertising campaign to attract new consumers to contact lenses. The main appeal of the campaign was to the affective motives—"What would you look like without your glasses?" A third step was to take advantage of the trust consumers have in the Bausch & Lomb name and produce a line of products—cleaning solutions, lubricants, and disinfectants—for use with contact lenses.

Bausch & Lomb and its competitors are introducing new products to bring non-contact lens wearers into the market. One product is the extended-wear soft lens that can be worn for approximately one month without having to be removed. This type of lens eliminated one of the strongest barriers that had kept people from buying contact lenses. The regular soft lenses must be cleaned daily and sterilized overnight, a process that many consumers wanted to avoid. Contact lens manufacturers do have to overcome two perceived problems with the extended-wear lenses, however. First, some of the lenses are very thin and have the reputation of tearing easily. An-

other problem is that some extended-wear lenses made of silicon caused eye damage; although the problem has now been corrected, consumers are still reluctant to try these lenses.

The newest type of lens to be developed is the tinted lens, which is designed to appeal to consumers who want to change the color of their eyes. A sizable percentage of the consumers of these lenses actually need no vision correction; they are just purchasing the lenses for cosmetic reasons.

Bausch & Lomb and its competitors see the contact lens market as in its infancy and are continuing to develop new products to draw new customers to try them and purchase them.[1]

Chapter 6 described buyers, the buyer decision process, and buying situations. In this chapter, we will deal with factors that influence the behavior of one category of buyers—consumers.

The phrase "consumer behavior" is often used to describe any buying behavior, whether it occurs in consumer markets or industrial markets. There is some justification for this usage: Whatever the type of market, there is consumption of products. However, we are using the phrase "consumer behavior" in a narrower sense to refer to the purchase of products for individual or household use and consumption. This excludes the purchase of products for use in business settings or production processes or for resale; these situations are classified as organizational buying behavior and are discussed in chapter 8.

Factors that Influence Consumer Behavior

The factors that influence consumer behavior are divided into two categories—internal and external. The **internal factors** include the *psychological factors* of needs and motives, personality, perception, learning, attitudes, and involvement.

The **external factors** are sociocultural factors and demographic characteristics. The *sociocultural factors* include societal values, economic factors, the media, and reference groups that strongly affect consumer behavior. *Demographic characteristics* identify groups of people who exhibit certain types of consumer behavior. The characteristics are age, gender, income, educational level, occupation, social class, ethnic group, and place of residence. All of these factors are shown in figure 7–1; they are described in the sections that follow.

Figure 7–1 Factors that influence consumer behavior

Internal Factors

- Needs and motives
- Personality
- Perception
- Learning
- Attitudes
- Involvement

External Factors

- Sociocultural factors
  — societal values
  — economic factors
  — the media
  — reference groups
- Demographic characteristics
  — age
  — gender
  — income
  — educational level
  — occupation
  — social class
  — ethnic group
  — place of residence

The Internal Factors: Psychological Influences on Consumer Behavior

At the core of any individual's consumer behavior is his or her own psychological makeup. There are a number of concepts from the fields of psychology and social psychology that are critical to an understanding of consumer behavior.

Needs and Motives

In psychology, **needs** and **motives** are distinct concepts. As we saw in chapter 1, needs are more basic than motives and can be defined as a discrepancy between an actual and a desired state of being. Motives are the forces that activate behavior aimed at fulfilling those needs. Maintaining a clear distinction between these two concepts in attempting to understand consumer behavior, however, is difficult and impractical.

The implementation of the marketing concept involves understanding consumers' needs and how a particular product can meet them. The marketer, then, is concerned with understanding the forces that cause consumers to take action to achieve some goal.

The number of specific motives that can be identified is almost unlimited. One theory categorizes motives as either *cognitive or affective*.[2] Cognitive implies knowledge and deliberation; affective suggests an emotional response. One type of cognitive motivation is the attempt to maintain consistency in a set of beliefs or actions. A dieting consumer who purchases a Weight Watchers frozen dinner is exhibiting cognitive motivation. That same consumer on the same shopping trip may be overcome by the sight of the fresh eclairs in the bakery window and purchase one for dessert. That is an affective motive.

The same theory states that motives can be either *active or passive.* Active motives imply a self-initiated action. Passive motives represent a reaction to some stimulus. The shopper who gives dinner guests kiwifruit for dessert may be actively motivated to express the self-concept of "fashionable gourmet cook." Another shopper may look at the kiwifruit but decide not to buy any. The passive motive may be to avoid admitting that he or she does not know how to serve this strange-looking fruit, an admission that could be threatening to the shopper's ego.

According to this classification, motives can also have as their focus either *preservation or growth.* Motives that preserve cause individuals to seek to maintain the status quo. Growth, on the other hand, implies self-development. The shopper who rejects the kiwifruit may be attempting to preserve self-esteem. A marketer of kiwifruit aware that many consumers may have this motive for rejecting this product may create a promotional campaign designed to turn a problem into an opportunity. Learning to love kiwifruit, serving them to family and friends, could be portrayed as an opportunity for broadening culinary horizons and for self-expression. The marketer can lead consumers to see this as an opportunity for growth.

Figure 7–2 Do consumers want to taste a delicious food product? Do they perceive themselves as purchasers and servers of light and nutritious foods? Both motives may lead consumers to buy kiwifruit.

The final category for motives is *internal or external*—internal states of being or external relationships with the environment. Consumers frequently have a mental picture (an internal state of being) of an ideal product or store that they can compare with their actual experiences. The supermarket manager who knows that the ideal store for the targeted customers has an expanded deli counter where a working person can purchase an entire meal at the end of a busy day may be able to develop that kind of deli. Consumers may correctly attribute the existence of the expanded deli to the rise in the number of two-worker households, thereby showing an understanding of the external environmental forces surrounding them.

Personality

For many years marketers have tried to relate some of the major personality theories proposed by Sigmund Freud, Carl Jung, Karen Horney, and Erich Fromm to consumer behavior. In general, "a few studies indicate a strong relationship between theories of personality and consumer behavior, a few indicate no relationship, and the great majority indicate that if correlations do exist they are so weak as to be questionable or perhaps meaningless."[3] Among the reasons that have been

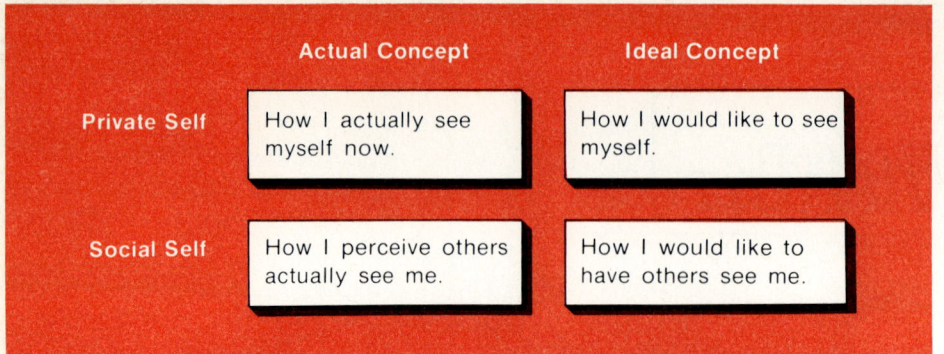

Figure 7–3 The identifiable parts of a person's self-concept

Source: Based on Del I. Hawkins, Roger J. Best, and Kenneth A. Coney, *Consumer Behavior: Implications for Marketing Strategy* (Plano, Texas: Business Publications, 1983), p. 383.

given for the lack of a more definite relationship are inappropriate use or modification of psychological concepts and lack of thought given to why particular aspects of personality should affect a particular type of consumption behavior.[4] Two concepts related to personality—self-concept and lifestyle—have been useful to marketers in understanding consumer behavior.

Self-concept. Self-concept consists of the attitudes a person holds about himself or herself. There are four identifiable parts of a person's self-concept, as can be seen in figure 7–3. These parts describe the private versus the social self and the actual versus the desired image.

In chapter 1, we explained that products are not desired for their tangible attributes but for the need-satisfying benefits they provide. Another way of saying this is that many products, especially those that are visibly consumed, serve as social symbols. Consumption of those products communicates a message, or conveys an image, to the person consuming the product and to others around the consumer. The consumer therefore often chooses products that maintain or enhance his or her self-concept. A product or brand that matches the aspect of self-concept that the consumer is attempting to convey is accepted. Products or brands that do not match are rejected.

In many product categories, the many competing brands have few perceptible differences to the average consumer. For example, numerous marketing research studies have shown that consumers cannot tell the difference between brands of beer in a blind taste test. Thus, virtually all beer advertising is image-oriented rather than oriented toward characteristics of the product. Schaeffer beer established itself as a good, hearty working-class beer by being "The beer to have when you're having more than one." Miller Lite avoided being stigmatized as a beer for weight-conscious women through advertising featuring macho athletes and personalities. At the same time, though, consumers received the message about light taste and fewer calories. In an advertisement for its Signature beer (see fig. 7–4), Stroh's is establishing itself as a beer for achievers with "something extra."

Figure 7–4 Stroh's Signature—a beer for people with "something extra." Consumers often purchase products that they perceive match and reinforce their self-concepts.

Reprinted by permission of The Stroh Brewery Company

Lifestyle. A person's self-concept serves as the basis for his or her preferred **lifestyle.** The term **psychographics** is sometimes used in place of lifestyle. The product and brand choices that reflect self-concept create a lifestyle within the constraints of everyday living. An example is shown in table 7–1, which gives a comparative profile of light versus heavy male beer drinkers using four lifestyle aspects. The profile suggests that the venturesome, successful male is a light beer drinker, while the more conservative, less successful male is a heavy beer drinker.

Many experts on lifestyles and psychographics argue that the more closely related the lifestyle measures are to the product category being studied, the better they will explain category-related consumption behavior. The National Product Diary study of actual consumer eating habits presented in focus 5–1 is a good case in point. Studying generalized concern about health and natural products would have been less likely to uncover the seeming contradictions in food consumption than were the specific measures of actual food consumption used in this study.

TABLE 7–1   A Comparative Profile of Light versus Heavy Male Beer Drinkers

	Scale Values[a]	
Psychographic Scales	Light Drinker[b]	Heavy Drinker
I. *Risk-taking*		
I like to fly.	6.1[c]	3.4
Buying stocks is too risky.	4.8	8.7
I often try new brands.	5.7	3.9
Taking chances can be fun.	5.1	2.2
II. *Permissive society*		
Hair length and clothing styles describe the nature of a person.	2.1	4.2
Hippies should be dealt with severely.	3.4	7.2
Discipline is lacking in people.	4.1	6.7
Marijuana smokers should not go to jail.	6.8	2.4
III. *Optimism*		
I approach a new day with excitement.	7.4	3.9
My best life accomplishments have yet to occur.	6.2	4.7
I do not do well at most things I've tried.	2.4	5.6
IV. *Active life*		
I look for an active stimulating life.	4.7	6.2
I go hunting.	3.5	4.4

[a] Ten-point rating scale: higher numbers indicate a higher score on the scale.
[b] Light drinker consumes 1–9 bottles per week and the heavy drinker consumes 10 or more bottles per week.
[c] Mean scale values are reported: All reported scores are significantly different at the .01 level by a z-test for differences between means.

Source: Thomas C. Kinnear and James R. Taylor, "Psychographics: Some Additional Findings," *Journal of Marketing Research*, November 1976, p. 422. Used with permission of the American Marketing Association.

Perception

Perception refers to the manner in which a person selects, organizes, and interprets the stimuli to which he or she is exposed. In other words, perception is the process by which a person gives meaning to the things he or she sees, hears, touches, tastes, and smells. The perceptions developed through exposure to a stimulus are the result of more than just the stimulus itself. They are affected by the person's mood, motives, personality, and the social and physical context of the exposure, among other variables. The presence of so many variables leads to two problems for marketers. First, the manner in which consumers develop perceptions as a result of exposure to marketing stimuli, such as advertisements, packages, and in-store displays, is difficult to understand. Second, it is not unusual for two individuals who have been exposed to the same marketing stimuli to have very different perceptions about the product.

Two aspects of perception have been identified as being of particular importance to marketers. They are perceptions of price and perceived risk.

Chapter 7 / Consumer Buying Behavior

Perceptions of price. There is a positive relationship between consumer perceptions of price and quality—the higher the price, the higher the perceived quality and vice versa, within reasonable limits.

Another taste test illustrates this point. The test calls for giving a group of tasters glasses containing the same beer. The glasses are identified as containing different-priced beers, however—highest-priced, moderately priced, and rock-bottom-priced. The tasters are then asked to rate each beer on several scales—strong to weak, full-bodied to watery, good taste to poor taste. The ratings for the "higher-priced" beers tend toward the more favorable end of each rating, the lower-priced toward the less favorable. When asked to tell what brand they think each beer is, the tasters will most likely suggest brand names that correlate highly with the supposed price.

The point is that price serves as an indicator when it is difficult for consumers to evaluate quality. If other cues are available, price becomes a less important determinant of quality. When consumers cannot accurately judge physical differences in the product, brand image may well determine the price that can be charged and the perception of quality. When Farberware introduced its innovative Ultra Chef

Figure 7–5 The high price, the appeal to an affluent lifestyle, and the presentation of gourmet foods contributes to consumers' perceptions of the innovative Ultra Chef as a high-quality product.

electronic cooker, for example, consumers had no experience with that type of product. For them, the high price ($450) indicated the quality of the product, and the good reputation of the Farberware brand name confirmed that perception (see fig. 7–5). In many product categories, however, consumers seem to believe that differences in quality are either nonexistent or meaningless. This may well account for the popularity of some generic, "no-brand" items in supermarkets. For some food items where differences in taste, color, and uniformity were readily apparent, however, the generic "brands" were short-lived.[5]

Another aspect of the perception of price is the perception of value. R. J. Reynolds has identified consumers with a strong perception of value as the targets for their new Century cigarettes. When the price of a pack of cigarettes in this country rose to over $1, sales of generic cigarettes took off. To reach consumers interested in lower-priced cigarettes, Reynolds produced a discount cigarette, Century. The consumers purchasing Century are proving to be those "interested in getting the best value for his or her money . . . the kind of person who buys a Volvo or brand-name clothing at an off-price retailer because it makes good sense economically."[6]

Perceived risk. Every buying situation has some degree of risk associated with it. The consumer may make the wrong choice among alternatives; the chosen product may not function properly; use of the product may have unintended or even injurious consequences. In general, the consumer perceives a high degree of risk if he or she believes that there are wide variations in product quality or does not feel competent to judge between alternatives. Consumers may respond to the risk in several ways:

1. They can reduce the amount of risk by searching for additional information. This should decrease the amount of uncertainty they feel regarding the situation.
2. They can reduce the amount they have at stake. For example, they can take advantage of a free trial offer, buy a smaller size, or buy a product with a warranty or guarantee.
3. They can be slower to accept or buy new products or brands.
4. They can develop a loyalty toward a particular brand and purchase only that brand.
5. They can be guided by price in choosing among unfamiliar products or brands.

Such actions reduce the possibilities of undesirable consequences associated with risky decisions.

The types of perceived risk go beyond the possibility of a product not working properly (**performance risk**). A buyer may recognize a **psychosocial risk**—the possibility of looking foolish or feeling stupid for having made a wrong decision. A recent television commercial advertising Commodore 64 computers capitalized on this type of risk. It showed computer owners confessing that they had purchased the wrong computers (that is, not Commodore 64s); they were able to confess only because they were wearing blindfolds, and therefore, were reducing psychosocial risk.

Another type of risk is **financial risk.** The more expensive a product, the greater the effect of financial loss from making a wrong choice. Consumers contemplating an expensive purchase will probably search for much information and take steps to try to reduce the risk.

The final type of risk is **physical risk.** When a product has the potential to cause actual physical harm to a buyer, such as certain types of medicines or medical procedures, the buyer, again, will spend more time searching for information and evaluating alternatives before purchasing the product.

If a marketer knows that there is a high degree of perceived risk inherent in the product category (as seems perennially true with automobiles and presently true with personal computers), strategies can be developed to minimize either the degree of uncertainty consumers feel or the consequences they will suffer as a result of an inappropriate purchase decision.[7]

Learning

Learning is an essential element of consumer behavior; virtually all consumer behavior is learned behavior. Psychological definitions of learning, and theories that support them, are quite complex. For our purposes it is adequate to consider learning as "a relatively permanent change in behavior occurring as a result of experience."[8]

The three buying situations discussed in chapter 6—extensive problem solving, limited problem solving, and automatic response behavior—have learning theory as their basis. When the consumer has little or no relevant experience on which to draw in making a purchase decision, he or she will generally engage in extensive problem solving unless the purchase is trivial and unworthy of the effort involved in complex decision making. As satisfactory experience with the brand increases, the consumer will first use limited problem solving and, with more experience, finally move to automatic response behavior, or essentially habitual behavior.

The description of the learning process in consumer behavior makes one crucial assumption: that the product purchase and use experience is a *satisfactory* one. Learning theorists refer to this as *positive reinforcement.* If the buying behavior is positively reinforced, the probability that it will be repeated is increased. A satisfactory experience with the product is positive reinforcement. So is the approval of one's family or friends when the product is being purchased or used. Another form of positive reinforcement is marketers' use of mass media advertising to remind buyers what a wonderful product they have already purchased. In figure 7–6, for example, Good Seasons is using positive reinforcement. It is reminding consumers about the quality and zesty flavor of its salad dressings, and it is showing how delicious a salad with its dressings can be.

Figure 7–6 By reminding consumers about their product's characteristics and showing an attractive use of the product, Good Seasons is using positive reinforcement to encourage further purchases.

Good Seasons® advertisement reproduced with the permission of General Foods Corporation

If the purchase behavior is not regularly reinforced, it can become *extinct*. Extinction causes a rapid decline in the probability of a repeat purchase of a product. *Forgetting* refers to the loss of material previously learned about the product and leads to a more gradual decrease in the probability of repeat purchase of a product. A marketer can combat forgetting on the consumer's part by repeating advertisements. The trick is to repeat advertisements enough to keep the stimulus alive, but not enough to seriously annoy consumers. Even more importantly, the marketer can ensure that the brand continues to deliver the need-satisfying benefits to the target consumers, thereby continually providing positive reinforcement. The marketer's desired goal in relation to consumer learning is to create consumer loyalty to a particular product or brand.

Attitudes

An **attitude** is "a learned predisposition to respond in a consistently favorable or unfavorable manner with respect to a given object."[9] Attitudes are formed or adjusted by what is learned from families and other social groups, from information received, and from behavior.[10] Attitudes are affected by the personality of the individual,[11] and they differ in their intensity and importance to the individual.

Attitudes are generally thought to be made up of three components—*cognitive* (knowledge or beliefs), *affective* (feelings or emotions), and *conative* (behavioral intentions). The attitudes of a college-bound high-school senior as portrayed in figure 7–7 illustrate each of the three components.

Attitudes can also be described as fulfilling particular functions for an individ-

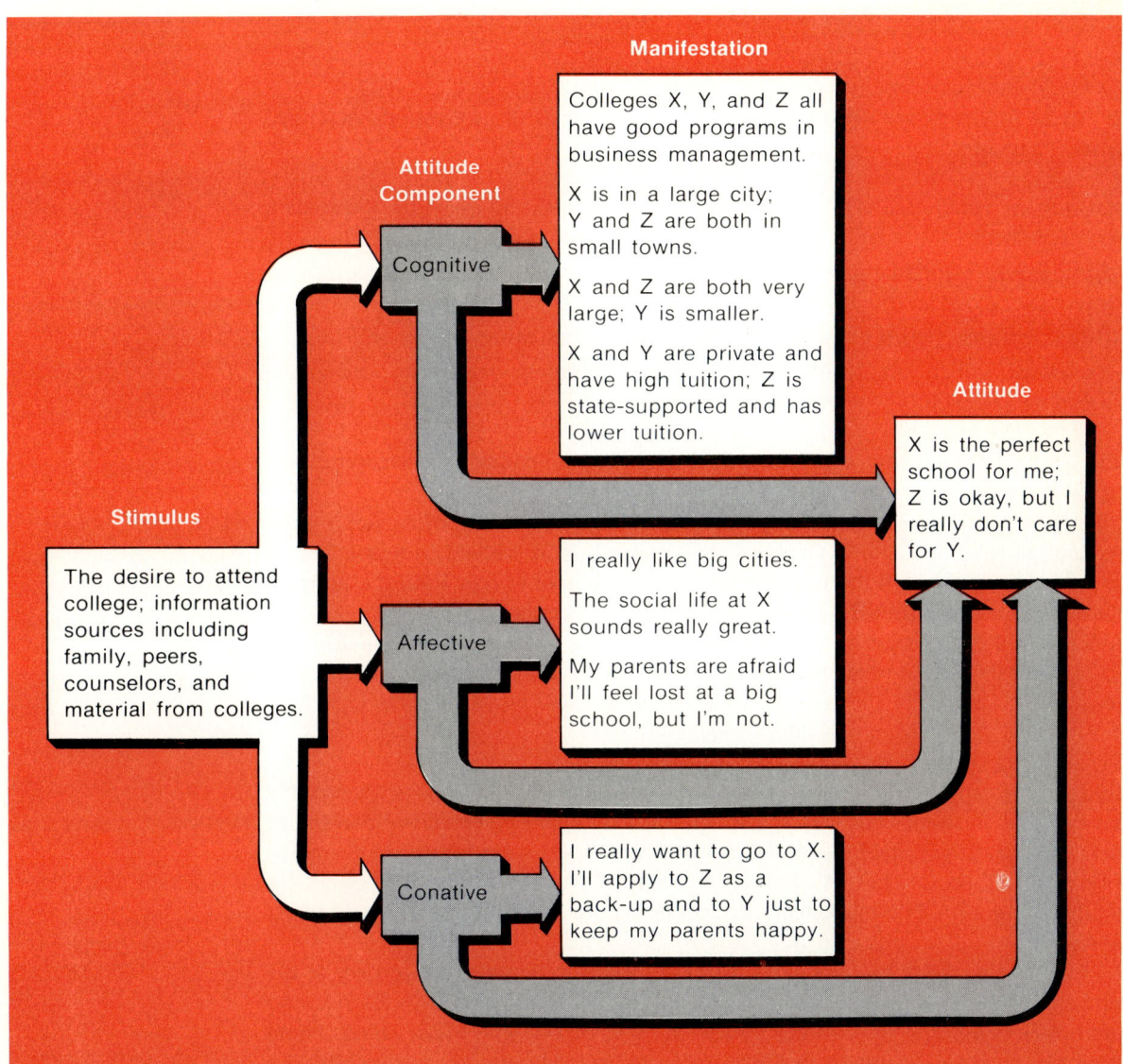

Figure 7–7 The attitudes of a college-bound high-school senior

TABLE 7–2 Promotional Appeals for a College that Utilize the Four Attitudes Functions

Function	Appeal
Utilitarian	The college offers degrees in these particular fields.
Ego-defensive	Our students are a select group of bright, highly motivated individuals.
Value-expressive	Our students are preparing for careers in various professional and managerial settings.
Knowledge	Our degrees are accredited by a variety of prestigious accrediting agencies.

ual. These functions are very closely related to the types of motivations described earlier. They are:[12]

—*Utilitarian*, which are ways of achieving desired goals or avoiding unpleasant consequences
—*Ego-defensive*, which help an individual defend his or her own self-image against internal or external threats
—*Value-expressive*, which express the individual's central values and/or self-image
—*Knowledge*, which supply frames of reference useful in organizing and giving meaning to beliefs

Table 7–2 illustrates how a college might use these functions in developing promotional appeals.

It is important for marketers to recognize that attitudes are often not a good predictor of later behavior.[13] Consider the college-bound student in figure 7–7. If the student's parents refused to pay tuition to any school except Y on the grounds that a small college offered a better educational experience, the student's own attitudes are likely to take a back seat to the parents' wishes. Other situations in which attitudes do not predict behavior will be explored in the section on involvement.

Involvement

Marketers become totally immersed in their products and their markets. Everything that happens to them is of critical importance to marketers. From the marketer's point of view, this is understandable. Sales of automobiles and parts are estimated to be $144 billion in 1984. A one percent share of the market is $1.4 billion. No wonder the automobile marketer is concerned about everything that could affect the market!

In the case of automobiles, consumers are likely to be quite concerned, as the purchase of an automobile involves high social, financial, and physical risk. An automobile is a major item in the budget of most consumers. Many things could cause the automobile not to perform properly. In addition, an automobile is a highly visible product and is often used to convey status or achievement. In other words, performance risk and psychosocial risk may both be quite high. Making the "right" decision is therefore important, and the consumer is likely to be quite involved in the purchase decision.

Often this is not the case. A pack of gum, a vegetable for tonight's dinner, and a box of facial tissues are all low-priced, quickly consumed items with little or no risk of any kind attached to the purchase. For the marketer these products still represent multi-million-dollar markets. For the consumer they are likely to be considered not worth investing time and effort—physical or cognitive—in the purchase process.

These two examples typify high and low involvement situations. **Involvement** is the intensity of interest with which consumers approach the marketplace.[14] It is a characteristic of the consumer, not of products. Consumers react to marketing stimuli very differently, depending on whether they are highly involved or not. The higher the degree of involvement, the greater the time, attention, and activity the consumer will give to each step in the buyer decision process described in chapter 6.

Sports Marketing Group at Jacobson Advertising

Figure 7–8 Serious, highly involved cyclists are deeply interested in the design of the frame, the innovative features, and the product specifications described in this advertisment.

Involvement can occur at several levels. Issues are more involving than products; world peace as a concept is more involving than, say, frozen dinners. Considering just products, however, a consumer may be very involved with the product category or brand. Most runners feel very strongly about the importance of a "good" shoe and about which brand is appropriate for the particular types of running situations. Most cyclists want to know about features that will help them choose the most appropriate bicycle for them (fig. 7–8).

Marketers often attempt to create a condition of high involvement from what had previously been low involvement. If consumers care little about the product category, this may not be easy. The marketer faced with low involvement may be better advised to use a more appropriate strategy, such as running frequently repeated, highly visual image-oriented advertising, usually on television.[15] The marketer who caters primarily to highly involved consumers may use both messages and media that require more cognitive activity on the part of the recipients.

The External Factors: Sociocultural Factors

The overall society in which a consumer lives has a considerable effect on consumer behavior. The beliefs and values and, indeed, the world view that an individual holds are learned and transmitted within that societal framework. The effect of those values is often difficult to assess because they are deeply, almost unconsciously, held. They are also enduring, changing slowly, even in the face of major technological and social change. The various sociocultural factors, then, have a tremendous effect on people's behavior as consumers.

Values are desired end-states, or the states of being individuals desire to achieve. As such, they describe the goals of society and of sub-groups within that society. Values also play an important role in defining what we as individuals and as a society *should* do.

Values

Values can be identified at several levels (see table 7–3). At the deepest and most enduring level are cultural values, which are held by a majority of people in a society. These values include ideas about security and freedom. At the next level are values specific to consumption activities. They describe attributes wanted in relation to products and buying situations, such as convenience and service. At the most superficial level are values specific to a particular product or product category. They describe attributes or benefits that a product should possess.

For the individual marketer, values that are specific to the buying situation and to the product are generally the most useful in helping to understand the behavior of a particular target market. A number of ongoing surveys conducted by public opinion research firms, trade associations, and individual companies assess the current state of values in the American populace.

Chapter 7 / Consumer Buying Behavior

TABLE 7–3 The Types and Levels of Values

Values	Definition	Examples
Cultural values	Enduring beliefs concerning desired modes of behavior	Security Happiness Freedom Social recognition
Consumption-specific values	Beliefs relevant to specific social, personal, and other activities	Prompt service Accurate information Convenient stores Nonpollution
Product-specific values	Evaluative beliefs about product attributes	Quiet Easy to use Durable Inexpensive

Source: Henry Assael, *Consumer Behavior and Marketing Action*, 2nd ed. (Boston: Kent Publishing, 1984), p. 288. © 1984 by Wadsworth, Inc. Reprinted by permission of Kent Publishing Company, a division of Wadsworth, Inc.

Economic Factors

Demand for a product or service is created by two **economic factors:** *ability* to buy and *willingness* to buy. Ability to buy is affected by consumer income, which, in turn, is affected by the level of economic activity. The attitudes that consumers hold toward current and future economic conditions play a major role in their willingness and intentions to spend, to save, or even to dis-save (to spend money previously saved). These consumer intentions are so important that they have been identified as a leading indicator of national economic well-being.

Individual concerns may override the effects of general economic considerations. For instance, even when consumers in general are pessimistic about the economy and intend to save rather than spend, a family with a child entering college will probably be forced to dis-save to fund college expenses. This could appropriately be described as *planned* dis-saving. On the other hand, a parent with several small children whose washing machine breaks beyond repair is facing an unexpected situation of almost crisis proportions. A working washing machine is necessary to the maintenance of the parent's lifestyle and sanity. The parent is likely to forgo many other current expenditures and even spend from savings to replace the appliance quickly. This kind of *unplanned* dis-saving is a frequent occurrence in American households.

The economic factors that have a direct impact on consumer plans to spend or save include:

—*Income*. When consumers expect their income to increase (as do college students nearing graduation), they spend more freely. They spend in advance of current income, dis-saving to make high-ticket purchases such as appliances and auto-

mobiles. When consumers expect income to decrease, they save for the "rainy day" they are anticipating.
- —*Prices.* When consumers expect prices to go up, they engage in anticipatory buying, stocking up in advance of the price rises. Similarly, when they expect prices to decline, they postpone purchases in anticipation of lower prices.
- —*Cost of credit.* When interest rates are high, consumers forgo purchases. When interest rates are down, consumers purchase high-ticket items, such as houses and automobiles, in greatly increased numbers.

Economic factors, then, have the greatest impact on postponable, or discretionary, purchases—mainly durable goods such as appliances, automobiles, and houses. Intentions to purchase nonpostponable, or nondiscretionary, goods such as food and clothing change much less dramatically. Even so, the *amount* that consumers plan to spend on nondiscretionary items may increase or decrease depending on consumers' sense of economic well-being. In good times, they "trade up" to more expensive items and in bad times they look for bargains.

Media

Marshal McLuhan says that "the medium is the message."[16] While that may be an overstatement, it makes an important point: the media vehicle chosen by advertisers (whether television, radio, magazine, newspaper, billboard, or other form) conveys a message to the consumer that goes beyond the actual advertising content (see fig. 7–9).

McLuhan classifies media as either "hot" or "cool." A hot medium like television provides a great deal of both auditory and visual sensory data. Movies, another hot medium, can be produced in 3-D, adding an even greater impact to visual stimuli. Cool media like a newspaper or the telephone convey less data, because they usually involve only one sense—visual for the newspaper, auditory for the telephone. The use of a hot versus a cool medium clearly regulates the amount of information the marketer can provide for the targeted customers. The manufacturers of food products, who are trying to build awareness or brand loyalty, usually choose television and magazine advertising because food products appear much more appetizing in color. On the other hand, supermarkets usually advertise in newspapers, as they have much information about prices and product availability to convey. Television advertising by supermarkets usually has a different objective—to build the image of the store(s) by stressing quality and customer service.

Another aspect of McLuhan's hot/cool classification is the degree to which the medium requires participation on the part of the recipient of the message. A hot medium leaves little or nothing to the imagination. The data are all provided, and the viewer is a passive recipient of the information. As little involvement is required, the television viewer will be less likely to internalize, and therefore remem-

Figure 7–9
Sebastiani's decision to place its advertisement in a magazine allows it to present a visually splendid use of the product. It also allows Sebastiani to involve the reader in the history and attitudes of the vineyard.
Sebastiani Vineyards/Offenbacher Advertising

ber, the information. A cool medium may require a great deal more involvement on the part of the reader. The reader can attempt to visualize the product and its possible uses. The thinking that is required in the attempt to visualize means that the reader is much more likely to retain the information in memory and have it available for later retrieval.

The medium itself is not the only factor that influences a consumer's reception of the message the advertiser wishes to convey. As we have seen, characteristics of the recipient are also important. Still, the pervasiveness of the mass media in a highly developed economy means that the media themselves will have a major impact on consumer behavior.

Reference Groups

A **reference group** is "that group whose presumed perspectives or values are being used by an individual as the basis for his or her current behavior."[17] While we often think of reference groups as consisting of persons who have face-to-face

Chapter 7 / Consumer Buying Behavior

181

interaction with one another, this definition correctly implies that an individual need not have personal contact with a group used as a reference point. Any group whose mere existence affects the way the individual thinks and behaves is a reference group.

Three types of reference groups are especially important to an understanding of consumer behavior. **Membership groups** include family, friends, peer groups, work associates, professional associations, and so on. These groups involve frequent interpersonal contact and are very important in the transmission of beliefs and values. The family has the strongest influence because of its unique role in early childhood socialization. As the child grows older, peer groups become more important than the family in influencing consumer behavior. Larger, more diffuse membership groups such as professional organizations are usually less effective in influencing consumer behavior.

Aspirational groups are groups to which an individual desires to belong. An individual will strive to be accepted by such a group, and its attitudes and values may then assume overriding importance to the individual. Adopting the consumption habits of the group is a highly visible way of demonstrating the aspirant's qualifications for group membership. The criteria used by executives in choosing work apparel is a good example of this aspirational mechanism at work. Figure 7–10 shows the lifestyle of one possible aspirational group and suggests how to become a member.

Avoidance groups may have an equally strong effect on an individual's consumption behavior, but in a negative sense. The individual who desires to avoid being categorized as a member of a particular group may go to great lengths to avoid the patterns of speech, dress, or consumption behaviors that characterize that group.

Not all product or brand choices are equally susceptible to reference group influence. There are at least three characteristics that influence the degree of susceptibility:

—*Visibility of the consumption situation.* When consumption is visible to others, product or brand choice is more likely to be susceptible to reference group influence.[18] Consumers frequently buy a foreign or premium brand of beer to serve to guests that is different from the one kept on hand for personal consumption.

—*Cohesiveness of the group.* The more attractive the group is to its members, the more likely they are to develop close ties to it. Members then tend to feel that the group is better than other groups and that its members are very supportive of each other. Such feelings encourage frequent communications among members, resulting in a high level of knowledge about one another's consumption-related beliefs and activities. The likelihood that group membership will influence consumption, then, is great. One study found, however, that the effect of group cohesiveness varied across product categories. The authors hypothesized that the reasons products were not equally susceptible to the influence of even a cohesive

Chapter 7 / Consumer Buying Behavior

Figure 7–10
Consumers aspiring to the consumption habits presented in this advertisement may be inspired to become members of the group of "Money readers."

group were related to the extent to which consumers perceived differences among products; the importance of personal taste in product choice; and the extent to which product use conveyed a desired self-image and social satisfactions.[19]

—*Similarity of group members.* The more similar group members are in terms of buyer behavior, the more likely they are to influence one another. The influence can be in two ways. One way is for one member to ask directly for information or for an evaluation of his or her own activities. The other way is for one member to observe the behavior of other group members toward consumption of the product. By observing other group members, the individual can evaluate his or her own activities.[20]

The preceding discussion revolves around the idea that groups with which an individual personally interacts can exert considerable influence on consumer behavior. However, many promotional appeals are based on the idea that individuals or groups with which a person does not interact can provide an important frame of reference. The use of movie stars in advertisements is an example of this sort of appeal. These are referred to as **socially distant reference groups.** This type of comparative influence occurs quite frequently. One study suggests that the more favorable consumers' attitudes are toward the activities of members of a socially distant reference group, the more likely they are to be influenced by that group.[21]

The External Factors: Demographic Characteristics

Demographics is the study of the characteristics of human populations. A number of demographic characteristics affect behavior. We will consider two aspects of each characteristic: the current status of the population for that popular characteristic, and how the status is changing; and how that particular characteristic affects consumer behavior.

Age

Because **age** is directly related to a variety of biological and sociological processes, it strongly affects the consumption of a wide variety of products and services. A number of products, such as dentures and rental of vacation condominiums in Florida for the winter season, are produced and marketed for older age groups, as these groups have certain health problems and a greater amount of leisure time. Jogging shoes and ski trips to the Austrian Alps are produced and marketed more for younger age groups because of the greater ability of these groups to engage in strenuous physical activity.

Age is assuming increasing importance to marketers at present because the age composition of our population is changing.[22] The 1980 census brought forcefully to our attention the fact that the U.S. population is aging. The median age in 1970 was 28 years; by 1980 it was 30 years, a sizable change in a single decade.[23] Figure 7–11 shows how the population is aging in the United States.

This has created a major upheaval in a youth-oriented culture. There are many ways in which marketers are reacting to an aging population. Many are recognizing this factor as an opportunity and are creating products for older consumers. A major manufacturer of jeans has added a line for the "mature" figure, with the advertising slogan, "You're not getting older; you're getting better." One of the largest single-product advertising expenditures in recent years has been for the skin-care cream Oil of Olay, clearly aimed at the "maturing" market. Johnson & Johnson has recently introduced Affinity shampoo aimed at the woman over 40; the product is specifically designed to treat the coarse and brittle hair of older consumers.

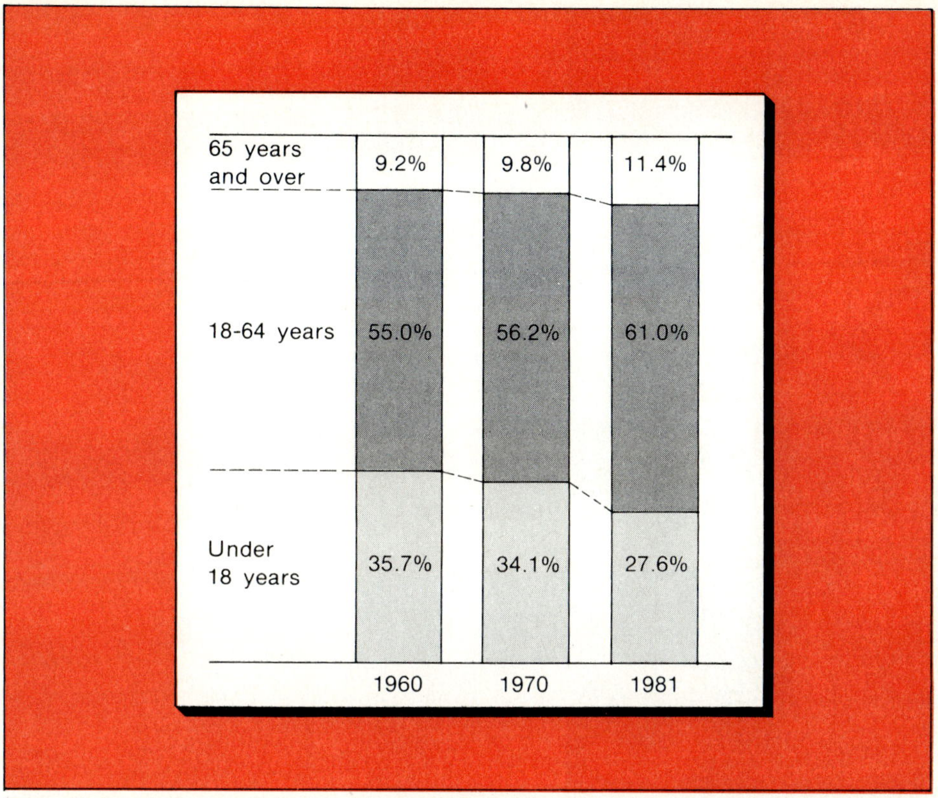

Figure 7–11 The aging of the U.S. population

	1960	1970	1981
65 years and over	9.2%	9.8%	11.4%
18–64 years	55.0%	56.2%	61.0%
Under 18 years	35.7%	34.1%	27.6%

Source: *Statistical Abstract of the United States, 1982–83* (Washington, D.C.: Bureau of the Census, 1983), p. xviii.

Gender

Biological **gender** also has a great impact on consumer behavior. Beyond products serving the obvious physiological differences in males and females, it exerts influence in two ways: by prescribing certain culturally ingrained ways of thinking and behaving, and by its effect on an individual's sense of self, or self-concept.

Women outnumber men in the U.S. population 117 million to 110 million. That majority is increasing slowly over the years for one simple reason: women outlive men. In 1981, the life expectancy was 70.3 years for men and 77.9 years for women. The difference becomes most apparent in the older age groups. In the 65-years-and-older age group, there are only 67.3 men for every 100 women. Marketers who concentrate on the older consumer market, then, are dealing with a market that is predominantly female.

When we look at men and women as consumers, the greatest effect of all has been caused by the increasing number of women in the labor force. As we saw in chapter 3, nearly half of all women 16 years of age and older worked in 1982, accounting for 43 percent of the civilian labor force in the United States. This

Figure 7–12 The increasing number of women with discretionary income form a lucrative market, and marketers are directing advertising toward these consumers.
W. A. Taylor & Company/J. Walter Thompson

change creates new opportunities for marketers, as working women are an important market segment for many products. They tend to purchase more clothing, more cosmetics, more hair-care products, and more leisure-oriented products and services than do non-working women. In general, their discretionary expenditures are high and marketers are directing advertising to these consumers (see fig. 7–12).

Marketers realize also that products and services that help save time are very attractive to working women. They do tend to be loyal to particular stores and brands, which cuts down on shopping time.

Income

The **income** for an individual or a household clearly determines ability to spend for consumer goods and services. Those in the lower income categories spend a large portion of their earnings on subsistence items, such as food, housing, and clothing. Those in higher income categories have greater amounts available for discretionary spending and are a prime target for marketers of a wide variety of goods and services. People in lower income categories are disproportionately less well

7-1 Focus on Consumer Behavior
HOW THE DUAL-INCOME FAMILY SHOPS

An increasingly important influence on buying behavior is the dual-income family. Today in more than half of all U.S. husband-wife households, both spouses earn incomes, and demographers predict that the number will increase in the coming years. Marketers are examining this growing market segment to learn how having two incomes affects families' buying behavior. A recent survey focused on dual-income families' shopping habits, attitudes, and lifestyles to aid marketers in understanding their needs and wants.

The first and perhaps most obvious difference between one- and two-income families is that those with two incomes tend to earn more. Dual-income families average around $25,000 per year as compared with an average of $20,000 for the single-income family. Many dual-income families say that the reason both husband and wife work is to be able to afford a more comfortable lifestyle. Other dual-income families continue to feel financial pressures despite the two incomes, especially those who have several children.

When both husband and wife work, often both take part in daily household tasks and shopping. The most common reason given for this behavior is that neither spouse has the time to do all these chores. When husbands and wives shop for groceries alone, their buying habits differ. The survey found that husbands are less likely than wives to buy impulse items or try new and unusual products. Wives are more likely to buy products in large quantities than are their husbands. Shopping habits tend to change when couples shop together. The survey found that wives adapt more to their husbands' shopping styles than the reverse. Wives are generally more experienced shoppers than husbands and tend to prefer shopping alone more than their husbands.

Some couples enjoy sharing the shopping and cooking because it provides opportunities to be together. For marketers this sharing of the workload offers a number of marketing opportunities. First, dual-income families are likely to be attracted by convenient, time-saving products. Second, marketers can aim grocery and household products at husbands as well as wives. In fact, about one-third of the couples surveyed reported that the husband cooks at least one dinner per week, while one-third also reported that both husband and wife prepare at least one dinner together. Based on this finding, marketers could emphasize the evening meal as a time for togetherness, as it is the meal for which dual-income families report sharing both the preparation and the meal itself. Dual-income families also eat out more often than single-income families.

Source: M. L. Roberts, L. J. Kirshbaum, and L. R. Cooper, "Two-Income Shoppers," *American Demographics*, March 1984, pp. 40–41.

educated, older, and single heads of households, especially women. Dual-income households are making up an increasing proportion of affluent households. Focus 7–1 describes the shopping behavior of dual-income households.

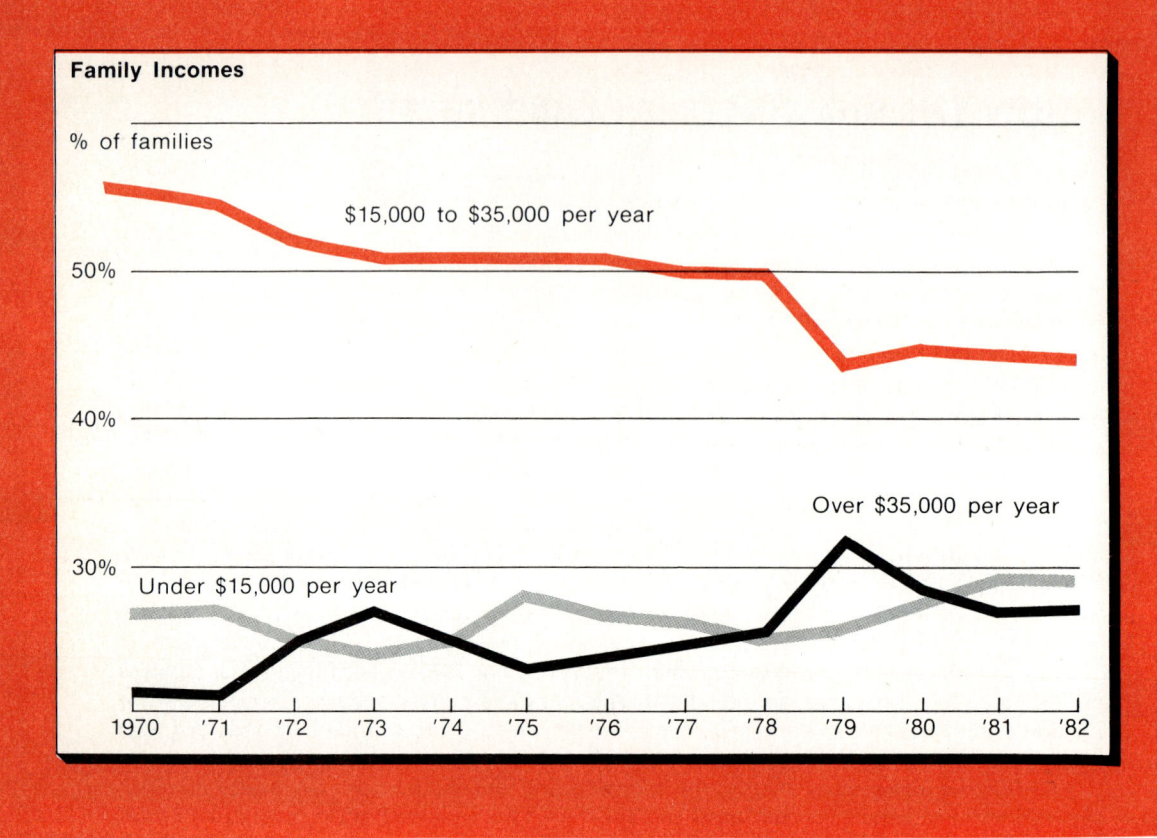

Source: Bruce Steinberg, "The Mass Market Is Splitting Apart," *Fortune*, November 28, 1983, p. 78. © 1983 Time Inc. All rights reserved.

Figure 7–13 The decline of the middle-income market

When affluence is defined as household income of $40,000 or more, the importance of high, absolute, and discretionary income becomes quite clear. In 1980, only 10 percent of all adults and 7 percent of all households fell into the affluent category, but their influence was much greater. Affluent households had more than 11 times the discretionary income of the remaining households in the population, owned more than twice as many cars per household, spent five times more on major appliances, thirteen times as much on single-lens reflex 35mm cameras, and drank seven times as much wine as did the less affluent households.[24] No wonder marketers consider them such a desirable target market!

Of great concern to the marketers of many categories of products is the fact that the mass, middle-income market is shrinking. In 1982, families with incomes between $15,000 and $35,000 per year made up only 44 percent of total families as compared with 51 percent in 1973. At the same time, the percentages of families making less than $15,000 or more than $35,000 grew (see fig. 7–13).[25] Manufacturers of products such as expensive clothing, home furnishings, and electronic gadgetry benefit from this trend, but marketers of mass-market products, such as moderately-priced clothing, may suffer.

Educational Level

The **educational level** of the U.S. population continues to rise. Ten million persons were enrolled in institutions of higher education in 1980 as opposed to 7.4 million in 1970. Sixty-nine percent of the population had completed high school in 1980 as opposed to 55 percent a decade earlier.

A consumer's level of education has both direct and indirect effects on his or her buying behavior. Some products and services, such as personal computers and opera tickets, are more heavily consumed by better-educated consumers. Consumption of other products, such as beer, is heavier among less well-educated consumers. In general, the educational level influences tastes, lifestyle preferences, and the ability to search for and process information.

Occupation

Occupation is strongly related to level of education. Just as the U.S. population is becoming better educated, it is increasingly being employed in white-collar jobs. Figure 7–14 shows the increase in white-collar jobs between 1970 and 1980. The trend is expected to continue due to increasing automation of production processes and the declining number of unskilled and semi-skilled jobs.

Occupational level, too, has both direct and indirect effects on consumer behavior. Clothing appropriate for a particular work situation is one direct effect. The indirect effects are probably an outcome of both the types of people and situations

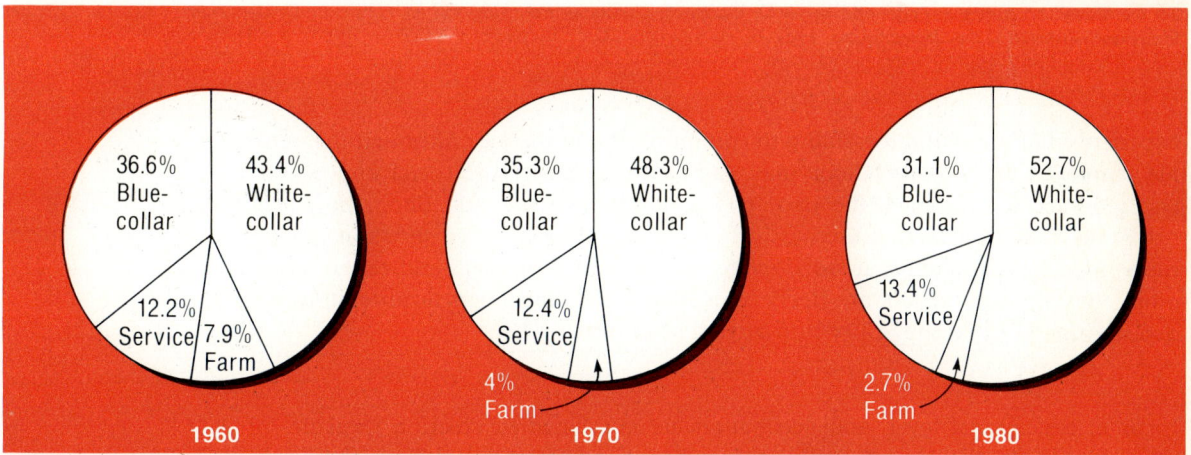

Figure 7–14 Percentages of workers employed in white-collar, blue-collar, service, and farm jobs

Source: *Statistical Abstract of the United States, 1982–83* (Washington, D.C.: Bureau of the Census, 1984), p. 386

Chapter 7 / Consumer Buying Behavior

TABLE 7–4 Social Classes in the United States and Their Typical Buyer Behavior

Social Class	Distribution in the Population	% Distribution of Family Income	Characteristics	Typical Buyer Behavior
Upper-Upper	Highest 5%	15.7	Social elite Inherited wealth	Consumers of high quality but unostentatious products Products purchased become standards for other classes
Lower-Upper	Highest Fifth	25.8	High-income professionals Social position earned, not inherited *Nouveaux riches*	Conspicuous consumers Buyers of expensive homes, automobiles, and luxury products Innovators
Upper-Middle	Fourth fifth	24.2	Career-oriented professionals Highly educated	Consumers of high-quality products that reflect family's success and position Interested in gracious lifestyle Experimenters with styles and designs
Lower-Middle	Middle fifth	17.5	"Typical" Americans—respectable, hard-working, conscious of cultural norms and standards	Consumers of products that make home neat and pretty Heavily influenced by standard styles and advice Careful shoppers; may be price-sensitive
Upper-Lower	Second fifth	11.6	Blue-collar workers Moderate education and level of skills	Impulsive, but brand-loyal consumers Self-perception as unskillful shoppers
Lower-Lower	Lowest fifth	5.2	People near or below poverty level	May be impulsive, unskillful shoppers May pay too much for products or pay high interest on credit purchases

Source: Based on James F. Engel and Roger D. Blackwell, *Consumer Behavior*, 4th ed. (Chicago: Dryden Press, 1982), p. 129; and *Statistical Abstract of the United States, 1982–83* (Washington, D.C.: Bureau of the Census, 1983), p. 431.

experienced at work and the ability to communicate on the job. Although the people employed on a factory floor may come from a variety of social and ethnic backgrounds, for instance, the pace of assembly-line work and often the sheer noise make communication next to impossible. The typical office situation allows more informal and often non-work-related communication. Ideas and experiences, often consumption-related, are freely transmitted, and consumers acquire attitudes and information that they carry into buying situations.

Income, educational level, and occupation are combined to create a measure of **social class.** In the United States, there are six major social classes; these are shown in table 7–4, along with descriptions of typical buyer behavior.

Social Class

One study of the effect of social class on food-related buyer behavior found that lower-class families placed less emphasis on the quality and taste of foods, middle-class families served canned juice and domestic wine more frequently, and upper-middle and upper-class families consumed the most ground coffee, frozen juice, and imported wines. In addition, lower-class homemakers were most likely to look for grocery ads in newspapers and to read them carefully.[26] Social class does not seem to be as influential in other product categories. The same study found that income alone, unconnected with such factors as social class and education, provided a better explanation for expenditures on major appliances that were not considered status symbols.

Since the income, educational, and occupational levels of the U.S. population are all increasing, it seems possible that more people are moving into the upper social classes and marketers may suspect that social class will have less effect on consumption behavior. This is not the case. There is "a basic continuity in the American status structure. Fundamental differences among the classes in self-image, social horizons, and consumption goals continue despite changes in income distribution, the demographics of family composition, and life styles."[27]

There is another important relationship between social class and income. That is the relationship between one household's income and the median income of other households in the same class. Overprivileged households have incomes higher than others in their occupational class while the underprivileged households have lower relative incomes. One study found that the buying behavior of overprivileged blue-collar workers was closer to the buying behavior of overprivileged white-collar and professional workers than it was to the buying behavior of other blue-collar workers.[28]

Ethnic Group

The ethnic composition of the United States is shifting, according to the 1980 census. Blacks and Hispanics make up an increasing proportion of the population. Immigration, especially of Hispanics, Caribbeans, and Asians, has increased greatly, and the proportional representation of these groups in the total population will increase.[29]

If the United States were truly a "melting pot" and these ethnic groups were quickly assimilated into the total population, their impact on marketing would be slight. However, the "melting pot" syndrome was probably overstated in the past, and the current emphasis on ethnic consciousness makes ethnic groups a strong influence on consumer behavior.

Differences in consumer behavior that are related to ethnicity may go far beyond product preferences. Ethnicity has also been linked to exposure to information, innovativeness, and patterns of information transfer.[30] It may also be related to the importance and meaning consumers attach to various products.[31] In addition, the foreign-language media, both national and local, give marketers the ability to reach ethnic groups with culturally appropriate appeals for mass-market or specialized products. In light of these factors, ethnic groups will be an important con-

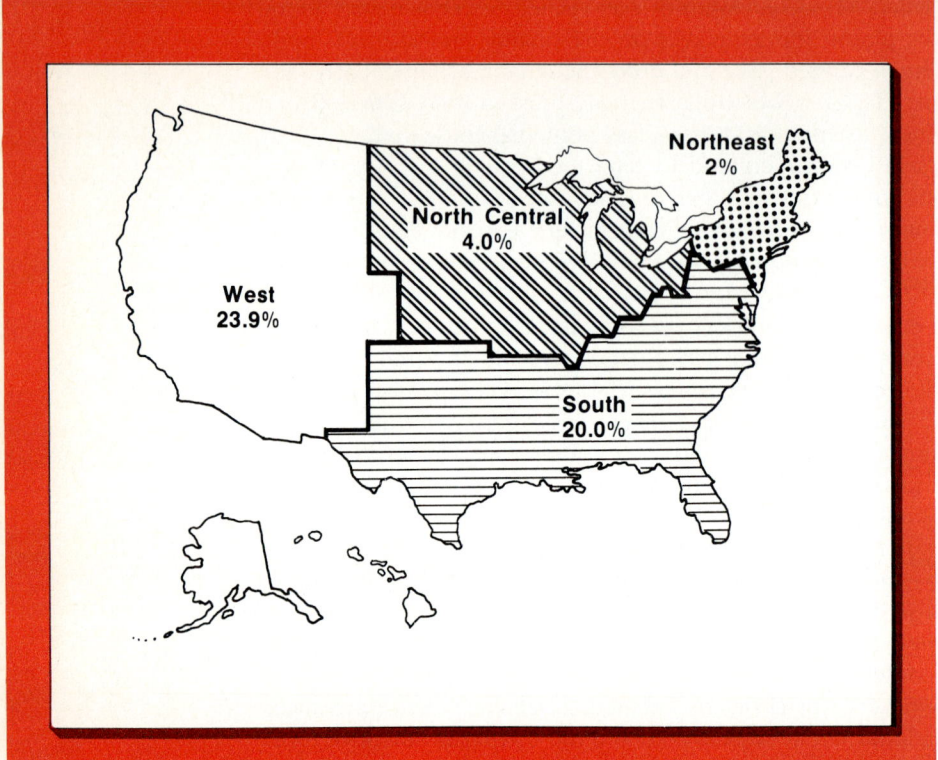

Figure 7–15 The rates of population growth in different areas of the United States

Source: *Statistical Abstract of the United States, 1982–83* (Washington, D.C.: Bureau of the Census, 1983), p. xvii.

sideration in forming marketing strategy for a wide variety of products long into the future.

Place of Residence

In the United States, **place of residence** can designate a region of the country, or it can refer to the urban/suburban/rural concentration in an area.

The population of the different geographical regions in the United States are growing at different rates. The older, industrial states in the East and Midwest are growing slowly, if at all. The Sun Belt states of the South and West are growing much more rapidly (see fig. 7–15). Since the lifestyle of the population of the Sun Belt states is based to a considerable extent on outdoor living and a generally slower pace, the implications for consumer behavior are enormous. For example, as we saw earlier, the products purchased and the motivations for those purchased are partly based on lifestyle, and marketers must be aware of lifestyle trends to provide the products that consumers want.

Almost since the Revolutionary War, the proportion of the population living on farms has been shrinking and that living in or near cities has been increasing. Suburbs are still the fastest growing geographical unit, although during the 1970s there was a trend toward moving back to rural areas. Except for some cities in the Sun Belt, most urban areas lost population during the 1970s.

Marketers will need to look carefully at the composition of urban/suburban/rural areas in the 1980s and beyond. Some of the sharp lines dividing the type of consumer found in each area are blurring. Many rural dwellers are not unaffluent, unsophisticated country folk, but are refugees from the city who brought with them affluent lifestyles and sophisticated tastes. The cities are no longer the haven of only the poor and a few extremely rich. **Re-gentrification** describes the movement of affluent singles, childless couples, and even some families into revitalized areas such as the South End of Boston. These population shifts are partly responsible for the fragmentation of the U.S. marketplace—the tremendous growth of different segments of our population, some of whom may have similar incomes, education, and occupations, but who differ greatly in tastes and lifestyles.

Factors that Influence Household Buyer Behavior

American households can also be described in terms of a number of characteristics that affect their consumption behavior. These are: composition of the household, stage in the family life cycle, changing family lifestyle, and changing family roles and behavior.

Composition of the Households

There are approximately 82.4 million households in the United States, an increase of 30 percent since 1970. Of these households, 60.3 million are considered *family households,* containing related persons living together. The number of family households increased by 17 percent between 1970 and 1981. There were 22.1 million *non-family households,* composed of singles or nonrelated persons living together. The number of this type of household increased by 85 percent between 1970 and 1981. The reasons for the dramatic increase in non-family households can be traced in part to changes in population demographics. Delayed marriage, the high divorce rate, and the increasing differences in longevity between men and women have all helped cause the increase in the number of non-family households.

Sales of some categories of consumer goods are directly affected by the number of households. The more households, the more housing units and appliances sold. Many other types of goods are affected, although less directly. Non-family households are less stable than family households and generally invest less in all types of

TABLE 7–5 Marketing Implications for the Stages in the Family Life Cycle

Stage in Family Life Cycle	Lifestyle	Buying Decision	Products Purchased	Promotion
Single:				

Young	Transitional	Individual	Basic furniture
			Records
			Fashionable clothing
			Travel
				Messages:
				  Special interest
				  Me-oriented
				Media:
				  Magazines, radio

Mature	Patterned	Individual	Condominiums
			High-quality furnishings
			Beter restaurants
			Financial planning investments
				Messages:
				  Quality
				Media:
				  Personal selling

Couples:				

Cohabitating	Impermanent	Independent	Low-cost furniture
			Lower-budget travel
			Individual financial services
				Messages:
				  "Buy now"
				Media:
				  Mass media

Married, without children	Hedonistic	Joint	Sensible furniture
			Insurance
			Career clothing
			Travel
				Messages:
				  Appeals to both spouses
				Media:
				  Mass media

Childless	Carefree	Joint	Smaller homes
			Sports cars
			Convenience foods
			Luxury travel
				Messages:
				  Quality, luxury
				Media:
				  Special interest

Married, with children	Child-centered	Complementary	Toys
			Larger homes
			Family-size packages
			Functional clothing
			Family restaurants
				Messages:
				  Family-oriented
				Media:
				  Women's magazines
				  Mass media

Divorced:				

Without children	Self-centered	Individual	Fashionable furniture
			Condominiums
			Small-size packages
			Small appliances
				Messages:
				  Me-oriented
				Media:
				  Mood magazines

With children	Constrained	Joint	Inexpensive furniture
			Low-cost housing
			Inexpensive clothing
			Discount foods
			Fast-food restaurants
				Messages:
				  Low price
				Media:
				  Mass media, especially television

Older:				

Married	Active or sedentary, depending on health and financial status	Complementary	Retirement homes
			Sports equipment
			Travel
			Brokerage services
				Messages:
				  "You owe it to yourselves"
				Media:
				  Television and newspapers

Unmarried	Active or sedentary, depending on health and financial status	Individual	Cruises
			Apartments
			Mass transportation
				Messages:
				  Enjoyment
				  Comfort
				Media:
				  Television

home furnishings. They may spend relatively little on many of the activities associated with "family life," including eating meals at home. Many family households are headed by single parents. The number of single-parent households doubled between 1970 and 1981 to 5.3 million. The women-headed single-parent households are more likely to live below the poverty line than are households of any other type.

A necessary corollary to the sharp increases in the number of households is that the average household size has decreased. In 1970, the average household contained 3.14 people; in 1981 it contained 2.73. Married-couple households had an average size of only 3.34 persons. Shrinking household size has affected everything from the size of dwelling units themselves to the serving size of convenience food products.

Stages in the Family Life Cycle

There was a time in the not-too-distant past when it could safely be assumed that most young people would marry soon after completing their schooling and quickly begin to raise a family. The children would grow up and depart to form their own households, leaving an "empty nest." At some point a sole survivor remained. This is the traditional family life cycle portrayed in table 7–5. The family life cycle was an important concept to marketers, as so much purchase behavior was directly correlated with the stages. In the 1980s, the traditional life cycle is no longer the standard for all people. Nevertheless, certain patterns of buyer behavior still apply to the stages in the family life cycle.

Each stage in the family life cycle has different consumption motives and activities. The stages do not necessarily represent homogeneous subgroups of people. For instance, young singles might be divided into those who are working and those who are still in school. The consumption styles of those two groups are likely to be quite different. Married couples with children include both couples whose children are all under six and those whose children are all over 18, with many variations in between. Consumption activities will vary greatly between these subcategories also. With this in mind, table 7–5 also presents some generalizations about likely consumption styles and activities for each stage.

Changing Family Lifestyles

The changes in household composition just described lead to major changes in the way households make buying decisions. The statistics on household size and composition alone do not tell the entire story, however. Changes in values regarding the family and family life are also undergoing profound change.

In a study conducted for General Mills, Yankelovich, Skelly, and White divided parents into two basic groups, "New Breed" and "Traditionalists."[32] According to them, "New Breed parents tend to be better educated and affluent. They . . . have rejected many of the traditional values by which they were raised: marriage as an

THE TRADITIONALISTS — 57%

Very Important Values:
- Marriage as an institution
- Religion
- Saving money
- Hard work
- Financial security

Characteristics and Beliefs:
- Parents are child-oriented — ready to sacrifice for their children
- Parents want their children to be outstanding
- Parents want to be in charge — believe parents should make decisions for their children.
- Parents respect authority
- Parents are not permissive with their children
- Parents believe boys and girls should be raised differently
- Parents believe old-fashioned upbringing is best
- Parents see having children as a very important value

THE NEW BREED — 43%

Not Important Values:
- Marriage as an institution
- Religion
- Saving money
- Patriotism
- Success

Characteristics and Beliefs:
- Parents are self-oriented — not ready to sacrifice for their children
- Parents don't push their children
- Parents have a laissez-faire attitude — children should be free to make their own decisions
- Parents question authority
- Parents are permissive with their children
- Parents believe boys and girls should be raised alike
- Parents believe their children have no future obligation to them
- Parents see having children as an option, not a social responsibility

WHAT BOTH GROUPS TEACH THEIR CHILDREN
- Duty before pleasure
- My country right or wrong
- Hard work pays off
- People in authority know best
- Sex is wrong without marriage

Figure 7–16 Characteristics and beliefs of New Breed versus Traditionalist families
Source: Yankelovich, Skelly, and White, *Raising Children in a Changing Society* (Minneapolis: General Mills, 1977), p. 8. Used with permission of Yankelovich, Skelly and White, Inc.

institution, the importance of religion, saving and thrift, patriotism, and hard work for its own sake. . . . New Breed parents question the idea of sacrificing in order to give their children the best of everything and are firm believers in the equal rights of children and parents. . . . They regard having children not as a social obligation but as one available option which they have freely chosen. Given the chance to rethink their decision, nine out of ten would still decide to have children." The New Breed and the Traditionalists have differing beliefs about the manner in which children should be raised. However, both types of parents are still transmitting a basic set of American values to their children (see fig. 7–16).

The New Breed approach to parenting suggests that children will be much more influential in choosing products and services for their own consumption. They are also likely to be more independent in thought and action than are children raised by Traditionalists.

The emergence of the so-called New Breed family is closely linked to the entry of women into the labor force and the increase in two-income families. There is concern over associated changes in family life coupled with the recognition that many family activities are handled differently. Another study conducted for General Mills in late 1980 found that a majority of those questioned felt that the negative aspects of both parents working outside the home outweighed the positive benefits. Working women, however, "feel that the fulfillment for women working outside the home, the added financial security, improved family communications, and independence for children outweigh negative effects on the family."[33] These families, irrespective of whether the wife worked or not, voiced strong disagreement with the traditional assumptions that raising children is solely the mother's responsibility, that the major wage earner should make major financial decisions, and that the secondary wage earner should make the decisions about housework and family activities. Marketers should recognize that American families increasingly believe that household decisions should be made jointly, by both husband and wife, and adjust their marketing activities to accommodate these changes. Increasingly, too, older children in these families are sharing in some aspects of family decision making.

Changing Family Roles and Behaviors

The fact that more married women now work outside the home is both a result and a cause of the demographic changes described earlier in the chapter. Looking at the effects of these changes on family decision-making behavior is another way of understanding the changes that are taking place.

One classic study found that husbands of liberated wives made fewer decisions concerning major appliances, automobiles, and vacations than did husbands of conservative and moderate wives.[34] This study classed husbands and wives as liberated, moderate, and conservative based on ten attitudinal items describing women's role in society. In general, it appears that when both husband and wife favor contemporary rather than traditional sex roles, they are more likely to share in decision making for a wide variety of products and services.

Summary

Motives may be either cognitive (involving knowledge or deliberation) or affective (emotional) and either active or passive. Motives can also focus on preservation (causing individuals to try to maintain the status quo) or growth (implying self-development). Finally, motives can be either internal or external.

A personality characteristic that is useful to marketers is self-concept, or a person's attitudes about himself or herself. Another is a person's lifestyle, or psychographics. Perception refers to the manner in which a person selects, organizes, and interprets the stimuli to which he or she is exposed. Important to the marketer are consumers' perceptions of price and risk.

Learning, or "a relatively permanent change in behavior occurring as a result of experience," is an essential element of consumer behavior. Three types of decision making—extensive problem solving, limited problem solving, and automatic response behavior—have learning theory as their basis. Positive reinforcement, or a satisfactory experience as a result of the product purchase, increases the likelihood that the consumer will buy the product again.

An attitude is "a learned predisposition to respond in a consistently favorable or unfavorable manner with respect to a given object." The process of learning attitudes occurs within families and other social groups. Attitudes are made up of cognitive, affective, and conative (behavioral intentions) components. Attitudes also fulfill many functions for the individual. Marketers use attitudes to predict behaviors.

Values are the states of being that individuals desire to achieve. On the deepest level are cultural values, at the next level are values specific to consumption activities, and at the most superficial level are values specific to a product category.

The two factors that create demand for a product are ability to pay and willingness to buy. Consumer plans to spend versus save are an important factor in predicting economic activity. Influences on plans to save or spend include income, prices, and cost of credit.

McLuhan classifies media as hot (providing a great deal of sensory data and requiring little participation) or cool (providing limited sensory data and requiring high participation). TV is considered a hot medium, while newspapers are thought of as cool.

A reference group is "that group whose presumed perspectives or values are being used by an individual as the basis for his or her current behavior." Three types of reference groups that are important to understanding consumer behavior are membership groups, aspirational groups, and avoidance groups. Three characteristics that influence a brand's susceptibility to reference group influence are visibility of the consumption situation, cohesiveness of the group, and similarity of group members.

Demographic characteristics that may influence consumer behavior are age, gender, income, educational level, occupation, social class, ethnic group, and place of residence.

Factors that influence household buyer behavior include composition of the households, stages in the family life cycle, changing family lifestyles, and changing family roles and behaviors.

Questions for Discussion

1. Identify and distinguish clearly between different categories of motivation.
2. What is the nature of the relationship between personality and consumer behavior? Explain your answer.
3. Examine the role of consumer perception in pricing men's shirts or women's shoes.
4. Discuss the types of risk involved in your seeking a college degree.
5. Explain how consumers' attitudes affect their buying behavior.
6. Based on your understanding of consumer involvement, identify and examine two decisions you made this week—one you are highly involved with and the other not so involved.
7. Identify and explain the role of any one demographic trend that seems to have the greatest impact on consumer behavior today.
8. Evaluate the relative roles of different reference groups in influencing consumer behavior.
9. Distinguish clearly the important marketing implications of one- compared with two-income families.
10. Develop a short list of products or services for which the demand will remain unaffected by the increase in non-family households. Explain your answer.

References

1. "Bausch & Lomb: Marketing Vision Bolsters Its Role in Contact Lenses," *Business Week,* November 17, 1980, pp. 173–84; and "Bausch & Lomb: Hardball Pricing Helps It to Regain Its Grip in Contact Lenses," *Business Week,* July 16, 1984, p. 78.
2. William J. McGuire, "Some Internal Psychological Factors Influencing Consumer Choice," *Journal of Consumer Research,* March 1976, pp. 302–19.
3. H. Kassarjian, "Personality and Consumer Behavior: A Review," *Journal of Marketing Research,* November 1971, pp. 409–18.
4. David L. Loudon and Albert J. Della Bitta, *Consumer Behavior: Concepts and Applications,* 2nd ed. (New York: McGraw-Hill, 1984), p. 504.
5. Bill Abrams, "Reports of Generics' Success May Be Greatly Exaggerated," *Wall Street Journal,* May 7, 1981, p. 29.
6. "Reynolds vs. Philip Morris: Dramatic Moves in Different Directions," *Business Week,* July 11, 1983, p. 101.
7. Raymond A. Bauer, "Consumer Behavior as Risk Taking," in *Dynamic Marketing for a Changing World* (Chicago: American Marketing Association, 1960), pp. 389–90.
8. Loudon and Della Bitta, p. 459.

9. Gerald Zaltman and Melanie Wallendorf, *Consumer Behavior: Basic Findings and Management Implications,* 2nd ed. (New York: Wiley, 1983), p. 429.
10. David J. Reibstein, Christopher H. Lovelock, and Ricardo de P. Dobson, "The Direction of Causality between Perceptions, Affect, and Behavior: An Application to Travel Behavior," *Journal of Consumer Research,* March 1980, pp. 370–76.
11. Henry Assael, *Consumer Behavior and Marketing Action,* 2nd ed. (Boston: Kent Publishing, 1984).
12. Daniel Katz, "The Functional Approach to the Study of Attitudes," *Public Opinion Quarterly,* Summer 1960, p. 163.
13. David J. Reibstein, "The Prediction of Individual Probabilities of Brand Choice," *Journal of Consumer Research,* December 1978, pp. 163–68.
14. Loudon and Della Bitta, p. 405.
15. Assael, p. 101.
16. Marshall McLuhan, *Understanding Media: The Extensions of Man* (New York: Signet, 1964), pp. 36–37.
17. Del I. Hawkins, Roger J. Best, and Kenneth A. Coney, *Consumer Behavior: Implications for Marketing Strategy* (Plano, Texas: Business Publications, 1983), p. 206.
18. Thorstein Veblen, *The Theory of the Leisure Class* (New York: Macmillan, 1912).
19. Robert Witt, "Informal Social Group Influence on Consumer Brand Choice," *Journal of Marketing Research,* November 1969, pp. 473–76.
20. George P. Moschis, "Social Comparison and Informal Group Influence," *Journal of Marketing Research,* August 1976, pp. 237–44.
21. A. Benton Cocanougher and Grady D. Bruce, "Socially Distant Reference Groups and Consumer Aspirations," *Journal of Marketing Research,* August 1971, pp. 379–81.
22. John M. McCann and David J. Reibstein, "Projecting Served Market Growth for Strategic Planning Decisions," in *Marketing Strategy/Controlling the Marketing Effort,* 7th International Research Seminar in Marketing, June 1980, pp. M1–M17.
23. Unless otherwise noted, the demographic statistics in this section come from *Statistical Abstract of the United States, 1982–83* (Washington, D.C.: Bureau of the Census, 1983).
24. *The Affluentials* (New York: Monroe Mendelson Research, 1980).
25. Bruce Steinberg, "The Mass Market Is Splitting Apart," *Fortune,* November 28, 1983, pp. 76–82.
26. C. Schaninger, "Social Class versus Income Revisited: An Empirical Reexamination," *Journal of Marketing Research,* May 1981, p. 201.
27. Richard Coleman, "The Continuing Significance of Social Class to Marketing," *Journal of Consumer Research,* December 1983, pp. 265–78.
28. William Peters, "Relative Occupational Class Income: A Significant Variable in the Marketing of Automobiles," *Journal of Marketing,* April 1970, pp. 74–77.
29. Leon F. Bouvier and Cary B. Davis, *The Future Racial Composition of the United States* (Washington, D.C.: Demographic Information Services Center, August 1982).
30. Elizabeth C. Hirschman,"American Jewish Ethnicity: Its Relationship to Some Se-

lected Aspects of Consumer Behavior," *Journal of Marketing,* Summer 1981, pp. 102–10.
31. Elizabeth C. Hirschman, "An Examination of Ethnicity and Consumption Using Free Response Data," *An Assessment of Marketing Thought and Practice* (Chicago: American Marketing Association, 1982).
32. Yankelovich, Skelly, and White, *Raising Children in a Changing Society* (Minneapolis: General Mills, 1977), p. 7.
33. Louis Harris and Associates, *Families at Work* (Minneapolis: General Mills, 1981), p. 9.
34. Robert T. Green and Isabella C. M. Cunningham, "Feminine Role Perception and Family Purchasing Decisions," *Journal of Marketing Research,* August 1975, pp. 325–32.

OBJECTIVES

1. To discuss the importance of studying organizational buying behavior.

2. To study the factors influencing organizational buying behavior.

3. To describe the steps involved in organizational buying behavior.

4. To explain the nature and structure of the industrial buying center.

5. To identify the implications of organizational buying behavior for industrial marketing strategy.

Organizational Buying Behavior

The Polaroid Corporation once had such strong products for the consumer—namely, the amateur photography market—that the company concentrated on the consumer market. Polaroid was responsible for the first cameras that could develop their own pictures, and the company still sells almost two-thirds of all "instant" cameras. Sales of these cameras are dropping rapidly, however, as 35-mm camera makers have simplified their products and 24-hour film processing is now widely available. In the late 1970s, Polaroid introduced another consumer-oriented product called Polavision, an instant home movie camera. Few home movie makers seemed to want the product, however, and Polaroid dropped it in 1980.

To improve sales, Polaroid's executives have overhauled the company's strategy and are developing products for and pursuing the industrial market. Pursuing the industrial market required that Polaroid acquire knowledge and experience in that area. The main factor was to recognize that organizational consumers, like individual consumers, have problems that must be solved. For Polaroid, this meant taking several steps. First, the company used their technological expertise to meet specific needs of industrial consumers. Second, the company invested in companies that had done work in such fields as fiber optics and computer printing to learn about different technologies. Third, the company hired engineers with backgrounds in optics, electronics, and physics to work on new types of products. Finally, the company reorganized itself into three divisions: consumer photography, industrial and technical photography, and magnetics. The industrial division is further divided into five profit centers that are each responsible for their own planning. Until these moves, Polaroid had been organized around its consumer photography division, the division that received most of the company's personnel and financial resources.

The result of all these changes in strategy and organization has been Polaroid's development of new products for industrial markets. One of these is the Palette computer-image recorder, a device that makes instant slides from computer images. The product works with personal computers, now so widely used in business, and users can choose the colors for their slides, even if the original computer image is black and white. In Palette's first year, experts predict that Polaroid will sell six million units.

A second industrial-oriented product is Autoprocess, a device that changes film from 35mm cameras into color slides instantly. When developing Autoprocess, Polaroid engineers responded to customer needs articulated during marketing research: They made a product that could be used with any brand of 35mm camera and that could produce high-quality pictures, and the product was offered at a competitive price. Sales of Autoprocess have been extremely good so far, and the product is expected to become a long-term success. Polaroid is committed to greater emphasis on industrial markets and in further product development based on a recognition of the needs of its industrial consumers.[1]

Organizations generally go through the same steps in the buyer decision process as do individual consumers. Organizations must recognize a need or problem, search for information, evaluate alternatives, make decisions about products and suppliers, and perform a postpurchase evaluation. Whether the organization is a manufacturing firm, a marketing intermediary such as a wholesaler or retailer, a nonprofit organization such as a hospital or a museum, or a governmental entity, the same steps apply. Why, then, is it necessary to look separately at organizational buying behavior?

To put it very simply, organizational buying behavior is generally more complex than is the behavior of individual consumers or even of households, as organizational processes are generally complex, and the products that are sold to organizations are sometimes highly technical.

A number of factors cause the organizational buying process to be complex.

—There are usually more people involved, each with a specific role to play.
—Organizational buying decisions generally take longer to make. The time required may be a function of the number of people involved in the decision, the complexity of the product or service, the degree of risk inherent in the decision, and the organizational procedures necessary to obtain approval for a purchase.
—Each organization is different from every other organization in the way they approach the buying decision process. While this is also true of consumers, in some industrial markets the much smaller number of organizations and the much greater size of their purchases means that marketing strategies must often be tailored to individual organizations.
—Organizational buyers are influenced by both "rational" economic motives and "emotional" motives, which are often associated with individual needs of decision makers for security and recognition within the organization. When the rational and emotional motives conflict, as is frequently the case, the task of the marketer is made more difficult.
—The products and services being purchased are often highly technical in nature. This calls for great skill on the marketer's part in providing information and helping prospective purchasers to evaluate the products.[2]

In spite of its complexity, the organizational buying process can be understood, analyzed, and applied to particular situations. Organizational buyers are in search of solutions to problems, and marketers can develop the ability to understand the problems of the organizational buyer. Essential to this understanding is a knowledge of the influences on organizational buying behavior.

Influences on Organizational Buying Behavior

The influences on organizational buying behavior fall into four main categories (see fig. 8–1):[3]

—The marketing environment
—The nature of the organization
—The nature and structure of the buying center
—The similarities and differences in the individual participants in the buying process

We will look at these influences in relation to the following example: The firm is called Liquid Filtration Systems.[4] Its high-technology filtration systems, ranging in price from $50,000 to several hundred thousand dollars, are sold to a variety of industries, including the food and dairy and pharmaceutical industries for use in

Figure 8–1 Influences on organizational buying behavior

- The marketing environment
- The nature of the organization
- The nature and structure of the buying center
- The similarities and differences in the individual participants in the buying process

manufacturing processes. One typical application is the clarification of apple juice by removing the tiny pieces of apple pulp to make a clear liquid with a long shelf life.

The firm was suffering from the problem faced by virtually all industrial marketers today: the high cost of sales calls. The cost of an industrial sales call is generally thought to be $200 and up. Because of the complexity of its products and their applications, Liquid Filtration Systems describes the cost of its sales calls as "really up."

To get the greatest number of sales from these expensive calls, the company's salespeople should contact only qualified prospects, or potential customers who are genuinely interested in their type of products. Liquid Filtration Systems was using advertisements accompanied by business reply cards in technical publications such as *Plant Machinery* to generate leads for its salespeople. The quantity of leads generated in this manner was satisfactory, but the quality was not. The company approached an advertising agency and gave them a single, straightforward task: Develop an advertising campaign that will generate high-quality leads for our sales force. The quantity does not have to be as great as that provided by our trade journal advertising, but the quality must be high—genuinely qualified prospects.

The agency realized that a campaign to support such a complex, expensive product must be based on a thorough understanding of buying behavior in the targeted industries. Together, Liquid Filtration Systems and the agency decided to develop a test campaign for a single division—the Oily Waste Water Division.

The Marketing Environment

An organization's marketing environment influences the nature and implementation of the buying process in a number of ways. Three trends are especially important in today's environment: technology and technological change, emphasis on quality, and an international emphasis.[5]

Technology and technological change. Not too long ago, it was reasonable to say that some industries were greatly affected by technological change and other industries were not. Industries that were thought of as being less affected by technological change were the older, mature industries, such as steel and textiles, and labor intensive industries, such as many types of business services. The pace of technological change has altered that. The major questions now concern the pace and the type of change, not whether this industry is changing and that one is not.

Emphasis on quality. It is no accident that a book entitled *In Search of Excellence* has been the runaway best seller in the early 1980s. The authors describe what they call "America's Best-Run Companies" as those that "provide unparalleled quality, service, and reliability."[6] The emphasis on product quality and reliability has had a profound impact on organizational buying. The requirements of buyers and product specifications have become tighter. The amount of tolerance, or deviation from specifications, allowed has become smaller. The role of technical experts in organizational purchase processes has become greater. In general, to the customer, "failure with tolerance" is still a failure.[7] Figure 8–2 shows one company's advertising based on the quality of its product.

Figure 8–2 An emphasis on quality in the marketing environment has led Hammermill to stress the high quality of its copier paper in its advertisements.
Reprinted with permission of Hammermill Paper Company

8–1 Focus on Marketing Strategy
SELLING AIRPLANES TO GOVERNMENT-OWNED THAI AIRWAYS INTERNATIONAL

Aircraft industry experts predict that during the next ten years over 3,500 airplanes will be sold to airlines around the world at a value of over $150 billion. Not surprisingly, the competition among the major aircraft manufacturers for sales of their planes is already becoming intense.

Two of the largest companies, Boeing Company and Airbus Industrie, recently battled one another for the sale of two aircraft to Thai Airways International. Making the initial sale of the two planes would lead to larger sales in the future. The two companies used practically every imaginable strategy to win this important account.

Thai Airways originally ordered the two planes from Airbus. These planes would be in addition to ten others that the airline had already purchased from Airbus. Thai Airways needed two planes that could travel longer distances than the original ten. General Electric Company (GE) had been contracted to develop engines for the planes, but design problems forced GE to postpone delivery of the engines for eighteen months. Here's where the competition began to get complicated. When Boeing heard about the GE delay, that company, together with the engine manufacturer, Pratt & Whitney, tried to woo Thai Airways away from Airbus. Then GE offered to sell a smaller engine compatible with Boeing's slightly smaller planes. Pratt & Whitney countered this move by promoting its more powerful engine to Airbus. Pratt & Whitney also offered to release the airline from a commitment to GE by buying a GE plant in Bangkok. GE had built the plant as part of an agreement with Thai Airways that the airline would buy more GE plane engines. GE heard about Pratt & Whitney's offer and rushed a representative to Bangkok to make a counteroffer.

International emphasis. International marketing in the 1980s is much broader than the importing and exporting of products, as we will see in chapter 20. It involves complex interrelationships between organizations throughout the world. The description of both sales competition and manufacturing cooperation in the jet plane industry presented in focus 8–1 is a good example. In the absence of restrictive international trade regulations, such relationships may become increasingly common. As a result, organizational buyers will be encouraged to think internationally (not in terms of national boundaries) when they choose suppliers.

The Oily Waste Water Division of Liquid Filtration Systems confronts an environment with one positive aspect and one negative aspect. The positive aspect is pollution control laws. Oily waste from industrial manufacturing processes cannot legally be disposed of in public sewers. It must be hauled off and disposed of in an environmentally safe manner.

The next phase of the Airbus-Boeing conflict involved competitive price slashing. Both companies made drastic price reductions; they offered to buy Thai Airways' used planes at prices that far exceeded their values; and they threw in free extras and services, including crew-training manuals and technical guides for the new planes. Thai Airways set a deadline for the two companies' offers. At the time of the deadline, the Boeing-GE partnership had made the best offer, according to Thai Airways.

Airbus continued to compete, though the battle appeared to have been lost. The company persuaded GE to agree to produce its more powerful engine in only 12 months instead of 18. In addition, Airbus launched a campaign to convince Thai Airways' executives that Airbus, not Boeing, could produce the superior product. Airbus also worked to get the Thai government on its side. French, British, and German officials met with Thai officials. The European representatives threatened to tighten conditions on loans to Thailand and controls on its exports to the Common Market if Airbus failed to win the contract. In the end, Airbus and Thai Airways signed an agreement.

The reason European governments became involved in the competition was that Airbus had developed a consortium, or an international alliance with several countries designed to increase sales, made up of manufacturers from France, West Germany, and Britain. This type of organization is particularly helpful in selling aircraft to the government-owned airlines in those countries. As we've just seen, a consortium can also unite several countries to use their influence on a country outside the consortium. Recently Boeing has formed a similar alliance with Japan. For a 15 percent partnership, Japan gains the opportunity to enter the commercial airliner market; Boeing anticipates increased sales to Japanese airlines.

Source: William M. Carley, "The Air War," *Wall Street Journal*, March 20, 1984, pp. 1, 18.

The negative aspect is the nature of the industries that produce the largest quantities of oily waste. These are established industries, including metalworking, machine shops, and can production, where the pace of technological change is relatively slow. These industries are generally slower to adopt technological innovations than are newer, technology-oriented industries. Liquid filtration is state-of-the-art technology, and few professional engineers are familiar with it. As a result, the most promising potential customers may be reluctant to purchase the product.

The Nature of the Organization

The nature of the organization itself and the amount of experience it has with a particular buying situation both have a great deal to do with its approach to the buying process. Three aspects of the organization must be considered: the buying situation faced by the organization, the structure of the organization, and the people involved in the organizational buying process.

The buying situation. As we saw in chapter 6, the three buying situations in organizational buying behavior are the *new task*, the *modified rebuy*, and the *straight rebuy*. These three buying situations and their characteristics are shown in table 8–1.

A new task arises when an organization has a problem with no standard solution or when there is a possible new solution (a new product or process, for example) to a recurring problem. Faced with a new task, the organization generally conducts an extensive information search and thoroughly evaluates its alternatives to reduce possible risks. The postpurchase evaluation provides information that will be used by the organization the next time a solution to the same problem is required.

A recent positive experience with a specific buying situation causes the succeeding similar purchases to fall into a modified rebuy situation. The organization seeks less external information and conducts a less extensive evaluation of alternatives, especially of new alternatives.

When the organization has sufficient experience to perceive little risk in staying with established suppliers, a straight rebuy situation exists. Straight rebuy situations may become so routinized that orders are generated automatically with no consideration of alternative products or suppliers. Such a situation exists when an office simply reorders stationery from its office supply vendor when it is running low.

In all of these buying situations, the industrial supplier's goal is to provide a satisfactory experience with a product, which includes the product or service itself, the terms of sale, and customer service. As the buying situation progresses from new task to straight rebuy, fewer products and supplier alternatives are considered. The end result is an organizational customer who is loyal to one product or brand.

While the newness of the buying situation is of critical importance, other attributes of the situation should also be considered. The product purchased—whether equipment, office supplies, or business services, for example—is related to the degree of risk in the decision. A major piece of equipment is not only expensive, it is possibly also critical to the functioning of the organization. The buying process will usually be thorough and lengthy. On the other hand, the decision to send out a single report to a typing service because the secretarial staff has no time

TABLE 8–1 Types of Organizational Buying Situations

Type of Buying Situation	Newness of the Problem	Information Requirements	Consideration of New Alternatives
New Task	High	Maximum	Important
Modified Rebuy	Medium	Moderate	Limited
Straight Rebuy	Low	Minimal	None

Source: Patrick J. Robinson, Charles W. Faris, and Yoram Wind, *Industrial Buying and Creative Marketing* (Boston: Allyn & Bacon, 1967), p. 25. Reprinted with permission.

available will be considered much less thoroughly, even if it represents a new task.

This discussion of the buying situation points out that not all organizational buying decisions are complex, expensive, high-risk decisions. The routine straight rebuy decision or the very low-risk decisions are usually made *autonomously,* often by a single individual called a **purchasing agent.** The less routine, more risky decisions are made by a *joint,* or group, process. This chapter concentrates on the decisions made by groups. One of the first questions asked by industrial marketers is always, "Will this decision be made *jointly* or *autonomously*?"

If the marketer is Liquid Filtration Systems, the answer seems quite clear. The decision will be made by a group process because a filtration system is technically complex, important to the industrial process for which it is purchased, and very expensive.

The structure of the organization. While each organization functions in a unique way, there are a few general characteristics of organizational structures that affect the buying process. As we saw in chapter 2, an organization has a formal structure represented by an organization chart. Most organizations also have informal structures that control the flow of communications within an organization. The informal structure is often quite different from the formal structure.

A *complex* organization with functional specialities and many different units may involve many people at many levels in the purchase decision. From the marketer's perspective, there are many influential people who must be contacted. Some of these influentials may be technical specialists who are likely to be very receptive to appropriate presentations of the right type of information.

The degree of *centralization* of the organization is also important. In a centralized organization, decision-making power is concentrated in relatively few individuals, and there are fewer influencers to contact. However, since these influencers have a great deal of power and responsibility, they may be protected by gatekeepers, who screen the information and the people, allowing marketers little direct contact with the decision makers. The decision makers themselves may be generalists who pay less attention to complex, technical information than do the functional specialists in a complex organization.

Also important is the extent to which an organization is *formalized.* A highly formalized organization adheres strictly to a prescribed set of policies and procedures. The more formalized the organization, the greater the number of people and different units who participate in the buying decision process. The process itself is often a highly structured written process, with less informal communications than might be expected among the participants. A marketer may find a highly formal organization quite difficult to approach and sell to, because new ideas do not flow freely and the organization tends to stick to established ways of doing things.

The communications network. Another aspect of the structure of the organization is the way both formal and informal communication flows through it. This can be seen by studying the workings of the communications network in a

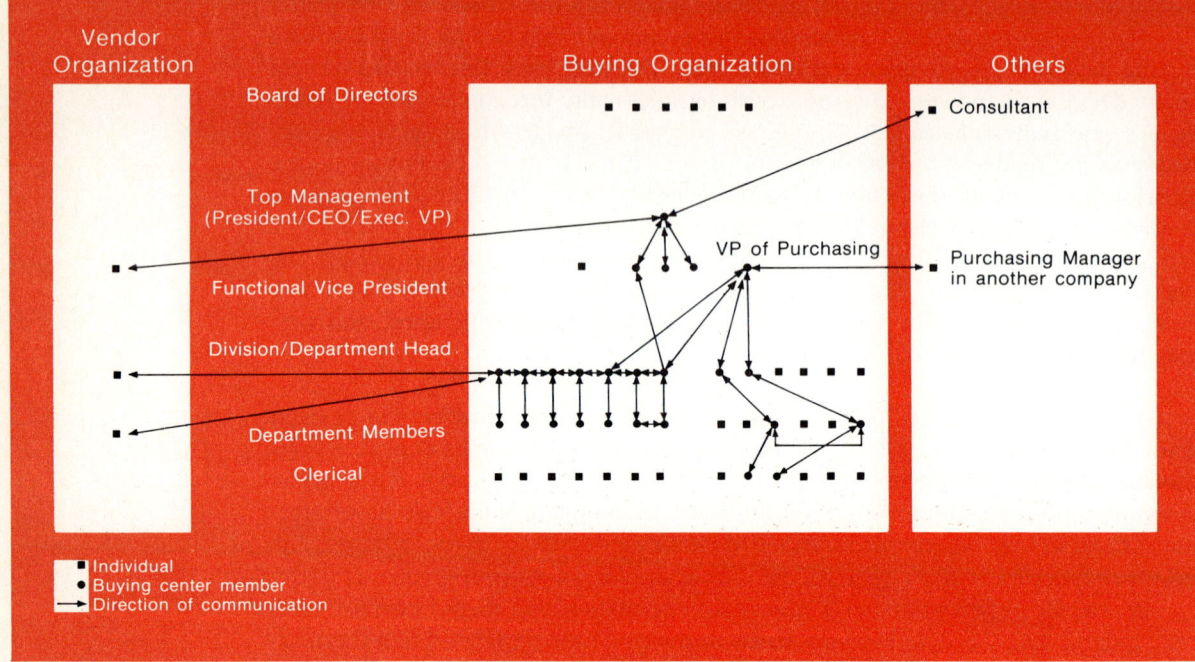

Source: Wesley J. Johnston and Thomas V. Bonoma, "The Buying Center: Structure and Interaction Patterns," *Journal of Marketing*, Summer 1981, p. 147. Used with permission of the American Marketing Association.

Figure 8–3
A possible communications network

particular buying situation. The communications network can be described on five dimensions:

1. The *number of levels in the organizational hierarchy* that send or receive communications concerning the purchase decision
2. The *number of different departments* within the organization that are involved in the purchase decision communications network
3. The *number of people* involved in the communications network
4. The *extent to which individuals involved in the process engage in communications* concerning the purchase process
5. The *extent to which the purchasing manager sends communications to and receives communications from* other people involved in the process

These dimensions cover the number of people involved, their status and affiliation within the organization, and the frequency and direction of communications that relate to the purchase decision process.

Figure 8–3 shows a possible communications network for a buying decision. Five levels of the hierarchy send or receive communication: top management, a vice-president, department heads, department members, and clerical personnel.

Chapter 8 / Organizational Buying Behavior   **212**

Eleven different departments are involved in the decision. Twenty-five people are in the communications network. The purchasing manager, in this case a vice-president of purchasing, is in a pivotal position in the communication.

Marketers who understand how the particular communications network works in a buying situation can develop an effective marketing strategy to reach it. Top managers in the buying organization must be approached by top managers in the selling organization. Junior salespeople are unlikely to gain access to top management or to make much of an impression if they do. Technical experts in the buying organization can be approached by technical experts from the selling organization. Users can be approached by salespeople with hands-on knowledge about the product.

Additionally, marketers who understand the type and frequency of communications in a customer firm will be better able to assess the amount and timing of information that is needed. An organization with a high degree of both formal and informal communication virtually does some of the marketer's work. An organization with less extensive communication will require the presentation of more information and is likely to need more time to make a decision.

The Nature and Structure of the Buying Center

The **buying center** is the name most frequently given to the decision-making unit involved in a specific organizational buying decision. A study of the buying center involves analyzing the roles its members have and diagnosing the influence its members have on one another as they engage in the process. Two factors are particularly important in understanding the nature of this interpersonal influence: the bases of power in an organization and the organization's conflict-resolving strategies.

Bases of power in an organization. Figure 8–4 shows five types of power that exist within an organization.[8] Each type of power has a different source, and each different type of power leads to a different type of influence in the purchase process. The influence can be positive and support a proposed decision, or it can be negative and veto the decision.

Reward power. Reward power refers to a manager's ability to encourage purchases and influence decisions based on the rewards—monetary, political, and so on—he or she can distribute. The reward may be quite direct, as in a pending salary increase or promotion. It may be indirect; only favored colleagues and subordinates are invited for a weekend cruise on his or her sailboat or are praised to others. Whether direct or indirect, all of these are important organizational rewards.

Coercive Power. The manager who can provide any rewards can also withhold them. This is *coercive power.* One direct way of coercing a subordinate is through performance evaluation. It is very difficult to argue often and loudly against a manager, especially as evaluation time draws near.

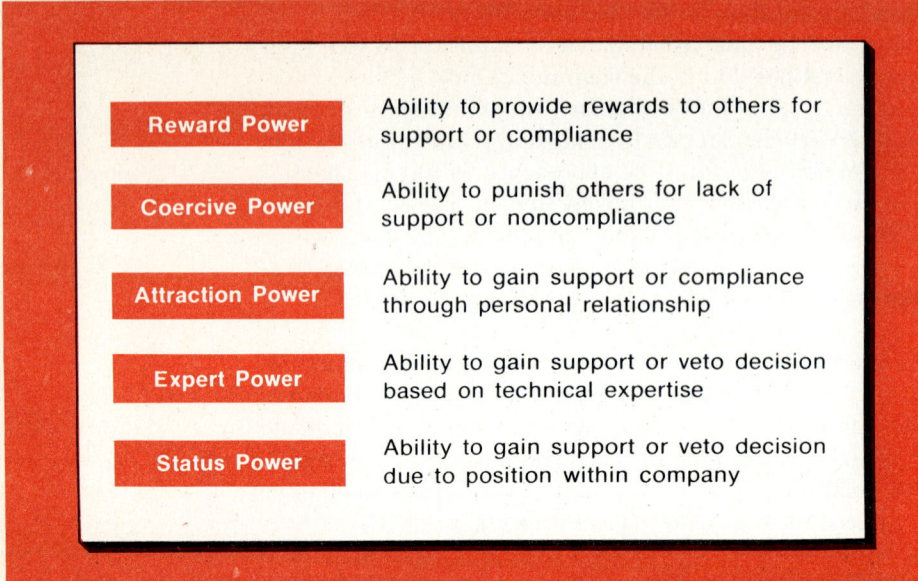

Figure 8–4 Bases of power in an organization

Source: Based on Thomas V. Bonoma, "Major Sales: Who Really Does the Buying," *Harvard Business Review*, May–June 1982, pp. 111–16.

Attraction Power. *Attraction power* describes a person's ability to influence others through sheer force of personality. This is sometimes called charm or charisma, and it is extremely potent. A person who gives advice on a friendly basis is very hard to resist.

Expert Power. *Expert power* is based on the technical expertise possessed by the individual, not on the individual's position in the organizational hierarchy. Technical expertise can, of course, be used either positively or negatively. If a technical expert does not support a decision, he or she often has the power to veto it. A technical expert's support of a product may work heavily in its favor.

Status Power. *Status power* comes from having a high-level position in the organization. It is similar to reward or coercive power, but it is often used to persuade rather than to enforce a decision. It is effective only if colleagues and subordinates are willing to let it be exercised.

The kind of power that a manager has or aspires to have affects his or her buying motives.[9] The top manager who wants a personal computer for status reasons has little interest in technical information about how the computer works. Its brand name and how it looks sitting in an office may be more important. On the other hand, information is power for the technical expert, who, therefore, wants to receive more technical information. Not only does the technical expert want different information from that desired by the top manager, the technical expert wants much *more* information.

Conflict-resolving strategies. Most purchasing decisions will cause some level of conflict within the organization, as not all members of the buying center will agree on one or more issues relative to the purchase.[10] The conflict may be resolved by the decision of one or more powerful participants, but more commonly, the organization will use a conflict-resolving strategy. The strategy used depends on whether the conflict pertains to an individual or to a group.

Individual Conflict-Resolving Strategies. An individual approaching a conflict can be either cooperative and attempt to satisfy other people's concerns, or assertive and attempt to satisfy his or her own concerns. These two approaches lead to the five different types of behavior shown in figure 8–5.

The individual who is both uncooperative and unassertive is engaging in *avoidance*. There is little reason for the marketer to attempt to inform or persuade such

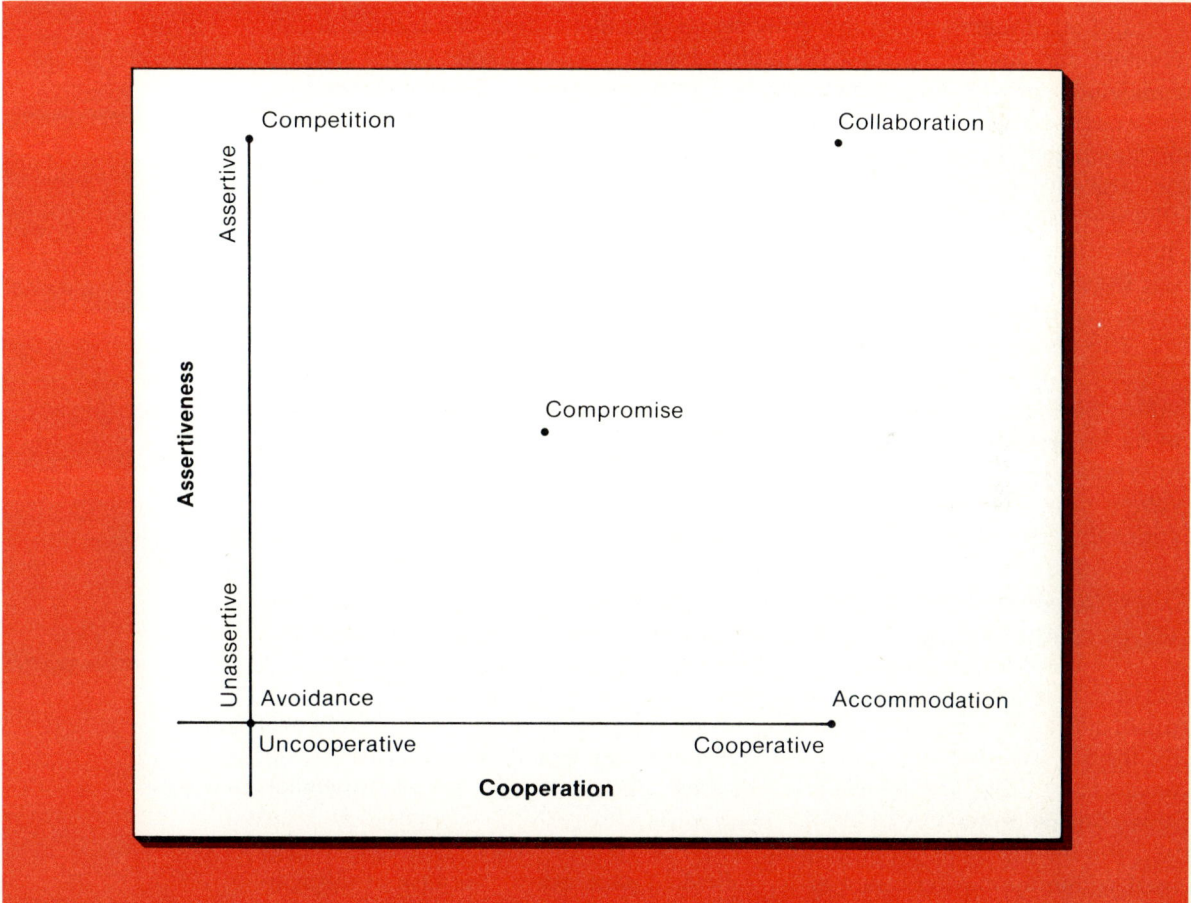

Figure 8–5 Types of individual behavior in approaching a conflict

Source: Adapted from Kenneth Thomas, "Conflict and Conflict Management," in *Handbook of Industrial and Organizational Psychology*, ed. Marvin D. Dunnette (Chicago: Rand McNally, 1976), pp. 889–935.

an individual. Whether from dislike of conflict itself or from fear of the consequences of being on the losing side, this individual is withdrawing from active participation in the buying center to the greatest possible extent.

The nonassertive but cooperative individual is engaging in *accommodation* to the desires of other members of the buying center. This type of individual, too, is of little value to the marketer. Bowing to the will of others, he or she will exert little influence on the purchase decision.

The individual who believes in *compromise* is attempting to strike a happy medium between being totally uncooperative and overassertive. This individual should receive some attention from the marketer, because he or she is having some influence on the purchase decision. This individual, however, will not be a strong advocate for the marketer's product or service within the buying center.

Advocates for a product are found among the assertive individuals in the buying center. The uncooperative assertive individual is engaging in *competition*. This individual is trying to get his or her own way, even at the expense of the preferences of other members of the buying center. For that reason, the competitive individual may not be the most desirable advocate for a marketer's products. The competitive individual may alienate other members of the buying center, and produce lingering resentment, which may spill over and affect perceptions of the product purchased. It may also affect future purchase decision processes.

The advocate the marketer would like to find is the individual who uses *collaboration*. This individual works with other members of the buying center to arrive at the decision that solves the organization's problem and simultaneously gives everyone the greatest possible benefit. This type of individual will make a good case for the marketer's product.

This discussion of individual conflict-handling situations assumes that the marketer's salesperson is active in the buying process. These behavioral styles can be understood only by engaging in face-to-face dealings with the individual members of the buying center. The salesperson who can best understand both the motives of individual participants in the buying center and the behavioral strategies that individuals use to deal with other group members will have a much better chance of positively influencing the final purchase decision.

Group Conflict-Resolution Strategies. The resolution of conflict within a group can be accomplished either through *negotiation* or the *use of power*. The strategies that are based on negotiation are the use of reason, ingratiation, and bargaining, plus the building of coalitions within the group. These strategies imply at least a reasonable level of cooperation among buying center members. The strategies based on the use of power—assertiveness, appeal to higher authority, and the use of rewards and punishments—suggest that there are one or more assertive members of the buying center.

The marketer can do little to influence the type of conflict-resolving strategy used within the buying center or by individual participants. The task of the marketer, though, is to understand the strategies and provide the most influential participants with the information they need to play their roles in the buying process.

When the advertising agency working for Liquid Filtration Systems analyzed the composition of the buying center for this type of product, they identified three key influentials—the plant engineer, the manufacturing manager, and the chief executive officer. The involvement of the plant engineer was obvious; this individual is responsible for all systems within the facility. The involvement of the manufacturing manager was only slightly less obvious. Even though filtration systems involve waste disposal, which is not a direct part of the manufacturing process itself, a defective or inefficient system could affect the manufacturing process, and the manufacturing manager is interested in seeing that an effective system is purchased. The chief executive officer was identified because a purchase of $50,000 or more had to be approved at the top level. The purchasing agent or purchasing manager was not considered influential in this type of decision. The decision is too technical, too complex, for most purchasing agents to wield much influence. The advertising agency decided that purchasing agents would be targeted in this campaign only if the position of manufacturing manager did not exist in a particular firm.

The Similarities and Differences in Individual Participants in the Buying Process

The activities and motives of specific members of the buying center can best be understood by looking at factors related to their professional backgrounds and to their own individual psychological makeup.

Professional background. An individual's professional background is formed by his or her educational background and professional contacts. The formal *educational background* of an individual will provide clues about his or her likely approach to the buying decision process. An engineer most likely will think in terms of technical specifications; managers with MBA degrees are often overly cost-conscious; a graphic designer is critical of color, shape, and visual appeal.

The extent to which a professionally-trained person associates with other professionals, especially ones outside his or her own organization, also has an effect on the approach to the buying decision process. In general, an individual who engages in professional activities and has many professional contacts will turn to other professionals for information about a product.[11]

Psychological influences. All of the psychological influences on individual consumer behavior that were presented in chapter 7 are also relevant to the understanding of individuals as organizational buyers. We will examine three of these influences—motivation, learning, and perception—in relation to organizational buying behavior.

Motivation. The motives of organizational buyers can best be understood by dividing them into *task-related motives,* which are directly related to the buying situation, and *non-task-related motives,* which are only indirectly related to the buying situation.

Figure 8–6 Advertising to task-related and non-task-related motives. Caterpillar is rationally setting forth the characteristics and capabilities of its compact lift trucks. Harvard Software is appealing to buyers' desires to perform their jobs well and to look good to management.

Reprinted with permission of Caterpillar Lift Trucks (left) and Harvard Software Inc. (right).

Task-related motives, sometimes called "rational" motives, relate to the price, quality, and services provided by the supplier for the product.[12] The importance of each of these characteristics in meeting the goals of the buying organization is clear. The mistake made by many marketers is to assume that these are the *only*, or even the primary, motives for an organizational purchase.

Each individual member of the buying center is just that—an individual. He or she has personal goals and objectives, such as security, promotion, and recognition, which affect certain transactions as much or more than do organizational goals. A manager, for example, may require that subordinates remove their shoes before entering his office because he does not want his white carpet to become soiled. He must have been motivated by other than "rational" goals to purchase that carpet.

Non-task-related motives do not always predominate. Clearly they do not. The point is that the marketer must be sensitive to the existence of non-task-related motives. It is the well-conceived product and marketing strategy that allows the organizational buyer to satisfy both organizational and personal objectives. Figure 8–6 shows advertisements directed to the different types of motives.

Learning. As with consumer buying behavior, organizational buying behavior involves a great deal of learning. Understanding an organization's learning process is complicated, however, as many individuals are involved, each with differing information requirements and differing degrees of involvement in the learning process.

The result is a more formal process, which organizes factual material and communicates it as required to various participants in the process. Techniques developed to help buyers evaluate products (discussed later in this chapter) contribute to learning within the organization. They also contribute to a much more formal postpurchase evaluation than is usually conducted for consumer purchases. This, too, increases the organization's store of formal knowledge about purchase decisions.

Perception. Because there is much to be learned in the process of organizational buying, the members of the buying center develop many types of perceptions. The critical ones are perceptions of the seller, of the seller's sales representatives, and each participant's perceptions of his or her own role in the process.

The *perceptions of the seller* involve the seller's corporate image. While the company name or brand name should not matter, a non-task-related motive to reduce or avoid risk may lead the members of the buying center to choose a well-known and highly regarded seller. If the product fails, they can point out that they went with the best. If the vendor is unknown or has a poor reputation, the buying center is open to much greater criticism if the product is ineffective.

The buyers' perception of the seller's sales representatives relates directly to the choice of seller. A recent study identified 17 attributes that have been found to be important in customers' ratings of industrial salespeople (see fig. 8–7).[13] The two key characteristics, empathy and expertise, seem to be the most important. Other research has indicated that the most successful salespersons are those who best understand the organizational buyer's own decision process.[14] Once again, the message to marketers is clear. Successful marketing strategies are based on a thorough understanding of the organizational buyer. The buyer is able to recognize attempts to simply "sell" a product. The buyer is looking for genuine assistance in solving his or her own problems.

A final perception is the *perception of the individual's own role in the buying decision process.* Each individual tends to believe that he or she plays a central role in the process, although that perception is not necessarily true. It is only human nature for an individual to overstate his or her importance in this process, and the marketer can be seriously misled by taking one individual's perceptions at face value.

Organizational buyers have perceptions of many distinct elements of a marketer's overall program, and some of those elements may interact with one an-

**Figure 8–7
Attributes that affect the perception of industrial salespeople**

1. Understanding of other people
2. Willingness to go to bat for the buyer within the supplier firm
3. Knowing how to listen
4. Knowledge of firms selling to
5. Knowledge of buyer's product line
6. Imagination in applying supplier products to buyer's product line
7. Confidence
8. Self-reliance
9. Product knowledge
10. Preparation for sales presentations
11. Understanding of buyer's problems
12. Follow-through on deliveries
13. Regularity of sales calls
14. Having a personalized presentation for each buyer
15. Providing technical assistance
16. Presenting many new ideas to the buyer
17. Willingness to handle rush orders

Source: Adapted from John E. Swan et al., "Industrial Buyer Image of the Saleswoman," *Journal of Marketing*, Winter 1984, p. 111.

other. A classic experiment determined that "respondents are more likely to favor the products of salesmen whom they rank low in trustworthiness when these salesmen represent well-known companies than they are to favor the products of salesmen whom they rank relatively high in trustworthiness but who represent unknown companies."[15] Similarly, a good sales presentation by the representative of an unknown company was a very positive factor when the decision involved a high degree of risk, but was less important for a low-risk decision.[16]

The individuals involved in the buying center for the products of Liquid Filtration Systems were divided into several groups by the advertising agency. The plant engineer and the manufacturing manager were both likely to have engineering backgrounds. They would require technical information. For them, the same basic promotional package, containing a letter, a technical brochure, and a reply card, was used. The envelope and letter were individually typed and addressed to the engineer or manager by name, not just by title, to increase the likelihood that they would read it and return the card requesting a sales call. Additionally, the plant engineer received a small bottle to collect a sample of the plant's oily waste water. When the salesperson called, he or she brought a briefcase-sized working model of the system. While the salesperson made the presentation, the sample was poured in, and the model worked. In approximately 20 minutes, the model produced water that could be discharged into a sewer, with only a minute quantity of oily slime remaining.

The chief executive officer, whether an engineer by training or not, was a generalist and needed less detailed and technical information. The real problem was getting any information to him or her. The agency knew that secretaries or gatekeepers tended to throw out all promotional material. What could they send that would not be sidetracked? The answer was a drum of popcorn delivered by a freight service directly to the chief executive officer's office. On it was a label modeled on the hazardous material sign used when transporting dangerous cargo. This one featured a "smiley face" and the legend, "Not Hazardous to Your Health." Inside the container of popcorn was a small bottle of unpopped kernels accompanied by a letter. It explained that oily waste water was like the popped kernels; there was a large quantity of it. The bottle of unpopped kernels was compared to the oily slime remaining after filtration. There was only a small quantity, which could be disposed of economically. There was also a business reply card in the drum, even though no one seriously expected chief executive officers to return it.

The agency reasoned that not even a chief executive officer could resist opening the drum. The craziness of the scheme should prompt the officer to call the plant engineer and say, "Who's this firm called Liquid Filtration Systems who just sent me a drum of popcorn?" The plant engineer, who had received the promotional package, should be impressed by such a strategy.

Did it work? Yes, it did. Each lead generated cost approximately $60, compared with the $80 per lead cost of trade journal advertising. Liquid Filtration Systems estimates that almost $400,000 in sales have resulted from these leads, while the campaign itself cost less than $16,000.

There was an additional and unexpected side benefit from the campaign. The level of customer awareness and interest proved to be highly motivating to the sales force of Liquid Filtration Systems. "Management has finally done something to really give us some help," was their attitude.

Focus 8–2 presents another example of organizational buying behavior.

The environmental, organizational, interpersonal, and individual influences on the organizational buying process are indeed complex. Yet, at the same time, as one sales manager recently said, "People sell to people." It is important to realize that these complex influences can be broken down, analyzed, and understood. It is also crucial to realize that influencers are human beings with goals, preferences, personal needs, and even insecurities. Looked at in this manner, the organizational purchase decision process becomes a little less formidable.

8–2 Focus on Organizational Buying Behavior
HOW B. F. GOODRICH BUYS

B. F. Goodrich Company has a shopping list of over 350,000 items and spends millions of dollars on its annual purchases. A few years ago, Goodrich reorganized its buying system so that one centralized department handles all of the company's purchases.

Prior to the reorganization, plant managers in many locations made their own purchases as needs arose. Goodrich executives discovered, however, that having one department of people whose primary job is to purchase led to tremendous savings. One example is the purchase of forklifts, previously one of the many responsibilities of the plant managers. Now that the purchasing department handles these orders, Goodrich is saving about $400,000 per year, as full-time buyers can spend the time and energy necessary to research the options in a particular product area, locate alternative suppliers, and negotiate prices and contracts. A centralized buying department also purchases in larger quantities, thereby often reducing prices. Goodrich estimates that in its second year the reorganized purchasing department saved the company over $18 million, and the company anticipates the savings could reach $30 million. These savings translate directly into increased company profits.

One change that was necessary in order to get these savings was to elevate purchasers' status within the company. Pay for several jobs was increased to attract talented job candidates. The company has also raised the status of several purchasing positions to the executive level, giving the buying department a great deal more authority than it had in the past.

Goodrich's purchasing department handles every purchase the company makes, from heavy equipment, such as forklifts, to routine office supplies. The department is broken down into sections that specialize in buying one kind of item; one section handles the buying and leasing of office copier machines, for example, while another unit concentrates on buying materials used for manufacturing Goodrich tires. By focusing on specific areas, the separate sections can study each company buying problem and the available solutions more deeply, company executives say.

Source: Based on Thomas C. Hayes, "At Goodrich, Buyers Help Raise Profits," *New York Times*, July 2, 1981, pp. D1, D6.

Steps in the Organizational Buying Process

We have already established the fact that the five basic steps in the buying decision process apply to organizational buying decisions just as they apply to individual and household decisions. Even so, because organizations usually carry out a more

Figure 8–8 Steps in the organizational buying process

1. Identification of needs (problem recognition)
2. Establishment of objectives and specifications
3. Identification of suppliers and obtaining bids
4. Evaluation of alternative suppliers
5. Selection of the supplier
6. Evaluation of the supplier

formal process, it is useful to look at a more detailed set of steps that organizations usually follow[17] (see fig. 8–8). These are:

1. Identification of needs (problem recognition)
2. Establishment of objectives and specifications
3. Identification of suppliers and obtaining bids
4. Evaluation of alternative suppliers
5. Selection of the supplier
6. Evaluation of the supplier

Identification of Needs

Identification of needs can come from anywhere in the organization. For rather routine purchases, primarily those that fall into the modified or straight rebuy situations, a need is often signaled when the purchasing department receives a requisition from a user department within the organization. The requisition may or may not specify a preferred supplier.

Not long ago, a hospital supply firm placed its first female salesperson in an established sales territory. The sales manager experienced considerable anxiety over this move, knowing he was in for a great deal of criticism if sales performance in the territory faltered. To his delight, not only did sales not fall off, they began a steady upward climb. After several months of satisfying sales increases, he decided to investigate the situation. He found that the new salesperson was spending a great deal of time on the floors of the hospitals, clinics, and nursing homes in the territory, discussing the problems the nurses faced and explaining how her products could help solve them. The result was that nursing supervisors were sending requisitions to their purchasing departments with strong recommendations that this specific brand of supplies be ordered. When last seen, the sales manager was interviewing other prospective female salespeople.

For the more risky modified rebuy or new task situations, identification of needs is more likely to originate at middle- to upper-managerial levels. For example, the comptroller decides that everyone in the accounting department needs on-line access to the organization's computer system and begins to investigate the merits of intelligent terminals versus personal computers. Or the chief executive officer of a rapidly growing firm decides that the success of the business and his own desire for recognition require the purchase of a company jet. Think for a few minutes about the decision process that is likely to occur in each situation, including who and how many people are likely to make up the buying center.

It is important to recognize that the trends discussed at the beginning of the chapter, especially the concern about quality, may be causing organizations to pay more attention to the identification of needs at lower levels of the organization. This broadens the group of people that marketers need to reach and to influence in behalf of their products or services.

In some instances, identification of needs may originate with the marketer, not the purchasing organization. This occurs when the marketer has developed a product, process, or service that can improve some operation of the organization. Industrial robots, which can be used in a wide variety of routine production operations, are a good case in point. The manufacturers of industrial robots have found it necessary to identify organizations that can benefit from robotic technology and to conduct extensive informational campaigns to acquaint potential buyers with the nature and benefits of this new technology.

Establishment of Objectives and Specifications

When the purchase being considered is a routine rebuy, specifications for the required product or service should already exist and are unlikely to be modified. In any other buying situation, the organization will engage in a process of establishing objectives to be accomplished by the purchase and developing specifications.

The formality and extensiveness of the process of establishing objectives and specifications depend on the organization's typical procedures as well as the degree of risk attached to the particular purchase situation. The specifications for a proposed purchase describe in more or less technical detail the precise characteristics of the product or service desired. The marketer who is aware of an impending major purchase can attempt to provide input into the process of developing specifications. This can result in the marketer's product being specified as the preferred purchase.

Identification of Suppliers and Obtaining Bids

The description of the organizational purchase process makes each of these activities seem to represent a discrete step in the process. In practice, this is often not the case. In particular, the development of specifications and the identification of suppliers are often done simultaneously. In order to write specifications, the organization needs to know what products or services, and consequently what suppliers, exist in the marketplace. After obtaining this information, the organization may conclude that no existing product or service meets its exact needs. If that is the case, the organization will search for a supplier who will design and manufacture a new product or will modify an existing product to meet their specifications. The starting point in either instance is a thorough knowledge of existing product offerings.

What are the sources of information used by the organization? They include:[18]

—Suppliers' sales representatives
—Exhibitions and trade shows
—Direct mail
—Press releases
—General news magazines and trade publications
—Journal advertising
—Professional and technical conferences
—Feature articles in the trade press
—Word of mouth

The sources of information available to the organizational buyer are more diverse than those commonly used by the consumer. However, like the consumer, the organizational buyer often receives information about a new product or service from a number of sources. Properly timed and coordinated, the cumulative effect of information from many sources can be much greater than if the marketer had relied on a single source.

For example, your instructor may have first heard of this textbook through a single direct mail piece or the Prentice-Hall catalog, a call from a Prentice-Hall salesperson, or an advertisement in *Marketing News* or in a professional journal such as the *Journal of Marketing*. He or she may also have had an opportunity to examine the book at the exhibition during the yearly American Marketing Association Educators' Conference and to talk to an editor or even the author of the book. While at the conference, your instructor may have discussed teaching materials and approaches with other marketing educators. All of these sources of information are important in the potential adoption of a textbook.

Three sources of information are of prime importance in organizational buying: media advertising, publicity, and informal communication.

Media advertising. Advertising aimed at organizational buyers rarely makes a sale, but it creates awareness and offers information that often provides a "foot in the door" for the marketer's sales force. (This topic is covered in detail in chapter 14.) Like advertising aimed at consumers, media advertising can focus either on the overall corporate image or on a specific product.

Corporate image advertising can have one or more of numerous objectives, depending on the nature of the firm's existing image and current marketing strategy. Typical objectives include creating awareness of the firm and its basic business or establishing the firm's reputation.

The advertisements used to establish corporate images are general. They are appropriate for any influential member of the buying center. They are especially appropriate for top managers who want to see "the big picture" and have little

Chapter 8 / Organizational Buying Behavior

Figure 8–9 Motorola is using both general corporate advertising and product advertising. The corporate advertising (above) reinforced Motorola's reputation as a leading electronics company. The product advertising (left) describes Motorola's Four-Phase System, lists present users and applications, and tells buyers where they can get more information about the product.

Reprinted with permission.

concern about the technical details. As such, they are most appropriate for the general business press and even television.

Product advertising focuses on one offering of a firm. For example, according to Federal Express advertisements, "If it absolutely, positively has to be there on time"—and if it weighs two pounds or less—the company's Courier Pak is the answer. This type of advertising may or may not attempt to make a sale. As it focuses on a specific product, more detailed and specific information is presented. These advertisements often appear in professional publications and the trade press. Figure 8–9 presents advertisements that demonstrate both types of advertising.

Publicity. The sponsorship of advertising is clear, and therefore the information advertisements contain is often viewed with some skepticism. Publicity, such as articles in the general or trade press, generates much less skepticism and tends to receive a "halo effect" from the credibility of the publication in which it appears. Consequently, marketers expend substantial sums on public relations efforts designed to encourage favorable trade press coverage.

Informal communication. Marketers generally agree that there is less informal communication in organizational markets than there is in consumer markets. However, when it does occur, it has a great deal of influence on purchase decisions.

There are several reasons why informal communication is infrequent. One is the ever-present concern that sharing of information could result in charges of collusion and draw unwanted attention from regulatory agencies or even result in lawsuits. Second, individuals who have narrowly defined jobs in an organization may have little contact with their counterparts in other organizations unless they are active in specialized professional organizations. Third, there is the perception that each organization is unique, and the experiences of one may be of little value to another. Finally, there is a degree of reliance on information from the industrial salesperson that usually does not exist in consumer markets. Not only is the industrial salesperson a frequently used source, he or she is often considered the most *trusted* source.[19]

The need for information is so great and the sources of information are so numerous that the information gathering process is often extremely time-consuming. The need to collect, organize, and disseminate information to the various members of the buying center often accounts for a substantial portion of the time in the buying decision process.

When a set of potential suppliers has been identified, the organization may or may not send out formal invitations to bid. Competitive bidding is frequent, although not universal, for high-cost, high-risk purchases. (Competitive bidding is discussed in chapter 12.)

Evaluation of Alternative Suppliers

Suppliers may be evaluated a number of times during the buying decision process; each evaluation involves an increasing degree of detail and specificity. For a major purchase, an evaluation is likely to be conducted at least twice—once to cut the number of firms actually asked to bid on the purchase down to a manageable level and a second time to select the actual supplier. The evaluation criteria include total cost, product performance, ordering convenience, the supplier's reputation, and accompanying services. The same criteria are used each time, but the thoroughness of the analysis may change as the buyers become more experienced with the suppliers and their products. At the end of the evaluation, the supplier is selected.

Well-managed organizations routinely evaluate the performance of suppliers. Usually, the results of the evaluations are provided to the suppliers, as it benefits both buyer and supplier for the purchase to be fully satisfying. In other terms, "a healthy supplier-buyer relationship is not adversarial or arms' length; long-term supplier-buyer relationships are mutually dependent and beneficial."[20] That statement goes to the core of good marketing and good management in the 1980s and beyond.

Evaluation of the Supplier

A Model of Organizational Buying Behavior

In order to organize the factors in organizational buyer behavior, a number of models have been created. The following model is made up of four influences on organizational buying behavior: the marketing environment, the organization, the buying center, and the individual participants.[21] Within these categories are *task-related variables,* or those directly related to the purchasing situation, and *non-task-related* variables, or influences that are only indirectly related to the buying situation. Organizational buying is shown as a process that involves many individuals, objectives, and decisions (see fig. 8–10).

Environmental influences. In the category of environmental influences are a wide variety of factors described in chapter 3 that can affect the buying decision—the technological, economic, political, legal, and cultural factors. Also included are institutions that influence the buying decision, such as governmental agencies, unions, and trade associations.

Organizational influences. Organizational influences include all those factors that are unique to a particular business. These include the organization's goals, resources (financial, human, and technological), and its policies.

This category can be further broken down into the variables affecting the buying situation, including identification of need, establishment of specifications, identification of alternatives, and evaluation of suppliers.

Another set of variables concerns the *organizational structure.* One important aspect of an organization's structure is its communications network: the way in which information is passed between individuals and departments; the way commands and instructions are issued; and methods of influence, persuasion, and integration. The system of authority in an organization is another important influence on organizational buying, as are the systems of status, rewards, and work flow. These systems within the organization are all vital to understanding the organizational influences on the buying decision.

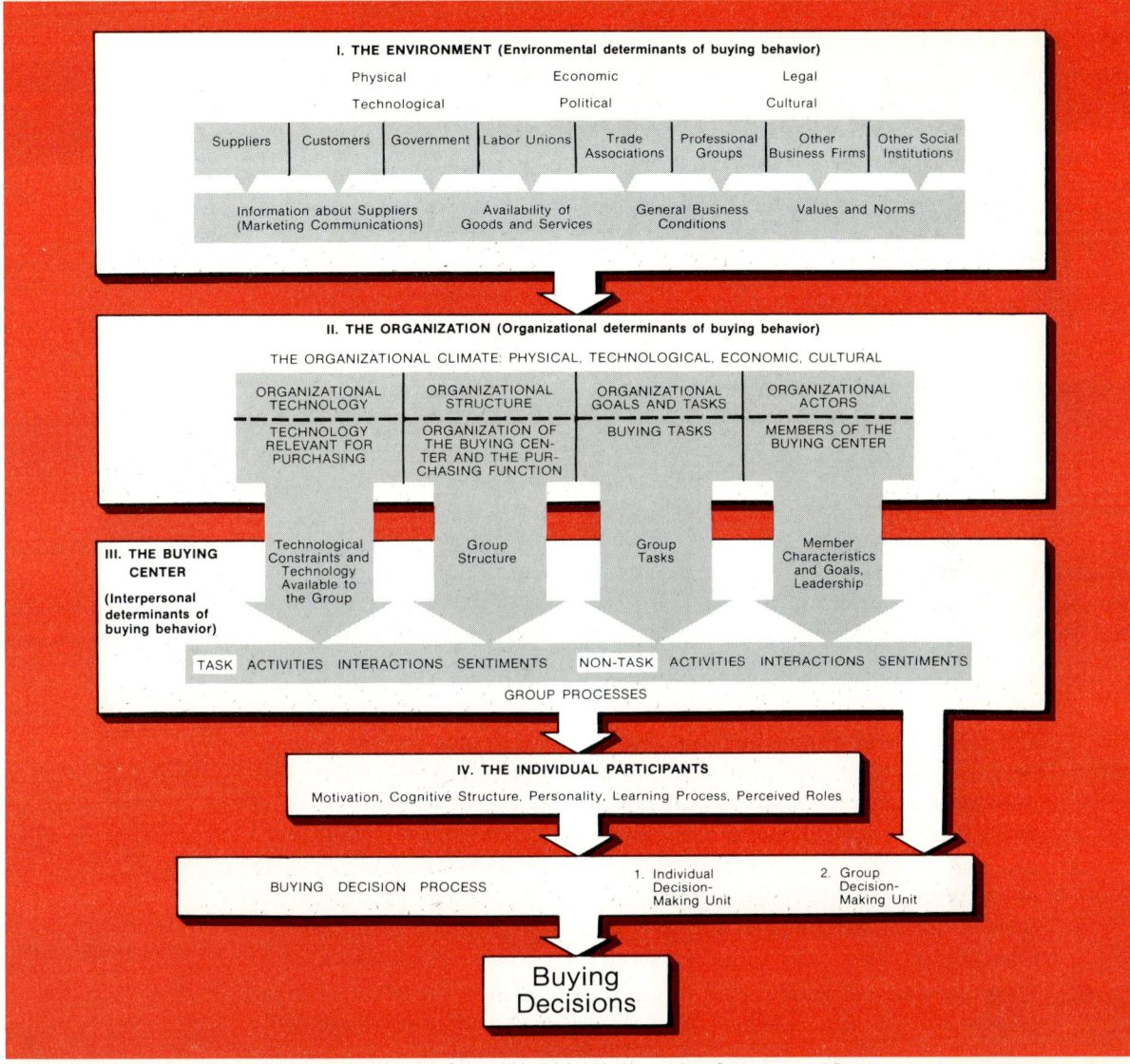

Source: Frederick E. Webster, Jr., and Yoram Wind, "A General Model for Understanding Organizational Buying Behavior," *Journal of Marketing*, April 1972, p. 15. Used with permission of the American Marketing Assocation.

Figure 8–10
A model of organizational buying behavior

Buying center. Interaction between individual members of the buying center, in their various roles, affects the organization's buying decisions in a way that is unique in every business. As buying is a group process, it involves interactions between members of the buying center, between the individual buying center members and outside salespeople, and between all the participants as a group. The group itself is affected by a number of variables: members' goals and personalities, group leadership, group structure, the group's tasks, and external influences. Very often the buyer or purchasing agent is a key member of the buying center because this individual is the supplier's sole contact with the organization.

Individual participants. Organizational buying ultimately depends on the behavior of individuals. Marketers often focus their efforts on specific individuals, rather than on the organization as a whole. These efforts focus on individual purchasers' characteristics—product preferences, decision-making processes, and psychological traits—in much the same way that marketers approach consumers. The organizational buyer, however, is restricted by the policies and resources of the organization.

As we have seen, all of these factors affect the steps in the buying decision process and thus affect the outcome of that process, the buying decision.

Similarities between Organizational and Household Buying Decision Processes

At the end of chapter 7, we saw that the buying behavior of individual consumers and households is similar. Here we look at the similarities between organizational and household buying decision processes. There are six main similarities:

1. Decisions may be either joint or autonomous. In the organization, autonomous decisions are usually routine and low risk. In the household, in addition to being routine and low risk, the reasons may include a member's lack of time or lack of interest in participating in the decision. Discussions of which floor wax to purchase are likely to be considered boring and a waste of time by many, if not all, members of the household.
2. For joint decisions, the composition of the decision-making unit is likely to vary from one decision to another in both households and organizations. Children, for example, are likely to be consulted about family vacations but not likely to be consulted about the purchase of insurance.
3. There are different family types or styles, just as there are different organizational types. The traditional families discussed in chapter 7 have some of the characteristics of centralized, and perhaps formalized, organizations.
4. Each individual, whether in a household or an organization, brings to each decision a different background and set of experiences and motives. Because of this, disagreement and conflict frequently occur.
5. The same set of conflict-resolution strategies are used in households as well as in organizations.
6. Most important of all, the marketing environment for both households and organizations is changing rapidly. While many of the changes may improve the quality of life, most present some difficulties at least in their initial stages.

The following story shows the connection between households and organizations. It is a true story of a major corporation versus the personal computer. About two years ago, top management decided it was time that all major executives should learn to use personal computers. To this end, they bought approximately one hundred personal computers. The executives were encouraged not to keep them in their offices, but to take them home. The theory was that they would have more free time to learn to use them at home than they would in their offices.

The executives did so, to the intense delight of their children. The children, already computer literate, were quickly giving virtuoso performances on the computers. Their parents, in most instances, were still trying to figure out how to turn them on.

By now the punch line of this story is probably quite obvious. Few, if any, of the executives have mastered the personal computer. They could not tolerate being upstaged by their own children and are likely to avoid personal computers for quite some time.

Providing a nice fringe benefit for the executives' children was hardly what the corporation intended when it spent a large sum of money on the computers. Any retail computer store manager who has watched the disaster that occurs when a nineteen-year-old computer genius tries to assist a middle-aged computer novice could have explained the likely attitudinal and behavioral problems to the corporation.

There is a single unifying theme that runs through both consumer and organizational markets today: the fragmentation of markets. There are few, if any, homogeneous markets, either consumer or organizational, left. The markets continue to splinter into more and more segments, each with somewhat different problems and desired solutions. The marketer who has an in-depth understanding of buyer behavior will be the most aware of emerging as well as dying market segments and best equipped to service them.

Summary

The organizational buying process is more complex than consumer buying because more people are involved, buying decisions take longer, each organization is unique, buyers are influenced by both rational and emotional factors that may be in conflict, and the products and services being considered may be highly technical.

Influences on organizational buying behavior fall into four main categories: the organization's environment, the nature of the organization, the type and structure of the buying center, and the similarities and differences between the individual participants.

Three environmental trends are important factors in organizational buying decisions: technology and technological change, emphasis on quality, and international emphasis.

Three aspects of the organization have a major influence on the organization's buying process. One is the buying situation and its degree of newness to the organization: a new task involves extensive information search and evaluation of alternatives, a modified buy involves less extensive information search and evaluation of alternatives, and a straight rebuy is simply a routine reorder. The structure of the organization, the second influential aspect of the organization, consists of its informal structure (communications networks) and its formal structure. The third aspect is the people involved in the organization's buying decision process. Personnel may be categorized by the levels in the organizational hierarchy, the number of departments, the number of people in the communications network, the extent to which individuals communicate, and the extent of communication.

Influences on the buying center (or decision-making unit) include the bases of power: reward, coercive, attraction, expert, and status power. The manner in which conflicts are resolved is another important influence on the buying center. Types of conflict resolution strategies include individual conflict-resolving and group conflict-resolution. Individual participants also influence the buying center through their educational backgrounds and psychological makeups.

There are six steps in the organizational buying process. The first step is identification of needs (problem recognition). The second is establishment of objectives and specifications. The third step is identification of suppliers and obtaining bids. Sources of information include suppliers' sales representatives, exhibitions and trade shows, direct mail, press releases, general news magazines and trade publications, journal advertising, professional and technical conferences, feature articles in the trade press, and informal communication. The fourth step is evaluation of alternative suppliers, followed by selection of the supplier, and a final evaluation of the supplier after the purchase has been made.

There are several similarities between organizational and household purchase decisions. These include the fact that decisions may be joint or autonomous; for joint decisions the composition of the decision-making unit is likely to vary from one decision to another; there are different types and styles within both kinds of groups; each individual brings to each decision a different background and set of experiences and motives; the same set of conflict strategies applies to both; and the fact that the environments for both change rapidly.

Questions for Discussion

1. Why should we study organizational buying behavior?
2. Examine the effect of the structure of an organization on its buying behavior.
3. Explain in what way the bases of power affect managers' buying behavior.
4. Identify the different strategies used to resolve conflicts in a buying center.
5. Can marketers influence the type of conflict-resolution strategies employed in a firm? Explain.
6. Illustrate how task- and non-task-related motives are both important in organizational buying behavior.
7. In what way is the sales presentation of a less well-known company different from that of a well-known company?
8. How are an organization's needs identified in modified rebuy, straight rebuy, and new task situations?
9. Why is there less informal communication in organizational than in consumer markets?

References

1. "Polaroid Sharpens Its Focus on the Marketplace," *Business Week*, February 13, 1984, pp. 132–36.
2. Frederick E. Webster, Jr., and Yoram Wind, *Organizational Buying Behavior* (Englewood Cliffs, N.J.: Prentice-Hall, 1972), pp. 5–7.
3. The discussion of influences on organizational buying behavior is based in part on Webster and Wind.
4. This example is based on the case study "Liquid Filtration Systems, Inc.," Direct Marketing Management Center, Boston University. Used with permission.
5. The discussion on the current environment is based on the insights of Professor Jeffrey Miller of the Operations Management Department at Boston University.
6. Thomas J. Peters and Robert H. Waterman, Jr., *In Search of Excellence* (New York: Harper & Row, 1982), p. 14.
7. Ibid., p. 181.
8. The discussion on bases of power is based on Thomas V. Bonoma, "Major Sales: Who Really Does the Buying?" *Harvard Business Review*, May–June 1982, pp. 111–16.
9. Ibid., p. 116.
10. The discussion of conflict is based on E. H. Bonfield, Carol Kaufman, and Sigfredo Hernandez, "Household Decision Making: Units of Analysis and Decision Processes," in Mary Lou Roberts and Lawrence H. Wortzel, *Marketing to the Changing Household: Management and Research Implications* (Cambridge, Mass.: Ballinger Publishing, 1984).
11. Gerald Zaltman and Melanie Wallendorf, *Consumer Behavior: Basic Findings and Management Implications*, 2nd ed. (New York: Wiley, 1983), p. 429.
12. Thomas V. Bonoma, Gerald Zaltman, and Wesley J. Johnston, *Industrial Buying Behavior* (Cambridge, Mass.: Marketing Science Institute, 1977).
13. John E. Swan, David R. Rink, G. E. Kiser, and Warren S. Martin, "Industrial Buyer Image of the Saleswoman," *Journal of Marketing*, Winter 1984, pp. 110–16.
14. Barton A. Weitz, "Relationships between Salesperson Performance and Understanding of Customer Decision Making," *Journal of Marketing Research*, November 1978, p. 501.
15. Theodore Levitt, "Communications and Industrial Selling," in Stewart H. Britt and Harper W. Boyd, *Marketing Management and Administrative Action* (New York: McGraw-Hill, 1973).
16. Ibid.
17. Henry Assael, *Consumer Behavior and Marketing Action*, 2nd ed. (Boston: Kent Publishing, 1984), p. 601.
18. Jagdish N. Sheth, "A Model of Industrial Buyer Behavior," *Journal of Marketing*, October 1973, pp. 50–56.
19. Frederick E. Webster, Jr., "Informal Communication in Industrial Markets," *Journal of Marketing Research*, May 1970, pp. 186–89.
20. B. Charles Ames and James D. Hlavacek, *Industrial Marketing for Industrial Firms* (New York: Random House, 1984), p. 60.
21. Frederick E. Webster, Jr., and Yoram Wind, "A General Model for Understanding Organizational Buying Behavior," *Journal of Marketing*, April 1972, pp. 12–19.

OBJECTIVES

1. To define market segmentation.

2. To identify the advantages of and criteria for segmentation.

3. To discuss the different bases for segmenting consumer and industrial markets.

4. To explain the attributes used in selecting target market segments.

5. To describe positioning and how marketers can position products.

9

Segmentation and Positioning

A victim of the ailing auto industry, American Motors Corporation (AMC) developed a new marketing strategy to increase sales. AMC set its sights on the affluent baby boomers and planned to reach that market by selling automobiles from its French partner Renault. This was a sensible tactic, as Renault had planned a line of sporty front-wheel drive cars to compete with Japanese models. However, AMC removed its own name and logo from most Renault cars and promotion in this country.

Why? AMC desperately needed to attract a new and more monied customer. Young, upwardly mobile professionals were perfect targets for these efforts, but such buyers were not likely to take a second glance at cars carrying an AMC logo. The company's image had become unglamorous. Partly because of this reputation, AMC had, in fact, carved out one of the least profitable niches in the market. AMC customers were older, with a lower income, and they purchased cars infrequently. Special options on a car didn't appeal to their wallets, nor did flashy, expensive sports cars. The traditional AMC buyer had little in common with the young professional that the company wanted to attract into its showrooms. AMC hoped that a low profile would help it to reap success from the new line of Renault autos.[1]

Another victim of the troubled industry, General Motors is also trying to reach a specific class of buyers more efficiently. The company has recently reorganized its design and manufacturing divisions into two groups, one for large cars and one for small cars. Customers who desire large, expensive models can choose from the Buick, Oldsmobile, and Cadillac lines. Those who drive smaller cars can turn to the less expensive Chevrolet, Pontiac, and GM's Canadian subsidiary brands. Right now, each brand offers both large and small cars.

The move is designed to give each line a sharper image, one that will more readily appeal to groups of buyers with similar tastes. At the moment, customers looking at GM's recent "X," "J," and "A" models, for example, complain that they don't see much difference between the lower-priced and higher-priced models. Managers at GM also believe that this move will enable them to respond more quickly when car buyers develop new preferences.[2]

In the middle 1970s, when the high cost of gasoline created a demand for small fuel-efficient cars, GM and other American auto makers couldn't respond. They have only recently begun to change their marketing strategies to meet the changing needs of a growing set of customers, or *segment* of the market. In this chapter, we look at how and why companies segment the market and at how they position products to appeal to chosen market segments.

Segmentation

A **segment** is a group of customers who desire specific features from a class of product. Both AMC and GM are redesigning their products so that models will appeal more precisely to particular segments of the market. **Market segmenta-**

tion is based on the assumption that not everybody will want the same features or services from a product class. Nor will they buy it in the same place, pay the same price, or be influenced by the same pieces of information about it. When segmenting a market, companies must bring out distinct marketing mixes that will answer the needs of targeted segments of customers.

Until recently, many businesses overlooked the fact that groups of customers may look for different characteristics from a product class. Remember Henry Ford's effort to sell one product, a standard black car, to an entire market. America's first major automaker discovered that by attempting to satisfy the market in general, it could not satisfy any one particular group or segment within the market. Ford's success was partially founded on efficiently producing a standardized product, a strategy that worked in the absence of competition. The market for automobiles was simply too diverse for one product, however, and other automobile manufacturers offering a range of products were able to enter it successfully. Segmentation is a concept that recognizes the diversity within markets. For marketers, there is a trade-off between finding a large enough market segment containing customers seeking the same features and recognizing that not all customers are seeking the same features.

How Segmentation Works

When competitors enter a market, a business must be more precise than ever in pleasing market segments. Let's see how that process works.

Figure 9–1 represents two dimensions of the automobile market. The horizontal line represents customers' tastes in cars, from conservative to sporty. The vertical line spans another range, from luxurious to subcompact. Dots scattered in the four sections stand for an existing market, sets of customers who purchase cars to suit various preferences. The dots in the upper right-hand section represent the market segment that is looking for a sporty, relatively luxurious car. The market segment in the upper left-hand section is attracted to a different car, one that is conservative and luxurious. The market segment in the lower left-hand section drives a conservative and compact car, and the market segment that drives sporty, compact cars is represented in the lower right-hand section.

These groups of customers are different segments of the market. But if a company looked at all consumers as one general market, it might decide to satisfy all of them by offering a "middle-of-the-road" car that is not too sporty or too conservative or overly luxurious or overly compact. This car is automobile A near the center of the figure.

If automobile A were the only car on the market, then all the customers from the four sections of this graph would have to buy automobile A or simply do without a car. They would be forced into that purchase even if automobile A lacked features—such as a sunroof or more leg room—that they were eager to have. Most likely, consumers from each of the four sections would indeed buy the car, but only the customer right in the middle would be truly pleased with automobile A.

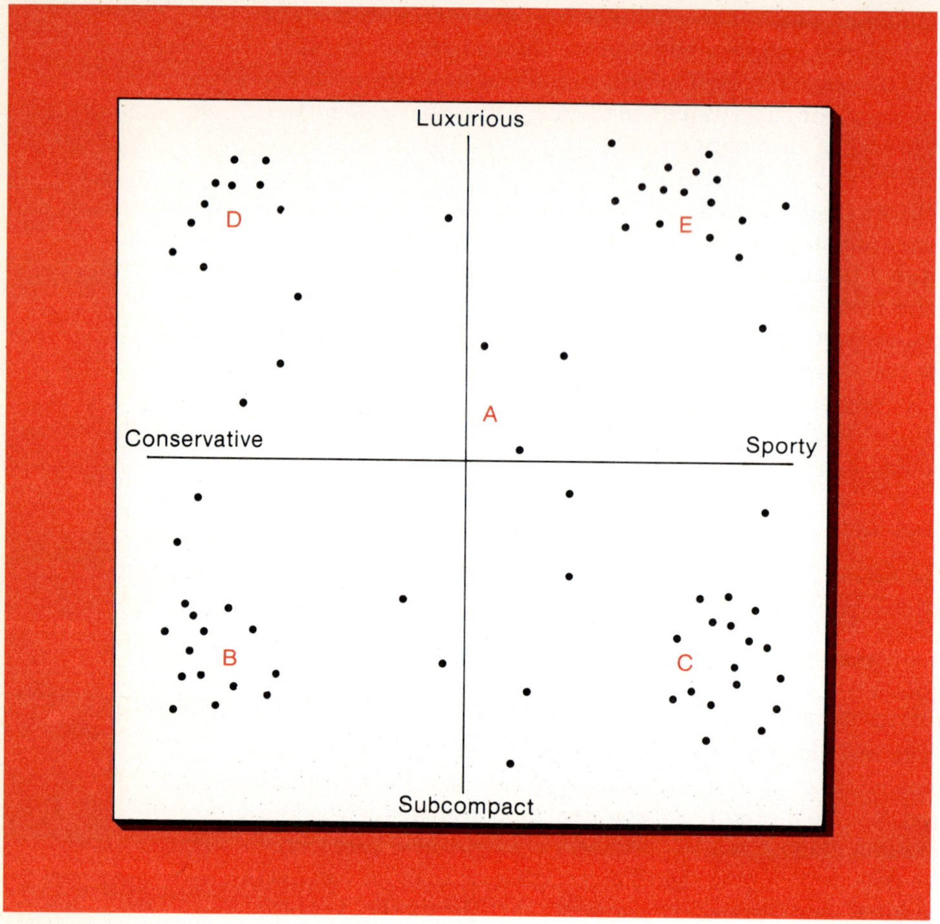

**Figure 9–1
Segmentation in the automobile market**

What happens when a competitor enters the market? Suppose that a different manufacturer offers automobile B, a conservative and compact car, located in the lower left-hand section of figure 9–1. Customers from that section will find that this entry satisfies their needs more precisely than automobile A does. Automobile A will likely also lose customers from the lower right-hand section. Although this market segment is looking for a sporty car, they will prefer automobile B's compact size to automobile A's medium size. Automobile B may even draw some sales from those with fancier tastes in the upper left-hand section. These customers may welcome the conservative style, even though they are still seeking a more luxurious model.

As additional competitors—like automobiles C, D, and E—enter the market, automobile A is left with very few customers. It has rapidly declined in popularity because it was not designed for a particular market segment but tried to please all customers. Competitors that have targeted and pursued a market segment have all been successful at taking away most of automobile A's business. A profitable marketing strategy, then, is often to aim for parts of the market, rather than for the entire market. When competitors appear, a company can maintain its position by selecting and satisfying a particular segment of the market.

Advantages of Segmentation

There are four major advantages to segmenting a market: Customers can be satisfied more precisely, communication and distribution are easier, the product can be tailored to the customers' needs more accurately, and competitive pressure can be reduced (see fig. 9–2).

Satisfying customers. One advantage of segmenting the market is that businesses can meet specific customers' needs more accurately by developing a product designed just for them, as competitors of automobile A were able to do.

Creating more efficient communication and distribution. When a business introduces a product developed for one set of customers, only those customers need to receive information about the product. At the same time, the business can distribute the product so that it is available to just that particular group. The company does not have to promote the product to the entire market, nor do all consumers have to be able to find the new product. As a result, by appealing to a specific market segment, a company can gain efficiencies in both communication and distribution.

Tailoring the product. Another advantage is that marketers can tailor their product to the exact needs of the targeted market segment. This strategy also allows a business to charge a higher price for its product, as customers are generally willing to pay more for a product with the precise desired characteristics.

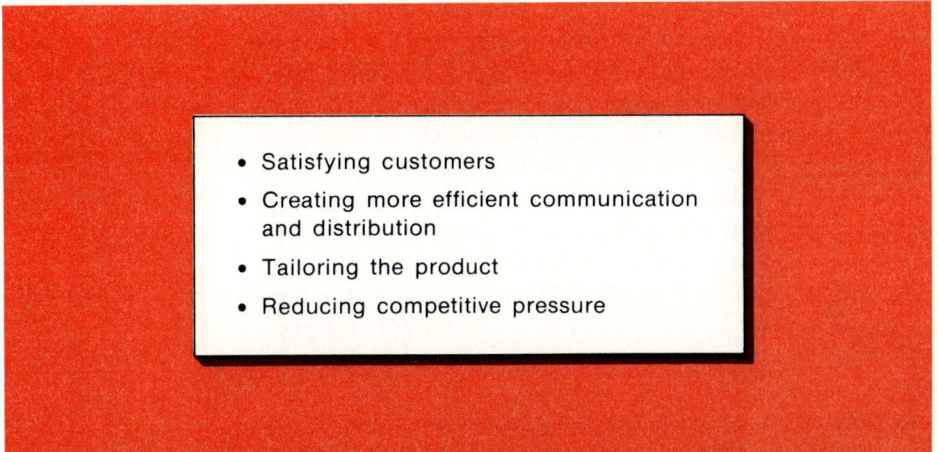

Figure 9–2 Major advantages of segmentation

Chapter 9 / Segmentation and Positioning

As an example, consider the toothpaste industry. For a long time, only Pepsodent and Gleem appeared on drugstore and grocery shelves. Then Crest was introduced, advertised with the famous shout from a grinning child, "Look, Mom, no cavities!" Crest targeted one market segment—young parents concerned about preventing tooth decay and keeping their children's teeth healthy. By tailoring its product to that set of customers, Crest was extremely successful. When the baby-boom children grew into teenagers and young adults, marketers adapted their strategy. Toothpaste was promoted for its ability to whiten teeth and thereby heighten the user's sex appeal, and brands such as Ultra Brite, Macleans, and Close-up rapidly appeared. Brushing with one of these products, the ads implied, would not only make customers' smiles brighter and sexier, but would enhance their social lives.

The toothpaste market seemed fairly saturated with little chance for a new entry to be successful, but recently another toothpaste, Topol, was introduced. Topol was designed for a unique set of customers with unique needs—smokers who wanted to remove nicotine stains from their teeth. Smokers, faced with the choice between a toothpaste that was made for a broader class of people and one made strictly for them, chose Topol. For the benefit of a stain-free smile, they were willing to pay twice as much for Topol as for regular brands. By segmenting the market and tailoring its product to that segment, Topol had also carved out a niche with no competition.

Reducing competitive pressure. Still another advantage of segmenting the market is that companies can reduce competitive pressure by creating and offering a unique product, like Topol, in a market that competitors had not previously discovered. For example, when Breck first introduced its different shampoos for normal, dry, and oily hair, it offered customers features not available from any other shampoo. Until then, all shampoos, like automobile A in figure 9–1, were produced for the average customer. Breck gave people the opportunity to purchase a shampoo made specifically for them; now consumers with any type of hair—from tinted to Afro to graying—can walk into a store and purchase a shampoo that's created precisely for them. Even though a market is highly saturated, products can still gain a competitive edge by appealing to a specific segment.

Criteria for Segmentation

Several guidelines will help businesses determine whether a market can be divided into groups of customers that can be profitably pursued. For a company to segment, there must exist differences among customers' needs, a set of customers' with common needs, enough people within each set or segment, an ability to design a marketing mix targeted at a specific subset of the market, and identifiable customers (see fig. 9–3).

Differences. As we pointed out earlier in this chapter, a segment might exist if some customers are looking only for *different qualities* in a product class. If everyone buys hand soap simply to wash away grime, for example, then the market

Figure 9–3 Can this market be segmented?

- Are consumers looking for different qualities in this product class?
- Do a significant and profitable number of consumers have common needs that can be satisfied by a product?
- Are there enough consumers in the proposed market segment?
- Can the company develop a marketing mix that will appeal to the proposed market segment?
- Can the company identify the particular customers who belong to the proposed market segment?

can't be segmented. If some people buy hand soap to wash away grime and other people buy hand soap to soften skin, then the market can be segmented.

Commonalities. Although differences in needs must be present, *commonalities* must also exist. The buyers within each market segment must share certain needs that can be satisfied by the same marketing mix. Otherwise, each segment of the market would be made up of an individual customer with unique demands. In such a case, a company would have no feasible way to produce and sell a product that would satisfy a significant and profitable number of customers.

Enough people. To market a product profitably, there must also be *enough people* in a particular group to justify the costs of designing a specific marketing mix. In some product categories, people use an item so infrequently that the market can successfully support only one or two brands. Such a brand must then appeal to the entire market, rather than to a tiny segment.

Additionally, there may not be enough people in a segment if heavy users account for a major percentage of sales in a product class. They are the customers to whom marketing efforts are best directed, yet they may be too small a group to segment further.

Marketing mix. If a company cannot develop a product that its targeted customers will want to rush out and buy, then time and money will be wasted by aiming for that group. That is, the company must possess the resources that will enable it to develop the right *marketing mix*, capable of appealing to the chosen segment.

Identifiable customers. Finally, marketers must be able to *identify the particular set of customers* that are looking for the same characteristics in a product class. This information is crucial in planning strategies to promote and distribute the product.

Bases for Segmentation

When creating marketing strategies, companies should segment a market before they develop and introduce a product, not after the fact. After targeting a market segment, companies can develop a marketing mix to appeal to that segment. If companies wait until after introducing a product to segment, they may find that the marketing mix is incorrect or does not attract the targeted customers.

Let's consider the case of a bank in a northeastern city that recently provided its customers with automatic teller machines (ATMs), an increasingly popular innovation. Other banks, upon introduction of their ATMs, have given them names like "Mac" or "George" to personalize the customer-bank interaction. The name chosen by the northeastern bank happened to draw college students to its machine. As a result, the bank concluded that college students formed its targeted segment for the new product. Yet college students—who rarely hold steady jobs, often keep low balances, have a high number of small transactions, and move before earning a regular income—are not the best customers for a bank. Instead, the bank should have segmented the market beforehand by determining which customers it would like to attract. As with any business, the new product could then be designed and promoted precisely for these customers.

The bases used to segment differ in consumer and industrial markets. We will look at these separately (see fig. 9–4).

Consumer bases. In deciding how to separate groups of individual consumers from others interested in the same product class but for different reasons, a marketer can choose from several methods or *bases* of segmentation. The main **consumer bases** are geographic location, socio-demographic variables, psychographics, behavior, buying habits, and benefits.

Geographic Location. Geographic location is a fairly common base, as it gives businesses an efficient way to reach a market. Distribution costs can be controlled as the product need only be available in the targeted market. Additionally, marketers can limit their communications strategy to that geographic area. Certain products, such as clothing and recreation items, lend themselves more to this approach than others.

Defining the market geographically may, on some occasions, be mistakenly confused as the segmentation approach itself. Instead, the geographic area may only constitute a "market" definition, as the territory in which the company will operate. For example, the Butcher Wax Company distributes its product in New England, Coors beer has been distributed strictly in the Midwest, and AT&T has developed many of its products only for the United States market. These are not definitions of segments, but rather markets of operation. There is no pretense that

Figure 9–4 Bases for segmentation

Consumer Bases
- Geographic location
- Socio-demographic variables
- Psychographics
- Behavior
- Buying habits
- Benefits

Industrial Bases
- Geographic location
- Product use
- Frequency of use
- Size of company
- Psychographics
- Method of purchase
- Type of industry
- Benefits

there are unique sets of needs within each of these geographic areas. This is not to say that their strategies were inappropriate. Rather, such geographic restrictions provide many operational and distribution efficiencies. This is not, however, a segmentation strategy.

This approach has often been used simply to cut costs rather than to segment a market according to sets of needs. Depending on the product, customers' needs may not differ simply because they live in various parts of the country. In contrast to the above examples, potato chip manufacturers produce various versions (more or less salty or oily) of their chips for different regions, are clearly cognizant of differing geographically-based needs (tastes), and have tailored their products accordingly.

Socio-demographic Variables. Another strategy for segmenting the market for consumer goods is to group buyers according to characteristics such as income, age, education, and size of family. These are known as *socio-demographic variables* and are effective ways to classify customers' needs.

In adopting this base, K mart has recently chosen to target more affluent customers. K mart customers are now greeted with camera and jewelry displays, rather than with the traditional popcorn stand, and can shop for other expensive items such as German wines and gourmet cookware, both new to K mart shelves. This strategy has already boosted slumping sales.[3]

Such an approach offers the marketer several advantages. People with specific socio-demographic characteristics are easily identified and counted, as several government and private sources publish this information. Furthermore, the media measure their audience along these lines, allowing marketers to make straightforward decisions about where to advertise.

Psychographics. As we saw in chapter 7, *psychographics* is a term including a person's self-concept, personality, and lifestyle. Political candidates use psychographics to create messages to appeal to specific groups of voters.[4] In business, psychographics draws human portraits of consumers as alternatives to lists of demographic data. These psychographic portraits, often supplemented by demographics, can offer sharper insights into why people buy what they buy.

There can be certain drawbacks to the use of psychographics, as in an unsuccessful attempt to distinguish Ford owners from Chevrolet owners on the basis of their personalities. But under certain conditions, psychographics can be useful in segmenting the market. Certain types of people might buy, or be interested in buying, brands or products different from other types. Introverts, for example, may buy differently from extroverts. These traits must also clearly relate to patterns of buying. Additionally, a reliable method must be used to measure the personality variables that form the psychographic portrait.[5]

Behavior. Buyer *behavior* is another valuable base for segmenting the market. *Rate of usage* is the most common behavioral characteristic that's used. In this case, marketers would identify the heavy and light users, as well as the light-to-medium users and nonusers of a product. Presumably each group would seek different qualities from a product class, and would thus respond to different advertising. Another behavioral characteristic useful in segmenting markets is *brand loyalty*. Some customers stay with a favorite product, while others like to switch from one to another. A marketer should consider what qualities entice a customer to purchase one brand over and over.

In some cases, however, the answer may be elusive. No one really knows why pickup truck drivers in the upper Midwest consistently favor Fords, while those in Texas, Kansas, and the Gulf states drive Chevrolets in overwhelming numbers. Tradition, rather than specific behavioral qualities, may be the only answer.[6]

Buying Habits. Some people shop only at premium stores like Neiman Marcus; others hunt for bargains at K mart. Some buyers rush out for the latest products as soon as they hit the shelves, while others wait to see what their friends bring home before making a purchase. These people can all be classified according to where and when they buy. Such *buying habits* can be an effective means of segmenting

FIGURE 9–5 Pepsi has used psychographics to segment the market; it is targeting the new generation of young and active consumers.
Reproduced with permission © PepsiCo, Inc.

the market, as long as the habits indicate that customers are looking for different qualities in a product class.

Benefit Segmentation. In the approaches we have just discussed, marketers look for characteristics that correlate with the needs consumers want satisfied by a class of product. An alternate method is to ignore these characteristics and instead group people according to the *benefits* they are seeking. Some customers, for instance, may want a personal computer in order to play games, while others want one for word processing. Still others look for a machine that can display intricate graphics. The most effective approach may be to divide these buyers into groups that desire similar benefits from the product class.

As another example, examine table 9–1, which shows how the toothpaste market can be segmented according to benefit—from attractive flavor to attractive price.[7] Of course, many people might welcome all these benefits in their toothpaste. But marketers can define segments by observing the *relative* importance that people attach to specific benefits.

Here, the toothpaste benefit segments were further identified by demographic and psychographic variables, including age, personality, and lifestyle. The segments are given names to match their personality; for example, people who tend toward hypochondriasis are called "The Worriers." A logical and detailed pattern emerges from this data, showing, for instance, that "The Worriers" are conservative, brush their teeth often, and seek the chief benefit of decay prevention from their toothpaste. The product that suits them best is, of course, Crest.

This additional information offers a valuable supplement to the insights gained from benefit segmentation. Knowing the benefits that customers seek does not, of course, explain how to identify and reach a given segment. Marketers can use the demographic and psychographic data provided in table 9–1 to purchase media and to draw a fuller picture of each segment. But the demographic and psychographic variables are merely descriptive, while the benefits actually explain why people make certain purchases.[8] Additionally, knowledge of benefits can help advertisers

TABLE 9–1   Benefit Segmentation in the Toothpaste Market

Segment Name	The Sensory Segment	The Sociables	The Worriers	The Independent Segment
Principal benefit sought:	Flavor, product appearance	Brightness of teeth	Decay prevention	Price
Demographic strengths:	Children	Teens, young people	Large families	Men
Special behavioral characteristics:	Users of spearmint-flavored toothpaste	Smokers	Heavy users	Heavy users
Brands disproportionately favored:	Colgate, Stripe	Macleans, Plus White, Ultra Brite	Crest	Brands on sale
Personality characteristics:	High self-involvement	High sociability	High hypochondriasis	High autonomy
Lifestyle characteristics:	Hedonistic	Active	Conservative	Value-oriented

Source: Russell I. Haley, "Benefit Segmentation: A Decision-oriented Research Tool," *Journal of Marketing*, July 1968, p. 33. Used with permission of the American Marketing Association.

Figure 9–6 Louis Rich has identified a market segment interested in the health benefits of less fat and stresses that its products have that benefit.
Courtesy of Oscar Meyer & Co.

to produce ads that directly appeal to consumers looking for those specific benefits (see fig. 9–6).

Industrial bases. The **industrial bases** for segmenting markets are somewhat different from those just covered. It is possible, however, to group industrial customers by *geographic location* or by *how the product is used*. For example, a business that sells line printers can group its customers into those that use a printer to print output from a mainframe computer or hard copy from a computer screen, or to aid telephone communication, or to provide plotting devices. Another way to segment by usage is to consider which products would be used in production or for resale by a retailer or wholesaler.

The *frequency of use* and *size of a company* are further bases that can be correlated to the needs industrial customers may have. Norwich Eaton Pharmaceuticals used both these bases to identify a new and profitable segment. Until recently, it has promoted its Vivonex and Dantrium, drugs used for feeding postoperative patients, only to doctors with private practices. When considering frequency of use and size, however, the company saw that hospitals, with their large numbers of patients, were the primary market as they purchased larger amounts of the drugs more frequently. Thus hospitals were identified as a new market segment, much to the delight of the salespeople at Norwich Eaton.[9] (Also see fig. 9–7.)

If marketers choose to use *psychographics,* they can group purchasing managers according to their attitudes. This information could help explain why the managers purchase certain products instead of others.

Method of purchase is also a base for segmenting industrial markets. For example, Federal Express was the first of overnight carriers to realize that secretaries and executives decide how to send out rush letters and packages, not shipping departments and purchasing agents. To appeal to this target segment, Federal Express used a large advertising budget to air clever television commercials, a practice competitors soon followed.[10] Other methods of purchase that could be used to classify industries are requests for bids and straight rebuy situations.

Type of industry is another base for segmentation. Standard industrial classifications will pinpoint the industry to which a company belongs—whether it is manufacturing, transportation, wholesale/retail, or another type. Marketers can then promote their product to companies in the targeted industry.

Research shows that *benefit* segmentation can be useful in industrial marketing, although this approach has not been widely adopted. So far it has been used only

Figure 9–7 Northern Telecom has used the size of a company to segment the industrial market and is showing how its Vantage phone system can help small businesses.
Courtesy of Northern Telecom Inc.

to supplement traditional bases. For example, a marketer might sell perishable produce to trucking firms, a type of industry. But the market for perishables can also be grouped according to benefit. In this case, the benefits that trucking firms most desire are speedy delivery and reliable refrigeration.[11] Using these benefits as only supplementary information, however, does not enable the marketer to find out what other industries might welcome these same advantages.

As is apparent, there are a number of ways to segment a market, not all of which are equally viable. Simply dividing the market into subsets is not the equivalent of segmentation. There is a difference between segmenting the market and partitioning it. Partitioning refers to dividing the market into subsets or regions for which individuals, such as a midwestern regional sales manager, are responsible. Partitions are not based on consumers' needs.

No matter which segmentation base is used in either consumer or industrial markets, it must meet two criteria in relation to the market. First, the people in the segment must be seeking the same characteristics or respond similarly to the marketing mix (and differently from people in other segments). Second, marketers must be able to identify who belongs in what segment. With these two criteria in mind, we can turn to the attributes used to select the segments.

Attributes Used to Select Target Segments

After a company has divided the market for its product class into segments, it must then select which segments to target. Marketers can, in fact, direct their efforts toward only one segment or toward multiple segments. In the second case, different marketing mixes would most likely be created for different segments, even though the marketers may be promoting the same product to each.

When selecting segments, marketers consider a number of attributes of a segment: size and strength, competition, growth, value, acceptability of product to consumers, ease of company's entry into the market segment, ease of competitors' entry into the market segment, and number and strength of competitors. Each of these attributes contributes to a further definition of each segment, which not only helps marketers choose the most appropriate segment or segments but also leads to the creation of a marketing mix that will appeal to the segment.

Size and strength. Marketers can evaluate the *size* of a group of buyers, determining if the number of buyers and the amount they buy justify the costs of distribution and media. Frequently companies are attracted to very large segments, which promise high profits but also strong challenges due to many competitors.

Let's take the case of Hart Schaffner and Marx, a prestigious men's clothier, which decided to move toward a larger group of customers. Its new Playboy-brand suits are priced around $130, certainly affordable to many more men than are its luxurious Christian Dior suits. Competition is tough, however, as both Levi Strauss and Haggar Company (the nation's largest manufacturer of men's pants) are also developing lower-priced suits for this sizable segment.[12]

Chapter 9 / Segmentation and Positioning

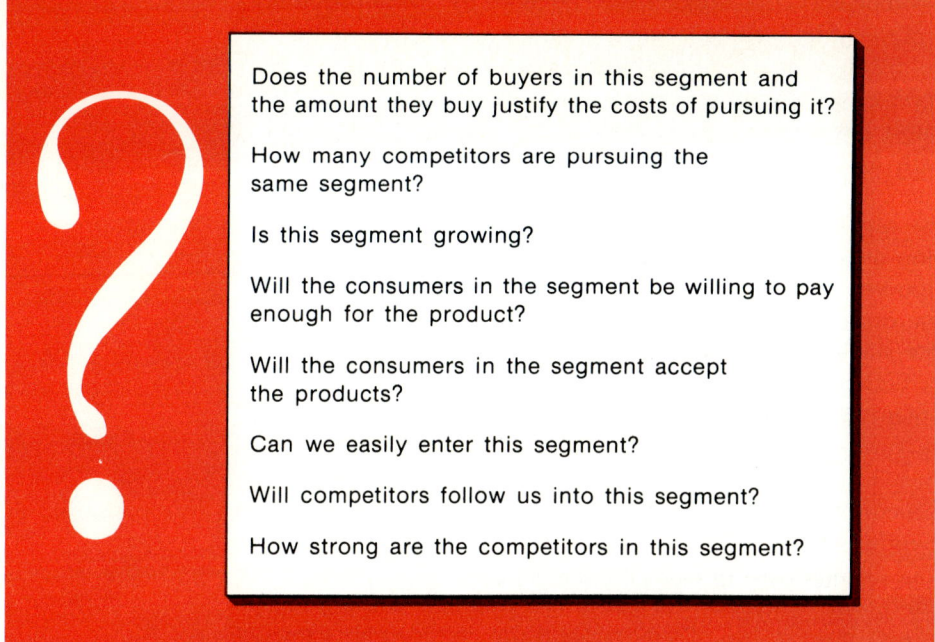

Figure 9–8 Should our company pursue this market segment?

The amount the consumers buy, or the *strength* of their purchasing power, is also important. In a dramatic climb, Tylenol increased its share of the analgesic, or painkiller, market from 4 percent to 37 percent. This increase was accomplished by targeting a new segment that exhibited much strength, or the capacity for a heavy volume of sales. In this case, Tylenol's makers, McNeil Pharmaceutical of Johnson and Johnson, switched its targeted segment from pharmacists and physicians, a relatively small segment, to consumers, a strong segment consisting of many buyers with much purchasing power. When Tylenol had been sold only by prescription, the first target was appropriate. Tylenol became an over-the-counter drug in 1966, however, and its manufacturers realized that they could earn substantial profits by promoting their product to the stronger segment of consumers. A. H. Robbins Company, sellers of Robitussin cough syrup, also benefited from selecting a segment on strength. Retail sales of the cough medicine quadrupled in four years to an estimated $77 million after Robbins advertised its product to ailing consumers. Robitussin's first market had also been pharmacists and physicians.[13]

Competition. Another way to evaluate the attractiveness of a segment is to choose one that is small but lacks *competition*, as Johnson's did with its Baby Shampoo when it marketed its product to parents of young children. By carving out this niche, it could control an entire segment, uncontested. If marketers are selecting a segment for a new product, they may choose one with a few or no competitors; if the segment has many competitors, the struggle may be fierce as the competitors go after smaller chunks of the same segment.

Growth. The *growth* of a segment is also an important attribute when selecting a segment. The most attractive marketing opportunities are in segments that are expanding, particularly at a quick rate. As an example, many businesses have recently changed their marketing strategy in order to appeal to the growing number of working women. The travel industry is paying special heed; United Airlines found that the proportion of women among its business travelers surged from 4 percent to 18 percent in seven years, and United employees are now told to assume that traveling women are executives. Hotels are also changing their practices. Following businesswomen's suggestions, they've tightened security and instructed waiters to place checks between male and female diners, since waiters can no longer assume that the men will always pick up the tab.[14]

Value. Another way to select a segment is by evaluating its *value*. That is, marketers look for a segment with customers that will pay enough for the product to make the campaign worthwhile economically. Or, with the same goal in mind, a company can search out the segment that can be reached by an expenditure low enough to justify the effort. The makers of Robitussin, for example, chose a segment that promised not only a great deal of strength but also considerable value, as customers were both willing and able to spend to purchase the product.

Acceptability of product to consumers. The Swiss watch industry has an image for quality and success that gives the industry *acceptability*, or assurance that its products will be favorably greeted by customers. But in the early 1970s, the Swiss saw sales of their mechanical watches drop under the powerful assault of Japanese electronic watches. To recover, Swiss watchmakers Tissot and Omega introduced their own line of expensive electronic watches. They promoted these watches by stressing the Swiss reputation for excellence, assuming that buyers would readily accept the new electronic timepieces, clearly marked "Made in Switzerland." As it turned out, even the Japanese bought Omega watches for their prestige.[15]

When identifying the right segment for a product, marketers must consider how receptive customers will be to the company's products. Success is more likely when a company enjoys a reputation that will readily draw favor, or acceptance, from targeted buyers.

Ease of company's entry into the market segment. When selecting the best customers to target, a marketer should consider the *ease in entering a particular market segment*. The decision may rest on whether the company can offer a product that will appeal to the targeted buyers and how effectively the company can advertise the product and distribute it to the targeted segment. Furthermore, the company's image must be evaluated to determine whether it is attractive to the segment or a hurdle that must be overcome.

Ease of competitors' entry into the market segment. Marketers must also consider the *ease of competitors' entry into the market segment*. In an ideal situation, the marketer's company could easily enter and succeed in a particular segment, but competitors would find it difficult to reach those customers. If a marketer decides that other companies can enter a segment easily, the marketer may want to choose another segment.

Number and strength of competitors. Finally, in selecting a segment, a company must be aware of the *number and strength of competitors* already in the market segment. A marketer might ask, for example, "Can the market segment support another brand?" or "How loyal are customers to competing brands?"

Marketers of Puffs, a facial tissue like Kleenex, were especially interested in answering the second question. When Puffs was first introduced, marketers thought that people who switch brands regularly make up the only worthwhile target for a new brand. Those who are loyal to one product, they thought, would not be interested in another product. Yet, the makers of Puffs found that the competition was vulnerable even in segments characterized by loyalty to a single brand. A study of the success of Puffs among several segments revealed that the new tissue drew significant sales from both customers who like to switch brands and those who prefer to stay with one brand. Many buyers, in fact, changed their loyalty from products like Kleenex to Puffs.[16]

When marketers have selected the market segment they want to pursue, they should take actions to create a marketing mix that will appeal to that segment. These actions fall in the category of positioning.

Positioning

What Is Positioning?

Men used to choose their barbershop by the location (or by which magazines it stocked). There was little variation in price, styles, or quality from barbershop to barbershop, and convenience of the location was the main consideration. When longer, more stylish men's haircuts came into fashion, the situation changed. Men started to choose their barber by reputation and by styling skill, and they were willing to pay the higher prices charged by these stylists. How could one barbershop develop a reputation that would set itself apart from others?

Barry Leonard calls himself a crimper, not a barber. He has opened a "high-tech," high-service barbershop in downtown Philadelphia. When customers (male or female) walk in, they can have some munchies or wine at the bar, make airline reservations, read the latest stock prices on the computer terminal, look at the latest haircuts on a slide show, or talk to the Japanese Koi fish. An individual's haircut is recorded on a video/computer system so that the customer's hairstyle can be duplicated or changed the next time. Leonard's philosophy is that his customers should get the best possible haircut and enjoy themselves at the same time. This approach was designed to position the barbershop as a place for young professionals; the approach has been highly successful (see fig. 9–9).

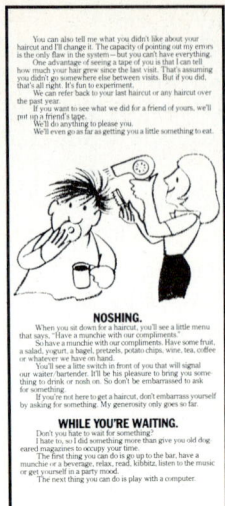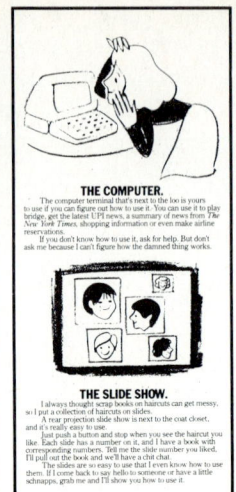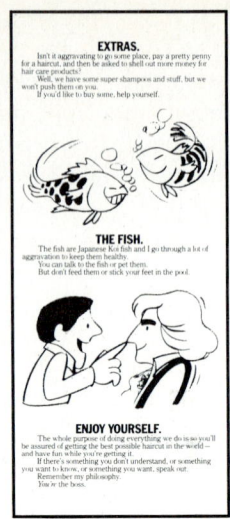

Figure 9–9
Elliot Carson
Advertising/Philadelphia

A barbershop can be seen as having positive or negative qualities, as being traditional or up-to-date, as giving crew cuts or blow-dries, and as serving children or young professionals. The customer's perception of a product is its **position,** or "the place a product occupies in a given market, as perceived by the relevant group of customers."[17] When marketers work to create a perception of a product, they are **positioning** the product.

A product's position can be created by a number of factors, including product characteristics, price, distribution channel, and promotion campaign. At Barry Leonard's, customers can get the latest, stylish haircuts at a high price. The barbershop itself is flashy and decorated and provides many carefully-thought-out services. The promotion campaign pushes the philosophy and style of the barbershop. All of these factors combine to form a position for Barry Leonard.

As another example, consider the way K mart and Bloomingdale's are positioned. Both are large stores selling a wide variety of merchandise, but their individual characteristics work to create distinct positions. K mart sells standard low-priced, but good-quality merchandise. The many outlets are located throughout the United States in suburbs and smaller cities. The stores themselves are clean and attractive, but functional. The promotion campaign stresses the low prices and the range of merchandise. The store's image appeals mainly to cost-conscious suburban and rural families.

Bloomingdale's has quite a different image. It sells high fashion and designer clothing and furnishings at top prices. The few outlets are located in large cities or exclusive suburbs. The stores themselves are showy and carefully designed to present a brilliant and top-of-fashion image. Bloomingdale's promotes itself as "like no other store in the world," and as the place where fashion trends begin. The store's image appeals to fashion-conscious upper- and upper-middle-class professionals and socialites.

There are seven basic ways a marketer can create an image or position for a product:[18] by attributes/benefits; by price/quality; by use/application; by product user; by product class; by the competition; or by a combination of these ways.

Ways to Position a Product

Positioning by attributes/benefits. The *attributes* of the product itself and the *benefits* to be gotten from it will tell consumers a great deal about its position. In the automobile market, Volkswagen has "value for the money," BMW stresses "handling and engineering," Datsun and Toyota emphasize "economy and reliability," and Volvo has "durability." In some cases, a new product can stress an attribute that competitors have ignored. Until Viva stressed durability, paper towels had emphasized only absorbency. And until Heinz started to say that it sold the slowest ketchup, no one thought about this attribute (also see fig. 9–10).

Positioning by price/quality. Few consumers believe that a fake fur coat and a real mink one have the same position. Nor do consumers believe that dime-store stainless steel cutlery is equal to Tiffany's sterling silver. The *price* and *quality*

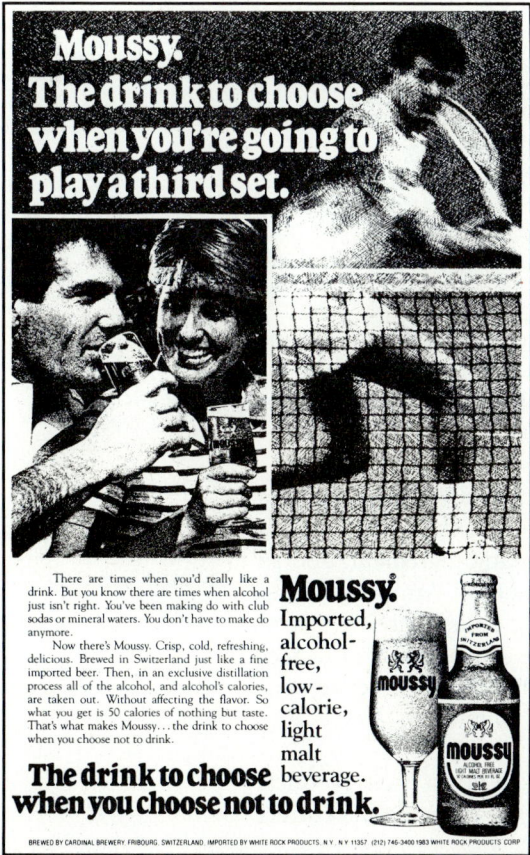

Figure 9–10   Alcohol-free Moussy—the drink to have when you don't want to drink—is being positioned by its attributes and benefits.
Courtesy of White Rock Products Corporation

Chapter 9 / Segmentation and Positioning

Figure 9–11 Reed & Barton silver, shown with other classic products, is positioned as a top-quality product.

Courtesy of Reed & Barton, Silversmiths

of the two create two different positions. In some cases, the quality is found in the materials used to make the product (as in real linen tablecloths or solid gold jewelry) or in the workmanship (as in a fine Swiss watch or a hand-knit sweater), and the price reflects it (see fig. 9–11).

Positioning by use/application. Finding a new *use* or *application* for an old product is a good way to create a position for it. For example, baking soda was once widely used in homes as a toothpaste, deodorant, baking ingredient, and so on. New products, however, had replaced many of its functions. Arm & Hammer then started to sell its baking soda as a way of eliminating odors in refrigerators, sink traps, and garbage cans. Campbell's sells its soups as ingredients for sauces and gravies. Gatorade, originally introduced as a summer beverage for active people, has tried to position itself as a drink for wintertime flu sufferers.

Positioning by product user. Marketers often try to direct their products toward a certain *product user* or segment of the market and try to create the correct image for the product in the eyes of that segment. Beer, for example, can be positioned for the upscale drinker (Michelob and Heineken) or for the blue-collar worker (Budweiser and Miller). Miller was once positioned as "the champagne of bottled beers" and aimed at an upper-class, largely female segment, until the position was changed to go after the larger segment of heavy beer-drinking, working-class men.

Various brands of perfume are aimed at different market segments. Some perfumes are positioned for elegant, monied, fashionable women. Others, like Charlie, are positioned for those with a young, active lifestyle.

We have already seen how K mart and Bloomingdale's have worked to create images that position the stores for different segments of the market.

Positioning by product class. A product can be positioned as similar to another type of *product class*. Parkay Margarine, for example, is advertised as tasting just like butter. Or products can be positioned as not similar to others, especially when they are new and unique. Aspirin-free Tylenol, Michelin radial-ply tires, and lead-free Amoco gasoline were all once new types of products that were positioned to stress how they were not similar to other products in their class.

Positioning by the competition. Products may now be positioned as having different attributes or benefits directly in relation to their *competition*. Avis, for example, built an entire advertising campaign around the slogan "We're number two, we try harder," implying that they were willing to provide more service than Hertz, the number one car rental company. Scope mouthwash positions itself as giving minty-fresh breath as opposed to Listerine's "medicine breath." A messenger service may position itself as faster or more reliable than its competition. In the early 1970s, 7-Up successfully positioned itself as the "un-cola." Its anticaffeine campaign ("Never had it, never will"), which implies that the caffeine in cola drinks is bad for consumers, has been equally successful.

Positioning by a combination of ways. Marketers can use any *combination of these ways* to create a position for their product.[19] For example, the California Prune Board, trying to create a more favorable image for prunes, has recently promoted prunes as good-tasting (positioning by attribute), as good for snacks or for breakfast (positioning by use), and as being eaten by all sorts of people, including baseball-playing eight-year-olds, wholesome-looking teenagers, and adults (positioning by user).[20]

After marketers have chosen the way to position the product, they plan exactly how they will use the elements of the marketing mix to create the position. The elements must be designed to contribute to the chosen image of the product. We have seen, for example, how Barry Leonard has created a total product and advertised that product to make his barbershop appeal to his target market of young professionals. The next nine chapters in this book discuss the elements of the marketing mix and show how they relate to the position of the product.

Summary

A segment is a group of customers who desire specific features from a class of product. Market segmentation is based on the assumption that not everybody will want the same features or services from a product class, nor will they buy it in the same place, pay the same price, or be influenced by the same pieces of information. Market segmentation must bring out distinct marketing mixes that will meet the needs of targeted groups.

There are four major advantages to market segmentation: Customers can be satisfied more precisely, communication and distribution are easier, the product can be accurately tailored to the customers' needs, and competitive pressure can be reduced. Companies can also reduce competitive pressure by offering a unique product.

For a company to segment, there must be differences among customers' needs, enough people with a set of common needs, an ability to design a marketing mix targeted at a specific subset of the market, and identifiable customers. When devising strategies, companies should segment a market before they develop and introduce a product.

Marketers can choose from several bases of segmentation. Geographic locations and socio-demographic/economic variables are two bases. Psychographics is a method of segmentation based on a portrait of consumers through their interests, attitudes, personalities, and lifestyles. Buyer behavior is another base of segmentation that most often includes rate of use and brand loyalty. Buying habits, such as where and when consumers tend to buy, can also be an effective base for market segmentation.

Another method is to define segments by observing the relative importance that people attach to specific product benefits.

Marketers can group industrial customers by geographic location, how the product is used, frequency of use, size of a company, psychographics, method of purchase, type of industry, and product benefits.

In selecting a market segment, marketers must consider the following attributes: size and strength, competition, growth, value, acceptability of the product, ease of entry, ease of competitive entry, and number and strength of competitors. After marketers have selected the market segment, they create a marketing mix to position the product for that segment.

A product's position is "the place it occupies in a given market, as perceived by a group of customers." Positioning is the marketer's effort to create a perception of the product. A product's position can be created by a number of factors: product characteristics, price, distribution channel, and promotion campaign. The seven ways to position a product are: by attributes/benefits; by price/quality; by use/application; by product user; by product class; by the competition; or by a combination of these ways.

After choosing the way to position the product, marketers design a marketing mix that will contribute to the position or image of the product and appeal to the target market.

Questions for Discussion

1. Explain the importance of market segmentation in business.
2. Identify the advantages of market segmentation to marketers.
3. Discuss the bases you would employ to segment the market for the following products: (a) residential carpet; (b) marketing textbook; (c) bed linens; and (d) mouthwash.
4. Discuss the differences in the bases employed in segmenting consumer and industrial markets.
5. What are the attributes used to select target market segments?
6. What is positioning?
7. Discuss the importance of psychographics as a base for segmentation.
8. How would you differentiate between positioning and market segmentation?

References

1. Douglas R. Sease, "American Motors Is about to Blot Itself Out to Build New Image Around Jeep, Renault," *Wall Street Journal,* May 14, 1982, p. 35.
2. John Holusha, "GM Serts Change to Two Groups," *New York Times,* January 11, 1984, p. D1; and Urban C. Lehner and Robert L. Simison, "GM Unveils Plan for Realigning Auto Making," *Wall Street Journal,* January 11, 1984, pp. 3, 24.
3. Charles W. Stevens, "K mart Beset by Steady Drop in Earnings, Tries to Attract Higher Income Shoppers," *Wall Street Journal,* August 10, 1982, p. 29.
4. "Selling Hard in 'Bohemia,'" *Sales & Marketing Management,* October 23, 1982, p. 37.
5. James F. Engel and Roger D. Blackwell, *Consumer Behavior,* 4th ed. (Chicago: Dryden Press, 1982), pp. 214–22.
6. Eugene Carlson, "Personality of Area's Drivers Offers Key to Auto's Success" *Wall Street Journal,* December 13, 1983, p. 33.
7. Russell I. Haley, "Benefit Segmentation: A Decision-Oriented Research Tool," *Journal of Marketing,* July 1968, p. 33.
8. Ibid., p. 31.
9. "Norwich-Eaton Checks into the Hospital," *Sales & Marketing Management,* April 6, 1981, p. 14.
10. Bill Abrams, "Purolator Courier's New Ads Take Aim at Federal Express," *Wall Street Journal,* September 29, 1983, p. 33.
11. Rowland T. Moriarty and David J. Reibstein, *Benefit Segmentation: An Industrial Application* (Cambridge, Mass.: Marketing Science Institute, 1982).
12. "Hart Schaffner & Marx: Expanding Boldly from Class to Mass Markets," *Business Week,* October 20, 1980, pp. 74–75.
13. Dennis Kneale, "Over-the-Counter Sales Give a Lift to Some Old Medicines," *Wall Street Journal,* September 16, 1982, p. 33.
14. Michael Doan, "Business Shifts Its Sales Pitch for Women," *U.S. News & World Report,* July 6, 1981, p. 46.

15. Walter Galling and Robert Ball, "How Omega and Tissot Got Ticking Again," *Fortune*, January 14, 1980, pp. 68–70.
16. Robert C. Blattberg, Thomas Buesing, and Subrata K. Sen, "Segmentation Strategies for New National Brands," *Journal of Marketing*, Fall 1980, pp. 59–67.
17. Yoram Wind, "New Twists for Some Old Tricks," *The Wharton Magazine*, Spring 1980, pp. 34–39.
18. The first six ways and some of the examples in their section come from David A. Aaker and J. Gary Shansby, "Positioning Your Product," *Business Horizons*, May–June 1982, pp. 56–62.
19. Wind, p. 36.
20. Erik Larson, "Admen Try to Make Juice-Loving World Swoon for a Prune," *Wall Street Journal*, February 15, 1983, p. 1.

CASES FOR PART II

3 Pepsi-Cola's "New Generation" Campaign

In 1984, the Pepsi-Cola Company launched a particularly expensive new advertising campaign geared to repositioning its flagship product, Pepsi-Cola, as a product for teenagers. The campaign was built around the theme: "Pepsi—the choice of a new generation" and featured rock superstar Michael Jackson in two of the campaign's seven commercials.

Both of the Michael Jackson commercials combine the techniques of music videos with traditional commercial techniques. One of the commercials features Michael Jackson in concert singing Pepsi lyrics to the music of the hit "Billie Jean." In the other, a very young teenage breakdancer and his friends bump into Michael Jackson on the street, and they all dance and drink Pepsi together.

The Jackson commercials cost Pepsi over $12 million dollars, including $5 million dollars for the rights to identify itself with Jackson, $2 million dollars to produce the two commercials featuring Jackson, and $5.5 million dollars to Jackson as the performance fee for the two commercials. All this money "had to" be spent before Pepsi spent a single dollar to air the commercials.

Other commercials in the campaign also featured young teenagers in takeoffs of movies that were particularly popular among teens. These include an *E.T.* spoof where a little alien hiding in the basement of a home is discovered because he has been drinking the family's Pepsi. Also in the campaign are commercials that are spoofs of *Close Encounters of the Third Kind* and *Jaws*.

As another part of its repositioning of Pepsi, the company signed pop singer Lionel Richie to a two-year contract at an estimated cost of over $5 million. Richie, the producer of Jackson's hit album "Thriller," will appear in Pepsi commercials beginning in 1985 and will compose and perform a new Pepsi theme song. Moreover, Pepsi will be the sole sponsor of Richie's concert tours through 1985.

The new commercials will be supported by an increased level of media budgets in both conventional and unconventional channels. In traditional media channels, Pepsi increased its network television spending in the first quarter of 1984 to just over $3.5 million (double its spending in the first quarter of 1983). This will be supplemented by spot and local advertising of $5.3 million. Pepsi has also bought a partial sponsorship (for $72,000) in Educational News Service's package of filmstrips entitled "Campaign '84: The Primaries." The filmstrips that were distributed to 16,000 high schools nationally during the spring of 1984 featured taped interviews with presidential candidates along with a Pepsi commercial.

The new campaign garnered much free publicity both when it signed Jackson and when the star was injured in the filming of the commercials. Indeed, the commercials have proved so popular that teenagers were reported to be calling television stations to find out when the commercials were going to be run. On the other hand, critics have questioned whether the popularity of the commercials will help Pepsi's sales among Jackson's fans, who know that for religious reasons their idol doesn't drink any products that include caffeine—including Pepsi.

Because of the importance of advertising in the highly competitive soft drink market, Pepsi has a lot riding on the impact of the "new generation" campaign. Research has shown that in blind taste tests consumers are unable to correctly identify Pepsi versus Coca-Cola. Thus, the key to success in the $27 billion dollar soft drink market has been image advertising. The key companies have long employed image advertising to give consumers an image that they can identify with. Coca-Cola has traditionally identified with Middle America, portraying Coke as the all-American drink and the necessary adjunct to good times ("Things go better with Coke," "Coke adds life," and "Coke is it"). Pepsi, on the other hand, achieved its greatest success in the early 1960s with a campaign based on the theme "The Pepsi Generation." Their ads showed that the Pepsi generation consisted of stylish young adults and college students. Industry observers pointed out that the campaign skillfully had identified the portion of the market that drinks the most soft drinks and focused on them. On the strength of the "Pepsi Generation" campaign, Pepsi began to challenge the dominance of Coke in the marketplace. By the end of the 1970s, Pepsi had the largest share of supermarket sales, and Coke maintained its market lead only by virtue of its extensive network of restaurant and self-service machine sales.

The Coca-Cola company also featured celebrity endorsements. Celebrities, including Paul Anka, Bill Cosby, Robert Klein, Telly Savalas, and Ted Turner, were a prominent part of the campaign used to launch Diet Coke, which by the beginning of 1984 was the number-three soft drink in America (following Coke and Pepsi).

Sources: Based on Fred Danzig, "Pepsi-Cola Gambles on the Young," *Advertising Age*, March 5, 1984, pp. 3, 62; and John Koten, "New Generation: PepsiCo Gambles on Ads Featuring Michael Jackson," *Wall Street Journal*, February 28, 1984, pp. 1, 16.

Questions

1. What is the likely effect of the "New Generation" campaign?
2. Is the focus on teenagers and a teenage superstar likely to affect the traditional Pepsi market? If yes, how? If no, why not?
3. Is the money that Pepsi is spending on Michael Jackson and Lionel Richie a good investment? How could the effects be measured?
4. Is Pepsi using the concepts of segmentation and product differentiation in the correct way? Why?
5. What are the key market segments for Pepsi? How have these segments changed over time?
6. To what extent should advertising be viewed as an entertainment "medium"?

4 Schlitz Beer

In 1980, the Joseph Schlitz Brewing Company faced a 25 percent decline in sales of Schlitz Beer. In only four years, Schlitz had slipped from its place as the second largest selling beer nationwide to a virtual tie for third place: Sales of Schlitz followed both Budweiser and Miller Brewing Company's Miller High Life, and were nearly tied with Pabst Blue Ribbon Beer.

In 1979, Schlitz suffered a $51 million deficit—its first deficit ever. After cutting costs by selling one of its breweries, the company earned a profit of $30 million in 1980, but sales continued to decline in an overall industry climate of growth.

Many customers had defected from Schlitz in 1974, when the company changed its brewing process. To cut costs, the Schlitz company used more corn syrup and less barley malt. Barley malt is the relatively expensive ingredient that gives beer flavor and body. At the same time, the price of Schlitz rose steeply. The result was a halt in the growth of sales by 1976, when production of Schlitz peaked at 24 million barrels. Production in 1980 fell to 15 million barrels. If the trend continued, more and more brands of beer would surpass Schlitz in sales volume by the end of 1982.

During 1977, Schlitz Beer was reformulated again. More barley malt was added to the mix, and a slower brewing process was instigated. After these changes even Schlitz's competitors admitted that Schlitz offered a quality product. But customers remained unconvinced: Former Schlitz Beer drinkers were not returning to the product, and the beer's tarnished reputation and image discouraged new customers from trying it. Production in 1980 fell to 15 million barrels. If the trend continued, more and more brands of beer would surpass Schlitz in sales volume by the end of 1982.

The crisis required a solution. One suggested option was an advertising campaign featuring nationally televised taste tests, to be broadcast live during the halftimes of four professional football playoffs and the Super Bowl in early 1981. The last of the five commercials, to be shown during the 1981 Super Bowl, would cost $1.7 million. The cost of backup ads—to be shown in the event of a technical problem with the live broadcast—and other expenses would total another $1.3 million.

The proposed campaign posed a big risk for Schlitz. If many beer drinkers were to decide in front of a live television audience that they prefer the taste of a competing brand over Schlitz, the advertising might backfire.

Schlitz was aware of consumer research which showed that beer drinkers cannot distinguish among major brands of unlabeled beer, on an overall basis or on selected characteristics. The specific characteristics tested included such factors as aftertaste, aroma, body, and strength.

Conducted with groups of at least 100 beer drinkers (defined as males who drank beer at least three times a week), the tests indicated that, according to the general ratings in the blind tests, drinkers of none of the brands rated the taste of "their" beer as superior over the others. In fact, in the blind tests, most participants could not even identify "their" brands of beer.

When participants were given bottles with brand labels, the overall ratings improved for all the brands of beer tested, and participants rated "their" brands of beer higher than the others. Perceptions of product differences, then, seemed to result primarily from participants' receptivity to the marketing efforts of the various breweries involved. Most American beers have a subtle flavor, and only a trained palate can distinguish among the various brands. It is estimated that perhaps no more than one person in a hundred has such a palate.

Sources: Based on Ralph I. Allison and Kenneth P. Uhl, "Brand Identification and Perception," in Harold Kassarjian and Thomas Robertson, *Perspectives in Consumer Behavior* (Glenview, Ill.: Scott, Foresman, 1968); and "Schlitz's Crafty Taste Test," *Fortune*, January 26, 1981, pp. 33–34.

Questions

1. Should Schlitz run the taste test commercials? What risks are associated with the campaign?
2. The test may be difficult to administer for two reasons: First, the FCC does not allow consumption of any alcoholic beverage before a television camera. This means that the tasters will not be shown tasting the product. Second, as the research indicates, part of the "taste" of a beer is psychological. Another factor is whether the beer has enough "head" as opposed to too much or too little. How would you handle these problems?
3. What steps can be taken to assure that viewers will believe the test if it comes out in Schlitz's favor? Do you expect Miller and Budweiser drinkers to believe the test?
4. What can probability theory tell you about the likely outcome of the tests?
5. What advertising strategy would you recommend to Schlitz?

5 American Express and the Women's Market

In 1983, marketing managers at the financial services company, American Express, were concerned about their penetration of the growing (and potentially lucrative) women's market. Their ongoing marketing programs had been effective in winning over about 40 percent of its traditional target market—affluent, frequent flying businessmen—whom the company perceived as meeting its criteria for potential customers. However, male cardholders outnumbered female cardholders by a ratio of four to one.

The company felt that its product (the American Express Card) was more than a charge card. Rather, American Express felt that its product was a fulfillment of its customers' need to feel successful. For many years, the American Express company had identified this need for professional success and achievement as a need for prestige. For this reason, it positioned the American Express Card as a tangible symbol of prestige. This message was the focus of the American Express Card advertising campaign that featured prominent (that is, successful, prestigious) businessmen, artists, and celebrities asking television audiences: "Do you know me?" American Express managers attributed much of the increase in the number of cardholders to this award-winning campaign.

While American Express was solidifying its market dominance among business travelers in general, the potential market of women cardholders was expanding. The company estimated that its 2.5 million female cardholders represented only about 20 percent of the women who met its financial, occupational, and lifestyle criteria.

Executives at American Express decided to launch a campaign targeted directly toward women. In designing this campaign, the company's executives realized that the women's market had changed. More women than ever before are working; single women often own their own homes and use their own credit lines. Indeed, women often fill numerous roles simultaneously. Many women, for example, successfully manage companies at the same time as they raise families. Despite the wide range of women's lifestyles, family situations, and occupations, their needs as consumers often merge. Not surprisingly, women base their purchasing and consumption decisions on need, desire, and ability to pay.

Company-sponsored marketing research showed that these "new style" women were aware of the American Express Card and had a favorable impression of it. Unfortunately, they did not see the American Express Card as being "for women."

As the first step in developing their women's strategy, the American Express managers examined the characteristics of female cardholders (and women, in general). The research showed that the typical female American Express card user was between 25–35 years old, was on the fast track to achievement, earned $20,000 or more annually, and held a professional, managerial, or sales position.

The research also indicated that both men and women in this age group had a definition of prestige that diverged from the company's traditional position. They seemed to define success as "leading an interesting, varied, unexpectedly rich life." Characteristics of this prestige might include having interesting skills or hobbies, living in diverse places, and pursuing more than one career.

The research also showed that this diversity of interests was reflected in the use of the American Express Card. American Express cardholders were using the card for local dining with friends, local shopping, and a range of personal, non-professional uses.

As the company executives were developing their approach to the women's market, they remembered the first time the company had targeted women. In the late 1970s, the company had run a timid ad to appeal to women without offending its male customers. The campaign attracted little attention and was quietly phased out. While realizing that the new campaign had to aggressively pursue the women's market, the executives remained concerned about offending male cardholders. The managers were also concerned that many advertising campaigns directed toward "the new women" either patronized women or ignored the special characteristics of the market. The managers clearly wanted their new campaign to avoid these pitfalls.

Sources: Based on Nancy Josephson, "Interesting Lives Are in Their Cards," *Advertising Age*, April 2, 1984, pp. M9–12; and Bill Abrams, "American Express Is Gearing New Ad Campaign to Women," *Wall Street Journal*, August 4, 1983, p. 23.

Questions

1. Is there a separate market for American Express Cards for women? Why isn't it just sufficient to say an American Express Card is the same thing to everyone in the marketplace, and therefore whatever works for men will work for women?
2. How should the company position itself to maximize its effectiveness in the women's market?
3. Should the company be concerned about the effects of their new campaign on their traditional male cardholders?
4. What steps should the company take in terms of changing the nature of the establishments that accept American Express Cards? Is any change necessary?
5. Develop a general advertising campaign targeted at the women's market. Include a general discussion of the appeals and the media that you would use.
6. How specific is this problem to American Express? Would other companies profit from the kind of market examination that American Express is going through? Is the issue only the changing nature of the American woman?

6 IBM PC and PC*jr*

In the spring of 1984, managers at IBM came to a startling conclusion. While their Personal Computer (PC) was a resounding success, their home computer PC*jr*) was beginning to look like a failure. The managers decided to re-examine their product and rethink their strategy.

Within two and a half years of its introduction in 1981, IBM's personal computer, PC, captured 34 percent of the personal computer market, and 60 to 70 percent of the corporate segment of that market. While technically the PC was far from revolutionary, it was backed by the reputation of IBM. Customers trust the IBM name and expect the company to endure and to service its machines. Consumers feel that many new, small computer companies may not survive an industry shakeout.

IBM is a profitable company with a reputation for continuing success based on a marketing strategy of attending to customers' needs. In 1982, the company's profits of $4.4 billion on sales of $34.4 billion made it the most profitable U.S. industrial company. In 1983, IBM commanded some 40 percent of the worldwide market for computing equipment and made about two-thirds of all mainframe computers.

After the microprocessor—the "computer on a chip"—was developed, Apple Computer Company produced and marketed the first microcomputers (positioned as products for a small number of computer hobbyists). Its sales jumped from less than $1 million to $582 million between 1977 and 1982. Although IBM monitored the personal computer market during this time, it waited to enter the market until a broad business demand for personal computers was apparent.

In its strategy for introducing the PC, IBM broke many of its traditional marketing procedures. In contrast to its usual product policy, IBM built the PC largely from parts purchased from outside companies. Similarly, it deviated from its usual distribution strategy by distributing and selling the PC through retail outlets such as Sears and Computerland. Moreover, IBM is offering discounts on the PC and developing new PC-compatible products at a faster rate than that for their other products.

The large advertising budget for the PC marks a departure for IBM, as well. The company spent only $4 million for advertising to launch the system/360 series of computers in 1964. IBM ran no television advertisements for any product until 1972. The advertising campaign for the PC, featuring a Charlie Chaplin look-alike, has been successfully used in all advertising media to make consumers aware of the PC. IBM's advertising expenditures on the PC alone in 1983 amounted to over $25 million.

The PC has transformed the personal computer industry. Although Apple had a four-year head start in the market, IBM's PC equalled its sales volume by 1983. With a few months after the introduction of the IBM PC, it has become the industry standard for the personal computer market. In 1982, IBM sold an estimated

200,000 PCs; in 1983, sales were projected to be 850,000; in 1984, sales of over 2 million units were expected.

In 1983, IBM introduced its home computer, the PCjr. PCjr was designed as a less flexible, less capable version of the PC. It has an internal memory large enough to perform tasks such as word processing and preparing tax returns, and it is compatible with and contains the same microprocessor as the PC. IBM made the PCjr partially compatible with the office PC, so that it could attract customers who already have a PC in the office and wants to run some of the software at home.

IBM faced a strange, new market with the PCjr. Although it had always produced office computers and sold to business customers, it was entering the mass market and, for the first time, selling directly to consumers.

The PCjr is sold in two versions. The basic version has 64,000 characters of internal memory, runs cartridge programs, displays 40 characters per line, and sells for $700. The enhanced version has 128,000 characters of internal memory, runs both cartridge and disk programs, displays 80 characters per line, includes a disk drive that stores an additional 360,000 characters of memory, and sells for $1,300.

While executives knew they were taking a risk in introducing a machine that was more expensive than most home computers, they believed that customers would be willing to pay the relatively high price for the IBM logo. With a price aimed at appealing to the elite of the home market, IBM promoted the PCjr on the basis of the company's reputation and the machine's versatility, rather than on the basis of competitive price.

Another consideration in positioning the PCjr was that if it proved too versatile, there was a risk of customers buying it instead of the more expensive PC. PCjr has a 16-bit processor, similar to that of the PC. The PC with 64,000 characters of internal memory and a disk drive sells for $1,900, while the PCjr, with twice the internal memory capacity and a disk drive, sells for $1,300. To prevent PCjr from replacing the PC, IBM needed to restrict PCjr's capabilities.

The answer IBM chose was to make the PCjr unappealing for serious business computing. Its keyboard is not suitable for extended typing; rather than full plastic keys, the machine has rubberized keys (which have been derisively compared to pieces of Chicklet gum). Whereas the PC has 83 keys, the PCjr has 62 keys. Both perform the same functions, though some tasks that require two keys to be pressed on the PCjr can be performed by pressing one key on the PC. The PCjr memory is not expandable beyond 128,000 characters, which prevents some popular software (such as Lotus 1-2-3, which requires more memory to run) from being used.

The color and sound capabilities of the PCjr, however, are superior to those of the PC. Moreover, its remote-control, lightweight keyboard enables the user to sit as far as 20 feet away from the processor.

IBM has controlled the distribution of the PCjr to keep it off the shelves of discounters. The PCjr is sold through dealers who already carry the PC and through company representatives, rather than through toy and department stores.

Advertising is especially important in the competitive home computer market, and for its *PCjr* ads IBM has employed the same Charlie Chaplin look-alike character who was so successful in the PC ads.

By the spring of 1984, *PCjr*'s sales were lower than predicted. Part of the problem appeared to be in positioning. Priced at between $800 and $1,600, some analysts believe that the *PCjr* has proved too expensive for casual home users, but not powerful enough for serious users who can afford a more capable machine. Research indicated that 59 percent of home-computer business is for those machines priced at $750 or less; 27 percent of the market is for those machines costing $1,500 or more; and that the least demand, only 14 percent, is in the middle of the market, the *PCjr* position.

Another problem facing the *PCjr* marketers is IBM's image as a supplier of office equipment. Since IBM does not have a reputation in the home, consumers may not understand that the *PCjr* is for the home. Moreover, there may be an even more basic obstacle of convincing people that a home computer is useful (an obstacle facing all home-computer marketers).

Sources: Based on "The Colossus That Works," *Time,* July 11, 1983, pp. 45–54; Myron Magnet, "How to Compete with IBM," *Fortune,* February 6, 1984, pp. 58–71; Andrew Pollack, "The Debut of IBM's Junior," *New York Times,* November 2, 1983, pp. D1, D4; and David E. Sanger, "IBM's Problems with Junior," *New York Times,* May 17, 1984, pp. D1, D5.

Questions

1. What is the market for the IBM PC? Who are the competitors of the PC?
2. Is the *PCjr* market the same as the PC market?
3. What mistakes, if any, did IBM make in the design and introduction of the *PCjr*?
4. What changes, if any, would you make in the *PCjr* itself and in its marketing program?
5. Is it too late for IBM to correct the problems it has encountered with the *PCjr*?
6. Is there a market for home computers (as opposed to personal computers)? What is it? Does that market exists today?

PART III
The Marketing Mix

OBJECTIVES

1. To furnish the definition and components of a product.

2. To provide the classifications of consumer as well as industrial goods.

3. To explain the nature of the product line and product mix decisions made by marketers.

4. To highlight the role of branding and the alternative approaches to branding a company's product.

5. To describe how packaging influences the marketability of a product.

6. To identify the importance of the service component in a product.

10

Products and Their Characteristics

With the introduction of the Apple II personal computer, Apple Computer, Inc., of Cupertino, California, changed the computer industry. In 1977, the Apple II was the first and only computer small enough, cheap enough, and easy enough to use to be available to people with limited space, funds, and computer experience. The Apple II fit easily on a desk top and cost less than $3,000, and most people could operate it without a graduate degree in computer science. This product put Apple among the top manufacturers of personal computers.

Apple marketers noted that the product's brisk sales weren't entirely due to purchases by individuals. The computer was selling well to businesses, too. At this point, Apple executives, planning to expand the company's product line, had a choice between further development of the home market or deeper involvement in the business market. Apple decided to try to attract additional business customers because of the greater profit potential in that market. In 1981, Apple introduced the Apple III. The new product was a more powerful—and more expensive—computer designed for business applications.

Apple's executives also decided that continued success for the company would depend on software that was easy to use, particularly if Apple wanted to gain a larger business clientele. The solution was the development of a "user-friendly" computer and software. In 1983, Apple introduced Lisa. With a $10,000 price tag, this computer offered a wide range of office functions—word processing, graphics, project scheduling, data base management, and so on.

What distinguished Lisa from other computers was the fact that users could master its programs in hours instead of days. And instead of learning complicated sets of commands to be keyed in, Lisa users had the

"mouse," a small plastic box with which sending commands involved merely pressing a button. Lisa's commands were represented in pictures: a wastebasket indicating the discard command, a picture of a file for storing material in the computer's memory, and a picture of a clipboard for storing data temporarily.

In 1984, Apple introduced the Macintosh and Lisa II. The Macintosh uses the same picture commands and the mouse but is less powerful and much less expensive than Lisa, designed for individual users, rather than businesses.

Meanwhile, IBM introduced its own personal computer, known simply as the IBM PC. The product has been highly successful. Two important factors have worked in IBM's favor in the success of the PC. First, the company has an established name that customers associate with long experience in the computer industry. Second, IBM offers its customers excellent repair and maintenance service. By 1983, IBM had taken over the number-one position in personal computer sales; Apple had dropped to the number-two spot. Other companies had also developed their own personal computers, so that Apple no longer had a stranglehold on the market.

Another problem for Apple has been with one of its own products, the Apple III. Product failures forced the company to recall many of these computers, and sales were not nearly as high as expected. The company reengineered the product, but sales never picked up. The Apple III may also have been priced too high. Many analysts believe that putting out a product that didn't work well may have hurt the Apple brand name.

Recently, Apple has made several product decisions to try to recapture some of its lost momentum. The company has divided its products into two distinct product lines. The Apple line contains Apple IIe, Apple III, and the new Apple IIc, a portable home computer based on the original product. The Lisa-Macintosh line features Apple's new technical achievements in user-friendly equipment. The two product lines are managed and marketed separately within Apple. Executives believe the company's success in the future will be the result of establishing technical leadership in this fast-changing, competitive industry. Another important factor in Apple's future, marketers believe, will be its development of distinct product families for separate computer markets.[1]

Since 1977, Apple has had to make numerous marketing decisions about its products and their characteristics. It has had to consider which types of new products to add to its line, what to call those products, which markets—home or business—to pursue, what auxiliary products and services to offer along with its computers, and so on. The actions Apple took were based on a consideration of how markets react to various aspects of a product. This chapter looks at products and their various characteristics and at what marketers consider when making decisions about them.

What Is a Product?

A **product** is any idea, service, or tangible good that a customer can acquire through a monetary transaction or an exchange. Not only tangible goods are considered products; intangibles like services and ideas are also included. A Sony Walkman, a Stouffer's frozen dinner, and a box of Band-Aids are all products, and so are a stay in the Plaza Hotel, a Greyhound bus ride, an advertising campaign by Doyle, Dane, Bernbach, Inc., and dry cleaning by One-Hour Martinizing. A product, then, is the potential satisfier of a consumer's or industrial market's want or need. But a product is not just the essential item; it is made up of a number of components that contribute to its ability to satisfy needs and wants. Components that are included in a product are its package; its name and the name of the company that produces it; and perhaps a warranty, guarantee, or the availability of maintenance service (see fig. 10–1). The total product is the sum of all physical and psychological features that aid in satisfying a customer's wants or needs. The success of a product is judged by how well it satisfies those needs and by how well it sells.

What makes a computer a total product? A piece of hardware needs software for it to run, training for its operators, and maintenance service in case of trouble.

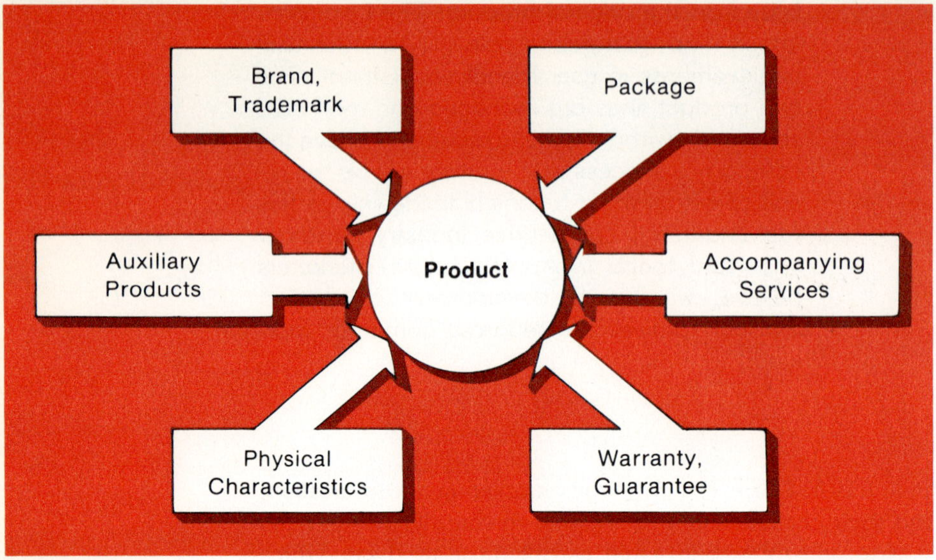

Figure 10–1 The characteristics of a total product

[Diagram: Product at center with arrows from: Brand, Trademark; Package; Auxiliary Products; Accompanying Services; Physical Characteristics; Warranty, Guarantee]

Apple has stressed additional characteristics that augment its products: The advertising for the Lisa-Macintosh line features ease of operation; the Apple IIc was designed to look good in homes; the variety of software available for the Apple II is featured. All of these components add to the computer's ability to satisfy needs and thus have been chosen by the company to be part of the total product.

Classification of Products

Products fall into two main categories, depending on the type of customer likely to buy them. The first type of buyer is the *consumer*, or someone who buys a product for personal use. The second type of buyer is the *organizational customer*, or the business, government, or nonprofit organizations that buy industrial products for commercial uses or to carry out their activities. (See fig. 10–2).

Consumer products are purchased by consumers for their personal use. They fit into three categories: convenience goods, shopping goods, and specialty goods. One product may fit into all three categories, depending on the situation. These categories primarily refer to the amount of effort used to acquire the product, the amount of effort used to compare various alternatives, and the amount of influence a particular brand has on the consumer's choice.

Consumer Products

Convenience goods. **Convenience goods** are those that sell mainly because they are widely available and usually involve little comparison shopping or

Chapter 10 / Products and Their Characteristics

272

effort. One type of product within the convenience goods category is **staple goods**, or products that consumers purchase frequently, including such grocery items as flour, milk, and butter. When shopping for these items, customers generally buy whichever brands the store happens to carry or they buy familiar brands. They do not usually compare prices with those of other stores before making a purchase.

Another type of convenience goods is **impulse goods**, or items that the consumer buys without planning the purchase in advance. Retailers often place impulse goods near the checkout counter, where customers waiting to pay will pick up these items on impulse. Examples include chewing gum, razor blades, and magazines. Again, the key factor in these items' purchase is their availability. Price is relatively inconsequential. Awareness of a particular brand makes purchases more likely when there are no other choices, but it is not a major factor.

A third type of convenience goods is **emergency goods**, or items for which there is an immediate need. Snow shovels during the first snowstorm of the season would be considered emergency goods. Price is not an important factor here either, but availability is. Hardware store owners might place snow shovels in the window on a snowy day so that passersby would be aware of their availability.

Consumers seeking convenience goods are not likely to shop at several stores and compare prices and quality. Instead, they are going to buy what is available. Manufacturers of convenience goods, then, must distribute the goods widely.

Shopping goods. **Shopping goods** are those that usually involve a fair amount of preplanning. Consumers often compare quality, brands, and prices in a

**Figure 10–2
Classification of products**

Consumer Products	Industrial Products

• Convenience goods
    Staple goods (milk, eggs)
    Impulse goods (razor blades, candy)
    Emergency goods (snow shovels)
• Shopping goods (personal computers)
• Specialty goods (Porsche, Godiva chocolates)
	• Installations (factories, computers)
	• Equipment (ovens, sewing machines)
	• Raw materials
	    Natural resources (petroleum, diamonds)
	    Farm products (wheat, eggs)
	• Processed materials (vinyl, flour)
	• Supplies (nails, paper)
	• Components (buttons, car radios)

number of stores before making a decision on shopping goods. Clothing is a shopping good. A consumer who needs a winter coat, for example, may go to several stores to compare many alternatives before making a final decision. Shopping goods generally cost more than convenience goods. Other items in this category include furniture, automobiles, and personal computers. A consumer interested in the Apple IIe is likely to compare its price, service record, and capabilities with IBM's PC and other brands. The financial risk involved makes consumers more cautious about these purchases. Time is not a significant factor here, so availability is not as important as it is with convenience goods. Knowledge about the product's price, specific features, and value are more important factors.

Specialty goods. The third category is **specialty goods**, or products for which a certain group of consumers has a preference. Here, price and availability are both insignificant factors, and the brand or certain features of the product are more important. Porsche customers pay a great deal of money for an automobile because they prefer that particular brand and the product's unique characteristics. Specialty goods may require the consumer to expend considerable time and effort to acquire them.

The same product can fall into all three categories of consumer products. For example, hotels are convenience goods for business travelers; the price of the room is usually insignificant, but the availability of the hotel is very important. Vacationers may treat hotels as shopping goods, considering several before making a decision. Convention planners treat hotels as specialty goods; the ones chosen must meet very specific standards as to facilities such as ballrooms, meeting rooms, and banquet service.

Industrial Products

Industrial products are marketed to organizations for commercial use, or to carry out their activities. Organizations may use these products in the manufacturing process itself, or the goods may have an indirect role in some other aspect of the business. Industrial goods usually fall into one of six categories: installations, equipment, raw materials, processed materials, supplies, and components.

Installations. **Installations** consist of the buildings and factories used by the organization and the major, heavy equipment. If Apple sold a network of its Lisa computers to a company, the computers form an installation.

Equipment. **Equipment** is the machinery and tools used to manufacture goods. A baker purchases ovens to bake bread, a furniture manufacturer buys table saws to cut the wood to build bookshelves, a publishing company purchases typewriters to type manuscripts, and a clothing company purchases sewing machines to make dresses.

Raw materials. **Raw materials** are items that are reformulated to go into the product. Included in this category are **natural resources**, or materials that come from the earth and are used in a manufacturing process. The petroleum used to make vinyl is a natural resource for manufacturers of record albums. **Farm products** are another type of raw material. These include items such as wheat and eggs used in baking, for example.

Processed materials. **Processed materials** are made from raw materials and are then used in the manufacturing process. The vinyl made from petroleum and the flour made from wheat are processed materials.

Supplies. **Supplies** are used less directly in the manufacturing process. Some examples are the items used to maintain manufacturing equipment and the items used to keep records of productivity. Supplies can include a wide range of products from machine oil, screws, and nails to computer paper, pens, pencils, and invoice sheets.

Components. **Components** are items that a company purchases to resell as part of its total product. A clothing manufacturer might purchase accessories or notions to become part of a dress. Belts or buttons, for example, could be purchased from another company. Also, an automobile manufacturer usually buys radios for its cars from another company.

How a company classifies its products has a tremendous effect on other parts of the marketing mix and on the company's marketing strategy. The Lisa-Macintosh line of computers is generally considered industrial and is aimed at business markets. It is higher priced than the Apple line, generally has more memory storage capacity, is advertised in the business press, and is distributed through business-oriented channels. The Apple line is generally considered consumer and is aimed at the home market. The prices are lower, the advertising heavier on television and in children's magazines, and the products distributed mostly through retail stores.

Product Mix and Product Line

Companies generally offer a number of different products to the market. The **product mix** is the total group of products one company sells, whether or not they are related to one another. For example, Owens-Corning Fiberglass has flame-resistant fabric in its product mix, as well as Tuff-N-Dri, a material for waterproofing basements. Bristol-Myers' product mix includes deodorants, pain relievers, drain openers, infant formulas, and medical and dental equipment.

A **product line** consists of several slightly varied but closely related products that a company groups under one brand name. Dannon Milk Products Company has a low-fat yogurt line that has several flavors. A product line can be very long or very short. WD-40 Company has only one product in its line, the very successful lubricant and rustproofing compound known as WD-40. Apple Computer's Lisa-Macintosh line includes Lisa, Lisa II, and Macintosh, while the company's product

TABLE 10–1 Apple Computer's Product Mix

Machine	Suggested Retail Price	Standard Memory	Primary Markets
Apple IIe	$895	64K	Schools, small businesses, and with price reduction, more home users
Apple IIc	$1,295	128K	Homes, offices, traveling professionals
Apple IIIPlus	$2,695	256K	Industry-specific businesses, especially agricultural and professional
Macintosh	$2,495	128K	General purpose businesses, universities, graphic-artists
Lisa	$3,495–5,495	512K	Users who need extra storage and memory

Source: Thomas C. Hayes, "Apple Is Banking on New Portable: The IIc Computer," *New York Times*, April 24, 1984, p. D23. Copyright © 1984 by The New York Times Company. Reprinted by permission.

mix includes all the computers under the Apple brand as well. Table 10–1 shows Apple's product mix, including both the Apple and Lisa-Macintosh product lines. The comparison of price, standard memory, and target market indicates how the members of each line do not conflict in terms of characteristics, but, rather, complement each other.

A company's product mix has both width and depth. The **width of the product mix** is measured by the number of different product lines in the mix. The **depth of the product mix** is measured by the number of different products in each product line. Figure 10–3 shows part of the very wide product mix of Beatrice Companies.

Courtesy of Beatrice Companies

Figure 10–3 The product mix of Beatrice Companies ranges from a number of lines of food products to Coca-Cola bottlers to Stiffel lamps to Samsonite luggage.

Modifications and Extensions of the Product Line

For most companies, the product line is not fixed. Companies can decide to add to their lines in order to achieve certain goals. They can also drop products that have failed or that have declined in profitability. Here are some of the main reasons for modifying or extending a product line.

To offset gains of a competitor. One reason for adding a new product might be to offset gains of a competitor. When a competitor introduces a new product that has strong influence in a particular area, a company might want to match it with a similar new product of its own. During the 1930s and 1940s, Lever Brothers had the top laundry soap, Rinso. When Procter & Gamble introduced a quickly successful new detergent, Tide, Lever Brothers reacted by introducing Rinso Blue and Surf.[2] Recently, soft-drink manufacturers, such as Coca-Cola, Pepsi, and 7-Up, have been struggling to keep up with one another's new sugar-free, caffeine-free product introductions. IBM responded to the success of Apple II with its introduction of the PC. When a new product threatens to take away a group of customers, companies often decide to introduce a new and similar product of their own.

To attract a particular market segment. Another reason to expand the product line is to attract a particular market segment. Dannon Milk Products had this objective in mind when it introduced a new product for children. The product is called Dannon Kids Style and is being marketed for the 34 million children in the 3- to 12-year-old age range. Executives at Dannon believed that they could not attract this group with their existing products, so they created something new.

Dannon Kids Style is made from whole milk instead of low-fat milk, giving the product a smoother consistency that is more appealing to children. Dannon also uses juice instead of fruit pieces to flavor the product, also contributing to the smooth texture of Kids Style. The packaging for this line is also different from Dannon's others. Each Kids Style flavor has its own character pictured on the container, including outer space creatures called Strawberrians, cheerleaders called Cherry Champs, and a rock group called the Bluesberries. The containers are smaller (4 ounces) than those designed for adults and are sold in packs of four.[3]

To broaden the appeal of an existing product. A third reason to expand a product line is to broaden the appeal of an existing product. A common practice among food companies is to add flavors to a product line or to introduce an additional form for the product. Coffee manufacturers often introduce decaffeinated and instant versions of a particular brand. Makers of frozen juices might begin with orange juice and later expand into other fruit juices. Deodorant manufacturers sometimes offer their products in a number of different scents as well as in spray and roll-on forms. Makers of shampoo might offer different forms of their product for those with dry, normal, or oily hair.

To enter new market areas. Sometimes a company introduces a new product that is very different from its existing line. This extension allows the company to enter into completely new market areas, another goal of product line extension. Polaroid Corporation recently used this strategy to enter the 35mm camera and computer graphics markets. The instant camera market was declining, so Polaroid executives decided that, to remain profitable, the company should move in other directions. Part of the solution was to offer a product that would appeal to the large number of 35mm camera owners. Polaroid developed the Instant Slide System that develops color slides inexpensively and instantly. Another new product, known as Palette, produces slides from computer graphics displays. The Instant Slide System is designed for a consumer market, while the Palette is aimed at businesses. With these two products, Polaroid is entering into areas of the market that its instant cameras could not reach.[4]

To capture distribution. Another reason to extend product lines is to capture a larger share of available distribution capacity. For example, as Campbell's kept expanding the variety of soups it was offering, grocers had to either expand the total space given to soups, drop the soups produced by another company, or not offer the full Campbell line. Since adding more varieties of soup did not increase the total consumption of soup, most grocers, who wanted to give customers the full range of choices, chose to stock the new Campbell varieties and drop competing lines. Now, Campbell's has captured most of the canned soup market, as it dominates the allotted shelf space. Similarly, as Pepsi was expanding its product line with Pepsi Free (both sugared and dietetic), Coca-Cola was forced to respond with caffeine-free brands to keep its share of shelf space. The losers in these competitive battles were the other "players."

To replace declining products. Still another motivation for developing new products is the fact that a successful product will not stay profitable forever. We have already seen several examples of products reaching the decline stage in their life cycles. The Polaroid camera, once a big seller because it offered immediate results for amateur photographers, lost its appeal when 35mm cameras became easier to use and quick film processing became more commonplace. The Apple II offered unique advantages when first produced, but now there are several smaller, cheaper, or more capable alternatives. Some new products are simply new models designed to replace old ones. Clothing manufacturers produce a new line of products once or several times per year as the fashions and seasons change. Automobile manufacturers are also continually updating their products to reflect changes in consumer needs, federal regulations, advances in technology, and competitive products that threaten sales.

The problem of cannibalization. One problem with product extension that companies try to avoid is **cannibalization.** This happens when a new product gets its sales at the expense of an existing product. For example, Coca-Cola had to consider whether Diet Coke would take sales from Tab, its other diet cola drink. The company tried to avoid the problem by positioning the two products for different markets. All new products must be evaluated in terms of their effects on the whole product line. If the product is clearly an increment to that line, then it is probably a worthwhile product extension.

Branding

Branding is a means of identifying a product and ensuring that consumers will recognize it. Today most products are purchased under some particular brand. However, this was not always the case. Products were once considered to be simply **commodities**, or goods differentiated only by their uses and not by their suppliers. One vendor's flour, cloth, soap, chickens, and other goods were considered by the end user as the same as those of other vendors. The one factor that might distinguish different vendors' products of the same type was price. Commodities are generally thought to be highly price-sensitive because when one merchant lowers the price on a commodity, others are forced to follow. Commodities' prices depend primarily on the available supply at a given time. Plentiful supply will result in price reductions, while scarcity will raise prices.

However, many marketers, including the author, feel that there is no such thing as a commodity.[5] Today's marketers recognize that the total product is greater than simply the physical good itself and believe that all goods and services can be distinguished by their own unique qualities. One way to recognize and reinforce the differentiation of similar products is through their brands. The American Marketing Association defines **brand** as "a name, term, sign, symbol, or design, or a combination of them intended to identify the goods or services of one seller or group of sellers and to differentiate them from competitors."[6] A **brand name** is "a word or group of words that identifies the product's seller to the consumer."[7] The brand name can be spoken. A **brand mark** cannot be spoken; rather, it is a symbol or design that represents the company. Figure 10–4 shows the Apple brand, containing both its brand name and Apple brand mark.

A product's brand carries a good deal of information, reducing or eliminating the need to find out about a product before buying it. Consumers confronted with a familiar brand have information about the product's image as promoted by the company. Even products that are very similar are now considered distinguishable by brand.

Perdue Farms has succeeded in enabling consumers to choose its chickens

Courtesy of Apple Computer, Inc.

Figure 10–4 The words "Apple Computer Inc." form the brand name. The apple itself is the brand mark.

from others by connecting the basic product (chicken) with several desirable components. Frank Perdue learned that consumers associate yellowness with high quality in chicken. To make his chicken more yellow, he feeds them marigold petals. The dye in the petals yellows the chickens' skin. Perdue's radio, television, and print advertisements (with the slogan "It takes a tough man to make a tender chicken") familiarize consumers with his product. His promise of a money-back guarantee contributes to consumers' trust in the quality of his brand. To identify the Perdue name, each Perdue chicken bears a tag clearly identifying its brand name. By associating his product with *reliably* high quality and the other features, Perdue is able to differentiate his chickens and thereby charge 15 percent more for his chickens than other companies charge for their nonbranded ones.

An industrial example of distinguishing products once thought of as commodities has occurred in the field of electrical components. The development of a unique production process enables Corning Glass to deliver orders much faster than other producers of the components. The shortened waiting time between order and delivery differentiated Corning's products from others and allowed the company to command a premium price in what was traditionally considered a commodity market. An additional result was an increase in the brand's market share. The ability to differentiate the product came from the recognition that the total product was more than the raw materials, that delivery time was an important part of the product.

The Importance of a Brand

A brand conveys an image for its products and brings to mind certain expectations on the part of consumers. The brand can reduce the amount of information processing in the decision process. When faced with a choice between several brand-name products, consumers make decisions based on their own needs and the attributes and their expectations of that brand. Ivory and Caress soaps are brands that convey two different sets of information. Consumers expect Ivory to be a pure soap without deodorants, perfumes, or other additives. They expect Caress to give them softer skin because this is the soap they've seen advertised as "the beauty bar with bath oil."

A brand also implies consistency. Consumers who have had a particular experience with a brand expect to have the same kind of experience the next time they purchase that brand. Of course, this can work two ways—bad experiences can be as influential on future brand choice as good experiences. People who bought faulty Apple IIIs may be hesitant about buying another computer under the Apple brand name, even though such a failure may never occur again.

When a company introduces a new product, it has to decide whether or not to use an existing brand name. Apple turned to the names Lisa and Macintosh to distinguish these computers and their technology from the Apple line. A successful brand name that connotes high-quality products, reliability, safety, or some other positive attribute can help a new product to succeed. However, if the new product fails, it can damage the reputation of other products under the same name. Also, many marketers feel that if the new product is not closely related to established

Figure 10–5 Family branding allows a company to advertise a number of products on the strength of the brand name.

Courtesy of R. Dakin & Company, San Francisco

products of that brand, the company should place it under another brand name. A well-known paper company that puts out a new line of soft drinks might be perceived by consumers as entering an area where it has no expertise. In this case, the paper company would probably create a new brand for the new product line. Generally, when the success or failure of a new product is highly uncertain, companies tend to protect the credibility of the existing brand by placing the new product under a different brand name.

Family Branding vs. Individual Branding

The main advantage of **family branding**, or grouping many products under one brand name, is that advertising and promotion for any of the products extends to the others in the family. The familiar name will appeal to customers, and companies do not have to spend as much to establish and create awareness of a new name. Some companies advertise the brand as a whole without stressing a particular product. General Electric has used an advertising campaign with the slogan

10–1 Focus on a Marketing Practice
GENERIC PRODUCTS

In 1977, Jewel Cos., a supermarket chain based in Chicago, introduced an alternative to brand-name products. The supermarket presented **generic products**, a choice that, at that time, was unknown to American consumers. Generics are lower-priced, usually lower-quality products that carry no brand name. During the next few years, most major supermarkets began to offer an aisle of generic products. This bargain section features items priced up to 49 percent lower than their brand-name counterparts. Generic packaging is literally of the no-frills variety. A package of paper towels, for example, bears only the words "Paper Towels" printed in black letters.

When generics first became widely available, many industry experts predicted that they would have no significant impact on brand loyalty. These experts reasoned that brand-loyal buyers would not trade reliable product quality for savings. In this case, the experts were wrong. Generics became widely available at the time of a national economic recession. One of consumers' primary concerns during this period was saving money. The generic products took off in a way that even their most optimistic proponents hadn't dared to predict. By 1981, many generics had reached about a 10 percent market share.

The first generic products were in household product and food categories. Commonly available items were generic detergents, paper products, pet foods, coffee and tea, snacks, and canned goods. As the years passed and generics became more successful, supermarkets became more bold about the generic products they offered. Some products once thought to be inseparable from their brand names now appeared brandless on grocery store shelves. Liggett & Myers Tobacco Company began offering generic cigarettes that supermarkets could present under three names: "Quality Lights," "Filter Lights," and "Flavor Lights," all of which, the company admits, are basically the same product. Alcohol producers began producing "California Champagne" or "Scotch."

Companies most hurt by the generics movement were those whose products were not the top-ranking brand in their category. The strongest brands retained customer loyalty, presumably because those customers didn't mind paying extra for quality. The brands ranked third or fourth in popularity—and also priced lower than top brands—lost ground to the even less expensive generics.

More recently, industry observers have seen generics lose some ground. As the economy showed some signs of recovery in 1983 and 1984, consumers started to return to their favorite brands. There are some indications that the sale of generics is now taking customers away from the stores' own house brands, rather than from the independent brand names. However, many experts believe that a significant portion of consumers will continue to buy generics. Even in a strong economy, these observers believe, brand loyalty will not reach the pre-1977 level while generics remain available.

Sources: Suzanne Bauschard, "Evolution May Hasten the End," *Progressive Grocer*, March 1982, pp. 31–32; Bill Abrams, "Brand Loyalty Rises Slightly, But Increases Could Be Fluke," *Wall Street Journal*, January 7, 1982, p. 23; "Mum's the Word for the New Generics," *New York Times*, May 5, 1981, p. F17; "No-Frills Food," *Business Week*, March 23, 1981, pp. 70–73; Mary McCabe English, "Calm after the Storm," *Advertising Age*, March 15, 1982, pp. M18–19.

"GE: We bring good things to living. We bring good things to life." The message is designed to apply to all GE products. If each were under a separate brand name, a strategy called **individual branding**, this type of generalized advertising would not be possible.

Gillette has used its name as the family brand of several, but not all, of its products. Gillette Foamy shaving cream featured the name, as did Gillette Blue Blades and Trac Two and Lady Gillette razors. But when the company introduced a new disposable cigarette lighter, the new product carried the name Cricket. The company logo appeared on the product to convey Gillette's reputation. Gillette tends to use its own name as the brand only for shaving products. Other products receive their own brand names—Right Guard for an anti-perspirant and Silkience for a shampoo and conditioner.

A company may also choose not to give a new product an existing brand name when the new product might take some of the firm's own customers away from another of its products (cannibalization). When Procter & Gamble introduces a new detergent, instead of putting it under the Tide brand name, the company gives it an entirely new name. Customers who like Tide might otherwise want to switch to the new Tide product. Procter & Gamble would prefer to attract customers of other companies' products with its new laundry detergent.

Another occasion when companies might want to choose a new brand name is when the existing brand name is designed to attract a particular market segment and to emphasize product features. The company may want to stress new features in a new product through a new brand name. The Tandy Corporation has devel-

Figure 10–6
Gillette uses different branding strategies for its products. Right Guard has its own brand name but is identified as a Gillette product. Silkience has its own brand name and is not identified as a Gillette product.

Courtesy of The Gillette Company

oped its Radio Shack brand to stand for inexpensive electronics products. The brand name works for that product line, but Tandy executives felt that the bargain image was wrong for its line of computers. The solution was to introduce the computer line under the Tandy name. When a company introduces a less expensive product line than the existing one, often it will put the new line under a different name to prevent its own customers from abandoning the higher-priced product in favor of the cheaper one.

Having distinct brands for different products also protects a company from damage to its entire product mix due to problems with one product. When Procter & Gamble's Rely tampon was connected with a serious illness, toxic shock syndrome, sales of the product plummeted. However, other Procter & Gamble brands, such as Duncan Hines and Tide, were unaffected. In contrast, McNeil Laboratories' entire product line was temporarily damaged when several people died from poisoning by cyanide that had been placed inside some Extra-Strength Tylenol capsules.

Brand Loyalty

The goal of many of these branding decisions is to develop brand loyalty among customers. **Brand loyalty** is the tendency for a customer to intentionally purchase a product repeatedly. There are two components of brand loyalty. One is the consumers' behavior, or the relatively consistent purchasing of a particular brand. The other is the customers' attitude about the product, or the intention to buy that product.[8] In other words, brand-loyal customers include those who buy the product consistently as well as those who would like to buy it but whose store may often be out of the brand. Most often, though, companies are interested in consumers' consistent purchasing of their product.

Both consumers and companies have reasons for developing brand loyalty. Consumers tend to buy the same brand because they know what they are getting in terms of quality and other attributes. They do not have to search for information about other products to find something that they want. Companies that have built and reinforced brand loyalty can use it as a way to reduce the threat of competition; loyal consumers may resist offers from competitors. Similarly, if consumers want to buy a certain brand, they may be willing to search for that brand and to pay a little more for it. High levels of brand loyalty serve as a barrier to entry into the market by a competitor.

Measuring brand loyalty. There are three general ways of measuring the amount of brand loyalty for a product (A). The first is to analyze purchasing patterns of that product (A) by consumers in relation to purchases of brands B, C, and D. If a consumer purchases a brand consistently (a pattern of AAAAA), that consumer is loyal to that brand. If a consumer's buying pattern is ABCDA, that consumer buys randomly and is loyal to no brand. A buying pattern of AAABA indicates a high degree of brand loyalty; perhaps the B indicates trying a new product or a discount on a competing product. A pattern of AAABBB indicates that a consumer has probably switched loyalty to a different brand.

A second way to measure brand loyalty is to analyze buying patterns and note the percentage of the time a consumer buys one brand.

The third way to measure brand loyalty is to experiment and see how much more a consumer is willing to pay for that particular brand. This is known as the "dollarmetric" method.[9]

Reasons for brand loyalty. Research on brand loyalty and brand switching has shown some general trends in the area, though there is no sure way to predict consumer behavior in a given situation. One trend suggests that conditions in the market are often more influential than the features of a particular product. When one product dominates a market, consumers are more likely to remain loyal to that brand, despite the introduction of attractive alternatives.

Another observation is that whether or not consumers tend to be brand-loyal seems to be unrelated to their personality characteristics and socioeconomic status. Also, people who tend to be loyal to a particular store, or shop there consistently, tend to be more brand-loyal than people who like to shop around for their purchases. Some researchers have found that if a purchase involves a good deal of risk, consumers will tend to be more brand-loyal.[10] This is because consumers know what they are getting. The conservative choice may be the most familiar one.

Perhaps the most important finding about brand loyalty is that consistent patterns for one product do not seem to hold true for another.[11] Consumers who demonstrate brand loyalty when they are purchasing a brand of coffee may not demonstrate brand loyalty when they are buying toilet tissue, soap, automobiles, or clothing. For this reason, marketers tend to be cautious about making general brand-loyalty predictions.

Creating brand loyalty is a major concern when marketers are deciding whether to use a known brand name for a new product. Placing many similar products under the same brand can reduce brand loyalty by diluting the image of the brand when the goal is to keep the loyal customers and attract new ones. For many years the Coca-Cola Company placed the Coca-Cola and Coke brand name on just one product. Its other products—Tab, Sprite, Mellow Yellow—received their own brand names. The company wanted to protect its most successful brand by not spreading the name too thin. Recently, Coca-Cola changed its policy, though, by introducing the Diet Coke soft drinks. The reason for using the Coke brand name at this point was that PepsiCo's products were beginning to threaten Coca-Cola's number-one sales position in the soft-drink industry.

Variety switching. The opposite of brand loyalty is **variety switching**. Consumers may be bored with familiar products, may want a change, or may just want to try something different. They may then switch to another brand for variety. This behavior happens even in stable markets with established competitors. In the soft-drink market, for example, drinkers of Coca-Cola and Pepsi may temporarily switch to 7-Up for the variety of a noncola drink; they will not switch back and forth between Coca-Cola and Pepsi. Enough switching goes on constantly for the market shares of the major competitors to remain stable.[12]

It is important for marketers to assess the amount of brand loyalty or variety switching to determine the desirability of entering certain markets. If the brand loyalty is lower or the variety seeking higher, entering the market and gaining customer trial of the product is easier.

Trademarks

A brand's **trademark** is its legally protected portion of the brand that distinguishes it from others. The trademark can be a brand name, brand mark, or package—any distinctive feature that helps to identify the product and to which the company has exclusive rights. A brand's trademark is what enables consumers to recognize it and select it easily from others. The Morton's Salt trademark is the picture of a little girl carrying an umbrella that appears on its packages; the Quaker Oats trademark is the picture of a Quaker on its packages. All of Apple's computers bear its symbol: a rainbow-colored apple with a bite out of it. The Coca-Cola bottle is a trademark of that product. Having a recognizable trademark assures customers that they are purchasing a product from a known source.

A company with a highly recognizable trademark is Mack Trucks, Inc., with its bulldog trademark that has been mounted on hood assemblies since 1931. The company uses its logo in just about every conceivable way, not only on its trucks but also on souvenirs available at a company store, executive neckties, stationery, and a flag outside company headquarters. The biggest buyers at the Mack store are foreign visitors who take souvenirs home as gifts. Mack Trucks believes that the bulldog functions as an effective promotional device, making the brand recognizable all over the world.[13]

The trademark is a legal concept, a way for the company to protect legally its brands from being copied and sold by others. Successful products are often involved in fierce legal battles with companies that infringe on their trademarks. One problem occurs when the brand name becomes the generic term for the product. Several words that are now generic names for a kind of product were once legal trademarks. These include cellophane, kerosene, and aspirin. A recent case of a company's loss of exclusive rights to a brand name involved Parker Brothers, a division of General Mills, Inc., and the name Monopoly for its well-known board game. Anti-Monopoly, Inc., challenged Parker Brothers' exclusive right to use of the word *monopoly* as the name of a game by marketing the real-estate game called Anti-Monopoly. Upholding several lower-court decisions, the Supreme Court ruled that the word *monopoly* had come to mean a type of game, rather than referring to the makers of a specific game.[14]

Chessie System Railroads has instituted policies to protect the trademark that appears on its railroad cars (a picture of a kitten asleep on a pillow). Chessie's trademark had been copied in the past by clothing and china manufacturers and a motel owner. The solution, as Chessie's lawyers saw it, was to charge high licensing fees for use of the trademark and require inspections by Chessie employees of the product carrying the trademark. Drawn up as protection for the company's trademark, these policies created some public relations problems for the company.

Figure 10–7 The Xerox Corporation conducts an active advertising campaign to protect its registered trademark.

Courtesy of Xerox Corporation.

Firms most affected were small businesses that manufacture miniature railroad cars and engines, some of which gross only $25,000 in sales per year. Many of the manufacturers simply stopped making Chessie cars. Several other railroad companies feel that was a loss for Chessie, as miniature railroads provide valuable exposure for the companies they imitate. Chessie is reviewing the policies and may drop the fee to $1 for miniature train manufacturers.[15]

Another legal conflict involved the makers of Tic Tac mints, Dynamints, and Mighty Mints. Ferrero, makers of Tic Tac, complained that makers of Dynamints (Warner-Lambert) and Mighty Mints (Life Savers) had copied its distinctive packaging and product. A clear plastic box with a label that wrapped over its top characterized all three products, though Tic Tac had been introduced earlier. In an out-of-court settlement, Warner-Lambert agreed to change its product significantly. Life Savers withdrew Mighty Mints from the market after unsuccessful market tests.[16]

Chapter 10 / Products and Their Characteristics   287

10–2 Focus on a Marketing Decision
WHY CAMPBELL'S IS CHANGING ITS SOUP PACKAGE

One of the most familiar product packages in the United States is the Campbell's soup can, whose red and white label has been a corporate symbol since 1897. Up to 2 billion of these familiar cans are produced and sold each year, but they may be becoming a thing of the past. The company has decided that the can is no longer so appealing to consumers, and it is planning to package its products in different forms—perhaps a dish that can be put into a microwave oven, perhaps a plastic container similar to the ones currently used by some instant soup manufacturers.

Campbell's hopes the new packages will expand its market by attracting as customers people who have so far avoided canned soup, particularly single people in search of convenience. Marketing research has shown that consumers don't like having to use a can opener, add water, and then clean several utensils just to have a bowl of soup. Younger people associate the can with artificial ingredients and believe that cans do not preserve vital nutrients properly. And the can has lost what was once its major advantage over other forms of packaging—extended shelf life for its contents. New plastics are almost completely impervious to oxygen, thus providing the same vacuum-packed preservation capability. Moreover, cans cannot be used in the microwave ovens currently found in one-third of all households in the United States. Furthermore, many other companies have begun repackaging their products. Beverage companies, for instance, have introduced "camibloc boxes"—rectangular boxes made of a waterproof and airtight combination of cartonboard, aluminum foil, and plastic—and aseptic packages.

Increasing the public's appetite for packaged soup, in general, as opposed to aiming for a larger share of the existing market, is especially important to Campbell's, because the soup maker already has about 80 percent of that market. It stands to reason that if the company can succeed in making packaged soups more generally appealing, it will get the major portion of any increase in sales. So a 17-member task force is undertaking the thorough, lengthy, and expensive process of evaluating alternative containers in consumer surveys and conducting tests on different types of containers. The possible new containers include squat, rectangular boxes; long, lean cartons; yogurt-type cups; a stand-up aluminum foil pouch shaped like a tetrahedron; and, perhaps the most conventional, a plastic container shaped just like the old metal can, including the red and white label. At the moment, the leading contender seems to be a microwave bowl, capped by an easy-open top (also made of plastic), which was highly praised in a 1983 market test.

Campbell's is proceeding slowly and does not intend to introduce new packages for its products before late 1984, and then only in selected regional markets. It also intends to phase out metal cans only gradually. However, it believes that other packages will eventually account for more than 80 percent of all soup sales.

Source: Paul A. Engelmayer, "Campbell Plans to Drop Its Tin Soup Can, Reflecting New Emphasis on Convenience," *Wall Street Journal*, March 28, 1984, p. 35.

Packaging

A product's **package**, consisting of its physical container and label, serves several functions. First, it simply protects the product during shipping and often serves as a storage container after the product has been purchased. In addition, the package also has a number of communication roles. One is to promote the product. An eye-catching and attractive package can help consumers to notice the product and might even result in unplanned purchases. The package can also convey an image for the product. General Sportcraft of Bergen, New Jersey, a sporting goods marketer, found that its package designs looked cluttered and dated. The company redesigned packages that distinguished Sportcraft's products from those of other companies. With a white box and red with blue stripes, the company conveyed the idea of athletics and patriotism. The company logo was changed so that it would look simple, clear, and striking. The company's president reports that the new design has helped to get the products into more stores and has encouraged impulse buying, particularly in large stores with minimal sales staff.[17]

Innovative packaging can sometimes stimulate sales. Super Glue of Glendale, New York, designed a package that invites consumers to try the product. The product is SuperKlip, a self-adhesive plastic clip. The SuperKlip package is a card with three clips encased in a clear plastic bubble. A fourth clip is left outside the plastic so that consumers can try it. At a recent hardware show, the package made the product an overwhelming success in comparison with its previous performance in a less innovative package. The manufacturer sold one million cards to retailers.[18]

Packaging can also influence the appeal of the product by making it more convenient. The soft-drink industry has witnessed a number of changes in packages. First there were one-serving glass bottles; then larger, multiserving bottles; then cans; then nonreturnable bottles; and, finally, plastic bottles. Each new container has been introduced to add to the product's convenience, to appeal to new market segments, or to reduce costs. The new aseptic paper and foil containers used for fruit juices and milk are another example. They employ a new technology that enables consumers and distributors to purchase perishable foods and drinks that will last much longer without refrigeration.

An important function of all packaging is to convey certain information to the consumer about the product. Government regulations require that manufacturers provide certain information about a product's contents. The Food and Drug Administration requires that food packages or labels list ingredients in order of their amounts (the ingredient used in the largest quantity comes first). Food packages also contain nutritional information, such as the amount of specific vitamins and minerals contained in a serving of the product, the number of calories, and the amount of fat. Manufacturers often emphasize features of their products that they think will help them sell. Campbell's Soup has recently relabeled a group of its soups to emphasize the fact that they are low in calories. Life Savers has done the same with its candies' labels by printing "Less than 10 calories in each piece" on every roll. Figure 10–8 presents a label that shows the types of information contained on packages. Regulations concerning labeling practices are designed to ensure that packages do not carry any deceptive information about products' sizes, uses, or the results to be expected from them.

In some circumstances packages can have a vital role in the product's marketing. The 1982 poisonings caused by Tylenol capsules laced with cyanide have brought about major changes in the packaging of medicines and cosmetics. "Tamperproof" packages became a legal requirement as well as a selling point for many kinds of products, as wary consumers looked for assurance that their medicines and cosmetics were safe.

In some marketers' view, the Tylenol incident created a new marketing segment, people concerned about the possibility of tampering.[19] Shortly after the incident, McNeil Laboratories, a division of Johnson & Johnson and the makers of Tylenol, began sealing Tylenol bottles so that consumers would know if the bottle had been opened. Bristol-Myers introduced a pop-top package for its product, Excedrin. Marketers have found that the new packages have had a positive impact on sales.

Tamperproofing can add significantly to the cost of the product, however, and marketers have been concerned that costs may outweigh benefits. One inexpensive method is Diamond Salt's cellophane tape over the package's pour-spout. Once the tape is pulled back, it cannot be restuck. Marketers are also cautious about making claims that their product is tamperproof. If there were an incident of tampering involving a product about which such an advertising claim had been made, the manufacturer would probably be held responsible.[20]

Figure 10–8 Labels convey much information about a product. This label contains the producer's brand name and brand mark, a photograph of the product, a description of the product and of product benefits (Crisp! In Very Little Water), nutritional information, a list of ingredients, directions for use, the producer's name and address, and a note to consumers.

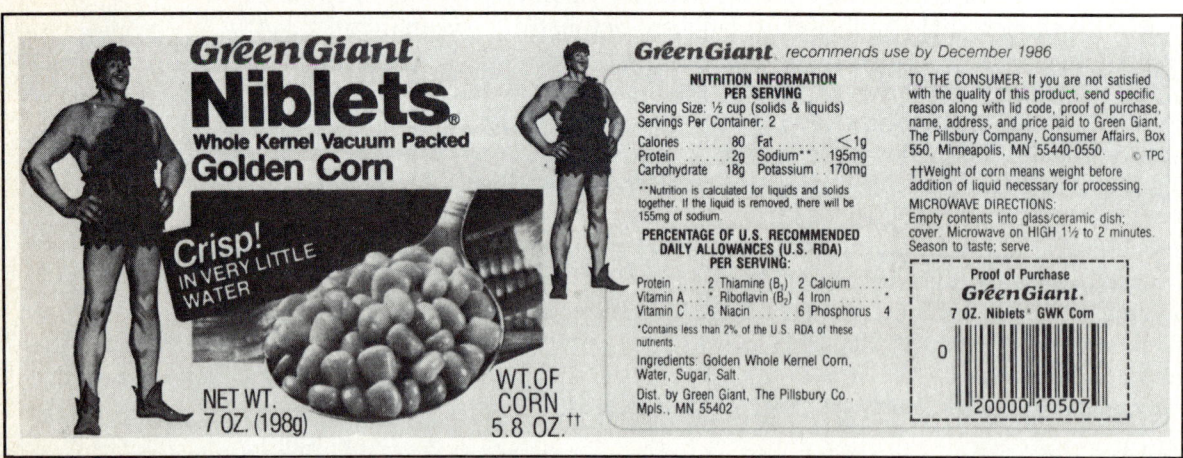

© Green Giant Company. Used with permission.

Services

As we mentioned in the beginning of this chapter, not all products are tangible goods. Services can be products in and of themselves, such as banking, airlines transportation, and dry cleaning. Services as products are discussed in chapter 21. Here we discuss **services** as components of tangible products. When considering which services to offer with a product, companies try to determine which would augment the particular product in terms of satisfying consumers' needs. Executives at Apple, for example, look at the possible services they could offer and choose the ones—training, software, installation, warranties—that make consumers more willing to try and purchase their products.

Many companies offer maintenance service on tangible products as a selling feature. Automobile manufacturers usually offer free repairs and replacement of parts for a limited time after a consumer buys a new car. Other manufacturers, such as watchmakers and appliance manufacturers, offer free repairs or replacement of the product if it fails within a certain time. **Warranties**, or assurances from the manufacturer about product qualities and offers to provide repair service, are also common. Service agreements and guarantees are particularly important when consumers perceive the purchase as involving a high amount of risk. When the product is new or unfamiliar, such as a computer, consumers may purchase an Apple IIe with all of its available services rather than a brand with few services. Purchasing an expensive television set seems like a smaller risk if customers know they can have the set repaired at no cost. The ultimate insurance against this kind of risk is the money-back guarantee, or the promise that if customers are dissatisfied, they can return the item and be reimbursed.

Another form of customer service for tangible goods is training in the use of the product. Singer offers customers free sewing lessons with the purchase of a new machine. One area for which this type of service is particularly important is the computer industry. For many people, buying a computer and the necessary software is not only a financial risk but also involves the risk of not having enough knowledge to operate them. Several software companies are adopting marketing strategies that address just this problem. Softsel Computer Products, Inc., offers dealers a toll-free phone number to call for technical advice on customers' questions. The company also offers its products only to authorized dealers in order to ensure that retailers have sufficient technical expertise to handle customers' questions. Context Management Systems tests retailers on computer knowledge before accepting them as dealers. When Polaroid introduced its SX-70, it opened an 800 telephone number to handle questions about the product.

Delivery and installation of a product are other services that are provided. In many cases a product has no value to the customer until it is delivered and installed. A customer may purchase wall-to-wall carpeting, but cannot use the carpeting until it is in place; in this case, the retailer who sold the carpeting often provides this service. Usually, the larger the product is, the more important it is to the customer that it be delivered. Similarly, the more complicated a product and the greater the probability that the customer would make errors in installation, the

10–3 Focus on Marketing Strategy
WHY COMPANIES PROVIDE SERVICES

An increasing number of businesses are recognizing the advantages of offering strong services to support their tangible products. In addition to helping customers and creating good will, service programs can provide information about customers themselves, alert manufacturers to problem products, provide a measure of the impact of an ad campaign, and provide ideas for new products and modifications of existing ones.

Procter & Gamble now has a toll-free 800 number listed on packages for all of its products. Customers can call the number to complain about problems with a product, to ask for information about its use, and to talk about how they have used it. P&G has a 75-member staff to handle calls, answer letters, and record information from customers. Product codes enable P&G to identify the item's manufacturing source in case of a problem and to correct it immediately. Calls from customers have prompted P&G to add a recipe for wedding cake on the package of its cake mix and to add high-altitude baking instructions on a brownies mix. P&G views the toll-free call-in lines as a way to find out about problems immediately and to correct them weeks or months sooner than would otherwise be possible.

At American Express, customer service is a very costly but, executives feel, an invaluable part of the business. A recent incident points up the lengths to which American Express will go to aid a customer. A midwestern cardholder's sister, Lebanese by birth, was stranded without money in war-torn Beirut after her bank closed. The cardholder contacted American Express to request that money be sent to his sister so that she could leave Lebanon. Over the course of one day, customer service personnel at American Express sent 28 telexes to Beirut, and arranged for special authorization for a check to be cashed for the woman. Their efforts were successful; the woman received $3,000 cash and was able to leave the country.

American Express places the costs for customer service phone lines, computers, personnel, training, and data banks at $150 million. Executives of the company view these services as one way American Express can differentiate its product from others in the market. Therefore the expense of such services is worthwhile as the primary way that American Express directly communicates with customers.

General Electric has established an Answer Center to respond to customers' questions about products. GE reports that 25 percent of its calls come from people interested in buying a GE product who want more information about it; 25 percent ask trained technicians for appliance repair information. The prepurchase calls provide GE with the opportunity to communicate directly with customers and possibly increase the number of sales. Calls for repair information enable GE to make product modifications and to learn which parts in old models are most likely to fail.

Other companies that have made similar efforts to improve services are Sony, IBM, Toyota, General Motors, Westinghouse, and Noxell. All agree that, though costs can be high, adding services can be a real selling feature for their products.

Source: "Making Service a Potent Marketing Tool," *Business Week*, June 11, 1984, pp. 164–70.

more likely that the service of installation will be provided. If a company purchases many Lisa computers for its offices as an installation, the company will arrange to deliver and install them.

As we mentioned earlier, some services are themselves products. We might view products as forming a continuum from the purely tangible to the purely intangible.[21] Of course, most products have some amount of each of these dimensions. In the purely tangible category are food products. Virtually all of what customers pay for when buying a loaf of bread is the physical product to be consumed. Yet even food can provide some intangibles. The current popularity of gourmet foods like Godiva chocolates suggests that food products can give consumers some intangible benefits like status.

Other tangible products offer a larger intangible component. An example of this type is a camera. In addition to the physical object, camera manufacturers are offering the possibility of recording an intangible, the memory of an experience, through photographs. The instant cameras offer a less abstract intangible, fast film processing within the camera itself.

Transportation is an example of a more pure service product.[22] An Amtrak passenger pays to get from one place to another. A relatively insignificant physical feature of the trip is the type of train used. Banking is also a service industry. The choice of checkbooks offered to customers could be considered a tangible aspect of the product but would not influence customers' choice of banks. Though there is considerable overlap between tangible and intangible products, marketers usually think of products as either tangible or intangible.

Summary

A product is any idea, service, or tangible good that a customer can acquire through a monetary transaction or exchange. A product is the sum of all physical and psychological features that aid in satisfying a customer's want or need. Elements of the product include its physical features, package, service provided by the manufacturer or dealer, brand name, company reputation, and its guarantee or warranty.

Products can be classified by the type of customer who buys them. Consumer products are those that people buy for personal use; industrial products are purchased by an organization for commercial purposes.

Consumer products fit into three categories: convenience goods (those that people buy mainly because they are available), shopping goods (those that involve preplanning and comparison of alternatives), and specialty goods (products of a certain brand for which a certain group of consumers has a preference).

Industrial goods are of four types: equipment, raw materials, supplies, and components.

The product mix is the total group of products one company sells, whether or not they are related to one another. The product line consists of several slightly varied but closely related products that the company groups under one brand name. Companies may decide to extend a product line for several purposes: to offset gains by a competitor's new product, to attract a particular market segment, to broaden the appeal of the line, to expand into new market areas, or to replace products declining in profitability.

Branding is a means of identifying a product and ensuring that consumers will recognize it. Commodities are goods differentiated only by their uses, not by their suppliers. A brand is "a name, term, sign, symbol, or design, or a combination of them intended to identify the goods or services of one seller or group of sellers and to differentiate them from competitors." The main advantage of family branding (grouping many products under one name) is shared advertising and promotion.

Reasons not to group a new product under an existing brand name include the fact that the new product may take away some of the company's customers for another of its products, market segments attracted by two different products may conflict, and to protect the product mix as a whole from problems caused by a single product.

Packaging can be a valuable marketing tool. Innovative packages can help to target the product at a particular market segment and can add to the usefulness of the product itself. The package also serves to convey important information to consumers about the product. Government regulations concerning labeling practices are designed to protect consumers from misleading packages.

Services are often an important element of a product. These can include guarantees, maintenance, and instruction in the use of the product. Many products have tangible as well as intangible features. Few products are purely tangible in nature.

Questions for Discussion

1. How does the text define the term *product*? In what way is it different from the layman's use of the term?
2. Discuss critically the criteria used in classifying consumer goods into different product categories.
3. Distinguish the characteristics of shopping goods and specialty goods and discuss their implications for marketers.
4. Illustrate the difference between product line and product mix with reference to a local company you are familiar with.
5. Numerous reasons may prompt product line modification and extension. Which of these reasons are really valid today? Which are not valid?
6. Discuss the marketing implications of the differences between brand, brand name, and brand mark.
7. Imagine a situation in which you, as a marketer, are not allowed to use a brand name on the product you sell. Examine the nature of marketing problems facing you.
8. Take the example of any company that employs family branding on its products. Evaluate why such a company should not use individual branding instead.
9. What are the marketing functions performed by the packaging of a product?

References

1. "The Personal Computer's New Job in the Lab," *Business Week,* August 22, 1983, pp. 116J–116L; Peter Nulty, "Apple's Bid to Stay in the Big Game," *Fortune*, February 7, 1983, pp. 36–41; "Apple Computer's Counter Attack Against IBM," *Business Week,* January 16, 1984, pp. 78–81; "Personal Computers: Smaller and Smarter," *Business Week,* March 28, 1983, pp. 134–38; "Apple Is Banking on New Portable: The IIc Computer," *New York Times,* April 24, 1984, p. D1; "Next Apple Computer Blends Old Design, New Technology," *Wall Street Journal,* March 23, 1984, p. 35; "Apple Faces Challenge Selling New Computer for Home Use," *Wall Street Journal,* May 3, 1984, p. 31.
2. N. R. Kleinfeld, "Lever's Battle to Rise Again," *New York Times,* March 12, 1983, p. 29.
3. "Dannon Whips Up Serving for Kids," *Advertising Age,* October 25, 1982, p. 88.
4. "Polaroid Sharpens Its Focus on the Marketplace," *Business Week,* February 13, 1984, p. 132
5. Theodore Levitt, "Marketing Success Through Differentiation—Of Anything," *Harvard Business Review,* January–February 1980, pp. 83–91.
6. *Marketing Definitions* (Chicago: American Marketing Association, 1960), p. 9.
7. Ibid., p. 10.
8. James F. Engel, Roger D. Blackwell, and David T. Kollat, *Consumer Behavior*, 3rd ed. (Hinsdale, Ill.: Dryden Press, 1978), p. 441.
9. Edgar A. Pessemier, "A New Way to Determine Buying Decisions," *Journal of Marketing,* October 1959, pp. 41–46.
10. Engel, Blackwell, and Kollat, *Consumer Behavior,* p. 449.
11. Ibid.
12. David J. Reibstein, "An Experimental Study of Brand Choice and Switching Behavior" (unpublished dissertation, Purdue University, 1975).
13. Del Marth, "How the Top Bulldog Learned His Way Up," *Nation's Business*, December 1981, pp. 56–60.
14. Pamela G. Hollie, "Monopoly Loses Its Trademark," *New York Times,* February 23, 1983, pp. D1, D4.
15. Daniel Machalara, "This Christmas Tale Pits Toy Railroads Against Little Kitten," *Wall Street Journal,* December 20, 1983, p. 1.
16. George Miaoulis and Nancy D'Amato, "Consumer Confusion and Trademark Infringement," *Journal of Marketing,* April 1978, pp. 48–55.
17. Norm Skarewitz, "If the Corporate Image Calls for a Facelift," *Inc.,* December 1982, pp. 111–12.
18. Ibid.
19. "Safe Packaging: Worth the Cost?" *Marketing News,* November 12, 1982, pp. 1, 15.
20. Ibid.
21. G. Lynn Shostack, "Breaking Free from Product Marketing," *Journal of Marketing,* April 1977, pp. 73–80.
22. Ibid.

OBJECTIVES

1. To explain why companies develop new products.

2. To describe the process of new-product development.

3. To illustrate the manner in which companies design new products to meet the specific needs of consumers.

4. To introduce the concept of the product life cycle and explain the different stages of the product life cycle.

5. To highlight the implications of the product life cycle for marketers.

11

Product Development and the Product Life Cycle

Frito-Lay, Inc., longtime leader in salted snacks, is getting serious about cookies. Nabisco, Inc., the nation's biggest cookie producer, has some heavyweight contenders for the salted snacks arena. Hershey Foods Corporation is working on developing candy that causes fewer cavities. Researchers at General Foods are trying to learn how rats lose weight in hopes of developing foods to aid human weight loss. Campbell Soup Company has introduced a line of low-sodium soups. What all these companies have in common is an active involvement in new-product development.

Some of Frito-Lay's most recent additions to the grocery store shelves are a product called Ta-Tos and one called O'Gradys. Both are variations on potato chips, but Ta-Tos are "super-crispy wavy," while O'Gradys are "extra-thick and crunchy." Developing these products wasn't as simple as it might seem. To fry potatoes so that they are both extra-thick *and* crunchy, Frito-Lay needed special machinery. Thick potatoes, when fried, usually brown on the outside but their insides stay white and soft. The new machines cut deep ridges in different directions on each side of the chip, allowing more even frying. A problem with the equipment is that it only accepts potatoes 4 inches long or shorter, meaning potatoes have to be presorted.

In 1981, Frito-Lay dominated the salted snack food market with sales of approximately $1.9 billion, but this was not enough for the company. As the company controlled 75 percent of the corn chip market already, its potential for growth within the market was limited. The company did, however, have strengths in packaging, production processes, and distribution channels that could be transferred to other markets, so it decided to pursue the attractive $2.5 billion a year retail packaged cookie market. Entering this market would not be easy, though, as Nabisco already had a 35 percent share of the market.

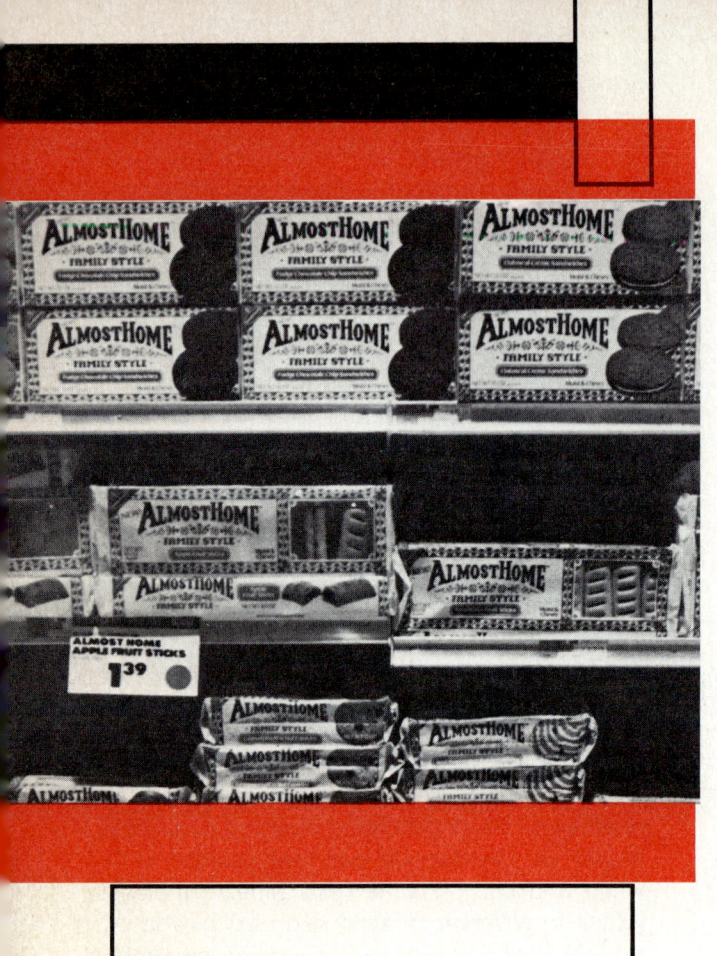

Having decided to enter the packaged cookie market, Frito-Lay was faced with the decision of which product to introduce. There were a variety of different styles, shapes, and flavors of cookies that could be developed. Should Frito-Lay enter the market with luxury cookies as Campbell's did with its Pepperidge Farm line? Should the company enter with simpler cookies, such as vanilla wafers? Or should it choose another product?

Frito-Lay decided that, rather than make this decision internally, it would get reactions and information from consumers. Thus, the company conducted marketing research in the form of customer interviews to find out what shoppers felt about the products already on the market. One message stood out—consumers found the existing cookies hard and dry and not worth the price. The company decided, then, to develop a soft and moist ready-to-eat cookie.

Just making that decision was not enough; the company now had to develop the product. Frito-Lay's research and development department was able to generate a variety of cookies that tasted great directly out of the oven, but were tooth-breaking after a few weeks. As the company itself could not develop an acceptable product, it looked outside. It found a company, Grandma's, whose cookies were preferred by consumers in taste tests, and immediately acquired it.

There were two problems, though. First, the costs of producing Grandma's cookies were significantly higher than Nabisco's costs. Second, the moisture content in Grandma's cookies was four times that of the competition, reducing the shelf life from six to less than four months. The second problem could be solved by using Frito-Lay's extensive distribution system for its salted snacks. The first problem could not be solved. Frito-Lay then had the choice of either lowering the quality of the cookies, thus lowering production costs;

building massive production facilities in anticipation of high future demand; pricing competitively with Nabisco; or hoping that customers would be willing to pay higher costs.

Frito-Lay found the first three choices unacceptable and the high-price strategy uncertain. Thus, the company decided to test both the product and the price in a Kansas City test market. The preliminary results gave Frito-Lay 15 to 20 percent of the market, taking away from the market shares of both Nabisco and Keebler.

Nabisco, however, with cookie sales of $11.4 billion in 1981, was not about to let this happen. It took two actions. The first was to develop its own soft cookies, called Almost Home. The second was to attack Frito-Lay in the salted snack market by introducing its own corn chip.

Procter & Gamble was also active in these markets. It had entered the salted snack market with its Pringles potato chips, and its Duncan Hines cookie mixes were strong in the cookie, although not ready-to-eat cookie, market. It then extended the Duncan Hines line by introducing a soft and moist ready-to-eat cookie under that brand name.[1]

Frito-Lay, Hershey, General Foods, Campbell, Procter & Gamble, and Nabisco have decided to expand their product mixes and are actively pursuing product development. In this chapter, we look at why companies develop new products, the process they follow and decisions they make while developing new products, and the marketing strategies they pursue for new products and products moving through their life cycles.

Product Development

Why Develop New Products?

All markets change over time as customers' needs change, as competitors present new challenges, and as technological advancements occur. Companies develop new products to meet these changes in the market. Some products with long histories on the market have been changed so many times that they no longer resem-

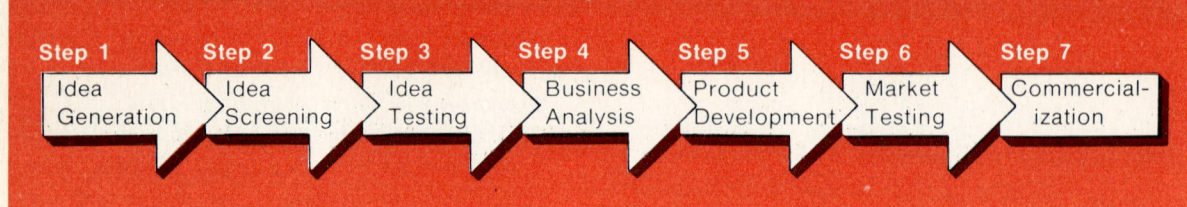

Figure 11–1 The new-product development process

ble their original forms. An example is Procter & Gamble's laundry detergent Tide, a product that has been on the market since 1946. The company has made more than 40 modifications in Tide to keep up with competition and to meet consumer demands. The Tide offered almost 40 years ago would not be acceptable today. To survive in today's competitive markets, companies must continually generate and test new-product ideas and present them to consumers. This **new-product development process** consists of seven steps: idea generation, idea screening, idea testing, business analysis, product development, market testing, and commercialization. These are shown in figure 11–1 and are discussed below.

Step 1: Idea Generation

The first step in the new-product development process is **idea generation.** Development of one successful product might come as the result of the generation of a hundred ideas. Most ideas will not work out for one reason or another, so companies encourage many different people to suggest ideas. Many large firms have entire departments devoted to conceiving and developing new products. But ideas can also come from sales and repair personnel, factory workers, outside inventors, competitors, office staff, retail dealers, and even from consumers themselves.[2] Companies set up a system for submitting ideas (such as a suggestion box or an official suggestion form for submitters to fill out) and give rewards for those adopted. These practices encourage the continual flow of ideas necessary for the company's growth and survival.

Regardless of who suggests the idea, the impetus for new-product ideas comes from two general sources. One is from a technological development; the other is from the recognition of a new consumer demand. A firm's research and development department might introduce a technological development in the form of an entirely new product or a new way to produce an existing product. Frito-Lay's research and development department invented a new snack, O'Gradys, from the combination of its idea for a thick, crunchy potato chip and its development of the machinery to produce it.

On the other hand, a product can come from a need that the company has found in the marketplace. Campbell Soup Company developed its low-sodium line when it learned that too much salt was a worry among a significant number of consumers. Estēe Lauder, Inc., created its Clinique division and product line based on knowledge of a health-conscious market segment's desire for fragrance-free cosmetics. Its new products are developed by Lauder's heavily funded research and

11-1 Focus on Successful Marketing
MEETING NEEDS FOR SPECIAL CLOTHING

Some clothing manufacturers are designing new products to meet the specialized needs, and wants, of well-defined groups of consumers.

Mothers Work sells maternity clothes for businesswomen. The company's founder, Rebecca Matthias, felt the need herself when, as a pregnant employee of a computer company, she resorted to buying business clothes two sizes too big. At the time, Matthias says, she was unable to find maternity clothes suitable for the business environment. Now she runs a company that manufactures them.

Matthias and others, including several leading clothes designers who have recently introduced maternity lines, are taking advantage of a profitable opportunity: an increasing high-income group of pregnant women who need to dress well. The group of professional pregnant women is one that is not only growing in terms of dress size but also in number, as more women enter professional careers and business and as the 1980s bring a small baby boom.

Big people need big clothes. Truckers, for the most part, are big people. Lots of truckers were unhappy with the way their jeans fit until Long Haul started making jeans that stretch to ease those climbs up to and down from the cab. The jeans also have extra room in the seat and thighs because truckers spend a lot of time sitting down and care more about comfort than about the snug fit of designer and conventional jeans. The makers of these trucker-inspired wonders have found just the right retail outlet for them too: the truck stop. Nowadays when a trucker stops off for a fill-up and a hot meal, he or she might also pick up a couple of pairs of jeans for the road.

Some people care a lot about fashion, on the other hand, even when it comes to the kind of underwear they choose. Several men's underwear companies have taken advantage of this preference by developing lines of chic briefs. The companies have found that most (70 percent) of men's underwear is purchased by women, and many don't mind paying extra for flashy colors or a sexy cut. Hanes, Jockey International, and Fruit of the Loom are among the brands now profiting from the consumer preference for chic briefs.

Sources: Claudia Ricci, "Now, for the Expecting Executive: Women's Suits with a Fuller Cut," *Wall Street Journal*, February 11, 1983, p. 23; Dennis Kneale, "Now, the Latest in Truck-Stop Chic: Big, Stretchy 'Long Haul' Jeans," *Wall Street Journal*, p. 35; Claudia Ricci, "Chic Briefs for Men Win More Buyers," *Wall Street Journal*, November 4, 1982, p. 33.

development department that includes several dermatologists. For Frito-Lay, the idea for soft cookies came from consumers, who identified the problems—hardness, dryness, not worth the price—that they found with existing products. Focus 11-1 describes how three clothing companies successfully developed products to meet needs they identified in the marketplace.

An essential part of the product development process is communication between company technicians (research and development) and the consumer market. If the new-product idea originates within the company, the firm must test it on consumers to find out if anyone wants the product. If the product idea originates in the market, the firm must find out from its technicians whether such a product is feasible.[3] In other words, can it be developed at a reasonable cost and can it do what it's supposed to do? Throughout product development, the company will check with both of these sources to make sure the development process remains "on track."

Step 2: Idea Screening

The second step in the new-product development process is **idea screening,** or reducing the number of new-product ideas to those that fit best with the company's objectives and that are practical, given the firm's financial, technical, and personnel resources. Screening involves clear identification of the customer benefits that the new product will provide and the specific market segment the company will aim for. For example, Frito-Lay had to determine that enough consumers wanted soft and moist cookies, that the company's strengths in packaging, production processes, and distribution channels supported the idea, and that the financial risk was acceptable to the company.

Usually, the person or department developing a product idea submits it in the form of a proposal. The company considers the practicality of the idea before beginning work on it. One element the proposal should include is an examination of how the product is expected to benefit the company. For example, the proposal might estimate the profits the company could expect and other advantages for the firm, such as involvement in a new market area. A related consideration is whether or not this product would offer the market benefits that cannot be found elsewhere. A company would probably decide against developing a new product that was offered elsewhere unless the new product could be produced simply and cheaply or potential gains were especially great.

Another important consideration in the proposal should be whether or not the company currently has the capacity to produce and market the suggested product. The company needs to consider whether its design and engineering staffs are equipped to handle the product, whether it has the equipment and facilities to produce the product, and whether the product can be marketed within the constraints of the company's resources. If the company is lacking in one of these areas, the decision makers will need to consider whether the product is worth the prospect of acquiring additional resources.

The proposal should also analyze the financial risk involved, an important consideration when deciding whether or not to adopt a new-product idea. Finally, the proposal should provide a detailed outline of the suggested product's physical characteristics.[4] (These considerations are summarized in fig. 11–2.)

The more specific the proposal is on each of these points, the easier it will be for the company to decide whether to continue consideration of this product or to abandon the project in favor of other ideas.

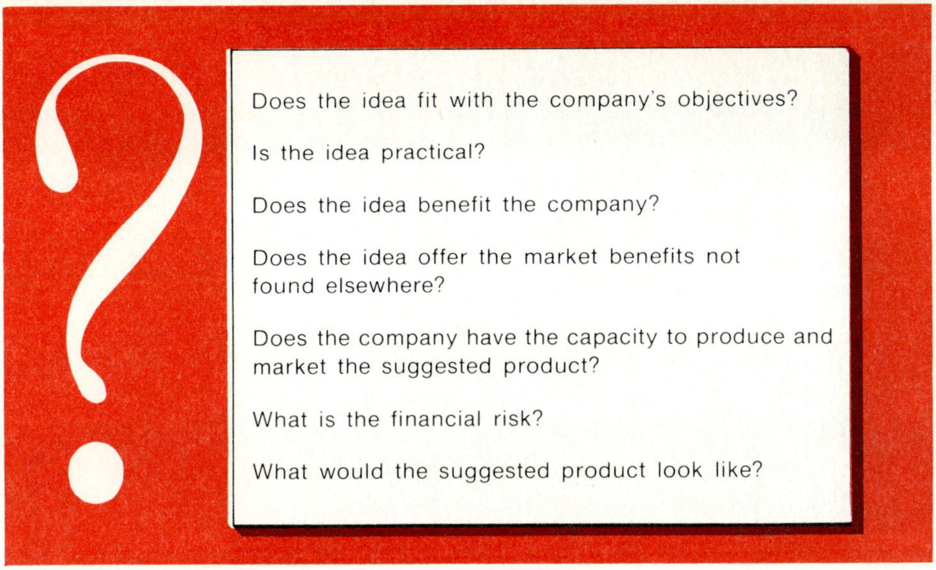

**Figure 11–2
Questions considered in idea screening**

Does the idea fit with the company's objectives?

Is the idea practical?

Does the idea benefit the company?

Does the idea offer the market benefits not found elsewhere?

Does the company have the capacity to produce and market the suggested product?

What is the financial risk?

What would the suggested product look like?

Step 3: Idea Testing

The third step in the new-product development process is **idea testing.** In the initial stages of developing a product idea, several tests are necessary to determine if the company should continue with the project. These early tests can take several forms. One type of test involves a discussion panel at which the company presents a list of the product's features, its proposed uses, and the benefits to be gained from it. A number of typical customers form the panel and are asked to consider this presentation and give their opinions on the item. Consumers are also asked to discuss whether they would be willing to buy the product. When the item is for an industrial market, testing is more difficult. Asking potential customers about the idea might result in exposure of the new-product plans to competitors.

An important part of idea testing is the development of a **prototype,** or a sample product that test groups can try. A prototype can give the test group a much clearer notion of what the product would be like than merely a description of it. The company, in turn, will receive more specific information about consumers' response. The prototype is especially important where product safety is a concern, where the product is complex, and where it has many attributes. Drug, cosmetic, and food companies are often required to test prototypes on animals before allowing consumers to try them. A maker of a "child-proof" bottle cap for medicine containers may give prototypes to several toddlers to test the item's safety.

The purpose of testing at this stage is to determine whether the idea will be accepted in its target market, whether the proposed product will actually perform the way it is supposed to, and often to identify any safety hazards. The form of the tests is determined primarily by the type of product. For a publications company's new magazine idea, a discussion panel might be most appropriate. For Frito-Lay's new tortilla chip, taste tests involving company employees might serve the com-

Published courtesy of General Mills, Inc.

Figure 11–3 A test kitchen. Two home economists in one of the Betty Crocker Kitchens are working on tolerance testing of cakes, measuring the heights of cakes baked under varying conditions.

pany's needs better. For Hershey, tests on laboratory animals may show whether a candy does cause fewer cavities.

Companies test ideas to increase the likelihood of their products' success. Thorough, detailed testing can also pay off when the company can work out problems early and develop a good product. The more thorough the testing, though, the more time it takes. The longer the research continues, the more likely it is that competitors will be prepared with their own similar products when the new product is introduced. The company must weigh the benefits of thorough testing against the benefits of rapid introduction of innovative ideas.

Step 4: Business Analysis

The fourth step in the new-product development process is the **business analysis**—a thorough examination of the company's policies and goals in relation to the proposed project. The decision of whether or not to proceed with a new-product idea will be based on business analysis. A project that risks too much for the company and has a low likelihood of a payoff will most likely be abandoned. The amount of risk involved is measured by the demands of each project. A high-risk venture would be one that required the company to purchase a great deal of new equipment to produce the new product and that would take the firm into an unfamiliar market area. A medium-risk project would be one in a familiar market that would employ some new technology. A low-risk project would involve small changes on an existing product, requiring no new equipment.

Frito-Lay's entry into the cookie market is considered a high-risk venture because it has involved acquiring new manufacturing equipment, adopting new production methods, developing new marketing strategies, and entering an unfamiliar market area. The company had to assess also whether the market was large enough and growing and whether they could capture enough market share to justify producing a new product. A less risky venture for Frito-Lay has been its development of new types of corn chips and potato chips. Here the company can employ many of the procedures and much of the technology it already uses for similar products. Of course, the degree of risk also depends on a company's financial, technological, and personnel resources.

Step 5: Product Development

The fifth step in the new-product development process is **product development.** Once the product has passed the preliminary stages of tests and analyses, the company begins work on producing it. The company's research and development (R&D) department is in charge of making the product idea a reality. Even during the product development process, though, the company evaluates R&D's progress at regular intervals to decide whether continuation of the project is worthwhile. Most important, at this stage the company makes its plans and actually finds out whether it can produce the product.

In this step, the company sets goals for the product. The company needs to define specifically how much time, money, and labor it is willing to spend on developing the new product. At the same time, the company states what returns it expects—in terms of profits from this product, increases in sales for related products, perhaps a boost in the company image, as well as any other gains that, realistically, the product could bring. The company must also set a point at which the product, if not successful, should be abandoned. In other words, the company can decide it will spend a certain amount of money and time on the product, at which point, if no progress has been made, it will not continue to develop the idea.

Another important consideration is what would happen if another company develops this product first. If the new product is complex, such as a computer or innovative medical equipment, customers may be slow to adopt it. In this case, it may actually be better to be the second entrant in a market, letting the first entrant educate customers about the product.

Research within a company is usually aimed at solving a problem. That is, the research department works with the idea of a specific type of product in mind, one that will solve a recognized consumer problem. Rarely is research within a company pure research, or the search for greater knowledge in a particular area with no specific goal in mind. As the project unfolds, company researchers keep in mind how compatible the developing product is with company goals, whether it can be produced within the financial limitations, and how much risk is involved in this solution.

Product development within a company is an ongoing process. Often employees in this area are not working on product innovations but on modifications of existing products. R&D at Frito-Lay has developed new flavors for its original line of Doritos corn chips. A car manufacturer might redesign the back seat of last year's best-selling model to provide more legroom. In most companies, product development involves working on many products at once to keep products in line with customer demands and to remain in a competitive position.

11-2 Focus on a Marketing Practice
CARNATION TESTS ITS CAT FOODS

Like most food manufacturers, Carnation Company needs groups who resemble potential consumers to taste its products before it produces them in large quantities. Based on test results, the company's research and development department adjusts the products' recipes. Taste testers of an important group of Carnation products happen to be cats.

The company is the second most successful manufacturer of pet foods and takes its fussy felines' opinions very seriously. In 1983, cat-food sales in the United States were about $1.6 billion; Carnation's total pet-food sales were about $486 million, of which 60 percent came from its cat foods. And as an increasing number of people are acquiring cats as pets, the market is growing. Carnation recognizes that the profit potential in the cat-food market is enormous.

The biggest hazard in the cat-food market is the cats themselves. Cats are picky eaters; their taste preferences change from day to day. And, if cats don't like a brand of cat food, their owners (the actual buyers) will probably buy another brand. To keep its products in line with this rather tricky market, Carnation maintains a cat-food research and development center, complete with computerized data banks, expert researchers and technicians, and lots and lots of cats. In 1983, the cats taste-tested about 250,000 cans of moist cat food and 70,000 pounds of dry cat food.

Carnation's cat-food taste tests have several purposes. First, the company wants to develop products that cats find consistently tasty. Carnation's R&D team works on maintaining a strong line of products that cats will choose as permanent favorites. At the same time, the team is working to find out what makes cats sniff and walk away from a food that they recently relished. Second, Carnation's R&D department continually develops new flavors to add to the product line and keep cats interested. Third, because cats are so taste-sensitive, the team presents existing products in which minor changes have been made (because one ingredient or another is unavailable) to the cats for approval. Finally, Carnation uses its cats to test competitors' products. If the cats prefer a competing brand, Carnation analyzes the food's contents and may make adjustments in its own recipes.

Carnation keeps 550 cats in its R&D department. The cats are allowed to play together during nonfeeding times, but they are fed in their cages to enable researchers to measure the exact amount of food they eat. This ongoing research is computerized at Carnation. Each cat has a computer number as well as a name. At feeding time, the cats receive a measured amount of a particular food. The food is weighed before and after the feeding, and the figure for the amount each cat eats is stored in the computer. Based on analyses of the Carnation cats' preferences, the company attempts to predict the kinds of flavors the nation's cats will prefer.

Source: Ken Wells, "How 500 Cats Play Guinea Pig in Pursuit of the Purrfect Food," *Wall Street Journal*, April 20, 1984, pp. 1, 13.

The sixth step in the new-product development process is **market testing.** Before the new product is introduced to the public, the company usually tries it out in limited areas. Market testing involves manufacturing the product on a relatively small scale and then measuring sales, repeat purchases, and the effectiveness of marketing strategies in order to predict profitability and market share when the product is introduced on a large scale. (Many of the procedures discussed in this chapter are the same as those discussed in chapter 5 on marketing research.)

Step 6: Market Testing

Marketers choose test markets that are as similar as possible to the national market or the total market where the product will be sold. If the test market is very different from the national one, results will not be an accurate prediction of a product's future success. One aspect of the market that should be considered is consumer demographics. Characteristics such as community members' average age, income, type of employment, as well as the area's climate and population, are important considerations.

Companies also need to take into account the conditions of the market. Often, when a product is being market tested, it is the only one of its kind available. By the time the results are in, however, other companies have seen the product and perhaps have imitated it. They may also offer discounts on similar products to try to dull the impact of the new product. So marketers need to view their products' success with caution, especially if there is relatively little direct competition during the market test.

Even when marketers are careful about choosing test market areas, results are not completely reliable predictors of a product's success. If the test predicts product failure, then the company will almost certainly drop it. Even when the test predicts product success, there is still only about a 50 percent chance the product will succeed in the national market.[5] Factors that can interfere with the test's predictability include the fact that marketers may have paid extra attention to the new product while it was being tested. In the actual market, special treatment of the product will be impossible, causing sales to be lower under natural market conditions. The time lag between the test and the product's introduction may also be a factor. Unpredictable events, such as changes in consumer attitudes, the entry of another competitor, or the emergence of new fads, can also affect response to a product.

Methods of market testing. A company can choose from several methods of measuring a product's success in the test market. One is to use a store audit, or simply record the product's sales in particular stores in the test area. Store audits will give marketers information about volume sales of the product and its market share. Marketers might want to conduct discussion panels. By questioning consumers over a period of weeks or months, marketers can learn about consumers' awareness of the product, repeat purchasing patterns, and brand switching. Sometimes marketers will also conduct telephone surveys to determine the effectiveness of the marketing strategy. Interviewers can find out how and where consumers learned about the product, what they like and dislike about it, how often they use it, and other details about responses to the product.

Time and cost of market testing are two factors that marketers must weigh against its potential benefits. Tests that take a long time to complete and analyze—perhaps up to a year—give competitors ample time to react with moves of their own. On the other hand, tests conducted too hastily may not have sufficient depth to be useful. Thorough testing is also expensive. Costs include manufacturing expenses (and perhaps the acquisition of new machinery and factory space to do so), advertising and promotional expenses, distribution, and the cost of collecting and analyzing the data. Considering the fact that many projects will be abandoned when the results are in, these expenses seem very great indeed. But the costs of actually introducing the new product will be far greater, so marketers see the testing stage as a very necessary one.

One of the benefits companies may gain from these costs is the ability to modify marketing strategies or even the product itself. Market testing pulls together all the plans for a product and enables marketers to evaluate how effectively they work together. This is the final opportunity to alter the product or marketing plans before the national introduction. Marketers view market testing as a vital step before making that final commitment to the product in time, money, and work.

Above all, the purposes of market testing are to allow the company to decide whether or not it should introduce the product on a national basis and, if the decision to introduce the product is positive, which marketing mix strategies to use. To assist in the latter decision, marketers may use different approaches or combinations of features, such as different product packages or levels of promotion, in different test markets. The approach that proves to be most successful at the market testing stage is then used in the general introduction of the product. This allows the company not only to avoid suboptimal product introductions but also to create and use the best marketing mix strategy. Marketers' goal at the market testing stage is to gather enough information to make these decisions, while not spending more time or money than is necessary.

Step 7: Commercialization

The seventh step in the new-product development process is **commercialization**, or the launch of a new product. This occurs after all the marketing data have been analyzed, the product has been approved for large-scale introduction, and the marketers have chosen appropriate market segments to which they direct promotion and advertising. The marketing mix strategy that worked best in step six will be used by the company, although it will have to be constantly analyzed and revised to keep up with the market.

Studies by the consulting firm Booz·Allen & Hamilton conducted in 1968 and 1982 indicate that the great majority of ideas generated do not reach the stage of commercialization. The 1968 study showed that, of 58 ideas generated, only one reached commercialization; the 1982 study showed that seven new ideas were considered for each commercialized product. Booz·Allen notes that the drop in the number of ideas generated is due to companies' increased attention to the market and to potential new applications of technology and to a clearer definition

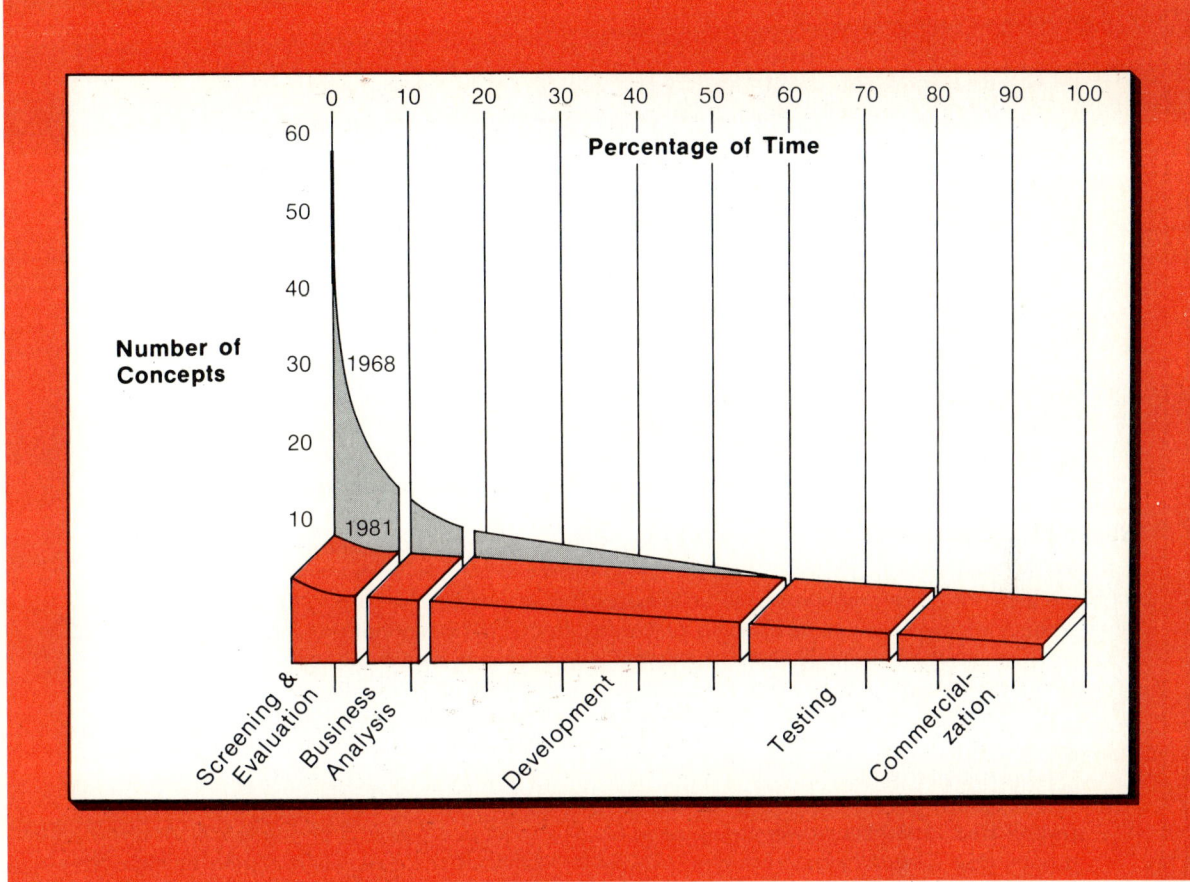

Source: Reprinted from *New Products Management for the 1980s* with permission of Booz·Allen & Hamilton Inc.

Figure 11–4
Survival of ideas through the new-product development process

and focus of ideas that are generated.[6] (The results of the studies are shown in fig. 11–4.)

Usually, companies do not introduce the product in the whole country at one time but use a **rollout**, or the gradual introduction of the new product into one area, or a few, at a time. The company selects what it feels is the best time to begin the rollout, given market conditions and improvements needed on the product. If Frito-Lay hears that Nabisco is planning to introduce a new product in three months, then the company may try to get its product out in one month. On the other hand, if Frito-Lay is confident of little competition, then it may decide to pay more careful attention to the details of its development, testing, and commercialization plans to be more sure of a success.

Focus 11–3 presents ongoing new-product development in the automobile tire industry.

Chapter 11 / Product Development and the Product Life Cycle   **309**

11–3 Focus on Marketing in Action
THE DEVELOPMENT OF NEW TIRES

The automobile tire industry has been working to develop new kinds of tires to solve old problems. Their efforts have focused on four problem areas: the need for increased tire durability; the need to reduce the risk of hydroplaning, or the tendency for tires to skid on wet surfaces; the need to increase bead retention, or to increase the likelihood that a punctured tire will remain on the wheel; and the need to reduce or eliminate the necessity for a spare tire.

Tire manufacturers are continually searching for a way to make tires last longer. Several years ago, the steel-belted radial tire was an innovation designed to do just that by reinforcing the rubber tread with steel belts. The belts increase the life of the tire, but they also contribute to one of the radial tire's major causes of failure. The belt portion of conventional radial tires is made up of a series of belts laid side by side. With continued use, the belts can become separated from one another. Armstrong Rubber Company has developed an idea for a different kind of belt using Dupont's Kevlar® Aramid fiber. By weaving the belts together instead of simply laying them side by side, Armstrong's new Tredloc® tire eliminates the problem of the belts becoming separated. Armstrong believes the new product will also reduce the chances of tire failure due to underinflation.

One of the biggest dangers associated with tires is hydroplaning, or skidding on wet surfaces when driving fast. When this happens, the tire literally loses contact with the road and is riding on a surface of water. The driver has no control over the car until it is again in contact with the road surface. The higher the speed in wet conditions, the more likely hydroplaning becomes.

A Hungarian engineer, Jerry Juhan, got the idea for how to attack this problem when several small, low-horsepower cars passed his expensive and powerful performance car on a rainy day. The difference between the controllability of the cars when driving at high speeds seemed to be the width of their tires. Small, less powerful cars have narrow tires, while more powerful cars have wider ones. The engineer reasoned that creating a way for water to escape from the center of a wide tire would reduce the chance of hydroplaning. Using two thin tires would be even better than one wide one, he thought, because the space between them would naturally draw water.

Juhan enlisted the help of an Italian company, Speedline of Padua, to create a special wheel on which to mount two tires instead of just one. Then he convinced Goodyear's research and development center in Luxembourg to create a twin-tire prototype for use at high speeds. The next step was to test the new tire on different kinds of cars. Porsches, Opels, and a Volkswagen Golf GTI were fitted with the new tire prototype. Tested in wet conditions at high speeds, the twin tires seemed to eliminate hydroplaning. The twin tires will probably be most appealing for high-performance cars, such as the Audi, Porsche, and Mercedes-Benz. Another benefit of the dual tire is that it is proving to be slower-wearing.

Many companies are working on the problem of bead retention. The bead of a tire is the edge of the inflated tire that is held by metal hoops against the rim of the wheel (see illustration 1). But when a tire is punctured while the car is moving, the air immediately escapes, and the tire can come off the wheel. The result is that the wheel suddenly crashes onto the road, perhaps causing the driver to lose control of the car. Even if the driver

Developing a new type of belt for Armstrong's Tredloc tire.
Courtesy of The Armstrong Rubber Co.

Goodyear's new twin tire.
Courtesy of The Goodyear Tire & Rubber Co.

maintains control, driving any distance on a flat tire will ruin it and the wheel. Again, tire makers are trying to develop a product that will eliminate this dangerous problem. At the same time, if they could develop a tire on which it is safe to drive even after the tire is flat (as in illustration 3), they could also eliminate the need to carry a spare.

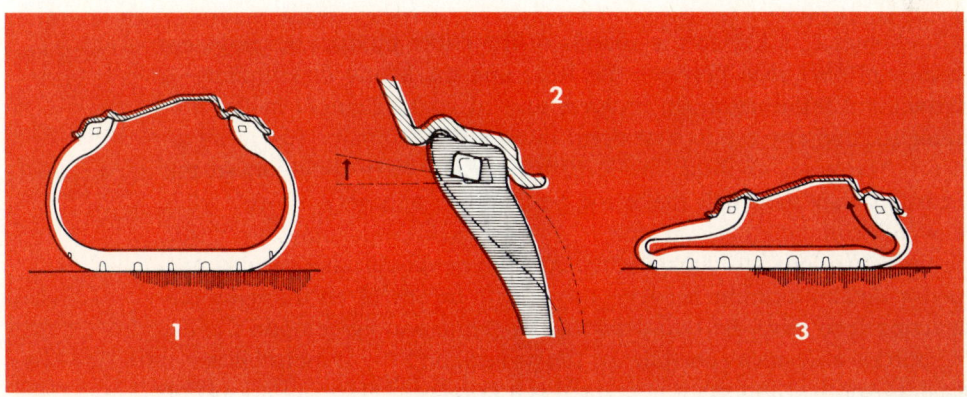

Bead retention
Reprinted from *Popular Science* with permission © 1984, Times Mirror Magazine, Inc.

(continued)

There are several different approaches to the bead-retention problem. Dunlop and Michelin's idea is to make deep grooves in the rim. When deflated, the sides of the tire collapse outward and the bead slips into the grooves to hold the flat tire onto the wheel and allow the driver to maintain control of the car. If necessary, the driver can continue driving at 40 miles per hour for 10 miles.

A German company, Continental, has a different idea. Continental wants to change the way the tire fits onto the wheel. Instead of attaching the tire to the outside of the rim, Continental proposes attaching it internally. In addition, the company has designed the sidewalls of the tire to be highly flexible so that it is less likely to pop off the wheel when the tire is deflated. The Continental Tire System, skeptics maintain, will have a great deal of trouble gaining acceptance because it requires a new kind of wheel as well as a new kind of tire.

Uniroyal's approach is to make the tire and wheel rim one piece. Bonding them together, the company feels, eliminates the danger of the tire coming off the wheel. A prototype of the new Uniroyal tire can run flat at 50 miles per hour for 50 miles.

Goodyear and Pirelli have joined forces to come up with their solution to the problem. The companies have designed an asymmetrical wheel rim with an especially high ridge to hold the bead, even after the tire deflates. The safety ridge gradually tapers off on two sides of the wheel. An advantage of this solution is that the asymmetrical wheel accommodates any kind of tire. The wheel keeps the flat tire in place at about 60 miles per hour on a straight road.

Each of these tire manufacturers is facing the same set of problems and developing unique ideas for solutions. Creating and testing prototypes are particularly important here, as there is a critical safety factor involved.

Source: Stuart Marshall, "Coming Your Way: Revolutionary New Tires," *Popular Science*, May 1984, pp. 100–2, 162–64.

Interaction between Marketing and Research and Development

As we saw in chapter 2, a key to the success of the entire product development process is continual *interaction* between the R&D and marketing departments—a constant exchange of information on progress toward goals, changes in the project's requirements, and any events that occur outside the company that could affect the project. The goals of these two departments are often different, so this interaction ensures that they will make the best of one another's efforts, while keeping the overall company goals in view.

Because these are separate departments, companies should take care to promote productive communication between them. One means of encouraging this kind of interaction is to have the two departments define and agree upon the use of allotted resources, a detailed schedule for the project, and the responsibilities of each department. Another important ingredient is a format for airing and resolving disagreements and problems.

Members of the two departments often feel there is a kind of "cultural" separation between them. This is because the type of work they do and their objectives are different in nature. These differences can be minimized if the two departments are not also physically separated. Very large companies sometimes have their various departments located in different cities. Fewer communications problems arise, however, when marketing and R&D departments have immediate access to one another. Productive interaction is also encouraged by the development of feelings of partnership, collaboration, and teamwork between the two departments.

Each product development situation is unique, so it is impossible to prescribe one system of interaction that will work for all of them. A successful new product depends on the marketing department's knowledge of market conditions and customer demands as well as the R&D department's knowledge of technological possibilities, costs, and time and labor requirements of the project. Consistent and thorough interaction between the two departments will aid in the efficient completion of the project.

The Product Life Cycle

When companies introduce new products, they do so with the knowledge that no product sells forever. Every product has a life cycle. The **product life cycle** (PLC) consists of four stages: introduction, growth, maturity, and decline. Each stage is characterized by a certain pattern of expenditures, distribution, prices, sales, growth, profits, and advertising and promotional strategies. Sales, for example, follow a pattern that goes from none at all, at the earliest part of the introduction stage, through a high point, and then back down to a low point, during the product's decline (see fig. 11–5). While the progression of a product through these

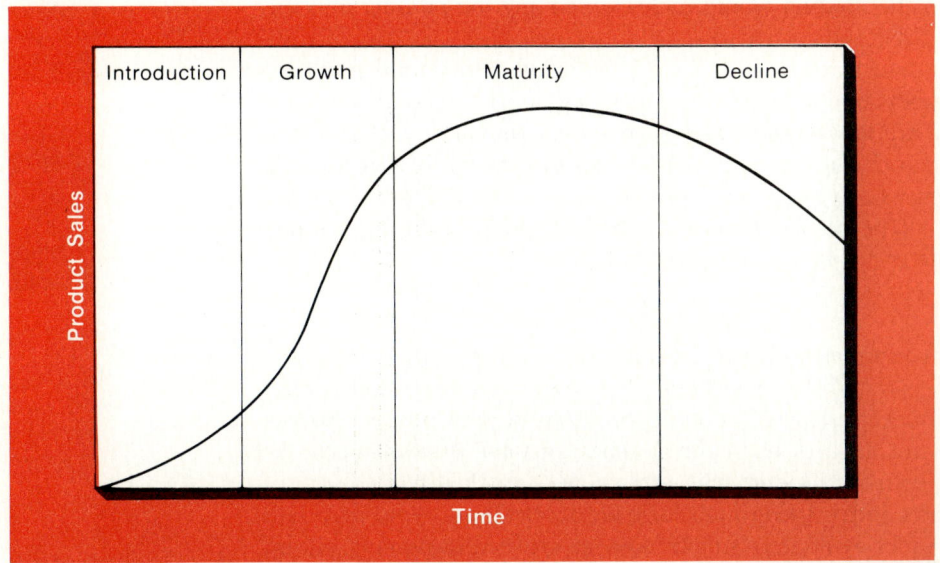

Figure 11–5 Sales throughout the product life cycle

stages is predictable, what is unknown is the length of time that each stage will take. Different types of products take different amounts of time to pass through these stages.

Individual product brands follow a life cycle, as do product forms and product classes. A **product class** includes any number of brands and forms of a product to satisfy one kind of a consumer need. The typewriter is an example of a product class. Examples of **product forms** include the manual typewriter, the electric typewriter, and the electronic memory typewriter. Examples of the combined product forms and brands would include the Hermes 2000, the IBM Selectric, and the Olivetti Praxis 35. A form or a brand might have a relatively short life cycle of, say, five or ten years, while the product class might live longer than the people who started it. For the most part, the discussion that follows will focus on brands within a product class.

Stage 1: Introduction

The **introduction stage** of the PLC begins as the new product first becomes available for sale. As we have discussed, national distribution takes time to achieve. At first, distribution will cover only a few areas. One reason for this is that during the introductory phase, most consumers are unaware of the product, as are retail stores, so demand for the product is very low. For this reason advertising and promotion in the introduction stage are quite heavy and are designed to develop consumer awareness of the product. Figure 11–6 shows an advertisement for Nabisco's Almost Home cookies, designed to build awareness. Since awareness is at a zero point at the beginning of this stage, the process could be a lengthy one.

In the introductory stage, the company has few competitors in this product category, particularly if the product is a unique one. If a competitor should introduce a similar product during this phase, the introduction would be shortened. Consumer awareness of the product would increase, sending the product into the next phase.

Expenses for the product are high during introduction. The company is still working out the best production system and is spending large sums on promotion and advertising. Profits are low or nonexistent, and the company may even lose money in its effort to launch this product. Sales begin to pick up toward the end of this stage. Customers who buy the new product in the introductory stage are known as **innovators.** (The percentages of adopters of products in the various stages of the product life cycle are shown in fig. 11–7.)

Stage 2: Growth

In the **growth stage**, consumer awareness has increased a great deal, and distribution has brought the product to most areas. By now the product has several competitors, so advertising stresses its merits in comparison with others. Product development, at this point, focuses on slight modifications and improvements, as all the major problems with the product have already been worked out.

Most important, sales during the growth stage are accelerating. Word of mouth helps to increase consumer awareness still further, as satisfied customers inform

Figure 11–6
Nabisco is building awareness of its Almost Home cookies through an extensive advertising campaign promoting its product's benefits.
Copyright Nabisco Brands, Inc.

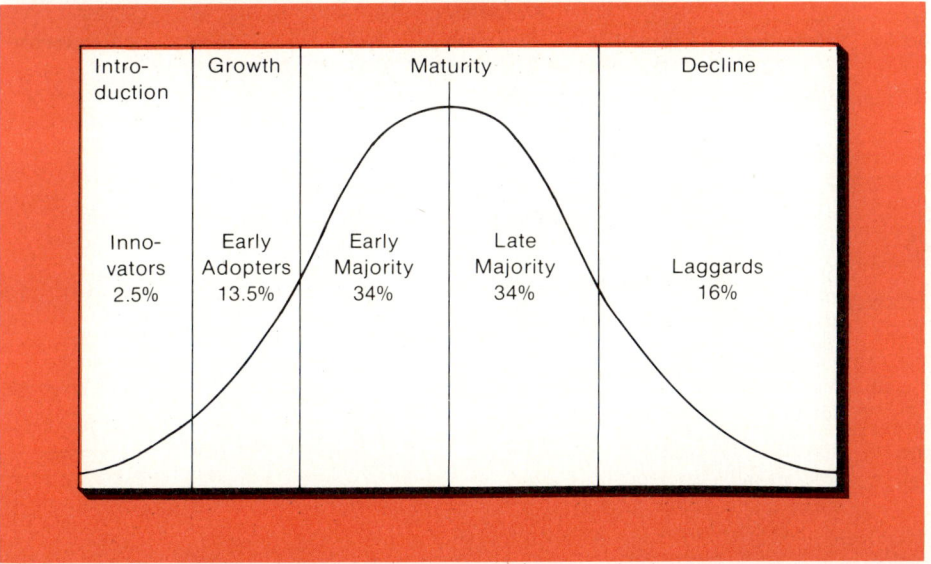

**Figure 11–7
Percentages of adopters through the product life cycle**

Source: Adapted from Everett M. Rogers, *Diffusion of Innovations* (New York: Free Press, 1962), p. 162. Copyright © 1962 by The Free Press of Glencoe.

others of the product's benefits. Customers who adopt the product during this phase are known as **early adopters.**

Because most of the product's problems are resolved, the advertising blitz of the introduction phase has been relaxed, and sales are increasing, the company is beginning to see profits. Production costs are also lower because the manufacturing process has been refined to increase efficiency and to reduce expenses. The company is now starting to see returns on its investments. In fact, the company will see its greatest profitability during the latter part of this stage.

Stage 3: Maturity

The **maturity stage** of the PLC is characterized by intense competition, as many companies now have products entered in this market. Advertising stresses the unique features of this product and attempts to differentiate it from similar ones.

Most consumers are now aware of the product. Demand will reach its highest point during this stage, as almost every customer who is going to use the product will do so before the end of the maturity phase. Costs for the company are now at their lowest point. The price may be driven down by competitive pressure. Product development might now come up with some new versions of the product—new flavors, sizes, or uses.

Customers who adopt the product during this stage are known as the **early majority** (if they adopt during the first half of this stage) or the **late majority** (if they adopt during the latter half).

Table 11–1 Characteristics of the Stages of the Product Life Cycle

Stage of the Product Life Cycle	Distribution	Promotion	Competition	Production Expenses	Profits	Sales	Consumers
Introduction	Limited	Heavy; designed to build awareness	Few, if any, competitors	High	Low or nonexistent	Low	Innovators
Growth	Almost throughout target market area	Heavy; stresses comparative merit	Several competitors	Lower, through increased efficiency	Growing; eventually greatest profitability	Growing rapidly	Early adopters
Maturity	Throughout target market area	Stresses product differentiation	Intense competition	At lowest level	Begin to drop	At highest point	Early majority; late majority
Decline	Decreases	Reminds consumers about product	Heavy competition, often from new products	Rising	Dropping	Dropping	Laggards

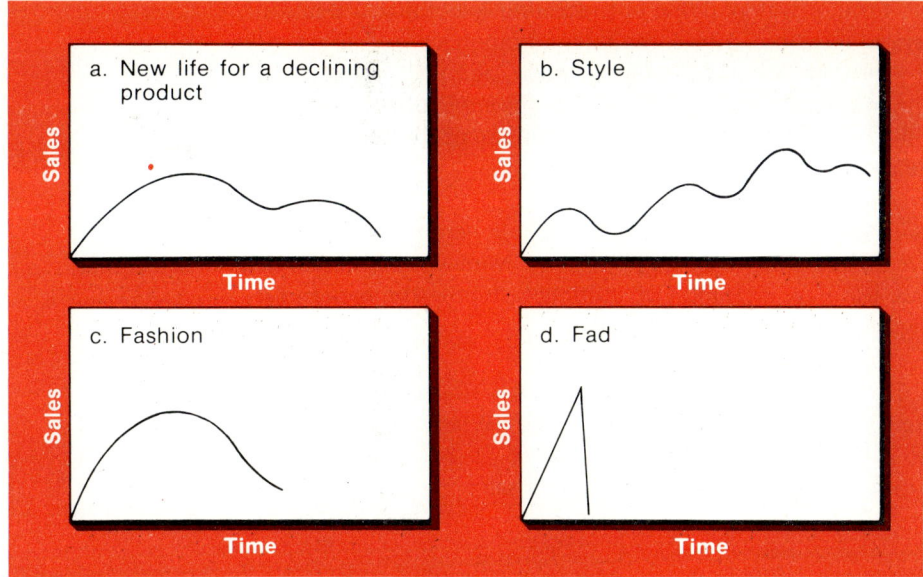

Figure 11–8
Variations in the standard product life cycle

The **decline stage** is the final stage for the product. Consumer demand decreases during this phase because of changes in market conditions, the introduction of other products, and changes in consumer demands. Distribution of the product also decreases, as some retail outlets drop the product. Customers who adopt the product during this phase are known as **laggards.** A product can retain a loyal group of consumers who continue to buy it, but eventually, if profits drop low enough, the company will stop producing it.

The characteristics of the stages in the product life cycle are summarized in table 11–1.

Stage 4: Decline

The product life cycle just described is a typical pattern for most products. There are, however, a few standard variations in the pattern as when a company gives a declining product new life or with a style, fashion, or fad.

Variations in the Product Life Cycle

New life for a declining product. When a product is in its decline stage, companies can take steps to increase sales. One step is a strong promotional push. Another is the repositioning of the product to attract new users or to sell in new markets. Johnson's Baby Shampoo, for example, was successfully repositioned as a product for adults, even male athletes, who wash their hair every day. A third step is to modify products or add characteristics that attract new customers. The pattern for this variation is shown in figure 11–8a.

Chapter 11 / Product Development and the Product Life Cycle

Style. A **style** is a form or way of doing or presenting something. There can be styles of clothing, design, literature, music, thought, automobiles, and so on. At various times, different styles are prevalent; they can then fade and return many times. This pattern is shown in figure 11–8b. Convertible automobiles, for example, were quite popular in the 1950s and 1960s, but not popular in the 1970s. Now some automobile manufacturers are reintroducing convertibles.

Fashion. A fashion is a short-lived style. A fashionable item becomes popular for one or several years and then loses its popularity. Miniskirts, Eisenhower jackets, and patched blue jeans are examples of clothing fashions. The pattern for a fashion is shown in figure 11–8c.

Fad. A **fad** is more intense and shorter-lived than a fashion. Suddenly everyone is wearing stickers, playing video games, or asking "Where's the beef?"—and then no one is. The pattern for a fad is shown in figure 11–8d; it is characterized by a meteoric rise in sales and an equally fast drop in sales.

Marketing Strategy in the Product Life Cycle

Marketers often compare the life cycle of the product to that of a living organism. Though this is a convenient concept in many respects, it also has its drawbacks. The decline stage and eventual death of the product are not necessarily inevitable. Some products have outlasted the people who originated them. Others have been saved through clever marketing strategies.

When demand for a product seems to be declining, companies have several choices. First, as we have mentioned, they can stop producing it. This decision is most appropriate when a new technology has rendered an existing product obsolete. Recently, typewriter manufacturers stopped making manual typewriters because the demand for electric models is so great that making manual ones is no longer profitable.

The second option is to promote additional uses for the product in order to boost sales. The makers of Arm & Hammer Baking Soda increased sales by showing in advertisements that the product could absorb cat litter box and refrigerator odors.[7] Procter & Gamble did the same for Ivory Soap by promoting it for adult uses, instead of as a product just for babies.[8] Fast-food chains have recently been beckoning customers tired of hamburgers with additional offerings—breakfast, dinner, and a more varied menu.[9] Hosiery manufacturer Hanes revitalized its sales of women's stockings by offering L'eggs panty hose in supermarkets and drugstores.[10] The new type of retail outlet for the product made it a convenience product, rather than a shopping good, and encouraged impulse buying. Michelob beer has been promoted as a beer for special occasions and weekends with the slogan "Weekends were made for Michelob," because of its slightly higher price. Marketers later encouraged everyday purchase of the beer, promoting the idea that Michelob could make even a weekday special with the slogan "Put a little weekend in your week."

These examples of life extension for products show that the concept of PLC is not a rigid one or one over which marketers have no control. When a product seems to be reaching a plateau in sales, that may be just the time to introduce innovative strategies to promote the product more vigorously. Although new-product development is vital to the company's competitive survival, existing products are equally important. New-product development is costly and takes a good deal of time, effort, skill, and often luck. Existing products that have shown strong performance in the past should not be abandoned too readily at times when they seem to be failing. Often it is more advantageous for a company to breathe new life into an existing product with an established name and reputation rather than conceive something entirely new. Usually, though, companies need to do both: Support existing products with careful attention to sales, growth, competitive actions, need for improvement, and promotional efforts; and, at the same time, create promising new products with innovative research and development methods.

Summary

Companies develop new products to meet new customer needs, to counter competitors' moves, and to take advantage of technological advancements.

Many ideas must be generated before the company finds one that will lead to a successful product. Product ideas come from two kinds of sources: technological developments and consumer demands.

Screening is reducing the number of new-product ideas to those that fit best with the company's objectives and that are practical, given the firm's financial, technical, and personnel resources. Idea proposals should include an examination of the ways the company will benefit from the project, whether or not the product is offered elsewhere, whether or not the company has the means to produce it, and the product's physical characteristics.

Idea testing can use consumer discussion panels or a prototype (sample product) to get consumer reactions to the idea. Idea testing is for measuring the product's acceptability, whether it works the way it should, and to identify potential safety hazards.

A business analysis is a thorough examination of the company's policies and goals in relation to the proposed product.

Even during product development, the company evaluates R&D's progress at regular intervals to decide whether continuation of the project will be worthwhile. Research within a company is usually aimed at solving a problem, rather than being pure research. Product development is usually an ongoing process.

Market testing involves manufacturing the product on a small scale and measuring consumer response to it in a few carefully selected regions. Market test areas should be as similar as possible to the national market or to the total market where the product will be sold.

Throughout the product development process a continual interface between the R&D and marketing departments is essential.

The product life cycle consists of four stages: introduction, growth, maturity, and decline. Introduction is characterized by low sales, profits, and consumer awareness of the product, as well as high expenditures for the company in advertising and promotion and a high price for consumers. The growth stage is characterized by accelerating sales and profits and dropping expenses for the company. During the maturity stage, demand and profits peak. The decline stage is the gradual drop in sales, profits, and distribution of the product, leading to its removal from the market.

There are many ways to control the product's life cycle. Companies need to concentrate on keeping successful existing products alive as well as developing new ones.

Questions for Discussion

1. Discuss the importance of developing new products, especially in the background of today's market conditions.
2. Identify and explain in your own two examples each of the sources providing impetus for the generation of new product ideas.
3. What are the criteria employed by companies in screening new product ideas?
4. Compare the objective and nature of testing in the idea testing and market testing stages of the product development process.
5. "Market testing presents promise as well as problems for the marketer." Comment.
6. Examine the nature of conflict that generally exists between the research and development and the marketing departments in a company.
7. Discuss the product life cycle concept and its important marketing implications.
8. Identify and explain under which particular stage of the product life cycle the following products and services fall: (a) rock music; (b) home computers; (c) a home movie project; (d) Softsoap; and (e) higher education.
9. How would you differentiate the marketing implications of style, fashion, and fad?

References

1. Janet Guyon, "Fixing a Snack," *Wall Street Journal,* March 25, 1983, p. 1; Betsy Morris, "Some Food Companies Bet on Bolder Research That Goes Well Beyond Tinkering with Recipes," *Wall Street Journal,* August 11, 1983, p. 44; Pamela Hollie, "Marketing Foods with Lower Salt," *New York Times,* April 9, 1983, pp. 29, 31; "Nabisco: Diversifying Again, but This Time Wholeheartedly," *Business Week,* October 20, 1980, pp. 74, 76; and Ann M. Morrison, "Cookies Are Frito-Lay's New Bag," *Forbes,* August 9, 1982, pp. 64–68.
2. Eric Von Hippel, "Successful Industrial Products from Customer Ideas," *Journal of Marketing,* January 1978, pp.39–49.
3. "Lauder's Success Formula: Instinct, Timing, and Research," *Business Week,* September 26, 1983, pp. 122, 124.

4. Edgar A. Pessemier, *Product Management: Strategy & Organization*, 2nd ed. (New York: Wiley, 1982), p. 4.
5. Yoram J. Wind, *Product Policy: Concepts, Methods, and Strategy*, (Reading, Mass.: Addison-Wesley, 1981), p. 403.
6. *New Products Management for the 1980s* (New York: Booz·Allen & Hamilton, 1982).
7. "Ten Ways to Restore Vitality to Old, Worn-Out Products," *Wall Street Journal*, February 18, 1982, p. 31.
8. Ibid.; see also Morrison, "Cookies Are Frito-Lay's New Bag."
9. Ibid., *Wall Street Journal*.
10. Ibid.

OBJECTIVES

1. To discuss the definition and meanings of price.

2. To identify the different objectives of pricing and the appropriate situations for each.

3. To identify five methods of pricing and discuss their advantages and disadvantages.

4. To describe how the choice of pricing method is influenced by the pricing objective.

5. To examine specific pricing myths in regard to the pricing objectives and the methods of achieving those objectives.

12

Pricing Objectives and Methods

The days when location alone determined which hotels and motels attracted guests are long gone. With the construction of many new lodging facilities in the last decade, competition has intensified to a new pitch.

To a greater extent than in most industries, the rate structure, or pricing, of hotels and motels is directly related to the benefits and services they provide. Motels that provide a mattress, clean sheets, and a functional bathroom charge the lowest prices. Middle-priced hotels might provide additional services, such as color television sets in every room and a comfortable dining room. Luxury hotels provide a stately or fashionable or classic ambiance, as well as such services as meeting facilities for business travelers, a free bottle of champagne on check-in, and a range of bars, cafés, and well-furbished restaurants.

Recognizing this, several national hotel chains with established market niches are aggressively striving to maintain their current status while expanding into new markets. In a number of cases, one hotel company now owns several groups of hotels, differentiated by the services they offer. For example, those that offer more services command a higher rate structure. The thrust of competition is especially keen in the deluxe hotel and budget motel segments of the market.

At one end of the market in the lodging industry are the high-priced luxury hotels. Partly due to the efforts of independent entrepreneurs, many deluxe hotels opened in the early 1980s aimed at the uppermost segment of the lodging market and offering an array of specialized services. The result has been a growing oversupply of high-priced hotel space that has sparked fierce competition throughout the United States. Newly built hotel rooms that were expected to bring more than $110 per night are being rented at half that rate in some areas.

At the same time, established hotel chains continue to move into the deluxe hotel market. Toronto-based Four Seasons Hotels has moved into the United States and has built ten top-quality hotels. Holiday Inns, Inc., has opened several Crowne Plaza Hotels and has plans for more. Ramada has launched a new chain called Ramada Renaissance Hotels. In addition, the Hyatt Hotels Corporation, which became a leader in the upscale hotel market in the 1970s, is trying to attract a clientele in the price range a cut below its traditional market—the upper-middle sector of the market—in addition to its upper-class clientele.

Cecil B. Day, an Atlanta real-estate developer, decided to enter the motel industry in the 1960s. The question was: Where to enter? Which market segment was stable or growing and not adequately served? The choice was among the luxury market, either business or resort, the middle market, and the economy market.

Day decided to pursue the economy market. This was accomplished initially in the form of six southeastern Days Inns by 1972; by 1983, there were over 300 Days Inns. Most of this growth was centered in Florida to attract family travelers visiting Walt Disney World and vacationers.

A critical question facing Days Inns was the price to charge for a room. If rooms were priced too high, the motels might not attract the targeted customers. If rooms were priced too low, it would not be possible to recover costs or make a profit.

Days Inns had been able to keep their costs low by using standard designs and by not having costly space devoted to large lobbies, meeting rooms, and fancy restaurants. Even so, the typical costs for the land and construction were up to $35,000 per room. The price which would eventually recover that cost obviously depended on the demand for the room. Complicating the picture was the surge in the number of competitive hotels.

Days Inns decided to charge an average room rate of $29.75, which is slightly higher than that of most of its competitors. Now Days Inns seeks to expand to a national level. And the economy motel market is facing new competition from Holiday Inns, which launched an economy chain in 1984. As the industry capacity expands or the travel market changes, Days Inns must be prepared to alter its prices.[1]

The pricing methods and strategies used by hotels (and by other companies) are directly related to overall marketing strategy. In this chapter, we are going to explore what companies want to achieve through their pricing strategies and the basic methods they use to set prices in relation to their goals and marketing plans.

Definition and Nature of Price

The second part of the marketing mix, the **price** is the amount that is paid to purchase a product. It is also the means through which the company recovers its costs and makes a profit. Pricing is the marketing variable that offers the most flexibility. Whereas the product, the distribution network, and even advertising decisions are relatively difficult to change over the short term, in most cases price can be altered more frequently. As examples, consider prices that change daily—the prices of stocks, of gold, of raw materials, and many food products. Price dictates what the company selling the product will receive in return for its efforts.

Price defines the value of a product or service to the customer: How much the customer is willing to give in order to have a particular product indicates how much that item is worth to the customer. When viewed from a broader perspective, price serves as an important guide to the value that society places on individual products and services.

Price has different meanings for different people. There is no single definition of price, and a number of myths pertaining to price exist. One of these myths is that a product is a "bargain" because it carries a low price tag or that another product is overpriced because it is expensive to buy.[2] It must be remembered, however, that a low price for some items and a very high price on others may represent the price that attracts a sufficient number of buyers so that the seller has incentive to provide it. The price is where the value of a product to the customer and the company's compensation for producing the product intersect. Price changes, then, provide indicators of changes in resource allocation by both consumers and producers.

This chapter will discuss other specific pricing myths in relation to pricing objectives and methods of achieving those objectives.

Pricing Objectives

Companies have objectives they are trying to achieve as they set prices for products. There are seven alternative pricing objectives that can be used (see fig. 12–1), and the objective chosen affects the price that is set. Defining pricing objectives for a product often involves choosing between short-run profits versus targeted levels of sales and market share that may enhance long-term profits. This section will describe specific pricing objectives. In its pricing strategy for a product, a company

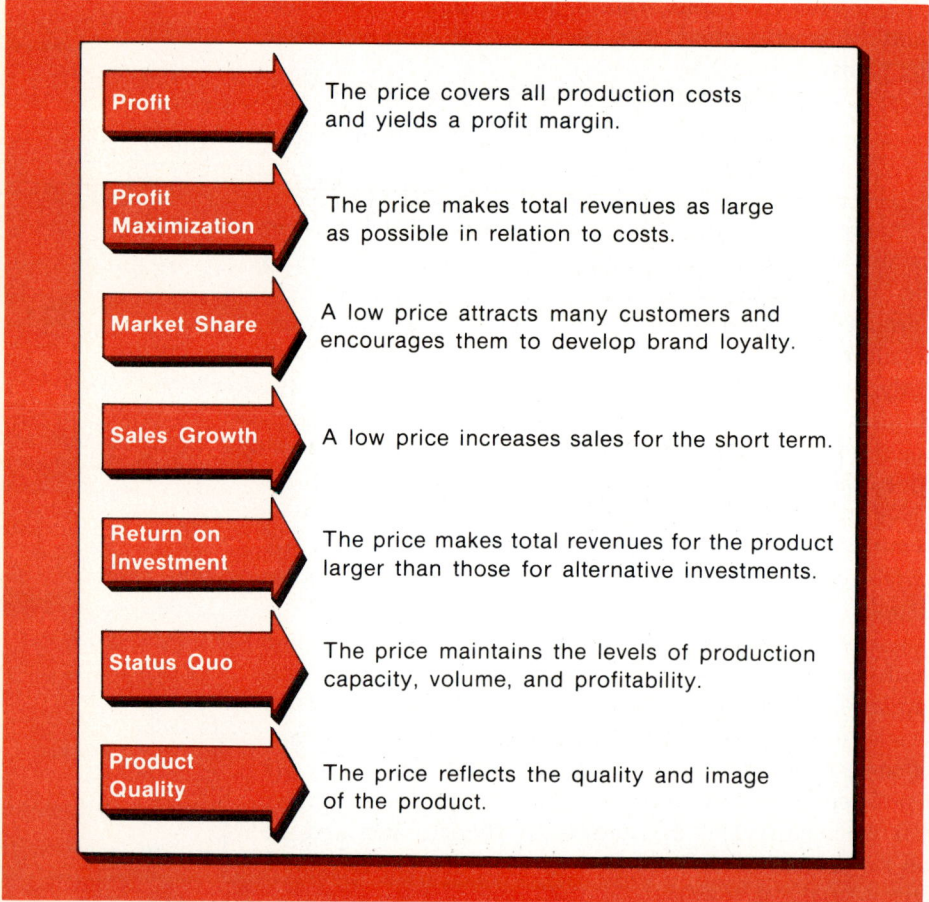

Figure 12–1 Pricing objectives

may have more than one objective at a time. Also, the dominant pricing objective for a particular product often changes as the product moves through its life cycle. (The product life cycle—introduction, growth, maturity, and decline—was discussed in chapter 11.)

Profit

Most companies have the objective of **making a profit** when they set prices. This involves determining the level at which the price will cover all production costs and also yield a profit margin. The profit objective is often set in the mature stages of a product's life cycle, when, having recovered development costs of the product, the company seeks to make money on it.

Profit Maximization

Profit maximization is another pricing objective often seen in the mature stages of a product's life cycle. When profit maximization is the pricing objective, the company sets prices that make total revenues as large as possible in relation to costs, in order to achieve for the firm the greatest overall profit on the item at that particular time for the short term.

There is a pricing myth that a company can always raise the price of a product in order to make a larger overall profit. In reality, it is possible that higher prices will yield lower overall revenues. If the increase in price causes the level of sales to decrease significantly, the company's profits are likely to decrease. The change in sales that results from a higher price is referred to as the **price sensitivity** of the market for a given product. This concept will be further examined in the section of this chapter on demand-oriented pricing. A number of the new deluxe hotels offering specialized services are finding the uppermost market segment to be more price-sensitive than expected and are thus realizing far lower revenues than anticipated.

Market Share

Obtaining market share is an alternative pricing objective, often found in the early stages of a product life cycle, as the company attempts to attract customers for the new product and keep them for the long term. Initial low prices may attract many customers, encouraging them to develop brand loyalty. When obtaining market share is the pricing objective, the company's intent is to make it difficult for other sellers to compete for a particular market, often by setting relatively low prices initially, in order to maximize profits over the long term.

As an example, the Gillette Company, which controlled about 60 percent of the U.S. razor and blade market in the 1970s, fearing that its share of the market might be eroded when the Bic Company introduced an inexpensive, disposable razor, rushed to bring out its own disposable razor, called Good News. Although the Good News razors, introduced at a retail price of 25 cents, were priced much lower than Gillette's other razors and were more expensive to produce, thus yielding a much smaller profit margin, Gillette's management felt it important to face directly the competition from Bic. As a result of this market share objective pursued by Gillette, Bic spent approximately $25 million between 1977 and 1980 on advertising to attain the 9 percent share of the market that Bic held; in 1980, Bic was reported to be losing money on its razor.[3]

When a company is threatened by a decreased market share, price is frequently used to remedy the problem. The pricing policies of airlines can be used to demonstrate this. In 1983, for example, United Airlines added 27 daily flights to its scheduled arrivals and departures at the San Francisco airport. The move triggered a reaction from other airlines; AirCal and Pacific Southwest Airlines increased their number of flights and slashed prices up to 50 percent, especially on the Los Angeles–San Francisco corridor, the nation's biggest airline market, to maintain their market shares.[4]

In attempting to gain market share, a company may set prices for a given time period so low that production costs are not even covered. Companies sometimes take this action in the belief that costs will be recovered over the life cycle of the product or service, thus trading short-term profits for market share and anticipated long-term profits. This strategy may reduce the number of competitors over the long run, thereby lowering marketing costs. (This strategy may run afoul of antitrust laws, though.) Distribution costs or advertising costs, for example, may be lower than they would be in a more competitive market. Without competition from Gillette, the costs of marketing the Bic disposable razor would have been much lower. Moreover, it is possible that producing a higher number of units will result in economies in production, enabling the seller to decrease costs rather than raise prices to customers. In the case of airlines, such as Peoples Express or AirCal, that lower prices to achieve greater market share, thus enabling the company's planes to fly with fuller loads, the long-term result might be lower costs and a lower rate structure.

Sometimes an early low price can backfire on a company. Coca-Cola Company found this strategy unsuccessful in selling wine. Entering the wine industry in 1977 with Wine Spectrum, Coca-Cola introduced its low-priced Vivante line in the summer of 1983, to compete in the economy wines market. Shortly afterward, it dropped the price of Vivante wine, using coupon and rebate promotions. (For further discussion of promotion techniques, see chapter 15.) During the same period, the profits in the wine business disappeared, and with a lesser return than expected, Coca-Cola sold its wine properties.[5]

Sales Growth

Sales growth may be a company's pricing objective. This approach gives little consideration to the competition, profit making, or the marketing environment, as long as sales are increasing. This is a short-term objective, often employed by companies with an excess inventory to sell off. If, for example, the oil industry has excess capacity, it may simply lower prices for a time.

Other examples of a sales growth objective include after-Christmas or seasonal department store sales and clearance sales on products when new models are introduced. At other times, buyers receive cash rebates from sellers, which provide a means of maintaining list prices while increasing sales at a lower price.

Figure 12–2
Companies with the objective of sales growth may conduct sales.

Teri Leigh Stratford

Maximizing a company's **return on investment (ROI)** is another pricing objective. It is not all that distinct from maximizing the profit on a particular product. This is a long-term strategy, used especially by financially-oriented managers and geared toward examining the use of money invested in a product. As discussed earlier, a profit maximization objective requires examining the revenues earned by a product in relation to the total cost of making those revenues—including capital, advertising, production facilities, and so on. To carry out an ROI objective, however, involves comparing the use of money to make the profit on a product, on the one hand, with alternative uses of that money, on the other. To justify selling a product, the product's total revenues must provide a bigger return on investment than could be realized from alternative investment opportunities. Prices are then set to reflect this objective.

An ROI objective is often an important part of new-product planning. By analyzing potential ROI from a proposed product, companies can respond flexibly and quickly to take advantage of fast-moving opportunities and continually revise their plans to work on the most attractive long-term opportunities. Once the purpose of the proposed new product is defined, the company can assign numerical values to the factors involved and thus measure the expected return on the product against its ROI objectives. This can give management a clearer idea about the effectiveness of new-product programs.[6]

ROI pricing objectives are applied to a broad spectrum of pricing decisions. A company considering the purchase of new equipment to produce a product might,

Return on Investment (ROI)

for example, ask: Will the increased efficiency and cost savings from the use of the equipment be great enough to justify diverting the money from alternative uses? Companies continually make decisions with such questions in mind.

Status Quo

Maintaining the status quo is another pricing objective; it involves adjusting the price to fit with the flow of the marketplace and with actions taken by competitors. The intent of this objective is to maintain the level of production capacity, the level of volume, and the level of profitability that existed in the past. This is clearly a "safe" strategy and is used for products in the mature stages of the product life cycle.

Product Quality

Another pricing objective is tied to **reflecting product quality.** First, this objective involves setting the price of a product or service commensurate with the quality of the product or service that the seller wishes to offer. If, for example, an extremely high-quality product, which will be costly to produce, is produced, then the price will have to be high enough to enable the use of high-quality materials and production. If, on the other hand, a company wishes to produce a relatively low-quality product, with relatively low production costs, then the price charged for the product will probably be lower as well.

The second aspect of product quality as a pricing objective relates to the image of a product that is sometimes created by the price itself. In some cases, when customers have few ways of determining quality for themselves, the price serves as an indicator to them. This is one of the main pricing objectives in the hotel industry. Customers' perceptions of product quality will be discussed further in the section of this chapter on customer-oriented pricing.

Methods of Setting Prices

Having looked at pricing objectives, we now turn to a discussion of the four methods used to achieve them. These are the cost-oriented, the competition-oriented, the demand-oriented, and the customer-oriented methods (see fig. 12–3).

Cost-Oriented Method

The **cost-oriented method** of pricing is closely associated with the profit objective, as well as the product quality objective, which were described in the previous section. Using this method, a company establishes a standard **profit margin.** After the company figures the cost of producing a given item, it determines the price to charge for that item by adding the standard profit margin to the costs of production. This method is demonstrated in figure 12–4.

How are costs determined? Two basic kinds of costs must be considered. The first are **fixed costs,** often called overhead costs, that include all expenses that are incurred regardless of how many units of a product are produced. Examples of

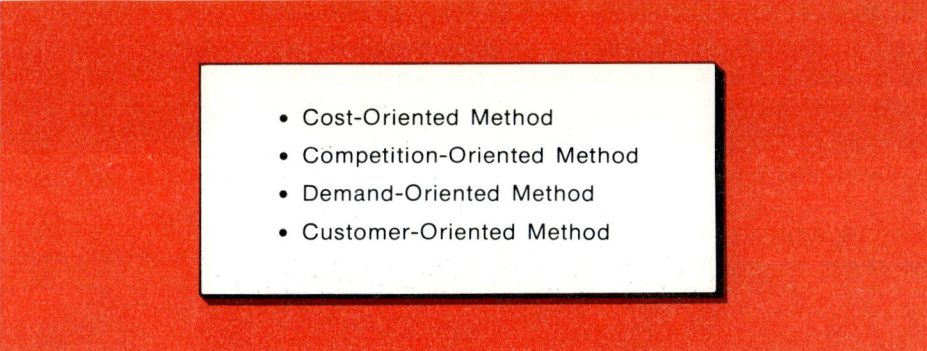

Figure 12–3 The four pricing methods

fixed costs are the cost of real estate for a production facility and the costs of employee salaries. The other is **variable costs,** the expense that increases directly with each additional unit that is produced, such as raw materials used to make a product. The total costs of production are the sum of fixed costs and variable costs.

Suppose, for example, a company that produces hi-fi's can produce a certain model at a variable cost of $400 for each hi-fi. If the company's standard policy is to **mark up** all items it sells by 25 percent of the cost of producing the item—that is, the variable cost—then the hi-fi with production costs of $400 would be priced at $500. If the variable cost of making a set of speakers is $100, then the company would sell that set of speakers for $125. Headphones that cost the company $20 to make would sell for $25. The company thus makes a profit of 25 percent of vari-

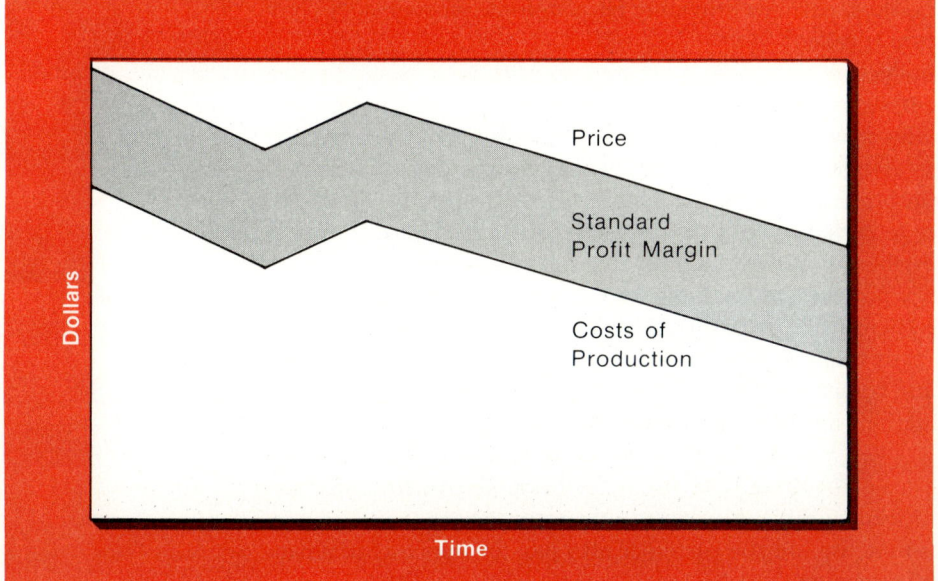

Figure 12–4 The cost-oriented method

Chapter 12 / Pricing Objectives and Methods

able costs—$100 profit on the hi-fi, $25 profit on the set of speakers, and $5 profit on the headphones. It is hoped that the volume sold will be great enough to more than cover the fixed costs as well, but what is ensured is that the variable costs of each item are covered. (The arithmetic of markups and markdowns is discussed further in appendix A.)

One version of this pricing method was developed at General Motors during the 1920s. While the GM pricing policy considered volume fluctuations through the business cycle and the cost of capital involved in running the business, prices to meet profit targets were based completely on internal company costs, rather than on the market.[7]

Advantages of cost-oriented pricing. The main advantage of cost-oriented pricing is that it provides a relatively clear-cut decision rule for setting prices. Moreover, when this method is strictly applied, it virtually guarantees that the company will make a profit on each item it sells.

This was a traditional pricing policy in the United States for many years. Companies such as General Motors would set prices they believed would provide a desired long-run profit at a given production volume. The intention was to achieve and maintain a pricing structure designed to change gradually and predictably, with a very few price changes made only to meet competition or to respond to other changing market conditions. Pricing decisions, as well as other marketing decisions, were tied to long-run aims.

Cost-oriented pricing also enables a company to take maximum advantage of its cost structure, allowing the firm to build on its own strengths. For example, it is likely that a company with a highly automated manufacturing facility geared to volume and with a large, well-paid sales force would approach pricing with the aim of generating large orders, perhaps providing large-volume discounts. A company with such a structure is called **volume-sensitive.**

In the case of the budget motel segment, where low price is the selling point, costs must be kept low. Days Inns excludes expansive lobbies, meeting rooms, and swank restaurants and thus avoids the cost of expensive public areas. In constructing new facilities, it uses standard designs in order to save on architecture fees. It clusters its new motels into one region—seven have recently been built in the San Francisco area—in order to cut advertising and service costs through economies of scale. Thus, this chain establishes a low-cost structure and prices accordingly.

Computer technology provides another tool for cost-oriented pricing. Complex automated monitoring systems give firms the capability of reviewing accurate, up-to-date information on costs of labor, raw materials, and energy used in producing a given commodity. Some companies have instituted cost-monitoring systems that can report on cost fluctuations monthly and even daily.

Disadvantages of cost-oriented pricing. Cost-oriented pricing also has disadvantages. First, it is usually difficult to determine accurately the costs of producing an item. For example, should the customer also pay for the costs of advertising or research and development?[8]

Figure 12–5 One way Days Inns of America keeps costs low is to use an attractive but standard design for its motels.

Courtesy of Days Inns of America, Inc.

Another disadvantage of cost-oriented pricing is that costs are frequently affected by the volume of items sold, and it is often difficult to know what the volume will be until the selling price has been determined. The calculations thus become caught in a circular pattern: Volume strongly influences cost, which in turn helps determine price, which in turn affects volume. For example, the per unit cost of producing 200 hi-fi's is generally less than the per unit cost of producing 25 hi-fi's; but more customers are willing to buy a hi-fi at a lower cost than at a higher. Given this situation, managers generally try to estimate cost and volume and then base prices on their best guesses.

One of the major drawbacks to cost-oriented pricing in today's market is that it is completely inward-looking: It in no way reflects what customers in the marketplace are willing to pay for a particular item.[9] In the example of the hi-fi company, a certain model hi-fi is sold for $500. If, however, a considerably greater number of customers are willing to buy the hi-fi for $475 than for $500, then the company has cut itself off from a substantial part of the market and has received lower overall revenues than could have been attained. If, on the other hand, a great many customers would be willing to pay $550 for the hi-fi, then the company is earning less revenues for the hi-fi's than it could have. For Days Inns, if customers are willing to pay more for their rooms, the chain is missing an opportunity to recover costs or make a profit.

If increased production costs threaten to reduce the profits earned by a prod-

Chapter 12 / Pricing Objectives and Methods

uct, raising the price of the product to cover the increased costs is not necessarily the best decision for management. Recall the pricing myth discussed earlier in this chapter, that raising prices always results in an overall increase in revenues. If many more customers are willing to buy the hi-fi at the lower price, the total revenues would be greater at the lower price.

Some companies have encountered problems by passing their costs of production plus a markup along to the customer regardless of the level of price sensitivity. U.S. Steel, which kept prices at a level high enough to allow several other companies to take a substantial share of the market, watched its market share dwindle from 48 percent in 1910, to 34 percent in the mid-1950s, to 23 percent in the late 1970s.[10] An alternative could have been to focus on lowering costs.

Before deciding whether or not to raise prices, marketers must gather all the information possible about the product's customers and try to determine the effect of a price rise on future sales. (The relationship between price and demand will be further discussed in the section on demand-oriented pricing in this chapter.)

The features of cost-oriented pricing are summarized in figure 12–6.

Competition-Oriented Method

Using a **competition-oriented pricing method,** a company sets its prices relative to—above, below, or equal to—those of the competition in general or the primary competition, based on its desired position or relative perceived value. This method is often used to achieve an objective of maintaining the status quo or of maintaining market share. A chain of bargain-priced motels, for example, could not raise its prices above those of other bargain-priced motels, or the chain would lose both its image as a bargain and a large number of customers. Similarly, a luxury-priced hotel could not lower its prices substantially, or it would lose its high-class image and its luxury-seeking customers to other higher-priced hotels.

When market share has fallen or has not risen as desired, and a firm suspects that its prices are out of line in relation to its competitors, then pressure is created for an adjustment in price. One should recognize that competitors may also be using a competition-oriented pricing strategy. If one hotel lowers its prices, the competition may do the same, resulting in lower profits for all and no change in market shares.

In developing a new product or service and employing competition-oriented pricing policies, a firm must consider whether it offers a differentiated product, functionally unlike any other product or service in the marketplace, or whether competitors offer similar commodities. For a unique product, the firm may adopt a price that is substantially different from that offered by the competition. For a product that is functionally similar or identical to competing products, the firm will probably adopt a pricing policy relatively similar to that of its competitors.

Competition-oriented pricing might be considered the salesperson's approach to pricing. Typically, salespeople feel that prices are too high, and they will attempt to lower prices to attract more customers. In some cases companies actually give price-setting authority to their sales forces. There are certain market conditions that are especially conducive to having this capability of making adjustments quickly to

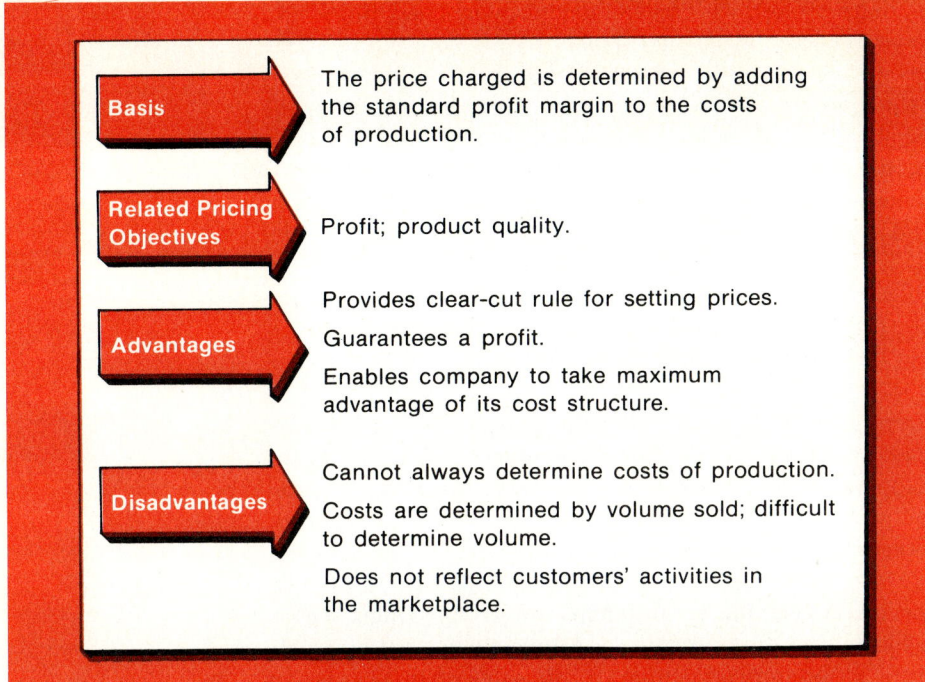

Figure 12–6 A summary of cost-oriented pricing

respond to actions of competitors. These include, for example, when the level of sales is highly dependent on price; where different customers are faced with different competitive offerings; where types of customers and their priorities vary widely; and where prepricing is difficult because of the size and continual changes in the product line.

Research indicates that, given pricing authority, sales personnel will use it to discount prices, and that as the sales force's pricing latitude increases, the amount of discount also increases.[11] This study found that firms that delegated little or no pricing latitude to salespeople generated higher revenues. Based on this, researchers have suggested that in cases requiring pricing flexibility, the sales force be allowed to recommend specific deviations from list price, but that management make all final pricing decisions.

It is reported that many companies have centralized their pricing decisions in their corporate headquarters. At U.S. Elevator Corporation, for example, top management now allows its salespeople to price only jobs that fall under $100,000. All other pricing is handled by an "estimating group" at headquarters, which has increased significantly in size since the mid-1970s.[12]

Let's take a look at competitive pricing in the hotel industry. The Hyatt Corporation established itself firmly in the upscale hotel market in the 1970s with luxury hotels in major cities and near airports that boast spacious atriums and plentiful greenery. Now, however, Hyatt is being seriously challenged. Holiday Inns is moving into the deluxe hotel market, with several new Crowne Plaza Hotels and plans for more. The Crowne Plazas aim to offer quality rooms with many of the same services Hyatt offers at rates just below Hyatt's. Westin Hotels, which owns New York City's Plaza Hotel, is planning to compete with Hyatt in the upscale market for airport hotels: It scheduled the opening of a new 450-room facility in 1984 at Chicago's O'Hare International Airport.

In the budget motel sector, Days Inns is seeking to expand beyond its stronghold in the Florida corridor and challenge other regional budget chains. At the same time, Holiday Inns is preparing to move into this market with a chain of budget motels. Although price has been the selling point for budget motels, the increased competition is expected to change the competitive strategy of proprietors in this market sector. Days Inns already offers room telephones and color television sets, which most budget motels do not. In general, whatever Days Inns charges is relative to the prices of other hotels in the area. If, for example, Days Inns is positioning itself below Ramada Inn, it will set the price accordingly. Moreover, as the number and nature of competitors change, Days Inns may have to adjust its prices.

Competition-oriented pricing is being increasingly used in the United States. Because of worldwide unused production capacity and increasingly stiff competition that began in the 1970s, prices geared toward target profits (the strict cost-based pricing described in the last section of this chapter) were no longer viable. The automobile industry illustrates how changing conditions are generating a new pricing strategy. As a result of foreign competition in the sales of small cars, for example, General Motors slashed the price of its subcompact Chevrolet Chevette in 1977. Moreover, both G.M. and Ford Motor Company priced their 1978 subcompacts on the West Coast, where Japanese foreign competition is stiffest, less than the price elsewhere.

Price leadership seems to be disappearing in many industries. In the past, companies such as U.S. Steel and IBM set the prices for their industries and smaller companies adopted identical prices. Smaller companies now, however, appear to be cutting prices to challenge industry leaders. There is evidence that even companies with such well-known names as Zenith, RCA, and Singer now face tough competition from smaller enterprises with lesser-known names.[13]

Advantages of competition-oriented pricing. A major advantage of competition-oriented price setting is that it may provide a perspective on the company's product and its relationship to competitors' products that is similar to the viewpoint of customers. Marketers need to be aware of the choices their competitors are offering, that is, the environment in which customers are evaluating their product or service. In situations where the market is competitive, customers will tend to be more sensitive to price differences than to the actual level of prices, although the level of this sensitivity varies from case to case.

Disadvantages of competition-oriented pricing. Competition-oriented pricing does have disadvantages. The company may not make enough profit on its product if it bases its prices on competitors' prices that are too low relative to the company's costs of producing the product. This fact requires that companies treat information obtained from salespeople with some caution. It is in the interest of the salespeople to keep prices low, and this bias can create imaginary market pressures. Furthermore, after the company bases its prices on those of the competition, the competition may change their prices. When taken to the extreme, actions of this sort may lead to price wars that hurt all the companies involved. The airline industry exemplifies an industry that feels the effects of price wars, as illustrated by the example given in the section of this chapter on market share pricing objectives. Eventually, though, the market generally stabilizes so that the relative price differential between a company and its competitors becomes clear.

Another weakness of competition-oriented pricing is that it presupposes that the competition has some intelligent means for setting prices and takes into consideration what customers are willing to pay for a product in the marketplace. In reality, such may not be the case. Thus, the actual value of a product in the marketplace may be ignored.

Moreover, basing prices relative to the prices of a competitor does not necessarily take into account what one company's products offer relative to the products of its competitors. Managers need latitude to build on their products' and their company's unique strengths or to adjust to their own unique weaknesses, and pricing strategy should support this capability.

The features of competition-oriented pricing are summarized in figure 12–7.

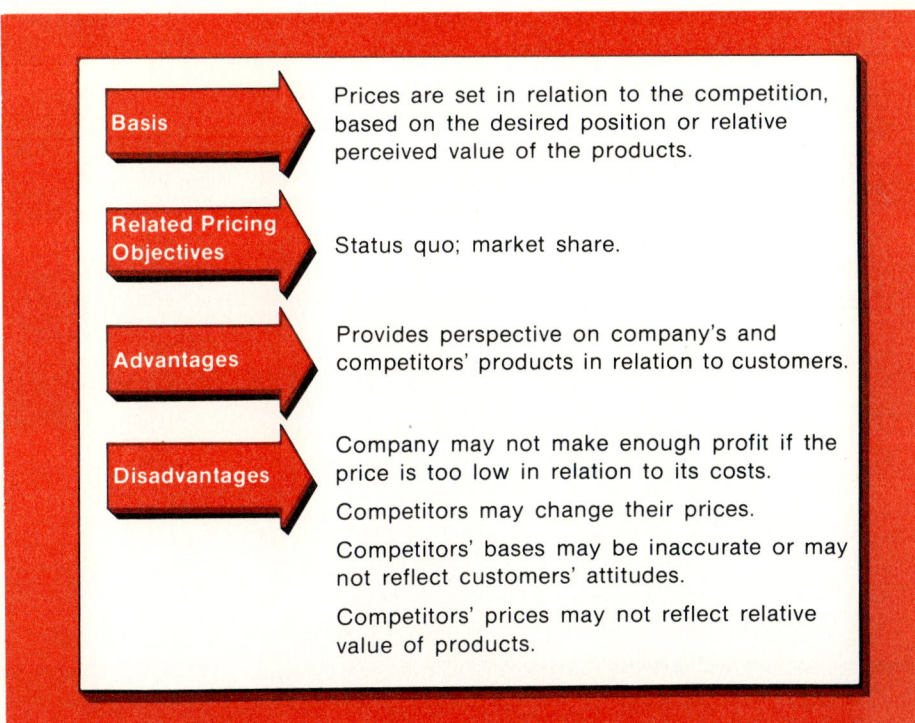

Figure 12–7 A summary of competition-oriented pricing

The **demand-oriented method** of setting prices, here referred to as the economist's approach to pricing, is used with profit maximization objectives.

In economic theory there are basic laws of supply and demand. The **demand curve,** or demand schedule, for any given item shows how much of that item customers are willing and able to buy at various prices during a given time. It is usually illustrated as a two-dimensional graph (see fig. 12–8), with the price per unit being drawn on the vertical axis and the quantity of units that would be purchased at each price drawn on the horizontal axis.

According to the law of demand in classical economic theory, the quantity of a given product demanded by customers varies inversely with the price of the product: As the price goes down, the quantity demanded goes up. The law of supply states that the quantity of the product supplied by sellers varies directly with the price: As the price goes up, so does the quantity supplied. If the price mechanism is to operate to the mutual advantage of the buyer and seller, then, it must settle on a price at which the quantity consumers are willing to buy is equal to the quantity suppliers are willing to supply.

The demand for some products changes greatly as the price changes, while there is less variation in the demand for other products as price changes. The degree to which the volume of a given product demanded is dependent on that product's price is referred to as the **price elasticity of demand.** More specifically, the price elasticity of demand is the percentage change in the number of units demanded divided by the percentage change in the price charged. When this figure is less than −1, that is, if demand increases when the price is dropped, the demand is considered **elastic** (see fig. 12–9a). In elastic demand, if the price is decreased, the total revenue will go up.

Demand-Oriented Method

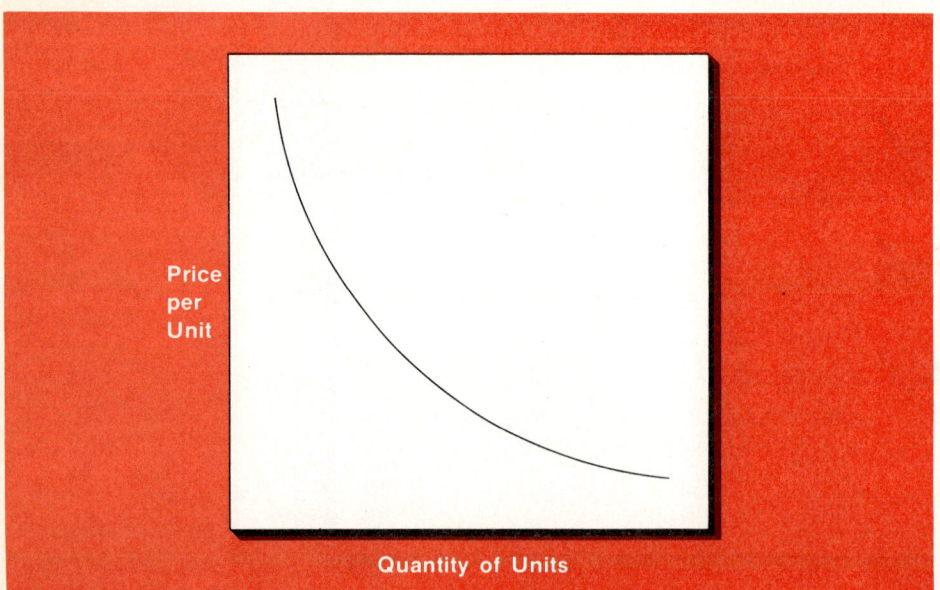

Figure 12–8 A classic demand curve

Chapter 12 / Pricing Objectives and Methods

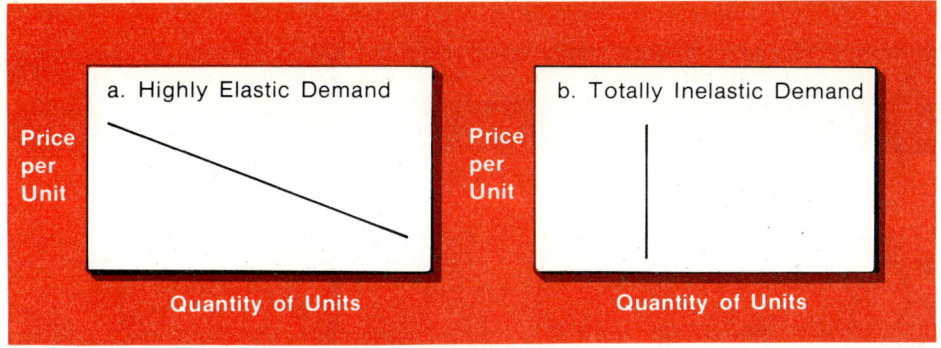

Figure 12–9 Price elasticity and inelasticity

When the percentage increase in demand is equal to the percentage decrease in price, there is a **unitary elastic;** that is, the total revenue does not change. When total revenue goes down as prices are lowered, the figure is greater than −1, and the demand is considered **inelastic.** In other words, demand remains constant when the price is raised (see fig. 12–9b).

By considering how price will affect the level of demand, this pricing method focuses on finding the price where, given the overall level of demand at that price, total profit will be the greatest. Ideally, Days Inns would set a price relative to demand. Sometimes they may do this, as in charging higher prices during summer vacation time. In practice, though, it is difficult to determine the demand curve.

Advantage of demand-oriented pricing. The advantage of demand-oriented pricing is that it enables a company to maximize profits. In theory, it ensures the marketer of setting prices at the level that will yield the highest total profit for the firm at a given time.

Disadvantages of demand-oriented pricing. This method is very difficult to put into practice, and few, if any, companies actually employ it. No one has yet developed a completely reliable or accurate method to estimate the demand curve for a particular brand of a product. It is still a very uncertain matter in most industries. Moreover, price can be used to shape demand, but not to change it radically. Demand curves are affected by a number of factors that are beyond the control of the pricing policymakers, and they are not always easy to predict or measure.[14]

First, demand is affected by consumer attitudes, personalities, and behavior, which are not always predictable. These factors tend to affect customers' perceptions of price and product. Also, the amount of real or perceived differentiation among different brands of a product will affect demand. Both of these factors will be discussed further in the next section of this chapter, on customer-oriented pricing. In this same context, because of differences in personalities, different customers will react differently to various sales personnel.

In addition to the personal tastes and attitudes of consumers, the level of personal income can change the demand curve. For example, as the level of personal income falls, fewer goods are demanded at every price.

Figure 12–10 A summary of demand-oriented pricing

Basis	The price charged is based on the demand for and supply of the product.
Related Pricing Objective	Profit maximization.
Advantage	Enables a company to maximize profits.
Disadvantages	Difficult to use. Depends on uncontrollable factors.

Local conditions are another factor that will influence demand. Local promotion, the local reputation for service, and the timing of the exposure of the customer to the product will make a difference. Many of these factors seem to be a matter of chance. Is the consumer exposed to an ad for winter coats after he has just ruined his old coat, or after he has just purchased a new one?

Finally, prices of other goods may also shift the demand curve for a given product. This is referred to as **cross-elasticities.** The clearest example is that of substitute goods. If more tangerines become available on the market, for example, or if their price falls, then the demand for oranges is likely to decrease.

More a theory than an actual practice, demand-oriented pricing can provide a valuable analytical tool to marketers as they make pricing decisions.

The features of demand-oriented pricing are summarized in figure 12–10.

Customer-Oriented Method

The **customer-oriented method** for setting prices is a relatively new way of thinking about pricing, and it reflects the acceptance of the marketing concept. It involves assessing the value of a product or service to the customer and using that value as a ceiling in determining price. This pricing strategy is usually aimed at maximizing profits: determining the maximum value of a product or service to the customer and charging that price.

Sometimes referred to as **benefit pricing** or **value pricing,** a customer-oriented pricing system requires that the marketer understand the total use of the product or service from the customer's point of view. It is the customer's perception of the total of costs and benefits—including both monetary and nonmonetary factors—that is important.[15]

Courtesy of Days Inns of America, Inc.

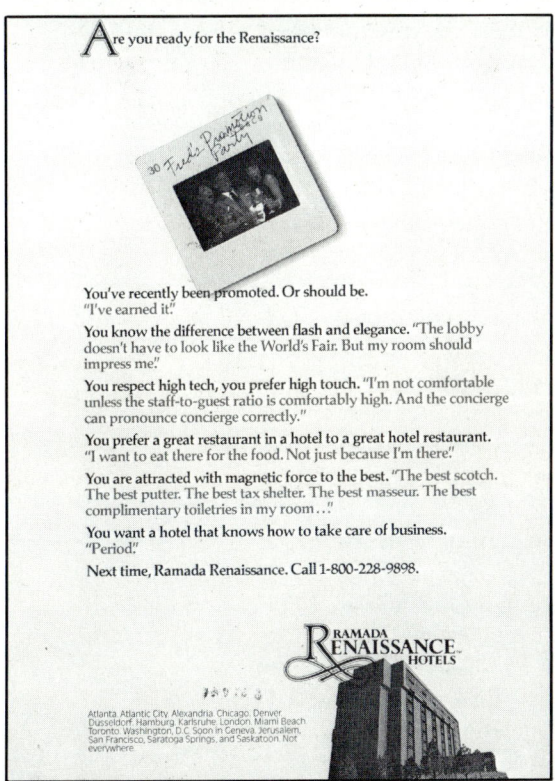

© Ramada Inns, Inc. 1984

Figure 12–11 Days Inns and Ramada Renaissance Hotels advertise the benefits and images that contribute to their pricing systems.

Chapter 12 / Pricing Objectives and Methods 341

The marketer must recognize the price may have more than one meaning to customers and that benefits are perceived differently by different customers. The most important benefits to the customer might be functional, as in the case of the customer who is building a set of bookshelves and is concerned with getting materials that are strong enough to support the planned weight; operational, as, for example, the family looking for a new washing machine that is concerned with reliability and durability; or financial, such as the customer on a tight budget who is attempting to make the smallest cash outlay possible in exchange for the purchase.

Real benefits might include prompt delivery of an appliance that is needed immediately, a reliable service contract available with a new computer system, favorable credit terms available for a new automobile, or the prestige perceived by the customer in owning a shirt with a particular label, of staying at a hotel in a prestigious location. The task of benefit pricing is to determine the monetary value of such tangible and intangible features to the customer at or slightly lower than this level.

In analyzing real costs to the customer, the marketer looks beyond the purchase price and includes those of installation, labor, energy usage—all the costs incurred over the life of the product. Other costs of a product might include inconveniences resulting from product failure, losses caused by late delivery, or the value of things that must be foregone as the result of purchasing the item.[16]

Prices can be an emotional issue for buyers. More than an investment of money, a purchase is also an investment of the customer's judgment and energies. In setting prices, marketers must consider the sensitivity and focus of customers' feelings—their joys and enthusiasms, as well as their fears and dislikes. Specific emotional and cultural beliefs can determine what customers accept as just.

Advantages of customer-oriented pricing. The marketer tries to view this trade-off between costs and benefits from the customer's viewpoint, recognizing that the customer will buy the product or service that he or she perceives as having the best relationship between costs and benefits. This, then, is a major strength of the customer-oriented pricing strategy: It is realistic and strives to be consistent with customers' needs and with the way customers make decisions about purchases.

Because needs, beliefs, and priorities vary among customers, marketers must decide to which customers they wish to appeal with the services they offer. Days Inns focuses on the budget-minded family market, and the chain's pricing structure encompasses successful promotional programs, such as discounts on food and lodging for senior citizens and allowing children of guests to dine free in the motel coffee shops.

Ramada pursued an upscale market by installing gambling facilities in 1979. To bolster its thus-far weak casino business, in order to reinvest revenues in its medium-priced and luxury hotel business, Ramada offers an air shuttle from New York City to its Atlantic City Tropicana Casino and Hotel.

To attract the very top segment of the market, Hyatt is experimenting with exclusive European-style hotels, with more services and higher rates. The Park Hyatt in Chicago, the first of this group, has a concierge and provides flowers, fresh fruit, and bathrobes in each room for guests. The rates are $125 and up, as compared with the rate of $94 and up charged by the Hyatt Regency in Chicago. Four Seasons Hotels, with an average room rate of $117, keep records of frequent guests' requests, so a guest can be given a favorite room or type of soap on the next visit.

Customer-oriented pricing is being used in a variety of industries. Companies in the moving industry, which in the early 1980s offered discounts to individual customers that ranged as high as 25 percent, announced in 1983 that price cutting and discounting were being slowly phased out, and that customer service would be emphasized as much as pricing. The new policies include such services as Allied Van Lines, Inc.'s, "coming home service," which sends a company representative to a customer's home two days after the move to make sure that all went smoothly; and United Van Lines's "golden umbrella" program, which, for a small premium, replaces damaged goods at full current market value.[17]

Disadvantages of customer-oriented pricing. A major weakness of a customer-oriented pricing strategy is that it is difficult to implement. To use this method successfully, the marketer must consider the total marketing mix—including advertising, promotion, and packaging. Other significant factors in this approach to pricing include the image of the manufacturer or other organization providing the product and the nature and image of the retail outlet, including its location and general clientele. Perhaps the greatest difficulty comes with identifying the benefits consumers want. If customers are not interested in the concierge, flowers, bathrobes, and fresh fruit provided by the Park Hyatt Hotel, a pricing strategy that calls for higher prices due to these services will not work.

The features of customer-oriented pricing are summarized in figure 12–12.

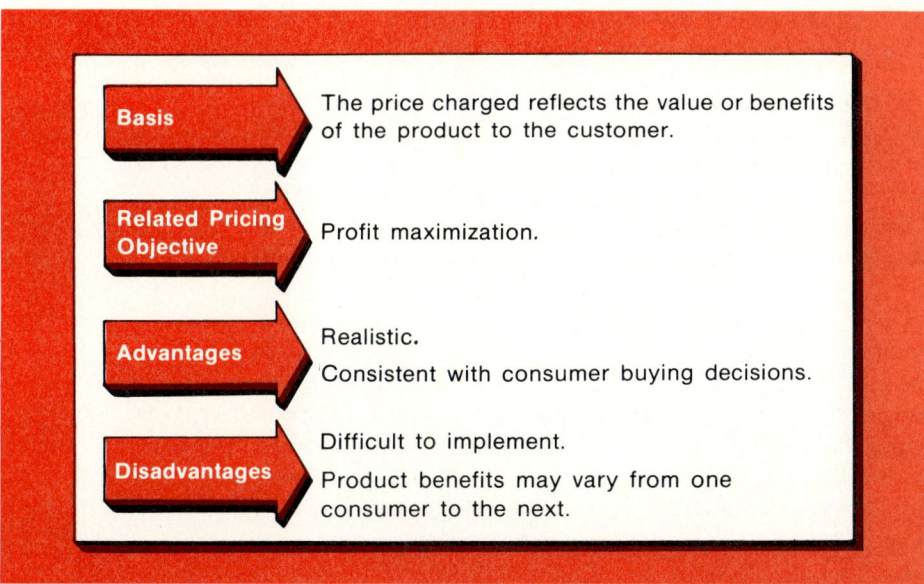

Figure 12–12 A summary of customer-oriented pricing

Basis	The price charged reflects the value or benefits of the product to the customer.
Related Pricing Objective	Profit maximization.
Advantages	Realistic. Consistent with consumer buying decisions.
Disadvantages	Difficult to implement. Product benefits may vary from one consumer to the next.

Bidding and Negotiated Pricing

Bidding and negotiated pricing provides a fifth and different type of method by which the seller and buyer of a product or service can agree upon a price. When this method is used, a product or service does not carry a fixed price in the marketplace; rather, the seller and buyer work out between themselves a price for it. The product itself and its accompanying services are often adjusted for that particular buyer.

By definition, then, this method provides a flexible approach to pricing; it is generally used with the objective of maximizing profits.

Examples of negotiated pricing include the purchase of automobiles—there is usually a base price from which negotiations between the buyer and seller begin. Another example is that of an auction where there is an opening bid. Prices for houses are usually negotiated. A number of industrial products and many products sold to the government are priced on a bid-type basis.

In determining whether or not to bid on a contract, the decision maker must clarify company objectives, then analyze how the prospective contract would fit with those objectives.[18] The firm's capacity and how it would be affected by a contract of the size under consideration are important factors. It is essential to obtain as much information as possible about the customer's sensitivities and about the bids that are likely to be submitted by competitors. In examining the bid, the manager should also consider alternative opportunities for the firm: What opportunities would the firm have to turn down if it were to receive the bid? Also, what follow-up opportunities might be made available as a result of obtaining this bid? How do the delivery requirements—timing and method of delivery—fit with the firm's capabilities?

Since this method of pricing is usually tied to profit maximization objectives, the worst position to be in is that of the second-lowest bidder. The company in that position not only loses the job but also signals to others in the industry how low it is willing to bid.

Computerized cost-monitoring systems are an obvious aid to this means of pricing. The relevance, timeliness, and flexibility of the analysis provided by some of these systems facilitate cost analysis of complex problems, even for smaller jobs for which detailed analysis would not have been financially feasible previously. Even in bids that require complicated analytical arithmetic, managers are able to try out many different ideas and test hunches quickly. These systems will never replace the need for careful thinking and decision making, however. The computerized results are merely a tool for making decisions, not in themselves decision makers.[19]

This method of determining price is advantageous for buyers because all bids are laid in front of them so that they can make a choice. To sellers, it provides an opportunity to customize prices for individual customers. Moreover, such factors as the quality of the work and the time involved can be considered in setting prices.

We have just looked at various methods of setting prices to achieve pricing objectives: cost-oriented, competition-oriented, demand-oriented, and customer-oriented. How do these methods apply to the hotel market discussed at the beginning of the chapter?

12–1 Focus on Marketing Strategy
FLEXIBLE PRICING

Rather than adhering to a set price for a product, some companies adopt a **flexible pricing** strategy. Flexible pricing means basing a product's price on conditions in the market and raising and lowering it in response to fluctuations in those conditions. The purpose of flexible pricing is to increase or maintain market share by offering a product at a price that differentiates it from the competition. Most often, companies set prices lower than the competition in order to attract additional customers. In 1978, General Motors and Ford both lowered the prices of their subcompact cars in the West to try to gain a competitive advantage over the Japanese manufacturers. A company may also raise prices under this system. GM raised the prices of its luxury cars at the same time it lowered prices on subcompacts.

    Flexible pricing contrasts sharply with the other pricing methods in which the company develops objectives and then sets prices to meet them. By these methods, an industry leader often establishes prices for smaller competitors. Using flexible pricing, however, the smaller competitors often try to price their products lower than the big companies in order to gain some of the market share. When Owens-Illinois, Inc., the largest manufacturer of glass containers, increased its bottle prices, smaller companies lowered theirs to keep brewery customers interested in using bottles. Armco Steel cut its structural prices by 20 percent to combat foreign competition. Other steel manufacturers had a similar goal in mind when they eliminated extra charges for cutting and treating their products. Dow Chemical's pricing strategy is to offer low prices in times of low demand and to raise prices when demand is high.

    Other companies, such as Hewlett-Packard Company and U.S. Elevator Corporation, try to provide products that are so distinct from competitors' that they do not need to follow other companies' pricing leads. Hewlett-Packard has charged high prices for its pocket calculators by offering unique features; when other companies match these features at a lower price, Hewlett-Packard introduces new models. U.S. Elevator is looking outside of the competitive construction industry and emphasizing special projects such as shipboard elevators. A data processing company develops unique services tailored directly to individual clients' needs and processes and continually tries to develop new services that give it a competitive advantage in keeping clients and attracting new ones and allow it to maintain its prices.

    One development that makes flexible pricing a more feasible pricing option today than it was in the past is the availability of computerized marketing information systems. U.S. Elevator and many other companies continually monitor costs of labor, materials, and so on, and adjust their prices accordingly.

Source: "Flexible Pricing," *Business Week*, December 12, 1977, pp. 78–88.

It appears that costs must be a consideration to all hotel marketers, but particularly to those aiming at the budget market, where price is the key selling point. As we have discussed, keeping costs low is crucial in this market.

It is an increasingly competitive market, however. The regional chain Days Inns is extending its market geographically, and strong national chains already entrenched in the medium-priced market, such as Holiday Inns and Ramada, are expanding into the budget motel market. In this environment, gaining market share can become an important objective. It is reasonable to speculate that these chains might begin to price competitively, perhaps trying to undercut each other slightly. Or they may focus increasingly on added services that they can offer to guests for the economy price. Using this latter strategy, they would enact customer-oriented pricing methods to some degree.

It appears that deluxe hotels will continue to build upon customer-oriented pricing strategies, with the hotels offering more and varied services to customers for the highest price customers are willing to pay. This will require careful analysis of the desires and priorities of the customers they seek to attract, and how much customers are willing to pay for those services.

The increasing number of luxury hotels makes it seem likely that competition-oriented pricing will continue to be a factor in these markets as in all others. Given such competitive conditions, the importance of gaining market share often increases. With the plethora of services and benefits available to deluxe hotel guests, even these hotels may seek to undercut the prices of competitors that offer the same level of services.

Demand theory can continue to provide an analytical tool to assist marketers in setting prices in all markets.

Summary

Pricing is the component through which management attempts to recover all the costs of its marketing efforts and is the variable that offers the most flexibility. Price is where the value of a product to the customer and the company's compensation for producing it intersect.

Pricing objectives include profit, profit maximization (setting the price to make the largest possible revenues), market share (obtaining as many potential customers as possible), sales growth, return on investment (or ROI, a long-term strategy involving maximizing the revenues earned by a product in relation to the total cost of earning those revenues), maintaining the status quo, and matching price and product quality or price and consumers' perceptions of product quality.

The cost-oriented method of pricing is based on a standard profit margin. The company figures its total costs and bases the product price on that amount and its standard profit margin. The advantage of cost-oriented pricing is that it provides a clear-cut decision rule for pricing. Computerization provides a tool for automated monitoring of the cost-oriented pricing system. Disadvantages include the fact that exact costs are difficult to determine, costs fluctuate with volume sold, and it is insensitive to customers' price demands.

The competition-oriented method involves setting prices relative to those of competitors. An advantage of this method is that it may provide a perspective on the company's product and its relationship to competitors' products that is similar to consumers' viewpoints. The use of competition-oriented pricing is increasing in the United States. Disadvantages include the fact that the company may not make enough profit if it bases its prices on competitors'. This method can also trigger price wars and does not necessarily take into account the features of the individual products.

The demand-oriented method is based on the laws of supply and demand in economic theory. Price elasticity is the degree to which volume of a given product demanded is dependent on that product's price. This method focuses on finding the price at which, given the overall level of demand at that price, total profit will be greatest. Advantages of this method include the fact that it enables companies to maximize profits, though this is difficult to achieve. Demand is affected by a number of factors, including customers' attitudes and tastes, local conditions, and cross-elasticity, or the shift of other goods. This method is more a theoretical concept than a practical one.

The consumer-oriented method for setting prices involves assessing the value of a product or service to the customer and using that value as a ceiling in determining price. A strength of this method is that it strives to be consistent with the way customers make decisions about purchases. A weakness is that this strategy is difficult to implement. A major difficulty is identifying the benefits that customers want.

In bidding and negotiated pricing, the buyer and seller work out a price between themselves. This is a flexible approach to pricing used with the objective of maximizing profits. Computerized cost-monitoring systems are an aid to this means of pricing.

Questions for Discussion

1. Discuss the different meanings attached to price.
2. Examine the importance of price to a marketer.
3. Explain the meaning of price that you would attach to the following: (1) a donation to the United Way; (b) a ticket to a Michael Jackson concert; (3) a famous painting, and (d) a college education.
4. Under what conditions would you choose profit maximization compared to obtaining market share as the pricing objective?
5. How appropriate is it to employ maximizing the return on investment as the objective of pricing? Explain.
6. "The cost-oriented pricing method involves a circular logic." Discuss.

7. Examine the current relevance involved in employing the "competition-oriented" method of pricing.
8. Examine the problems involved in employing the "customer-oriented" method of pricing.
9. Identify clearly how the product life cycle affects the pricing objective chosen for a product.

References

1. The discussion of hotels here and throughout the chapter is based on "Four Seasons Finds Room in a Crowded Market," *Business Week,* April 2, 1984, p. 85; Subrata N. Chakravarty and Anne McGrath, "Room at the Top?" *Forbes,* March 12, 1984, pp. 58–61; "Hyatt Hotels: Putting Out the Welcome Mat for a Broader Clientele," *Business Week,* October 31, 1983, pp. 68–69; "Days Inns: Looking for a Berth in a Crowded National Field," *Business Week,* October 31, 1983, pp. 70–72; "Two Weary Innkeepers Try to Renovate," *Business Week,* December 13, 1982, pp. 106, 109.
2. "Pricing Policy Based on Myths," *International Management,* May 1979, p. 9.
3. Linda Snyder Hayes, "Gillette Takes the Wraps Off," *Fortune,* February 25, 1980, pp. 148–50.
4. "War in the West's Crowded Skies," *Business Week,* September 26, 1983, pp. 72, 74.
5. "Why Coca-Cola and Wine Didn't Mix," *Business Week,* October 10, 1983, p. 30.
6. Philip A. Scheuble, Jr., "ROI for New-Product Planning," *Harvard Business Review,* November–December 1964, pp. 92–102.
7. Benson P. Shapiro and Barbara B. Jackson, "Industrial Pricing to Meet Customer Needs," *Harvard Business Review,* November–December 1978, p. 120.
8. F. E. Brown and A. R. Oxenfeldt, "Should Prices Depend on Costs?" *MSU Business Topics,* Autumn 1968, pp. 73–77.
9. Andre Gabor, "How to Price," *Journal of Purchasing and Materials Management,* Spring 1982, p. 29.
10. "Flexible Pricing," *Business Week,* December 12, 1977, pp. 78–83.
11. P. Ronald Stephenson, William L. Cron, and Gary L. Frazier, "Delegating Pricing Authority to the Sales Force: The Effects on Sales and Profit Performance," *Journal of Marketing,* Spring 1979, pp. 21–28.
12. "Flexible Pricing," p. 81.
13. Ibid., pp. 80–81.
14. This discussion based on William P. Albrecht, Jr., *Economics,* 2nd edition (Englewood Cliffs, N.J.: Prentice-Hall, 1979), pp. 406–11.
15. Shapiro and Jackson, pp. 119–27.
16. Ibid., p. 120.

17. Agis Salpukas, "Moving Industry's Revival," *New York Times,* March 15, 1984, p. D1.
18. Stephen Paranka, "Competitive Bidding Strategy," *Business Horizons,* June 1971, pp. 39–43.
19. Michael S. Morton and Andrew M. McCosh, "Terminal Costing for Better Decisions," *Harvard Business Review,* May-June 1968, pp. 103–12.

OBJECTIVES

1. To describe the various approaches to modifying prices.

2. To study the different pricing policies used by companies.

3. To examine the effect of the product life cycle and the product line on pricing decisions.

4. To understand the conditions that favor price modification.

5. To recognize the legal issues involved in making pricing decisions.

13

Pricing Modifications, Policies, and Considerations

In the early 1980s, a proliferation of home and personal computers led manufacturers and distributors of these products to engage in pricing modifications and policies to increase their market shares, profits, or sales or simply to stay in business. A number of actions were taken; the following examples show some actions and the reasons for them.

In the summer of 1983, home computer manufacturers used a combination of price reductions and rebates to compete. Atari, Texas Instruments, and Commodore computers that had previously sold for $200–300 now could be bought for $99. Tandy introduced two new computers that cost less than $200. Timex computers could be bought for $45; this same computer had long been the least expensive at $99.

IBM had already made its move into the microcomputer market with the introduction of the IBM PC, aimed at the business market. When IBM introduced the PC*jr* aimed at the home market, it had to decide on a price level.

Some aspects of the decision were clear. The PC*jr* had to be priced lower than the PC itself, as the PC*jr* was cheaper to make and the home computer market was more price-sensitive than the business market. At the same time, IBM did not want to set too low a price. IBM recognized that people would be willing to pay more for the IBM name, and they did not want to tarnish that name with a low-priced product.

An obvious decision may have been to price the PC*jr* at $2,000, as IBM traditionally prices at the high end of the market. A high price would give IBM a generous profit margin and would leave them with the option of lowering prices at a later time.

Choosing a low price of approximately $400 would allow IBM to have a greater effect in the market. Most of the competitors were already pricing at the low end of the market; going directly against the competition would give IBM deeper penetration of the market.

Another decision concerned the level of advertising expenditures. Heavy advertising would create a high level of consumer awareness, but it might cause competitors to reduce prices, making the PC*jr* look all the more expensive by comparison.

The decision was finally made to introduce the PC*jr* at a mid-point of approximately $1,200 and to support the introduction with heavy advertising expenditures.[1]

Why were many of these actions taken? The makers of home and personal computers found themselves in a market with rapid changes in competition, types of products offered, and the nature of distributors and customers. All these factors led manufacturers and distributors of home and personal computers to consider their pricing strategies, modify prices, and use various pricing policies.

In chapter 12 we looked at the nature of pricing, the pricing objectives companies can follow, and the basic methods for setting prices. In this chapter, we will look at the modifications and policies used to pursue the objectives and at factors to be considered in setting prices.

Various Pricing Modifications

When sellers are setting the prices they actually charge, they can use a number of pricing modifications. These include discounts, geographic pricing, and psychological pricing.

Discounts, or reductions in prices, are common in most industries. They can be directed either toward members of the distribution channel or toward final customers. Discounts directed toward members of the distribution channel are given to encourage the channel members to carry or assist in the marketing of the product. Discounts directed toward final customers are given to encourage purchases. The types of discounts are discussed in the paragraphs that follow and are summarized in table 13–1.

Discounts

Quantity discount. One common form of discount is the **quantity discount.** Sometimes a manufacturer or a wholesaler offers a quantity discount to a retailer. If the buyer—in this case, the retailer—purchases a large enough volume of a product, the seller—in this case, the manufacturer or distributor—will provide it at a discount. Offering a quantity discount has two advantages for the seller. First, it can lower the seller's costs by making possible greater efficiencies in production and distribution. Second, by serving as an incentive to the buyer to purchase bigger quantities, the discount can increase the seller's overall sales volume.[2]

Trade discount. Another kind of discount, the **trade discount,** is generally offered to a distribution channel member, who, in turn for the reduced price on a product, assumes some of the responsibilities for marketing it. The retailer might, for example, agree to display the product in a prominent place—at the end of an aisle or near the checkout counter—thus helping the manufacturer to promote the product to customers. This form of discount is sometimes known as an **allowance** or a **functional discount.**

TABLE 13–1 Types of Discounts

Discount	Offered to	Definition
Quantity Discount	Distribution channel members; final consumers	Discount offered for purchasing large quantity of product; for example, "Buy ten, get one free."
Trade Discount (Allowance; Functional Discount)	Distribution channel members	Discount offered for taking on marketing responsibilities.
Cash Discount	Final consumers	Discount offered for paying with cash rather than with credit card.
Seasonal Discount	Distribution channel members; final consumers	Discount offered for purchasing product at end of season or during off-season.
Cash Rebate	Distribution channel members; final consumers	Rebate given for purchasing particular product at a particular time.

Figure 13–1 Some retailers, such as this food store, pass the savings from manufacturers' discounts along to their customers.

Laimute E. Druskis

Cash discount. A **cash discount** involves offering a lower price to those customers who pay cash as opposed to those who use credit cards. The **Cash Discount Act,** an amendment to the Truth in Lending Act, permits retailers to offer unlimited discounts to their customers to encourage cash payment.[3] The major advantage of the cash discount is that the seller is spared the costs of maintaining cash receivable records and carrying the accounts. Gasoline stations are major users of cash discounts, offering lower prices to customers who pay cash to reduce the use of credit cards. Providing the discounts is considered especially important in this market, as it is estimated that the cost of providing credit runs from 6 cents to 9 cents per gallon.[4]

The effect of a cash discount on retail prices depends upon customers' credit card behavior. Some customers will always pay cash or always use credit cards, regardless of whether or not a cash discount is offered. The cash discount, however, will only be an effective marketing tool in cases where a relatively high proportion of credit customers switch to cash or check when offered a discount for doing so or when it attracts new business when competitors are not offering similar discounts. For example, the Atlantic Richfield Company (ARCO) was the first oil company to offer cash discounts. Previously, most gasoline stations accepted bank cards or their own credit cards. ARCO chose to pay the customer to get cash at the time of the purchase. This led many of ARCO's own credit card customers to use cash, and it lured many customers away from competitors. It took a while for other credit card issuers to recognize the advantages of the cash discount. Otherwise, for the cash discount to be profitable, the retailer must initially have a relatively high proportion of credit sales. If the number of credit card sales is already low, the retailer would be giving a discount to too many customers who would have paid cash anyway. The retailer must also ensure that the costs of the discount program do not exceed the benefits gained from it.[5]

Seasonal discount. Some manufacturers and retailers offer **seasonal discounts,** lowering prices at the end of a season or during off-seasons. The advan-

Chapter 13 / Pricing Modifications, Policies, and Considerations **354**

13–1 Focus on Marketing Strategy
DISCOUNT MEDICINE

"Lowest prices in town," "Bargain discounts"—these are familiar advertising slogans that promise that the vendor sells similar items at a lower price than the competition. This form of marketing, called discounting, has long been used by manufacturers and retailers. Now, discounting has reached the medical profession, and the result may change the methods of providing medical care.

Doctors are overcoming their past opposition to marketing their services due to a number of problems: competition within the medical profession is increasing (the number of new doctors grew by 40 percent from 1970 to 1980); many hospitals, particularly older ones in inner cities, have lost revenue as the populations they serve have dwindled and federal funding has been slashed; medical costs have been rising faster than the inflation rate; and businesses across the country are burdened by costs of providing medical insurance benefits to their employees.

The answer to these problems may be the *preferred provider organization*, or PPO. In a PPO arrangement, a group of hospitals or doctors or both joins together and offers to provide comprehensive medical services to businesses at a lower cost than they would otherwise pay. In short, they discount their prices. How does this work? In Cleveland, for example, the Ameritrust Bank found that its employee health-benefit costs had increased by more than 700 percent over an eight-year period to approximately $5 million per year. So the bank signed agreements with three local PPOs.

Ameritrust employees could choose any of the PPOs or continue with their existing health insurance plan. Those choosing to use PPO doctors would have no medical expenses beyond their monthly contributions; those using other doctors would pay the first $150 to $300 of charges each year and then 20 percent of their medical bills up to $2,300. The bank's health plan would cover the rest. The bank would continue to pay the same monthly premium per employee ($140) as it had before, but the employee's monthly contribution would be only $35, up to $25 lower than in other health plans. The agreements allow Ameritrust to conduct frequent reviews of costs and to compare the prices charged by doctors and hospitals to make sure that costs are under control.

What are the results? Critics warn that savings from discounts in the prices of services may be illusory if consumers are encouraged to purchase more of the services. Critics also fear that the quality of services may decline.

Supporters of PPOs argue that hospitals and doctors will now have an incentive to operate in a cost-efficient manner. Many doctors see PPOs as a way of building up their practices. And patients and businesses seem pleased at the idea of spending less for their medical services.

Clearly, only time will tell if PPOs indeed provide the best for less.

Source: Michael Waldholz, "To Attract Patients, Doctors and Hospitals Cut Prices to Groups," *Wall Street Journal*, November 22, 1983, pp. 1, 18.

tages of seasonal discounts are that they can smooth out the sales cycle by lengthening the selling season, and they can reduce the remaining inventory of the discounted items. At the end of the winter season, for example, winter clothing and ski equipment are sold at a discount to make room for summer products and, eventually, next year's styles.

Cash rebate. Another form of discount is the **cash rebate,** in which the seller maintains the list price but gives the buyer a partial rebate for buying a particular product at a particular time. Rebates have become a common pricing policy in the automobile industry, and their use appears to be increasing. Rebates are also used as competitive tools. For example, Sony offered a $50 rebate on its Betamax videocassette recorder to maintain its market share in the face of competition. In another example, Gillette offered the high rebate of $1 per package of three erasable-ink pens; in order not to be beaten in the market, Scripto had to match the offer.

A. C. Nielsen, the marketing research firm, found in a 1980 survey that 45 percent of households in the United States had responded to rebate offers compared with 27 percent in 1977.[6] This rise may have been due both to greater consumer price sensitivity and to the increase in the number of rebates offered.

Geographic Pricing

When a seller is shipping a product to a buyer—whether distribution channel member or final customer—the seller may modify the price, based on the buyer's geographic location or the distance to be traveled. This is **geographic pricing,** and there are a number of policies that can be pursued. These are shown in figure 13–2 and described below.

The most standard one is **freight on board,** or **FOB,** in which case there is a standard price for the product, not including shipping, and the buyer absorbs the shipping costs. The greater the distance is between the buyer and seller, the higher the shipping costs are that the buyer must pay. In buying from mail-order firms, for example, the buyer normally pays for the product and pays an additional shipping charge.

Freight absorption is another means of determining shipping charges. In this case, the seller absorbs the cost of shipping, and there is no additional transportation cost to the buyer.

Uniform delivered is a policy in which the shipping cost for a product has been established and the cost is the same regardless of the buyer's location—all buyers pay the same shipping costs. Using this procedure, the seller usually determines a general shipping charge based on the average cost of shipping the product.

Zone pricing is another commonly used method of determining shipping charges. When it is employed, concentric circles—or zones—are usually set up from one shipping location; the farther a zone from the shipping location, the higher the shipping charge. Everybody within the same zone pays the same charge. The U.S. Postal Service uses this system.

Psychological Pricing

As we saw in chapter 12, there is always a psychological factor involved in pricing. The price chosen for a product depends in part upon what the seller wishes to convey to the customer.

Odd/even pricing. Retailers sometimes follow a policy that incorporates the concept of **odd/even pricing.** Evidence suggests that setting an odd price at slightly less than an even one can suggest a substantially lower price. Many customers seem to perceive the difference between $9.99 and $10.00 as being much greater than 1 cent, although they perceive little difference between $9.98 and $9.99. Odd/even pricing has been traditionally used in selling automobiles. For a long time, the barrier was $10,000, and each auto manufacturer priced its cars at

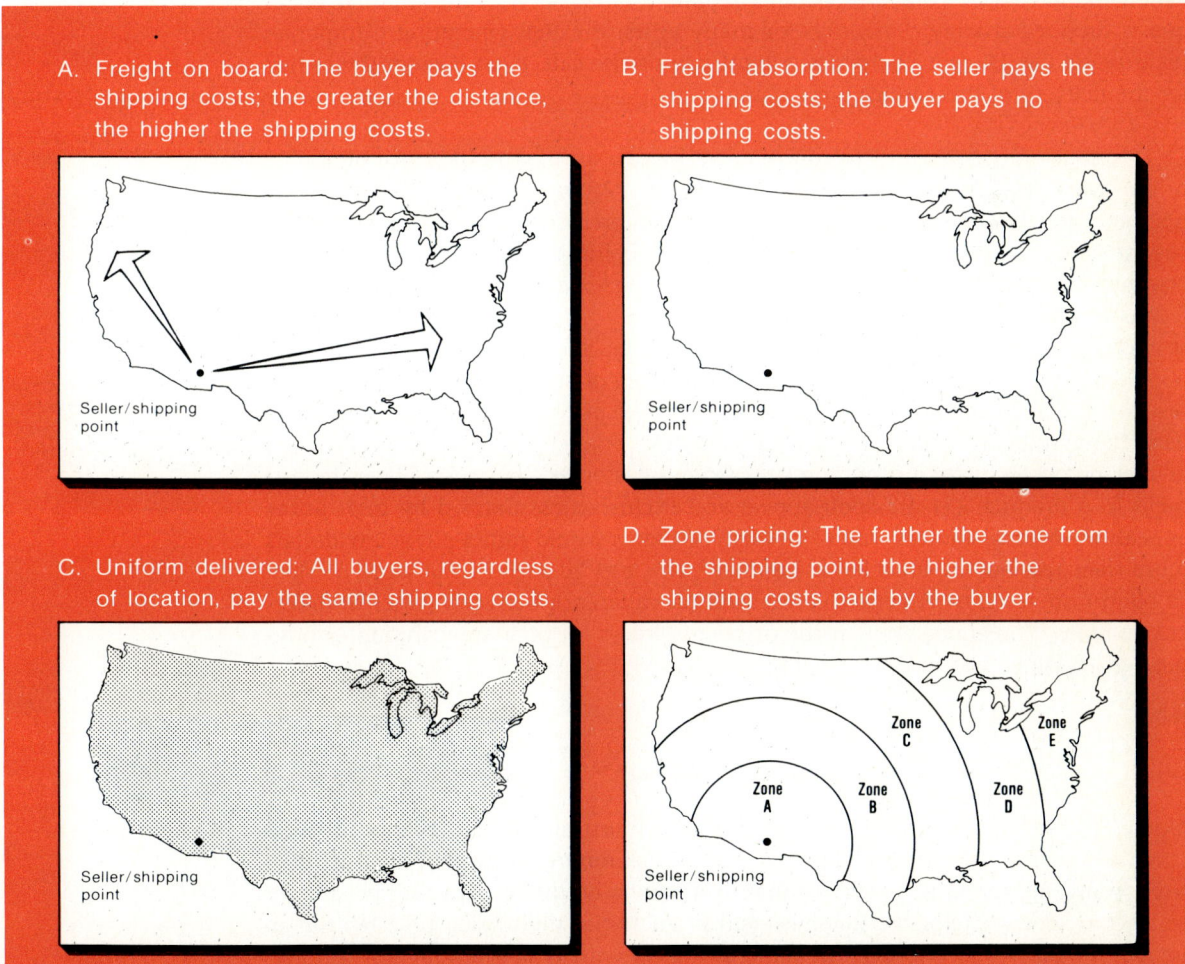

Figure 13–2 Types of geographic pricing

Chapter 13 / Pricing Modifications, Policies, and Considerations

under $10,000; the cars would be listed at, perhaps, $9,995. On the other hand, if the seller wishes to convey an image of selling a premium product, it is often considered best to use the even price. Items in an exclusive shop are often priced at $10 or $10,000.

Customary pricing. The term **customary pricing** means pricing according to what the customer would expect the price to be for a particular product, based on custom and tradition. The seller recognizes the importance of those customer expectations, and even though the costs of producing a given product might change, the seller continues to charge the amount that customers expect to pay for it.[7] As an example, customers in the United States have traditionally thought of telephone information requests as a free service provided by a telephone company. When the telephone company began charging for this service, the number of requests dropped sharply. Similarly, for many years, the Bell Operating Companies maintained the 10-cent charge for a local pay phone call, even though their costs for the delivery of this service were rising.

Price as an indication of quality. Price can serve as an indicator of quality in the minds of customers as we saw in chapter 12. The impression may or may not be correct, but when they lack other bases on which to form a judgment, customers often perceive a higher-priced item as being a higher-quality item. Sellers, then, may set a high price to indicate that theirs is a high-quality product (see fig. 13–3). This is sometimes known as **prestige pricing**.

The perception of a correlation between price and quality is essentially rational. It implies that customers trust in the forces of supply and demand, and it rests on the assumption that the prevailing market prices exist because they have been found to be fair and rational. In general, this pricing policy works because (1) greater product satisfaction often results from a customer's having a bigger investment in a product, (2) the snob appeal and exclusiveness implied by high prices appeals to some customers, and (3) many customers would rather pay a few dollars more than risk buying an inferior product.[8] This can be seen in the wine market. In blind taste tests, most people cannot tell the difference between wines of different qualities. Consumers look at the prices to "know" if they are drinking or buying a good wine.

Skimming and Penetration Pricing

One of the strategic questions that the marketer must answer is whether to use a **skimming** or a **penetration** pricing policy. A skimming strategy, which is often used in pricing a product or service that is functionally unlike any other product or service in the marketplace, involves setting an initial high price to establish an image of quality and also keep demand at a level with which production facilities can keep up. If the product is a high-technology, complex, or scientific one, the initial high price may help the firm recover development costs. After a time, when

Figure 13–3 The high price of Tanqueray Gin reflects its high quality, prestige, and perfection.

competition has entered the market, the firm may lower the price and make it more available to a wider market. While the price is kept high, the company is able to maximize profits by getting as many sales as possible—"skimming" the top of the market—from those customers who are relatively price insensitive; then, by lowering prices over time, it expands the market for the product or service.

For a product that is functionally similar or identical to competing products, the firm will probably adopt a penetration pricing policy, which involves setting a low initial price that does not cover the firm's costs, but enables the marketer to gain quick entry into the marketplace, gain a large market share, perhaps drive competition off, and ultimately reduce costs through the larger volume that would presumably result.

One of the issues involved in this decision to use skimming or penetration is whether to try to maximize profits immediately or to build market share for the future and try to make more profits over the long term. The skimming policy is one of making a profit on each item sold, from the beginning; the penetration policy is a long-term policy that leads to profits in the future.

The advantages of a penetration strategy are the gaining of as much market share as possible and opening new markets, driving competition out of the market, and lowering long-term costs because of the economies of scale made possible by

TABLE 13–2 A Comparison of Skimming and Penetration Pricing

	Skimming	Penetration
Definition	Initial price is high to recover development costs, establish high-quality image, or keep demand level with production	Initial price is low to gain entry into market, gain large market share, drive off competition, and reduce costs through large volume
Objectives	Profit maximization immediately	Market share; greater long-term profits
Advantages	Immediate profits Immediate recovery of costs	Large market share Rapid development of new markets Reduction of competiton Lower long-term costs

producing a larger volume. This relates to a concept known as the **learning** or **experience curve.** The learning curve emphasizes that production costs decline as output rises, partly because of the economies that come from producing a high volume of the product but more important because workers learn over time how to produce products more efficiently.

The main advantage of a skimming strategy is the immediate profits the seller can make from the market. It is a particularly useful strategy when there are high cash outlays involved with introducing a product, when there is a market segment that is not overly price-sensitive, and when competition is limited.[9] In these conditions, a low price would give the product away, as consumers are willing to pay the extra amount.

As was mentioned in chapter 12's discussion of competition-oriented pricing, Hewlett-Packard has successfully employed a skimming strategy in the highly competitive pocket calculator market. The company equips its new products with special features and prices them higher than the industry average. By the time a product has competition, Hewlett-Packard has changed its product line.

Texas Instruments (TI), on the other hand, employs a penetration pricing strategy, continually lowering prices at higher levels of output for a relatively unchanging product. When a number of companies seemed on the verge of entering the digital watch market, TI again employed a penetration pricing policy and discouraged competition; for example, when TI announced plans to introduce a digital watch that would sell for $10, Gillette and other companies abandoned plans to make digital watches.

Table 13–2 compares the characteristics of skimming and penetration pricing.

Product Line Pricing

Most companies offer more than one product in their product line. The makers of toothpaste, for example, offer different sizes of the same brand, and the price per ounce decreases as the size increases. If there are three classes of tickets on an airline flight—tourist, business, and first class—and tourist-class tickets are more easily sold than are first-class seats, then the airplane's tourist section will probably be larger than its first-class section. Marketers must consider how the price of one product in their product line may affect the price of others in the line. The point is that there is **price cross-elasticity** in product line pricing.[10]

Texas Instruments introduced its model TI 99/2 computer in January 1983, with a suggested retail price of $99.95. By May, it reduced the price of the more powerful 99/4A to $99. The model 99/2 was caught in the price squeeze. In another example, the low prices of IBM's 4300 series, introduced in 1979, hurt overall sales and profits. One of the 4300 machines that sold for $69,000 exceeded the computing power of an existing $560,000 machine.

Figure 13–4 shows another example of product line pricing. Apple is advertising the prices for the different models of its Lisa and Macintosh computers based on differences in memory and product features.

Usually firms produce and distribute a number of products in a line either because there is a relationship between demand or the costs of production for the

Figure 13–4 The prices of the computers in Apple's product line are based on differences in memory and product features.

Courtesy of Apple Computer, Inc.

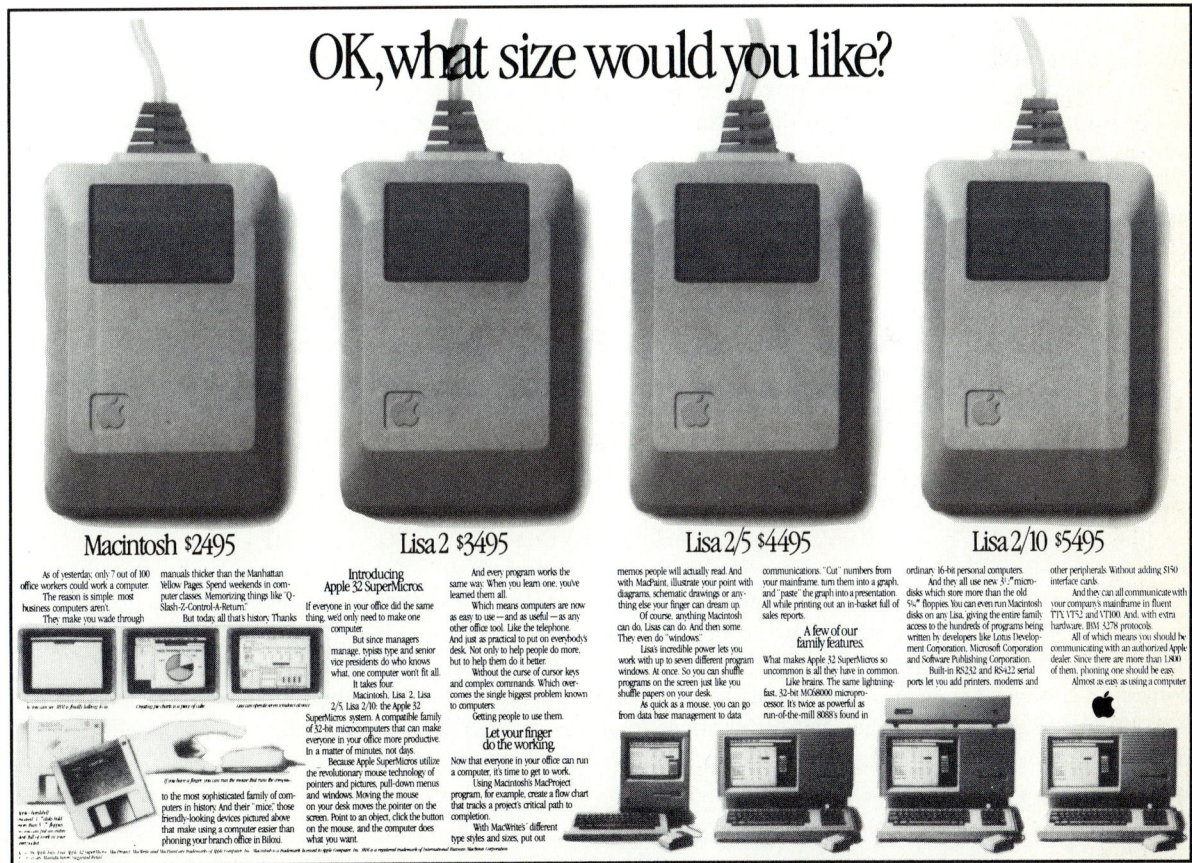

Chapter 13 / Pricing Modifications, Policies, and Considerations

361

various products or because the firm wishes to appeal to several diverse market segments with their different products. If the firm's products are related by both cost and demand, the quantity of any particular product produced and sold affects both the sales and costs of the other products in the line.[11] Changing the price of one product to increase its sales may or may not increase the overall sales revenues of the firm; the sales for related products in the line may drop.

Marketers also consider the effects of prices charged on the other items in the line. Adding a new, prestigious, or expensive item to a product line may enhance the image of the entire line. At the same time, evidence suggests that the lowest-priced item in the product line ordinarily affects the total sales of the line far more than does the price of any other product in the line.[12] Actual sales of this lowest-priced item may be a small percentage of the company's total sales, but lowering the price of this item often increases the overall sales of the company's products. The lowest price seems to be the one most frequently remembered by customers. It contributes to the company's image and often serves as the basis customers use for comparing the prices of similar products offered by two firms. The lowest-priced item in the line might also influence marginal buyers—those who are uncertain about whether to make the purchase—to buy.

Finally, in pricing items in the product line relative to one another, the marketer must decide whether the differences in features and additions justify the price differentials. Ideally, the different prices are determined by differences in production costs and demand for each product. But this information is often not available and marketers must estimate the differences. For assistance, they may look at the relationship between products in their other product lines and between product lines offered by competing companies for indications about the comparative value of various features.[13]

For example, when No Nonsense Fashions introduced its new Ultra Sense pantyhose, it set a price of approximately $2.99, which was much higher than the approximately $1.59 charged for its No Nonsense brand pantyhose. Its rationale was that the features of better fit and increased sheerness possessed by Ultra Sense would attract customers willing to pay the higher price.[14]

Pricing and the Product Life Cycle

The price charged for a product changes over time and as the product moves through its life cycle. (The stages in the product life cycle—introduction, growth, maturity, and decline—were discussed in chapter 11.) Throughout the life cycle, continual changes occur in promotional strategy and in the costs of production and distribution, and these changes call for changes in prices as well. The pricing of a new product begins at its birth, and pricing modifications continue throughout its life cycle.

Pricing in the introductory stage. In its introductory stage, a product generally enjoys protection from competition. Marketers are faced with the decision about whether to use penetration or skimming pricing, as discussed previously in this chapter. Generally, marketers examine consumer preferences and establish the feasibility of the product, then mark out a range of prices that will make the product attractive to buyers, and estimate the probable sales that will result from various prices. If the company's lead time over its competition is lengthy, the company has more latitude to use a skimming strategy. If the competition is about to introduce its own product, however, the company may have to use a low price to establish a competitive advantage.

Pricing in the growth stage. In the growth stage, competition is increasing but still limited. The company may start to enjoy the benefits of the learning curve described earler in this chapter and may either reduce prices or enjoy high profits due to reduced costs.

Pricing in the mature stage. In the mature stage, competition intensifies, providing customers with more alternatives. Prices are generally lowered at this stage as competitors struggle for market share. The efficiencies of producing the product increase, and costs also decrease, affecting prices if the company is using cost as the basis for setting prices.

Pricing in the decline stage. In the decline stage of the product life cycle, the company often tries to make as great a profit from the product as possible. The company may lower the price of the product to attract more customers or to hold on to its remaining customers. An alternative strategy may be to lower prices, such as advertising costs. As we will see in chapter 19, it is not advisable to invest heavily in low-growth markets.

There are two general trends that can be noted in pricing through the product life cycle. The first is that, in general, there is a steady decline in a product's price. The second is that, as a company becomes more efficient in producing the product over its life cycle, production costs will drop, affecting the product's price if the company is using a cost-based pricing method.

Price Discrimination

Since different customers have different sensitivities to price, the marketer sometimes wishes to offer one price to one segment and another price to another segment. This policy is called **price discrimination** and is viable when different market segments will react differently to prices. Under some circumstances, this type of strategy is illegal; generally, a company cannot charge different customers different prices for the same commodity. But there are cases, usually when the different markets are clearly identifiable and able to be clearly separated, in which this strategy can be successfully used within legal boundaries.

Consider how the airlines have been able to separate the business market from the tourist market. The business market is generally less sensitive to price and pays regular established fares. The tourist market, on the other hand, tends to be more sensitive to price and willing to observe restrictions, such as flying at certain times or staying at a destination for a prescribed number of days. By observing these restrictions, these customers can be legally eligible for a lower fare. Other legal examples of price discrimination are the telephone company, which charges set rates during business hours and reduced rates during evening hours, and the reduced rates that are offered to children and the elderly for many services.

Motivations to Modify Prices

There are a number of reasons for sellers to modify their price. These include responses to actions by competitors, excess production capacity, falling market share, demand exceeding production capacity, increasing costs, and inflation (see fig. 13–5).

Response to Actions by Competitors

As we saw in chapter 12, some companies base their prices on the prices charged by competitors. For these companies, it is important that their prices be in line with those of competing products. When competitors modify their prices, then, these companies may feel that they have to modify theirs. Under competition- or consumer-oriented pricing, the prices of similar products affect the value of a given

- Our competitors have lowered (or raised) their prices.
- We have excess production capacity.
- Our market share is falling.
- Demand is exceeding our production capacity.
- Our costs are increasing.
- We are being affected by inflation.

Figure 13–5 Should we modify our prices?

product to customers; one product becomes more valuable to customers at its current price if the price of a competing product has risen. This may enable the marketers of the more valuable product to raise their prices. Conversely, if the competition lowers its price, the product is of less value to customers because another product is readily available at a lower price. In the personal computer market, for example, a number of companies have produced models that look like and have features like the IBM PC, but cost less. When IBM simultaneously cut the prices of the PC models by up to 23 percent and increased their capabilities, the makers of the "lookalikes" found increased pressure in the already highly competitive market.

At some times, though, the best response to competitors' actions is no response, as happened in the beer market. In 1980, at the beginning of an economic recession, Miller, which was already the price leader, increased its prices. Competing breweries did not follow, but rather held up their own price increases. The result was that Miller's sales volume dropped, while the market shares and sales volumes of the competitors rose. Anheuser-Busch, for example, saw its market share rise from 27.8 percent to 29.5 percent in 1981.[15]

As we saw in chapter 3, deregulation has led some competitors to drop their prices and other competitors to drop theirs in response. The "price wars" created by these moves have occurred in the airline, trucking, and bus line industries.

Excess Production Capacity

A company that has excess production capacity might choose to lower its prices. In this case, producing more units of a product would not lead to additional fixed costs, as all the facilities are in existence. Any hotel or airline may find it useful to lower its prices to sell space, for example, as the capacity already exists. If warehouse capacity, production facilities, and/or the labor force are not fully utilized, it would be best to use those resources to help absorb fixed costs.

Falling Market Share

A company may also choose to reduce prices when its market share is falling. If it seems likely that the marketplace will be responsive, reducing prices to increase market share is often a good strategy. Before choosing to reduce prices, however, a company should estimate as closely as it can the elasticity of demand. Since prices communicate product quality to many consumers, potential buyers may not respond as expected to lower prices.

When Demand Exceeds Production Capacity

If demand exceeds production capacity, it may be wise to increase prices. The company may have priced too low in relation to what people are willing to pay for the product. Reducing the demand by increasing prices brings the demand more in line with production capabilities. Rather than frustrating customers by not having enough stock, the company simply sells to those customers who are able to pay the higher price. At the same time, the company may make higher profits on the quantity of the product that is produced.

Increasing Costs

Increasing costs are another reason for raising prices. This is especially true when a company is employing a cost-based pricing strategy. But this situation poses a dilemma—while rising costs without price increases can ruin profits, price hikes can be costly to a firm in terms of customer goodwill and long-term market share. It is essential that a company ensures the high quality of its product if it is raising prices.

Inflation

An inflationary economy poses additional complications for price setters. It may be necessary to estimate what costs are going to be and set prices in anticipation of inflation. Many companies have become more formal and structured in their pricing policies, moving responsibility for pricing decisions higher in the corporate organization.[16] It is reported that more and more companies are employing an ongoing price review, with adjustments coming in some companies as often as every two weeks.[17]

Companies are adopting an array of price-setting methods in response to uncertainties about costs and markets. Some companies are adopting **delayed-quotation pricing,** setting a final price only when items have reached the stage of finished goods. **Escalator clauses** are employed in some pricing policies—price increases are automatically implemented based on a previously stated formula, such as increases in wholesale price indexes or listed price increases of raw material suppliers.[18]

The policy that some companies follow to cope with inflation is to drop their low-priced products. But the risk here, as discussed earlier in the chapter, is that low-priced products often serve as a stimulant to sales throughout the company's product line. Eliminating them may decrease overall company sales.

Some companies are attempting to eliminate discounts, allowances, and special services which complicate price-setting by making it difficult for a company to know what its products are selling for.[19] But, if used creatively, discounting and promotional allowances can stimulate demand for products not requiring critical resources and boost company profits.

Separating the cost of services from the price of the product is another response to inflation and increasing costs. Using this policy, a firm that has priced a major product to include special services or peripheral equipment shifts to a policy in which each element of the product-service mix is priced separately. Usually, the sum of the prices is higher than the old, single price. In contemplating this policy, however, it is important for the company to ascertain the importance of each service to customers. If charging separately for each service causes total sales to decline, the company's overall profits may fall.[20]

When marketers consider employing any of these policies, they must consider possible effects. Cumulative price increases, for example, may reduce the amount of consumers' disposable income, which reduces the number of products they can buy. Another consideration is that concentrating on high-profit products and improving the company's cash flow may not be consistent goals. Focusing on high-profit products may reduce the company's cash flow as a result of reduced sales of low-profit items.[21]

The Relation of Pricing to the Marketing Mix

As price is one element of the marketing mix, it is related to the other elements. For example, one area of concern is the relationship between prices and advertising. There is an ongoing argument about the effect of advertising on prices: Are the costs of advertising passed along directly to the consumer? Or does advertising ultimately lower prices by facilitating market efficiency?

Some argue that the more a company advertises, the more it must charge to cover the cost of that advertising. Thus, advertising causes higher prices. The counterargument is that the cost to consumers of choosing products by using alternative sources of information, without advertising, exceeds the costs of using advertising. Advocates of this viewpoint believe that the availability of low-cost advertising gives manufacturers an incentive to produce higher-quality products; in other words, those manufacturers offering the best value and price have an opportunity through advertising to increase sales.[22]

Some studies have indicated that when a company increases its advertising relative to competition, the price that the company charges is higher relative to the competition. This happens because as a company increases its advertising, demand for its product rises, and competitors must sometimes lower their prices in response in order to maintain market share.[23]

The evidence seems inconclusive. It appears that there is validity to both arguments. Studies of retail advertising find that advertising increases consumer price sensitivity.[24] Studies of manufacturer advertising find that advertising decreases price sensitivity.

With regard to distribution, another element of the marketing mix, price is often a determining factor in the decision about which retailers will carry a product. Certain retailers will not carry products that do not fit into their price range. On the one hand, many retailers who are trying to establish or maintain a prestigious image are willing to carry only high-priced items. Moreover, since the distributor may influence customers' perceptions of the manufacturer, some manufacturers are reluctant to distribute their product through mass-market or inexpensive retailers for fear of damaging their overall image.

There is an obvious correlation between price and product. Generally, as the quality of the product goes up, so does the price. Partly this is because the price

Figure 13-6 An advertising campaign for J&B Scotch whisky is enhancing its image as a high-quality (and thereby high-priced) product.

Courtesy of The Paddington Corporation, New York

must incorporate the higher costs of producing quality goods. Higher prices may also influence the perception of higher-quality products in the minds of customers, as we have seen. As discussed earlier in this chapter, in setting a product's price, the prices of other products in the line must also be considered. Pricing new products inconsistently with other products in the line may negatively affect overall sales.

The relationship between price and the marketing mix can be seen in the liquor industry. Sales of distilled spirits have been dropping in recent years, especially in the middle-price range. With this in mind, distilleries are adjusting the elements in their marketing mix to position themselves as either top- or bottom-level products. J&B Scotch is having its image enhanced through a $15 million ad campaign. Crown Royal has been given a chic new package and has been designated as an "import," instead of the less impressive "Canadian" whiskey. At the other end, some brands are using sales promotion tools, such as coupons and contests, to increase sales.[25]

Legal Issues in Pricing

There are a number of legal constraints on pricing activities. Three of the major areas of legal concern—the Robinson-Patman Act, price-fixing, and unfair trade practices—are discussed below.

The Robinson-Patman Act

The **Robinson-Patman Act** makes it illegal to charge different customers different prices for the same product. There are, however, exceptions, as we saw in the discussion of price discrimination. Pricing policies are considered discriminatory only if the customers are in competition with one another. Thus, it is not discriminatory for a marketer to sell to wholesalers and retailers at different prices, since the two are not in direct competition. Moreover, charging different prices to different customers for the same product is legal as long as the same discount, such as a quantity discount, is made available to all customers. The Robinson-Patman Act also makes it legal for a marketer to charge different prices for the same product if it is more costly to provide the product to one customer than to another. Factors such as different shipping costs justify charging different prices to different customers. Thus, the Robinson-Patman Act allows market segmentation and varied prices for the same product in instances such as those described earlier in this chapter.

There appears to be a trend for the courts to interpret the Robinson-Patman Act less literally than they have previously, thus giving sellers significantly more latitude in developing and administering their promotional programs. As an example, McNeil Laboratories, makers of Tylenol, sold Tylenol at a discount to buyers who agreed to perform advertising services for the Tylenol purchased. Amster, a wholesaler, ordered an amount of Tylenol that McNeil judged to be in excess of Amster's advertising capability. McNeil supplied Amster with a substantially lesser quantity than Amster had ordered, an amount that McNeil believed to be in line with Amster's advertising capability. When Amster brought suit against McNeil, the court found that McNeil's selective granting of the discount was based on "valid business considerations" and did not violate the Robinson-Patman Act.[26]

Price-Fixing

Any collusion between competitors in setting prices, a practice known as **price-fixing,** is highly illegal. Sometimes companies try to avoid this law by announcing in advance what their prices are going to be, to give that information to the competition. But it is strictly forbidden by law for companies to meet with their competition and try to determine what the commonplace price in U.S. markets for a given product will be.

Research indicates that certain conditions appear to be more conducive to price-fixing than others.[27] Some of these factors are industry characteristics, namely, where there are many competitors for the same market; where each job is priced individually, and pricing decisions are made at low levels of the organization; and where products are largely undifferentiated. Other factors that can con-

Chapter 13 / Pricing Modifications, Policies, and Considerations

tribute to price fixing relate to companies themselves. These include company environments where a great deal of pressure is put on executives to achieve profits and volume and where price setting is decentralized.

Unfair trade practices are pricing actions taken by wholesalers and retailers to sell products below cost or with a very low markup to attract customers. These practices are illegal, as their intention is to destroy competition. The main users of these practices had been larger distributors who were able to sustain the costs of these actions to drive smaller competitors out of business.

Unfair Trade Practices

Summary

A common form of discount is the quantity discount. If the buyer purchases a large volume, the seller reduces the product's price. A trade discount is offered to a distributor or retailer who, in return for the reduced price on the product, assumes the responsibilities for marketing it. A cash discount makes the product available for a lower price to customers who pay cash. A seasonal discount is a lower price in an off-season. A cash rebate is a discount practice in which the seller maintains the list price but gives the buyer a partial refund for a particular product at a particular time.

Freight on board (FOB) is the most standard way of pricing a product. FOB is the practice of charging the wholesaler, retailer, or customer the standard price for the product itself plus shipping charges. Uniform delivered is a policy in which the shipping cost for a product has been established and is the same regardless of the buyer's location. In zone pricing, concentric circles (zones) are set up from one shipping location. The more distant the buyer is, the more costly the shipping.

An odd/even pricing strategy is the practice of setting a price just below an even dollar amount to give the impression of a bargain or at the even dollar amount to give the impression of a premium product. Customary pricing means pricing according to what the customer would expect the price to be.

A skimming strategy involves setting an initial high price to establish an image of quality and also to keep demand at a level with which production facilities can keep up. A penetration policy involves setting a low initial price that is perhaps not justified by the firm's costs but that enables the marketer to gain quick entry into the marketplace, gain a large market share, perhaps driving competition off, and ultimately driving costs down through the large volume that would result. Criteria used to determine which of these strategies to adopt for a new product include the number of potential customers and the price they are willing to pay, the right combination of price and promotion, and choice of distribution channel.

Marketers should establish prices that will expand the sales of highly profitable items and contract sales of relatively unprofitable products within the same line.

Products may be related in one of three ways: two products may be competitive, complementary to one another, or the relationship may be neutral.

In the introductory stage of the product life cycle, the product generally enjoys protection from competition and the price is often high. In the growth stage, competition is still limited, and the price remains high. In the mature stage, competition intensifies, and prices are generally lowered as are costs of production. In the decline stage prices are lowered still further.

Product prices should be in line with those of competing products. A company that has excess capacity may decide to lower a product's price to increase demand because more units will not entail additional fixed costs. Reducing a product price may also reverse a falling market share. Raising a price helps to reduce demand when production facilities are operating at capacity and offsets rising costs.

Prices may also be increased due to inflationary costs. Strategies designed to help companies respond to inflationary costs are delayed quotation and escalator strategies and unbundling of services.

Studies of retail advertising show that it increases consumer price sensitivity, while studies of manufacturer advertising show that it decreases price sensitivity. With regard to distribution, price is often a determining factor in a retailer's decision about whether or not to take the product. Generally, as the quality of the product goes up, so does the price.

The Robinson-Patman Act specifically prohibits price discrimination, although there are exceptions. Collusion between competitors to try to fix prices is highly illegal. Conditions conducive to price-fixing include situations where there are many competitors for the same market; where each job is priced individually, and pricing decisions are made at low levels of the organization; and where products are largely undifferentiated.

Questions for Discussion

1. Differentiate between the nature of price discounts provided to members of the distribution channel and to the final consumers.
2. What conditions generally promote the use of the cash discount in marketing a product?
3. What explains the use of "freight on board" and "uniform delivered price" methods of pricing by companies?
4. "Price rarely functions as the indicator of product quality." Comment.
5. What are the advantages of a skimming pricing policy?
6. "Penetration pricing works in certain conditions, not in others." Comment.
7. Explain how appropriate it is to use product line pricing in the case of the following products or services: (a) men's neckties; (b) women's cosmetics; (c) dairy products; and (d) legal services.
8. How do companies generally price their products in the face of inflation?

9. Are the following price discriminations legally permissible? Why or why not?
   a. Different ticket prices ($9, $12, $15, etc.) for a baseball game.
   b. Different rates (consumer vs. commercial rates) for local telephone services.
   c. Auto companies selling spare parts at different prices to auto dealers and body shops.
10. What conditions seem to generally favor price-fixing by companies?

References

1. The computer examples here and throughout the chapter are based on "A Price War Blasts Open the Home Market," *Business Week,* June 13, 1983, pp. 104–9; David E. Sanger, "IBM Cuts Prices on PC Line," *New York Times,* June 8, 1984, pp. D1, D4; and "How IBM Made 'Junior' an Underachiever," *Business Week,* June 25, 1984, p. 106.
2. John F. Crowther, "Rationale for Quantity Discounts," *Harvard Business Review,* March–April 1964, p. 73.
3. Charles A. Ingene and Michael Levy, "Cash Discounts to Retail Customers: An Alternative to Credit Card Sales," *Journal of Marketing,* Spring 1982, p. 92.
4. "Gas Credit Starts to Evaporate," *Business Week,* May 10, 1982, p. 111.
5. Ingene and Levy, pp. 93, 95.
6. Ronald Alsop, "Hoping to Ease Economic Pinch, Many Avidly Pursue Refund Offers," *Wall Street Journal,* October 18, 1982, p. 37.
7. Benson P. Shapiro, "The Psychology of Pricing," *Harvard Business Review,* July–August 1968, p. 18.
8. Ibid., p. 22.
9. Joel Dean, "Pricing Policies for New Products," *Harvard Business Review,* November–December 1976, pp. 85–87.
10. Hubert Gatignon and David J. Reibstein, "Optimal Product Line Pricing: The Influence of Elasticities and Cross-Elasticities," *Journal of Marketing Research,* August 1984, pp. 259–67.
11. Kent B. Monroe and Andris A. Zoltners, "Pricing the Product Line During Periods of Scarcity," *Journal of Marketing,* Summer 1979, p. 50.
12. Alfred R. Oxenfeldt, "Product Line Pricing," *Harvard Business Review,* July–August 1966, p. 140.
13. Ibid.
14. Pat Sloan, "No Nonsense Tries on a New Niche, *Advertising Age,* February 1, 1982, p. 10.
15. "What Blew the Head Off Miller's Profits," *Business Week,* February 15, 1982, pp. 39–40.
16. "Pricing Strategy in an Inflation Economy," *Business Week,* April 6, 1974, p. 43.
17. "How Price Tactics Feed Inflation," *Business Week,* March 10, 1980, p. 36.
18. Joseph P. Guiltinan, "Risk-Averse Pricing Policies: Problems and Alternatives," *Journal of Marketing,* January 1976, pp. 10–11.

19. "Pricing Strategy," p. 44.
20. Guiltinan, p. 11.
21. Guiltinan, pp. 13–14.
22. Paul W. Farris and Mark S. Albion, "The Impact of Advertising on the Price of Consumer Products," *Journal of Marketing,* Summer 1980, pp. 17–35.
23. Mark S. Albion and Paul W. Farris, *The Advertising Controversy* (Boston: Auburn House, 1981).
24. Farris and Albion, "The Impact of Advertising," p. 28.
25. "Why Spirit Sales Are Slipping a Bit," *Business Week,* May 17, 1982, p. 141–42.
26. "Legal Developments in Marketing," *Journal of Marketing,* Fall 1981, p. 136.
27. Jeffrey Sonnenfeld and Paul R. Lawrence, "Why Do Companies Succumb to Price Fixing?" *Harvard Business Review,* July–August 1978, pp. 147–49.

OBJECTIVES

1. To provide an overview of marketing communication decisions.

2. To identify the objectives of communication and how they affect promotional decisions.

3. To describe the process of communication and the different models of communication.

4. To study the different forms of marketing communication.

5. To examine the factors affecting the promotional mix.

14

Communication and the Promotional Mix

While Polaroid was introducing its instant movies and foreign competitors were making inroads into the camera and film markets, Kodak was developing a new technology in order to maintain its dominance in the photography industry. By 1982, Kodak had developed its newest product line, disc system cameras, which were designed to simplify amateur photography more than ever. The disc cameras use a disc of film instead of a roll, are pocket-sized, advance automatically, set exposure automatically, and have an automatic flash with a battery that recharges in one second and is expected to last the camera's lifetime. Models are available that focus as close as 18 inches and have a self-timing device to take pictures automatically.

Kodak viewed this new technology as its most significant development in 20 years. Having developed the product line, the next question was how best to introduce it to the public. As disc system cameras were totally unfamiliar to consumers and distributors, a considerable effort was needed.

The overall decision for Kodak was how best to introduce its new technology to gain acceptance in the marketplace. One aspect of this decision involved choosing the recipient of the message. Should the effort involve only consumer promotion? Even if Kodak could interest consumers in the cameras, the effort would be inconsequential if consumers could not find them in outlets. Kodak could hope that the consumer interest would stimulate retailer interest, or it could direct its promotional effort also toward distributors.

In presenting the line of cameras to the marketplace, Kodak used all aspects of the communication mix. The campaign opened on February 3, 1982. Kodak's vice-president John Robertson introduced the camera line on the national news program, "Good Morning America." The company received additional

publicity by holding news conferences in all major U.S. cities. Newspeople were given the opportunity to try the camera by photographing models in picturesque settings. Kodak's representatives explained the technical features of the products and answered newspeople's questions. In New York, Kodak's top executives spoke with reporters from the most influential media—network television, major business publications, and photo industry trade publications. The result of this portion of the campaign was that Kodak's new product line received coverage on every major television and radio network and in several articles in such important publications as *The New York Times*, *Time*, *Business Week*, *Fortune*, and *The Wall Street Journal* and many others.

The campaign also included sales promotion. Retailers received discounts if they ordered disc products early. Consumers who purchased the disc cameras received free rolls of film.

Kodak also used personal selling methods in this early portion of its communications campaign. Two weeks after the product's introduction, Kodak representatives were highly visible at the annual Photo Marketing Association convention. Here, Kodak's focus was on dealers and photofinishers, or people in the business of developing and printing photographs. Success in this portion of the photo industry is perhaps more important to Kodak than is selling cameras. At the convention, Kodak made several audiovisual presentations to groups of dealers and photofinishers and, in addition, gave live demonstrations to the disc product line. Kodak also sent salespeople to talk with professional groups about the disc product line and to demonstrate specific uses relevant to the groups. These organizations included the Rochester Engineering Society, the Optical Society of America, and Photographic Scientists and Engineers.

Advertising was one of the most important aspects of Kodak's communications campaign. The total advertising budget was $45 million, a record for Kodak, with a major portion of the advertising dollars going for television air time. The company's goal was to reach 95 percent of the public with an average of 18 messages per person by Christmas of 1982. Efforts to meet that goal included presenting commercials on the most popular prime-time programs of the year. Disc commercials ran for 30, 60, or 90 seconds on popular programs such as "M*A*S*H," "Mork and Mindy," and "Little House on the Prairie." The 90-second commercials during prime-time viewing hours were a first for Kodak. The company also broke tradition by showing the camera to 1,000 consumers before its introduction. Their responses helped to develop the theme for the ad campaign: "decision-free" photography. Commercials introduced the technology behind disc photography and featured vignettes in which the disc camera could take an excellent photograph, one that a conventional camera would miss. In major magazines, such as *Time*, *People*, *Sports Illustrated*, and *TV Guide*, Kodak later ran a special ad campaign designed especially for summer. The theme was "Get it while it's hot," featuring uses for disc cameras in summer settings, such as picnics and beaches. These ads were designed to show consumers that summer picture-taking is fun and easy with a disc camera.[1]

Before creating so extensive and integrated a promotional campaign, Eastman Kodak had to make a number of decisions concerning how and what it would communicate to various groups of people. In this chapter, we are going to look at how companies make these decisions, including how they develop promotional messages, how they choose the promotional tools they use, and how they combine the various tools to create a promotional mix.

An Overview of Marketing Communication

In a basic sense, **marketing communication** involves the sending of information. What that information is depends on three factors:

1. The recipients of the information
2. The nature of the message
3. The form of the communication

The Recipients of the Information

The recipients of the information can consist of all consumers, or of all the potential consumers in the targeted market segment, or of the people who are already consumers. The recipients can be the members of the distribution channel—retailers and wholesalers—who will sell the product. The recipients can also be people in a decision-making unit who are not involved in the final purchase decision, such as gatekeepers, influencers, and users. Finally, the recipients can be people not related to the purchase decision, such as the company's stockholders, business analysts, opinion formers, and technical specialists.

When Eastman Kodak was preparing its promotional campaign, it wanted to reach a number of these recipients—the consumers who would be purchasing the products, the dealers who would be selling them, scientists and engineers, and the news media who might write favorably about the new cameras and create an air of excitement around them. Others Kodak may have wanted to reach could have included the business and financial communities who would see Kodak as an attractive investment and the company's own employees to create a sense of teamwork and to boost morale.

The Nature of the Message

A company can be communicating a number of messages. It can be trying to make people aware of the company and its characteristics or of the company's products. The message can also try to interest consumers in the product and lead them to purchase it. The nature of the message depends on who the recipient is and how complex the product is. Different explanations of a product would be given, for example, to a consumer who just wants to take a photograph and to a scientist who is interested in the technology behind the disc camera. Similarly, different messages would be created for a simple-to-use camera, such as the disc camera, and for a complicated microscopic camera that would be used in only a few high-technology industrial or educational settings.

Eastman Kodak had a number of messages that it wanted to communicate. One was to consumers to tell them that a new camera based on a new technology existed and that it would let them take better photographs. Another message was aimed at dealers; it let them know how the product worked and also tried to convince them that consumers would want to buy this product. Another message—the scientific principles behind disc photography that make it a better way to take photographs—was aimed at scientists and technical specialists.

The Form of the Communication

There are four basic forms of marketing communication: advertising, sales promotion, publicity, and personal selling (see fig. 14–1). The characteristics of each of these forms of communication make each more suited for communicating a certain type of message to a certain audience. For example, Eastman Kodak used advertising to introduce the cameras to a wide audience and the one-on-one communication of personal selling to explain the details of the technology to scientists.

Communication Objectives

The decisions about each of these factors are based on the objectives or goals of the communication. What can a company be trying to achieve through its marketing communication? Some of the possible objectives include creating awareness, explaining or demonstrating the product, creating a positive image, convincing the buyer to make the purchase, shaping the buyer's attitudes about the product, or drawing an initial response from the buyer.[2] These individual objectives fall into a general objective of making an unaware buyer conscious of the company and leading that buyer to make some form of purchase. Eastman Kodak, for example, had the goal of creating awareness of its new technology among consumers, and it sent an introductory message to the mass audience through advertising.

Marketing communication, then, involves identifying the audience for the communication, deciding on the nature of the message, and choosing the form of the communication. Decisions about each of these factors are based on the objectives of the communication, as set by the company. These ideas will be discussed later in this chapter.

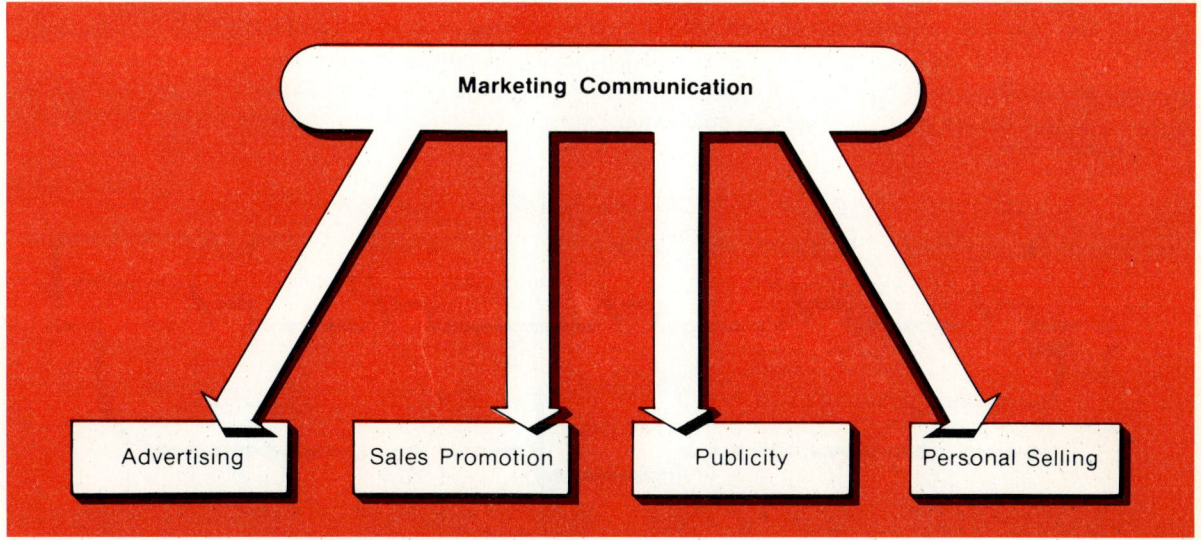

Figure 14–1 The forms of marketing communication

Models of Communication

We have just looked at the factors in marketing communications, but we have not discussed what marketing communication is. **Marketing communication** is "the sharing of information, concepts, and meanings by the source and receiver about products and services and the organizations that sell them."[3] Understanding this definition requires looking at the elements in the process of communication. We will look first at a basic model of communication and then at how the model has been adapted to marketing communication.

A Basic Model of Communication

Figure 14–2 presents a basic model of communication consisting of seven elements: a source, the message, encoding, transmission, the receiver, decoding, and feedback.[4] These elements are described in the paragraphs that follow.

The source. The **source** of any communication is the person or organization who generates the message and decides on its content. The source will have an image of credibility that will determine how the rest of the communication is perceived. The source is also often judged by its traits; that is, if a person considered a role model is the source of the message, then that message is more likely to be listened to.

The message. The **message** is determined by the communications objectives and is the sum of the information the source is trying to send to the receiver. The message consists of words, copy, photographs, and artwork.

Encoding. **Encoding** is the process of putting the information in the message into a form that will be understood by the receiver. The words, copy, photographs, artwork, and other means chosen must mean something or convey images to the receiver that correspond to what the source is trying to communicate. The process of encoding requires an understanding of the needs and behavior of the receiver so that an effective message can be created.

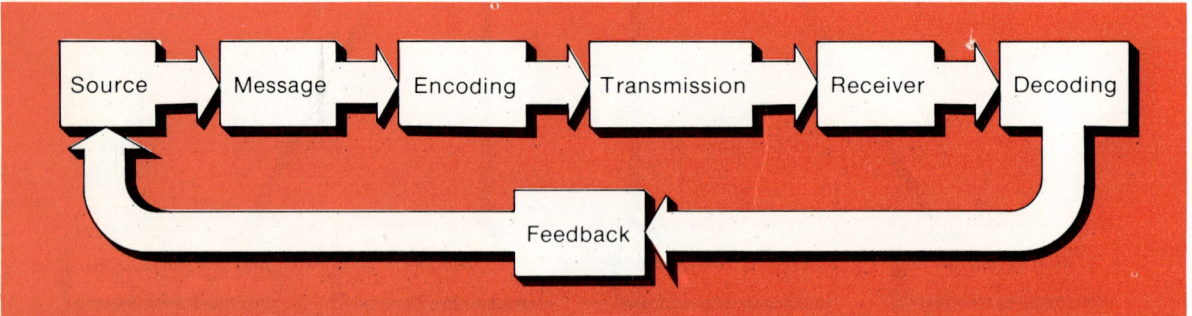

Figure 14–2
A basic model of communication

Source: Richard E. Stanley, *Promotion*, 2nd ed. (Englewood Cliffs, N.J.: Prentice-Hall, 1982), p. 138. Reprinted by permission of Prentice-Hall, Inc., Englewood Cliffs, N.J.

Transmission. **Transmission** is the carrying of the message from the source to the receiver. The transmission can be through one or a number of channels. During the transmission, **noise** can interfere with the reception of the message. The noise can come from the environment, as with other transmissions, or physical factors that block communications, or it can be internal, as when the receiver is distracted.

Receiver. A **receiver** is a person who perceives and listens to the message. No receiver listens to every message. Rather, receivers choose among the various messages selectively and retain only those that interest them. How the receiver interprets the message is determined by the beliefs, attitudes, and factors that make up consumer behavior (see chapter 7).

Decoding. **Decoding** is the process of taking the message and putting it into familiar terms. For the message to have the intended effect, it must match the meaning the receiver gives it during the decoding. The receiver decodes and interprets the message through the factors covered in the discussion of consumer behavior (see chapter 7).

Feedback. **Feedback** is the message the receiver sends back to the source. In one-on-one communication, it can be a gesture, an expression, or a verbal response. In mass communication, it can take the form of some action. By observing the feedback, the source can determine whether the message was received and decoded as was intended.

These seven elements combine to form the basis of communication. Now let us turn to another model that shows how these elements combine to form a marketing communication system.

A Marketing Communication System

Figure 14–3 presents a marketing communication system that contains the same elements of the basic communication model, although the elements may have different names.[5] We will look at these elements.

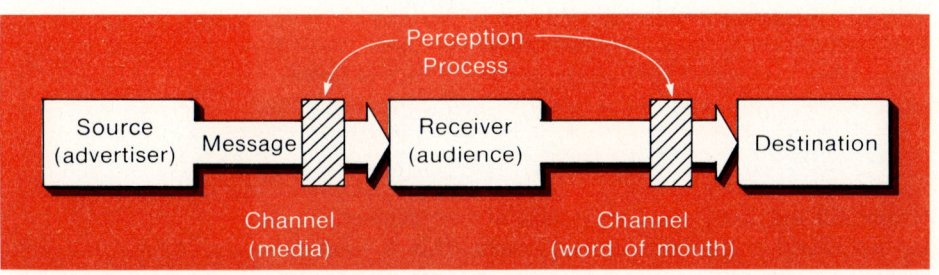

Figure 14–3
A marketing communication system

Source: David A. Aaker and John G. Myers, *Advertising Management*, 2nd ed. (Englewood Cliffs, N.J.: Prentice-Hall, 1982), p. 234. Reprinted by permission of Prentice-Hall, Inc., Englewood Cliffs, N.J.

The source. The source of the message is the company that wants to send information to consumers. In personal selling, the salesperson is considered a source; in publicity, a public relations director can be the source; in advertising, a spokesperson who appears in the advertisements can appear to be the source. As we saw earlier, the source is judged on credibility and on the traits perceived as belonging to the source. Eastman Kodak itself was a source of information about disc photography, as were its executives in talking with the news media and appearing on television and its salespeople in talking with technical specialists about the product.

The message. The message is the advertisement, sales presentation, press release, or other form of communication that transmits information. The message consists of the copy, the visual presentation, the mood or image created, and the approach used, such as comparative, informative, or humorous. The content of messages will be discussed further in chapters 15 and 16. The messages that Eastman Kodak was sending to its different audiences was that it had created a new technology, that its new disc cameras created "decision-free" photography, and that it is an innovative company and an attractive investment.

Figure 14—4 A top athlete, such as basketball star Isiah Thomas, is a highly credible source for an advertising message about athletic shoes.

The channel. The channel used to send the message can be one or more of the forms of communication—advertising, sales promotion, publicity, and personal selling. Each form is more effective than others under certain conditions, and the message received is affected by the channel used to send it. For example, the news stories generated by publicity lent importance and credibility to the introduction of the new technology. The use of personal selling by specially trained salespeople helped to spread the message about the new technology to technical specialists as the salespeople could demonstrate the cameras and answer direct questions. Mass communication through advertising was the best way in which to reach a wide audience to tell them about the new type of cameras.

The receiver. The receiver is the target market segment. As each segment has certain characteristics, the message must be formulated to appeal to that audience so that it has the desired effect on that audience. Telling a technical specialist that it's fun to take pictures with a disc camera would not fulfill the company's objectives, nor would it be appropriate to tell a consumer about the inner workings of the camera. The message must also mean something to the receiver in terms of attitudes, behavioral characteristics, and steps in the buyer behavior process, as we will see.

Destination. Communication does not always end at the receiver, as the receiver may pass along information and attitudes to others. This is known as **word-of-mouth** communication. For example, a dealer may have been told about

Chapter 14 / Communication and the Promotional Mix

the features of the cameras and may pass that information along to a potential buyer. Or a satisfied buyer may tell a friend about the new camera.

Perception process. At two points in the marketing communication system—before the message reaches the receiver and before the message reaches the destination—there are perception processes. Before a message can achieve its objective, it must pass through the factors that contribute to the receiver's perception. These factors include the willingness to listen to the message, the nature of the message itself, and the set of behavioral characteristics, including culture, values, and information needs, that influence the effect of the message. For example, if a consumer has no intention of purchasing a camera, the message would be ignored.

A main theme running through the discussion of the communication process is that the nature of the message is affected by the form and interpretation of the communication. In the next section, we will look at the factors that marketers consider when they are developing the means that will get the intended message to the receiver.

The Nature of the Communication Message

We now come to the question of what the message should be. In general, the message should be related to the communication objectives, and the information contained in the message should have the desired effect upon the consumer. The question then becomes: What should the company's communications objectives be? A number of theorists have considered this question and have developed ways in which to understand and identify communications objectives. We will now look at these ways.

The Hierarchy of Effects

One set of ways to develop objectives is to consider the **hierarchy of effects,** or the progressive thoughts and opinions consumers have about a product. A standard way to look at the hierarchy is to consider the AIDA model (see fig. 14–5). This model suggests that buyers pass through steps in a hierarchy before they make a

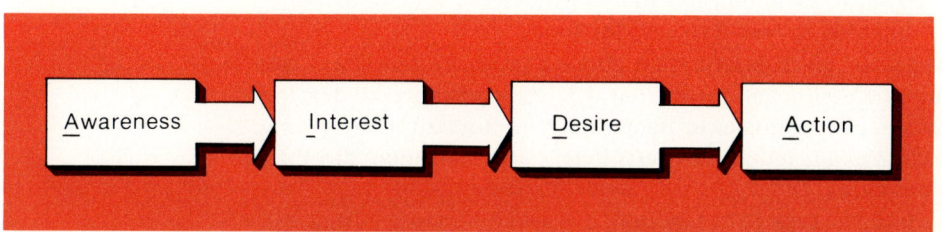

Figure 14–5
The AIDA model

Figure 14–6 An advertisement creating awareness.

Reprinted with permission of Ralston Purina Company

purchase. First, consumers become *a*ware that the product exists. Then, they develop an *i*nterest in the product and may try to find out more about it in an information search. Then, they develop a *d*esire for the product and form a purchase intention. Finally, they take *a*ction; they actually purchase the product.

The importance of this model to marketers is that, if marketers can recognize where the consumer is in this progression, they can identify exactly what must be communicated and can create a message that will appeal to and affect consumers.

Do consumers have to be made aware of the existence of a new product? Then marketers can create messages that introduce the product and describe its benefits. In figure 14–6, for example, Ralston Purina is telling consumers about its new fish-flavored dog food. Moreover, it communicates that dogs love the taste of fish and, indeed, prefer this new dog food to beef-flavored dog food.

Do consumers have to be given information about a product? Marketers can present facts, arguments, and product attributes that will lead consumers to develop an interest in their product. For example, in figure 14–7, Motorcraft is presenting information that shows that its FL-1A oil filter lasts longer and traps more dirt than do three of its main competitors.

Must the purchase desire be created? Marketers can develop messages that will make consumers want to purchase a product. In figure 14–8, the marketers of

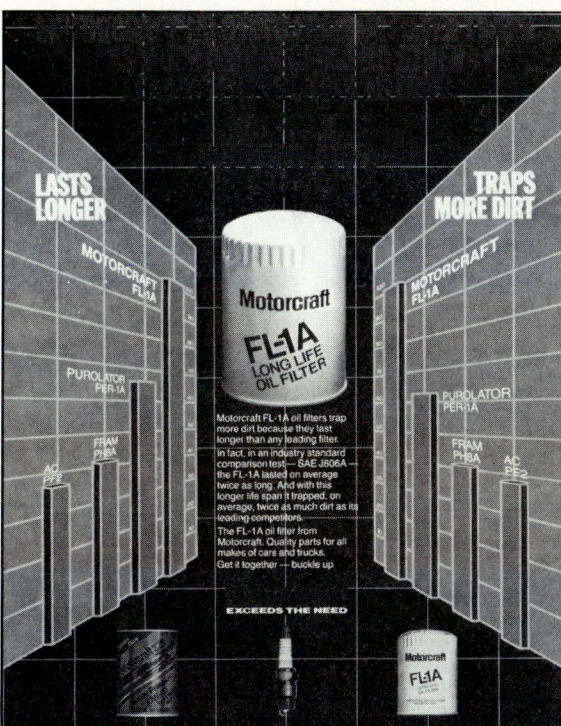

Figure 14–7 An advertisement presenting information.
Ford Motor Company

Figure 14–8 An advertisement creating the desire to purchase.
Copyright Nabisco Brands Inc.

TABLE 14–1 A Hierarchy of Effects

Related Behavioral Dimensions	Movement toward Purchase	Types of Promotion or Advertising Relevant to Various Steps
Conative: the realm of motives. Ads stimulate or direct desires.	Purchase ↑ Conviction ↑	Point-of-purchase Retail store ads Deals "Last-chance" offers Price appeals Testimonials
Affective: the realm of emotions. Ads change attitudes and feelings.	Preference ↑ Liking ↑	Competitive ads Argumentative copy "Image" ads Status, glamour appeals
Cognitive: the realm of thoughts. Ads provide information and facts.	Knowledge ↑ Awareness	Announcements Descriptive copy Classified ads Slogans Jingles Sky writing Teaser campaigns

Source: Robert J. Lavidge and Gary A. Steiner, "A Model for Predictive Measurements of Advertising Effectiveness," *Journal of Marketing*, October 1961, p. 139. Used with permission of the American Marketing Association.

Fleishmann's Light Corn Oil Spread and Borden Lite-line Cheese Product have chosen three ways in which to create desire. First, they demonstrate an attractive and delicious-looking use of the products. Second, they present a recipe that gives consumers a direct reason to purchase the products. Finally, they include a coupon that allows consumers to save money on the products.

Another way to look at the same idea is to consider the hierarchy of effects in table 14–1.[6] In this hierarchy, the buyer moves up through five steps before making the actual purchase. The first step is *awareness;* consumers just know of the existence of a product. At the second step, buyers are developing *knowledge* about the product and the benefits it offers. At the third step, this knowledge has created a *liking* for the product. The liking develops into a *preference* for the product over all other similar products in step 4. In step 5, the consumer develops a *conviction* that is eventually turned into the actual *purchase*.

You will also note in table 14–1 that these steps are related to the three types of attitudes described in chapter 7: the cognitive, the affective, and the conative. Each attitude can be influenced by a certain type of message (also shown in table 14–1). The implication is that marketers who want to influence a person at a certain point in the hierarchy holding a certain type of attitude can develop a type of communication message directly for that situation. For example, if marketers have the objective of creating a preference for their product, they can recognize that an effective way to do this is to create a message that appeals to affective, or emotional, attitudes. Advertisements that present the image or status of a product are communicating this type of message. On the other hand, if marketers have the objective of stimulating the actual purchase, their message can appeal to the conative attitudes or motivations. The message may be in the form of a final push, such as a sales promotion offering a deal on the purchase.

The DAGMAR Model

Another way of looking at how a hierarchy of effects influences a communication message is the DAGMAR model, shown in figure 14–9.[7] (DAGMAR is an acronym of the title of a book, *Defining Advertising Goals for Measured Advertising Results,* by Russell H. Colley.) The major premise behind this model is that there is much waste in advertising due to a lack of a fully defined objective of what is to be communicated to whom. Having a specific, written, measurable goal allows marketers to create messages that will move people from their stage in the hierarchy through the remaining stages to making the purchase. The DAGMAR model presents five stages and the marketing forces, or forms of communication, that can be used to carry out the various possible objectives, such as creating awareness or establishing the conviction to buy. The model also notes the countervailing forces that marketers must consider when preparing their message. For example, if the competition is making certain attractive claims about their product, a message that tries to establish conviction to buy may not have its intended effect.

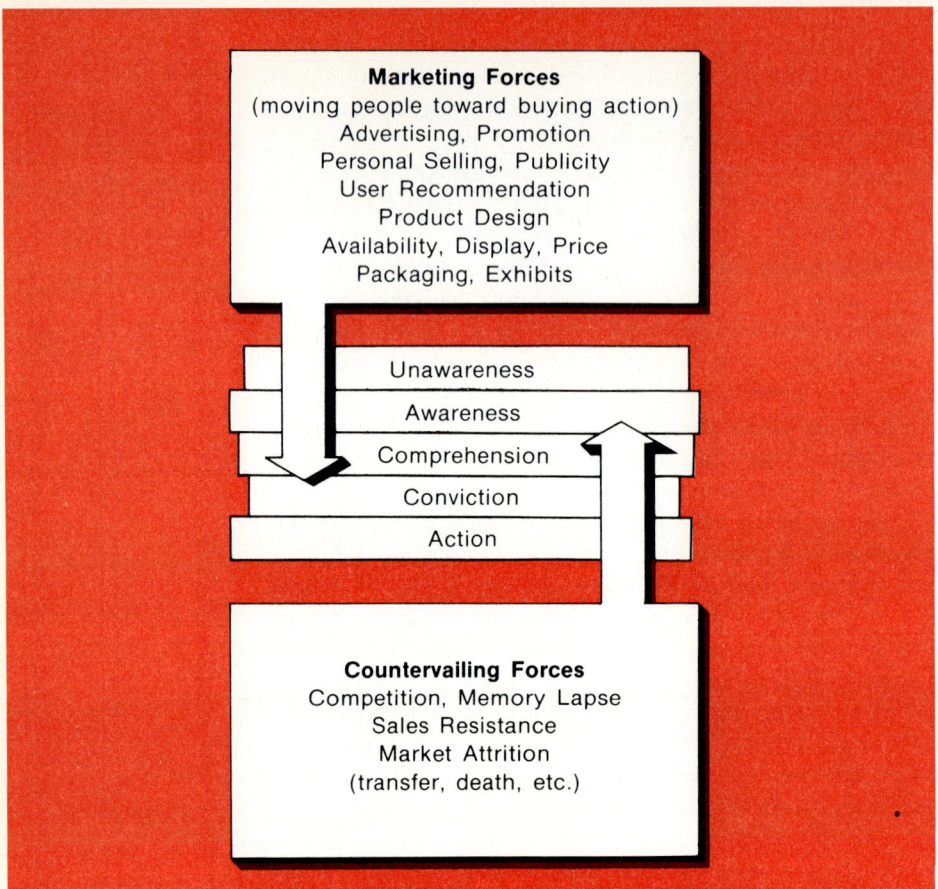

Figure 14–9 The DAGMAR model

Source: Russell H. Colley, "Squeezing the Waste Out of Advertising," *Harvard Business Review*, September–October 1962. Copyright © 1962 by the President and Fellows of Harvard College; all rights reserved. Reprinted by permission.

The Low-Involvement Hierarchy

A final way in which to consider the nature of the message is to look at the low-involvement hierarchy[8] (see fig. 14–10). This hierarchy was developed as an attempt to explain the effect of television advertising. The model suggests that few television viewers are involved with the products or with the communication. The products, in addition to having low involvement, are also little differentiated from competing products, are best promoted through mass advertising, and are in the mature stages of their life cycles.[9] The model suggests further that, because of the low involvement, the advertisements do not lead to any changes in attitudes about the products. Rather, they eventually lead to the consumer remembering the name of the product and perhaps taking the action of purchasing it. After the purchase, if the product is satisfactory, the consumer would then go through an attitudinal

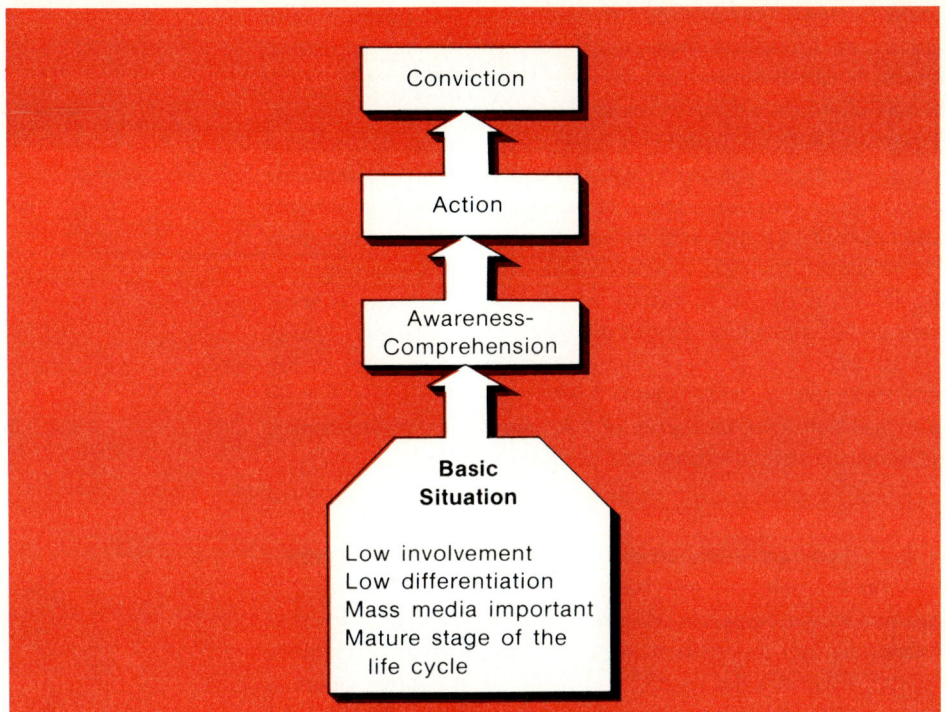

Figure 14–10 The low-involvement hierarchy

Source: Michael L. Ray, *Advertising and Communication Management* (Englewood Cliffs, N.J.: Prentice-Hall, 1982), p. 187. Reprinted by permission of Prentice-Hall, Inc., Englewood Cliffs, N.J.

change, having learned through use that the product performs in a certain manner and provides certain benefits. This sequence is a reversal of the latter stages in the other hierarchical models, as it involves action by the consumer before the consumer develops conviction about the product. The implication of this model for marketers is, perhaps, that in a low-involvement situation, the message must be communicated repeatedly if it is to have its intended effect on consumers.

The Forms of Marketing Communication

Marketers carry out their plans to achieve their promotional objectives by using one of the forms of marketing communication: advertising, sales promotion, publicity, and personal selling. As indicated, each of these forms has characteristics that make it appropriate for communicating a certain type of message and for reaching certain consumers. The forms of communication are described next.

Advertising

Advertising is "any paid form of non-personal presentation and promotion of ideas, goods, or services by an identified sponsor."[10] Advertising can appear in newspapers and magazines, it can be broadcast through television or radio, or it can appear outdoors as on billboards. Other forms of advertising include circulars, direct-mail pieces, and posters. A main feature of advertising is that it reaches a mass audience, which makes it the best form to use when trying to communicate with as many people as possible. Another feature of advertising is that it presents a standardized communication: all people will be presented with the same message. Advertising is best at communicating a limited amount of information to a large number of people. In terms of the hierarchy of effects, advertising is most effective at creating awareness of a product. Remember that when Eastman Kodak had the goal of creating awareness of its new disc cameras in 95 percent of the general population, it conducted a widespread advertising campaign largely through televised commercials featuring its theme of "decision-free" photography. (The types and methods of advertising are discussed in chapter 15.)

Sales Promotion

Sales promotion includes "those activities, other than personal selling, advertising, and publicity, that stimulate consumer purchasing and dealer effectiveness."[11] Sales promotions fall into two major categories. There are *trade promotions* aimed at members of the distribution channel to get them to carry a product or carry more of the product. Some of the discounts discussed in chapter 13 are forms of trade promotions, as are bonus packs, trade allowances, and trade shows. The second category is *consumer promotions*, aimed at consumers to get them to make a purchase. Coupons, premiums, bonus packs, and samples are all kinds of consumer promotions.

As you can see from these examples, sales promotion is a combination of pricing and advertising. It is trying to communicate something about the product, but it also provides an incentive, usually financial, for making the purchase. In terms of the hierarchy of effects, sales promotion is often used to move a person from conviction about the product to actually making the purchase.

The message conveyed to consumers by sales promotion is standardized, and sales promotion reaches a mass audience. It is the fastest-growing form of communication, with more effort going toward it than to any other form. (Sales promotion is discussed further in chapter 15.)

Publicity

Publicity is "non-personal stimulation of demand for a product, service, or business unit by planting commercially significant news about it in a published medium or obtaining favorable presentation of it upon radio, television, or stage that is not paid for by the sponsor."[12] Companies do not directly control publicity. They can actively seek it as Eastman Kodak did in holding news conferences and demonstrating the new disc cameras, but they could not control what, if anything, would be said or written as a result of these activities. The general purpose of publicity is

Figure 14–11 Trade shows and exhibitions are one form of sales promotion.
Marc P. Anderson

to create goodwill for a company or interest in a product. Eastman Kodak, for example, hoped that favorable news stories would create interest in its cameras. (Publicity is discussed further in chapter 15.)

Personal Selling

Personal selling is "oral presentation in a conversation with one or more prospective purchasers for the purpose of making sales."[13] Personal selling differs from the other forms of communication in that it is personal—the message can be customized to appeal directly to specific customers. It is a very effective way of relating a product to the particular needs of any one customer and of communicating directly with, including answering the questions of, specific consumers. Personal selling is expensive for a company, but it is a valuable way of moving customers from a state of interest or conviction to making the actual purchase. Personal selling is also different from the other forms in that it is direct two-way communication. Not only is the company communicating a specific message to a consumer, it is also receiving direct feedback about its products. For Eastman Kodak, personal selling was an effective way in which to communicate directly to the dealers and photofinishers who would be carrying or handling the new disc cameras. (Personal selling is discussed further in chapter 16.)

Creating the Promotional Mix

Organizations generally do not rely on just one form of communication. Rather, they will choose among and create a mix of the forms based on the communication objectives and the nature of the receiver. This mix is known alternatively as the **communication mix** or the **promotional mix.**

The question then arises: How does a company decide which form or forms to use? The first consideration is what resources are available to the company. Does the company have its own sales force? Is one of the advertising media available? What budget does the company have to pursue promotion? Once these questions are answered, the company moves on to three other considerations: the type of product, the stage of the product's life cycle, and the consumer's stage in the buying process.

The Type of Product

Simple products, such as types of food, clothing, or office supplies, do not need much of an explanation. Generally, consumers just have to be aware that the products exist and where they can purchase them. For these products, advertising and sales promotion may be the most appropriate forms of communication.

As products become more complex and consumers search for more and detailed information about them, the company may find that two-way communication is necessary. The product may require a customized explanation or demonstration that must be provided through personal selling. Many types of industrial products and equipment, for example, are promoted through personal selling.

The Stage of the Product Life Cycle

Different forms of communication are appropriate for different stages of the product life cycle and the different objectives the company has for each stage. In the introduction, for example, a main objective is to make consumers aware that the product exists, and advertising, with its ability for mass communication, is the most effective form. Another objective may be to get retailers to carry the new product, and the company may decide to use trade promotions. A third objective may be to get consumers to try the product, so the company may use consumer promotions.

In the growth stage, the company may want to make more people aware of the product, so it may continue advertising. Consumers, however, may find the need to get more information about the product; the company may thus find that it needs to use personal selling.

In maturity, consumers are repurchasing the product. An objective may be to remind them that the product exists and that it has certain features. Mass communication through advertising may be the best way in which to accomplish this. In maturity, there is also increasing competition, and the company may have to use the incentives of various forms of sales promotion to keep consumers purchasing their product.

14–1 Focus on Marketing Strategy
PROMOTING CAMERAS AND FILM

In 1976, Canon introduced its AE-1 camera into the American market. The AE-1 was a technological advancement—a simple-to-use 35-mm camera with an internal microprocessor that helped amateur photographers find the proper exposures for their pictures. The promotional campaign for the camera was extensive. Canon developed the catchy slogan "So advanced, it's simple" to stress the technological features. Advertisements appeared on television and in magazines, showing athletes such as tennis players John Newcombe and Tracy Austin and figure skater Peggy Fleming taking action photographs with ease. This was the first time that 35-mm cameras had been advertised on television. Canon also launched a sales promotion campaign by contributing to athletic organizations and, consequently, becoming the "official camera" of the New York Yankees, the National Football League, and other sports groups. The entire promotional campaign has paid off for Canon, as it now controls approximately 30 percent of the 35-mm camera market. This success has led Canon to continue its promotional strategy.

Canon's AE-1 was the first camera of its kind, so Canon was faced with the task of establishing the market and maintaining its leadership in face of later competition from such companies as Olympus and Minolta. Fuji was faced with the opposite problem, as it tried to establish itself in the American film market. It found itself competing against Eastman Kodak, which was willing to counter any moves Fuji made to hold on to its 85 percent share of the market.

Faced with a shrinking market in Japan, Fuji decided to move into the United States in order to grow. It already had an excellent reputation due to the high quality of its tapes and other video products, which made its entry into the film market easier. It made a number of moves: It cut the price of its print paper, and it introduced a new type of high-resolution film. Kodak countered with lowered prices, its own high-resolution film, and an extensive promotional campaign. Fuji then became the official film of the 1984 Olympic Games in Los Angeles; the company planned to publicize its connection with the Olympics to gain greater market share. Kodak countered this move by becoming a sponsor of the U.S. Olympic Team and by conducting extensive television and print advertising campaigns and a sales promotion campaign featuring Olympic athletes. Fuji's future promotional plans include heavy advertising and promotion of the Fuji name, with the hope that greater brand recognition will lead to greater sales. Fuji cannot forget, however, that Kodak wants to hold on to its market share and will probably conduct heavy advertising and promotion campaigns of its own.

Sources: Based on Louis Kraar, "Japan's Canon Focuses on America," *Fortune*, January 12, 1981, pp. 83–88; and "Fuji Photo: Sharpening Its Image in the U.S. as It Develops New Products," *Business Week*, October 24, 1983, pp. 88–89.

In the decline stage, the company may want to use sales promotions to increase sales of the product. The company may also reposition the product along a different attribute or use and may use advertising to communicate this to a new audience.

The Consumer's Stage in the Buying Process

As we have seen, different communication messages are used to create different states in and lead to different actions by consumers. Similarly, the forms of communication are suited to deliver certain types of messages. When creating the mix, marketers consider what they want to communicate to consumers at different stages (for example, create awareness in unaware consumers) and use the appropriate combination of message and form.

Figure 14–12 The forms of communication complement each other. Advertising creates an awareness that makes personal selling easier.

Reprinted with permission from McGraw-Hill Publications Company

Interrelationships among the Forms of Communication

The forms of communication are by no means independent of each other. Rather, they work together as part of the communication mix to achieve the company's objectives. For example, consider figure 14–12. The point of this advertisement is that the awareness of a company and its products created through advertising (in this advertiser's magazine, it is hoped) makes the job of the sales force in personal selling much easier. Similarly, it has been suggested that an integrated program of advertising and sales promotion is more successful than either form used independently in creating long-term success for a product.[14] Thus marketers create the total communications mix based on the attributes of each form and its ability to accomplish the company's communications objectives.

Summary

The purpose of marketing communication is to send information to consumers. What that information is depends on the audience for that message (consumers, stockholders, the business community, and so on) and what that message is supposed to achieve.

A model of communication involves a *source* sending a *message* through a *channel* to a *receiver* who then provides *feedback* to the source. The message passes through *perceptual processes,* during which the receiver analyzes and interprets the message according to his or her needs or according to the factors that affect his or her consumer behavior.

The nature of the communication message is related to the communications objectives of the company. There are a number of ways to develop the objectives. One is to consider the hierarchy of effects. The *AIDA model* proposes a hierarchy in which a consumer must become *a*ware that the product exists, must then become *i*nterested in the product, must then develop the *d*esire to purchase the product, and finally must take the *a*ction of making the purchase. If marketers can recognize where consumers fall in this hierarchy, they can develop a message that will directly work toward meeting their objectives.

Another hierarchy was proposed in the *DAGMAR model,* in which consumers must also be moved through the cognitive, affective, and conative attitudes through messages created to influence directly consumers' stages in the hierarchy.

A *low-involvement model* has also been proposed that reverses the steps in the hierarchy under certain conditions. This model suggests that the repetition of the message may lead a consumer to purchase a product in a low-involvement situation and that successful use of the product then leads the consumer to develop a favorable image of the product.

The forms of communication used to transmit the message are *advertising, sales promotion, publicity,* and *personal selling.* Each of these forms has characteristics that make it appropriate to transmit a certain type of message to certain customers at specific stages in the hierarchy of effects.

Marketers use a *communications* or *promotional mix* of the forms of communication based on the resources of the company. Other factors considered in creating the communications mix are the type of product, the stage of the product's life cycle, and the positioning of people in the buying process. The forms of communication in the promotional mix are interrelated and assist one another in achieving the communications objectives of the firm.

Questions for Discussion

1. What are the different objectives used by companies in making communication decisions?
2. How would you describe the basic model of communication?
3. Evaluate the critical role of decoding in the communication process.
4. What are the practical promotional implications of low-involvement decisions by consumers?
5. Examine the functional usefulness of the DAGMAR model of communication.
6. Explain the importance of sales promotion in selling the following products: (a) photographic films; (b) photographic cameras; (c) automobiles; and (d) women's cosmetics.
7. "Personal selling is a rather unique form of promotion." Explain.
8. In what way does product life cycle shape the promotional mix of companies?
9. Discuss the importance of publicity in promoting a product.

References

1. The discussion of Eastman Kodak here and throughout the chapter is based on Barnaby J. Feder, "Kodak Shows New Disc Cameras," *New York Times,* February 4, 1984, pp. D1, 2; Gay Jervey, "Kodak Unloads Big Film, Disc Ad Drives," *Advertising Age,* July 4, 1983, pp. 1, 32; "Kodak Disc Aims, Shoots, and Wins," *Sales Marketing Management,* January 17, 1983, p. 1; Scott Hume, "Kodak Promo Develops Ad Awareness," *Advertising Age,* August 29, 1983, p. 3; and "Tight Focusing by Kodak," *Public Relations Journal,* November 1982, pp. 16–21.
2. Michael L. Ray, *Advertising and Communication Management* (Englewood Cliffs, N.J.: Prentice-Hall, 1982), p. 176.
3. Richard E. Stanley, *Promotion,* 2nd ed. (Englewood Cliffs: N.J.: Prentice-Hall, 1982), p. 136.
4. The description of the model is based on ibid., pp. 138–43.
5. The description of the model is based on David A. Aaker and John G. Myers, *Advertising Management,* 2nd ed. (Englewood Cliffs, N.J.: Prentice-Hall, 1982, pp. 234–35.
6. Robert J. Lavidge and Gary A. Steiner, "A Model for Predictive Measurements of Advertising Effectiveness," *Journal of Marketing,* October 1961, pp. 59–62.
7. Russell H. Colley, "Squeezing the Waste Out of Advertising," *Harvard Business Review,* September–October 1962, p. 81.

8. Herbert E. Krugman, "The Impact of Television Advertising: Learning Without Involvement," in Harold Kassarjian and Thomas Robertson, eds., *Perspectives in Consumer Behavior* (Glenview, Ill.: Scott, Foresman, 1968).
9. Ray, *Advertising and Communication Management*, p. 187.
10. *Marketing Definitions: A Glossary of Marketing Terms* (Chicago: American Marketing Association, 1960).
11. Ibid.
12. Ibid.
13. Ibid.
14. Roger A. Strang, *The Relationship between Advertising and Promotion in Brand Strategy* (Cambridge, Mass.: Marketing Science Institute, 1975).

OBJECTIVES

1. To identify the different components of advertising decisions.

2. To discuss the different objectives of advertising.

3. To explain the nature and characteristics of the different advertising media.

4. To describe the different objectives and methods of sales promotion.

5. To describe the different objectives and methods of publicity.

15
Advertising, Sales Promotion, and Publicity

The Whopper versus the Big Mac; flame broiling versus frying; "Aren't You Hungry?" versus "You Deserve a Break Today." The battle of the burgers is in full swing.

In 1983, McDonald's had 41.5 percent of the hamburger fast-food market, Burger King 16.2 percent, and Wendy's 9.4 percent. The first missile was launched when second-place Burger King claimed that a survey showed consumers preferring the Whopper to the Big Mac. Furthermore, Burger King claimed, Big Macs had 20 percent less meat than Whoppers, and Big Macs were fried rather than flame-broiled. McDonald's responded by suing to block the ads, claiming that they were false and misleading. While the courts were deciding whether Burger King's claims were legitimate, McDonald's had to decide whether to ignore the direct attack or to counterattack. A response might draw more attention to the Burger King claims, while silence might indicate that Burger King's flame-broiled burgers really do taste better.

If a counterattack were to be launched, a decision had to be made about the target. Historically, McDonald's was the leader with Middle American, middle-income families with young children. Burger King appealed more to adults, a market segment that may be more influenced by the better-taste campaign. Should McDonald's continue to focus their attention on the young family market, or should it strike directly at the adult customer?

Once the target audience was chosen, McDonald's had to decide what to say. Should McDonald's say that frying really is better? Should it stress other aspects of its food quality? Or should it run a taste test of its own? An alternative was to ignore the hamburger argument altogether and put more emphasis on its Chicken McNuggets.

Should this battle lead McDonald'a to increase its advertising budget? It was already spending $300 million a year on advertising.

Would more of the same type of advertising exposure be beneficial, or should the current funds be used to respond to Burger King? An increase in McDonald's advertising budget may prompt a similar increase in Burger King's.

Burger King's promotional campaign was conducted mostly through television. Should McDonald's also use television, or should it select a different medium? Perhaps a magazine advertisement would permit a more detailed rebuttal of Burger King's claims.

The battle became more complicated when Wendy's took two actions. First, it opened a legal suit of its own against Burger King; second, it launched its immensely popular "Where's the beef?" promotional campaign.

The battle did not stop with advertising. Both Burger King and McDonald's use all sorts of promotions to draw customers. Both ran a price promotion in January 1984, charging only 39 cents for a hamburger. McDonald's offered Olympic mugs at a low cost and was a sponsor of the 1984 Olympic games. In an earlier promotion, McDonald's offered a set of glasses featuring Peanuts comic strip characters. Burger King has made Tuesday "Family Night" and charges only 99 cents for a Whopper. Both have mascots—Ronald McDonald and the Burger King—who promote their respective restaurants. Both do special birthday parties for children. McDonald's is a sponsor of the Ronald McDonald houses, residences for children who are suffering from severe illnesses.

Wendy's campaign became a fad in itself. Wendy's licensed manufacturers of towels, mugs, T-shirts, and bumper stickers to use the question. There is even a talking doll that asks, "Where's the beef?" The publicity surrounding the question included newspaper and television stories about the commercials and interviews and appearances by the advertisement's stars.[1]

The top three hamburger fast-food restaurants are using a combination of the communication forms—advertising, sales promotion, and publicity—to carry out their communication objectives. The use of these forms involves deciding on the objectives and the messages and, based on a knowledge of the methods, possible uses, and effectiveness of each form, deciding on which form or mix of the forms to use. In this chapter, we are going to look at the methods, possible uses, and effectiveness of advertising, sales promotion, and publicity.

Advertising

As we saw in chapter 14, the American Marketing Association defines advertising as "any paid form of non-personal presentation and promotion of ideas, goods, or services by an identified sponsor." While advertising is one important facet of the business world, it is big business itself. In 1982, nearly $55 billion was spent on advertising. Of this, approximately $30 billion was spent by major corporations on national advertising and approximately $25 billion by small companies on local advertising. Even more striking is the percentage of expenditure on advertising in comparison with profit. For example, in 1979, advertising expenses as a percentage of after-tax profits were 177 percent for General Foods, 277 percent for Miles Laboratories, 90 percent for Procter & Gamble, and over 400 percent for Unilever-U.S.[2]

Advertising Objectives

Why do advertisers think it worth their while to spend so much money on advertising? Companies can have one or more objectives to achieve through advertising (see fig. 15–1). One is to *publicize a brand*. The public's perception of products

- Publicize a brand
- Increase demand
- Create an image
- Influence or support an issue
- Enhance the company's financial position
- Create enthusiasm in a company's work force
- Increase distribution for a product

Figure 15–1
Advertising objectives

Figure 15–2
Beatrice is publicizing its ownership of a wide variety of brands.

Beatrice Companies, Inc./ Marsteller, Inc.

comes from direct observation or from what they have read, seen, or heard. As early as 1959, evidence suggested that advertised brands are perceived as being superior to nonadvertised ones.[3] Advertisers want to get the brand name in front of the public, show how this brand can meet a consumer's needs, and say something about the product's attributes so that consumers can evaluate the product. Sometimes this kind of advertising is for a particular product, as for a specific detergent, messenger service, or restaurant. At other times, advertisers are promoting an entire product line; General Electric, for example, ran a popular series of commercials for its product line with the slogan, "GE. We bring good things to life." Beatrice ran a series of television commercials and print advertisements (see fig. 15–2) tying the Beatrice name to its broad product mix.

A second objective of advertising is to *increase demand* for a product. The company might want to increase sales volume through increased demand. The company may feel that it can raise its prices if there is an increased demand for its product. Also, increasing demand for its product is a way of taking business away from competitors. Burger King has been stressing this aim by advertising that millions have switched to it from McDonald's.

A third objective of advertising is to *create an image* for the company. A company may want to appear as socially aware or as a technological leader or as "good guys." Advertisements showing the Ronald McDonald Houses remind customers that McDonald's is a concerned and responsible company.

A fourth objective of advertising is to *influence or support an issue*. American steel companies have been running ads that call for a limit on the amount of foreign steel that can be imported. Mobil Oil has been running a series of advertisements that explain its views on a range of topics.

A fifth objective is to *enhance the company's financial position*. An advertising campaign by the Grace Company stressing the breadth and success of its business attracted a number of new investors in the company. Such a campaign can also raise the price of the company's stock.

A sixth objective is to *create enthusiasm in a company's work force*. Employees like to work for companies that advertise, especially when the advertising creates a favorable image for the work force. Ford's campaign that stressed "Quality Is Job 1" portrayed its work force as dedicated, caring, and thoroughly competent, which the workers liked. The sales force, too, is enthusiastic about successful advertising campaigns, as it becomes easier for them to sell products that consumers are already aware of.

A final objective is to *increase distribution for a product*. If consumers see a product advertised and ask for it in stores, more stores will carry a product. (This is known as a *pulling strategy* and is discussed further in chapter 17.) Even before the campaign begins, a company can tell retailers that the product will be advertised and that consumers will be asking for it. Stores will then want to carry the product to be ready for the consumers.

Advertising Decisions

Once a company has decided to advertise, it has four decisions to make: which segment to advertise to, what message to communicate, which media to select, and how to determine the effectiveness of the campaign.

Which segment? As we saw in chapter 9, companies will divide a market into various segments. Choosing a specific segment to advertise to will help the company to direct the rest of its advertising campaign. The company should have gathered enough information about the segment to know what messages will appeal to it and through which media the segment can be reached.

As an example, let us look at a Mississippi company in the business of advising and negotiating for timberland owners. Its market segment was timberland owners. The message it wanted to advertise to this very specific audience was that it could provide them with certain services. But when it came time to place the ads, it forgot its market segment. It decided to run its ads on the CBS "Evening News." When asked why it wanted to run the ads on that program, management replied that it would reach a large number of consumers. The flaw in this reasoning was that the company would be reaching a large number of irrelevant consumers and would thus be wasting its money.

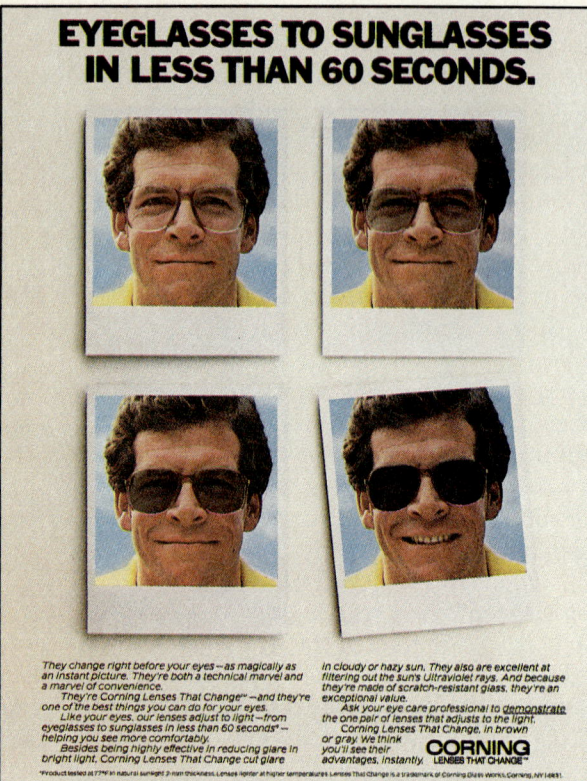

Figure 15–3 Corning is using a demonstration structure to inform consumers about its Lenses That Change. The demonstration effectively shows the lenses in the process of changing.
Corning Glass Works/Calet, Hirsch & Spector

What message? As we saw in chapter 14, the type of message the advertiser communicates depends on the communication objectives, the market segment, the consumer's stage in the buying process, and the product's stage in its life cycle. While there are many individual messages that can be sent, they fall into four main categories: introductory, informative, persuasive, and reminder.

When a company wants to publicize a new brand, it will use an **introductory message.** The company wants to gain attention for its product. The words "new," "introducing," or "now at your store" may appear prominently in the ad, along with reasons or incentives to try the product. Introductory messages are used to create awareness in the hierarchy of effects.

When a product is in its growth stage and a company wants to increase demand for it, the company may use an **informative message.** The ads may say "Do you know that . . . ," or they may point out that the product has certain attributes that can solve consumers' problems. Informative advertisements are used to create interest or conviction in a hierarchy of effects. This type of advertising is useful for a product in a very competitive market. For example, when Topol toothpaste tried to establish itself in the crowded toothpaste market, its promoters focused on the product's ability to whiten tobacco-stained teeth. Its ads feature people who successfully used Topol to correct this problem. The campaign itself has been highly successful, as Topol has gained a significant share of the market. In the burger wars, McDonald's created new demand for Chicken McNuggets by creating the excitement of McNugget Mania and by telling people about new ways to use McNuggets, including food for office parties.

The third type of advertising is **persuasive advertising.** The purpose of this type is to convince consumers that they would be making the correct choice if they purchased the mouthwash that four out of five dentists use or the analgesic that nine out of ten doctors recommend. Comparisons between products are forms of persuasive advertising. If a company can show that one hamburger has more beef or that the hamburger is broiled rather than fried, consumers may be persuaded to try the product. This type of advertising is often used in the product's growth and mature stages; it leads to conviction or a purchase intention in a hierarchy of effects.

A fourth type of advertising is **reminder advertising.** This type serves two purposes. First, it reminds consumers about a product that is in the mature stage of the life cycle. Second, it acts to reinforce consumers who have just purchased the product; it reconfirms that they have made the correct choice.

Figure 15–4 Stouffer's is using a slice-of-life structure to remind consumers about its side dishes.
Reprinted by permission of Stouffer Foods Corporation

Chapter 15 / Advertising, Sales Promotion, and Publicity

The content of the advertisement consists of copy and art, which are developed to carry out and emphasize the message. The six basic structures for ads are the *story*, the *slice-of-life* ad, the *testimonial*, the *announcer*, the *demonstration*, and the *song and dance*.[4] An advertiser may use a story to introduce a product or remind consumers about it, a demonstration to inform consumers about the product's characteristics, a testimonial to persuade, and a song and dance to remind. Any structure, though, can be successfully used with any message.

The three combatants in the burger wars use different types of advertisements. Burger King tends to show delicious-looking food—golden-brown french fries, succulent Whoppers, ripe tomatoes and lettuce being prepared, sizzling burgers flame broiling—while appealing to people's eyes and stomachs. McDonald's tends to use slice-of-life ads, showing happy families and groups of friends eating at McDonald's or cute children bringing McDonald's food to their hungry meat-and-potato fathers. Wendy's "Where's the beef?" campaign uses humor to make its point.

Decisions about the Media

There are four main advertising media: television, radio, the out-of-doors, and print. When planning their advertising campaign, marketers must select which medium or media to use and how to schedule their advertisements. These are the main decisions to make about the media.

Media selection. By now, the advertiser knows which market segment to go after and what message to present to that market. The next step is to choose the medium or media that will carry the message. The most common media are television, radio, out-of-doors media such as billboards, newspapers, and magazines. Each medium has its strengths and weaknesses that must be considered when deciding which to use. Although it is possible to use only one, most advertisers use a combination of these.

The main criteria used to select the media are selectivity, penetration, coverage, flexibility, cost, and editorial environment[5] (see fig. 15–5).

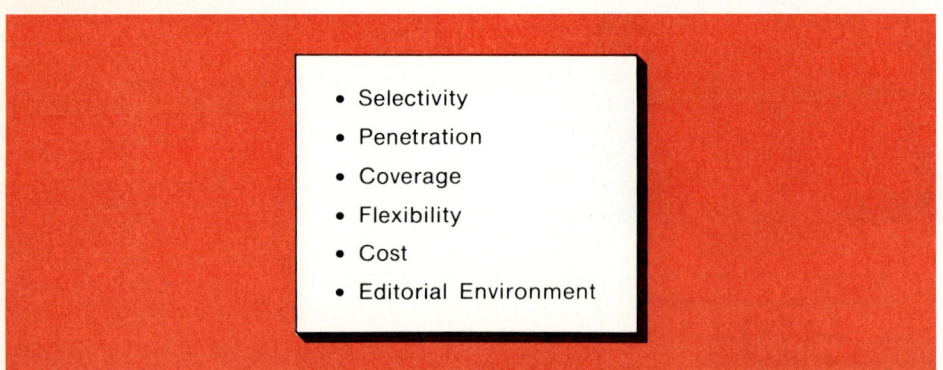

Figure 15–5 The criteria for media selection

Selectivity. **Selectivity** refers to the medium's ability to reach a particular geographic area or a specific class of people. A local newspaper or radio station, for example, can reach a certain geographic area with little waste, and a local restaurant or store may choose to advertise through these. Specialized magazines, such as *Car and Driver, Popular Photography,* or *Food & Wine,* can reach a certain group of people. If a camera company wants to introduce a new type of lens or a food company a new type of gourmet product, it can choose an appropriate magazine to reach its customers. General interest magazines, such as *Life,* may attract general, national advertisers, such as Burger King or MacDonald's, but they probably will not attract more specialized advertisers. Network television, similarly, attracts a general audience. Advertisers might be more interested in choosing a more specialized cable television station, such as ESPN, that attracts a specific market segment. The media are also selective in terms of demographic characteristics. *Good Housekeeping* magazine reaches more women than men, and rock radio stations a younger audience than do classical ones.

Penetration. **Penetration** is the extent to which the medium reaches the target market. For example, if an advertiser wants to reach sports buffs, it can choose a televised event, such as the Super Bowl, which every sports buff watches. Similarly, *Business Week* penetrates the business market better than *Money,* which is aimed at a more general consumer market.

Coverage. **Coverage** is the percentage of the total market a medium is able to reach. In a particular geographic area, with 2.5 million households, a newspaper with a circulation of 600,000 is covering 24 percent of the market. Brewers advertise heavily on televised sports programs, for example, since these programs cover a sizable percentage of beer drinkers.

Flexibility. The **flexibility** of a medium can be measured by how far in advance an advertising commitment must be made. Newspapers and radio stations are relatively flexible and allow advertisers to react to a timely event or competitive challenge. A sudden change in the weather, for example, may lead a retailer to advertise winter coats or umbrellas in the newspaper. The other media are less flexible. Time on television must be purchased long in advance, and most magazines are printed long before they appear.

Cost. The **cost** of a medium is one of the most important criteria for selection. The cost may be absolute; no matter how much an advertiser may want to appear on network television or in a national magazine, the high cost may prohibit it. The cost may also be relative and take into account the audience's size and quality. The cost of a full-page ad in two different magazines may be the same, but an advertiser would probably choose to appear in the one with the higher circulation. Advertisers also relate the cost to the ability of the medium to reach the target market. In absolute terms, for example, it might cost 1 cent per viewer to advertise on network

Figure 15–6 An advertisement for a local lottery will be placed in media that reach that local market. This advertisement for the DC Lottery appeared in *The Washingtonian* magazine.

Figure 15–7 A medium's editorial environment affects how an advertisement is perceived. *The Washingtonian* is promoting its award-winning editorial environment.
Courtesy of *The Washingtonian* magazine

television and 1.5 cents to advertise on a cable television station. The cable station, however, will deliver a more selective audience, so an advertiser who wants to reach that particular audience may consider the higher cost worth it.

Editorial Environment. The **editorial environment** of a medium sets the tone in which an advertisement appears and is perceived by the audience. People associate *Good Housekeeping* magazine with product quality ("The *Good Housekeeping* seal of approval"), so they may look more favorably on products advertised in it. Many magazines and newspapers run campaigns promoting themselves as media with good editorial environments for products. In figure 15–7, or example, *The Washingtonian* is not only promoting its excellence as reflected in its status as a finalist for the National Magazine Awards, but it is also showing itself in the company of other acclaimed magazines.

Now, let us look at the characteristics of the specific media.

Television. Television is the newest, but perhaps the most pervasive, medium. Most people watch television. On an average evening, 60 percent of American households watch television. The average American watches approximately 6 hours of television a day.[6] In 1983, advertising expenditures on television were approximately $15.1 billion.[7]

When advertisers approach television, they pay attention to the type of program, the nature of the audience watching the program, and the number of viewers. Certain types of shows are known to attract certain segments of the population, and advertisers wanting to reach those segments advertise heavily on those shows. Sports programs, for example, attract large numbers of male viewers, so "male" products such as beer and razor blades are promoted heavily on them. Products such as detergents and floor waxes that interest homemakers are advertised during daytime soap operas. Recently, advertisers are targeting the young professional audience and are putting a premium on advertising on the shows that that audience watches.

Advertisers get information on the composition and size of the audience for a show from a number of sources. The best known, perhaps, is the A. C. Nielsen Company. The Nielsen ratings tell advertisers what percentages of the viewing audience and television set owners are watching various programs. The ratings are obtained through electrical devices wired into television sets in cooperating homes that register the percentage of homes tuned to a particular show. A show with a rating of about 29 or 30 means that 29 or 30 percent of all homes with television sets watched that show. Nielsen and other rating companies, such as Simmons and Arbitron, can also provide demographic information about a show's viewers.

The ratings and audience determine the rates paid by advertisers. Often, the cost of an advertisement is based directly on rating points, with a cost of so many dollars per point. Advertisements shown during special programs with large audiences, such as the Super Bowl or the Olympics, are more expensive than usual. Advertisements shown during prime time are more expensive than are those shown late at night. Advertisements shown during shows like golf tournaments, which tend to be watched by higher-income executives, are more expensive than are those that reach an equal number of blue-collar workers, such as commercials shown during televised bowling tournaments. Advertisements shown nationwide are more expensive than are those shown on local stations.

In the early days of television, advertisers sponsored programs by themselves. Now, except for occasional specials, advertisers co-sponsor programs along with other advertisers. Each advertiser produces its own commercials and buys a certain amount of time—60, 30, or 15 seconds—on the appropriate program.

Advertising on television has two distinct advantages. First, because it is a visual medium, television is ideal for advertisements that demonstrate something or that try to create an image or a mood. The **storyboard,** or prepared plan of the advertisement, for a television commercial in figure 15–8 demonstrates this. Dannon yogurt is promoting itself as a healthful food; showing active, athletic, and attractive people eating Dannon yogurt helps to create and reinforce that image.

Figure 15–8 A storyboard for a Dannon Yogurt television commercial.

Second, television advertising can reach a broad, nationwide audience very quickly and efficiently.

The second advantage can also be a disadvantage. Because it is a very broad audience, a large number of the viewers will not be interested in the product. The growth of cable television may solve this problem in the future, as advertisers can go after more specialized market segments. (Narrowcasting and split-cable television are discussed in chapter 22.)

Another disadvantage is that advertisements sometimes get lost on television. Stations may string several ads together so that any single ad does not stand out; this is known as **clutter.** Also viewers tend to ignore ads. Sometimes, advertisements look so similar to viewers—soft drink ones have happy songs, those for analgesics make scientific comparisons—that it is difficult for a viewer to remember exactly which product is being advertised.

Radio. Radio has been an important medium for advertising for over 50 years. During television's explosive growth period in the 1950s, some predicted the death of radio. But radio audiences grew, and the amount of advertising on radio grew correspondingly. Total advertising expenditures on all radio stations were approximately $5 billion in 1983.[8] Today 99 percent of American homes and 95 percent of cars have radios.[9] The average total listening time per person is 3½ hours a day.[10]

Advertisers approach radio much as they approach television. Radio stations and programs have different audiences. Advertisers study the audiences to decide on which stations and programs to place their messages. Rock stations, for example, are a particularly efficient medium for reaching the youth market. Radio talk shows and all-news stations, on the other hand, tend to attract older, middle-income, male listeners.[11]

There are many advantages to advertising on radio. It is still a relatively low-cost medium, so advertisements can be longer or run more frequently than can those on television. Scheduling on radio is highly flexible, so announcements can be timed to promote special events and offers. The narrowness of the geographic area served by a radio station makes radio the perfect medium for retailers and small businesses who do not want or need broader coverage. Finally, radio reaches consumers at specific times of the day, which makes it ideal for advertising certain types of products to specific listeners. For example, Maxwell House coffee has been advertised at breakfast time, Campbell's Soup at lunch, and Datsun during rush hours, when it used the slogan, "Put your money in the bank, not in the tank."

The main drawback of radio as an advertising medium is the obvious one—products cannot be shown visually. Radio, then, will not be used to promote the latest fashions or delicious-looking food. Radio advertisers, however, have developed clever "dialogue" advertisements to promote such products as *Time* magazine and Blue Nun wine.

Out-of-Doors. Signs, or out-of-doors media, are the oldest type of advertising, dating back to Egyptian times, when pharaohs carved their names on temples. Until the nineteenth century, when advertisers turned heavily toward newspapers and magazines, signs and posters were the main advertising vehicles. Today, still, our-of-doors media play a valid role in the media mix.

Out of doors is a catchall category for anything not on the airwaves or in print. It includes standardized **billboards** (which alone accounted for $160 million of advertising dollars in 1980), transit advertising, roadside signs, and even printed shopping bags.

Billboards have traditionally come in one of two forms: a **poster** or a **paint.** The poster is a large printed sheet of paper that is pasted onto an outdoor billboard. A paint is handpainted onto a wall, billboard, or other surface. In recent years, electronics have become widely used for billboards.

Companies using billboards determine the location by studying traffic patterns, nearness to distribution outlets, and other factors. Since viewers usually have little time to look at the ads, they tend to have little copy but feature the product's name and an attractive design or illustration.

The main advantages of out-of-doors media are that the cost is relatively low

Frank Siteman/Stock, Boston

Figure 15–9 A variety of billboards and signs advertise the motels, restaurants, and services available on this street in Las Vegas.

in relation to the exposure and the ads tend to be close to the distribution outlet. The main disadvantages are that it is impossible to convey much information, that the viewers may not be in the chosen market segment, and that many people feel the ads are not environmentally healthy.

Print media. The print media—newspapers and magazines—are the most effective in reaching specific audiences in terms of income, occupation, education, and interests.[12] Most magazines and newspapers are produced for certain types of people with special interests, and advertisers wanting to reach these people can be sure to do so by appearing in carefully chosen ones. For example, manufacturers of sporting goods may advertise in *Sports Illustrated,* haute couture designers in *Vogue,* and software companies in *Business Week* or *Personal Computing.*

There are advantages, too, in having an advertisement appear in print rather than as a passing image on radio or television. The content of the advertisement can be more in depth and longer. Facts presented in it can be read, re-read, analyzed, and even clipped out.

Both newspapers and magazines use audited circulation figures to set advertising rates and to promote themselves to advertisers. Every six months, publications submit statements of circulation to the Audit Bureau of Circulation (ABC). ABC verifies circulation, and these figures are then passed on to advertisers. The figures also show subscription sales, single-copy sales, and sales of various regional and demographic editions.

Newspapers. Newspapers are printed primarily in black and white on inexpensive, disposable paper. They come in standard and tabloid sizes and are printed daily or weekly. They are generally considered a local advertising medium, as most circulate in limited geographic areas. Approximately 1,710 of them appear daily and another 7,626 of them appear weekly.[13] A small number of newspapers have a nationwide circulation; these are often aimed at specific ethnic or religious groups.

Newspaper advertisement rates are based on the size of the ad, whether the advertiser is local or national, and the circulation of the paper. Usually, the higher the circulation, the more expensive the ad. Also, national advertisers are charged more than are local ones. Approximate newspaper advertising expenditures in 1983 were $19.6 billion.[14]

Magazines. Although magazines and newspapers are both print media, they offer different advantages to advertisers. Newspapers, by their nature, offer a current, spot news format and appeal most to people in a particular area. They are also usually thrown out after one day, so their ads do not last longer than that day.

Magazines, on the other hand, take a more leisurely, feature format and appeal to a particular kind of person through the country. *Good Housekeeping,* for example, appeals to homemakers, whether they are in New York, Iowa, or Oregon. Magazines are usually produced monthly, although there are also weekly, biweekly, and quarterly ones. As magazines are usually kept for a period of time, ads in them "live" and produce results over a period of time. Magazines are also printed on slicker paper that allows color reproduction; the ads in magazines, then, can be more artistic and creative than can those in newspapers.

There is a vast array of magazines published in this country. They tend to fall into one of two categories: trade or consumer. **Trade magazines** are produced for a specific business or profession. They may be edited to appeal to all employees in a certain industry; *Advertising Age* is an example of this kind. They may also be edited to appeal to a certain level of employee in all industries; *Management Review,* for example, is prepared for managers in all fields.

Trade magazines may be professional ones, such as *American Journal of Nursing* or the *Journal of Marketing.* Another group caters to various merchandising or marketing functions, with such publications as *Sales & Marketing Management.* There are institutional magazines, such as *School Library Journal,* industrial ones, such as *Chain Store Age* or *Discount Store News,* and general business ones, such as *Business Week* and *Fortune.*

Figure 15–10 Trade magazines carry specialized advertisements for selective audiences. This advertisement, for example, appeared in *Radio-Electronics* magazine.

Courtesy Tektronix, Inc.

Advertisements appearing in these publications reach a highly selective audience and are not wasted on nonrelevant customers. Advertisements in these publications can also be used to "sell to the seller" before selling to consumers. For example, an advertisement for a new food product in *Progressive Grocer* may persuade a supermarket to carry the product. Thus, the product is on the shelves when interested consumers attracted by later ads first look for it.

Consumer magazines are popular, nationally distributed magazines with large circulations. There is a trend away from general interest magazines, such as *Look*, *Life*, and *The Saturday Evening Post*. And many of these went out of business because their audiences were too general to attract advertisers interested in specific market segments. In their place rose the many special interest magazines that focus on such topics as science, cars, photography, gardening, or specific cities. As these magazines are read by specific market segments, advertisers can appeal to their target consumers with little waste of advertising dollars. Because advertisers are so interested in segmenting the market, even the general, nationwide magazines offer special regional editions. *Time* offers a special edition that reaches households with incomes over $25,000 a year.

Magazine advertising rates are based on the size of the ad, the number of colors in it, and the guaranteed circulation. Advertisers will look at the **CPM rate,** the cost per thousand, of delivering a full-page black and white ad to 1,000 homes. This figure provides a good basis for comparing various magazines. The CPM usually drops as the circulation of the magazine rises, but higher costs may be justified if the advertiser wants to reach a very select audience. If a camera manufacturer is advertising a new type of lens, it may be more efficient to pay more to appear in a photography magazine than to pay less to appear in a general interest one. Magazine advertising expenditures reached $3.42 billion in 1982.[15]

The characteristics of the advertising media are presented in table 15–1.

Media scheduling. Advertising dollars are generally allocated on an overall budget, usually by the fiscal year. How the dollars are spread out over the year is called **media scheduling.** Decisions about scheduling are usually based on the product's characteristics and the communication objectives.

TABLE 15–1   The Characteristics of the Advertising Media

	Forms	Advantages	Disadvantages
Television	Local television Network television Cable television	Good for product demonstrations, image or mood advertising Reaches broad audience quickly and efficiently	Broad reach brings message to uninterested consumers Ads may be lost in clutter Consumers may ignore ads
Radio	Local stations	Low cost Flexibility Narrowness of geographic area served for local advertisers Consumers reached at specific times of the day	Product cannot be shown

Out-of-doors	Billboards
	  Poster
	  Paint
	  Electronic
	Transit advertising
	Roadside signs
	Printed shopping bags
		Low cost
		Located close to distribution outlet
			Cannot carry much information
			Viewers may not be in chosen market segment
			Environmentally unhealthy

Print Newspapers	Standard size Tabloid size Dailies Weeklies	Can carry much information Narrow market segment served	Ads do not "live"
Magazines	Trade magazines Consumer magazines Weeklies Monthlies Quarterlies	Color reproduction of ads Can carry much information Narrow market segment served Ads "live"	

Some products sell heavily in certain seasons and are advertised heavily at those times. Perfume, jewelry, and small personal appliances, which are often given as Christmas presents, are advertised heavily in November and December. Candy is advertised heavily before Halloween, flowers before Mother's Day, and children's clothing in August for the back-to-school selling season.

Products that are less seasonal are advertised in a number of patterns, often based on when consumers are going through the buying decision process. People buy soap detergents continuously throughout the year, so these are advertised continually. A pattern called **flighting** calls for a product to be advertised heavily and then not advertised at all. The heavy advertising coincides with the period when consumers are deciding which type of a product to buy. For example, a sizable proportion of sales of motorcycles are in the spring. Yamaha did a study that showed that while the sales are in the spring, consumers are gathering information about types of motorcycles and making the decision about the type in the winter and early spring. Thus, Yamaha concentrates its advertising in the winter and early spring. Flighting is considered the most effective pattern in terms of the effect on the consumer.

A pattern between continuous and flighting is **pulsing**. In this pattern, an advertiser has a certain amount of continuous advertising with pulses of heavy advertising. Both Burger King and McDonald's use pulsing. They both advertise continuously but step up the frequency of their advertising when they want to introduce a new theme or support a specific promotional activity.

A number of factors influence the media schedule. One is the irritability of certain ads or advertising themes. Some run so often that advertisers may create a negative response to the product. Some advertisers feel that there is no such thing as negative response, though. Two of the campaigns considered the most irritating—the Wisk detergent "ring around the collar" and the Charmin "Mr. Whipple"—are also among the most successful. At the same time, some advertisers try to reduce the possibility of irritation by producing a number of different ads, although they all have the same theme. AT&T used this strategy for its "Reach Out and Touch Someone" campaign.

Another factor is the clutter of surrounding ads. Certain television and radio stations run a string of ads together so that any one ad can get lost. Advertisers try to get around this problem by choosing the station or program carefully or by creating an ad that stands out.

Measuring Advertising Effectiveness

Retailer John Wanamaker said that half of all advertising is wasted, but no one knows which half that is. Unlike other, more tangible aspects of business, the effectiveness of advertising can be hard to measure. In general, though, the effectiveness of a campaign can be judged by how well the campaign's objectives are met. If the objective was to increase sales, looking at the sales figures is a way to measure effectiveness. Wendy's, for example, may judge it's "Where's the beef?" campaign a success by noting that its sales jumped by 17 percent following the airing of the 1984 commercials.[16]

Figure 15–11 Does this advertisement featuring breathtaking scenery and camping vacationers make people want to visit Idaho? One way to tell is to count how many people do call the 800 number or write for more information.
Idaho Travel Council

Advertisers can use a number of additional, specific methods to measure advertising effectiveness. One way is to get consumers to react in some way, perhaps by writing for more information, ordering a recipe, or sending in a reader response card. Advertisers can also test the comparative effectiveness of two versions of the same ad by seeing how many consumers react to each.

A number of experimental techniques similar to those described in chapter 5 can also be used. In a controlled experiment, people can be taken into a theater and shown various print or televised ads; later, they are asked whether or how well they recall the ads. In a field experiment, people can be called, asked whether they saw a specific show, and then asked about the commercials on the show. Advertisers are also turning to a number of laboratory experiments that test consumers' physiological responses to various ads. One of these is described in focus 15–1.

15–1 Focus on a Marketing Development
CAN ADVERTISING EFFECTIVENESS BE MEASURED THROUGH PSYCHOLOGICAL RESEARCH?

Advertisers are always looking for ways in which to measure the effectiveness of their ads. One concern is how effective the various advertising media are in comparison with one another. Advertisers would like to know if a particular medium is more likely to make people remember a product. Recently, a group of psychologists who specialize in research on the human brain has offered advertisers some help with this task.

The brain is divided into two parts, a right hemisphere and a left hemisphere. Although there is some communication between the two hemispheres, to a large extent they function separately. The left hemisphere controls the right side of the body, while the right hemisphere controls the left side of the body. Not only are the two sides of the body handled by separate hemispheres but so are intellectual abilities. The right side of the brain appears to be the source of creativity, abstract thinking, and spatial perception; the left hemisphere handles written and spoken language and logic.

One method psychologists have used to make these discoveries about when each side of the brain is working is by using an electroencephalogram (EEG) to measure brain waves. By attaching electrodes to the scalp, researchers can obtain a reading of each hemisphere's activity level while a person performs some task. For example, psychologists might monitor brain activity while someone reads a book. A high level of activity in the left hemisphere and a low level of activity in the right hemisphere would indicate that the left hemisphere is predominantly responsible for reading.

Psychologists believed that recording subjects' brain activity while they viewed magazine and television ads could help to compare the effectiveness of the ads in these two media. Because the left hemisphere handles language, the researchers thought this side of the brain would be more active when people were viewing magazine ads. The researchers also felt that a higher level of brain-wave activity would appear when people were paying

Sales Promotion

As is advertising, sales promotion is a form of sponsored communication, part of a planned strategy to put the name of a product in front of the consumer or member of the distribution channel. While advertising is aimed at changing attitudes toward a product or company over a long-term period, sales promotions aimed at consumers are targeted toward stimulating immediate sales, are tied to limited time periods, and have expiration dates. The emphasis of advertising on a product's attributes brings long-term payoffs; in contrast, consumer promotions help to facilitate greater attention to an ad. Further, the researchers believed that people would remember this ad better than others for which lower levels of brain activity had been recorded. The researchers made three specific predictions about television versus magazine ads. First, they expected that magazine ads would stimulate more brain activity than would television ads; second, they believed that the left hemisphere would be more responsive to magazine ads than to television ads; and, finally, they expected that people would be most likely to remember those ads that had generated the highest levels of brain activity.

The participants in this study were hooked up to an EEG so that, while they looked at each medium, the researchers could monitor their brain waves. Participants were told that its purpose was to get their reaction to a new television movie and to a new magazine. Actually, the researchers were only interested in brain activity while subjects viewed television commercials (for such products as mayonnaise, hair coloring, and cat food) and magazine ads (for a soup, a store, and a coffee). After subjects had been exposed to both media, they answered a questionnaire that tested their memory of the various brands they'd seen advertised.

The results of the experiment showed that magazine ads did generate more brain-wave activity, confirming the researchers' first prediction. This higher level of brain activity suggested to the researchers that subjects had paid closer attention to the magazine ads than to the television commercials. The data also confirmed the second prediction that magazine ads would stimulate more activity in the left hemisphere. Contrary to the researchers' predictions, however, was the fact that, although participants showed more brain-wave activity when viewing magazine ads, they did not necessarily remember those brands better than others. Unfortunately, then, the results of this study are inconclusive. Even considering the findings that confirmed the psychologists' expectations, the overall results showed that the EEG readings could not help advertisers predict better memory of a product. Advertisers will have to stick with more traditional methods for predicting the success of their ads and, for now, leave brain-wave measurement to the psychologists.

Source: Based on Sidney Weinstein, Valentine Appel, and Curt Weinstein, "Brain-Activity Responses to Magazine and Television Advertising," *Journal of Advertising Research*, June 1980, pp. 57–63.

distribution of a product in the present and give the consumer incentives to purchase *now*. Trade promotions may bring short-term payoffs, but they are also designed to create a long-term working relationship and goodwill.

Advertising and sales promotion can be used to complement each other in a company's marketing strategy. Studies indicate that money spent on a combination of advertising and promotion produces higher sales and profits than does the same amount of money spent on either of those components alone.[17] Advertising and sales promotion can have common themes and can help each other meet the communication objectives.

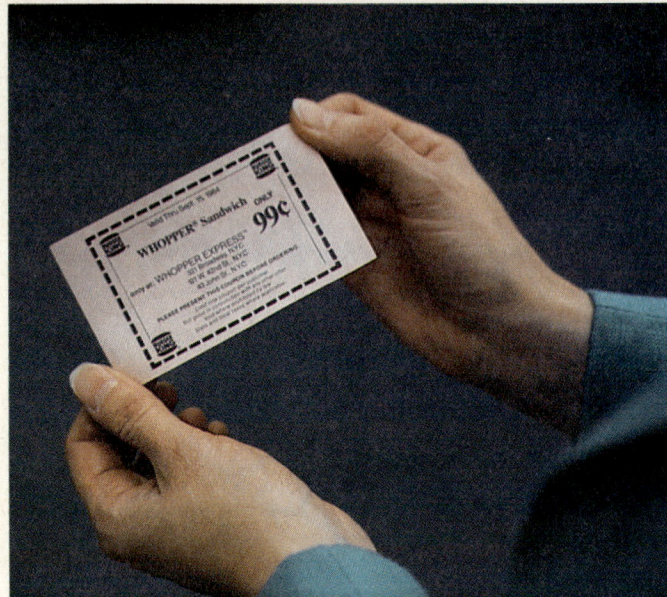

**Figure 15–12
Coupons were one form of sales promotion used in the burger wars.**

Anita Duncan

The use of sales promotion is growing. A report published in 1975 indicated that, on the average, promotion spending increased twice as fast as did that of advertising between 1969 and 1975. While advertising was reported to have increased by 6 percent, from $16.4 billion in 1969 to $30.5 billion in 1976, promotion was reported as increasing 9.5 percent, from $14.6 billion in 1969 to $20.5 billion in 1976.[18] Other studies have confirmed this trend, although it is sometimes difficult to measure the amount spent on sales promotions. A number of reasons have been offered to explain the growing use of promotion: it is being increasingly accepted by management; marketing personnel are better qualified in developing promotions; and the increased number of brands requires the use of promotions.

Sales Promotion Objectives

As with advertising, the communication objectives determine the type of sales promotion. *Stimulating immediate sales* is the objective of many sales promotions; this is often achieved by temporarily lowering prices. Six-packs of a soft drink, for example, sometimes carry a sticker advertising a special "cents-off" price for a limited time. Or a health club might sponsor a special February promotion, featuring a reduced membership rate to those who join during that month.

Some promotions, especially those for new products, have the objective of *persuading consumers to try the product.* Often, a free sample of the product—perhaps shampoo or dishwashing detergent—is sent to the homes of potential consumers. Publishers sometimes send two or three free issues of a magazine to potential subscribers, to encourage them to read it, and then offer them a subscription if they wish to continue receiving the publication.

Figure 15–13 Sales promotion objectives

- Stimulate immediate sales
- Persuade consumers to try the product
- Persuade consumers to reuse a product
- Encourage consumers to buy a greater quantity
- Appeal to price-sensitive consumers
- Create a more even sales cycle

Some promotions have the objective of *persuading consumers to reuse a product.* A familiar example is a coupon inside a jar of coffee, offering a discount off the regular price for purchasing the next jar of the same brand of coffee. When a customer brings in a roll of camera film to be developed, the film-developing company sometimes provides a free roll of new film for each roll developed, thus encouraging the reuse of the film-developing service.

Encouraging consumers to buy a greater quantity of a particular product is the goal of some promotional campaigns. Promoters may simply want to increase sales volume. They may also want to provide incentives for consumers to shift their normal purchases forward to an earlier time and to keep a larger supply of the product in their homes. This kind of promotion is also often launched prior to the introduction of a new product by a competitor for another reason—by giving consumers incentive to stock up on their product before the new product enters the market, the promoters hope to avoid losing any market share to the competitor. When No Nonsense pantyhose was about to enter the market, L'eggs pantyhose launched a special promotion, a dual-pack—two pairs of stockings at a special low price. As a result, consumers were already well supplied with pantyhose when No Nonsense entered the market. In 1983, Procter & Gamble lowered the price of Downey Fabric Softener in markets, mostly in the Midwest, where Lever Brothers was introducing a new lower-priced competing product, Snuggle.

Some promotions have the objective of *appealing to price-sensitive consumers.* The product may be offered at the regular price to its target market and offered, under specified conditions, at a lower price to consumers who comply with the conditions of the promotion. A supermarket may sell frozen dinners at the regular price to most consumers, for example, but sell them at a lower price to consumers who use coupons. Airlines often feature a regular fare for flights during the week, when business travel is heavy and planes are usually filled, and a lower fare specifying weekend travel or other restrictions to stimulate the purchase of tickets that might otherwise remain unsold.

Some promotions have the objective of *creating a more even sales cycle.* These often take the form of price incentives. Department stores, for example, frequently sponsor White Sales in January to stimulate sales of sheets and towels during one of the slowest periods in the annual retail business cycle.

Decisions about Sales Promotion

The major decisions about sales promotions involve choosing among the possible types of sales promotion, which are described below.

Consumer promotions. The main types of consumer promotions are free samples, price incentives, contests, premiums, point-of-purchase displays, coupons, and bonus packs.

Free Samples. Some manufacturers promote a product by providing a **free sample** of the product itself to the consumer. Often, this is done by mailing a product or a group of products—such as household cleaning supplies—directly to the homes of targeted consumers. A variation of the sampling method occurs when the manufacturer sends a salesperson to a retail store to distribute free samples of a product—a taste of cheese in the supermarket, for example, or a cosmetics sample in a department store—to shoppers.

Price Incentives. **Price incentives**—ranging from a few cents off the regular price on a can of soup to a several-hundred-dollar reduction in the price of a stereo system—are a common form of sales promotion. The incentives may be initiated by any distribution channel member to stimulate demand for a particular product among consumers or persuade consumers to buy more of the product at a specific time.

Contests and Sweepstakes. **Contests** and **sweepstakes,** an increasingly popular form of promotion, stimulate excitement and interest in products. While the bonus being offered might not be appealing enough to consumers if it were divided among all the people who buy the product, the possibility of winning a big prize enhances the attractiveness of the overall purchase. The 1984 Summer Olympics were the focus of numerous promotional events; a number of companies—ranging from Fuji Film to Miller Brewing—sponsored contests with free trips to the Olympics for the winners.

Premiums. Offering **premiums** to consumers who purchase a product is another means of stimulating sales by enhancing the attractiveness of buying it. Sales promotions involving premiums may be initiated by any distribution channel member. Boxes of children's cereals commonly contain a free toy or include a coupon enabling consumers to buy a toy at a reduced price. Aim toothpaste in 1984 offered a calculator at a reduced price to consumers who sent in proof-of-purchase seals from the product's box. Cunard cruise company in 1984 offered a free flight back

Figure 15–14 Sweepstakes are an increasingly popular form of sales promotion. The Grand Prize in this one is a trip to Hawaii.

©1984 Castle & Cooke, Inc.

to the point of departure as a premium to those who purchased a ticket to sail on the ocean liner, the *Queen Elizabeth II.*

Point-of-Purchase Displays. **Point-of-purchase displays** are sales promotions offered by the retailer to appeal to the final consumer. Evidence indicates that these displays have a tremendous impact on consumers; any display that catches the customer's eye increases the chances of a sale. Among the most effective displays are prominent signs and banners; end-of-aisle displays; and displays near the checkout register that customers can consider while waiting to pay for their purchases. Gillette has been successful in featuring widely recognized displays of its razor blades near checkout counters, especially in drugstores.

Coupons. Manufacturers' use of **coupons** as sales promotions has greatly increased over the past decade. Both the amount of discount given by coupons and the length of time for which they are valid vary widely. Many considerations shape a manufacturer's decision about the method of coupon distribution. Some are distributed through the mail to the target market. Others are distributed in newspapers and magazines. It has been found that coupons with the highest redemption rates are those distributed in or on packages—an effective means of encouraging consumers to reuse the product. If that consumer would have purchased the product anyway, then the manufacturer has just discounted the price when it was unnecessary. If, on the other hand, the consumer has been prevented from switching to another brand, the coupon has been valuable. Some coupons are distributed as flyers on the street. There continue to be new variations of coupon distribution. One promotional company in Canada began attaching coupons to plastic breadbag closures, allowing consumers to redeem the coupons inside the store before opening the package. It is claimed that the redemption rate was dramatically increased with the "instant coupons."[19]

Bonus Packs. **Bonus packs** are another means that manufacturers use to promote their products. The consumer who buys a particular product receives additional units or an additional quantity of the product at no additional cost; for example, buy three and get the fourth one free. More of the product for the same price is the message communicated to the consumer.

Trade promotions. Trade promotions are generally aimed toward one of two major objectives. The goal of manufacturers or distributors in offering the first kind of trade promotion is to persuade other channel members to carry a particular product, to carry a larger quantity of the product, or perhaps to share the responsibilities and costs involved in stocking inventory of the product. In the other kind of trade promotion, the channel member who offers the promotion intends it to be passed through the channel to the final consumer. The retailer has more direct contact with consumers than do other channel members—for example, consumers often seek the retailer's advice about stereo equipment, computer equipment, or jewelry. Thus the manufacturer or wholesaler often finds it effective to offer a trade promotion to a retailer to encourage favorable communication to consumers.

This section considers several methods of trade promotion: cooperative advertising, incentive programs, trade shows, and push money.

Cooperative Advertising. **Cooperative advertising** is one means by which the manufacturer can promote a product with the retailer's assistance. Under this type of agreement, the manufacturer helps to fund advertising that communicates information about the manufacturer's product and the fact that it can be purchased at the retailer's store. To qualify for cooperative advertising, usually the retailer must purchase a certain volume of the manufacturer's product. After demonstrating to the manufacturer that the advertising has been accomplished, the retailer is reimbursed for a portion of the advertising's cost.

Incentive Programs. **Incentive programs,** or **trade allowances,** enable the manufacturer or distributor to provide a bonus—a cash bonus, extra units of the product, or another kind of bonus—to a channel member who buys a certain vol-

Figure 15–15 A cooperative advertisement, sponsored by both clothing manufacturer Adolfo and retailer Saks Fifth Avenue.
Courtesy of Saks Fifth Avenue

ume of the product during a given time period. Incentive programs are an effective means of encouraging retailers to try carrying a product during the early stages of its life cycle or in an especially competitive market.

Trade Shows. Annual or semiannual **trade shows,** sponsored by various associations and organizations, give manufacturers and distributors a forum in which to display their products to a large number of potential distribution channel members. There is great diversity in the kinds of shows sponsored each year—such as gift shows, electronics shows, hardware shows, automobile shows, stationery shows, and gourmet food shows—that enable distribution channel members to see at one time all the products they may want to carry. Since the shows are aimed at stimulating immediate purchases by distribution channel members, special premiums and incentives are frequently offered to those distribution channel members who place orders for merchandise at the shows.

15–2 Focus on Marketing Practices
SALES PROMOTIONS

Marketers are always looking for new ways to promote their products. Often, conventional advertising methods are not the answer. Here are some of the original methods companies have found to promote their products.

Executives at Toro Company had a problem with low sales for its snow throwers. Consumers feared that buying a snow thrower would be an unnecessary expense if the winter proved to be a mild one with light snowfall. Toro came up with a solution: it promised to refund customers' money for the snow throwers if the snowfall for the year was below 20 percent of the average for their area. That sounded like a good deal to a lot of cautious consumers. Sales increased dramatically during this promotional campaign. (Meanwhile, snowfall was average or above average, releasing Toro from its refund obligation.)

The American Book Award (ABA) is the Academy Award of books in that it is an annual award for high achievement. The Association of American Book Publishers would like this honor to be even more like the Academy Award and work as a promotion for the books that are nominated. Each year as the Academy Award nominees are announced, moviegoers make a point to see them. To create a similar impact on book sales, the ABA committee now prepares catalogs of nominees available in bookstores. In addition, the ABA committee informs authors that they've won well in advance of the awards' presentation. This way, ABA authors are more likely to show up at the presentation, making the event more likely to attract newspaper and magazine coverage.

Many companies are finding that movies provide significant promotional opportunities. Marketers can pay moviemakers to use their product in feature films. Cheerios made a cameo appearance on a breakfast table in *Superman*, RC Cola in *Rocky III* and *North Dallas Forty*, Hawaiian Tropic suntan oil in *The Cannonball Run*. Marketers can't prove that this promotional strategy is effective, but feelings are positive about it, especially when the movie is a hit. The risk involved is that the movie may be a bomb, reducing the number of consumers who will see the product on the big screen.

Recent deregulation of the commercial airlines has created some fierce competition in

Push Money. **Push money** is an incentive given to retailers by other distribution channel members in exchange for promoting a product through retail displays. The incentive to the retailer might be, for example, a cash payment or a lower price for the product. The retailer, in turn, agrees to give the product a certain amount of shelf space where the product's label is clearly visible or a prime display such as an end-of-aisle display or one near the checkout counter.

Focus 15–2 describes some novel sales promotions being used by manufacturers and distributors.

the industry. To stay on top, the large airlines have come up with a number of promotional strategies to encourage both sales and loyalty to the airline. United Airlines gave its passengers coupons good for half the fare on a future United flight. (American Airlines quickly followed with a similar promotional campaign of its own.) Three airlines—Trans World Airlines, United, and American—used contests as a promotional tool. United's "Take-Off" game gave each passenger a tic-tac-toe scratch-card. The passenger rubbed the card with a coin to reveal nine pictures. The appearance of three airplanes in a row won the traveler a free round-trip ticket. American offered discounted blocks of seats to travel agencies and travel organizations like Club Med. This strategy encouraged sales to large groups of travelers. To attract families as customers, TWA offered free air fare for children accompanied by their parents.

Super 8 Motels of Aberdeen, South Dakota, discovered a new advertising medium: the sides of trucks. From National Truck Ads Ltd., the motel company rents 7′ × 20′ ad space on the sides of tractor trailers hauling loads all over the United States. For Super 8, advertising on trucks was an effective supplement to federally restricted billboard advertising.

Ortho Consumer Products Division of Chevron Chemical Company is the best known manufacturer of chemical plant-care products. Now Ortho publishes a book to aid in identifying plant problems and to recommend Ortho products to treat them. The 1,000-page book, *Ortho Problem Solver*, is available to retailers as a selling tool. Salespeople can help their garden shop customers more quickly and efficiently using this reference while promoting an Ortho product at the same time. Several years ago, Ortho counted on its reputation as an authority on plant care to aid in the promotion of books on the subject. Now the company is using the same process in reverse, publishing a book to promote its chemical products.

Sources: Bill Richards, "Executives at Toro Are Dreaming of a White Winter—Very White," *Wall Street Journal*, December 20, 1983, p. 33; "Bought a Good Book Lately?" *Sales & Marketing Management*, May 17, 1982, p. 31; "Now the Battling Airlines Try Mass Marketing," *Business Week*, April 28, 1980, p. 104; Steven Mintz, "You Oughta Be in Pictures," *Sales & Marketing Management*, September 14, 1981, pp. 38–40; "Super 8 Takes Its Ads on the Road—Literally," *Sales & Marketing Management*, February 8, 1982, p. 16; and "Ortho Sells by the Book," *Sales & Marketing Management*, October 11, 1982, p. 14;.

Measuring Sales Promotion Effectiveness

In measuring the effectiveness of a sales promotion, marketers analyze how well the sales promotion's objectives were achieved. For example, if the goal were to stimulate sales, then measuring the change in sales volume would be a logical way of analyzing effectiveness. It is important to analyze sales before, during, and after the promotions to determine whether effects are only temporary. A situation, for example, in which the number of sales increases during the month of a promotion but falls far below the average the following month—because the extra quantities purchased during the promotion have not yet been consumed—reflects no real gain for the manufacturer. It actually represents a decrease in sales revenue since the cost of the promotion must be considered. If the purpose of the sales promotion was to gain trial for the product, then it is appropriate to attempt to determine how many consumers tried the product, or how many retailers carried it, as a result of the promotion. If the sales promotion was designed to get reuse of a product, and if coupons were used as the method of promotion, then the coupon redemption rate can be studied.

Publicity

Publicity is a form of communication not directly sponsored by the company and, unlike the advertising and promotion components of the marketing strategy, is not directly aimed at stimulating sales. It involves exposure for the company, often by spreading information through the news media. Its general objective is to create a favorable image and reputation for the company—perhaps with the public; with investors and stockholders; or, in the case of lobbying for legislation favorable to the company, with Congress.

What should a company publicize? The firm must analyze what its assets are and what the public or other target group might find of interest. An unusual angle related to the opening of a new store might prompt publicity. In early 1984, Bijan, a retail store that sells exclusive designer fashions for men, opened a new store on New York's prestigious Fifth Avenue. The unique feature of the store—widely reported in feature stories in the local media—was that customers are admitted "by appointment only"; the store has locked doors and a customer cannot simply walk in off the street to browse.

Sometimes a product itself becomes news. The game "Trivial Pursuit" became the subject of numerous media stories when it was introduced in the United States in 1983. Some stories have focused on the social or psychological aspects of playing the game, and some radio broadcasters have even incorporated questions from the game into their programming, using the questions to stimulate listener call-ins. Cabbage Patch dolls also became news when the media produced stories about the tremendous demand for and appeal of these products.

A technological breakthrough may generate publicity for a company. When IBM researchers in the fall of 1983 developed a microchip with the potential for a memory capacity far exceeding any previous computer chips, the report became a national news story. New discoveries in medical laboratories can also produce positive publicity for a company.

Community service is another subject of publicity. American Express launched, in October 1983, a widely advertised three-month program during which one penny of each credit card transaction and one dollar for each new cardmember was donated to help restore the Statue of Liberty. The company reported a sharp rise in the number of sales transacted with its credit cards, and in new card membership applications. The promotion also raised an estimated $1.3 million for the

Julie Betts Testwuide

Figure 15–16 Press coverage of the award ceremony for the 1983 New York City Marathon generated publicity for marathon-sponsor Manufacturers Hanover Bank.

statue, and publicity about it earned a reputation for American Express as being public-minded and responsible.

Warner Communications, parent company of ATARI, Inc., received publicity in 1984 when it donated ATARI computer hardware and software for the Playing to Win Computer Center, located in a low-income area of New York's East Harlem. Helping give underprivileged young people an opportunity to gain computer experience contributed toward an image of ATARI as being concerned about education and the community.

In addition to media stories, as illustrated in the preceding examples, **press releases** and **press conferences** are other means of generating publicity. For example, much speculation and publicity preceded the introduction of IBM's personal computer in late 1983. News stories anticipating it appeared throughout the media. When IBM finally held a press conference to announce the introduction of the IBM PC*jr*, it was reported nationwide.

Providing information through seminars, workshops, and articles is another means of garnering publicity. A small bank in St. Louis has held physical fitness

Chapter 15 / Advertising, Sales Promotion, and Publicity 429

Figure 15–17 The use of publicity is not new. RCA attracted much attention for its unique television receiver by displaying it at the 1939 New York World's Fair.

seminars as a means of promoting business.[20] Some computer retail stores offer free word processing workshops to familiarize potential customers with their products. Department stores have been holding informational seminars aimed toward working women. Trade magazines often publish articles by individuals who have expertise in a variety of specific fields, thus giving the companies who employ these authors positive publicity.

Point-of-purchase displays can also be used to generate a positive reputation for a company. The Super Glue Corporation, which makes a kit enabling parents to fingerprint their children to have records in case of an emergency, supplies each retail outlet with a display including a poster of missing children's photos from the Child Find organization and a toll-free number where anyone having information about a missing child can call. Providing this public service gives Super Glue an image of caring about its customers and the community.[21]

New channels for publicity are never exhausted. Motion pictures have become an aid to publicity, as it has become increasingly common for brand-name products to appear on camera as props. Corporate clients can hire product placers, a new breed of entrepreneur in Hollywood, to persuade film makers to plant the clients' brand-name products in appropriate movie scenes, thus associating the product with popular movie characters.

Sometimes companies are faced with negative publicity. When bottles of Tylenol, made by McNeil Pharmaceuticals, a division of Johnson & Johnson, were tampered with in Chicago in 1982, Johnson & Johnson quickly withdrew Tylenol from the shelves and reissued the product in a new tamperproof bottle. The company focused its advertising and the efforts of its sales force on promoting this new safety feature. As a result, Johnson & Johnson was perceived as a responsible company concerned with the safety of its customers.

The Tylenol incident also caused 1982 sales of Halloween candy to plummet. To counteract the unfavorable publicity, the following year the National Confectioners Association and Chocolate Manufacturers of America launched a $500,000 campaign to promote Halloween, an effort that included pro-Halloween posters in grocery stores and a toll-free Halloween hotline with Dr. Joyce Brothers explaining the psychological benefits of Halloween for children.[22]

After the fuel "crisis" of the 1970s, the oil companies emerged with a reputation for being greedy and interested in huge profits at the expense of the consumer. Many oil companies engaged in public service activities aimed toward counteracting this image. Texaco, for example, began a program in 1980 to influence consumer and environmental groups. A constituency relations manager for Texaco holds regular workshops, refinery tours, and roundtable discussions with representatives of these activist groups. One result of the program has been support from several of the groups for some of Texaco's lobbying efforts in Congress.

Measuring Publicity Effectiveness

Measuring the effectiveness of publicity poses difficulties. It requires analyzing how well the objectives of the publicity were achieved. If, for example, making the public, or a more specific target group, aware of a new product or service was the goal, then analysts can try to determine how many people know about it. But if the purpose was to counteract negative publicity, it is impossible to know what the company's image would have been had no effort been made to place the company in a favorable public light.

One of the best ways of measuring the effectiveness of publicity is to note the total effect on society of the communication. The burger wars provided a strong

Figure 15–18 Publicity surrounding Wendy's "Where's the beef?" advertising campaign was so effective that *this* advertisement needed no explanation.

example of the effectiveness of the publicity surrounding the "Where's the beef" slogan in that the slogan permeated people's speech, clothing, and the political arena to the extent that it became a point of reference. For example, people knew exactly what was meant by the advertisement presented in figure 15–18.

Summary

Advertising is "any paid form of nonpersonal presentation and promotion of ideas, goods, and services by an identified sponsor." The purposes of advertising include publicizing a brand, increasing demand, creating an image for the company supporting an issue, enhancing the company's financial position, creating enthusiasm in the company's work force, and increasing product distribution.

Advertising involves four company decisions: which segment to advertise to, what message to communicate, what media to use, and how to determine the campaign's effectiveness. Four kinds of messages are introductory, informative, persuasive, and reminder. The main criteria used to choose the media are their selectivity, penetration (extent to which the medium reaches the target market), coverage, flexibility, cost, and editorial environment.

Television is the most pervasive medium: advertisers consider the type of program, the nature of the audience, and the number of viewers. Two advantages of television advertising are the fact that it is a visual medium and the fact that it can reach a nationwide audience.

Advantages to advertising on radio are its relatively low cost, the geographic narrowness of its audiences, and the fact that the audiences tune in at specific times of the day. The main disadvantage is that radio cannot show products visually.

Out-of-doors media include billboards, transit advertising, roadside signs, and printed shopping bags. The main advantages of out-of-doors media are low cost and close proximity to point of purchase. The main disadvantages are the limitation on the amount of information that they can convey and the fact that the viewers may not be in the target segment.

Print media include newspapers and magazines and are most effective in reaching a specific target audience. The content can be more detailed. Newspapers are considered a local advertising medium. Magazine ads produce results over a longer period of time. Trade magazines are produced for a specific business or profession, whereas consumer magazines are popular, nationally distributed publications with large circulations.

Media scheduling is the way in which a company's advertising budget is spread out over a year. Some products are advertised more heavily during a particular season. Three types of scheduling are continuous, flighting (heavy advertising during a known buying period followed by no advertising), and pulsing (continuous with periods of heavy advertising).

Advertisers measure the effectiveness of their campaigns by looking at how well their objectives have been met, by looking at customer response, and by using experimental techniques.

Sales promotion is a form of sponsored communication, part of a planned strategy to put the name of the product in front of the consumer. Promotion objectives can include stimulating immediate sales, persuading consumers to try or reuse the product, encouraging the purchase of greater quantities, or evening the sales cycle.

Consumer-aimed promotions include offering free product samples, price incentives, contests, and premiums. Point-of-purchase displays comprise sales promotions implemented by the retailer to appeal to the final consumer. Other forms include coupons, rebates, and bonus packs.

The purpose of trade promotions is for manufacturers and distributors to persuade other channel members to carry a particular product. Methods include cooperative advertising, incentive programs, trade shows, and push money (an incentive offered to channel members in return for promotional efforts).

Publicity is a form of communication not directly sponsored by the company that is not directly aimed at stimulating sales. Channels for publicity include media stories, press releases, press conferences, seminars, workshops, point-of-purchase displays designed to give the company a positive image, and movies.

Questions for Discussion

1. What are the different objectives of advertising?
2. Explain the nature and importance of the four categories of advertising messages.
3. What criteria are generally used in selecting advertising media?
4. Compare the appropriateness of using television and radio media in promoting products.
5. Discuss the media scheduling you would use for the following products: (a) recreation products; (b) automobiles; (c) cosmetics; and (d) home computers.
6. "The effectiveness of an advertising campaign cannot be measured." Comment.
7. Why has sales promotion become increasingly important in recent times?
8. Differentiate between the different methods of trade promotion.
9. What makes publicity so appealing to some companies?

References

1. The burger wars example here and throughout the chapter is based on "The Fast-Food War: Big Mac Under Attack," *Business Week,* January 30, 1984, pp. 44–46; "Burger Brawls," *Time,* October 11, 1982, p. 74; "Burger King Beefs Up Its Jabs and Jokes," *Business Week,* September 26, 1983, pp. 42–43; and "Burger King TV Spots Fry McDonald's Again," *Advertising Age,* March 7, 1983, p. 3.
2. David A. Aaker and John G. Myers, *Advertising Management* (Englewood Cliffs, N.J.: Prentice-Hall, 1975).
3. P. M. Carrick, "Why Continued Advertising is Necessary," quoted in Max Sutherland and John Galloway, "Role of Advertising: Persuasion or Agenda Setting?" *Journal of Advertising Research,* October 1981, p. 28.
4. Roy Paul Nelson, "The Design of Advertising," quoted in Ibrahim M. Hefzallah and W. Paul Maloney, "Are There Only Six Kinds of TV Commercials?" *Journal of Advertising Research,* August 1979, p. 59.
5. This section based on John S. Wright, Willis L. Winter, and Sherilyn K. Zeigler, *Advertising,* 5th ed. (New York: McGraw-Hill, 1982), pp. 134–40.
6. Ibid., p. 145.
7. "Industry Survey: Media, Basic Analysis," *Standard & Poor's Industry Analysis, Media,* June 9, 1983, p. 73.

8. Lawrence C. Soley, Jesse E. Teel, Jr., and Leonard N. Reid, "A Comparison of Influences on Fixed and Grid Ratio Advertising Rates," *Journal of Advertising*, Fall 1980, p. 15.
9. "Industry Survey: Media, Basic Analysis," p. 74.
10. *Radio Facts* (New York: Radio Advertising Bureau, 1980).
11. Wright, Winter, and Zeigler, p. 154.
12. Ibid., p. 167.
13. This statistic based on information provided by the American Newspaper Publishers Association, 1982.
14. This statistic based on information provided by the Newspaper Advertising Bureau, 1983.
15. This statistic based on information provided by the Publishers Information Bureau, 1982.
16. "Wendy's Second Quarter Net Income Leaped 36%," *Wall Street Journal*, August 1, 1984, p. 30.
17. Paul W. Farris and Robert Buzzell, *Relationships Between Changes in Industrial Advertising and Promotional Expenditures and Changes in Market Share* (Cambridge, Mass.: Marketing Science Institute, 1976); and Roger A. Strang, *The Relationship Between Advertising and Promotion in Brand Strategy* (Cambridge, Mass.: Marketing Science Institute, 1975).
18. Roger A. Strang, "Sales Promotion—Fast Growth, Faulty Management," *Harvard Business Review*, July–August 1976, pp. 115–24.
19. "Bread Bucks' Instant Dough," *Sales & Marketing Management*, October 12, 1981, p. 19.
20. "What's News," *Wall Street Journal*, July 16, 1981, p. 1.
21. "Super Glue Created the Help the Children Foundation and Introduces Precious Prints," *Entrepreneur*, February 1984, pp. 46–47.
22. "Public Relations Campaign Hopes to Undo the Harm Done to Halloween's Image by the Tylenol Scare," *Wall Street Journal*, May 10, 1983, p. 37.

OBJECTIVES

1. To identify the role of personal selling in marketing.

2. To describe the nature of the communication process involved in personal selling.

3. To explain the steps involved in the personal selling strategy.

4. To list the different types of sales representatives.

5. To discuss the roles of recruiting, training, motivating, compensating, and evaluating salespeople.

6. To provide different types of sales force structures.

16
Personal Selling

American Cyanamid's staff of industrial salespeople sell chemicals to other companies for use in manufacturing processes. The nature of the selling job has changed, though, in response to changes in the environment and the changing needs of the company.

Up to the early 1970s, American Cyanamid's salespeople were given a territory and instructed to sell as many chemicals as possible. They knew little about their company's goals and finances. The selling tools they used included establishing personal relationships with the customer's purchasing agent and just dropping in on potential customers.

Changes in the economic, political, and competitive environments led to a redefinition of the American Cyanamid salesperson's job. A number of competitors from Western Europe, Japan, and China were selling chemicals in the United States and fighting for larger shares of the market. At the same time, rising energy costs, periods of recession, and an increase in government regulation of the chemical industry made customers anxious to keep costs low and increase business efficiency. Gathering information—about customers' needs, competitors' actions, demand for new products, pricing levels—became vital to the company and has become the salesperson's main task. Other tasks include handling customer complaints, keeping track of government regulations about chemicals, monitoring the world chemical market, and developing financially appealing sales offers for customers.

The salespeople have also had to adjust to a more efficient and cost-conscious buying atmosphere on the part of customers. Purchasing agents are better informed and, in light of the competition, better able to ask for good deals on purchases. Another factor has been the growing use of computers in the buying process. Some companies routinely reorder

supplies, including chemicals, through their computers, making it very difficult for a salesperson to introduce new products to the company. All of these factors affect the nature and purpose of personal selling and the role of the salesperson for American Cyanamid.[1]

Personal selling is the fourth element in the communications mix. In this chapter, we will look at the decisions, and factors that affect those decisions, that companies make in relation to their personal selling program, including the roles of their salespeople, the selling process, and the organization and management of their sales force.

The Roles of the Salesperson

Salespeople have often been called the "spark plugs of civilization." Without good salespeople, the world would not know that a better mousetrap has been created, or that a new category of consumer needs has not been fulfilled. For example, without salespeople, how could a doctor learn about an important new drug that may be just the one needed to save a patient's life? Without salespeople, how could a grocer learn about a new line of frozen foods that may be just the product needed by busy working parents? Without salespeople, how could a manufacturer of office equipment learn that a new product is difficult for consumers to use?

In each of these examples, the salesperson serves as the eyes and ears of both the company and the consumer, conveying information about new products to potential consumers and about consumers' needs and potential satisfiers to the company. As the "eyes and ears," the salesperson has three main roles:

1. *Conveyer of information:* The salesperson conveys the information about the product mix offered by the company for the consumer and about the product mix sought by the customer from the company.
2. *Catalyst in the buying process:* The salesperson influences the buying process by showing how products can satisfy the consumer's needs.
3. *Service agent:* The salesperson can also be a delivery person, display arranger, provider of customer services, teacher, and performer of other functions needed by customer and company.

American Cyanamid's salespeople perform each of these selling roles. First, they convey information to both the company and consumers. The salespeople have become a main source of information for the company about customer needs and the various competitive and economic factors that influence the company. The salespeople also communicate to customers information about the company's products, prices, schedules, and other factors that affect the buying process. Second, as catalysts in the buying process, American Cyanamid's salespeople try to create selling offers that suit the customer's financial and production needs. Finally, as service agents, the salespeople handle customer complaints, settle customer disputes with the company, and answer customer questions.

By performing the three selling roles, American Cyanamid's salespeople fulfill the needs both of customers, by providing a desired product under satisfactory conditions, and the company, by providing revenue and the information needed to carry on business.

No marketing activity, of which selling is an important part, exists in a vacuum. The environment in which consumers live and in which companies operate is a dynamic one, as was described in chapter 3. Figure 16–1 shows the dynamics of personal selling, including the five environmental factors that salespeople must take into consideration as they carry out their roles.

For example, the chemical industry in the 1980s is providing a challenge for American Cyanamid's salespeople. A number of foreign companies are entering the United States and are providing serious competition. Economic conditions are making cost-conscious customers look for good deals from their suppliers. The use of computers has given customers an additional way to save costs and increase the

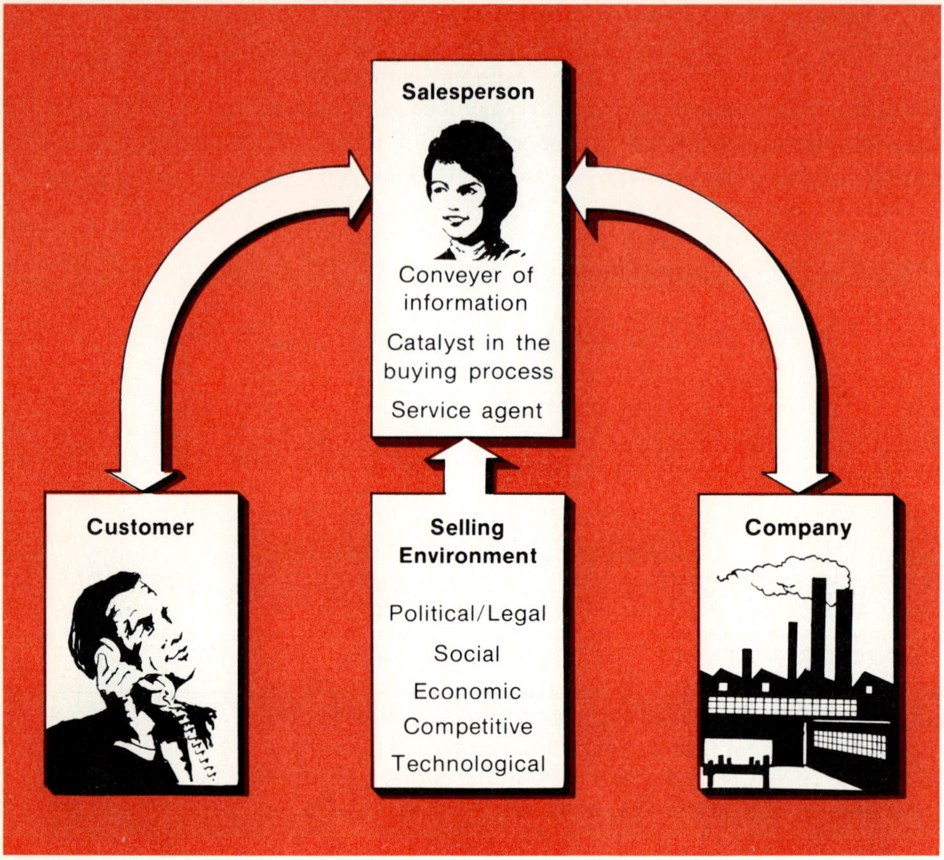

Figure 16–1 The dynamics of personal selling

Salesperson
- Conveyer of information
- Catalyst in the buying process
- Service agent

Customer

Selling Environment
- Political/Legal
- Social
- Economic
- Competitive
- Technological

Company

efficiency of their purchasing operations, but it has also made the selling process more difficult for salespeople.

Personal Selling Communication

Personal selling is a very complex activity. As we have seen in chapter 14, it is "the personal or impersonal process of assisting and/or persuading a prospective customer to buy a commodity or service or to act favorably upon an idea that has commercial significance to the seller."[2] Personal selling involves some form of communication between a producer and a consumer. It differs from the other elements of the communications mix—advertising, sales promotion, and publicity—because it involves communication between two people, often face to face.

The typical personal selling communication model is shown in figure 16–2. (This model is similar to the general communication model presented in chapter

14, but it has been adapted to fit personal selling.) In personal selling, because the salesperson addresses the customer in person, the sales presentation can be personalized to meet the customer's specific needs. The noise can be overcome by the salesperson adjusting for such distraction as it occurs. Communicating effectively requires a knowledge of what one wants the customer to know or do and an organization of material and words that will have meaning to him or her. In the model, feedback is immediate. That is, the customer can give an order on the spot or can indicate dissatisfaction with the seller or the product during communication. The salesperson can also listen to what consumers communicate about their needs and interests.

The sales presentation in figure 16–2 consists of nonverbal as well as verbal communication. Studies of communication have shown that as much as 50 percent of the attitudes that people develop in face-to-face communication result from nonverbal exchanges. The earliest impressions in a conversation come mainly from the subjective interpretation of nonverbal cues rather than from the importance of the spoken word. The skilled salesperson can make both elements work together effectively. In doing so, the salesperson considers the needs of the consumer first, and plans the total communication from the moment of approach through the listening process to the delivery of the final message.

A number of personal qualities aid in personal selling communication. Because selling is a transaction involving people, a successful salesperson must acquire the ability to empathize with customers. *Empathy* is the ability to stand in other persons' shoes, to feel their feelings and think their thoughts. In selling, the ability to

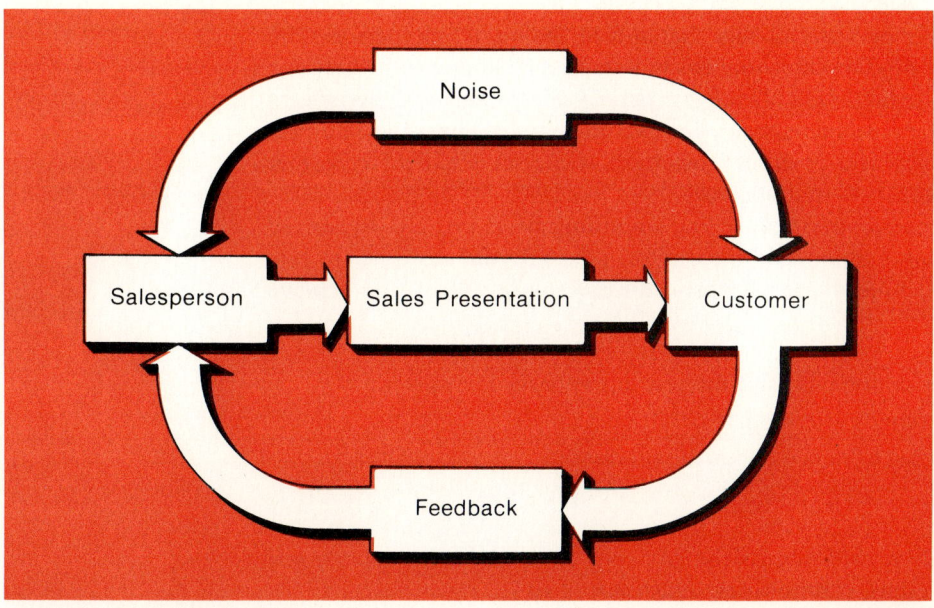

**Figure 16–2
Personal selling communication model**

Figure 16–3 The sales presentation, as conducted by this Fuller Brush salesperson, involves both verbal and nonverbal communication and allows for immediate feedback.
Courtesy of the Fuller Brush Company

understand customers in this way enables the salesperson to develop rapport with them and to establish credibility in their eyes. This empathy is a form of the marketing concept, as it is a recognition of the needs of consumers and implies a concern with meeting those needs.

Enthusiasm is another personal quality that aids in selling. A salesperson who is enthusiastic about the product can more easily interest a customer in it than one who views selling as a tedious task. Finally, a *flexible* salesperson will be able to adapt more readily to the customer's style. For example, a very outgoing salesperson may intimidate a shy and reserved customer, while an ebullient customer might find the quiet salesperson quite boring.

The two main purposes of personal selling communication are, first, to convey product and company information and, second, to persuade the customer to buy the product. In order to fulfill these purposes, the salesperson must first achieve four secondary goals:

1. Identify the key selling points of interest to the particular customer.
2. Attract the customer's attention.
3. Present convincing evidence about the product.
4. Ask for action.

In the next section, we will discuss the strategies through which salespeople achieve these goals and, thus, communicate effectively.

Sales Strategy

Much work is done before a salesperson can start selling. The company has to define its markets and businesses, as we saw in chapter 4. It will also have segmented the market to identify the types of customers it is pursuing. And it will have created a marketing plan that includes all of these decisions.

The company's salespeople are the implementers of its marketing plan. Their first step is to create a sales plan that identifies specific potential customers and their needs and wants. Having done this homework, the salesperson proceeds through the six main steps in personal selling: prospecting, approach, sales presentation, handling objections, closing, and follow-up (see fig. 16–4).

Prospecting

Prospecting is the sales activity in which the salesperson creates a list of potential buyers, or **leads,** for a product. Out of the total market of consumers, salespeople will focus on those consumers most likely to be interested in the product. The company has already defined its market, and the marketing plan has identified specific customers within that market whose needs are satisfied by the product. At times, however, the salesperson must develop his or her own leads. The most common sources for leads are:

1. *The cold canvas.* Knocking on every door is a nonselective but potentially effective way of uncovering possible buyers.
2. *Advertising returns.* People who respond to advertisements in appropriate publications that invite inquiries or offer a free sample are often good prospects.
3. *Referrals.* Satisfied customers and acquaintances may be able to name people or companies that have a need for or are interested in the product.
4. *Lists.* Lists purchased from other companies, made from specialized directories, or drawn from other collections of names contain a preselected group of prospects.
5. *Social contacts.* Friends or people met at social events are potential prospects.
6. *Center of influence.* Influential people in specific areas may be able to identify prospects.
7. *Company records.* The company's service records and inquiry files may identify potential prospects.
8. *Other salespeople.* Salespeople in the same company or for noncompeting companies may suggest prospects.

Each lead is then examined in terms of the customer's need for the product and ability to buy it. This examination creates the list of **qualified prospects,** the customers the salesperson will call on. The work of prospecting is time-consuming

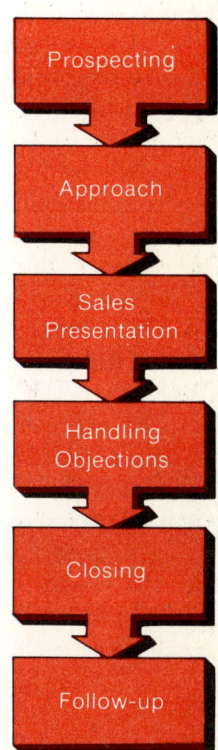

Figure 16–4 The six main steps in personal selling

and sometimes tedious. It is a present- as well as a future-oriented activity. Leads that do not become qualified prospects now may at some time in the future.

Approach

The second step is the **approach,** the method of initial contact with the qualified prospect. Some common ways to make an approach are telephoning for an appointment, sending an introductory letter followed by a telephone call, arranging an introduction to the qualified prospect by a mutual acquaintance, or calling "cold" at the prospect's office hoping for an opportunity to meet with him or her. Knowledge of the prospect and the situation will help the salesperson determine the best approach to use. The first few minutes of the initial meeting are included in the approach, as the salesperson must attract the prospect's attention, arouse his or her curiosity, establish rapport, and build the foundation for a mutually beneficial conversation.

Sales Presentation

The purpose of the **sales presentation** is to bring a message to the prospect. Because the main advantage of personal selling over mass selling is its ability to personalize the message, the sales presentation can discuss product benefits in terms of the prospect and his or her identified wants and needs. The marketing plan sets forth the need-satisfying characteristics of the product for each type of customer.

Figure 16–5 shows the AIDA model (discussed in chapter 14) in relation to a sales presentation. The customer's *attention* is gained through the sales presentation, including the use of special techniques such as visuals or a product demonstration. The prospect's attention cannot be held for very long without creating *interest* in the product. Customers will not be interested unless they can see some need-satisfying characteristic or benefit to them. They need evidence to create belief and *desire*. If the customer feels a need or want for the product, then a sense of desire is likely to develop. The evidence, benefits, and desire combine to persuade the prospect to take *action* and pursue the buying process.

The sales presentation is the core of personal selling communication. The salesperson asks questions and listens to the prospect's answers, incorporating expressed points of interest into the presentation. The product's characteristics relating to the prospect's needs, as well as relevant advantages and disadvantages, are discussed. The sales presentation appeals to the prospect's senses and helps him or her visualize the product in his or her life. Claims and evidence used to create desire should be believable to the prospect.

Handling Objections

Handling objections is another term for answering questions. For the salesperson, this part of the selling process is an opportunity to provide more product information of particular interest to the customer. Again, personal selling communication is essential. The key to handling objections effectively is listening to what the prospect is really saying.

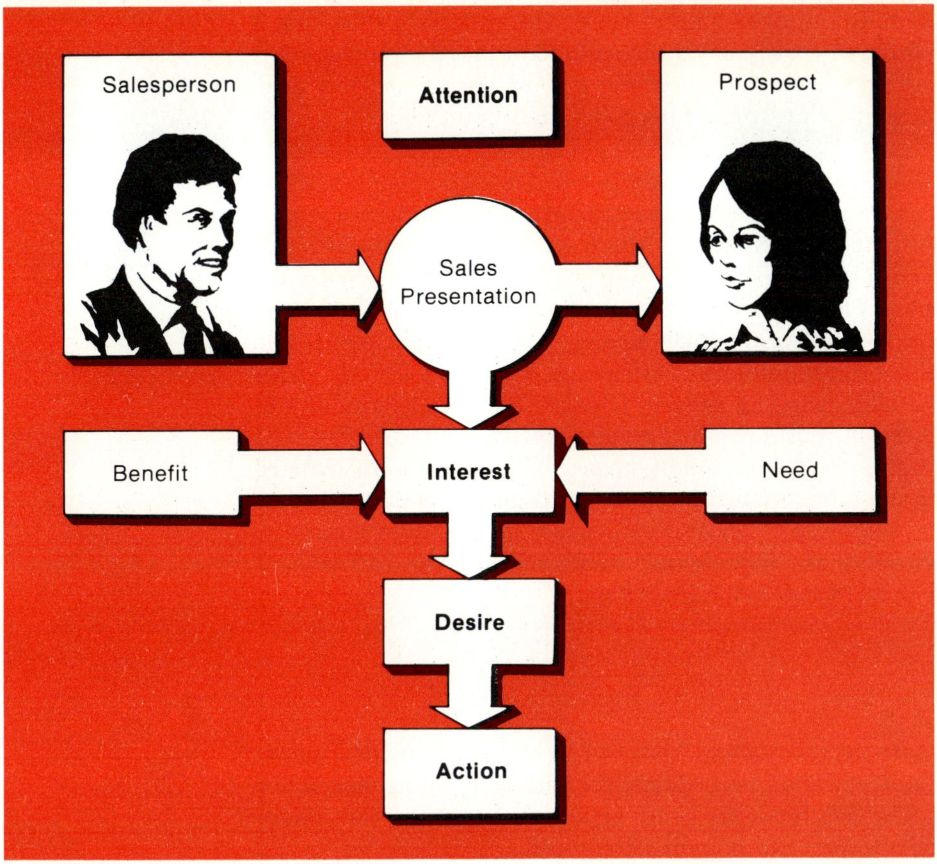

Figure 16–5 The AIDA model in a sales presentation

Understanding customer behavior helps explain why objections occur in many selling situations. Customers are frequently risk avoiders. Objections are the customer's attempt to delay making a commitment or to reduce risk related to the product. By meeting objections as they occur and answering them skillfully, the salesperson can make the sale with more certainty and satisfaction. One possible way is to refer buyers to satisfied customers, especially those who had similar uncertainties about the product.

Closing

Closing is the point at which the customer agrees to buy the product. If an effective sales presentation is made and objections are handled, then closing should follow naturally. By observing both verbal and nonverbal feedback, the salesperson can determine the prospect's state of readiness to buy. When a buying signal is observed, the salesperson can make it easy for the customer to make the purchase.

A trial closing at any point in the selling process can assist the salesperson in reading the pulse of the prospect. Asking the prospect's opinion about the product

Chapter 16 / Personal Selling

or the deal will help identify the right time to close. The real effect of asking a question, though, is to bring the customer to the realization that the purchase has been made. The actual closing may be made on minor points such as delivery date, installation, shipping method, color, size, return policy, and so on.

Follow-up consists of providing all the services attached to the product and analyzing a consumer's postpurchase satisfaction. These activities determine whether or not a customer who has bought once will buy again. They can also enhance the product's and the company's image, help develop a competitive selling edge, serve as a source of new referrals and testimonials to use in sales presentations, and provide important leads for future sales calls. Follow-up techniques include attention to the details of the sale, including delivery schedule and installation, awareness of service problems for the customer, and regular postsale contacts.

Follow-up

Important feedback also results from follow-up activities. Information gathered may be useful in selling the same product to another prospect or another product to this particular buyer. Salespeople can also gather information from customers about important market trends and new product needs that they can convey back to the company for use in its overall marketing effort.

Types of Sales Representatives

There are five types of sales representatives, classified by the functions performed, the amount of training and education needed, and the variety of selling techniques used in each situation. The five types are order getters, order takers, missionary salespeople, technical salespeople, and support salespeople.

Order getters serve customers who are making an initial purchase from the supplier. They identify prospects and the needs of the prospects and sell the prospects products that will meet their needs. Order getters set up displays, give product demonstrations, perform promotional work, make sales presentations, and handle objections. After the sale, they try to stimulate future demand for the product.

Order Getters

An upholstery salesperson is one kind of order getter. A customer who is redecorating an office may want to select fabrics to re-cover the furniture. The salesperson visits the customer in the office to help select the appropriate materials based on the customer's tastes and the purpose of the redecoration. The order getter may also measure the furniture to be re-covered and arrange for its pickup and delivery.

Order takers meet customers who already know what they need. The tasks they perform include being available and visible to take orders, providing delivery ser-

Order Takers

Chapter 16 / Personal Selling

Figure 16–6 Order getters sell consumers products that will meet their needs. This may involve demonstrating the use of some products, such as makeup.

Donald C. Johnson, Click/Chicago

Figure 16–7 Order takers meet and respond to customers who already know what they want.

Marc P. Anderson

vice, and offering the best deals. A salesperson for a liquor distributor is an order taker. By calling on various beverage retailers, this salesperson finds out which of the company's products are selling and need to be restocked; the salesperson may also arrange displays of the product and hand out promotional materials that could enhance the retailers' business.

16–1 Focus on a Marketing Practice
ELECTRONIC SELLING

In the horse-and-buggy days, a company used the traveling salesman as a major part of its marketing effort. The drummer, as he was called, would travel from town to town to meet personally with potential buyers, show them the wares in his battered trunks, and try to persuade them to place orders. Now, however, the same company's salesperson is likely to tote a video-cassette recorder to demonstrate the product, if he or she is on the road at all. Electronic devices, including personal computers, videodisc players, video-cassette recorders, and the telephone, have brought about great changes in the way products are sold.

The major forces behind this change are advancing technology, corporate emphasis on productivity, and the increasing technical sophistication of many new products. The cost of keeping a salesperson on the road has increased sharply (travel, food, and lodging can cost the company much more than the salesperson's wages). At the same time the cost of much of the technology used in telemarketing, teleconferencing, and computerized sales has fallen greatly, making sophisticated electronic marketing affordable and cost-competitive even for smaller companies.

Gould, Inc., a California company that manufactures medical products, found that sales personnel were not always able to convey the exact merits of some complicated products to potential customers. So Gould developed a video support system to help sell a new product—a disposable transducer that translates blood pressure into readable elec-

Missionary and Technical Salespeople

Missionary and **technical salespeople** do not necessarily make the actual sales. They function more as providers of advice, training, and educational services. They may prepare the proposals for certain types of technical or complex products that will be purchased through bidding. These salespeople usually work with another salesperson who actually initiates and closes the deal. A salesperson for a manufacturer of heavy equipment may initiate the selling process with a prospect. If the prospect has questions about how the machinery works or has objections that the order getter cannot handle, a technical salesperson may be called in.

College textbook salespeople are examples of missionary salespeople. These salespeople visit professors to tell them about new and existing textbooks and to find out about their interest in new course material. They provide review copies of books and convey ideas about new products from professors back to their companies. The actual order for the textbook is placed through the college bookstore. The salespeople then follow up later in the semester to see how the course is progressing and to determine the professors' future textbook needs.

tronic impulses. The system included two videotapes, one a sales presentation and the other a user-training film, and salespeople were equipped with videocassette recorders to take with them on calls. The results? In less than a year, Gould claimed to have captured 45 percent of the transducer market and had sales in excess of 25,000 units a month.

Videotapes do not supplant the outside salesperson, but the telephone and contemporary techniques of *telemarketing* often do. Telemarketing can involve as little as taking orders to actively going after business from potential customers. Telemarketing can also be a way for companies to cut costs. After Louisiana Oil and Tire Company set up a telemarketing system, the company's phone bill increased, but other sales expenses declined by more than twice as much, and sales doubled.

Technological progress is also making order taking an electronic task. More and more companies are buying mainframe computers that can communicate directly to another company's mainframe computer and can therefore be used for "paperless" ordering. The American Hospital Supply Corporation, for example, instituted a method called analytical systems automated purchasing (ASAP). Customers could enter purchase orders into their own computer and have it get in touch with American Hospital's computer, find out what is available and when it can be shipped, and place the order. All of this is done instantly, with no paperwork. American Hospital and other companies using electronic selling methods feel that their salespeople have become more productive and are able to spend more time on customer service and on promotional activities for the company.

Source: Based on "Rebirth of a Salesman: Willy Loman Goes Electronic," *Business Week*, February 27, 1984, pp. 103–4.

Support Salespeople

Support salespeople are not engaged in the actual sale, but rather support the other types of salespeople by performing such activities as arranging delivery, providing customer service, providing educational and training materials, listening to customer questions and complaints, and following up. These activities are often called **maintenance selling;** their purpose is to assist and keep the customers the company has.

The roles of the various types of salespeople may change as companies start to use new technology in the selling process, as can be seen in focus 16–1.

Sales Force Management

The characteristics of a successful salesperson were discussed earlier. Some of these characteristics already exist in an individual before he or she chooses a selling career, while other skills are obtained through training and experience. Qualified

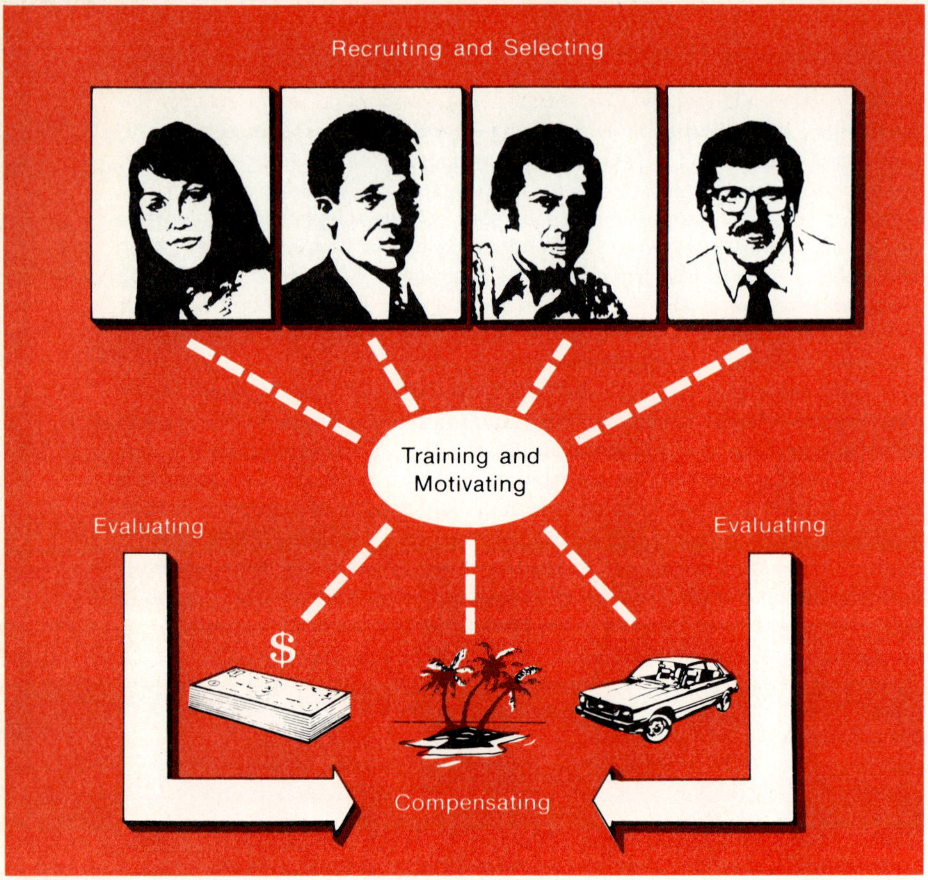

**Figure 16–8
Elements of sales force management**

salespeople must be recruited, trained, motivated, compensated, and evaluated (see fig. 16–8). We will look at each of these points in relation to Mary Kay Cosmetics, a company whose success and profits depend on the quality, size, and motivation of its sales force.[3]

Recruitment

Selecting the right people is essential to a company because much time, money, and effort are spent training new sales force members. A common problem faced by sales managers is recognizing talented and potentially successful people to hire for the sales force. Selection involves careful screening of the candidates.

Most recruiting is done through the use of campus interviews, in-house recommendations, employment agency referrals, classified ads in newspapers and trade publications, and convention contacts. Since the human element is more important than the written credentials of a candidate, personal evaluations are crucial to the screening process. The preliminary review of applicants and referrals often involves application forms; some type of testing, such as verbal and math intelligence tests, personality tests, or interest inventory tests; personal letters of recommendation; and other tangible evidence of the candidate's ability. However, these devices basically serve to eliminate persons who are obviously unsuitable for a selling position. Further evaluation is done through one or more personal interviews, usually conducted by the sales manager and sometimes by other members of the sales force with whom the candidate would be working. Thus, a combination of qualities and skills contributes to the identification of good sales potential (see fig. 16–9).

The two most costly aspects of sales force management are high turnover of salespeople and sales training. If recruitment is done skillfully and selectively, then these costs can be minimized.

The more salespeople Mary Kay Cosmetics has, the more sales it can make and the more revenue it gets. Therefore, the company has an active recruiting program. Salespeople at Mary Kay Cosmetics are called consultants. The consultants are encouraged to find other people to become consultants, often through the social network of friends and relatives. When consultants get eight recruits, they receive a commission of 8 percent on the orders of the recruits. When the consultants get 12 recruits, they become directors and receive commissions of 9 to 12 percent of their consultants' sales. If a director's consultants' sales are more than $72,000 in a six-month period, the director receives additional bonuses. These financial incentives lead many of the salespeople to engage in active recruiting for the company.

**Figure 16–9
Characteristics of sales potential**

A good potential sales force candidate should:

- Have oral communication skills.
- Be able to write clearly and concisely.
- Be well organized.
- Have the ability to plan.
- Be a skillful problem-solver.
- Demonstrate a high energy level.
- Exercise good judgment.
- Have a pleasant personality.
- Be a sensitive person.
- Have persuasive ability.

Training

There are four types of sales training:

1. Orientation for newly hired sales representatives
2. Presentation of product information and product demonstrations
3. Development of selling skills and strategy
4. Motivational training and peer group interaction

In order to be successful, salespeople must possess the necessary tools of the trade. These include knowledge about the company and its products, information about the market, knowledge of the competition, an understanding of the customer, organization skills, time management skills, and an understanding of the art of selling. Learning about these tools comes from a variety of formal as well as informal training experiences. Salespeople learn from each other as well as from the sales manager, and they become more knowledgeable as they develop in their jobs. The task of the sales manager is to recognize the training needs of the sales force members, and to plan activities and meetings to enhance their growth.

The effective use of the training function is exemplified by a program of Xerox Learning Systems.[4] More than 500 sales calls made by some 24 different sales organizations were analyzed in an effort to gather information to assist in the development of the company's sales training program. Certain key skills that contributed to selling success, as well as a number of common errors leading to failure, were noted. (These are shown in fig. 16–10.) Training sessions communicated this information to salespeople, who could use it to enhance their selling abilities and avoid some proven pitfalls in their selling activities.

Motivation

The key to achieving company profits is a highly motivated sales force. Supervision and support must come from the sales manager to assist in this effort. A company's motivation program involves the human element of frequent personal contact of the sales manager with every member of the team to provide individualized attention to salespersons' needs, as well as meetings, training sessions, and compensation packages to support the sales force.

American Optical's Vision Care Products Division offered a special motivation—its top salespeople were treated to a weekend at a luxury hotel.[5] Mary Kay Cosmetics has quite a large motivation program for its top achievers. Other than the financial incentives for recruiting new salespeople, Mary Kay also rewards its top sellers by giving them furs, jewels, vacations, and, for the very best, pink Cadillacs. The company also holds sales conferences at which top sellers are praised in front of their fellow salespeople.

Compensation

All forms of compensation are important in maintaining high levels of involvement by salespeople. Selling is an emotionally and physically demanding occupation,

FIGURE 16–10 Key skills and common errors in selling

Key Skills

1. Asking questions to gather information and uncover needs
2. Recognizing when a customer has a need and showing how the product can satisfy it
3. Establishing a balanced dialogue with customers
4. Recognizing and handling negative customer attitudes
5. Using a benefit summary and action plan requiring commitment when closing

Common Errors

1. Telling instead of selling; not asking enough questions
2. Not allowing the customer to express needs; asking too many closed-end questions
3. Not responding to customer's needs with product benefits
4. Not recognizing or handling negative customer attitudes
5. Not recognizing when or how to close

Source: Based on Mike Radick, "Training Salespeople to Get Success on Their Side," *Sales & Marketing Management*, August 15, 1983, pp. 63–65.

and many involved in it are motivated to produce high levels of sales through continuous reinforcement and recognition.

Compensation in the form of salary, commission, or bonus can be a powerful motivator in selling. Payment to salespeople can include any combination of money, insurance and health benefits, expense accounts, and nonmonetary benefits. A **straight salary** is a fixed payment to the salesperson on a regularly scheduled basis, and usually is a form of compensation for time spent on selling activities. A **straight commission** is a monetary reward based on the amount of sales made. Most firms use a **combination compensation plan**—part salary, which provides some financial security to the salesperson, and part commission, giving the salesperson a stronger incentive to make more sales. Some companies also offer benefits in the form of health and life insurance, a car, vacation pay, or cash bonuses. It is also common for salespeople to be paid for their expenses, either as a lump sum per month or on a reimbursement basis. Depending on the type of company, the nature of its clients, and the salesperson's rank in the company, part of the compensation plan can include such nonmonetary benefits as club memberships, special titles, and honorary plaques.

The form of compensation may be determined by the company's marketing strategy. Salespeople tend to plan their activities according to how much money they will make. If the company's marketing plan requires that its salespeople call on all types of customers and spend equal amounts of time and effort with them, a straight salary compensation plan makes the most sense. Such a plan holds no incentive to spend more time with the largest customers who produce the most sales and, consequently, the most commission. The same idea holds for a company's sales force placing products in wholesale or retail establishments. The salespeople may recognize that they would receive more money in the form of commissions if they placed an expensive watch, for example, in drugstores or five-and-dimes. The company, however, may want the watch to be sold only through the finest department stores; thus, a straight salary plan or a combination plan makes sense.

Companies that want to increase their sales volume may have a straight commission compensation program, as Mary Kay Cosmetics does.

Evaluation

In many organizations, compensation is tied to sales force evaluation. The sales manager, together with each sales representative, sets a **sales quota,** or a target dollar/sales volume expected to be achieved in a specific time period, based on the nature of the selling job as well as the experience and ability of the salesperson. During evaluation, the manager not only determines the benefits to be received as compensation, such as raises and promotions, but also identifies individual training needs and reviews the sales quotas and goals. The key to effective use of sales force evaluation is having set the sales quotas and goals in advance, so that the members can be goal-directed in their sales activities throughout the year.

Mary Kay Cosmetics sets sales quotas for its salespeople. Fellow salespeople can tell how well others are doing by the uniforms they wear. Consultants wear mufti uniforms until they meet their sales targets; then they are allowed to wear red blazers. When consultants become directors, they wear gray suits.

In 1983, there were more than 200,000 women and a few hundred men in the Mary Kay Cosmetics sales force, and they produced sales of approximately $305 million. The continued success of the company depends on maintaining and managing this sales force well.

Types of Sales Force Structures

One aspect of managing the sales force is deciding how the sales force is to be structured. Companies consider the types of products they are marketing and the nature of their customers and organize the sales force to best reach and serve the customers. The main types of sales force structures are by geographic area, by product, by type of customer, team selling, and national account management.

The sales force structured by geographic area. Structuring the sales force by geographic area is the most common type of organization. A salesperson is given a **territory** covering a geographic area in which there are a certain number of customers or potential customers, and the salesperson travels around the territory calling on the customers. The size of the territory may vary. For example, one salesperson for a stationery supplies company may have a territory covering two square blocks in mid-town Manhattan, while another salesperson for the same company may have a territory covering North Dakota, South Dakota, and Montana.

The salesperson in the territory sells the entire product line for the company. This form of structure allows the salesperson to develop business ties in particular areas and to adapt the sales presentation to meet the needs of customers in a particular area.

The sales force organized by product. Companies with more than one product line may choose to structure their sales force by product, with a separate sales force for each product line. Such an organization allows sales representatives to develop greater expertise about the products. When Pitney Bowes wanted to increase sales of its copier, it created a copier-specialist sales force separate from the sales force that sells other products in its product line. The copier-specialist sales force receives special training about copiers and sells only Pitney Bowes' three top model copiers. The extra expertise and the special attention given to copiers raised domestic copier sales by 17 percent in 1981.[6]

The sales force organized by customer. When companies are selling the same products to different types of customers, they may choose to structure the sales force by customer. The needs of individual consumers and types of businesses differ, so the sales forces concentrating on each can tailor their sales presentations according to those differences. For example, manufacturers of personal computers discovered the farm market and started to sell personal computers to farmers. But the needs of farmers are quite different from the needs of city-based small-business people. The manufacturers had to develop sales forces that understood farming and would know how to sell to farmers. Digital, for example, sets up booths at farm equipment shows where it demonstrates its Rainbow personal computer and the software that can be used in farm management.[7]

Team selling. Technical or complicated products may require a team of salespeople to make the sale. The team may be composed of an order getter, several technical salespeople, and any number of support people performing a number of activities. Each member of the team contributes particular expertise or performs a function necessary to making the sales. Focus 16–2 presents an example of the effectiveness of team selling.

16–2 Focus on Marketing Strategy
TEAM XEROX

Until recently, a Xerox Corporation photocopier salesperson couldn't sell customers a Xerox personal computer. For personal computers, the person to speak to was a Xerox personal computer salesperson. For a Xerox printer and a Star computer work station, customers had to contact two other salespeople. And the salesperson for one product might not help customers get in touch with a salesperson for another kind of product because the company offered no incentive for salespeople from one division generating sales in another. The company's sales divisions worked under different managements in separate offices, conditions that also discouraged cooperation among them. Branch sales offices had separate showrooms for the different types of products.

Xerox's 4,000 copier salespeople have been a key factor in keeping the company one of the top photocopier manufacturers. More than 70 percent of the company's annual revenues comes from copier sales. But Xerox's computer division has had several product failures due to low sales. Xerox recently discontinued its battery-powered personal computer because of poor sales; when the company introduced its word processor, the new product was quickly eclipsed by the best-selling IBM Personal Computer.

Xerox's approach to reversing its computer sales figures has been to create a unified sales force. The new sales system is called Team Xerox and is designed to encourage cooperation, rather than competition, among salespeople.

Copier salespeople, the backbone of Xerox's sales force, are learning about the company's personal computers and office systems over a two-year period. Salespeople specializing in the different kinds of Xerox equipment work together in sales teams. The company assesses the work of the team as a whole, rather than evaluating individual team members' performances. The sales teams share offices, and the branch showrooms display all types of Xerox products.

Early reports from the company indicate that the new sales approach will be a success. The University of Pittsburgh has recently purchased several million dollars worth of Xerox computers. The decision to buy the Xerox products instead of the many alternatives, according to the school's computer center director, was the direct result of the company's team-selling approach. Members of the sales team worked together to fit Xerox products with one another and to match the university's needs.

Team Xerox is the company's recognition that simply providing quality products to meet customers' needs is not enough. Xerox expects to demonstrate that a strong sales force organized to benefit the company as a whole is crucial to any product's success.

Source: Dennis Kneale, "Xerox Takes New Marketing Tack to Improve Poor Computer Sales," *Wall Street Journal*, May 5, 1984, p. 31

National account management. In some cases, one customer is large enough or important enough to have a salesperson assigned to that customer only. This is called **national account management;** a salesperson is responsible for one account with one company for the entire country. This form of structure allows the salesperson to specialize in the products used by that company and to understand fully the needs of the company. The salesperson will often work with the company to solve problems (usually using the salesperson's company's products).

Summary

The salesperson has three main roles: conveyor of information, catalyst in the buying process, and service agent. The American Marketing Association defines selling as "the personal or impersonal process of assisting and/or persuading a prospective customer to buy a commodity or service or to act favorably upon an idea that has commercial significance to the seller." Personal selling is the only face-to-face form of communication available in marketing. Nonverbal communication is also an important element in personal selling, as are emotional qualities, enthusiasm, and flexibility.

The salesperson has two primary goals: to convey product and company information and to persuade the customer to buy the product. Secondary goals include identifying key selling points of interest to the customer, attracting the customer's attention, presenting convincing evidence about the product, and asking for action.

Prospecting is the process of creating a list of potential buyers. An approach is the method of initial contact with the potential customer. The presentation is giving the message to the prospect. The AIDA model of personal selling is composed of four elements: gaining the customer's attention, creating interest in the product, developing the customer's desire for the product, and persuading the prospect to take buying action.

Handling objections is the part of the sales process that involves answering the customers' questions and reservations about the product.

Closing is the point at which the customer agrees to buy the product.

The follow-up involves postsale activities, such as phoning or writing to customers after the sale and being aware of service problems. The follow-up is a source of feedback for the salesperson and the company and can generate a positive product and company image.

For support salespeople, the existing customer receives most of the salesperson's attention. Key functions include order taking, delivery, service, education, and follow-up. For order getters, the salesperson's primary concerns are seeking prospects and converting them into customers. Salespeople are also classified as order takers and missionary and technical salespeople.

A sales manager serves as a liaison between the sales force and other aspects of the marketing function within the organization. Sales management tasks include recruiting, training, and motivating salespeople and providing forms of compensation that salespeople find satisfying. Most firms offer a combination of salary and commission as compensation for their salespeople.

In many organizations, compensation is tied to evaluation. Salespeople have goals for target dollar/sales volume expected to be achieved during a specific time period.

The sales force can be structured by geographic area, by product, or by customer. Companies can also choose to organize into team selling or into national account management.

Questions for Discussion

1. In what way is personal selling different from other types of promotional activities?
2. Explain the different roles performed in personal selling.
3. Identify the different sources for leads in finding sales prospects.
4. "Personal selling requires that the salesperson goes through all the steps in the selling strategy." Comment.
5. Show in what way the role of missionary salespeople is important in personal selling.
6. Compare geographic-based and product-based sales force structures?
7. Examine the importance of national account management in today's business conditions.
8. What are the most important qualities needed in the successful salesperson?
9. Based on your own personal experience as a buyer, evaluate the role of the sales presentation in concluding a sale.

References

1. Based on Hugh D. Menzies, "The New Life of a Salesman," *Fortune*, August 11, 1980, pp. 173–77.
2. *Marketing Definitions: A Glossary of Marketing Terms* (Chicago: American Marketing Association, 1960).
3. The Mary Kay Cosmetics example throughout this section is based on "Mary Kay Cosmetics: Looking Beyond Direct Sales to Keep the Party Going," *Business Week*, March 28, 1983, p. 130; and Dean Rotbart and Laurie P. Cohen, "The Party at Mary Kay Isn't Quite So Lively, As Recruiting Falls Off," *Wall Street Journal*, October 28, 1983, pp. 1, 12.
4. Mike Radick, "Training Salespeople to Get Success on Their Side," *Sales & Marketing Management*, August 15, 1983, pp. 63–65.
5. "Vision Care Keeps Its Goals in Focus," *Sales & Marketing Management*, March 16, 1981, p. 23.

6. "Pitney Bowes Sends in the Specialty Team," *Sales & Marketing Management*, August 16, 1982, p. 25.
7. Meg Cox, "Farmers Growing Demand for Computers Draws Many High-Tech Firms Into Market," *Wall Street Journal*, December 22, 1983, p. 27.

OBJECTIVES

1. To describe the complex, dynamic nature of channel decisions.

2. To examine the role and functions of different types of channel intermediaries.

3. To compare the alternative channel systems generally available to a marketer.

4. To discuss the role of physical distribution in marketing.

5. To explain the role and importance of different physical distribution functions.

6. To highlight the systems perspective involved in physical distribution.

17
Channels of Distribution and Physical Distribution

Sales of personal computer software topped $10 billion in 1984 and are expected to top $30 billion in 1988, a growth rate of 44 percent per year over the next five years. Where are consumers purchasing this software for their personal computers? This varies, depending on the source of the software, the customer, and the type of software.

Book and information publishers, such as Dow Jones and Dun & Bradstreet, are producing their own software or acting as distributors for other companies' software. They use their traditional distribution channels, often selling through bookstores or through mail-order advertisements.

Most software, however, is produced by computer manufacturers and software companies and is distributed through one of several outlets designed to serve specific types of customers. Computer hardware manufacturers with their own stores often sell software for those computers in the same stores. At Radio Shack, for example, a customer can purchase both a Tandy computer and its software. Similarly, IBM Product Centers sell both IBM computers and software.

Some stores, although independent of the manufacturer, sell software for only one brand of computer. Two former IBM employees opened a store in Dallas called SoftSource to provide software and assistance to owners of the IBM Personal Computer.

General software stores, some of which are franchises, sell a variety of software from both computer manufacturers and software companies. A software store can choose for its target market either business people or hobbyists. The type of software it carries depends on the customer. Business people are often interested in accounting, inventory management, and sales growth prediction programs. Hobbyists may be interested in personal finance and word processing programs

and games. Both types of customers may expect expert advice and help from salespeople in a software store.

There is a growing market segment of both professional people and knowledgeable customers who do not need assistance but are interested in purchasing software in a convenient location at a low price. Software wholesalers are reaching these customers by placing software in department stores, convenience stores, supermarkets, and shopping mall kiosks. Rack jobbers are placing racks by checkout counters in mass-merchandise stores, such as K marts. The prices at these locations are often substantially lower than those at software stores.[1]

Personal computer software can be distributed through a number of different channels, depending on the producer, the type of customer, the location, and the price. Each software producer must make decisions about these factors when choosing how it will distribute its products. Should it distribute through specialty software stores, or should it go after the mass market? Which types of marketing intermediaries are interested in distributing its products? Which are best suited for its products? Which are most efficient at reaching its target customers? This chapter looks at the possible distribution channels and at the factors producers consider when choosing among them.

Channels of Distribution

The **channel of distribution** is the series of intermediaries through which the product passes to reach the final customer. It can be very short and direct, as when IBM sells its own software in an IBM Product Center, or it can be longer, as when a software company sells its products through wholesalers, which sell to retailers, which sell to customers. There are many different types of **intermediaries,** including **wholesalers, retailers, agents, brokers, jobbers,** and **manufacturer's representatives.** The channel of distribution can consist of several levels of these intermediaries; some common channels are shown in figure 17–1.

Which channel or channels should be used to reach the target market(s) most effectively is an important decision for the marketing manager. When buying software, for example, different groups of consumers with different needs will buy the same product in different channels. Those who are unsure and less knowledgeable require help and a great deal of information before making their decision; they will shop in specialty software or computer stores where salespeople and brochures are available to assist in the purchase decision. Other segments of the market are quite comfortable purchasing computer software from a rack in a supermarket or drugstore.

The channel decision is a dynamic one. A particular channel may be perfectly

**Figure 17–1
Common channels of distribution**

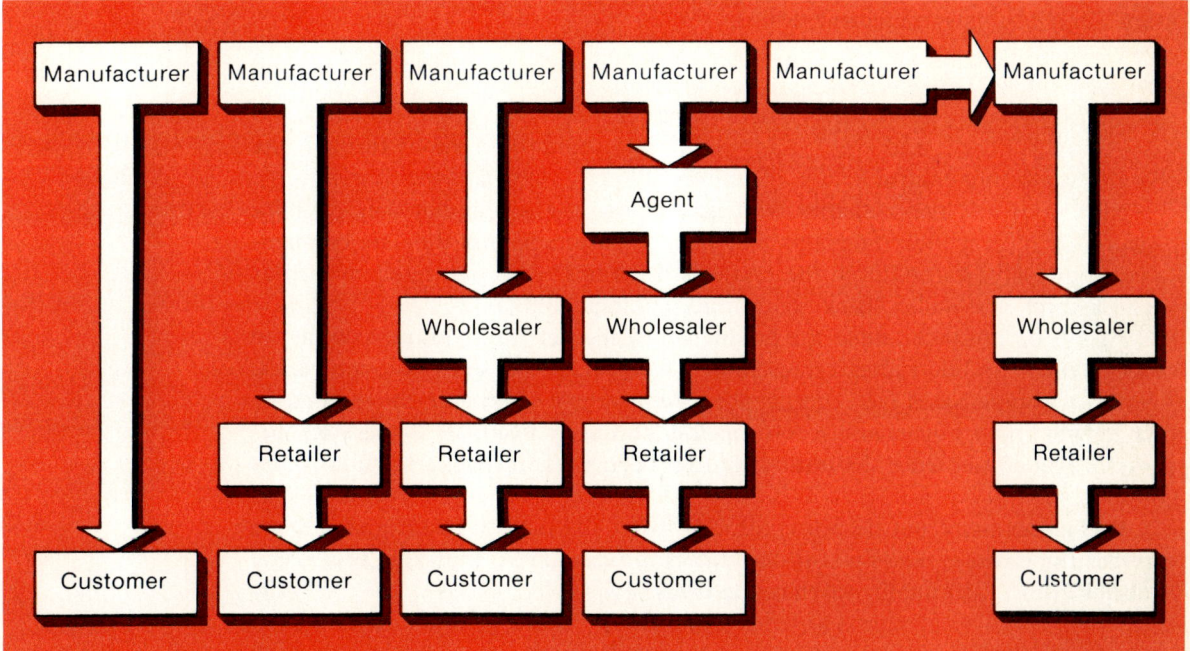

Chapter 17 / Channels of Distribution and Physical Distribution   463

appropriate today, but tomorrow it may lose its effectiveness because consumer needs change. For example, computer software was originally sold only through computer specialty stores. As the market and the number of products expanded, however, specialized software stores sprang up. As consumers become more knowledgeable about the product, and as the market grows even more, many people will be willing to satisfy their software needs from racks in supermarkets, drugstores, and discount department stores.

The type of channel used has significant implications for the other parts of the marketing mix. As software is moved from specialty stores to supermarket racks, changes in the product, price, and promotion may be necessary: The product will have to be standardized and simplified; the price will be lowered; promotion will shift from personal selling in retail stores to advertising to presell the product; and the packaging will become easily recognizable and contain information so consumers can understand what the product is and how to use it. Because each channel reaches a different target market, the marketing mix for each channel must be adjusted to meet the needs of each.

The computer software example also demonstrates that most firms will sell the same product in multiple channels to both industrial customers and consumers. Selling in multiple channels requires multiple marketing strategies. The product itself and the rest of the marketing mix may have to be modified to suit the nature of the channel. For example, Fieldcrest Mills, Inc., sells its high-priced, luxury quality Fieldcrest brand towels exclusively to department stores and its low-priced St. Mary's brand to mass merchandisers.[2]

Types and Functions of Intermediaries

Types of intermediaries. There are three basic types of intermediaries—**merchants, agents,** and **facilitators,** who ease the flow of goods through the channel but do not control it.

Merchants are intermediaries who take title to the goods that they offer for resale. That is, they own the goods they offer to customers and they are compensated from profits earned from the resale of the items. Common retailers such as Sears, K mart, and Radio Shack are examples of merchants.

Agents do not take title to the products they market. They do not assume the risk of ownership but, rather, represent an organization that does own the goods. Agents are compensated with commissions. An example of an agent is a real estate broker who brings buyers and sellers together and helps negotiate the sale or purchase of real estate. Once the transaction has been completed, the agent is paid a commission.

Facilitators assist but do not control or direct the flow of goods and services through the channel. Examples of facilitators are trucking companies, advertising agencies, banks, and public warehousing firms.

Why are intermediaries used? A manufacturer can market its products directly to final consumers, but it must use intermediaries of some sort. In using intermediaries, manufacturers give up some control over how their product or service is marketed. Why are they willing to do this? The answer can be found in an analysis of the functions that move the product and its ownership from the point of production to the point of consumption. Often, intermediaries can perform one or more of these functions more efficiently and/or more effectively than the manufacturer could. The following section describes the functions that intermediaries perform.

The role of intermediaries can be explained by examining the needs of producers and consumers. Producers usually specialize in the types of products they manufacture. They like to produce in large, economic quantities in large, efficient production facilities. These facilities are often located some distance from most of their customers. They usually produce a limited line of products according to their expertise in a way that is as efficient as possible. They also like to sell in large quantities because it would not be efficient to have salespeople calling on individual customers, and it would be very expensive to establish a chain of stores to sell directly to consumers.

Consumers, on the other hand, like to buy in small quantities, and they like to choose from large assortments so that they can compare the products of several producers or buy many different products in one shopping trip.

Intermediaries satisfy the needs of both producers and consumers. They adjust the discrepancies in quantity and assortment between producers and consumers. They buy in large quantities from producers and sell in small quantities to consumers. They buy products from many producers so that they can offer an attractive assortment of goods to their customers. They offer these goods at convenient locations near the consumers.

The computer software example demonstrates this process. The specialty software retailer seeks to buy an assortment of software packages from various producers to meet the needs of its customers. It buys from several manufacturers in quantity and sells to consumers, one package at a time, from locations convenient to those customers. A supermarket is another example of an intermediary buying in large quantities from many producers and offering a large assortment of goods to customers.

Functions of intermediaries. The specific functions performed in a channel of distribution can be categorized into three groups—transactional, logistical, and facilitating (see fig. 17–2).

Transactional functions include the actions that directly influence the transactions between manufacturers, intermediaries, and customers. They are *buying, selling,* and *risk-taking.* Intermediaries buy products from various producers to offer an assortment of goods to meet their customers' needs. This includes identifying potential suppliers, evaluating their products, negotiating the purchase, and arranging for the delivery of the products. Intermediaries must also sell the products they buy, including promoting the products through advertising, personal selling, and display. During this time, intermediaries absorb the risks of owning the products.

**Figure 17–2
Functions of intermediaries**

Transactional
- Buy products from producers.
- Promote and sell the products to customers.
- Absorb the risk of ownership.

Logistical
- Store the products.
- Transport products from producers to customers.
- Sort the products.
- Break-bulk quantities into smaller quantities.

Facilitating
- Assist with financing.
- Grade product quality.
- Provide market information.

For example, a computer software store takes the risk that a particular package in its inventory will become obsolete or be replaced by a new, superior package of software.

Logistical functions include the operations needed to get the products from the producer to the customer. They include *storing* the products until they are needed by their customers, *transporting* the products from the producer to a place that is convenient for their customers, and *sorting* the products by size, grade, or type and **bulk-breaking,** or breaking down bulk quantities of products into smaller quantities desired by customers. The scene at the Maryland Wholesale Produce Market in figure 17–3 shows many of the logistical functions. Growers (producers) deliver products, which are then transported to retailers at left; assortments of products are created at center; and the products are temporarily stored at right.

Facilitating functions ease the transfer of the products from producer to customer. Intermediaries often assist both producers and customers with *financing*. They offer credit to customers to make it easier for them to buy. Many retailers, for example, offer credit cards to customers. Intermediaries can also help to finance the operations of producers. Some intermediaries also *grade* products by judging their

United Fresh Fruit & Vegetable Association

Figure 17–3
A scene at the Maryland Wholesale Produce Market showing the transport, sorting, and storage of products.

quality and labeling them accordingly. Finally, intermediaries *obtain market information* from customers and pass it along to producers; the information could include such things as fashion trends and expected sales volume.

All these functions must be performed to fill the gap that exists between producers and customers. These functions cannot be eliminated, but can only be shifted among the producer, intermediaries, and customers. The marketing manager must decide who will perform which functions. Because many intermediaries are specialists at performing particular tasks, know the market, and enjoy economies of scale in their operations that cannot be matched by a manufacturer, they are often more efficient at these functions.

To get a sense of this efficiency, look at figure 17–4. On the left, each of four software companies is trying to sell to each of four customers; sixteen contacts are being made. On the right, the four software companies sell their products to an intermediary, a software store; the store then sells to the four customers. The number of contacts has been reduced to eight, creating a higher level of efficiency in the marketplace.

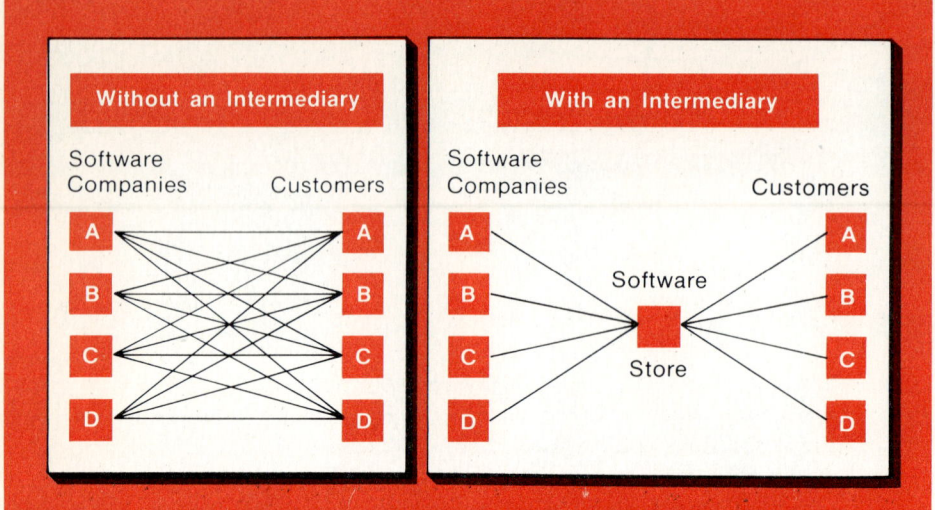

Figure 17–4
Intermediaries create efficiency in distribution

Types of Market Coverage

How many retailers should a computer software producer persuade to carry its products? This is a major decision for all producers and marketing managers. The answer depends on an analysis of both the buying habits of the target market segment and the characteristics and image of the product. The analysis will suggest one of three types of market coverage—intensive, selective, or exclusive (see fig. 17–5).

Intensive market coverage. **Intensive market coverage** involves the marketer's attempting to distribute a product in as many locations as possible. Convenience goods, such as cigarettes, candy, and newspapers, are distributed intensively. Most buyers are unwilling to stop at several stores for these products. If a

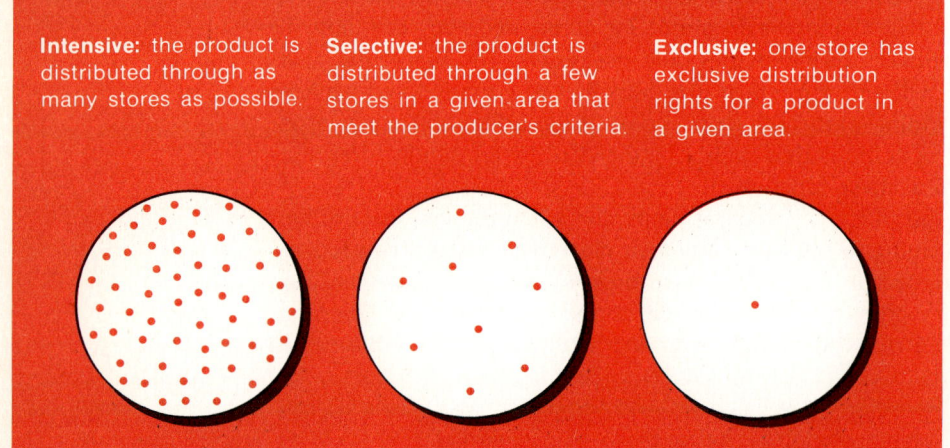

Figure 17–5 Types of market coverage

Chapter 17 / Channels of Distribution and Physical Distribution

particular brand is not available at one location, the buyers will buy a similar brand that is available at that location. Intensive market coverage has three main characteristics. First, the product's image is not affected by the widespread distribution. For example, the fact that Marlboro cigarettes are sold from machines in some sleazy bars does not tarnish the image of Marlboro. Second, the store itself does not promote the product. Third, the producer does not expect the store to give information or demonstrations about the product.

Exclusive market coverage. **Exclusive market coverage** involves an intermediary's being granted exclusive rights to sell a particular product in a territory. An automobile or farm machinery dealership is an example of this type of coverage. The buyers must be willing to travel to the exclusive dealer and, in so doing, pass by dealers carrying competing brands. The producer using exclusive market coverage expects a more aggressive selling effort from the retailer and to have some degree of control over the retailer's marketing efforts. The retailer is spared direct competition from retailers selling the same brand and is assured of a steady source of supply and a closer, more cooperative relationship. Consumers can expect the retailers to give them any information they may need.

Exclusive distribution is often used in the early stages of a product's life cycle. Consumers are not familiar with some new products, such as computer software, so they are dependent on the retailer. The producers recognize the importance of the retailer in the buying process and may be more willing to give the retailer exclusive dealership. In return, the retailer will probably make more of an effort to sell the product and explain its features to consumers. In later stages of the product's life cycle, consumers become more knowledgeable and need less support from retailers. Distributors are more willing to move to selective or, as we have seen with computer software, to intensive distribution.

Selective market coverage. **Selective market coverage** falls somewhere between intensive and exclusive. The producer attempts to distribute its product only through those retailers that meet its criteria as to image, location, or market segment served. The producer hopes for a good working relationship with the retailer and a fair amount of selling effort and exposure of its products by the retailer. The retailer is somewhat protected from competition from other retailers carrying the same product, although there may be some price competition. Selective distribution is used for shopping goods, such as clothing or appliances. The product does not have to be available in every store because the consumer will go to several.

Types of Channels

There are two basic types of channels—traditional channels and vertical marketing systems. These channels are shown in figure 17–6.

Traditional channels. Up to this point, we have discussed channels in which all of the members (producers, wholesalers, retailers, and so on) are inde-

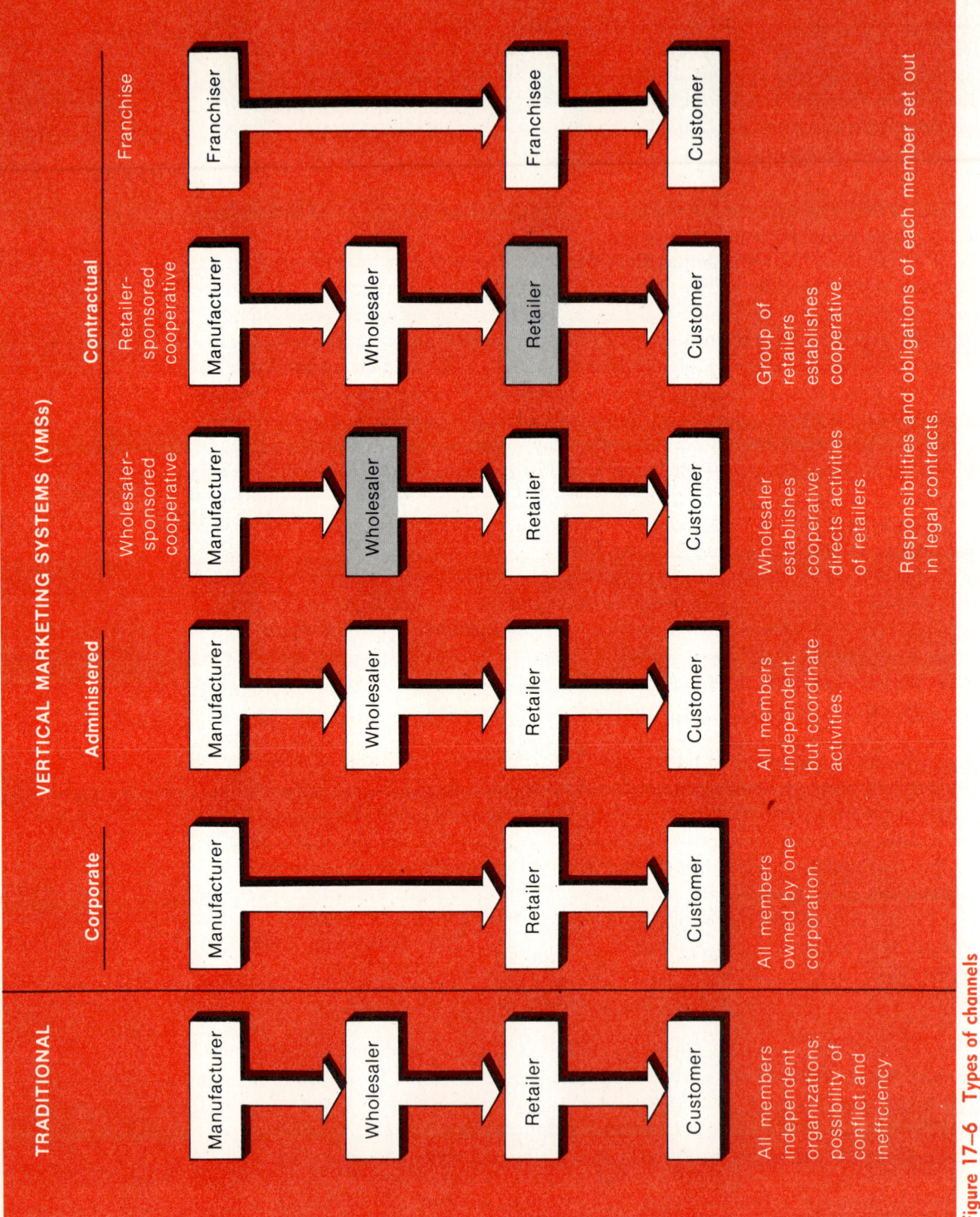

Figure 17–6 Types of channels

pendent organizations. These are **traditional channels.** In these channels, each member is seeking to maximize its own position in relation to the others. There is often no center of control or unified set of objectives for the entire channel. Sometimes one channel member may have more power than the others and may use the power to control the channel. At other times, channel members do not see themselves as part of a channel; they only see that they have suppliers and customers.

Let's look at a traditional channel in the software field. IBM produces software for its Personal Computers. The software is sold to consumers through a variety of stores. As there is a great demand for IBM software, stores want to carry it and want to be part of the channel. IBM then has the power to choose its distributors and thus could control the channel. A new software company, anxious to get its software in front of consumers, may have to persuade stores to carry it. In this case, the stores have the power and can control the channel.

In these traditional channels, functions can be performed by more than one member, leading to conflicts and a lack of efficiency. For example, a producer and a retailer may both mark prices on the same package, duplicating the work. There is also a waste of effort when a producer supplies point-of-purchase display materials that a retailer refuses to use.

Vertical marketing systems. **Vertical marketing systems (VMSs)** are distribution channels that are centrally managed as a total system. The parts or members of the channel do not operate independently; rather, their actions are coordinated so as to maximize the efficiency and effectiveness of the entire channel. Each unit of the channel is coordinated with all other units. IBM selling its own software through its Product Centers is an example of a VMS. Focus 17–1 presents another example of a VMS.

The use of vertical marketing systems has grown in recent years to the point where they now account for approximately 60 percent of all retail sales. There are several reasons for this growth. One is that because they are centrally managed, VMSs can overcome many of the inefficiencies of a traditional channel. Also, as marketing has become more complex, the need for specialists has increased. VMSs can provide expert staffs at all levels in many areas such as data processing, promotion, site selection, and inventory control that smaller, independent firms cannot afford.

There are three types of VMSs—corporate, administered, and contractual.

Corporate Vertical Marketing Systems. **Corporate VMSs** are organizations in which all the parts of the channel are owned and all functions performed by one corporation. This is known as **vertical integration.** Manufacturing, wholesaling, and retailing are all owned by the same organization. Coordination and control are easiest in this type of VMS, but it also requires the highest financial investment by the corporation. Examples of corporate VMSs are Sears, Roebuck, which owns at least part of many of its suppliers, Sherwin Williams, which produces the paint and owns the stores it is sold in, and Radio Shack, which manufactures and retails its

17–1 Focus on a Marketing Practice
COOPERATION IN A VMS

Caterpillar Tractor Co. has been a leading manufacturer of farm equipment for over 50 years. A key to the company's consistent success, even at times when other companies' sales have declined, is its policy of cooperation with its dealers. Each dealership is an independently owned business, but Caterpillar works hard at maintaining cooperation and its unusually close relations with dealers. Caterpillar's approach is to help its dealers sell to customers by meeting dealers' needs quickly and efficiently.

One way Caterpillar is able to smooth its operations is by providing a computerized distribution system that links all U.S. dealerships with a Caterpillar center in Illinois. When a dealer orders a part through this system, Caterpillar can usually deliver it the next day. One policy designed to please both the dealers and their customers is the company's commitment to provide any replacement part within 48 hours, or else give the part to the customer for free. The company goes one step further by buying back any parts that the dealers are unable to sell.

Caterpillar encourages its dealers to provide service and maintenance for its products in addition to selling new equipment. The company reasons that customers are more likely to buy equipment from dealers who can also provide repairs and upkeep. Caterpillar also offers rebuilt engines and restored tractor parts at half the price of new machinery. The rebuilt engines and parts will last almost as long as new ones. The company feels that providing this advantage to customers will further benefit its relations with dealers, though Caterpillar sacrifices the profits that would come with the sales of all new parts.

The company further develops its partnership with dealers by offering training programs designed to introduce dealers to new products or to compare Caterpillar equipment with that of competitors. Sometimes these involve bringing dealers to the United States or assembling groups in Europe. Again, the company views the expense of these programs as a worthwhile investment. Caterpillar even goes as far as encouraging dealers' children to enter the business, another policy that fosters a deeper, long-term dealer-manufacturer relationship.

Source: "Caterpillar Sticking to Basics to Stay Competitive," *Business Week*, May 4, 1981, pp. 74–80.

---

products in corporate-owned stores. Sometimes the vertical integration is only partial. Campbell's, for example, grows its own produce to make its products, but it then sells the products (soups) to wholesalers.

Administered Vertical Marketing Systems. **Administered VMSs** are very similar to the traditional channel, as the members are independent businesses. But the members have replaced the traditional adversarial relationship with a partnership relationship. The members work together to coordinate their efforts and maximize their effectiveness. This coordination is usually achieved by the strongest member, often a manufacturer, which is recognized by the other members to have a great deal of expertise in the marketing of that product.

Contractual Vertical Marketing Systems. **Contractual VMSs** are channels in which cooperation and coordination are achieved through legal contracts that clearly spell out the responsibilities and obligations of each channel member. There are three types of contractual vertical marketing systems—wholesaler-sponsored cooperatives, retailer sponsored cooperatives, and franchises.

In a **wholesaler-sponsored cooperative,** a wholesaler gets independent retailers to join the cooperative. The wholesaler buys centrally in large quantities and passes the savings on to the retailers. In addition, the wholesaler provides expertise in promotion, pricing, store location and layout, financing, inventory control, and merchandising. The retailers benefit from a recognized image promoted by the wholesaler. The wholesaler, in return, gets a large volume of sales from very little selling effort.

Retailer-sponsored cooperatives are very similar to wholesaler-sponsored cooperatives except that they are established by a group of retailers rather than by a single wholesaler.

Franchises are probably the best known type of contractual VMS. A franchise is an agreement between the owner of a business system, the **franchiser,** and another person or organization, the **franchisee,** that wishes to use the franchiser's business system. The agreement is spelled out in a legal contract. Examples of franchises are McDonald's, automobile dealerships, Century 21 Real Estate, soft-drink bottlers, and 7-Eleven stores.

Franchising is very popular in the United States because it solves problems for both the franchiser and the franchisee. Businesses often lack the financial resources and the management talent to expand quickly. Potential franchisees, on the other hand, lack a proven business system and accepted market image. In a franchising arrangement, each side meets the needs of the other. The franchisees provide the capital and management and get in return training, promotional support, the presence and support of a larger enterprise, and use of a proven business system. The franchisers provide support and expertise and get motivated manager/owners to expand their business. Some franchisers, though, find themselves losing control if the franchisees try to become too independent. At one time, for example, Dunkin Donuts wanted to add muffins to its product line, but some franchisees objected, and the idea was slow in developing.

Managing a Channel of Distribution

The challenge for the marketing manager is to achieve a satisfactory level of cooperation and coordination in the distribution channel to maximize its efficiency and effectiveness. This can be difficult, as the members of a channel have some measure of independence and may have diverse interests and conflicting objectives.

The distribution channel is not only an economic system but also a social system. Each member has a role to play according to its area of specialization, and each member expects the other members to perform certain tasks. For example, retailers expect suppliers to supply them with certain products and services, and manufacturers expect retailers to put forth a certain level of selling effort. If one member does a poor job, it hurts other members and can lead to conflict. The level of dependency between channel members is greatest if there is only one possible channel structure that can help the individual member achieve its objectives. For example, a retailer is dependent on a supplier if that supplier is the only source of a highly demanded product. In the computer software field, it is important for a software store to carry IBM software, as there is a strong demand for it. The greater the dependency, the greater the potential for conflict.

Power is an important concept in channel management. Power refers to the ability of one channel member to control the decisions of another member. For example, IBM may be able to tell the computer software retailer how IBM's products will be displayed and promoted within the store. The greater the dependence of channel member A on B, the greater the power of B.

In order to coordinate the activities of the members of the channel, one member must have the power to influence the decisions of the other members. There are five bases or types of power that can be developed by a channel member seeking to control the channel. The more of these bases of power one member develops, the more power that member has to influence the decisions of other members.

The first type of power is called *reward power*. Reward power is based on the benefits that can be expected if channel member A does what B wants. For example, a supplier (B) may promise a retailer (A) certain future trade allowances if the retailer sells a predetermined amount of the supplier's products. Another example is the case of a franchiser (B) who promises a certain level of profits to a prospective franchisee (A). Conflicts can develop between franchiser and franchisee if the profits do not reach that level.

Another type of power is based on *expertise* or *special knowledge* possessed by one member and desired by other members. For example, retailers may believe that a manufacturer has special knowledge about how their product should be displayed, priced, and promoted. They are therefore willing to follow the manufacturer's instructions concerning decisions in these areas.

A third type of power is called *legitimate power*. One channel member acknowledges that another member has the legitimate right to exert an influence on its activities. The acknowledgment may be involuntary, as when a franchisee is bound by contract to let the franchiser make certain decisions. The acknowledgment may also be voluntary, as when a retailer perceives that a manufacturer has the right to control the pricing strategies for its product.

Referent power is the fourth type. It is based on the desire of one channel member to be associated with another member. For example, a retailer may want to carry a particular brand that lends status to that retailer. Or it can work the other way; a clothing manufacturer may want to have its clothing sold in an exclusive store, like Bloomingdale's or I. Magnin.

The fifth type of power is *coercive power;* one member has the ability to punish another member. For example, a retailer that refuses to promote and display a supplier's product in the way demanded by the supplier may find that deliveries from that supplier become erratic and undependable. Coercive power is obviously negative. If exercised, it may make future cooperation difficult.

The marketing manager's ability to develop these bases of power and use them depends on the type of channel. It is often difficult to do with a traditional channel. It is easier in an administered VMS, where the marketing manager can shift the distribution functions and coordinate activities to create the most efficient distribution channel.

In the software field, a new producer may find that all the power lies with retailers. The producer may find it difficult to get the retailer to carry its products, and it may find that it has to open its own stores. Once a producer becomes known, the power shifts somewhat into its own hands, as retailers become more interested in carrying its products.

Pushing and Pulling Strategies. Implicit in the previous discussion are the concepts of push and pull. In a **pushing strategy,** a manufacturer promotes, or pushes, a product to wholesalers and retailers, who, in turn, push the product to their customers. The product, in effect, is pushed along through the distribution channel; the manufacturer puts a promotional effort behind the product and wants or expects wholesalers and retailers to do the same.

In a **pulling strategy,** the manufacturer promotes the product to consumers, who demand it from retailers, who, in turn, demand it from wholesalers. The product, in effect, is pulled through the distribution channel by the consumer demand created by the manufacturer's promotion. In the computer software field, consumers may demand IBM software, so retailers must carry it to satisfy the demand.

Conflict in the channel. Conflict between channel members may occur when there is a difference in objectives or perceptions of the marketplace. For example, Jordache wishes to sell its jeans for a relatively high price through retailers with a fashion image, while K mart wants to sell large numbers of a product at low prices. Therefore, Jordache became very upset when K mart was able to obtain a large number of Jordache jeans and sell them in K mart stores. Both parties took the other to court. Jordache claimed the jeans were counterfeit. K mart claimed the jeans were indeed genuine, that Jordache wanted to stop the sale of its jeans in K mart stores, and that Jordache was intentionally interfering with distribution relationships.[3] (The case has not yet been settled.)

Some conflict in the channel is bound to occur. To a point, it is even desirable. After a certain point, however, it can become damaging, as in the Jordache/K mart example. Both had to bear the legal costs and possible damage to their images.

Another source of conflict comes when producers use **multiple channels,** or more than one distribution channel to handle the same product. One or more distributors may not like it that others are also selling the product. When Bulova started selling its watches in department stores, drugstores, and discount stores, jewelers, previously the only distributors, became upset and spent less time pushing the watches. Not only did they have increased competition, but they also faced a change in customers' image of the watches.

Determining the Structure of Marketing Channels

Figure 17–1 shows possible channel structures of different lengths. Why do some manufacturers sell direct to customers, and others use intermediaries? Marketing managers consider several basic factors that determine why some channels are longer or have more levels than others.

Characteristics of customers. If a manufacturer's customers purchase in large quantities and are concentrated geographically, the manufacturer may choose to sell direct to them. In such cases the manufacturer can afford to send salespeople to call on customers, and the products can be shipped in large, economical quantities directly to the customer. Tire manufacturers, for example, sell large quantities of their tires to the few automobile manufacturers this way. On the other hand, if customers are geographically dispersed and buy in small quantities, the manufacturer will tend to use intermediaries. The intermediaries will buy in large quantities and make the product available to many consumers. Tire manufacturers sell only a few tires at a time to individual consumers through a variety of dealerships, automobile supply stores, and gasoline stations.

This example indicates that the channel structure can depend on whether the customer is an individual consumer or an organization. The automobile manufacturer is an organization and can purchase the tires directly from the manufacturer or from intermediaries who serve the needs of industrial buyers. If the products being purchased are more complicated, such as robots for an automobile assembly plant, the purchase may require the performance of more distribution functions, as described in chapter 8. Tires being sold to individual consumers are distributed selectively through channels that may include wholesalers and a variety of retailers who serve the needs of these consumers.

Characteristics of the product. Their characteristics may lead some products to be sold directly to customers by manufacturers. Complicated or high-technology products like mainframe computers are often sold directly because intermediaries may not be able to understand, explain, give adequate push to, install, or service the product. Perishable products like seafood and fresh fruit are often sold directly because they must be delivered to customers before they spoil. Inexpensive, bulky items like building materials are often sold directly because they cannot bear the expense of many handlings.

Products that must be delivered quickly to customers, such as hospital supplies, are best distributed indirectly. It is faster to ship the product from a warehouse near the customer than to ship directly from a distant factory. This is also true of easily substituted goods that customers are unwilling to wait for or to shop for. Such products must be available in many locations when they are needed.

New novelty products may need novel channels of distribution. When the Chipwich—a new type of ice-cream sandwich made with chocolate chip cookies—was introduced in 1981, the manufacturers created awareness and a personality for the product by distributing it through pushcarts decorated with a chocolate chip motif. Within only a few weeks, approximately 12,000 Chipwiches a week were being sold. This success led to selling Chipwiches through more traditional distribution channels; by 1983, approximately 80 percent of Chipwiches were sold in food stores.[4]

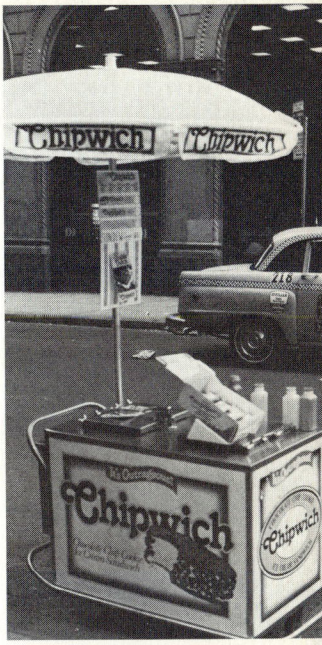

Figure 17–7 The Chipwich cart is more than a method of distribution; it creates a personality for the product.
Anita Duncan

Characteristics of the manufacturer. A financially secure manufacturer is better able to set up and control its own channel of distribution than a financially weak firm that cannot afford to build warehouses, open retail stores, and hire a sales force.

Firms that manufacture many similar products intended for the same market are in a better position to sell directly to customers. The manufacturer's sales force or stores can present several products to each prospective customer, thus spreading the cost of the sales effort over many products. For example, a manufacturer of a broad range of computer software would be more likely to consider establishing its own software stores than a manufacturer of only one software package.

Let's look at how three manufacturers of cosmetic products chose their channels of distribution. Cosmetics are bought in small quantities, and information about them and their use often has to be given directly to customers. Mary Kay Cosmetics chose to distribute its products directly to customers through its own sales force. Not only does this allow for direct demonstration of the products, but it allows the salespeople, or "beauty consultants," to establish direct relationships with customers. This approach has been highly successful for Mary Kay.[5]

A number of top-quality cosmetics companies, such as Georgette Klinger and Estée Lauder, are now producing cosmetics for men and distributing them selectively through their own salons (a vertical marketing system) or through top department stores (a traditional channel). Because cosmetics often do need demonstrations—especially in this case when new products are being sold to a new market segment—these channels make sense. Georgette Klinger feels, however, that men may feel more comfortable ordering cosmetics through the mail, so it is advertising its mail-order option in sports, business, and men's magazines.[6]

Noxell Corporation, producer of the Cover Girl line of cosmetics and of Noxema, also distributes through traditional channels, but its choice of channel members is different. It does not distribute its products through top department stores or cosmetics stores. Rather, it sees its customers as the mass market, and it distributes intensively through mass merchandisers and chain stores, such as K mart and Woolworth's. Usually its products are displayed and purchased from self-service racks; Noxell does not expect its distributors to demonstrate or give information about its products.[7]

Chapter 17 / Channels of Distribution and Physical Distribution

Physical Distribution

Merrill Lynch, Pierce, Fenner & Smith is one of the world's largest brokerage and financial services companies. The products the company distributes to 800 companies throughout the world, as well as to individual customers, are information, stock certificates, reports, and assorted explanatory material and documents. In order to handle the logistics of distributing this material in an efficient and economical way, Merrill Lynch set up an Information Distribution Group (IDG). The IDG has taken a number of steps to streamline the company's distribution system.

One step has been to recognize the savings from bulk deliveries. Most of the products sent by Merrill Lynch are small and must be transported quickly. Gathering small packages going in the same direction and forming one large package saves money. This is done on a companywide basis by the "Merrill Lynch Express." Material from the many New York offices is assembled at one location and grouped and sorted. The transporters, then, have to make only one pickup of a presorted, bulk shipment. As much of the distribution work has already been done by the company, much money is saved. The material for destinations in New York and nearby states is carried by truck. The material for other states and for overseas is carried by air forwarders.

Merrill Lynch is an international company and distributes many products overseas. To expedite overseas distribution, IDG is talking with foreign customs services and post offices. Some possible ways to improve distribution services include standardizing forms and procedures with these foreign organizations and packaging to improve handling.

The IDG also has the role of customer service department. It arranges for special distribution procedures when needed and solves distribution problems for customers as efficiently and economically as possible.[8]

Physical distribution is concerned with the movement and storage activities required to make the firm's products available to customers. Most products are not manufactured at the locations where they will be demanded when the customer will need them. Physical distribution fills the gap by moving the product to locations convenient to the customer and making them available when the customer needs them. If the customer cannot wait for the product to be produced and delivered, the product will have to be stored until it is demanded.

In economic terms, the physical distribution system provides **time, form,** and **place utilities** to products. For the physical distribution manager to create these utilities, the task is to provide the right product, to the right customer, at the right time, in the right quantity, at the right location, in the right condition, at the lowest total cost. These are known as the six "rights" of physical distribution. How effectively and efficiently these rights are accomplished can have a major impact on the level of demand for the product or service, on the degree of consumer satisfaction, and on the profitability of the firm.

In a broad sense, physical distribution is concerned with managing the flow of materials through the channel, starting with the sources of raw materials, parts,

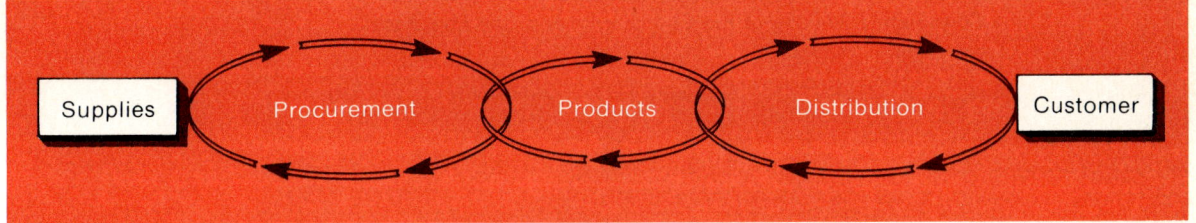

Figure 17–8 The business logistics system

components, and supplies, through manufacturing and processing, and then to the final consumer. The flow of materials and information from procurement of raw materials by the manufacturer to manufacturing/processing to the consumer as a total system is called **business logistics** (see fig. 17–8). The terms *physical distribution* and *business logistics* are often used interchangeably; physical distribution, however, is actually the segment of the logistics system from the end of the production line to the final consumer.

Physical distribution management is important to all organizations. This is obvious in companies that have large volumes of materials moving through the system, as in the manufacture of automobiles and steel. It is also important to service firms such as Merrill Lynch, where the availability of supplies and information is critical to the quality and availability of the service to be provided.

Functions of Physical Distribution

The definition of physical distribution used by the National Council of Physical Distribution Management (NCPDM) contains an extensive list of physical distribution functions:

> The term may not be familiar to you, but the function is something from which you benefit every day. Physical distribution is the movement of an item from the place where it was made or grown to the place where it is used or consumed. For example, because of the physical distribution process, there is fresh food in your local grocery store, regardless of the season.
>
> All of the activities involved in moving goods to the right place at the right time (as opposed to manufacturing them) can be described under the broad term, "distribution." The act of supervising or managing this far-reaching activity is generally known as "distribution management." Those persons who work in this industry are generally referred to as "physical distribution managers."
>
> The components of the physical distribution system are: customer service, demand forecasting, distribution communications, inventory control, material handling, order processing, parts and service support, plant and warehouse site selection (location analysis), procurements, packaging, return goods handling, salvage and scrap disposal, traffic and transportation, and warehousing and storage. A position in a small company may involve all of these, while working for a large corporation may entail being involved with only one of these areas.[9]

TABLE 17–1   A Comparative Ranking of the Characteristics of the Five Basic Transportation Modes

	Speed	Cost	Reliability	Availability	Capability
Air	1	1	2	2	4
Truck	2	2	3	1	3
Rail	3	3	4	3	2
Water	4	4	5	4	1
Pipeline	5	5	1	5	5

1 = highest.

Some of these functions are primary and some are supportive of the primary functions. The primary functions are transportation, inventory management, and order processing. These activities are considered primary because transportation and inventory management account for the bulk of physical distribution costs and because order processing is essential to the functioning of the whole system. We will discuss these first.

Transportation

The physical distribution manager can choose from five basic modes of transportation. They are air, truck, railroad, water, and pipeline. Each mode can be ranked in relation to the other modes as to its speed, cost, reliability, availability, and capability. Table 17–1 presents the rankings of these characteristics for each mode.

Speed refers to the average time taken to travel from origin to final destination. *Cost* refers to the relative level of expenditures that would be required to move the product from origin to destination. *Reliability* refers to the variability in the speed and service given. In very reliable service the transit time is always the same, for example, always three days. In unreliable service the time varies; on the average it might take three days, but it may take either one day or five. *Availability* refers to the firm's access to a particular mode. For example, water transportation is used most frequently by companies close to water. *Capability* refers to the ability of a mode to handle shipments of various weights and dimensions. For example, an ocean freighter can accommodate much larger and heavier products than an airplane can. Each mode has a unique combination of these characteristics that determines its suitability for particular products and for meeting the distribution goals of each company. Merrill Lynch, for example, wants fast and reliable delivery, so it uses air and truck transportation, depending on the distance to be traveled.

Air. Air transportation is generally very fast and reliable, but it is also very expensive. There are some exceptions to these characteristics, however. First, although no other mode comes close to the airport-to-airport speed of air transportation, the total transit time from origin to destination may be faster by truck, especially over relatively short distances of less than 200 to 300 miles. This is due to the time it takes to get shipments to, through, and from the airport.

Second, airlines generally provide very reliable service, but a service failure, for example, can greatly increase the transit time. When an airport is closed by inclement weather, a shipment may not arrive until the third day instead of the normal one day.

Finally, although the out-of-pocket costs paid for air transportation are very high relative to other modes, the fast service may make possible the reduction of inventory costs. This more than compensates for the higher transportation costs.

Due to these characteristics, air transportation is most often used for products traveling a relatively long distance with a high value per pound, such as electronic equipment and documents; emergency goods, such as machine parts or components to keep a factory from shutting down; or for perishables, such as cut flowers from Hawaii to the mainland.

Truck. Trucks provide relatively fast, moderately priced, and reliable door-to-door service. For these reasons, trucks tend to carry a large share of a broad range of manufactured goods over long and short distances and bulky, low-valued products such as sand and gravel over short distances. Because trucks can go almost anywhere they often provide the pickup and delivery service for many shipments that travel between terminals by one of the other modes.

Railroad. Railroads are best suited to moving large quantities over long distances at a low cost. As a result, low-valued, bulky items such as coal, grain, and industrial chemicals are often shipped by rail. Railroads were once the dominant mode of transportation, but over the past 60 years they have lost a large share of the market to water carriers, pipelines, and trucks. This trend can be seen in table 17–2, which compares the amounts of products shipped through the five modes.

TABLE 17–2 Estimated Distribution of Intercity Ton-Miles

Mode	1979 (billions of ton-miles)	Percent of Total		
		1979	1960	1940
Rail	918	36	44	61
Motor carrier	614	25	22	10
Air	6	—	—	—
Water	410	16	17	19
Pipeline	588	23	17	10
Total	2,536	100	100	100

Source: Transportation Association of America, *Transportation Facts and Trends*, 15th ed. (Washington, D.C., July 1979), p. 8; and Transportation Association of America, *What's Happening in Transportation*, Supplement, "Transport Review for 1979" (Washington, D.C., January 22, 1980).

Water. There are several water systems available to shippers in the United States. They are the inland waterways consisting primarily of the Mississippi and Ohio rivers and their tributaries, the Great Lakes/Saint Lawrence Seaway, and the oceans. Each system has its own unique type of equipment and vessels. For example, barges and towboats are used on the inland waterways, giant lake freighters are found on the Great Lakes, and ocean freighters are used for transportation on the oceans.

Regardless of the water system, water carriers are relatively slow and are susceptible to the vagaries of weather, such as floods, icing, droughts, and storms. They are used primarily for carrying large quantities of commodities over relatively long distances at very low cost. The products of mines, forests, and farms are often found on waterways. Water transportation is an attractive alternative for shippers of low-valued, bulky commodities that have access to a waterway.

Pipeline. Pipelines are the most specialized mode of transportation because they can only transport gases and liquids in large volumes. They are primarily used for the transportation of petroleum products, although there is currently a major effort underway in the United States to construct pipelines for coal slurry, a solution of 50 percent pulverized coal and 50 percent water. The construction of such pipelines so far has been successfully blocked by the railroads, but many expect such pipelines eventually to be built in some parts of the United States.

Electronic transportation. The five modes just described are the traditional and most widely used ones. A growing number of products, mostly services, are being distributed by a sixth mode—electronic transportation. Throughout the country, consumers are banking through automated teller machines through a process called electronic funds transfer. Consumers with personal computers can deal with stockbrokers and financial managers from their living rooms. Colleges are giving credit for certain educational programs seen on special television channels or in audiovisual centers. This mode of transportation will grow with the acceptance and spread of technological developments.

Intermodal transportation. The physical distribution manager can choose to utilize one mode exclusively or, in some cases, to use combinations of modes of transportation to capitalize on the unique advantages of each. **Piggyback,** or trailer-on-flatcar, and **fishyback** are two popular forms of intermodal transportation.

Piggyback involves putting truck trailers on railroad flatcars for long-distance transportation. Piggyback combines the ability of trucks to make door-to-door pickups and deliveries of shipments with the efficiencies of long-distance railroad transportation. The use of piggyback transportation is increasing, as can be seen in focus 17–2. Fishyback involves putting truck trailers or containers on water carriers, combining the wide availability of trucks with the low cost and carrying capability of water transportation.

Intermodal transportation has become easier due to the practice of **containerization,** or the use of large shipping containers resembling truck trailers without wheels. These containers can be stacked on board ships or placed on railroad flatcars or truck undercarriages. They can be interchanged between modes easily and efficiently by cranes. Containers have significantly decreased the costs of loading and unloading cargo as well as the costs of cargo pilferage.

Modal choice. It is the task of the physical distribution manager to choose the modes of transportation that best meet the service requirements of customers at the least total cost. The final choice will depend on the type of product, its value per unit, its density and dimensions, the available modes, the location and density of customers, the speed and consistency of the service provided, and of course the costs. For example, Agrexco, an Israeli flower-growing company, has a perishable product that must reach its distant customers in the United States quickly throughout the year. Considering the distance and the needs for speed and consistency, Agrexco ships by air. Every day, it packs 747s full of flowers and sends them on their way.

In addition to choosing the mode of transportation, the physical distribution manager must also decide whether the firm should provide the service itself as a **private carrier,** for example, buy its own trucks or aircraft; hire a transportation company, or **common carrier,** such as Delta Airlines or Consolidated Freightways on a shipment-by-shipment basis; or negotiate a long-term contract with a transportation company, or **contract carrier,** to provide a specialized service.

Deregulation. For many years the transportation industries have been regulated by federal commissions, such as the Interstate Commerce Commission (ICC) and the Civil Aeronautics Board (CAB). These agencies controlled such things as the geographic extent of a transportation company's operations, the prices or rates it could charge, and even whether a company could enter the industry at all. Recently, major changes in the laws regulating airlines, trucking companies, and railroads were passed by Congress. These laws have created a much more competitive environment for the carriers and have opened many more alternatives for the physical distribution manager. This new environment is particularly evident in the airline industry, where new carriers, such as Muse Air and New York Air, are entering the industry, and rate wars have broken out on major routes, such as between New York and Miami. Although not as evident to the general public, the effects on the trucking industry have been very similar to those in the airline industry. (The effects of deregulation in general and on the trucking industry in particular were seen in more detail in chapter 3.)

Inventory Management

Inventory management is another primary area of importance for the physical distribution manager. Most firms must produce products in anticipation of demand. They speculate that customers will buy the products produced today at some time

17–2 Focus on a Marketing Development
THE GROWTH OF INTERMODAL TRANSPORTATION

The six modes of transportation generally operate independently; in fact, there has frequently been competition among the modes for business. Now the reverse is coming to pass—intermodal transportation. One form of intermodal transportation, called piggybacking, is now bringing two traditional competitors, trucks and railroads, together. Piggybacking, or the shipment of highway freight trucks on railroad flatcars, has recently emerged as the railroad industry's fastest growing business. All kinds of cargo, from a Lincoln Continental packed in a load of watermelons to an entire container full of loose ball bearings, have been shipped in this manner. It is particularly popular for shipping over long distances along express rail routes.

How has this all come about? Primarily, according to railroad officials, because deregulation in 1981 gave railways more freedom to adjust freight rates, thus becoming more popular with shippers. Before that time, the Interstate Commerce Commission (ICC) had final approval over rates. Second, railroad mergers created fewer, larger railroad networks that could operate more efficiently because they had more control over their equipment and delivery time. Loads no longer had to be transferred frequently from railroad to railroad, a cumbersome, inefficient, time-consuming process. Finally, because deregulation has allowed them to become more economically competitive, railroads have been able to invest funds in improving their tracks, consequently making it possible for their trains to travel faster in safety.

For decades, railroads had been losing business to trucks, whose market share of intercity surface freight had grown from 23 percent in 1950 to more than 38 percent in 1982. While piggybacking has not yet reversed this trend, it has slowed it. In 1982, piggyback traffic grew 9.5 percent over 1981. In the first 45 weeks of 1983, piggyback traffic grew by 19 percent. Predictions are that by the turn of the century, piggyback traffic (which now accounts for only 12 percent of all railroad carloadings) will constitute as much as 50 percent of the freight carried over some rail lines.

Recognizing that piggybacking is a profitable and effective business, the Association of American Railroads is running an advertising campaign promoting it. The big winners, though, are shippers, who get lower rates and better service through piggybacking.

Source: Norman Thorpe, "Piggyback Rail Traffic Catching On," *Wall Street Journal*, December 27, 1983.

in the future. Inventories of raw materials and parts are held to ensure that production can occur and plant shutdowns can be avoided. These firms produce an inventory of finished goods for two reasons. First, customers may demand that products be immediately available, as is the case with supermarket items. Second,

In a series of advertisements directed at shippers, the Association of American Railroads is promoting the benefits of intermodal transportation.

Courtesy of Association of American Railroads

manufacturing economies can be achieved by producing a large quantity of a product in a single batch or production run. Inventory of finished goods is therefore held to increase demand for the product and/or to reduce production costs.

Although there are clearly advantages to holding inventory, there are also costs. Annual inventory carrying costs typically range from 25 to 30 percent of the value of the inventory. Thus, an organization that has an average inventory on hand throughout the year of $1 million would incur an annual inventory carrying cost of between $250,000 and $300,000. The costs of carrying inventory include the costs of the capital tied up in the products and the costs of storage, insurance, taxes, and the risk that the product will be damaged or become obsolete before it can be sold. Because these costs can be substantial, the physical distribution manager is always looking for ways to reduce or eliminate inventories without damaging demand for the products and production economies. Large stocks of inventory help to ensure that demand can be satisfied quickly, but there is also a cost penalty that must be minimized.

Inventory is also a major current asset for most firms. Typically, 20 to 35 percent of a manufacturing firm's assets are in inventories. Retailers and wholesalers often have an even higher proportion of their total assets in inventory. Therefore, inventory management can have a significant impact on the return on assets of a company.

Inventory management is complicated by several factors. First, demand is often very difficult to predict. Most firms experience variations in demand for their products that leave them with either too much or too little inventory.

Another factor is the large number of items that must be monitored and controlled. It is not uncommon for a single firm to have thousands or even millions of items held in inventory. For example, International Harvester has 345,000 items, a large grocery store can have around 15,000 items, Revlon offers 33,000 items, and a small menswear store may have upwards of 100,000 units. These large numbers reflect the need not only to have a basic product, such as a shirt, but also to carry all the combinations of sizes, colors, styles, materials, and so on.

The high cost of capital and vigorous foreign competition have forced many firms to take a very careful look at their inventory policies and procedures. Some of the actions that have been taken to make inventory management more efficient are to computerize inventory records, install optical scanners at retail checkouts to provide up-to-the-minute inventory counts, implement improved forecasting techniques, and install computerized materials requirements planning (MRP) programs that attempt to reduce incoming raw materials and parts inventories. Many of these techniques have proven effective in reducing inventory levels. For example, General Motors Corporation claims to have reduced its inventories by 21 percent through implementation of an improved warehouse flow system.[10]

Order Processing

Order processing is a primary physical distribution function. It is the customer's order that triggers the entire system. Also, the data on the customer order are fed into the company's information system and used to control and coordinate the physical distribution system.

A basic concept in order processing is the order cycle. The order cycle is the time that elapses from the customer placing the order until the shipment arrives at its final destination. The order cycle is composed of four distinct parts: (1) the transmission of the order from the customer to the firm; (2) the actual processing of the order, including checking for errors on the order, checking to see that inventory is available, and checking the credit of the customer; (3) shipment preparation; and (4) transit or delivery time, the time it takes to get the order to the customer.

Supporting Activities

The two most important supporting physical distribution activities are warehousing and protective packaging.

Warehousing. The **warehouse** is where the inventory is kept. Some warehouses are used primarily for storage of finished goods, while others, called **distribution centers,** are used primarily for breaking down large-volume shipments into smaller lots, putting together assortments of several products, and shipping them out to waiting customers.

The physical distribution manager has the choice of renting space and services from a **public warehouse** or building a **private warehouse** owned and used exclusively by the firm itself. The type and number of warehouses, their location, and their capacity depend on the needs of the manufacturer and its customers. Generally, a large private warehouse is chosen if the firm is certain of a high, steady volume of its products moving through the facility. A public warehouse is a better choice for a company if the location of its customers changes and demand for its products is erratic.

Finished goods warehouses located near the manufacturer's customers are used for two reasons. One is to provide faster service to customers, since it takes less time to ship to a customer from a nearby warehouse than from a distant factory. The other reason is to reduce transportation costs. If customers order in small quantities, it is cheaper for the company to ship in large quantities to the warehouse, break up the shipment, and ship in small quantities the short distances to nearby customers.

Protective packaging. As we saw in chapter 10, one of the functions of a product's package is protection. The basic problem in protective packaging is to balance the cost of the package with the cost of damage to products. A package that completely eliminates damage may cost more than the product.

Other issues in protective packaging involve the stackability of the package and pilferage. Stackability refers to how many packages can be placed on top of each other. Package shape and strength are often designed to facilitate stacking. The stronger the packages, the higher they can be stacked. The higher the stack, the greater the utilization of the space in the warehouse. Pilferage can be reduced by eliminating the name of the product or its description from the package, such as "color TV" but still being able to identify what it is for order picking and shipping purposes.

Customer Service

The functions that have been discussed so far are inputs to the physical distribution. The output of the system can be thought of as **customer service.** There are many parts to customer service, all of which contribute to the effectiveness of the physical distribution system. The two most common measures of this effectiveness are product availability and order cycle time. A physical distribution system that provides a high level of customer service is one that is able to fill nearly all orders from inventory, has a very short and consistent order cycle time, and makes few errors in products shipped and destinations. The elements and role of customer service in the physical distribution system are shown in figure 17–9.

Physical distribution systems producing high levels of customer service yield higher levels of customer loyalty and satisfaction and suffer fewer losses from canceled orders that could not be filled and thus fewer lost customers. However, systems that produce high levels of customer service need to carry large inventories, use faster and more consistent transportation, have more warehouses, and process orders faster. In other words, a physical distribution system that produces high levels of customer service will also require more costly inputs. The physical distribution manager must, therefore, consider costs and possible levels of customer service and find ways to produce an acceptable level of customer service at the least total cost.

Basic Concepts in Physical Distribution

There are three basic concepts in physical distribution—the systems concept, the total cost concept, and the concept of cost trade-offs—that managers make decisions about when creating their physical distribution program.

The systems concept. The basic, underlying concept for the successful management of physical distribution is the **systems concept.** Systems have the following characteristics:

1. The components or parts of the system are interrelated; that is, a change in one part will produce changes in other parts.
2. Optimizing the output of the entire system takes precedence over optimizing the output of each individual component.

All of the functions of physical distribution are interrelated and form a system. Changing one component will affect others. For example, switching from truck to rail transportation will increase inventory levels because railroad shipments are larger and slower. Also, the output of the physical distribution system will not be optimized by optimizing the individual components. For example, reducing transportation costs to a bare minimum by using very slow, inconsistent, high-volume carriers will cause inventory levels and costs to escalate, given that a certain level of customer service must be maintained. The transportation mode that minimizes the costs of the total system may very well not in itself be the cheapest.

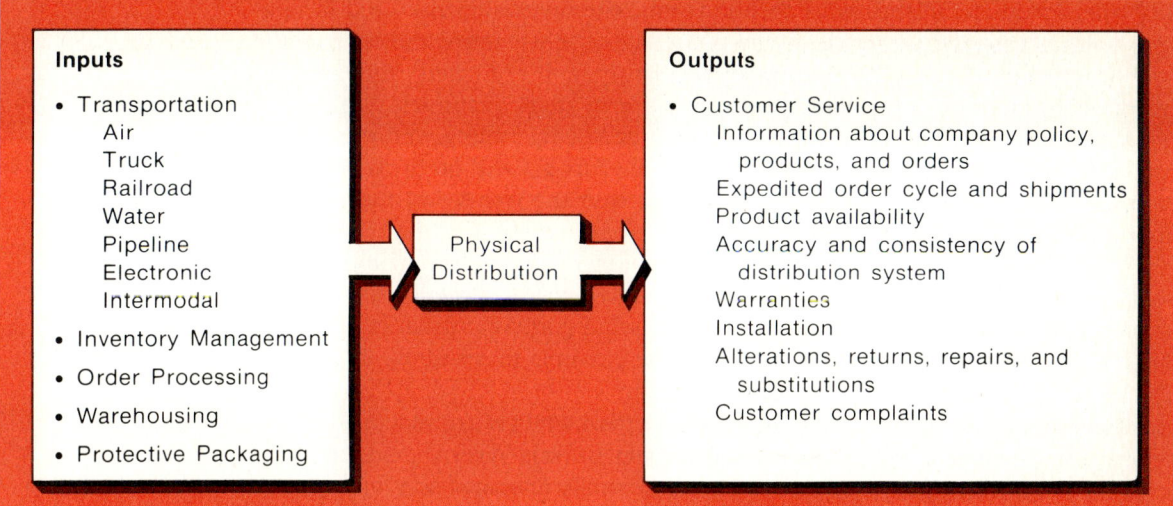

Figure 17–9 The inputs and outputs of a physical distribution system

The total cost concept. The **total cost concept** derives from the systems concept. It states that, because the physical distribution functions form a system of interrelated parts, any change proposed for one part of that system should be studied for its effects on the costs of other parts of the system. In other words, if managers want to increase the number of warehouses, they must first study the effects on transportation, inventory, and order processing costs. The challenge is to reduce the total costs of the system, not just the individual components.

The concept of cost trade-offs. The **concept of cost trade-offs** recognizes that the costs of these interrelated physical distribution functions are often in conflict. That is, very often, if one cost is reduced another will increase. For example, increasing the number of warehouses will reduce transportation costs but will also increase inventory costs. Ideally, the physical distribution manager will look for situations where increasing one cost will reduce another by an amount greater than the increase in the first one. For example, switching to truck transportation from rail may raise transportation costs by $500,000 but reduce inventory carrying costs by $1 million for a net reduction of $500,000.

Summary

A channel of distribution is the series of intermediaries through which a product passes to reach the final customer. Most firms sell the same product in multiple channels to both industrial customers and consumers.

The three types of intermediaries are merchants, who take title to the goods they offer for resale; agents, who do not assume the ownership risk; and facilitators, such as trucking companies, who assist but do not control the flow of the products through the channel. Intermediaries satisfy both producers' and consumers' needs by buying in large quantities and selling in small quantities.

Intermediaries' transactional functions include buying, selling, and risk taking. Logistical functions include the operations needed to get the products from the producer to the customer. Facilitating functions ease the transfer of the products from producer to customer.

Intensive market coverage involves the marketer's attempting to distribute a product in as many locations as possible. Exclusive market coverage involves an intermediary who is granted exclusive rights to sell a particular product in a territory. In selective market coverage, the producer attempts to distribute its product only through those retailers who meet its criteria.

Traditional channels are those in which all the members are independent organizations (producers, wholesalers, retailers, and so on). Vertical marketing systems (VMSs) are distribution channels that are centrally managed as a total system; the actions of the channel members are coordinated to maximize efficiency. The three types of VMSs are corporate, administered, and contractual.

There are five kinds of power involved in holding the distribution system together. These are reward, knowledge, legitimate, referent, and coercive power.

Manufacturers sell direct to customers when they purchase in large quantities and are geographically concentrated, when the product is perishable, and when the manufacturer is financially secure.

Physical distribution is concerned with the movement and storage activities required to make the firm's products available to customers. The physical distribution manager's goal is to provide, at the lowest possible cost, the six "rights": the right product to the right customer at the right time in the right quantity at the right location in the right condition. Business logistics is the flow of materials from procurement of raw materials to manufacturing/processing to the consumer.

One of the primary functions of physical distribution is transportation, including modes such as air, truck, railroad, water, and pipeline. The second primary function is inventory management, which involves speculating about customer demand and producing and storing a corresponding quantity of a product. Order processing, the third primary function, is putting the customer's demand for the product into the company's information system in order to control and coordinate the physical distribution system. Supporting activities include warehousing and protective packaging.

Customer service is the output of the physical distribution system. Two measures of the effectiveness of a physical distribution system are product availability and order cycle time.

The three basic concepts of physical distribution are the systems concept, the total cost concept, and the concept of cost trade-offs.

Questions for Discussion

1. Discuss the role of channel intermediaries in marketing products.
2. Identify the conditions in which intensive, selective, and exclusive methods of distribution are ideally employed by companies.
3. Distinguish the role of three categories of functions performed by channel intermediaries.
4. "Conflict is inherent in the very nature of channel relations." Comment.
5. Explain the reasons why the vertical marketing system has become so important in the fast-food industry.
6. Assume that you have successfully developed an effective and safe spray-on suntan lotion. Explain the nature of channels of distribution that you would employ for this new product.
7. Explain in what way the functioning of a physical distribution system can influence the overall success of marketing.
8. Explain which particular mode of transportation you would employ for the following products: (a) newsprint, (b) flowers, (c) a computer system, and (d) glass sheets.
9. Distinguish clearly between the primary, supporting, and customer service functions of physical distribution.
10. "Total cost concept is a natural extension of the systems concept considered so important in physical distribution." Comment.

References

1. Based on "Software Retailing: Quick Bucks—and Quicksand," *Business Week*, May 16, 1983, pp. 136–38; and "Software: The New Driving Force," *Business Week*, February 27, 1984, pp. 74–84.
2. "Fieldcrest: Saving Its Name for a Luxury Image," *Business Week*, January 9, 1984, pp. 112–13.
3. "K mart Hits Jordache Suit, Says Its Jeans Are Genuine," *Wall Street Journal*, December 15, 1982, p. 2.
4. "Pushcarts Give Sales of Chipwich a Shove in the Right Direction," *Sales & Marketing Management*, January 18, 1982, p. 57.
5. "Mary Kay Cosmetics: Looking Beyond Direct Sales to Keep the Party Going," *Business Week*, March 28, 1983, p. 130.
6. "Does He or Doesn't He?" *Sales & Marketing Management*, April 5, 1982, p. 28.
7. "Noxell Glows in the Mass Market," *Business Week*, February 14, 1983, pp. 148–50.
8. "Distribution . . . Merrill Lynch Style," *Traffic Management*, September 1983, pp. 51–54.
9. National Council of Physical Distribution Management, *Careers in Distribution* (Oak Brook, Ill, 1983), p. 3.
10. "But Experience Taught Firms Better Control Warehouse Flow," *Christian Science Monitor*, June 3, 1983, p. 9.

OBJECTIVES

1. To highlight the role of retailing in marketing.

2. To identify the components and the importance of retailing decisions.

3. To describe the methods of classifying retailers and the functions of different retailers.

4. To highlight the importance of wholesaling functions.

5. To identify the different types of wholesalers and describe the functions they perform.

6. To discuss the future of retailing and wholesaling.

18

Retailing and Wholesaling

The growth and success of Family Dollar Stores, Inc., a chain of retail stores, is based on its rock-bottom prices for consumer goods. There are now close to 600 Family Dollar Stores in 13 states, located mostly in working-class neighborhoods and small towns, close to their customers. Almost every item in Family Dollar Stores costs less than $15; any item costing more than $12 has to have the approval of a committee before it appears in any of the stores.

One way Family Dollar is able to keep prices down is by keeping its operating costs down. The company has just one warehouse where it stores merchandise, including appliances, automotive products, and housewares, for all its stores. Two major items that Family Dollar tries to provide at the lowest possible prices are socks and T-shirts. These are bought by the hundreds of thousands, thus enabling the chain to get volume discounts on the goods it later sells to consumers. The discounts leave room for a higher profit margin for Family Dollar. The stores take only cash and checks for merchandise, eliminating costly credit card charges.

Another factor that keeps the stores' costs down is their location. Because most stores are located in small towns, advertising and real estate costs are lower than they would be in large metropolitan areas. Family Dollar often rents store space at discount prices in small strip shopping centers that have lost business to the malls. Owners of these spaces are pleased by the fact that the Family Dollar Stores draw customers and by the fact that the company signs five- to ten-year leases. The stores have been placed over a wide geographic area and serve customers who work in a variety of industries. This strategy keeps Family Dollar from being severely affected by an economic depression or trouble in any one industry or area.

Family Dollar also keeps its stores' staff to a minimum. Some stores can run at off-peak times with only two salespeople; the stores rely on part-time help for busier times.

The company's success is based on the fact that it offers frequently needed goods in convenient locations for a very low price. The stores offer little in the way of fashionable goods, expensive products, or service. The company believes that with this formula it will continue to prosper.[1]

As marketing intermediaries, retailers and wholesalers make decisions about their target markets, the products they carry, the services and conveniences they provide, the nature of their outlets, and their roles in distribution channels. In this chapter, we will look at the different types of retailers and wholesalers and at the decisions they make as they carry out their functions.

Retailing

Retailing consists of activities that involve the sale of goods and services to the final consumer. Retail activities are conducted by businesses such as Dayton-Hudson, K mart, and Family Dollar Stores; by manufacturers such as Tandy that sell directly to consumers; and by nonprofit organizations such as museums and churches.

Retailing is often thought of as a quiet, unexciting, even static industry. Nothing could be further from the truth. Retailing is in a continual state of change, constantly recognizing and adapting to the changing needs of consumers. Retailing is also brutally competitive. First, as it is a relatively easy industry to enter, there are always plenty of actual or potential competitors. Second, most retailers sell branded goods, which are readily available at a competitor's store. Third, most consumers have a Sears', Penney's, or other mail-order catalogs at home and can easily make price comparisons. Finally, there is no effective way to prevent competitors from copying a successful retailing concept, since retailing processes cannot be patented.

The constantly changing retail environment makes it easy for new competitors to enter and for older ones to fail in the face of the new competition. In the past, large, supposedly secure retailers, such as W. T. Grant, Wickes, A&P, and E. J. Korvette, have faltered or even failed, while new retailers, such as The Limited, Wendy's, and Toys "Я" Us, have grown dramatically over very short periods of time. All of the successful retailers have been able to identify opportunities in changing environments and develop unique offerings to capitalize on them. Family Dollar Stores, for example, serves a primarily working-class market segment, with staple items at consistently lower prices than competitors. It remained profitable and even grew during a recession in which several competing discounters failed.

Retailers range in size from neighborhood mom-and-pop stores to large international organizations with billions of dollars in sales. Total retail sales in the United States were more than $1,038 billion in 1981, and retailing employs approximately 17 percent of the nonagricultural work force. In 1977 there were 1.85 million retail establishments in the United States with average annual sales per store of $390,000. There were 25 retail stores for every 1,000 households.[2] Table 18–1 shows the ten largest retailers in the United States and their 1983 sales figures. Table 18–2 shows a breakdown of the retail trade by types of businesses and their 1981 sales figures.

TABLE 18–1   The Ten Largest Retailing Companies

Retailer	Sales in 1983 (in thousands of dollars)
1. Sears, Roebuck	$35,882,900
2. K mart	18,597,900
3. Safeway Stores	18,585,217
4. Kroger	15,236,013
5. J. C. Penney	12,078,000
6. Southland	8,772,067
7. Federated Department Stores	8,689,579
8. Lucky Stores	8,388,155
9. American Stores	7,983,677
10. Household International	7,911,900

Source: "The 50 Largest Retailing Companies Ranked by Sales," *Fortune*, June 11, 1984, p.186. © 1984 Time Inc. All rights reserved.

TABLE 18–2   Retail Trade Sales by Kind of Business

Kind of Business	Sales in 1981 (in billions of dollars)
Retail trade, total	$1,038.8
Durable goods stores, total[a]	326.6
Automotive dealers	180.7
Motor veh., misc. automotive dealers	160.6
Motor vehicle dealers	151.7
Motor vehicle dealers, franchised	143.6
Auto and home supply stores	20.1
Building materials, hardware, garden supply, mobile home dealers[a]	53.2
Building materials, supply stores	44.5
Hardware stores	9.4
Furniture, home furnishings, equipment[a]	45.7
Furniture, home furnishings stores	27.9
Household appliance, radio, TV	14.3
Nondurable goods stores, total[a]	712.2
Apparel and accessory stores[a]	47.8
Men's, boys' clothing, furnishings	7.8
Women's clothing, specialty stores, furriers	17.8
Women's ready-to-wear stores	16.4
Family clothing stores	10.4
Shoe stores	8.5
Drug stores and proprietary stores	33.0
Eating and drinking places	94.0
Food stores	237.6
Grocery stores	219.3
Gasoline service stations	101.7
General merchandise group stores[a]	127.5
Department stores	103.6
Variety stores	9.0
Misc. gen. merchandise group stores[b]	14.9
Liquor stores	17.5
Non-store retailers	25.3
Mail-order houses (department store merchandise)[c]	4.9

[a] Includes kinds of business not shown separately.
[b] Includes catalog showroom stores.
[c] Includes sales made by mail-order catalog desks in department stores or mail-order firms.

Source: U.S. Bureau of the Census, *Current Business Reports*, series BR, *Monthly Retail Trade*.

Retailing Decisions and the Retailing Mix

When retailers are forming their overall marketing strategy, they make decisions about seven variables: location, merchandise, communications, price, services, physical attributes, and personnel. These variables are sometimes called the **retailing mix;** they are shown in figure 18–1. Like the elements of the marketing mix,

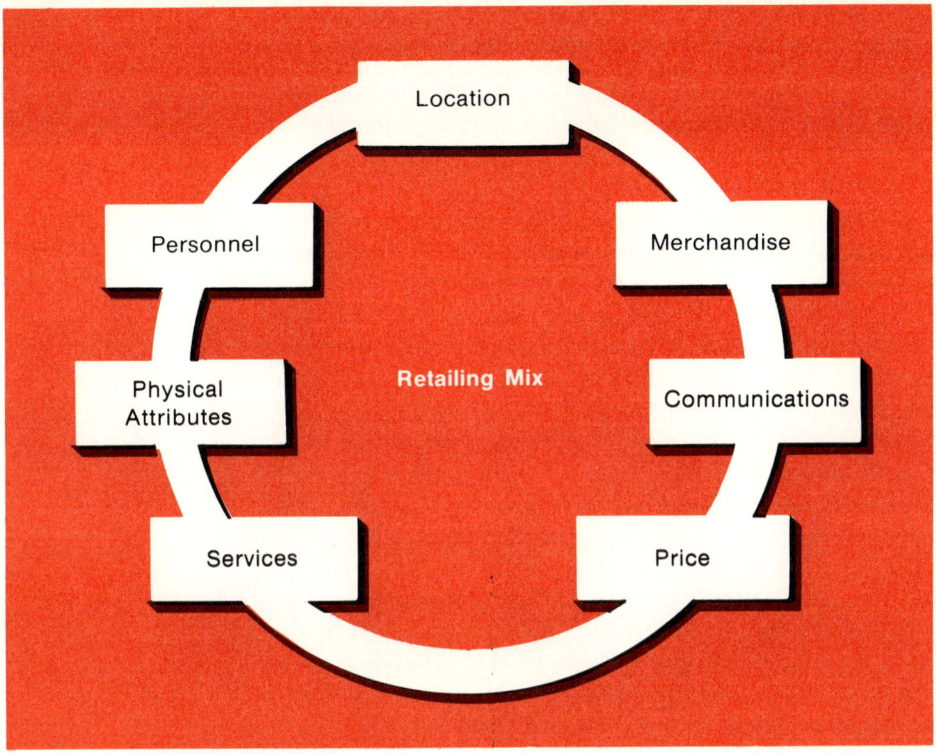

Figure 18–1 The seven variables in the retailing mix

[Diagram: Retailing Mix with seven variables arranged in a circle — Location, Merchandise, Communications, Price, Services, Physical Attributes, Personnel]

these variables are interrelated and coordinated to satisfy the needs of the target market.

Family Dollar Stores provides a good example of how a successful retailer coordinates variables. Family Dollar Stores has defined its target market to be working-class consumers located in small towns in the southeastern United States. It assembles an assortment of low-priced, staple merchandise, including apparel, automotive goods, and housewares, to appeal to its target market. It locates its stores in the working-class neighborhoods populated by its target customers. The store sites are relatively inexpensive, allowing Family Dollar Stores to keep its prices down. The stores are equipped with simple, inexpensive fixtures that are functional and help project an economical image. The number of salesclerks is kept low to reduce costs. Finally, the stores are near Family Dollar's distribution center so that distribution logistical costs can be minimized.

Family Dollar Stores has identified its target market and has put together a retailing mix in which each variable contributes to satisfying that target market and each variable is consistent with all the others. The total retailing mix allows Family Dollar Stores to project a clear image to its target market. Customers know what to expect from Family Dollar Stores, and as long as that image is consistent with the needs of its target market, it will continue to be successful.

Stores can also rearrange the variables in the retailing mix to change their images or broaden their target markets. Three of the nation's largest retailers are in the process of doing this:

—While keeping its traditional low-income customers, K mart is trying to attract more upscale customers. The range of merchandise its stores carry has become much broader. It has started to carry more fashionable clothing, including such name brands as Levi's and Wrangler. It has opened home improvement centers and electronic centers that sell computers and software in many of its stores. While K mart still carries inexpensive products, it prices some of its new merchandise at higher levels; the most expensive dresses it used to carry cost $13 to $17, while the most expensive ones now cost $45 to $55. To match the new merchandise and higher prices, K mart has redecorated with brightly colored interiors, new fixtures, fashionable displays, and clearly defined departments.[3]

—J. C. Penney is also trying to attract upscale customers. It made a highly publicized arrangement with top designer Halston to sell a line called Halston III clothing. The prices of this clothing are higher than traditional J. C. Penney prices, but customers can purchase a Halston coat for $200 rather than the $5,000 charged for a Halston original. The store is also dropping some of the products it carried, such as household goods, to make room for clothing. Store interiors have been remodeled to complement the new merchandise.[4]

—Sears is not changing its target market; it still sees itself as a family store for middle-class customers. It is, however, bringing "sparkle" into its stores to attract more of these customers and to get them to spend more money. It is dropping its slow-moving merchandise lines, such as automobile air conditioners. It has started to focus on apparel, offering Levi's and lines of clothing bearing the names of golfer Arnold Palmer, tennis player Evonne Goolagong, and model Cheryl Tiegs. The stores' interiors have been greatly restyled; merchandise is now displayed with flair. Sears has had to communicate this change, as many new customers could not believe that the sparkling "new" stores were Sears stores.[5]

Let's take a closer look at the variables in the retailing mix.

Location. Retailing is primarily a local activity. Most retailers, especially those that sell convenience goods, draw most of their customers from the surrounding area. The farther away customers are from the store, the less likely they are to shop at it than customers close by, because as the distance between store and customer increases, so do the number of intervening alternatives. For example, regional shopping malls have been found to draw 55 to 85 percent of their patrons from within 15 minutes' driving time of the mall. Smaller stores draw the bulk of their customers from an even closer area. Generally, the larger the shopping mall or area and the greater the variety it offers, the farther people will travel to shop there. People will also travel farther if they are looking for selectively or exclusively distributed products.

The retailer, therefore, must locate near its target market or devise ways to persuade consumers to travel to it. Low prices, immediate availability of products, or a unique product assortment may convince customers to travel farther than they would otherwise.

Merchandise. The retailer must also make decisions about the merchandise to be offered the target market. One decision concerns the width and depth of the product lines carried. The answer may depend on the type of store. Discount department stores often carry a wide but not deep assortment of products. Specialty stores, such as The Limited or the Athlete's Foot, carry a narrow but deep assortment of goods. Recently, the most successful retailers have carried either very narrow and deep assortments or very wide but shallow assortments. Retailers offering both moderate depth and width do not appeal to consumers' needs for variety, economy, or the convenience of one-stop shopping.

Retailers must also consider whether they want to carry certain types of merchandise. Each product has an image, such as cheap, well-made, or expensive, and the retailer must decide if the image of the product agrees with the image the store projects. When Halston started to sell clothing through J. C. Penney, Bergdorf Goodman dropped his clothing, as it no longer had the "right" image. On the other hand, certain manufacturers may not want their products carried in certain stores if the store's image does not match the products' image. A department store may want to carry the clothing of a certain top-quality designer, but that designer may feel that the store does not have an exclusive enough image and may want the clothing carried only in specialized boutiques.

Communications. The manner in which the retailer communicates with its target market affects how the store is perceived. The retailer must tell the target market about the merchandise it carries, the location of the store, special sales or offers, new products, credit policies, and so on. The promotional mix chosen, including the messages sent, the advertising media used, and the nature of the sales promotions, should project the desired image. Figure 18–2 shows advertisements for two stores with quite different retailing mixes. The styles of presentation convey strong messages about the merchandise carried, prices, services provided, and general image of each store.

Price. The prices and general price levels charged are a major concern of retailers. In chapter 12, we saw that prices are strongly connected with the image of a product and the benefits attributed to it. The price level chosen by a retailer, then, largely determines how customers perceive a store and its merchandise. Prices above general market level indicate that a store is exclusive and that it carries designer clothing, Rolls Royces, or sterling silver. Prices below general market level suggest that the store, such as Family Dollar Stores, provides fewer services and carries more functional, lower-quality merchandise.

Another pricing decision for retailers concerns price competition and the possibility of being underpriced by competitors. Many retailers try to find ways to

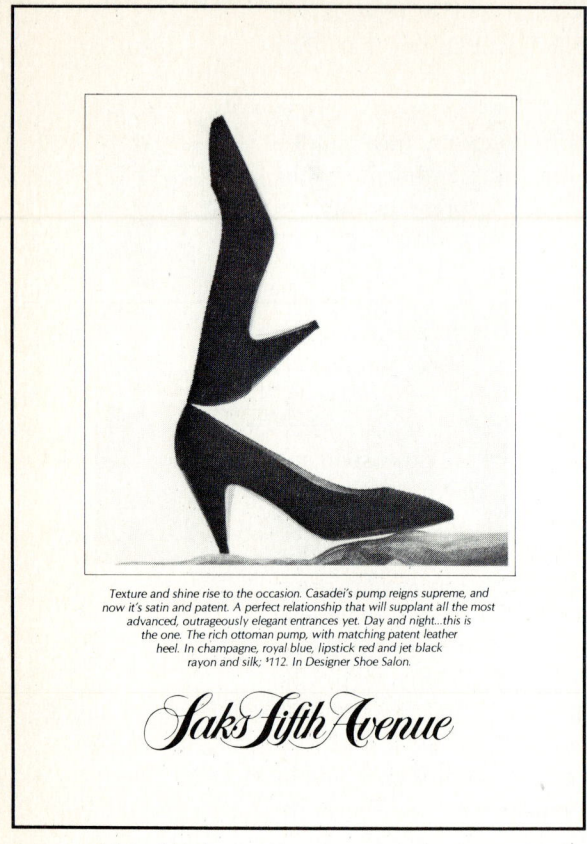

Courtesy of Saks Fifth Avenue

Courtesy of Trustworthy Hardware Stores

Figure 18–2 Saks Fifth Avenue's image as an exclusive department store is conveyed in this advertisement. The fashionable, exclusive merchandise is artistically displayed and supported by graceful copy. Trustworthy Hardware Stores's image as conveyed in its advertisement is of a functional, helpful hardware store with a wide range of practical merchandise at low prices.

protect themselves against price competition. One increasingly popular strategy is to carry store brands or private label merchandise at lower prices than those of nationally distributed brands.

Services. Retail services include credit, lay-away plans, alterations, gift wrapping, knowledgeable and helpful salespeople, home delivery, free parking, baby-sitting, and product demonstrations. The retailer must decide which services are considered essential to its target market and which it should provide. The retailer must also offer services that are consistent with its image. For example, it would be inconsistent for Family Dollar Stores to offer valet parking and washroom attendants at its stores. Credit and a liberal return policy, however, may be very important to its customers and could be offered while still maintaining its low-price image.

Physical attributes. The store's physical attributes and appearance contribute to the store's image. The facade should attract the target customers and encourage them to visit the store. The internal appearance, including level of lighting, style of decorating, and number and type of displays, confirm customers' impressions of the store and their expectations about merchandise, prices, and services offered. The layout of the store should encourage customers to stay and make purchases and expose them to as much of the merchandise as possible. For example, a well-laid-out store will place the items sought by most of its customers along the back walls and impulse items along the aisles leading to the popular items. Care must be taken not to make shopping in the store overly inconvenient for customers.

Personnel. Because the retailer's personnel have direct contact with consumers, they are an important part in conveying the store's image and providing the services the store offers. Salespeople in department stores with high-fashion images are usually tastefully and fashionably dressed and informed about fashion trends. Salespeople in cosmetics stores are beautifully made-up themselves and are skilled in the application of makeup. Salespeople in automobile dealerships are able to discuss gasoline mileage, comparative performances, and service requirements. Salespeople in computer stores should know how to operate the computers and be able to teach others.

Focus 18–1 discusses the decisions made by two successful hardware stores about their retailing mixes and shows how the decisions created different images for the stores.

Classifications of Retailers

There are several ways to classify retail institutions, none of which is mutually exclusive of the others. We are going to look at retailers, first, in terms of their retailing mix; second, in terms of store ownership; and, third, in terms of store location.

Retailers Classified by Retailing Mixes

Retailers can be considered convenience stores, specialty stores, department stores, mass merchandisers, catalog showrooms, or nonstore retailers. These retailers are discussed below and listed in figure 18–3.

Convenience stores. The number of **convenience stores,** like 7-Eleven, Get and Go, and U-Totem, have increased dramatically over the past 20 years. In 1960 there were only about 2,500 convenience stores; in 1982 the more than 38,000 convenience stores had total sales exceeding $15 billion and accounted for

Figure 18–3 Types of retailers classified by their retailing mixes

- Convenience Stores
- Specialty Stores
- Department Stores
- Mass Merchandisers
    Supermarkets
    Superstores
    Box stores
    Warehouse stores
    Combination stores
    Drive-throughs
    Discount stores
- Catalog Showrooms
- Nonstore Retailers
    Catalogs (mail order)
    Door-to-door retailing
    Vending machines

6 percent of the U.S. food market.[6] Convenience stores typically carry a rather limited assortment of food, health and beauty aids, snack items, and such miscellaneous goods as magazines. They are located in or near neighborhoods and are used by consumers for emergency purchases or fill-in purchases between regular trips to the supermarket. They are often located closer to consumers' homes than supermarkets, allow consumers to park right at the front door, have no checkout lines to stand in, and may be open 24 hours a day.

Convenience stores often charge higher prices than supermarkets and have high profit margins. Many convenience stores are currently adding additional services, such as gasoline pumps. Conversely, some oil companies, such as Arco, are getting into the convenience food store business by encouraging dealers to operate convenience stores at their gasoline stations.[7] Convenience stores typically do very little advertising. The most important parts of their retailing mix are convenient location and merchandise assortment.

Specialty stores. **Specialty stores** are retailers that concentrate on sales of one narrow but deep product line, such as clothing, appliances, jewelry, or rugs. Examples of specialty stores are Lane Bryant and The Limited for clothing, Sherwin-Williams for paint, Johnston and Murphy for shoes, and Radio Shack for elec-

18–1 Focus on Marketing Strategy
DIFFERENT RETAILING MIXES FOR HARDWARE STORES

Selling hardware used to be as straightforward as scooping a pound of nails out of a barrel into a bag. But with the tremendous growth in the number of homeowners and do-it-yourselfers doing home-improvement work, the market for hardware tools and building supplies has expanded. Sales are expected to reach approximately $43 billion in 1985. To reach this expanding market of customers who know little about home repairs (as opposed to the traditional market of builders and other skilled workers), hardware stores have developed different methods of selling hardware. Two chains of hardware stores—Home Depot, Inc., a four-year-old company based in Atlanta now operating 19 stores, and Lowe's RSVP, a 25-year-old chain of 235 stores based in North Wilkesboro, North Carolina—demonstrate two of the methods.

Home Depot appeals to bargain hunters. The stores spend virtually no money on furnishings and fixtures and look like large warehouses. At a typical store, products such as lumber, light bulbs, roofing materials, and tools are stacked in piles sometimes as high as the ceiling. Customers may have to dodge forklift trucks moving large quantities of materials. The focus is on low prices. Home Depot tries to peg its prices at 20 percent below competitors' by buying in large volume, by using the stores themselves as warehouses and thereby saving on secondary storage costs, and, of course, by minimizing costs. However, the store does emphasize help for untrained customers, and to that end teaches its salespeople how to answer questions and give advice.

In contrast to Home Depot's bare-bones approach, the Lowe's RSVP chain tries to create stores that attract new types of hardware customers, including women. Its stores are small, attractive, and well organized with carefully designed displays. They carry more consumer items that are not strictly hardware, such as appliances, and their products are packaged in plastic and contain complete directions. Like Home Depot, Lowe's has trained staff to give expert advice, and like Home Depot, Lowe's claims its prices are competitive. But unlike its rival, Lowe's does not consider pricing to be its primary focus—service, a wide selection of products, and quality are more important.

Both methods are working. In this expanding market, both chains are thriving, with rapidly rising sales and increasing numbers of customers.

Source: L. Erik Calonius, "Two Hardware Chains Try Different Ways to Attract New Do-It-Yourself Customers," *Wall Street Journal*, December 28, 1983, p. 31.

tronic products. Concentrating on one product line often targeted at a specific market gives the specialty store a more distinct image and greater expertise in marketing that product line than department stores, which are their main competition. By pinpointing specific target markets, they often enjoy strong customer loyalty and some pricing freedom. They are often located in heavily visited areas, such

TABLE 18–3   The Ten Leading Clothing Specialty Chains

Chain	Sales in 1981 (in thousands of dollars)	Number of Stores in Chain
1. Lerner Shops	$717,000	767
2. Petrie	529,800	791
3. U.S. Shoe Corp.	457,700	712
4. Hart Schaffner & Marx	442,000	310
5. Lane Bryant	419,160	274
6. The Gap	417,385	522
7. The Limited	364,900	430
8. Melville	333,721	1059
9. Woolworth (specialty stores only)	258,700	634
10. Allied Stores Corp. (specialty stores only)	245,034	69

Source: *Chain Store Age*, June 1982. Reprinted by permission. Copyright Lebhar-Friedman, Inc., New York, N.Y.

as large regional shopping malls. Table 18–3 shows the ten leading clothing specialty chains of stores and their 1981 sales figures.

Department stores. **Department stores,** such as Hudson's, Dillard's, Macy's, Sears, J. C. Penney, and the May Company, typically carry a wide product assortment of moderate depth. They are found in central business districts and regional shopping malls. Their price levels range from competitive and at the market level, at Sears and J. C. Penney, to high and prestige-oriented, at Bloomingdale's and Neiman-Marcus, depending on the image of the store. Most of the large department stores belong to chains, such as Sears and J. C. Penney, or they belong to ownership groups, such as Federated Department Stores, which owns Bloomingdale's, Lazarus, I. Magnin, Rich's, Burdine's, Bullock's, and Abraham & Straus, among others. Table 18–4 shows the ten leading department store chains.

TABLE 18–4   The Ten Leading Department Store Chains

Chain	Sales in 1983 (in millions of dollars)	Number of Stores in Chain
1. Sears, Roebuck & Co.	$25,089	813
2. K mart	18,598	2,547
3. J.C. Penney	12,078	2,014
4. Federated Dept. Stores	8,689	551
5. Dayton Hudson	6,963	1,075
6. Montgomery Ward	6,003	375
7. Wal–Mart	4,667	646
8. May Dept. Stores	4,212	1,584
9. ADG	3,718	382
10. Allied Stores	3,676	570

Source: "$100 Million Club," *Chain Store Age Executive*, August 1984, p. 33. Reprinted by permission. Copyright Lebhar-Friedman, Inc., New York, N.Y.

Courtesy of B. Altman & Co.

Figure 18–4 Both B. Altman (left) and Saks Fifth Avenue (below) are creating smaller "specialty stores" within their stores to display products that appeal to a particular group of customers.

Courtesy of Saks Fifth Avenue

There are two major trends in department store strategy. First, many large department stores with a traditionally local presence, such as J. L. Hudson's and I. Magnin, have been expanding and opening outlets throughout a region or the country. Second, department stores have been dropping or modifying their traditional departments to offer groups of different products designed to meet the needs of a particular group of customers. For example, a men's apparel department, formerly organized by suits, slacks, and shirts, may be divided into smaller separate departments offering complete outfits for businessmen, students, or vacationers. This strategy has been adopted to compete with specialty stores; the department store, in effect, becomes a collection of specialty stores, as can be seen in figure 18–4.

Mass merchandisers. **Mass merchandisers** are retailers that practice a two-part strategy of low profit margins and high turnover of merchandise. Their success depends on selling large volumes of merchandise and appealing to a mass market. There are seven types of mass merchandisers: supermarkets, superstores, box stores, warehouse stores, combination stores, drive-throughs, and discount stores.

Supermarkets. A **supermarket** is a large store that sells food and a limited range of household products. One of its main features is that customers serve themselves. The supermarket industry is dominated by such chains as Kroger, Safeway, and A&P (see table 18–5) and by such wholesaler and retailer cooperatives as IGA. Supermarkets account for approximately 75 percent of all U.S. grocery sales. Chain stores account for approximately 60 percent of supermarket sales.[8] Supermarkets are usually located near large residential areas because consumers will usually shop at the nearest one. Supermarkets also tend to be located far from competitors, because consumers usually shop at only one supermarket per shopping trip.

Competitive prices are important to supermarket customers, but it is often difficult to compare prices between stores. Prices, therefore, are not the customer's prime consideration when choosing a supermarket. Rather, the supermarket that is closer, cleaner, and has a better assortment of merchandise often gets the business.

Supermarkets typically carry 7,000 to 15,000 different items and are constantly bombarded with requests from manufacturers to carry from 100 to 200 new products weekly. Because they cannot accommodate all of these products, new products must be chosen and approved by a buying committee. In some chains an old product must be dropped before a new one can be added. The most important merchandise categories for a supermarket in terms of creating a competitive advantage in attracting customers are meat and produce. Packaged, branded grocery items are uniform from one supermarket to another, but the quality and price of meat and produce will vary. Often the supermarket with a reputation for fresher produce or a wider selection of cuts of meat will attract more customers.

TABLE 18–5   The Ten Leading Supermarket Chains

Chains	Sales in 1982 (in billions of dollars)	Total Number of Stores
1. Safeway Stores, Inc.	$17.0	1,888
2. The Kroger Co.	$11.5	1,258
3. Lucky Stores, Inc.	7.5	541
4. American Stores Co.	7.5	680
5. Winn-Dixie Stores, Inc.	7.0	1,220
6. The Great A&P Tea Co., Inc.	4.7	1,055
7. The Grand Union Co.	4.0	725
8. Albertson's, Inc.	3.5	412
9. Jewel Cos., Inc.	3.4	347
10. Supermarkets General Corp.	2.7	117

Source: Newspaper Advertising Bureau. Reprinted by permission.

The supermarket industry is very competitive, as profit margins for the industry frequently average less than 1 percent of sales. Supermarkets use various strategies to increase profit margins. One strategy is to carry products with higher profit margins, such as auto accessories, housewares, hardware, records, and even some apparel and appliances. Cost control is another strategy that supermarkets attempt to increase profits. The recent introduction of computerized checkouts with electronic scanners is one way of controlling costs, by making price marking of individual items unnecessary (except where marking is mandated by law). Electronic scanners also help with better control of inventories and analysis of merchandise to be carried, and they make fewer errors.

A final way supermarkets are competing is by positioning themselves for specific markets, instead of trying to serve all types of consumers. A number of stores have gone upscale. The Grand Union Co. has a six-year, $700 million renovation plan during which it is changing the merchandise its stores offer to include more healthful, exotic, or high-quality items. Some new offerings include live trout, imported cheese, "natural beef," and unusual fresh fruits, such as figs and persimmons. Safeway is testing departmentalization; one Texas store, for example, has a separate flower department that is arranged to look like a separate shop. A new Giant Food store in Maryland has a full-time chef, fresh pasta, and imported fragrances.[9]

Other supermarkets are moving in other directions and are becoming parts of combination stores or superstores, which are described below.

Figure 18–5
Shoppers in this Grand Union are offered the choice of a number of gourmet products, including unground coffee beans.
Laimute E. Druskis

Superstores. Compared to the typical neighborhood supermarket, **superstores** are much larger; have wider aisles; carry a wider range of merchandise, including garden supplies, clothing, and televisions; and have bakeries, pharmacies, and delicatessens on the premises. Their primary appeal is the larger merchandise selection and a "nicer" atmosphere to shop in. Prices are competitive with those of a regular supermarket.

Box Stores. **Box stores** appeal to price-sensitive shoppers. They offer few services or amenities in order to keep costs and prices down. Merchandise is displayed on plain racks, often in cut boxes. No checks are accepted. Fewer than 1,000 items are carried; there are no refrigerated perishables and very few sizes and brands per item. Customers may bring their own shopping bags or buy them at the store and pack their own purchases. The stores usually have a spartan, warehouselike appearance. Box stores attract shoppers from much greater distances than a traditional neighborhood supermarket due to the appeal of the lower prices.

Warehouse Stores. **Warehouse stores** are no-frills operations offering fewer products than a traditional supermarket but more than a box store. They use inexpensive displays, offer few services, and are located in inexpensive, often out-of-the-way locations. They appeal to the price-sensitive, one-stop shopper and may attract shoppers from a great distance.

Combination Stores. **Combination stores** combine two stores, a supermarket and general merchandise store, under one roof and with common checkouts. Examples are Shagg's, Alpha Beta, and Meyer Thrifty Acres. They feature a broad range of merchandise, competitive prices, and the convenience of one-stop shopping.

Drive-throughs. **Drive-throughs** are in their infancy. They offer customers the convenience of shopping from home. Shoppers telephone their orders to a warehouse where a computer compiles a shopping list for a worker at the warehouse. The order is gathered, and the customer drives up, loads his or her automobile, and pays for the order. Prices are very similar to those of a traditional supermarket because certain economies can be achieved from a warehouse operation. One potential problem in such an operation is that shoppers cannot look at and pick their own produce and meat. However, by providing consistently high-quality products, drive-throughs feel they can overcome this problem.

Discount Stores. **Discount stores,** usually members of a chain of stores, offer a broad but not very deep assortment of merchandise. They usually carry only the most popular, fastest moving brands and sizes of products. They provide fewer services and therefore have lower operating costs than a traditional department store. They also have relatively inexpensive buildings and fixtures and are located in less expensive areas. Lower costs allow them to keep prices low and encourage high sales volumes. In 1980, their total sales were just over $52 billion, up from only $6 billion in 1962. The ten largest discount store chains in the United States are shown in table 18–6.

The major growth of discount stores occurred in the 1960s, when they offered hard goods and staple items at lower prices than other types of retailers. In recent years, some discount stores have tried to trade up, offering more expensive merchandise and fashion goods. Trading-up has not always been successful for dis-

TABLE 18–6   The Ten Leading Discount Store Chains

Chain	Sales in 1983 (in millions of dollars)	Number of Stores in Chain
1. K mart	$18,758	2,188
2. Wal-Mart	4,744	747
3. Target	3,118	217
4. Gemco	2,135	79
5. Best Products	2,081	204
6. Zayre	1,902	288
7. T. G. & Y.	1,750	503
8. Service Merchandise	1,458	175
9. Toys "R" Us	1,320	199
10. Bradlees	1,183	132

Source: "The Discount Industry's Top 100 Chains," *Discount Stores News,* July 23, 1984, p. 17. Reprinted by permission. Copyright Lebhar-Friedman, Inc., New York, N.Y.

counters. By following this strategy, discounters can alienate their current customers, who seek low-priced, staple merchandise, fail to attract more affluent, fashion-conscious customers, and confuse their images. Such a strategy did not work for E. J. Korvette, which has now failed. K mart is in the process of upgrading the interiors of its stores and adding more fashionable merchandise. Family Dollar Stores is resisting the temptation of trading-up, as it feels it has the right retailing mix for its target market.

Off-price retail stores, such as T. J. Maxx, J. Brannam, Hit or Miss, Designer Depot, and Loehmann's, which offer fashion goods at discount prices, have been growing very fast recently. Off price retailing is discussed in focus 18–2.

A final type of discount store is the **factory outlet store.** This type of store is run by a manufacturer to sell its excess products. Clothing and furniture are often sold through factory outlets.

Catalog showrooms. **Catalog showrooms,** such as Service Merchandise, grew rapidly during the 1970s and had total sales of $8.4 billion in 1980. They work as follows: Consumers select and order merchandise from a catalog while in their homes, then they go to the catalog showroom, pick up the order, and pay for it. Catalog showrooms specialize in appliances, jewelry, and other hard goods. They usually do not carry such goods as apparel.

Catalog showrooms appeal to consumers primarily because of their low prices. These stores have lower operating costs than discount stores for four reasons. First, their costs of merchandise are low; they display only one model of each item they carry, and because inventory is warehoused out of sight, shoplifting losses are reduced significantly. Second, they require fewer employees. Third, they are usually located in relatively inexpensive locations, as customers preshop from the catalog and are willing to travel to the showroom because of the low prices. Finally, the catalogs are the primary promotional and advertising expense.

Nonstore retailers. We usually think of stores when we think of retailing, but a large and growing proportion of retail sales occurs outside of stores. The three major types of nonstore retailing are catalogs (also known as mail-order retailing), door-to-door selling, and vending machines.

Catalogs (Mail Order). **Catalog (mail-order) retailing** is a rapidly growing sector of retailing. There are two types of catalogs: general merchandise catalogs, such as those of Sears, Montgomery Ward, and J. C. Penney, and specialty catalogs, such as those of The Horchow Collection, L. L. Bean, and Lands' End. The primary appeal of catalogs is that customers, especially the growing number of dual-career families, can shop conveniently from their homes.

Recognizing the appeal of this market, mail-order retailers are providing merchandise for it. Department stores are broadening their mail-order operations by mailing catalogs to credit card holders and others on their mailing list. The Spiegel Catalog, whose traditional customers were lower-income, price-oriented shoppers, is now also going after upscale working women. Their main catalog features de-

18–2 Focus on Marketing Strategy
OFF-PRICE RETAILING

One of the rapidly growing trends in retailing is **off-price retailing**. Off-price stores offer brand name and designer clothing at 30 to 60 percent below the standard retail price. Since 1979, sales at off-price stores have doubled and have reached approximately $7 billion per year.

Off-price stores differ from discount stores in that the discount stores pay wholesale prices to suppliers but have a smaller markup than full-price retail stores. But off-price stores are often able to buy merchandise *below* wholesale prices, by buying manufacturers' overruns and end-of-season goods, often in large quantities. Their prices are not necessarily *low*, just *lower*. (Loehmann's, one of the oldest and best-known off-price stores, carries such items as sable coats for a mere $25,000.)

Although they have been around for many years, off-price stores only became popular a few years back, when inflation and recession made consumers, even affluent ones, very price-conscious. When these consumers found out they could get popular brands and designer clothes at a store like Loehmann's for half what they would have to pay at Marshall Field or Bloomingdale's, they bought.

Off-price stores have prospered at the expense of full-service department stores, and these stores are fighting back in a number of ways. Filene's, in Boston, has created a more extensive customer service program and has expanded its salesclerks' training program. Dayton's, in Minneapolis, has focused on the competitiveness of its prices and fashion lines. Others are eliminating unprofitable departments and placing more emphasis on private label merchandise sold only through their own stores.

Some stores are using more aggressive tactics. Bergdorf Goodman, in New York City, stopped carrying clothing designed by Halston after he created an inexpensive line of apparel for J. C. Penney. And some stores, such as Sakowitz, in Houston, are making no adjustments to counter the new trend. They believe their customers have expensive tastes and well-filled wallets, and will continue to pay more to shop in style.

Source: "Off-Price but on Target," *Time*, October 31, 1983, pp. 90–91.

signer clothing and home goods (see fig. 18–6). Their smaller specialty catalogs feature furs, linens, and gourmet cookware.[10]

Specialty catalogs appeal to specific market segments and, in addition to clothing, sell fruit, cheese, household items, luggage, jewelry, and even Christmas trees.[11] The growth and success of specialty catalogs depends on the development of a specialized mailing list of customers interested in their products. They often add to this list by advertising in specialty magazines that are read by members of their target markets.

Figure 18–6 The growing number of upscale working women are a main market for mail-order retailers, such as Spiegel, who are creating catalogs to appeal to them.

Courtesy of Spiegel, Inc.

Door-to-Door Retailing. **Door-to-door retailing** involves sending a salesperson to call on customers in their homes. Companies such as Avon, Mary Kay Cosmetics, Kirby vacuum cleaners, and encyclopedia companies have been very successful using this type of strategy.

There are four major problems with door-to-door selling. First, companies face high costs caused by low productivity of sending a salesperson to call on households rather than having prospective customers ready to buy coming to the salesperson in a store; at the same time, relatively high commissions are often paid to these salespeople. A second problem is the high turnover rates among salespeople; annual turnover rates of more than 100 percent are not uncommon for some companies. This means that the companies continually have the high costs of recruiting and selecting salespeople. A third problem is that many communities have ordinances prohibiting door-to-door selling. Finally, as the number of dual-career families increases, fewer customers are home to listen to salespeople when they call.

Figure 18–7 Types of retailers classified by ownership

- Chain Stores
- Independent Merchants
- Consumer Cooperatives

A variation of door-to-door selling is **selling parties** at which a salesperson displays and discusses a line of products and takes orders from the party attenders. This strategy has been popularized by Tupperware and has been adopted by other firms selling other types of merchandise.

Vending Machines. **Vending machines** eliminate personal selling and provide 24-hour service. The 16 million vending machines in the United States accounted for $14.6 billion in sales in 1981, or for 1.4 percent of all retail sales.[12] The major problems encountered by vending machine retailers are the high costs of the machines, breakdowns, theft, and vandalism. There is also a relatively narrow range of products sold from vending machines in this country; usually beverages, candy, snacks, and small personal care items are all that are sold. In Japan, where vending machines are more popular, such products as whiskey, magazines, toys, and worms for fishermen are sold.

Retailers Classified by Ownership

Retailers can be classified according to their ownership. There are three primary forms of ownership—chain stores, independent merchants, and consumer cooperatives (see fig. 18–7).

Chain stores. Any retailer that owns more than one store is considered a **chain.** Chains range from two units to several thousand. The largest chains by type of business are supermarkets, such as A&P and Safeway, gas stations, and variety stores, such as Woolworth. Tables 18–3, 18–4, 18–5, and 18–6 show the leading chains. Chains account for approximately 18 percent of all retail stores and 48 percent of all retail sales in the United States.

Chains enjoy several advantages over independent, one-store retailers. First, their buying is usually centralized. That is, buying for all of the stores in the chain is done by one central organization. Centralization of buying gives chains a lot of bargaining power with suppliers, not only in the buying of goods, but also for buying and leasing real estate, borrowing money, and buying advertising. This bargaining power leads to lower costs for the chain and potentially lower prices for customers. Chains can also centralize their staff work. They can hire experts in real estate, marketing research, inventory management, accounting and finance, and other areas; this expertise is extended to and used by all the members in the chain. Another advantage of chains is that they can attract talented personnel because they offer job security, more generous benefits, and more attractive advancement opportunities. A key advantage of chains is that member stores project a common image to the public. The stores and the merchandise in them are identical, and throughout the country, customers know what to expect from chains.

Chains also have some disadvantages. They have increased overhead costs from the layers of management required to supervise and manage their far-flung operations. Also, they are less able to adjust to changes in the general market and are not able to adjust their retailing mixes to local market conditions. Finally, it is often difficult to control their organization, as there are so many workers in so many stores throughout a wide area.

Independent merchants. Eighty-two percent of retail stores, accounting for 52 percent of total retail sales, are run by independent merchants.[13] In such stores the owner wears many hats—manager, chief buyer and merchandise planner, salesperson, stock clerk, and janitor. Independent merchants do not have large staffs of experts, but they also do not have the overhead such staffs require.

Independent merchants have a number of major problems. They may find it difficult to secure credit from suppliers, they can't promote employees very far, and they must purchase in small, uneconomical quantities. The failure rate of small retailers is very high. Finally, it is relatively easy to open a store, so there is always the potential for intense competition.

In spite of these disadvantages, small independent merchants do have some advantages. Many customers prefer to deal with the owner of a local store rather than a possibly disinterested manager hired by an impersonal corporation located at a great distance. The owner can often cultivate close, personal relationships with customers. Local independent merchants can adjust to local tastes and market conditions much easier than a large chain can. A final advantage is the entrepreneurial vigor often exhibited by an independent business owner with a large personal stake in the success or failure of an enterprise. Such enthusiasm is not often displayed by a hired manager.

Consumer cooperatives. **Consumer cooperatives** are retail establishments owned and operated by a group of consumers who invest, receive stock certificates, manage the operation, and share in the profits. Cooperatives are usually formed on the belief that the members can better fulfill their needs than existing retailers and that they can do it much cheaper.

Consumer cooperatives most often sell the staple grocery items that can be found in supermarkets, but some are formed to buy specialty goods, such as health foods. The typical cooperative works as follows: Each week members compile lists of products they want; then all of these lists are combined, and master orders are submitted to buyers who purchase on the wholesale market. When the shipments arrive, members break them down into the original orders first submitted by members. Finally, members pick up and pay for the orders.

Figure 18–8
Members of this food cooperative are picking up their orders of butter and cheese.

Laimute E. Druskis

The consumer movement spawned some growth in cooperatives, but they still account for a very small share of the retail market. This is because it takes a lot of work and initiative to operate one, and since supermarkets' profit margins only average less than 1 percent, savings for the members are not very large.

Retailers Classified by Store Location

Choosing a good location is a very important decision for a retailer because location is the least flexible element of the retailing mix. Because of the investment required, or the nature of the lease, a location is usually fixed for a long time. In general, a good location may compensate for other deficiencies in a retailer's mix, but the effects of a poor location may not be overcome by superior performance in other elements of the mix.

The location of the store will affect the retailer's overall strategy. For example, an inexpensive, out-of-the-way location will require heavy promotion or low prices or both to entice customers. Or a downtown location in a primarily business area will probably do most of its business during the day selling to office workers; weekends and evenings will not account for large sales volumes. The products carried must appeal to this market segment, and window displays may be the most important type of promotion to draw passersby into the store.

The retail location decision should be made on the basis of the needs of the target market. Family Dollar Stores seeks to appeal to blue-collar shoppers; thus their stores are located in neighborhoods where this target market lives and shops. Family Dollar Stores also employs a strategy of geographic concentration. It only locates stores in the regions surrounding its distribution centers. Such a strategy produces distribution economies and enhances control of the individual stores because none of them is very far from headquarters. Other advantages of a concentration strategy are those of visibility to their target market and promotion economies. The costs of advertising are shared by the many stores in the chain. Family Dollar Stores also chooses inexpensive sites, avoiding expensive shopping malls.

Once the location decision has been narrowed to a particular city, the retailer must choose between locations in the downtown central business district, shopping centers, or single-store sites (see fig. 18–9).

Central business districts. Central business districts (CBDs), or "downtowns," are attractive because of the large concentration of people, particularly during business hours. The CBD of large- and medium-sized cities has historically been the center of retail activity, but retail sales in the CBDs of most American cities have declined for a number of reasons. First, public transportation to many of the CBDs is no longer adequate. Many CBDs have decayed to the point where they are no longer attractive, although some cities are trying to rejuvenate their downtown areas. Second, higher-income shoppers have moved to the suburbs and now do much of their shopping at new, attractive regional shopping malls designed to appeal to just such customers. Many of these suburbanites also fear crime in the CBDs. In addition, real estate values in CBDs are quite expensive and perhaps difficult for a retailer to justify.

Figure 18–9 Types of retailers classified by store location

- Central Business District (CBD)
- Shopping Centers
  - Neighborhood shopping center
  - Strip shopping center
  - Community shopping center
  - Regional shopping center (mall)
- Single-Store Sites

In spite of the problems with a CBD location, many retailers still locate there. For example, specialty shops catering to office workers for clothing, snacks and tobacco items, stationery, gifts, floral products, restaurants, and taverns are often found in CBDs.

Shopping centers. **Shopping centers** are common throughout the United States and Canada. They are run as a business by the owner, who controls the assortment of stores in the center. There are four categories of shopping centers, based on their size and the market area they serve.

Neighborhood shopping centers. **Neighborhood shopping centers** usually contain a supermarket, a drugstore, and perhaps several other stores such as a card shop or Radio Shack. They serve primarily the neighborhood within a one-mile radius of the store.

Strip Shopping Centers. Rows of stores along a busy street are called **strip shopping centers.** The heavy traffic of the street itself and that generated by the other stores in the strip, combined with relatively low rents, make strip shopping centers attractive to some retailers. For example, service stations, auto dealerships, low-priced restaurants, bars, and convenience stores are often found in such locations.

Community Shopping Centers. **Community shopping centers** usually contain a large variety store or discount department store, such as K mart, Wal-Mart, along with all of the stores found in a neighborhood shopping center. They serve an area of one to three miles surrounding the center.

Regional Shopping Centers. **Regional shopping centers,** or **malls,** are the largest shopping centers and can contain up to eight large department or, increasingly, discount[14] stores, called **anchors,** and up to 250 specialty stores. They often serve a wide area, up to 30 or 40 minutes' driving time away. They have grown at the expense of the CBDs. The owner of the mall attempts to offer a balanced assortment of stores and to project a distinctive image. Anchor stores are chosen and sought based on the estimated amounts of traffic they generate. The specialty stores located between the anchors live off of the traffic generated by them. Rents for the specialty stores are very high compared to other types of locations, but promotional costs are low because of the large amount of traffic generated by the mall. Malls are usually built in locations with easy access to major highways, and they have ample parking space. The combination of anchors and specialty stores, along with the restaurants, decorative fountains, meeting areas, and special events, makes malls appealing and needs-satisfying places to shop.

The primary disadvantages of malls for retailers are the high rents, a very competitive environment, and the inflexibility of hours, since all the stores in a mall must be open at the same time. Some malls are so large that they are no longer very convenient to shop in. Also, many malls have been built in anticipation of future residential development, making the mall too large for the existing trading area and population. For this reason there are very few new malls being planned for suburban areas.

Single-store sites. **Single-store sites** are freestanding buildings with no adjacent stores. Their advantages are low rents, no competition, flexible hours, easy visibility from the street, and convenient parking. The major disadvantage is that they must usually advertise heavily to attract customers initially. Single sites work best for large retailers that have a strong market identity and offer a reason, such as low prices, a unique assortment of merchandise, or convenience, to draw customers to the site. Examples of retailers that commonly choose single sites are Kinney Shoes, Levitz Furniture Warehouses, K mart, and McDonald's.

Future of Retailing

Retailers in the future, as in the past, will have to contend with a constantly changing environment. Their success will depend on their ability to identify changes and adapt to them. Major changes will occur as a result of shifts in consumer demographics and advancing technology.

As we saw in chapter 7, the demographic characteristics of the United States are changing. The population is aging, the number of retired consumers is growing, and the number of working women and two-income families is rising. All of these changes will require adjustments by retailers in terms of merchandise carried, services offered, and retailing practices.

Technology will also have an impact on retailing. Electronic scanners and computerized management systems will be used even more widely than today. Such systems allow retailers to spot trends more quickly and to adjust their inventories of merchandise more quickly and accurately. Electronic home shopping will also increase during the next decade. The technology is available and is being manufactured now. Some examples are catalogs on video tapes and cassettes, cable TV shopping shows with call-in ordering, and home computers connected to cable TV for ordering products displayed and demonstrated in a TV store. Predictions as to the household penetration of these systems vary by system and forecaster, but the rapid expansion of home computers indicates that widespread use of such electronic home shopping techniques may grow quite rapidly. (The future of retailing is discussed further in chapter 22.)

Wholesaling

In the mid-1970s, Foremost-McKesson, the country's largest wholesale distributor, found that its traditional functions of distribution, warehousing, and transportation were not generating high profits or providing growth. The company decided, therefore, to move in two directions: It has brought new technologies into its functions and operations, and it has taken on new roles to add value to its distribution services. Its actions include the following:

—Automating warehousing
—Introducing data processing and using it to create stronger ties with suppliers and customers
—Designing stores for its customers
—Providing such services for its drugstore customers as acting as intermediary in processing medical insurance claims
—Providing rack jobbers to aid retail stores with stocking and displays
—Finding new uses for products from manufacturers
—Using computers to help customers manage inventory and plan marketing strategy.[15]

By taking these actions, Foremost-McKesson has increased its value as a member of a distribution channel and has created new vitality in its wholesaling activities. It has also led other wholesalers into the use of technology and the widening of functions and services performed. In this section, we will look at the functions of wholesalers and their roles in the distribution process.

A **wholesaler** is "a firm which buys and resells merchandise to retailers and other merchants and/or to industrial, institutional, and commercial users but which does not sell in significant amounts to ultimate consumers."[16]

There is a distinction between wholesaling and wholesalers. Manufacturers that sell to other manufacturers and to retailers directly are wholesaling their products, but they are not wholesalers. Wholesalers are independent organizations that buy products or services and then resell them to anyone but the final consumer. This section is concerned with wholesalers.

In 1977 (the last time the industry was surveyed), there were 383,000 wholesalers in the United States, with annual sales of $1,258 billion.[17] Except for a few large wholesalers, such as Foremost-McKesson, wholesale establishments are primarily small businesses. Only 147 of all wholesalers had 20 or more employees; the average number was only 11.

Wholesalers exist to perform a number of necessary functions. Their exact functions depend on their position in the marketing channel between production and consumption. They must perform services for both their suppliers and their customers

Wholesaling Functions

Figure 18–10
Services performed by wholesalers

For Customers
- Physical possession to aid rapid delivery of goods
- Ownership to absorb inventory carrying costs
- Financing
- Risk-taking
- Negotiating with many suppliers to create assortment of goods
- Ordering
- Assisting with promotion
- Assisting with store design
- Assisting with management procedures

For Suppliers
- Identifying customers
- Handling inventory
- Supplying small businesses
- Acting as sales force
- Providing financial services

Source: L. Stern and A. El-Ansary, *Marketing Channels*, 2nd ed. (Englewood Cliffs, N.J.: Prentice-Hall, 1982). Reprinted by permission of Prentice-Hall, Inc., Englewood Cliffs, N.J.

more efficiently and more effectively than those institutions could do themselves. Figure 18–10 lists some of the services a wholesaler might provide.

Services for customers. Foremost-McKesson provides an example of services performed for customers by a full-service wholesaler. It selects an assortment of goods from many manufacturers, simplifying the purchasing of goods by its customers. Its customers need only contact Foremost-McKesson rather than hundreds of potential suppliers. (The efficiency created by marketing intermediaries was discussed in chapter 17.) Foremost-McKesson also helps affiliated retailers choose store sites, design new stores, design the layout of stores, and plan and control inventories; it also provides rapid delivery of merchandise to its customers and purchases in large, economical quantities. Foremost-McKesson has a stake in its customers' performance. The more its customers sell, the more it sells.

Services for suppliers. A wholesaler also performs one or more of the following services for its suppliers:

1. Wholesalers have continuity in and intimacy with local markets. Being close to

customers, they are in positions to take initial steps in the sale of any product, namely, identifying prospective users and determining the extent of their needs.

2. Wholesalers make possible local availability of stocks and thereby relieve suppliers of small-order business, which the latter can seldom conduct on a profitable basis. Also, they tend to have an acute understanding of the costs of holding and handling inventory in which they have made major commitments.

3. Within their territories, wholesalers can provide suppliers with a sales force that is in close touch with the needs of customers and prospects. Also, by virtue of the fact that wholesalers represent a number of suppliers, they can often cover a given territory at a lower cost than could the manufacturer's own sales representatives.

4. Wholesalers perform financial services for suppliers by providing volume cash markets through which they can recover capital that would otherwise be invested in inventories.[18]

Two important points must be understood concerning wholesaling functions. First, not all wholesalers offer all of these services. Some do, but others specialize in one or several of them. Second, a manufacturer or retailer may decide to eliminate a wholesaler from its channel and perform the wholesaling functions itself. Wholesalers can be eliminated but not the functions they perform. Focus 18–3 discusses the functions performed by three different industrial wholesalers.

Types of Wholesalers

Wholesalers may be classified according to ownership of the enterprise, whether they take title to the goods, and the number of functions they perform. The types of wholesalers are discussed below and listed in figure 18–11.

Figure 18–11 Types of wholesalers

- Merchant Wholesalers
    - Full-function wholesalers
    - Limited-function wholesalers
        - Cash-and-carry wholesalers
        - Drop shippers
        - Wagon or truck jobbers
        - Rack jobbers
        - Mail-order wholesalers
- Agents
    - Manufacturer's agents
    - Selling agents
- Brokers
    - Commission merchants
    - Auction companies

18-3 Focus on Marketing Strategy
INDUSTRIAL WHOLESALERS

Industrial wholesalers compete to attract customers by providing the most attractive products and services. Some wholesalers use low prices, while others stress customer service and their ability to increase the efficiency of their customers' businesses.

The Vallen Corporation, in Houston, sells plant safety equipment to the petrochemical industry. Vallen's biggest account is Dow Chemical in Freeport, Texas. To earn the account, Vallen offered a combination of low prices, fast delivery, and a computerized ordering system. A Dow plant manager can place an order for needed safety equipment simply by entering a request into a Vallen computer. The nearby Vallen warehouse maintains a stock of the products most frequently requested by Dow and makes deliveries to the plant every two hours. Vallen's competitive advantage here is excellent service. Under this system, Vallen eliminates the need for Dow to operate and maintain its own plant safety stockroom. Without this system, plant safety managers or other Dow employees would have to phone several vendors in search of needed items. Waiting time between order and delivery would be greater, as would be the purchase price. For Vallen, the agreement with Dow means large orders for which payment is guaranteed within ten days.

Vallen's strategy is to provide convenient service for all its customers. In the company's early years, a major goal was to expand its product line so that it could supply all the equipment needed to meet all safety regulations. This policy is still in effect, as Vallen makes a special effort to keep pace with changes in safety regulations.

One advantage that Illinois-based Lawson Products does not offer its customers is low price. In fact, this hardware wholesaler has a 240 percent markup on many of the screws, nuts and bolts, and other replacement parts it sells. The company's founder and chairman points out that because Lawson hardware is used on and in expensive equipment, the additional cost of small parts is inconsequential to customers. What does matter to them,

---

Wholesalers can be classified as company-owned or independent. Often a manufacturer will take on wholesaling functions and establish its own sales branch and warehouse in a market. We are primarily concerned with independent wholesalers—**merchant wholesalers, agents,** and **brokers**—that operate independently of the suppliers they buy from and the retailers they supply.

Merchant wholesalers. Eighty percent of all wholesalers are merchants. Merchant wholesalers take title to the goods they market, while agents and brokers do not. Merchant wholesalers are paid through profits on the resale of the goods they purchase from suppliers. Their sales figures are broken down by type of business and can be seen in table 18–7.

Merchant wholesalers can be further classified as to the number of functions they perform. **Full-function wholesalers** provide the full range of functions pre-

though, are convenience, time, quality, and efficiency, and those features happen to be exactly what Lawson offers.

Lawson's five regional warehouses are 99 percent stocked at all times with its 17,000 replacement parts. In addition, Lawson employs 1,100 salespeople to make calls on clients, many of whom work in rural areas with little other access to parts wholesalers. A visit by a Lawson salesperson can eliminate a lengthy trip to a hardware store. Lawson's products are also of high quality so that customers are certain they are buying a reliable item. This company stresses efficiency in its own operations as well. Parts are counted and boxed under automated systems, and the company ships by UPS to ensure quick deliveries.

W. W. Grainger, Inc., of Skokie, Illinois, has a product line that includes electric motors, fans, posthole diggers, and garbage cans. Grainger is primarily a motor wholesaler, but the company's product line is designed to include almost anything that can save customers the time it would take to visit another store. Grainger has 165 "wholesale-only" stores where a customer who comes in to buy a replacement motor might also pick up a few other items—a pound of solder, for example, or a mop wringer. These items might cost more at a Grainger store, but buying them there will provide valuable time savings for the person rushing to complete a job.

Adding these items to the stores' stock has another advantage for Grainger. The expanded product line makes the company's distribution system more efficient. Grainger has a centralized warehouse from which assortments of goods are shipped at least once a week to the stores. The large number of Grainger products enables the company to ship full truckloads frequently, instead of having to resort to partially filled trucks or less frequent shipments. The company's chairman attributes the company's success to "Having the right thing in the right place at the right time."

For each of these companies, success hinges on providing service that enables industrial customers to operate more efficiently.

Source: William Baldwin, "Dollars from Doodads," *Forbes*, October 11, 1982, pp. 51–56.

TABLE 18–7   Merchant Wholesalers' Sales by Kind of Business

Kind of Business	Sales in 1981 (in billions)	Kind of Business	Sales in 1981 (in billions)
Merchant wholesalers	$1,179.1	Nondurable goods, total[a]	$674.1
Durable goods, total[a]	500.0	Paper and paper products	24.4
Motor vehicles and automotive equipment	94.7	Drugs, proprietaries, and sundries	15.8
Furniture and home furnishings	16.6	Apparel, piece goods, and notions	27.1
Lumber and construction materials	34.1	Groceries and related products	167.7
Electrical goods	54.2	Farm-product raw materials	125.6
Hardware, plumbing, and heating equipment	30.3	Beer, wine, and distilled beverages	35.9
Machinery, equipment, and supplies	148.2	Petroleum and petroleum products	187.1

[a]Includes kinds of business not shown separately.
Source: U.S. Bureau of the Census, *Current Business Reports*, series BW, *Monthly Wholesale Trade*.

Table 18–8   The Ten Leading Food Wholesalers

Wholesalers	Sales in 1982 (in billions of dollars)	Stores Served
Super Valu Stores	$4.1	2,118
Fleming Cos., Inc.	3.5	2,956
Malone & Hyde, Inc.	2.2	2,200
Wakefern Food Corp.	2.2	196
Wetterau Inc.	2.0	1,402
Certified Grocers of Calif., Ltd.	1.8	3,800
Associated Wholesale Grocers Inc.	1.4	722
S. M. Flickinger Co., Inc.	1.35	1,100
Nash-Finch Co.	1.25	2,073
Super Food Services, Inc.	1.2	823

Source: Newspaper Advertising Bureau. Reprinted by permission.

sented earlier, while **limited-function wholesalers** specialize in one or several of those functions.

Full-function wholesalers are the traditional wholesalers that perform all or most of the functions associated with wholesaling. They take title to the goods, store them until they are needed by customers, transport them, sell and promote them, make contact with and negotiate with both suppliers and customers, extend credit to customers, and assume the risks of ownership. They can be further categorized depending upon the merchandise assortment they carry. General merchandise wholesalers carry several different, but usually related, lines of products. Table 18–8 shows the ten leading food wholesalers in the United States. Single-line wholesalers carry a narrower line of merchandise, such as only frozen food. Specialty wholesalers carry a very narrow product line, such as fancy tropical fruit. Limited-function wholesalers provide only one or a few of the wholesaling functions. There are a number of kinds of limited-function wholesalers.

Cash-and-Carry Wholesalers. **Cash-and-carry wholesalers** do not offer financing to customers, nor do they deliver the products to customers or employ an outside sales force. They deal primarily with small retailers that pick up the goods they need and pay in cash. Cash-and-carry wholesalers are used most often by small food stores, markets, drugstores, and garages that buy in quantities too small for a full-function wholesaler to handle profitably.

Drop Shippers. **Drop shippers,** or desk jobbers, pass orders from customers to manufacturers to ship directly to the customer. Drop shippers do not maintain inventories or take possession of the goods. They are found most often in lines of trade where goods are bought and sold in carload or truckload quantities, such as coal, lumber, fuel, building materials, and chemicals. The costs of handling and transporting these goods are very high relative to their value, so avoiding extra handling saves money.

Wagon or Truck Jobbers. **Wagon or truck jobbers** are self-employed merchants that operate out of their own trucks. They often deal in perishable or semiperishable goods and handle smaller accounts. They deliver and sell tobacco products, snacks, fresh fruits and vegetables, and similar products.

Rack Jobbers. **Rack jobbers** are important in variety and specialty lines, especially in supermarkets and drugstores. Rack jobbers sell such goods as comic books, panty hose, health and beauty aids, housewares, records, books, and hardware. The rack jobber sets up racks in supermarkets or drugstores, stocks them with products it owns, and maintains them. The retailer provides the space and collects the money when they are sold. The rack jobber may or may not handle the financing function. Rack jobbers are largely responsible for the wide range of merchandising practices of supermarkets and drugstores, because they introduce new lines of products into these stores at little risk to the retailer. The displays of potato chips, popcorn, and other snacks often seen in supermarkets and drugstores are an example of a rack jobber's work.

Mail-Order Wholesalers. **Mail-order wholesalers** distribute catalogs of their product assortment to small retailers and industrial buyers often located in areas outside the larger metropolitan population centers. They are most often found selling hardware, sporting goods, and jewelry. Their primary market is retailers that are too small to justify a personal sales call.

Agents and brokers. Agents and brokers are wholesalers that do not take title to the goods, but are compensated with commissions upon the completion of a sale. They usually perform a very limited set of functions concerned with facilitating the buying and selling of goods. Many agents and brokers operate as field salespeople, offering customers a limited line of products from several manufacturers. Agents and brokers have tended to decline in importance in recent years relative to merchant wholesalers.

Manufacturer's Agents. There are two kinds of agents. **Manufacturer's agents,** or **manufacturer's representatives,** sell the products of a manufacturer in a specified geographic area. Functioning as the sales force for the manufacturer, they work under contracts to several noncompeting manufacturers and sell an assortment of products for them over an extended period of time. They are used by manufacturers too small to have a sales force or in a territory too small to support the manufacturer's own sales force. Some manufacturers will also use them to develop a new sales territory. They often do not take possession of the products they sell but pass orders back to the manufacturer, which then ships the products to the buyer. They are often found selling industrial products, automotive products, clothing, and food products.

Selling Agents. **Selling agents** normally handle the entire product mix of a manufacturer and determine the complete marketing program for that mix. They are given a great deal of responsibility over prices, territory, promotion, and terms of sale.

Brokers attempt to bring buyers and sellers together. They usually represent a principal, which is either a buyer or a seller. They do not take title or possession of the products, nor do they extend credit. They negotiate with customers based on limitations established by the principal. Brokers are often found in markets that buyers and sellers enter infrequently because they are unfamiliar with the market and seek out a broker that is knowledgeable. Brokers are not employed on a continuing basis but only intermittently, as needed. They are used to sell or buy real estate and seasonal food products. For example, a tomato canner only operates during the harvest season and hires a broker to sell its products for the year.

Commission Merchants. **Commission merchants** are brokers used by small farmers to sell their annual harvests. Commission merchants take possession of the commodities but not the title. They locate buyers for the commodities, negotiate the terms and price of the sale, and ship the commodity to the buyer. Once sold, the money paid by the seller (minus the commission) is sent by the commission merchant to the farmer.

Auction Companies. **Auction companies** are brokers in that they bring buyers and sellers together. They are important in the sale of such products as used automobiles, tobacco, fruit, furs, art and decorative objects, and livestock. These products must be examined before purchase, and their prices are set by the market. The auction company provides a forum for the examination of the products; they do not provide financing or assume the risks of ownership. They are paid a commission upon the completion of a transaction.

Future of Wholesaling

Throughout history, wholesaling has had its ups and downs. During the nineteenth century, wholesalers were the dominant business institutions. Retailers and manufacturers were usually small, and large wholesalers existed to serve them. As manufacturers and retailers grew in the first half of this century, they began to replace wholesalers with their own sales offices and purchasing and warehousing operations. Some even predicted the extinction of the full-service wholesaler.

Wholesalers have been maligned as parasites and often characterized as an unnecessary, costly institution that merely drives up the prices that consumers must pay for goods. As we have seen, however, the wholesaling functions must be performed to overcome the gap between production and consumption. Wholesalers can be eliminated, but not their functions. As long as wholesalers can perform these functions more efficiently and effectively than producers and retailers can, there will be wholesalers. Many manufacturers have found that they cannot do the job that wholesalers can. In fact, the wholesaling sector of the economy has been growing in recent years, and it is expected to continue to grow as new technologies and new roles broaden the range of services they can provide to suppliers and customers.

Summary

Retailing consists of activities that involve the sale of goods and services to the final consumer. Retailing is brutally competitive, though a fairly easy industry to enter.

The retailing mix consists of variables that the retailer can manipulate and coordinate to satisfy the needs of a target market. Such variables include location, merchandise, communications, price, services, physical attributes of the store, and personnel.

Convenience stores are located conveniently to neighborhoods, and consumers use them for fill-in purchases between regular trips to the supermarket; they are high-margin, high-turnover retailers. Location and merchandise assortment are the most important part of their mix. Specialty stores are retailers that concentrate on sales of one merchandise line with a narrow but deep assortment. Department stores carry a wide assortment of moderate depth and are located in central business districts and shopping malls.

Mass merchandisers are retailers that practice a strategy of low margins and high turnover. Supermarkets usually locate near large residential areas and far from competitors. Price is an important variable. Superstores are larger and carry more items than supermarkets. Box stores offer very low prices and few services. Warehouse stores are no-frills operations offering fewer items than supermarkets but more than box stores. Combination stores combine supermarket, general merchandise, and discount stores.

Discount stores offer a broad but not very deep assortment of the most popular, fastest-moving merchandise; they keep building and fixture costs down in order to offer low prices and encourage high sales volumes. In catalog showrooms, consumers select merchandise from catalogs in their homes, then go to the showroom and buy it; these stores can offer low prices because of low costs. Nonstore retailers include mail-order, door-to-door, and vending machines.

A chain is a number of identical stores with one owner. Buying is centralized so that its bargaining power may lead to lower prices. Independent merchants are one-store retail operations. Consumer cooperatives are retail establishments owned and operated by consumers. They are most often found in the food sector.

The retail location decision should be made on the basis of the needs of the target market. The retailer must decide between a central business district (CBD);

regional, community, or neighborhood shopping center; street location; or isolated, single-store site.

One key to marketing's future is demographics. At present the 35- to 44-year-old age group is very important to retailers. The over-65-years age group and working women will gain importance. Advances in technology will also have an impact on retailing.

A wholesaler is "a firm which buys and resells merchandise to retailers and other merchants and/or to industrial, institutional, and commercial users but which does not sell in significant amounts to ultimate consumers." Wholesalers' functions include services to customers (such as selecting an assortment of goods from many manufacturers and providing rapid delivery of goods), as well as services to suppliers (such as identifying prospective customers and providing suppliers with a sales force). Not all wholesalers perform the same services. A retailer or supplier can choose to eliminate the wholesaler.

Merchant wholesalers take title to goods. They can be full function or limited function. Agents and brokers are wholesalers that do not take title to the goods but are compensated with commissions. Manufacturer's agents sell the products of a supplier in a specified geographic area. Brokers attempt to bring buyers and sellers together.

Questions for Discussion

1. Evaluate the role of retailing in marketing.
2. Critically examine the importance of location in retailing decisions.
3. Differentiate between department stores and mass merchandisers.
4. What are some of the special problems facing nonstore retailers?
5. "Wholesalers can be eliminated but not their functions." Explain.
6. How would you explain the key retailing role played by chain stores in the United States?
7. Differentiate between merchant wholesalers and agents.
8. Explain why we need limited function wholesalers. Give examples.
9. Compare the future of single-store sites and shopping centers as retailing centers.

References

1. "Family Dollar Stores: As Rivals Fall, This Discounter Keeps Growing," *Business Week*, January 24, 1983, pp. 90–91.
2. *Statistical Abstract of the United States, 1982–83* (Washington, D.C.: U.S. Bureau of the Census), p. 801.
3. Steve Weiner, "K mart Upgrades Clothing Lines to Draw More Customers and Change Firm's Image," *Wall Street Journal*, April 4, 1984; and "K mart: The No. 2 Retailer Starts to Make an Upscale Move—at Last," *Business Week*, June 4, 1984, pp. 50–51.

4. Isadore Barmash, "Penney's $1 Billion Gamble on Chic," *New York Times*, July 10, 1983, p. 4F.
5. "New Look for the Top Retailer," *Time*, December 5, 1983, pp. 66–68.
6. *Progressive Grocer*, June 1982, p. 37.
7. "Atlantic Richfield: Marketing Muscle Has the Competition Reeling," *Business Week*, September 12, 1983, pp. 86, 88, 92.
8. *Progressive Grocer*, August 1983, p. 32.
9. "Supermarkets Change to Lure More Shoppers," *Wall Street Journal*, November 14, 1983, p. 33.
10. "Spiegel: From Mass to Class," *Business Week*, October 4, 1982, pp. 68, 72.
11. Susan Carey, "Can't Find the Right Christmas Tree? Now You Can Order One by Mail," *Wall Street Journal*, December 14, 1982.
12. *Vending Times*, July 17, 1983, p. 29.
13. *Progressive Grocer*, May 1983, p. 47.
14. "The Discount Twist in Suburban Shopping Malls," *Business Week*, July 7, 1980, pp. 94, 96.
15. "Foremost-McKesson: The Computer Moves Distribution to Center Stage," *Business Week*, December 7, 1981, pp. 115–21.
16. *Marketing Definitions: A Glossary of Marketing Terms* (Chicago: American Marketing Association, 1960).
17. *Statistical Abstract of the United States, 1982–83* (Washington, D.C.: U.S. Bureau of the Census), p. 810.
18. L. Stern and A. El-Ansary, *Marketing Channels*, 2nd ed. (Englewood Cliffs, N.J.: Prentice-Hall, 1982), pp. 121–22.

CASES FOR PART III

7 Polaroid and Polavision

In 1977, Polaroid Corporation introduced a new instant movie camera that enabled users to shoot home movies and view them within seconds. The new product included a lightweight, battery-powered camera, a half-inch-thick film cassette that held 2 minutes and 40 seconds of film, and a portable televisionlike viewer with a 12-inch screen.

The new technology making Polavision possible drew much attention. The same year Polaroid's main competitor, Eastman Kodak, added five projectors and five movie cameras to its home movie line rather than presenting new technology.

Although instant movie equipment was revolutionary, there was already a large and growing market for instant still cameras. In 1976, an estimated 4.5 million instant still cameras were sold in the United States. By 1978, the number had increased to 8.2 million cameras, 42 percent of all cameras sold, and it was estimated that Polaroid could have sold more cameras if production had been faster.

While the market for instant still cameras was still growing, the market for "non-instant" traditional home movie cameras and projectors had slipped. In 1978, only 560,000 home movie cameras were sold in the United States, compared with twice that number six years earlier. This decline was also reflected in market penetration, as only 1 percent of all U.S. homes had movie cameras and projectors. Thus, for Polavision to succeed, Polaroid had to expand the home movie market.

The emergence of home video and videocameras presented a growing challenge to movie cameras. Offering the advantages of reusable tape, long-playing cassettes, and immediate viewing on a television set, videocassette equipment had a promising potential market.

Polaroid defined the market for Polavision as the mass market, with users ranging from mothers recording and reliving moments in their young children's lives to amateur golf or tennis players using the instant replay to evaluate their swings. The company's strategy was to distribute Polavision as widely as it had the SX-70 instant still camera five years earlier. For example, as part of its promotional strategy in late 1978, Polaroid offered to have Polavision delivered to homes as a Christmas gift by a person dressed as Santa, or to provide a Santa suit to customers who purchased Polavision. Polaroid increased its advertising budget, including sponsoring 30-second television commercials to promote Polavision on family-oriented shows.

The company was perfecting the technology behind Polavision to add sound, which it expected to introduce in about a year. The company was also developing greater film capacity, a power zoom, and a faster lens for low-light filming.

Industry analysts outlined several drawbacks of Polavision. At $699 for the camera and viewer, it was priced high for the mass market. Its lack of light and sound capabilities limited its usefulness. Furthermore, it was necessary to finish shooting a roll of film before processing it. Finally, the necessity of carrying along the playback unit posed an inconvenience to users.

Faced with these promises and prospects, Polaroid executives had to decide how to proceed with Polavision.

Sources: Based on Peter W. Bernstein, "Polaroid Struggles to Get Back in Focus," *Fortune*, April 7, 1980, pp. 66–70; and "Instant Movies System Introduced by Polaroid," *New York Times*, pp. D1, D5.

Questions

1. How could Polaroid have decided whether or not to introduce Polavision?
2. What are the strengths and weaknesses of Polavision?
3. What is the market for Polavision? What are the needs of that market, and how can they be fulfilled?
4. What are Polavision's competitors? How does Polavision compare with them?
5. What steps could Polaroid take to market Polavision?

8 Lotus 1-2-3 and Symphony

In early 1984, managers at Lotus Development Corporation of Cambridge, Massachusetts, were wondering how to maintain their success. The company has been a winner in the competitive computer software industry since its inception in April 1982. To launch its first product, an integrated program known as Lotus 1-2-3, Lotus spent $1 million on advertising over a three-month period, an unprecedented amount in the computer software industry.

An integrated program is one that combines many of the most popular computer applications in one package. Lotus 1-2-3, the first commercially successful integrated program, combined financial analysis spreadsheets, graphics, and data file management capabilities in a single floppy disc that sold for $495.

Not only was Lotus 1-2-3 the hottest selling software package in 1983, it proved to be one of the best-selling computer programs ever. More than 110,000 copies were sold during the product's first nine months on the market. About two-thirds of all U.S. companies buying computers in 1983 chose Lotus 1-2-3 for making computerized financial projections and displaying the results in computer-generated charts and graphs.

In 1984, Lotus faced the challenge of trying to follow Lotus 1-2-3 with an equally successful second program. No computer software company had yet created and sold two leading products in a row. Producing the second success was crucial to Lotus's maintaining momentum.

A shakeout among computer software companies was expected in 1984. The precarious position of many companies was highlighted by estimates that 90 percent of revenues for computer software sales are being generated by fewer than ten companies.

It is unlikely that long-term price wars, such as those in the home-computer market, will strike the business software market, since the latter appears to be less price-sensitive. The businesses and professionals who purchase business software often have greater need for computer applications and more money to spend on software.

But the business computer software market is increasingly competitive. Several new companies have announced new products that will compete directly with Lotus. Moreover, as microcomputer software offers more computing power and more sophisticated capabilities, an increasing number of mainframe software manufacturers are entering that market.

Early in 1984, Lotus announced the introduction of Symphony, a package with Lotus 1-2-3's capabilities plus word processing, more sophisticated record-keeping, and the ability to communicate with other computers over the telephone. The program was sold for approximately $895.

Much is at stake: It is estimated that the business microcomputer software market is approximately $3 billion in 1985. The challenges facing Lotus are how to expand its share of that market and how to successfully expand its product line.

Sources: Based on David Wessel, "Lotus to Unveil Software Adding New Functions," *Wall Street Journal*, February 8, 1984, p. 5; and David E. Sanger, "The Next Big Test for Lotus," *New York Times*, February 13, 1984, pp. D1, D9.

Questions

1. What was the basis for the success of Lotus 1-2-3?
2. What must a computer software company do to maintain its market position?
3. Are the sales of software tied to the sales of computers? If hardware sales drop, will sales of software also drop?

4. What is the role of price in the computer software market?
5. Will Symphony be able to match the success of Lotus 1-2-3? Why or why not?
6. What marketing strategies would you suggest to Lotus for the marketing of Symphony?

9 Texas Instruments and the Home-Computer Market

Early in 1984, marketing managers at Texas Instruments (TI) were assessing the company's future in the home-computer market. In 1979, TI had been one of the first companies to market a computer for home use, as opposed to office use. Priced at $1,150, the machine proved too expensive for home users, and sales were limited. As technology advanced and the market grew, the price fell. The result was a home-computer market of over $1 billion in 1982. Although demand had grown rapidly, the supply had grown even faster, resulting in fierce competition, oversupply, and steep price cuts. By 1983, the prices of home computers had fallen 75 percent in 18 months.

Sales of TI's 99/4A home computer soared, but in the environment of severe price cuts, TI reportedly lost $50 for every machine it shipped. By the end of the third quarter of 1983, TI's home-computer operations had a deficit of more than $500 million.

Some suggested that TI simply quit the home-computer business. But others suggested that it would be foolish for the company to abandon its long-established distribution channels for products selling for less than $1,000.

TI overestimated the size of the market. TI had initially predicted that nearly 7 million home computers would be sold in 1983 and that the company would sell 3 million of them. In reality, only 5 million home computers were purchased by consumers in 1983, and only 20 percent of them were sold by TI.

TI's home-computer business was plagued by other problems. In February 1983, a technical problem with the 99/4A's transformer halted shipments of the machine for a month. At about the same time, the company lost track of what consumers were taking off the shelves and underestimated the number of its computers still held in stock by retailers.

At one time, TI had led the way in price cutting in the calculator and digital watch markets, basing its pricing on the learning curve, which states that per-unit costs decrease with increasing volumes of production. In 1983, Commodore cut the prices of its home computers. TI responded; the price of the 99/4A, $950 two years earlier, dropped to $199 plus a $50 rebate. When the rebate expired, TI permanently dropped the price to $149. Commodore countered with a price of less than $100 for the VIC 20. TI responded with another $50 rebate to lower the effective price of the 99/4A to $99.

The price cuts were enacted so quickly that TI didn't have time to bring out a new model designed to compete at the bottom end of the market. Thus, the company began losing money on every unit of the 99/4A it sold. Moreover, TI failed to lower production costs as prices were reduced, which led to a cost/price squeeze.

Faced with this situation, TI evaluated a number of marketing options. One plan was to reposition the TI home computer to compete against higher-performing models from other vendors. Another plan included increasing radio and television advertising, which would involve a complete rethinking and restructuring of its consumer ads. A third plan involved price. TI considered competing on the basis of price with peripherals, reducing the price of a package of four 99/4A peripherals—including disc drives and additional memory—from $1,200 to $550. Finally, TI considered expanding its distribution channels for the 99/4A. In marketing its professional personal computer, TI had set up and stocked a new distribution channel—computer specialty stores. This channel might be an effective outlet for consumer sales for home computers.

Sources: Based on "Behind the Shakeout in Personal Computers," *U.S. News & World Report*, June 27, 1983, p. 59; "Sudden Shake-up in Home Computers," *Fortune*, July 11, 1983, pp. 105–6; and "Texas Instruments Cleans Up Its Act," *Business Week*, September 19, 1983, pp. 56–64.

Questions

1. Why is TI having trouble in the home-computer market?
2. What was the effect of price cutting in this market?
3. What distribution channels would be most appropriate for TI's 99/4A?
4. Would you recommend that TI adopt the plan for the pricing of peripherals? Why or why not?
5. Do you think TI should stay in the home-computer market? Why or why not?
6. How would TI's withdrawal from the home-computer market affect the company itself, competitors, and the home-computer market?

10 The Miller Brewing Company and Meister Brau

In October 1983, the Miller Brewing Company (the second largest brewer in the United States), producers of premium-priced Miller High Life and Miller Lite, introduced Meister Brau. The market chosen for Meister Brau was the popular-price (or less-expensive) market, in which its main competition would be Old Milwaukee and a number of regional brands. The popular-price market accounts for 24 percent of all beer sales.

To promote its new beer, Miller embarked on a comparative advertising campaign based on a taste test comparing Meister Brau with Budweiser, the leading beer in the premium-price market (and the premier product of Anheuser-Busch, the nation's largest brewer). The taste test, conducted in 46 cities throughout the country, indicated that those tested felt that Meister Brau tasted as good as Budweiser. The test led to a series of print advertisements that carried the following message: "A nationwide survey has determined that Meister Brau tastes as good as

Budweiser. In all fairness, it also determined that Budweiser tastes as good as Meister Brau. You decide." The point of the advertisement was that Meister Brau gave consumers the same good taste they got from Budweiser, but at a better price.

Miller chose to use an advertising campaign based on quality and price as a way to attract consumers in the price-conscious, popular-price beer market. Price is important to these consumers, who tend to be younger blue-collar workers. Telling them that they can get a product of the quality of the leader in the higher-price, premium market at a low price is a great lure. Miller tested the lure in its test marketing of Meister Brau; it used a number of slogans and advertising approaches, and the one comparing Meister Brau to Budweiser in taste and price was the most effective.

The test marketing of Meister Brau proved so successful that Miller moved up the date for nationwide introduction of the product from 1984 to October 1983.

Source: Based on James Hammett, "Across the Country, Miller's Raising Some Braus," *Advertising Age*, January 16, 1984, p. M30.

Questions

1. What is the target market segment for Meister Brau?
2. Is the overall beer market price-sensitive? Is the market for permium beer, such as Budweiser, price-sensitive? Why or why not?
3. Is the Meister Brau message of "high quality, low price" a contradiction? Why or why not?
4. Do you agree with Miller's decision to market Meister Brau nationwide? Why or why not?
5. What further steps would you recommend to Miller in its marketing of Meister Brau?

11 Miller Lite

When Philip Morris (the country's most successful cigarette company) bought Miller Brewing Company in 1970, Miller was the eighth largest brewery in the country, and Philip Morris had no experience in the highly competitive beer market. By 1983, Miller had become the second largest brewery in the country, largely due to the success of Miller Lite.

Although Miller was the first company to make light beer a widespread commercial success, the concept of light beer was not new. The Meister Brau Brewing Company had introduced its light beer in 1967 but had targeted the product for diet-conscious female beer drinkers—a market too small for the beer to be successful. In the same year, Rheingold Brewing Company had introduced Gablinger's Beer, another reduced-calorie beer. Gablinger's was positioned as a chemical, laboratory breakthrough—not an appealing image for most beer drinkers. Both products failed to attract substantial market shares.

Executives at Miller knew that for their company to grow, it would have to reposition its products and introduce new ones. A decision was made to introduce Lite Beer nationally and target it to heavy beer drinkers, where the strength of the American beer market lay. Heavy beer drinkers are the 30 percent of all beer drinkers who consume 80 percent of the beer purchased in this country. Miller's decision to target this market segment for its light beer contradicted the prevailing belief in the beer industry that light beer would not appeal to heavy beer drinkers. They tend to be men aged 18 to 49, generally blue-collar workers, who drink at least eight 12-oz. beers per week.

Through their consumer research, Miller found that many male, heavy beer drinkers were willing to try a light beer despite the negative, feminine image associated with it. Initial tests of Miller Lite found that these beer drinkers reported being able to drink more Lite without feeling filled up. They also found that the taste of Miller Lite had to be improved.

After developing a light beer with a better taste, Miller found in test markets that repeat purchases were high. (Repeat purchases of Meister Brau's light beer and Gablinger's were low, as beer drinkers did not like the tastes.) But the problems of light beer's negative and feminine images remained. The solution was to change the images through advertising. Miller needed to masculinize the product, and heavy beer drinkers needed to be persuaded that Miller Lite was a real beer with an added benefit—that they could drink more of it.

Miller translated this solution into the advertising strategy for Miller Lite. The first aspect of the strategy was the message that low-calorie beer was less filling. The second aspect was that it tasted great. The slogan developed was: "Everything you always wanted in a beer. And less."

For spokesmen, Miller decided to use well-known personalities who were unquestionably male and with whom heavy beer drinkers could identify. By using humor in the commercials, Miller was able to create warmth and make the messages fun and entertaining. This proved to be the right tone, as Miller wanted to associate Lite with the social environment of "macho" men drinking beer together and having fun.

Lite Beer from Miller became the third largest selling beer in the country by 1980. By 1983, it accounted for 60 percent of all light beer sold. As Lite Beer was extremely successful, Miller executives had to contend with the natural consequence of success and defend their brand from competitors. In 1984, the marketing managers had to review their advertising campaign and protect their brand's market share.

Source: Based on material provided by the Miller Brewing Company.

Questions

1. What were the promotional problems for Meister Brau's light beer and Gablinger's?
2. What were Miller's promotional objectives?

3. What was the target market for Miller Lite? How was the advertising campaign shaped by this market?
4. What made the promotional campaign for Miller Lite work?
5. In light of increasing competition in the light beer market, should Miller change its promotional strategy? If you think it should, what changes would you suggest?

12 Comparative Advertising in the Fast-Food Industry

In 1981, McDonald's was by far the leader in the fast-food industry, with sales of $7.6 billion. Second-place Burger King's 1981 sales were $2.3 billion. Moreover, Burger King's growth rate had slowed down considerably over the previous few years. Introductions of new products, such as a veal parmigiana sandwich, had failed, and marketing strategy had not been consistent. Burger King executives developed an overall marketing plan to increase sales, even to take over first place from McDonald's. One part of this plan was the "Battle of the Burgers," a comparative advertising campaign.

Burger King commissioned a taste test comparing its hamburgers with those of McDonald's and Wendy's. The taste tests, according to Burger King, showed that customers preferred the taste of its flame-broiled hamburgers over the taste of McDonald's fried hamburgers. Moreover, Burger King pointed out that its hamburgers contained 20 percent more meat than McDonald's.

Using the results of this test, Burger King launched a $19 million television advertising campaign, the first comparative advertising campaign in the fast-food industry. The first round of commercials publicized the customers' preferences for Burger King and the Whopper over McDonald's and the Big Mac, and they stressed that Burger King burgers contained more meat. The spokespeople in the advertisements were children, who present the clear (at least to Burger King) results of the tests and said that they were switching to Burger King. A second round of ads stressed the preference for flame-broiling over frying and showed comparative shots of succulent Burger King burgers flame-broiling and less succulent McDonald's burgers frying.

The third round of ads presented perhaps the strongest direct comparative message. Burger King found a family named MacDonald that had actually switched from McDonald's to Burger King. The five-member family and their dog are shown in disguises, as they "can't show our faces anywhere." They explain that they have switched to Burger King and, in response to an announcer's question, recommend that every family also switch. The commercial ends with the whole family telling viewers that when they switch to Burger King, they can say that "The MacDonalds sent you."

Burger King is pleased with the results of the comparative advertising campaign and plans to run several more series of commercials featuring comparisons between the two chains. The purpose of the campaign, one Burger King executive said, was to get consumers to re-think their food consumption choices, a purpose that Burger King feels is being met by this type of campaign.

Sources: Based on Christy Marshall and Scott Hume, "Major Fast-Fooders Locking Horns Again," *Advertising Age*, September 12, 1983; "Burger Brawls," *Time*, October 11, 1982, p. 74; and "Burger King's Ads Cook Up a Storm," *Business Week*, October 11, 1982, p. 39.

Questions

1. What were the reasons for Burger King's decision to launch the "Battle of the Burgers" comparative advertising campaign?
2. How do the advertising approaches of Burger King, McDonald's, and Wendy's differ?
3. Do you think comparative advertising was an effective tool for Burger King to have used, given their comparative situation?
4. How does the humor in Wendy's advertising campaign compare with the comparative advertising technique of Burger King?
5. Has this advertising campaign made you rethink your own choice in burger consumption?

13 Levi Strauss

Faced with an increasingly competitive market, Levi Strauss made a dramatic change in its distribution strategy in 1982. Levi's jeans, which had traditionally been sold through specialty stores, were not to be sold through mass merchandisers, such as Sears and J. C. Penney. Due to this distribution change, managers at Levi Strauss had to predict and then respond to the reactions of their specialty store customers.

Until 1978, Levi Strauss dominated the jeans market with approximately a 33 percent market share. Its jeans were sold primarily in specialty stores for about $9 a pair. In 1978, however, fashion designers entered the jeans market, a move that disrupted all accepted wisdom about marketing blue jeans. The marketing revolution started with the introduction of Gloria Vanderbilt jeans by Murjani. The jeans were specifically designed to fit women, and they were marketed through television ads that connected Gloria Vanderbilt's glamorous, jet-setting image with the jeans. Department stores, such as Macy's and Bloomingdale's, had never carried jeans and remained uninterested in them, even with the Vanderbilt name. The television ads, however, prompted consumers to ask for the jeans at the department stores, which led the stores to carry them.

Advertising continued to be key to the marketing of designer jeans. Jordache's provocative ads focused on the "look" of their jeans; Calvin Klein's ads used sexual imagery. Advertising began to differentiate designer jeans from other jeans on the market, and designer jeans moved swiftly into major department stores. Total sales of both traditional and designer jeans increased and topped $5 billion in the United States in 1981.

In contrast to the price cutting customary in the traditional jeans market, designer jeans makers raised prices to convey the image of higher quality. The higher prices were welcome to retailers, as they provided larger profit margins.

Levi Strauss initially underestimated the effect of designer jeans. Believing that the designer jeans fad would disappear, the company continued to operate as it always had. It focused on the lower end of the market and offered no product targeted to the upscale market. The low-priced Levi's did not offer enough of a profit margin to be carried in better department stores, and the utilitarian image and widespread availability offered nothing to enhance the images of the exclusive stores.

Levi Strauss's sales had increased 500 percent between 1962 and 1970. By 1977, its sales had grown by another 500 percent; by 1980, sales exceeded $2.8 billion a year. But in the face of a changing market and an economic recession, sales in the period 1980–82 dropped 10 percent, and net income plunged 76 percent.

To combat the new competition from both traditional and designer jeans manufacturers and to reverse the downturns in sales and profits, Levi's management decided to increase the distribution base. In 1982, Levi's went on sale in Sears and J. C. Penney, expanding the Levi's distribution base by 2,600 units. These mass merchandisers had carried their own private label jeans that had been considered competitors to Levi's. Having changed their distribution, Levi Strauss had to try to minimize the effect of this change on their traditional distributors.

Source: Based on "Levi Strauss: A Touch of Fashion— and a Dash of Humility," *Business Week*, October 24, 1983, pp. 85, 88.

Questions

1. What are the risks in Levi Strauss's change in distribution strategy?
2. How would you expect specialty stores that have been the traditional outlets for Levi's to react to this change?
3. List the differences between specialty stores (such as The Gap) and mass merchandisers (such as Sears).
4. What steps would you recommend to Levi Strauss to reduce the risks of the change in distribution strategy?

5. Sears and J. C. Penney had traditionally avoided national brands but have sold their own private label brands. What is the basis for that strategy? Why would they change that strategy, for example, by selling Levi's?

14   Pricing in the Videocassette Market

Home videocassettes have created new markets for motion pictures. Shortly after theatrical release, films may be released on cassettes, enabling viewers who own videocassette recorders (VCRs) to buy or rent the cassettes for home viewing. These new markets for films have a great effect on the revenues of major studios. Videocassette sales reached $625 million in 1983, with strong indications that the market is still expanding.

Studios generally set a retail price for the videocassettes ranging from $79.95 to $89.95. This price tended to encourage consumers to rent rather than buy the tapes from retailers. But studios vary in their pricing strategies. In 1983, Paramount cut its prices to persuade consumers to buy the tapes. The studio offered box office successes such as *Flashdance* and *Raiders of the Lost Ark* at a retail price of $39.95.

The Paramount Video Group, formed in 1981, markets Paramount's home video products through 40 national distributors, which supply 10,000 video retailers. The video group considers many factors in deciding how to set prices and distribution strategies for videocassettes. The effects of these decisions are significant. If the cassette is purchased, rather than rented, by consumers, the potential market increases from the 10,000 video stores to the more than 8 million consumers who own VCRs. Moreover, copyright law prevents studios from collecting royalties or other revenues from retailers who purchase videocassettes and subsequently rent them to consumers.

Studio executives must also consider the effects of videocassettes on other film markets. It was predicted, for example, that strong sales of *Raiders* videocassettes might delay the film's appearance on cable television (another source of revenue for the studio). By delaying the cable showing, the studio could keep customers from choosing to record the film off cable television for $10 (the price of a blank tape) rather than choosing to buy it for $39.95. Another decision is whether to distribute the cassettes through traditional video retailers only or to involve mass merchandisers. For example, in 1983, Paramount was trying to persuade movie theater owners to sell videocassettes in their lobbies, alongside popcorn and candy.

In November 1983, when Paramount released its home videocassette of *Raiders* at $39.95 through traditional video retailers, it received initial orders for 500,000 units, representing $20 million in potential sales. The *Flashdance* home video release had attracted orders for 150,000 units in its initial shipment, and *Star Trek: The Wrath of Khan* sold 60,000 units in its first release.

The record number of sales was attributed to factors that included the increasing number of VCR owners, the low price, rising rental rates, and the Paramount promotional program. The company had supported the *Raiders* cassette with a $1 million advertising campaign, plus nationwide dealer and consumer promotions combined with in-store and point-of-purchase displays.

By the late spring of 1984, sales of *Raiders* at $39.95 were nearing 1 million units ($40 million in retail sales), providing $25 million in revenues to the studio. By comparison, Columbia Pictures sold 100,000 units of its film *Tootsie* at $79.95, grossing $5 million for the studio.

Advocates of the lower-priced cassettes point to the sales numbers to support their position. Moreover, many executives believe that high-volume sales of movies to the home market will keep interest high and thus help promote the films at the box office. Other studios resist the big price cuts, however, since few cassettes generate enough volume to be profitable at the lower prices.

Sources: Based on Laura Landro, "Movie Studios Put More Emphasis on Home-Video, Pay-TV Markets," *Wall Street Journal*, May 1, 1984, p. 37; and Tony Seidemann "'Raiders' Setting Sales Marks; Par Claims 500,000 en Route," *Variety*, November 23, 1983, p. 27.

Questions

1. Identify the major pricing strategies in the home videocassette market? How do they differ?
2. List the reasons for Paramount not pursuing a skimming strategy.
3. Do you think pricing strategies in this market would change if studios could collect royalties on rentals of videocassettes? Why or why not?
4. What factors affect the retail price of a videocassette?
5. Do you think Paramount's strategy of offering videocassettes at $39.95 was a good one? Why or why not?

15: R. H. Macy & Company

In the late 1970s, many New York stores were losing market share to boutiques, the increasingly successful Upper East Side department store Bloomingdale's, and other competitors. One of these was R. H. Macy's flagship store in New York City's Herald Square, which was considering plans for renovations that would update its image with customers and capture the sense of excitement that Bloomingdale's seemed to have.

One possibility considered by Macy's was to transform its basement into a fashionable retail area. Since about 1971, the basement had been a sales floor for budget clothing and was considered the "bargain basement"; before then it had displayed a wide variety of housewares and appliances. Macy's considered returning the housewares to the basement, adding new kinds of kitchenware and gourmet food, and marketing the merchandise in a new way.

A proposed plan for the basement included transforming the floor into a space to be called "The Cellar," designed like a street with a terra-cotta brick walkway down the center of the space. The sides of the street would be lined with boutique-like departments, each with its own ambiance and merchandise. The design featured lots of wood to give the space a warm effect, piles of varied and colorful merchandise, an arch design as a unifying element, and lower, softer lighting. To complete the image, The Cellar would have its own logo on shopping bags and wrapping paper.

The boutiques in this plan would include:

—A food area to be known as The Marketplace, in which popular and best-selling types of staples, such as biscuits, crackers, pickles, and jams, would be sold. The target market for these goods was the "middle-level gourmet" market, consisting of young adults aged 20–35. The prices and staples chosen would appeal to these consumers rather than to sophisticate upscale shoppers who might buy at exclusive gourmet shops.

—A cookware shop containing name-brand appliances, cookware and other food preparation items

—An old-fashioned apothecary

—A stationery shop

—A fabric boutique

—A replica of the popular East Side pub P. J. Clarke's

Macy's executives were concerned that such a renovation might affect Macy's image. They were worried that Macy's would no longer be known for low or comparative prices. Another worry was the risk involved. The renovation would be costly, and there was no guarantee that the store's image would be updated enough to attract more customers.

Another alternative was to adapt store hours to New Yorkers. A plan called for staying open on Sundays and opening at 8 A.M. on weekdays, one hour earlier than before. The plan also called for staying open until 7 P.M. on weekdays, but shortening night hours to close at 8:30 on the evenings the store stayed open late.

Sources: Based on Lisa Hammel, "One Basement That's Looking Up," *New York Times,* November 15, 1976, p. 36; and Isadore Barmash, "Retailer Plans to Remodel, End Bargain Basements and Limit Night Hours," *New York Times,* pp. 49, 52.

Questions

1. Is it possible for a retailer to change or update its image? Explain your answer.
2. Should Macy's consider Bloomingdale's a competitor? Why or why not?
3. How would changing the basement affect Macy's overall image?
4. How consistent is the fashionable image Macy's wants to acquire with the competitive pricing image Macy's wants to retain?
5. If "The Cellar" concept were implemented, what features should it include? Why?
6. What marketing strategies would you recommend to Macy's to update its image?

PART IV
Marketing Strategy and Planning

OBJECTIVES

1. To identify the role and importance of marketing strategy.

2. To explain the importance of and strategies for corporate growth.

3. To describe the factors considered in planning marketing strategy.

4. To discuss the different approaches employed in making marketing strategy decisions.

5. To show the relationship between strategy planning and budgetary planning.

19

Marketing Strategy

As recently as 1980, American Express was primarily a credit card and traveler's checks company. Opportunities for growth in these markets lay mainly in finding new customers to carry the card and new applications for the card. As fewer and fewer people left home without the card, American Express's potential growth opportunities were waning.

As American Express wanted to continue to grow, it faced the decision of whether to identify new markets and applications for the card or whether to pursue new businesses. If it chose to pursue new businesses, it then had to decide whether to develop the business internally or to acquire an existing business. Perhaps the most difficult decision was which new business to pursue.

American Express decided to pursue the cable television industry and the financial services industry. Acquiring existing companies in each of these industries would give the firm a quick entry and, depending on the specific companies acquired, an established level of customer awareness. Developing these businesses internally would allow the firm to develop its own programs, without being restricted by the direction and reputation of an acquired company.

After weighing these considerations, American Express decided to acquire companies. In the case of the cable television industry, American Express bought 50 percent of Warner Cable Communications, Inc. Renamed Warner Amex, it is one of the country's largest cable television networks. Moving heavily into financial services, in 1981 the company acquired Shearson Loeb Rhodes, a major diversified brokerage house. American Express's portfolio also contains Investors Diversified Services, which gives the company a door-to-door sales force for investment products.

To expand its financial services line further, in 1984 the company acquired Lehman Bros. Kuhn Loeb, a prestigious investment banking firm. Overseas, American Express has

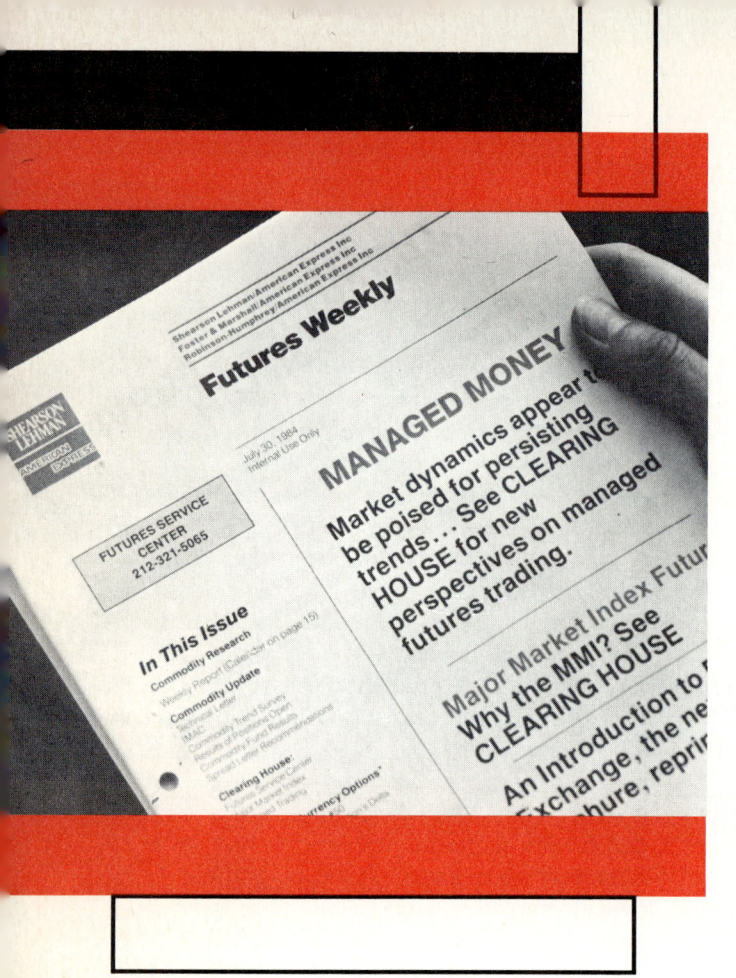

expanded the network of its American Express International Banking Corporation by acquiring several non-U.S. subsidiaries of the Trade Development Bank holding group in Europe and America.

This series of acquisitions is linked to a clearly defined company mission and goal: to become a financial services superpower. American Express is committed to serving distinct market segments: the upwardly mobile, affluent consumer as well as corporations and financial institutions with specialized needs. Both segments are well suited to the company's strategies for growth. For example, Shearson/American Express (the former Shearson Loeb Rhodes) is eager to benefit from Lehman's trading operations in bonds and money market instruments, as Shearson executives now predict a growing need for trading in investment banking. With Lehman filling out its portfolio, the company wants to become the top investment banking firm internationally.

To understand how these acquisitions have altered the scope and size of American Express, think about the following figures. In 1979, the company made profits of $151 million from travel-related services, $35 million from banking, and $186 million from insurance. Just four years later, these figures changed dramatically. Amex then made profits of $301 million from travel-related services, $175 million from investment services, $136 million from banking, and $30 million from insurance.[1]

Management at American Express defined the company's goal as becoming a financial services superpower. Reaching this goal requires a number of decisions: What moves can the company make to achieve this goal? Which specific alternative should they consider? What markets should they pursue? What factors must they consider in creating their marketing strategy? How can they evaluate the progress of their strategy? In this chapter, we look at these questions and at the decisions that marketers face in creating marketing strategies.

Introduction to Marketing Strategy

Marketing strategy involves matching a company's resources and skills with risks and opportunities in the marketplace. In shaping a marketing strategy, a company must first develop a firm grasp of the nature of its business. To define its business, as discussed in chapter 4, a company should specify (1) the market it plans to serve and (2) the general type of product or service it will promote to that market. Additionally, the company must identify the customer needs that its product or service should satisfy. It must also identify its competitors so as not to be upstaged by rival products or services. A sound business definition further helps a company to take stock of its strengths and weaknesses.

Many companies operate within several businesses, each with distinct markets and competitors. These businesses are known as **strategic business units,** or SBUs. An SBU is a freestanding unit within an organization, held together by its own customers, customer needs, and technologies. It is operated by its own management, which devises strategies for that particular unit.

Within the broad umbrella of the business definition is a carefully formulated set of general objectives known as the **company mission.** As we discussed in chapter 4, a company mission sets forth the company's product or service and the customer needs that this item will satisfy, and the general means the company will use to meet those needs. Executives rely on this mission to help them chart the long-range goals of survival, growth, and profitability. When formulating a marketing strategy, managers will need a clear sense of these goals to evaluate opportunities and risks within the marketplace.

As managers eye new markets and potential acquisitions, they consider the company's overall corporate strategy. This broad-based strategy reflects the goals of a company's divisions in technology, finance, human resources, and manufacturing as well as marketing. All these various divisions need to be coordinated in a consistent manner. Marketing strategy, because it links the company to its customers and to its competitors, is crucial in enabling the company to meet its general objectives.

Establishing a Competitive Advantage

One purpose of a sound marketing strategy is to guarantee a company's survival and success in relation to its competitors. To that end, the strategy will usually outline a number of tactics to help the company establish a **competitive advantage.** These may include lower costs, control over distribution, and product differentiation. Use of any of these tactics depends on the objectives established by the company.

Figure 19–1 People Express's lower costs allow it to establish a competitive advantage—even when offering premium service.

Courtesy of People Express/Plapler & Associates, New York

Lower Costs

In some markets, a company can establish a competitive advantage by operating with *lower costs*. With lower costs, a company can offer either an equivalent product at a lower price or a similarly priced product that is of higher quality than competing brands. With either advantage in cost, a company could eventually dominate the market.

People Express has done very well by adopting this strategy, for instance (see fig. 19–1). Having lower labor costs and flying more efficient aircraft have allowed People Express to keep costs low. Its competitors, however, are locked into expensive labor contracts and fly older, less efficient equipment. Pan Am, for example, has typically high costs that are more than double People Express's.

Control over Distribution

Exerting *control over distribution* is another way that a company can establish a competitive advantage. Remember how Campbell has effectively limited other soup makers' ability to enter the market. The channels of distribution are already loaded to capacity with varieties of Campbell's Soup, leaving no room for competitors. To take another case, Coca-Cola and Pepsi control the distribution channels for sodas. As a result, there is little room on grocers' shelves for other soft drinks. The already established access to retail grocers may partly explain why Coke and Pepsi have made such smashing profits from their caffeine-free and low-calorie colas, as they were able to demand and get shelf space for these products.

Product Differentiation

To establish a competitive advantage, companies can also carry out the strategy of *product differentiation*. That is, a company can identify a market segment that wants a product slightly different from other products in the same category. Marketers at that company can then develop a product precisely tailored to these specific desires. For instance, Gillette has recently introduced Body Flowers, a deo-cologne (another term for a scented deodorant in an aerosol can), designed to catch the attention of younger consumers interested in the combination of fragrance and deodorant. First-year sales in the budding market for deo-colognes were only $45 million, although Gillette has predicted a second-year boom of $80 million. The company wants to carve out at least a 19 percent share in this new niche.[2]

The Growth Matrix

One of the major purposes of marketing strategy is to determine the nature and direction of the company's growth. Most companies establish growth as one of their objectives and develop plans to pursue it. Why is growth so important to companies? There are three general reasons:

1. For a firm to attract investors, it must have growth, as few people are interested in investing in a company that does not have a growth strategy.
2. Growth is a good motivator of both employees and managers as it creates opportunities and challenges and boosts morale.
3. As we saw in chapter 11, all products have a life cycle, and some of a company's products will probably be in the decline stage. For a company just to maintain its position, it must pursue growth in some areas.

The question, then, is what is the best way in which to pursue growth. The growth matrix in figure 19–2 suggests four possible strategies: deeper penetration in the same market with the same products, offering new products to the same market, offering the same products to new markets, and **diversification,** or offering new products in new markets.[3]

Chapter 19 / Marketing Strategy

Figure 19–2 The growth matrix

	Product Dimension	
Market Dimension	Present Products	New Products
Present Markets	Market Penetration	Product Development
New Markets	Market Development	Diversification

Source: Igor Ansoff et al., *From Strategic Planning to Strategic Management* (Chichester, England: Wiley, 1976). Reprinted with permission of John Wiley & Sons, Ltd.

Deeper Penetration in the Same Market with the Same Products

In one growth strategy, a company takes its existing products and tries to penetrate the same market further. This strategy works best when there are a low number of users of the product, when the product is in an early stage of its life cycle, and when the company wants to increase the volume of production so that it can learn more about producing the product and, thus, create further production efficiencies. There are several actions a company can take to pursue this strategy. One is to establish or increase a promotional budget to communicate the features of the product to a wider range of consumers. A second is to reduce the price of the product to encourage price sensitive people to try it.

Offering New Products to the Same Market

If the market is already saturated with the existing product and the company cannot achieve deeper penetration, the company can offer new products to that same market. This strategy is often pursued when the company's existing products are in the mature stage of their life cycle and customers have established a high degree of brand loyalty to those products. This strategy can best be understood by considering the following example.

Levi Strauss had a major share of the college student blue jeans market, and it was very successful in that market. At a point that market became saturated, as every college student had and wore a pair of blue jeans. College students, however, were aware of Levi Strauss and had developed brand loyalty to it. The company, therefore, decided to pursue growth by introducing new products into this market. The first new products were also pants, but instead of the standard blue jeans, these had straight legs or bell bottoms or were pastel colored. The next step was to introduce new types of products—shirts, belts, hats, and so on. Because of the high degree of brand loyalty, it was relatively easy for Levi Strauss to succeed by offering new products.

Chapter 19 / Marketing Strategy

Offering the Same Products to New Markets

Another strategy is to offer the same products in new markets. This approach is often pursued when the existing market segment is saturated, when competition in that segment is intense, or when the company has a cost advantage in that it can create the products at lower cost levels than can the competitors. Implementing this strategy requires some changes in the company's marketing mix. The company may find that it has to modify its pricing strategy to attract customers in the new market, that it has to develop different ways to communicate with the market, and that it has to establish new distribution channels to reach the market. Levi Strauss also pursued this strategy by going after the female college student market. Its original customers had been college men, and although females wore Levi's, they wore products made for men. Levi Strauss took the same product—blue jeans—redesigned it, and aimed it at female college students. This same strategy was used to create blue jeans for children. Another example of this same strategy is the action taken by Johnson & Johnson in relation to its baby shampoo; after the baby market was saturated, the company sought adult buyers by advertising the product as "gentle enough to use every day" and by showing male athletes in their commercials as users of the product.

Figure 19–3 The first American Express headquarters, built in 1858. Since that time, the company has pursued a number of growth strategies.

Courtesy of American Express Archives

Chapter 19 / Marketing Strategy

Diversification: Offering New Products in New Markets

The final strategy that marketers can use to pursue growth is to diversify or offer new products in new markets. This is the riskiest and costliest strategy for a number of reasons. First, the company must set up new distribution channels and methods of promotion to reach the new market. Second, the company is dealing with a new set of customers; it does not know or understand the needs of those customers as well as those of its present customers. Moreover, the company does not have a reputation or image among the new customers and must establish awareness of itself. Third, the company may be providing new products that it has little experience with and knows little about; it is not known for selling these products, and it is not considered to be expert with them.

Why, then, do companies follow this strategy? For some companies, diversification may be seen as an opportunity to redefine the business or simply to survive. For other companies, it may be seen as the only possible way to grow as their markets are all saturated. Others who have products with cyclical sales may want to diversify into areas with a different schedule of cyclical sales; the overall result would be to even out the flow of business activities and revenue for the company. A final reason may just be that the lure of diversification is strong. Many companies pursued diversification for this reason in the 1970s, and many of the same companies have found themselves **divesting** themselves of these businesses in the 1980s.

There are two ways for companies to pursue diversification. The first is to acquire another company. For example, Coca-Cola decided to expand its mix of beverages and purchased Minute Maid. This approach works best when the company acquired is in an area in which the company has some expertise or when the acquiring and acquired companies can provide advantages—in technologies, markets, expertise, or finances—that support and enhance the other company. The other approach is to develop new products for new markets internally. AT&T pursued this approach in its development of computers; these were new products for them, and, while some of the consumers were the same, many of the targeted consumers were different from the existing customers of AT&T's communications products.

Focus 19–1 presents a discussion of how two companies are using a combination of these strategies to pursue growth.

Factors in Creating a Marketing Strategy

There are at least two popular adages that relate to marketing strategy. One is that gaining market share is generally the key to success in any business. A second is that it is easier to penetrate a market that is growing than one that is stagnant or shrinking. We will examine the bases of these notions as we review a variety of factors that are considered in creating marketing strategies.

19–1 Focus on Marketing Strategy
GROWTH STRATEGIES

R. J. Reynolds Industries, Inc. (RJR) is currently analyzing and rearranging its portfolio. At RJR's core is its tobacco business. RJR is investing the profits from cigarette sales in consumer companies, while it is considering pulling out of two businesses—Aminoil, Inc., an energy company, and Sea-Land Industries, Inc., an ocean shipper. RJR is expanding its involvement in its Del Monte Corporation, a food processing company; Kentucky Fried Chicken (KFC); and Heublein Inc., a spirits and wine company.

RJR is going after further penetration of the fast-food market by expanding the number of KFC outlets worldwide. From a current total of 6,000 outlets, there will be 7,800 outlets by 1988. The company is also working to improve quality and consistency of the outlets and the food served in them. Since 1982, the company has cut down the KFC menu and improved the training program.

Through Del Monte, RJR is seeking to attract diet-conscious customers with a new line of low-sodium and low-sugar products. RJR is using the same consumer-oriented strategy in Heublein by stressing the successful lighter-proof liquors, such as vodka and tequila. The company is also responding to consumers' wants in its cigarette business by reducing its operating costs in production to reduce cigarette prices.

By entering into food processing, fast-food restaurants, and the liquor business, RJR is diversifying from its tobacco business origins. Each of these acquisitions represents an entry into a new market area.

Another company, Dart & Kraft, Inc., is taking a different approach to growth. Dart & Kraft is now turning away from opportunities to enter markets that are very different from those for its core group of products. The company sees the key to future growth as expanding its strong brands, including Kraft cheeses, salad dressings, and Tupperware food-storage products, and acquiring related businesses, rather than diverse ones.

This view comes after several years of Dart & Kraft acquisitions in nonfood areas. During the late 1970s, company executives were attracted by the higher profit margins of businesses like Duracell, makers of batteries, and Hobart Corporation, kitchen appliance manufacturers. Disappointing sales and other problems, however, convinced Dart & Kraft to return its focus to food products. Executives now feel that the company's strong reputation with its food brands is its most valuable asset. Dart & Kraft is expanding its product line, offering new products to a strong existing market.

Dart & Kraft's latest acquisitions are also in the food area. The company recently purchased Celestial Seasonings, a profitable and growing business that makes herbal teas, and Lender's Bagel Bakery Ltd., makers of frozen bagels. Dart & Kraft is also expanding its cheese line with the acquisition of cheese manufacturer Churney Company.

Dart & Kraft's approach is to build on the areas of business it knows best, rather than to branch out into entirely new market areas. The company hopes to bring about higher profits by taking risks only in the areas where it has expertise and a good reputation.

Sources: "The Consumer Drives R. J. Reynolds Again," *Business Week*, June 4, 1984, pp. 92–99; and "Dart & Kraft Turns Back to Its Basic Business—Food" *Business Week*, June 11, 1984, pp. 100–5.

Gaining Market Share

An impressive volume of empirical data shows that market share correlates highly with a company's return on investment (ROI) and with other measures of profitability. Since market share is a measure of volume, a firm with a larger market share usually has a greater volume of business, a dominant brand name, and increased power to bargain with suppliers, distributors, and buyers. Gaining market share can thus be an important factor in marketing strategy.

Consider the following example. Coca-Cola began selling wine in 1977 through a division called the Wine Spectrum, which featured wines from New York State and California. But despite Coca-Cola's expertise in marketing, the new line failed to top the 27.7 percent market share held by the industry leader, E. & J. Gallo Winery. In fact, after six years in the business, Coca-Cola could muster only around 5 percent ROI, as compared with the 10 to 15 percent that the company earns on soft drinks and the 10 percent it earns on its Columbia Pictures. Given these results, Coca-Cola began looking for a buyer for the Wine Spectrum. At the same time, Seagram wanted to gain market share for its wine business, which includes the Paul Masson brand. Partly because many Americans have switched from drinking cocktails to wine, Seagram has watched its sales of distilled liquors slip. Anticipating greater profits by moving further into the wine industry, Seagram bought the Wine Spectrum. This acquisition immediately pushed Seagram up to the number two position in domestic wine, with an 11.2 percent share of the market. Diverse objectives of each company point out why Coca-Cola rid itself of an unprofitable venture while Seagram pulled in greater profits and market share from the same business.[4]

The experience curve. A heftier market share is also likely to enhance a company's experience curve. As we have seen, the experience curve demonstrates the fact that the more a company produces and sells, the better it becomes at those operations. As a result of this experience, a company develops greater efficiencies in production, in identifying sources of supply, and in other areas that reach well beyond the initial benefit of economies of scale.

For example, consider how the experience curve works at Boeing. Although the cost of manufacturing the first 767 aircraft will total nearly $100 million, the cost of making the fiftieth aircraft should slide to around $8 million. After making the first few planes, the company can reap more efficiencies as each successive 767 leaves the production line.

On the other hand, shaping a marketing strategy around the experience curve may cause problems for managers. What are the consequences of a steady doubling of production? What is the limit to which costs can be reduced? And after costs have been reduced as much as possible, what form should the company's next strategy take? These questions are important because if managers concentrate on cost cutting through increased production, the company may become vulnerable to changes in the market. For instance, this strategy gives a company little leeway to make changes in the product or match a competitor's innovative offerings.

Consider the case of NCR, which had invested heavily in the plant, equipment, and skilled workers to produce cash registers using the old electromechanical change boxes. When Burroughs introduced new machines featuring electronic change boxes, it took over NCR's position as market share leader.

To avoid the risks of this strategy and still enjoy some of its benefits, IBM has evolved a compromise. It remains the industry pace setter by bringing out products with major changes. However, in between new models, it relies on the experience curve for reducing costs. Although only companies with vast resources can manage this strategy, it does allow IBM to reap some efficiencies and still respond to new directions in the market.[5]

The profit impact of marketing strategies (PIMS). For strategy planners, a valuable source of information is the Profit Impact of Marketing Strategies (PIMS) data base of the Strategic Planning Institute. Gathering data from a number of major North American corporations, PIMS researchers seek to answer questions for marketing strategists. For example, how can managers estimate ROI in a new business? Although ROI fluctuates from year to year and industry to industry, PIMS research does show that ROI increases as market share expands. A recent study revealed that, on the average, businesses with market shares greater than 36 percent earned over three times as much, relative to investment, as did businesses that gained less than a 7 percent share of their markets. PIMS data thus show that, in companies typical of those surveyed, market share exerts a heavy influence on profitability.[6]

Market Growth

Another important factor in marketing strategy is the rate of growth within the targeted market. As the popular adage we mentioned earlier indicates, when a market is expanding slowly, it is difficult to gain market share. In such a market, competitors contend for relatively sluggish segments. As a company cannot expand its business by staying in a static market, marketers attempt to take sales from competitors in order to gain market share. The market will thus become intensely competitive, and companies may simply try to protect the market share they already have.

On the other hand, when a market is growing, companies can expect increased sales. Competitors are also likely to have increasing sales, so that everyone involved needs no longer to employ protective tactics, as in slow-growing markets. In growth markets, companies can increase sales without adversely affecting the competition. Thus, it is generally less costly to increase sales in markets that are growing than in those that are static or shrinking.

Consider the case of Sears. This middle-of-the-road retailer sells staple goods that are more practical than fashionable. "We're keenly aware that we're in a mature business," notes one top executive. While Sears still expects its retailing business to grow, it is investigating additional opportunities with strong growth potential. The success of Allstate Insurance, which Sears founded in 1931, suggested the potential of financial services. Sears purchased broker Dean Witter and real-estate

Courtesy of Sears, Roebuck

Figure 19–4
Perceiving financial services to be a market with strong growth potential, Sears acquired Dean Witter and Coldwell Banker to join with Allstate in its Financial Network.

firm Coldwell Banker in 1981, and these two firms, along with Allstate, form a financial network that sells financial services to Sears customers both in the Sears stores and through the Sears catalogue. Sears' large number of retail customers serves as a base for the financial services. Sears is also investigating other opportunities; industries in food and oil have been mentioned as likely candidates for future acquisitions.[7]

Portfolio Analysis

Sears' search for new growth markets demonstrates the importance of **portfolio analysis.** A **portfolio** is the collection of the businesses and products in which a particular company is involved. By studying the portfolio with a given strategy in mind, managers can decide which businesses should be continued and which should be sold. Portfolio analysis also guides the company toward appropriate new acquisitions. As we saw earlier in our discussion of American Express, a series of acquisitions can be highly profitable when a company's portfolio is managed carefully, following clear objectives.

Mergers and acquisitions are often made according to financial considerations, but marketing strategies can help to determine whether the latest addition to a company's portfolio will be a profitable one. When analyzing the portfolio, managers can ask several questions: Should the company enter this market? Should it

Chapter 19 / Marketing Strategy 554

drop an old product or business? Should it add a new one to its portfolio? Answering these questions involves marketers in identifying the current position of the firm's various products and in forecasting the demand for existing and proposed products. Additionally, marketers guide the company as it decides how to allocate marketing resources. Finally, marketers can aid corporate strategic planners by monitoring and communicating trends in the marketplace. Such new directions may require a change of strategy.[8]

As an example of the various marketing strategies for analyzing a company's portfolio, consider what happened at G. D. Searle & Co. This pharmaceutical company developed financial problems as it had made a series of unprofitable acquisitions. The company had gone on a purchasing spree that added such diverse businesses to its portfolio as medical drapes, instruments, and record forms. By selling off these unprofitable businesses, the company generated substantial amounts of cash that it put into its research department. Having severely limited its research efforts during the purchasing spree Searle was losing its grip on the drug business, its primary focus. By analyzing its portfolio and abandoning unprofitable businesses, Searle was able to push forward with new drug development, essential for achieving its overall objectives.[9]

The Boston Consulting Group (BCG) Matrix

A more specific technique of portfolio analysis has been developed by the Boston Consulting Group. This approach is generally known as the **BCG Matrix** (see fig. 19–5). The matrix shows that companies can divide their various businesses and product lines into four groups. The matrix itself is organized along two dimensions: market share and market growth.

Products in the upper left-hand corner, exhibiting high market growth and high market share, are known as *stars*. Stars are strong competitors in expanding

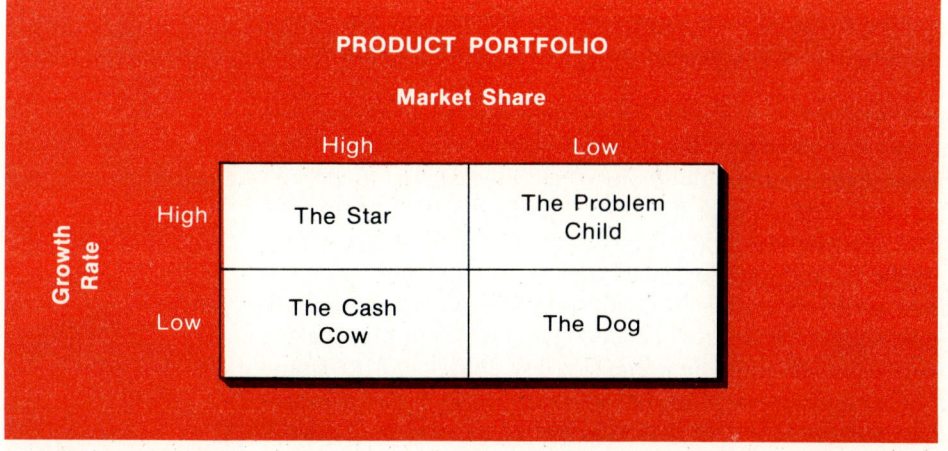

Figure 19–5 The BCG Matrix

© 1970 The Boston Consulting Group, Inc. All rights reserved. Published by permission.

Chapter 19 / Marketing Strategy

555

markets that are expected to contribute to the future profits of the firm. Those products in the lower left-hand corner, characterized by high market share but low market growth, are termed *cash cows*. They generate substantial funds used to finance new businesses. In the upper right-hand corner are products called *problem children*. Although the problem children are targeted at growing markets, these products have captured only a small market share in the face of competition. Finally, in the lower right-hand corner are the *dogs,* the unpromising products that compete poorly and are trapped in unattractive markets.

A strategy based on this matrix suggests several actions. Managers should try to gain more market share for their stars and for their problem children, possibly by investing in the product line or by making a promising acquisition. Energy would be wasted, however, by trying to increase the market share for the cash cows. Although they are highly profitable due to their high market share, the cash cows are either stuck in a mature market or are limited by the mature stage of their life cycle. An appropriate strategy for cash cows would be simply to maintain the market share already captured. The dogs should most likely be sold, allowed to atrophy, or dropped from the portfolio as they generate almost no cash and have no future.

The BCG Matrix suggests ways in which managers can generate funds to invest in the future. To accomplish this, a company should develop a portfolio that balances a herd of cash cows with a constellation of rising stars. With a balanced portfolio, the cash cows can provide substantial money to invest in the rising stars and problem children. As the company moves forward, stars may eventually become cash cows, while the cash cows may lose market share and turn into dogs. The problem children, also feeding off the cash cows, may eventually become stars. Any money made from selling the dogs can be used to aid the problem children.[10]

If a company's portfolio heavily favors one type of business over another, serious problems can arise. With too many stars, the company would constantly be searching for new cash to finance the stars' expansion. If the company has too many cash cows, the portfolio would look impressive for the present but would falter as the markets of the cash cows decline with the declining stages of the products' life cycles.

In helping managers to develop a marketing strategy, the BCG Matrix also highlights several important characteristics about each business. For example, dogs tend to operate with out-of-date equipment and only small investments in marketing and research and development. Despite their low market share, problem children tend to operate with modern plants and equipment, and they invest aggressively in marketing, research and development, and new products. Like the problem children, the competitive stars operate with modern equipment and substantial research and development expenses. Finally, the cash cows are like the dogs in that they use old-fashioned equipment and put few dollars into R&D and marketing campaigns.[11] This type of portfolio management marks a major transition from previous management policies that may have issued a mandate of growth to be applied equally to all products and businesses within the firm.

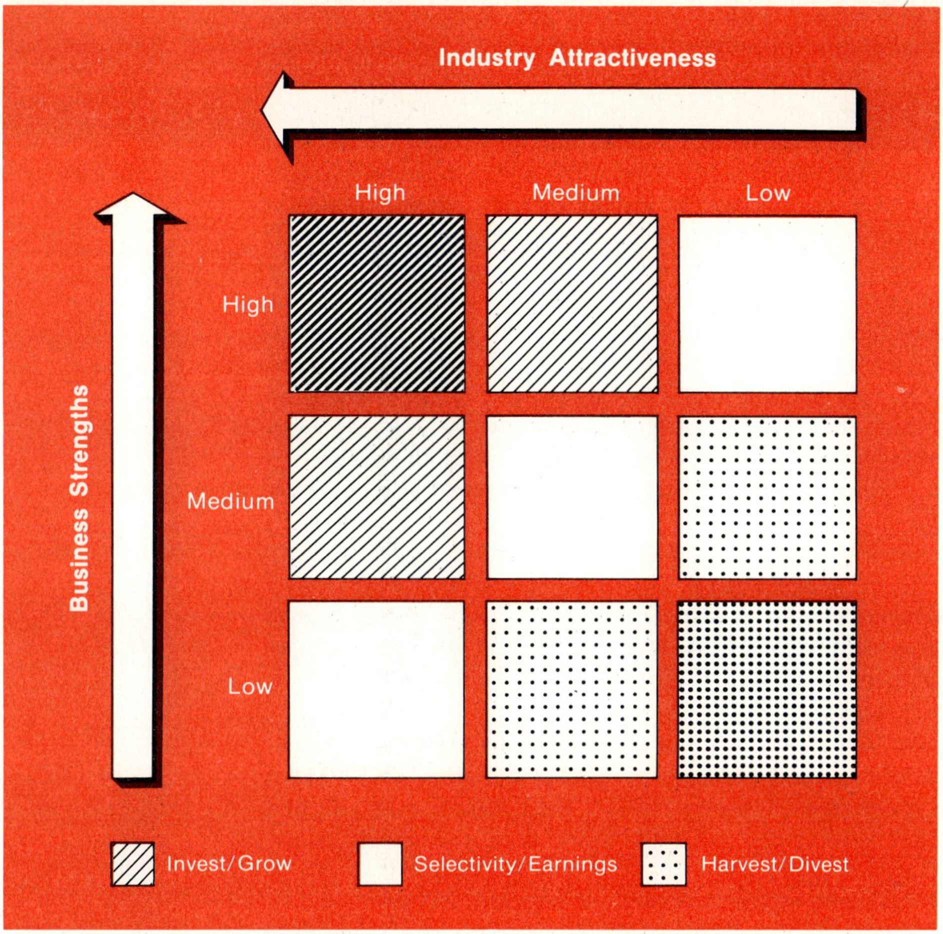

Figure 19–6 The General Electric Business Screen

Used with the permission of General Electric.

The General Electric (GE) Business Screen

The GE Business Screen is similar to the BCG Matrix. But rather than plan strategies around the specific dimensions of market share and growth, the GE Business Screen uses more general terms. As you will see in figure 19–6, the GE Business Screen plots the success of businesses along the horizontal axis of industry attractiveness, which is much like market growth. The vertical axis is determined by business strength, which is very similar to market share.

To see how the screen works, look at the upper left-hand corner, which represents those businesses that are investing and expanding. They are similar to the stars in the BCG Matrix. The products in the lower right-hand corner, as with the dogs of the BCG Matrix, can be sold or dropped from the portfolio.

The general terms used in the GE Business Screen are more appropriate to some businesses than are those in the BCG Matrix. For example, a market may not

Chapter 19 / Marketing Strategy

only be growing but also belong to an industry highly attractive for its generous profit margins. Additionally, business strength may not depend only on market share, but may come from competitive advantages. Some theorists thus recommend that marketing strategy depends not only on the potential of the market and product, but also on a firm's unique resources and abilities that may create the competitive advantage.[12]

When choosing a strategy on the basis of the GE Business Screen, managers can first evaluate a company's position on this screen. For example, a particular business might be in a very attractive industry, but the company may lack the strength to stay even or outpace the competition. In this case, managers can pull out of the business, invest heavily to develop a competitive advantage, or perhaps acquire a more promising company in the same industry. On the other hand, managers may find that a business is quite strong but that it does not belong to an attractive, profitable industry. In this instance, a prudent strategy would be to withhold investments and simply use the business to generate cash. If the business is neither strong nor in an attractive industry, then the best plan would be to abandon the market.

To Pioneer or to Follow

When deciding to introduce a product or acquire a new business, a company may choose to become a *pioneer* in the market. A less risky strategy is to wait for the competitors to enter and then *follow*, ready to learn from their mistakes. Each strategy offers advantages and disadvantages; let us consider them.

In becoming a pioneer, a company must weigh the risks involved. It is difficult, for example, to calculate the demand for a new product or to estimate the costs of entering and maintaining a position in a new market. The company may also find that it has heavy expenses in educating the marketplace about the benefits of the new product.

For aggressive and clever marketers, however, pioneering offers many attractions. In general, companies stand to earn even greater profits by pioneering than by playing the "me-too" imitators' game. As the pioneer, a company will have already benefited from the experience curve when competitors enter the market. With this benefit, the pioneering company can step up production, enjoy economies of scale, and cut costs while its competitors are still scrambling to develop a similar product. Once competitors' products are available, the pioneering firm can maintain its position by slashing prices or by refining product quality. A further advantage to this strategy is that the company can choose and control the best distribution channels. Additionally, the pioneer can mold the market's expectations of the product, shaping perceptions about price and quality. Finally, the first product will most likely appeal to a broad range of customers, allowing the company to develop a competitive and diverse product line.

Chesebrough-Pond's has profited by being a pioneer. When it introduced a new product, the "soft" home permanent called Rave, Chesebrough created and

Figure 19–7 Federal Express used a pioneering strategy by being the first company to offer a two-hour, door-to-door delivery service.

Reproduced with permission of Federal Express Corporation. All rights reserved.

proceeded to dominate a $100 million market. Rave is odorless and produces a soft curl, more fashionable than the tight curls associated with traditional home permanents like Gillette's Toni. Although Gillette and Procter & Gamble soon introduced their own soft home permanents, Chesebrough remained the market leader, capturing nearly a 27 percent market share.[13]

Many companies, however, deliberately adopt the strategy of following. For instance, the housewares division of General Electric had traditionally entered new markets soon after the pioneer had created a market. As a quick follower, GE often developed many new products but did not market them until a competitor educated the market and established distribution channels. Once the demand began to swell, GE introduced its products, ready to build on the groundwork laid by the first entrant. (The division was divested in 1984.)

The chief advantage of being a follower is that the follower can wait for the pioneer to find out whether a promising market exists. With this knowledge, the follower can then decide if the venture is worth pursuing. Also, the follower can more easily estimate the size of the market as well as the costs of entering it. In some cases, the follower may benefit from lower costs, as it can profit from mistakes made by the pioneer. Furthermore, the follower can wait to enter until the market swells to such a size that the company can immediately begin production with high economies of scale. The follower's strategy also permits a company to benefit from the advantages of segmenting a market. After the pioneer has established a broad base of customers, a company can then carve out its own niche by offering a product more precisely suited to the needs of a given segment. This strategy also permits the follower to choose a segment willing to pay a high price, if that is consistent with the company's objectives.

Barriers to Entry

Barriers that keep companies from entering a market can work in two ways. They can keep companies from being the first to enter a market. Or, once a pioneer has successfully established a position in a new market, barriers can keep rivals from entering and wooing away customers.

For example, consider how E. & J. Gallo Winery made business tough for Coco-Cola's Wine Spectrum, a division we discussed earlier. When Coca-Cola sought to establish a position in the wine business, Gallo set up several effective barriers by cutting prices and increasing advertising.[14] In another instance, Chesebrough fought off competitors to its Vaseline Intensive Care Lotion, a market leader. When Procter & Gamble and Nabisco introduced similar lotions, Chesebrough fought back by offering special pricing deals to retailers and two-for-one gimmicks to consumers.[15]

In addition to these approaches, there are other ways to bar competitors' entry. Various markets permit various kinds of barriers that allow companies to protect their domains. Some barriers are related to the concept of economies of scale; that is, companies must target a large enough market to make the investments in technology and production worthwhile. Pioneers can also hold off competitors by adopting the strategy of product differentiation. Advertising of special features, for instance, can help companies to create a range of unique products targeted for specific segments, eliminating most of the possible ways for competitors to differentiate their products. In the case of the detergent market, the main competitors—Colgate, Procter & Gamble, and Lever Brothers—have marketed such a range of products that it is very difficult for a new entrant to find and carve out an undiscovered niche. One example is the strategy used by Clorox to hold off competitors by differentiating its products; the company has recently test marketed a liquid bleach that is specially scented to hide the odor of chlorine.[16]

Some companies may simply choose not to enter a market because of the high investments of capital that are required. In other markets, already established companies have acquired tremendous cost advantages, often because of experience, knowledge about a specific technology, or ownership of raw materials. Take the case of foreign steel industries, which have developed new technologies. The U.S. steel industry would require a large investment to develop the same technologies, which thus erect a formidable barrier. Additionally, an aspiring competitor may find that the already established company has monopolized all the channels of distribution.

Competition

Competition in business requires managers to size up their rivals' strengths and weaknesses and be especially alert to market signals from competitors. A market signal is any covert or overt action that indicates a competitor's intentions. Although some signals are no more than bluffs, others may be warnings or smoke screens. It is not always easy to distinguish the true intention behind the signal. For instance, a larger firm may bring an antitrust suit against a smaller rival. But

Figure 19–8 By creating a shampoo and conditioner just for permed hair, Lamaur, maker of Perma Soft, has created its own niche in the highly competitive shampoo market.
Courtesy of Lamaur, Inc.

Chapter 19 / Marketing Strategy

the larger firm may not really be protesting an alleged infringement of the law. Instead, the company suing may actually want to punish the smaller company for stepping too far aground on turf already spoken for.[17]

Amid the forces of any given industry, only one or two companies generally survive. When several companies have targeted the same customers, eventually one firm will dominate due to a competitive advantage. More companies can, however, earn a profit in an industry if they carve out their own niches.

When evaluating the options for competing, managers should consider the virtues of "peaceful coexistence" among competitors. In such a state of relative peace, companies recognize the dangers facing all rivals when one competitor launches cutthroat tactics. These tactics can spark an often ruinous price war, as has happened in the airlines industry. Further, a company that does succeed in stamping out all competition must then be thinly spread across all segments, thereby open to attack from newcomers.[18]

Peaceful coexistence can also occur among competitors who have targeted different segments of the market. Each rival then carries a distinct advantage over the other, allowing the market to function with a balance of competition. On the other hand, when competitors are very similar to each other, the battles can turn bloody and exceptionally costly.[19]

Buyers and Suppliers

When planning marketing strategy, managers must also be aware of the needs of and the power held by buyers and suppliers. For example, the number and type of buyers influence the moves that managers can make. If a market is composed of only a few buyers, each buyer has power over the success of a product. Additionally, such a market is likely to support only a few brands, all aimed at the entire market rather than at a smaller segment, making the competition more intense. On the other hand, in a market with many buyers, each customer has only a small say in a product's success.

The type of buyers can further heighten or lower the intensity of competition. If buyers are flexible about the sort of product they choose, then they can exert a certain amount of pressure on their suppliers. But if companies depend on a product, then their suppliers have considerable power.

Similarly, as the number of suppliers increases, their individual capacity to exert pressure on buyers decreases. If the supplier's product is not essential to the buyer, then the supplier further loses clout. Furthermore, suppliers are at a disadvantage if substitutes for their products are readily available. However, if there are only a few suppliers of a product essential to the buyers, then suppliers can strike tough bargains.

The Marketing Plan

In formulating a strategy, marketing managers will develop a **marketing plan.** This plan functions as a road map, guiding the company along the best route to implementing a particular strategy. It identifies the company's businesses, target markets, and customers, as well as the services or products that the company will sell. In attempting to reach its chosen customers, the company will also use the marketing plan to establish the desired level of sales, percentage of market share, and profitability. The plan indicates how the company's product stands up to the competition. And, finally, a marketing plan outlines the specific marketing mix best suited to the firm's product.

As you will recall from earlier chapters, the marketing mix is a blend of the four P's—product, price, promotion, and place. In designing a marketing plan to capture a greater market share, managers need to analyze how each element contributes to this goal. That is, particular markets may require a greater emphasis on one of the four P's.

Throughout this book, we have discussed how various aspects of the marketing mix meet consumers' needs. For example, consumers purchasing morning newspapers may only be interested in how intensively they are distributed. Or consumers purchasing high-technology products may be most concerned about the accompanying services. Or consumers interested in gaining prestige may purchase only the most expensive products. Based on its knowledge of the needs of its consumers, then, the company shapes the marketing plan to allow for the creation of a marketing mix to meet those needs.

The marketing plan can also be shaped according to the company's chosen actions in relation to the competition. If the plan is to dominate rivals, then the company may create a marketing mix that gives it a competitive advantage in the particular market. If the company has decided to match competitors' actions, then the company will create and invest in a marketing mix that equals the competitors'.[20]

For any market, however, the marketing mix forms a cohesive package. Even if one element may require greater investments, managers must consider how each element relates to the others. Some elements do not work well with others, while other elements increase each other's effectiveness, producing a synergistic effect. Synergy can be briefly represented as $2 + 2 = 5$, an equation showing that the sum is greater than the parts. For example, companies may be able to grab a greater market share by combining the synergistic strategies of high price and heavy advertising. On the other hand, it is less profitable to combine high price with low advertising, since these tactics do not work well together.[21]

Budgeting

Traditionally, marketing strategies have played a limited role in **budget planning,** the process by which a company decides how to allocate resources. Marketers have usually been called upon only to provide sales forecasts, which have then been used by the financial and production departments to develop the specific amount of goods or services to meet the anticipated demand. As a result, a company's allocation of resources has been determined by the sales projections. However, alert budgeting and allocation of resources can further stimulate sales, even surpassing the expected level.

Let us look at the relationship between marketing and budgeting in more detail. The conventional practice, in which forecasted sales determine the budget, can stop the company from planning an optimum budget. Any sales forecast should be based on an assumed budget level. If the budget is changed, the amount of forecasted sales should be changed accordingly. The budget the finance department selects is based on what the forecasted sales would allow the firm to afford. This is not unreasonable. But the marketing department may not be able to meet the forecasted sales levels if the finance department does not give it the budget it based its forecasts on.

Above all, managers must bear in mind the company's mission and objectives and the corresponding objectives for the particular product. If these call for growth, then the budget can initially be high to promote increased sales. In addition, managers should decide (1) how much of the total budget will be given over to marketing expenses and (2) how the budgeted funds can be shared among various marketing efforts. To make these decisions, managers will need to evaluate how different consumers and markets respond to each effort strategy for the given product. For example, consumers are sensitive in varying degrees to the price of specific products. Consumers also vary from one geographic region to another in their responsiveness to different promotional campaigns and to different channels of distribution.

In each case, managers should try to estimate the effectiveness of specific marketing plans. Such information then permits a company to predict the results of a dollar spent on one product or in one particular region as opposed to the same dollar spent on another product or in another region or in another manner.[22]

Marketing Control

After a marketing plan has been established, a company cannot simply sit back and wait for the profits to roll in. Instead, a plan requires careful monitoring, or **marketing control,** to ensure that strategies are producing the desired results. In some cases, companies may have to take corrective action to guide their operations back to a profitable course. They may discover that some strategies have not been carried out properly or that others require changes, due to shifting trends in the competition, market, and economy.

Frequent review of a marketing plan is also important because any plan can become dated quickly. As an example, in the late 1960s, auto makers organized their factories to produce large numbers of big, gas-guzzling cars. Just ten years later, U.S. auto makers had to scramble and retool their factories to accommodate the new demand for small, fuel-efficient cars. Furthermore, marketing plans can go out of date in much less time than ten years. Competitors can introduce innovative products, government regulations may limit opportunities, and advertising costs may soar. A **strategy audit** helps companies to review their marketing plan and chart an altered course in response to these various trends.

To offer effective guidance, a strategy audit must meet several requirements.[23] It should cover a broad analysis of the company's marketing environment, objectives, strategies, and systems. It must be conducted by a person who is independent of the operation and can remain objective. And it must take a systematic approach. Additionally, it will incorporate a well-organized series of steps designed to diagnose specific problems, similar to an audit prepared by a public accountant. Finally, a strategy audit needs to be conducted periodically. Companies may lose valuable opportunities if they wait to audit their marketing plan only when business slumps. Instead, audits should be conducted when business is booming, as well as during slack times, to find ways of increasing business. By auditing strategies during prosperous periods, companies are also better equipped to prepare for changing demands and economic lows.

Figure 19–9 presents a strategy audit.[24] The audit is divided into two parts, the situation analysis and the planning profile.

The **situation analysis** gives companies the chance to take a hard look at all factors affecting the way in which strategies are shaped. These factors include the business definition and an assessment of a company's portfolio in terms of market growth and share. Also covered here are the critical factors that determine success in a given market with a specific product or service. For example, the critical success factors in the mainframe computer market once included technical expertise and customer service; now it is changing to include the availability of software and price. Other factors cover the competitive advantages that a company's product can offer.

In addition, the situation analysis draws a profile of the overall market as well as of specific segments. Following the steps of this audit, you will see that item F concerns the importance of ranking benefits sought by each segment. In the next three points of the audit, managers assess their competitors by first ranking them and then citing the major benefits that they offer. The next step is to analyze their key strengths. In the third step, item I, managers are to create a matrix that represents how well the product satisfies various customer needs. The last element in the situation analysis is the risk analysis, which asks managers to anticipate possible events and devise an alternate strategy.

Moving to the second part of the audit, you can see that the **planning profile** first covers objectives, which may be expressed in terms of profits, market share, or other goals. Next are strategic recommendations, which are tactics for achieving the stated objectives. The five-point marketing program design asks managers to outline tactics in specific detail. Finally, the last two stages of the planning profile require a manager's best estimate for revenues over five years and a method for measuring the effectiveness of the chosen strategy.

I. SITUATION ANALYSIS

A. Company Business Definition:

B. Company Portfolio (e.g., growth/share matrix):

C. Critical Success Factors for New Product/Service under Consideration:

D. Competitive Advantages and Uniqueness of New Product/Service:

E. Market Profile for New Product/Service (Total vs. Segments):

	Total	Segment A	Segment B	Segment C	Segment D
a. Size:					
b. Growth Rate:					
c. Projected Profitability:					
d. Technological Life Cycle Stage:					
e. Projected Market Share:					

F. Benefit Analysis:

Rank Order of Benefits Sought	Segment A	Segment B	Segment C	Segment D
(1)				
(2)				
(3)				
(4)				
(5)				

G. Competitive Analysis:

Major Competitors	Benefit 1	Major Benefits			
		Benefit 2	Benefit 3	Benefit 4	Benefit 5

H. Strength of Competitors by Segment:

Major Competitors	Segment A	Segment B	Segment C	Segment D

I. Competitive Positioning:

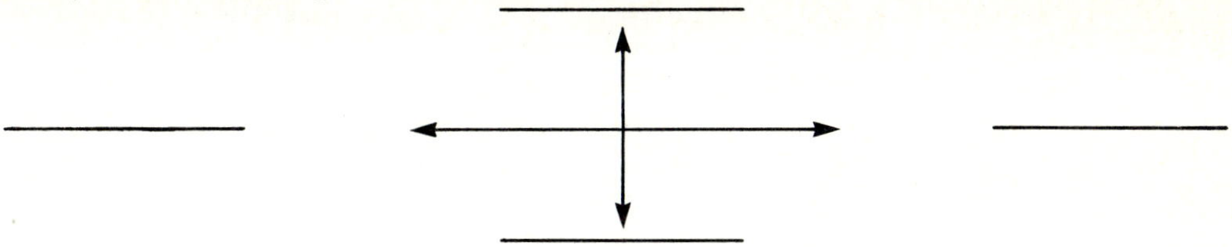

J. Risk Analysis:

    Event   Likelihood of   Possible
                               Occurrence   Impact
-
-

II. **PLANNING PROFILE**

    A. Objectives for New Product/Service (1984 vs. 1989):

    B. Strategic Recommendations for New Product:
-
-

    C. Marketing Program Design:
        1. Target Markets and Priorities
-
-

        2. Product Positioning
-
-

        3. Pricing Policy by Segment
-
-

        4. Promotional Program
-
-

        5. Distribution Program
-
-

    D. Revenue Share and Profitability Projections (by year, for 5 years):
-
-

    E. Measurement/Tracking System

Figure 19–9 The strategy audit
Used with the permission of David J. Reibstein and Thomas S. Robertson.

Summary

Marketing strategy involves matching a company's resources and skills with risks and opportunities in the marketplace. The general purpose of marketing strategy is to ensure a company's success and survival. One way to accomplish this is by establishing a competitive advantage through lower costs, control over distribution, and product differentiation.

Another major purpose of marketing strategy is to determine the nature and direction of the company's growth. There are four general strategies used to achieve growth. One is to take existing products and try to penetrate the same market further. The second is to offer new products to the same market. The third is to offer the same products to new markets. The final strategy is diversification, or offering new products in new markets.

A number of factors influence the creating of marketing strategy. Two major objectives of companies, gaining market share and market growth, lead companies to develop new strategies or analyze their present ones. Portfolio analysis, or the study of the company's collection of businesses and products, helps companies plan strategies for their present products, decide which products or businesses to develop or acquire, and recognize their unprofitable businesses. The Boston Consulting Group Matrix and the General Electric Business Screen are tools that can be used in portfolio analysis.

Another factor is whether the company should pioneer, or be the first to enter a market or develop a new product, or whether the company should follow, or wait for competitors to take these actions first.

Various barriers to entering a market and the actions of competitors and suppliers also affect a company's marketing strategy.

The formulation of marketing strategy leads to the development of the marketing plan, which identifies the company's businesses, markets, and customers, names the company's goals, and describes the strategy the company will follow.

Budget planning, or the process by which a company allocates its resources, is part of the development of marketing strategy. Marketing control, or the system a company uses to evaluate or revise its marketing strategy, helps the company determine the effectiveness of its marketing plan. The strategy audit is a tool that can be used in the marketing control process.

Questions for Discussion

1. Why is growth so important for companies?
2. Under what conditions would a marketer penetrate the same product or market deeper?
3. "Since diversification is the riskiest and costliest growth strategy, companies are well advised not to grow through diversification." Comment.
4. Examine the importance of portfolio analysis in making marketing strategy decisions.
5. Differentiate between the Boston Consulting Group Matrix and the General Electric Business Screen approaches to marketing strategy decisions.

6. Discuss the advantage of employing pioneering in marketing strategy.
7. Identify the different components of a comprehensive marketing plan.
8. Evaluate critically how strategy planning and budgetary planning can support each other.
9. Compare the "cash cows" and "dogs" in terms of the Boston Consulting Group Matrix.

References

1. Bill Abrams, "American Express Is Gearing New Ad Campaign to Women," *Wall Street Journal,* August 4, 1983, p. 23; and "The Golden Plan of American Express," *Business Week,* April 30, 1984, pp. 118–22.
2. Pamela G. Hollie, "Gillette Deodorant Strategy," *New York Times,* February 15, 1984, pp. D1, D4.
3. Igor Ansoff et al., *From Strategic Planning to Strategic Management* (New York: Wiley, 1976).
4. "Vintage Deal," *Time,* October 10, 1983, p. 53.
5. The discussion of experience curves is based on Walter Kiechel III, "The Decline of the Experience Curve," *Fortune,* October 5, 1981, pp. 139–46.
6. Sidney Schoeffler, Robert D. Buzzell, and Donald F. Heany, "Impact of Strategic Planning on Profit Performance," *Harvard Business Review,* March–April 1974, pp. 137–45.
7. "Sears' Strategic About-Face," *Business Week,* January 8, 1979, pp. 80–83.
8. Yoram Wind, "Marketing and Corporate Strategy," *The Wharton Magazine,* Summer 1982, pp. 38–45
9. "Searle: Rallying a Drug Company with an Injection of New Vitality," *Business Week,* February 8, 1982, pp. 98–99.
10. Walter Kiechel III, "Oh Where, Oh Where Has My Little Dog Gone? Or My Cash Cow? Or My Star?" *Fortune,* November 2, 1981, pp. 148–53.
11. Donald Hambrick, Ian MacMillan, and Diana L. Day, "Strategic Attributes and Performance in the BCG Matrix—a PIMS-Based Analysis of Industrial Product Businesses," *Academy of Management Journal,* September 1982, pp. 510–29.
12. Michael E. Porter, *Competitive Strategy* (New York: Free Press, 1980), p. 12.
13. "Chesebrough: Finding Strong Brands to Revitalize Mature Markets," *Business Week,* November 10, 1980, pp. 73–76.
14. "Vintage Deal," p. 53.
15. "Chesebrough," *Business Week.*
16. "Clorox: An R&D Game Is Brightening Its Profit Picture," *Business Week,* April 23, 1984, p. 113.
17. Michael E. Porter, *Competitive Strategy* (New York: Free Press, 1980), pp. 75–87.
18. Philip Kotler and Ravi Singh, "Marketing Warfare in the 1980s" *Journal of Business Strategy,* Winter 1981, pp. 30–41.
19. Bruce D. Henderson, "The Anatomy of Competition," *Journal of Marketing,* Spring 1983, pp. 7–11.

20. Victor J. Cook, Jr., "Marketing Strategy and Differential Advantage," *Journal of Marketing*, Spring 1983, pp. 68–75.
21. Paul W. Farris and David J. Reibstein, "How Prices, Ad Expenditures, and Profits Are Linked," *Harvard Business Review*, November–December 1979, pp. 173–84.
22. John M. McCann and David J. Reibstein, "Incorporating Marketing into Corporate Planning Models."
23. Philip Kotler, William Gregor, and William Rodgers, "The Marketing Audit Comes of Age," *Sloan Management Review*, Winter 1977, pp. 25–43.
24. This strategy audit was prepared by David J. Reibstein and Thomas S. Robertson and is used with their permission.

CASES FOR PART IV

16 RCA Videodiscs

In the spring of 1984, RCA Corporation announced it would stop making videodisc players, machines that play recordlike discs of movies or other presentations for viewing on a television screen. RCA began developing the product as early as 1970, and the players were once considered the company's most promising new product. Since 1981, RCA lost almost $350 million dollars, bringing total losses on the product to about $575 million. From the beginning, sales were disappointing, and market pressures forced the company to drastically reduce the price of the player. When they were first introduced, the players cost around $700; by 1984, their price had dropped as low as $150.

The failure of RCA's videodisc player could have been due to the company's interpretation of the market for rapidly changing video electronics technology. In the early seventies, the company chose to develop a product for the home-viewing market. At the time, RCA had a choice between developing a videocassette recorder (VCR) or a videodisc player. RCA chose to develop the videodisc player for three main reasons. First, the company believed that the technology involved in the VCR manufacturing process could not be significantly improved. Second, RCA thought that VCR prices could not be cut enough for the mass consumer market and that the lower-priced videodisc player would be more saleable. Third, RCA believed consumers would be more attracted to their videodisc player because movie disc prices ranged from $10 to $20, while movies on videocasettes cost between $80 and $90.

Unfortunately, RCA was wrong on all counts. Two Japanese companies, Sony Corporation and Matsushita-Kotobuki Electronics Industries, made important improvements in VCR production technology. Also, new miniaturization techniques allowed them to reduce VCR prices, shrinking both the equipment and the price gap between the VCR and videodisc player. Finally, RCA failed to anticipate the success of the movie rental industry.

In addition, RCA failed to develop the features of videodisc players to keep up with consumer demand. The company's videodisc player did one thing only: It played videodiscs. Other manufacturers developed a random-access function that allowed viewers to direct the player to any place on the disc, to start playback at any point. This function is particularly desirable in industrial and commercial settings. Stores using the player as a catalog of merchandise, for example, can access any group of items. European and Japanese manufacturers had included this feature for many years, while RCA introduced a less effective version of this feature as a last-ditch effort. All videodisc players lack another important function: the ability to record. A major reason consumers buy the VCR is because of its ability to record television programs for later viewing. The videodisc player has only the capacity to play prerecorded programs.

Even though RCA discontinued the player, the videodisc itself is still a living product. The company plans to continue producing the discs for about three more years for the 500,000 videodisc players that have already been sold and for the many thousands of remaining players the company hopes to sell before entirely shutting down this area of its operations. RCA says that its videodiscs have always sold well. While the company originally expected to sell an average of 11 discs per player, actual sales have been closer to 30 discs per player. CBS Inc. and other entertainment and movie companies also plan to continue producing new programs on videodiscs.

Sources: Based on "RCA's Rivals Still See Life in Videodiscs," *Business Week,* April 23, 1984, pp. 88–90; and Andrew Pollack, "Losses Lead RCA to Cancel Videodisc Player Production," *New York Times,* April 5, 1984, pp. A1, D25.

Questions

1. Why was the videodisc market important to RCA?
2. Is there a market for videodiscs? If yes, what is it? If no, why not?
3. What were the main reasons for RCA's failure in this market?
4. What could RCA have done to prevent its failure in this market?
5. How could marketing research have been conducted to improve the decision making in this market?
6. How similar is this situation to those faced by similar technologically advanced consumer products?

17   Dana Corporation

Dana Corporation, a manufacturer of parts for automobiles, trucks, and industrial machines, was regarded in the 1970s as one of the nation's best-run companies. Its ability to increase productivity while lowering costs contributed to its strong financial record. This financial success was clearly visible in the company's bottom line as profits catapulted from $62 million in 1975 to $164 million in 1979. Its sales were drawn from three general markets: original-equipment auto and truck parts, replacement parts, and industrial machine components.

The 1980 recession was particularly damaging to Dana, largely because of an overemphasis in one segment of the original-equipment market—light-truck parts. Dana's earnings for the nine months ended May 31, 1980, were reportedly down 32 percent from the previous year, to $85.7 million; sales over the same period had declined 8 percent, to $2 billion.

Light trucks, which had come to represent 35 percent of Dana's sales, lost customer appeal because of their heavy gasoline consumption. As Dana had taken on all the light-truck business it could, General Motors and Ford had come to represent two-fifths of its total sales volume. On the basis of its business in this market segment, Dana continued to order new equipment and to increase its light-truck parts production, thus increasing its dependence on auto parts.

In the first five months of 1980, Detroit's sales of light trucks were down 34 percent from 1979. Although Dana tried to cancel orders for and rid itself of $85 million worth of new equipment, it still found itself having to pay for $20 million worth. In May 1980, responding to the market slowdown, Dana permanently shut down 50 percent of its light-truck manufacturing capacity.

At the same time, Dana executives decided to diversify. In 1980, the company purchased a savings and loan holding company and a small insurance company, and set up a financial holding company under which it could operate its financial businesses. Executives at Dana believed that this expansion into financial services, a completely new area for the firm, was a natural development, given its success at cutting corporate expenses. A factor that contributed heavily to Dana's containment of costs was the internal financial services that Dana had initiated five years earlier in response to rising insurance rates, growing leasing costs, and foreign currency fluctuations. Having realized cash savings through these services, Dana executives believed that they had learned enough to offer them commercially.

From 1980 to 1982, Dana struggled to recover from the steep decline in light-truck parts. The financial services operation was not a focus of management attention. Dana's earnings in 1982 fell 46 percent below 1980 earnings, to $52 million, the lowest in ten years. Sales fell 11 percent in 1982, to $2.4 billion. Dana closed five plants and laid off one-third of its U.S. employees. In 1983, a rebound in the cyclical original-equipment parts market (which can fluctuate 40 percent in a year) bolstered Dana's sales, and company earnings rose to $112 million, on sales of $2.8 billion.

Under Dana's holding company, Diamond Financial Holdings, Inc., Dana's financial services had expanded by 1984 to include savings and loan, insurance, leasing, and real-estate development operations. Although the financial services remained only marginally profitable, Dana executives expected them to supply 10 percent of the company's 1984 earnings, and 20 percent of earnings by 1989.

The replacement market for auto and truck parts (which is considerably less cyclical than the original-equipment market) appeared as Dana's most promising market in 1984. By 1989, Dana set a goal of increasing its replacement parts business to account for as much as 40 percent of net earnings, up from less than 30 percent in 1984. Dana's marketing strategy also calls for original-equipment business to contribute about 30 percent of earnings in 1989, compared with an estimated 50 percent in 1984. Dana's industrial business is expected to generate the remaining 10 percent of 1989 company profits.

Sources: Based on "Dana: As Light Trucks Stall, A Push into Financial Services," *Business Week,* July 21, 1980, pp. 98–100; and "Dana: Repairing Its Profit Machine by Pushing Replacement Parts," *Business Week,* May 7, 1984, p. 63.

Questions

1. What was the cause of Dana's sales and earnings drop in 1980? Could it have been avoided?
2. What are the risks of concentrating sales in one or two industries (that is, focusing on businesses the company really knows well)?
3. Evaluate the decision by Dana to diversify.

4. Regardless of whether or not you believe Dana should diversify, evaluate its move into financial services.
5. Do you expect Dana to achieve its goals? Why or why not?
6. Evaluate Dana's marketing management. On the basis of the information in the case, are they good marketing managers?

PART V
Facets of Marketing

OBJECTIVES

1. To understand the nature and importance of international marketing.

2. To examine the role of and the problems in conducting marketing research before making international marketing decisions.

3. To identify the factors considered in making international marketing decisions.

4. To describe the different ways of entering international markets.

5. To recognize some of the special problems involved in international marketing.

20

International Marketing

President Reagan's 1984 trip to the People's Republic of China marked some significant improvements in relations between the two countries. At the same time, China is undergoing major political changes under the leadership of Deng Xiaoping. Deng's policies appear to be much more capitalistic than those of his predecessor, Chairman Mao Tse-tung. The current leader believes in offering "incentives" for labor, enabling Chinese workers to earn many times their annual income under Mao. Import and export regulations have also been relaxed. With more money to spend and more lenient trade regulations, China is becoming an increasingly important market for American products.

But the situation is complex. Minor fluctuations in Chinese-American relations can drastically change opportunities for trade. One sensitive point is this country's relationship with Taiwan. In 1982, Reagan agreed to reduce the sale of arms to Taiwan and eased export regulations governing American high-tech products. The result was a friendlier China and an expanded market for U.S. products. However, these doors could slam shut on trade between the two countries as quickly as they have opened.

In Mao's day, farmers worked in large communes under the authority of "team leaders." Today, Deng has dropped the commune system in favor of one that offers financial rewards to farmers for extra production. After producing a contracted amount for a set price, farmers can now sell surplus either for the going price on the open market or for a 50 percent markup to the government. The new system has increased both production and farmers' earnings. A Peking newspaper recently featured a story on the first Chinese farmer to own a car. Now earning $18,000 per year, chicken farmer Sun Guiying purchased his own brand-new Toyota.

Another key to increased consumerism in China is a new acceptance of outsiders and the government's desire to modernize. In the past, Chinese culture has emphasized deep respect for the country's history as well as mistrust of outsiders. Recently, China has increased the number of people permitted to study abroad from almost zero in 1974 to nearly 10,000 Chinese students in the United States alone in 1984.

The Chinese are admitting more foreign business also. A town that was once a small fishing village is now a home away from home for foreign businesses, including PepsiCo, Sanyo, and Citibank. Color television sets, stereo systems, and refrigerators are now common possessions for residents working for these companies. Many own their own homes as well.

In the cities, changes are even more evident. Residents dress in popular Western styles. Imported cars and buses have been added to the bicycle traffic. A large hotel is modeled after an American Holiday Inn. In Peking, close to 130 American businesses have set up shop. Trade between the United States and China is 50 times what it was in 1972, reaching $5.5 billion in 1984.

Despite the seemingly vast transformation, however, China is such a large country that many cities and more remote areas will not experience changes for many years to come. Also, many people distrust the government's recent support for enterprising individuals, fearing it will change, just as many other government policies have changed.

While these policies are in effect, however, many Western products are becoming increasingly popular with Chinese consumers. Cosmetics sales have increased 31.5 percent since 1983. Plastic surgery for women and permanent waves and aerobics classes for men are also on the rise. The Chinese are hungry for American and Japanese computers, television sets, and stereo equipment. China offers an expanding market for many U.S. businesses. In entering this market, however, Americans need to be aware of the influences of a foreign culture, international politics, and a government and country undergoing rapid and unpredictable change.[1]

In many ways, international marketing is not much different from other forms of marketing, and most of what has already been discussed in this book applies to it, too. The main difference is that the target market segments are outside of the United States, and the company's marketing strategy must be adapted to these different segments. This chapter is going to look at the factors companies must consider in moving into this new market segment. These include the marketing environment that affects the decision to go abroad, the factors that affect the choice of international markets, the possible ways to enter international markets, and necessary adaptations of the marketing mix to international markets.

The International Marketing Environment

For many companies, the trade environment of the 1980s requires taking advantage of international marketing opportunities. But international marketing is a complex and vast undertaking involving many managerial responsibilities, as the following definition suggests: **International marketing** spans researching, planning, and implementing all entry strategies—from exporting to culturally similar and physically proximate markets like Canada to producing and marketing out of a wholly-owned subsidiary in a culturally exotic, poor, and distant market like Bangladesh.

Moreover, a number of factors in the marketing environment affect international marketing. These include: saturated markets at home unable to absorb the products of American companies; the rise of international competition threatening market shares and profits of U.S. firms in product lines like textiles, automobiles, steel, and electronics; rapid technological advances in new products demanding aggressive marketing to retain customer loyalties in once comfortable, established markets at home and abroad; and economic realities.

To get a sense of the economic realities, consider the importance of export marketing to a healthy domestic economy. First, the share of U.S. productive output that is exported has steadily increased from 4 percent in 1950 to 8 percent in 1979, and to an estimated 13 percent for 1983. Second, exports create jobs: from

1977 to 1980, 79 percent of all new jobs in the manufacturing sector were directly linked to exports. Despite these factors, evidence abounds that the health of our export economy is shaky at best. The last time the United States had a **trade surplus** (more exports than imports) was in 1975; by 1982 the **trade deficit** (more imports than exports) surged to $42.7 billion, with $60–$70 billion estimated for 1983, and for 1984, $100 billion. The rising deficit may be traced partly to the fact that in their struggles to pay the interest on their staggering foreign debts, developing countries around the globe have cut back imports from 20 percent to 40 percent. For each $1 billion lost in exports, there are between 25,000–40,000 fewer U.S. jobs. Finally, the healthy surplus in services exported declined by 28 percent in 1982. The economic realities are becoming more complex with the growth in **countertrade,** as can be seen in focus 20–1.

The international marketer is confronted by a larger set of challenges when the firm opens production facilities overseas. Lower costs have motivated U.S. firms to invest directly in foreign countries, although they encounter problems when dealing with foreign economies and political systems. The debt crises confronting third world developing nations like Brazil and smaller, industrialized nations like Belgium add yet another stimulus to direct investment overseas. Government policy within these nations now discourages imports of foreign goods; instead, foreign corporations are encouraged to set up production facilities locally.[2]

This brief introduction shows that international marketing is shaped by environmental factors and economic realities both at home and overseas. By recognizing this, marketers can better make decisions about going abroad, select the best foreign markets to enter, and target the more profitable and appropriate segments within their borders.

Choosing International Markets

After the international marketer has made the decision to go abroad, the next step is to choose the specific markets to enter. The choice is based on the information collected about a number of factors.

Collecting information through marketing research is essential to identify the most attractive markets, to isolate the best segments within markets, and to gain an understanding of consumers' needs. As with marketing research in domestic markets, accurate, up-to-date marketing research is a critical step to successful international marketing.

There can be problems in conducting international marketing research. Data collection is often complicated by the sheer number of markets for which information must be collected, the availability and reliability of statistics, the researcher's inexperience with foreign marketing systems, language barriers, and simple physical distance. The small size of many markets, especially in the third world, may not

The Role of Marketing Research in Identifying and Segmenting International Markets

20–1 Focus on Marketing Practice
COUNTERTRADE

Countertrade is a system of exchange that uses goods for payment instead of money. We usually think of this practice as a primitive form of exchange that was long ago replaced by the use of currency. On the contrary, countertrade is increasing, particularly in international transactions. While companies most often prefer exchanging their products for cash, countertrade is sometimes a necessary alternative. Poorer nations are apt to have limited cash available, and a countertrade transaction may be the only way they can buy. One research firm estimates that countertrade accounts for up to 25 percent of all international trading.

General Motors Corporation's subsidiary company, Motors Trading Corporation, sells GM products in foreign markets. Often the transactions are part of a counterpurchase agreement: Motors Trading buys a country's goods on the condition that the country will purchase GM products. Motors Trading first finds buyers for the foreign goods or determines that GM can use them itself before entering such an agreement. In countertrade agreements with China, GM has bought low-priced industrial gloves and cutting tools that the company uses in its own production operations. GM has also received Chinese vacations for employees. Chrysler Corporation enters fewer countertrade agreements than does GM and then only after attempts to make a cash sale have failed. Jamaica recently paid for Chrysler vehicles in bauxite. The United States has also received Jamaican bauxite in return for surplus dairy products. McDonnell Douglas has struck a deal with Canada in which the company will buy parts from Canada and agree to find buyers for other Canadian goods. In return, the Canadians are buying $2.4 billion worth of McDonnell Douglas jet fighters over a 15-year period. A company in West Germany has sold $9 million worth of hydraulic truck cranes to the Soviet Union. In return, the Germans will buy a certain amount of Soviet goods.

Critics of the countertrade system believe that this kind of exchange increases the cost of goods up to 40 percent by adding the cost of extra paperwork and fees for intermediaries to negotiate the deals. At the same time, many companies maintain that they gain business through countertrade that would elude them otherwise.

Some countertrade deals backfire, however. As payment for jets sold to Yugoslavia, McDonnell Douglas received $3 million in canned hams for which the company had reportedly had difficulty finding a buyer. The company ended up using much of the ham in its own employee cafeterias. According to the Department of Commerce, only one in four countertrade contracts is fulfilled completely. Chemical Bank's Export Advisory Service recommends that businesses be entirely clear on the quality of the countertraded goods they expect to receive, as well as insuring that the agreement will be fulfilled within a short period of time.

Sources: Michael Doan, "As Barter Deals Spread, So Does U.S. Concern," *U.S. News and World Report*, January 16, 1984, p. 48; Philip Maher, "The Counter Trade Boom," *Business Marketing*, January 1984, pp. 50–56.

justify the "knowledge investment" required to overcome these research problems.³

Several research strategies offer partial remedies to these problems. First, marketing research must begin with a definition of the research problem, including creative identifications of markets and customers. For example, in third world markets where income distribution is highly skewed, a creative definition may lead to the identification of institutions rather than households as customers for costly durable goods. Second, the researcher should be flexible in selecting marketing research techniques and matching them to data limitations. Third, the data collection effort should not focus only on the foreign market. Factors within the U.S. market must be researched carefully to determine how they restrict the firm's freedom in shaping the international marketing plan. These factors include the products offered, foreign markets selected, financial resources available to launch and implement the international marketing strategy, and the economic and legal environments both in the United States and in the foreign market. For example, antiboycott regulations within the United States prevented U.S. firms from adhering to Middle Eastern nations' boycotts on trading with Israel; this limited the amount of business conducted between the U.S. firms and the Middle Eastern nations.

Factors to Consider in Choosing International Markets

The marketing research surveys study and analyze various factors within foreign markets and their importance to the decision about which foreign markets to enter. These factors include: economic-financial factors, political-legal factors, cultural factors, demographic factors, and trade agreements (see fig. 20–1).

Economic-financial factors. *Economic-financial factors* within a country affect the ability of a company to conduct business in it. The first and perhaps the most important economic factor is the *amount of foreign debt carried* by that country, especially if the country is an export destination. The effect of the third world debt crisis on U.S. exports over the past two years was termed "staggering" by U.S. Trade Representative William Brock.⁴ The reduction in U.S. trade with the eight largest debtor nations in Latin America contributed to some two-thirds of the enormous U.S. trade deficit over the past two years. The amount of foreign debt a country carries has a ripple effect on the economy overall and touches the country's foreign exchange position and exchange rates; for example, it may lead to tight government controls on wages and prices along with barriers on nonessential imports.

The second factor is the *income distribution within potential markets,* especially those within the third world. How income is distributed through the population may be useful in predicting the types of consumer needs and demands, as well as the types of products that may be sold there and the quantities that may be sold. For example, if the population of a country is divided into a tiny wealthy class and the rest of the population living at the subsistence level, the country probably has only a small target market for luxury, high-technology, and electrical products.

Economic-Financial Factors

- Amount of foreign debt carried
- Income distribution within the market
- Amount of foreign investment already in the market
- Natural resource base
- Inflation rate

Political-Legal Factors

- Role of government in business activities
- Stability of government
- Barriers to international trade
- Laws and regulations affecting the marketing mix
- Laws and regulations affecting business activities
- Stability of the work force
- Political relations with trading partner

Cultural Factors

- Style of business within the market
- Attitudes toward bribes and questionable payments
- Language, race and nationalities, geographic divisions
- Role of institutions, religious groups, educational system, mass media, family

Demographic Factors

- Number of organizations within the market
- Size and quality of work force
- Population size and growth rate
- Composition of households
- Geographic distribution and density of population

Trade Agreements

Figure 20–1 The factors to consider in choosing international markets

If a U.S. firm is considering investing overseas, the economic variables already mentioned may apply, especially when the products produced will be consumed locally. The firm might also analyze the third factor, the *amount of foreign investment already in the market,* as the successes of current foreign investors over time reflect the banking and financial environment and the tax structure in that market.

The fourth factor is the *natural resource base.* If the market is dependent on one natural resource for its export earnings, such as copper or silver, the long-term attractiveness of this market is questionable, as supply and demand relationships can shift. For example, the oversupply of oil and accompanying price drop in the early 1980s left some Middle Eastern countries that formerly had trade surpluses with trade deficits.

The fifth factor is the *inflation rate.* Inflation rates are nowhere more dramatic than in Argentina, which recorded the world's highest inflation rate of 433.7 percent for 1983 consumer prices. In December 1983, to cope with the problem, Argentina's new government reacted by freezing prices of some 30 essential items, including basic foodstuffs. This action had an incalculable effect on companies with product lines directly affected by the price freeze and on foreign investors who had to deal with inflationary effects on supplies, wage rates, and prices.

Political-legal factors. An analysis of the foreign market's **political-legal factors** begins with an assessment of the *role of the government* and whether it acts as a participator in or regulator of business activities. While the U.S. government qualifies more as a regulator, in the centrally planned economies of Eastern Europe and the USSR the government regulates and participates in business.

A second factor is the *stability of the government* and the laws, regulations, and policies it produces. For the foreign company operating in Italy, for example, there have been some 43 new governments between World War II and mid-1983.[5] However, with a market like Italy, dealing with changes in the political-legal environment has a somewhat routine quality, especially since all the governments up to 1981 were dominated by one political party. In contrast, the unexpected fall of the Shah of Iran essentially reinforced the need for a **country-risk analysis,** which is an analysis of the factors that increase the risk of doing business with a country.

The third factor concerns *barriers to international trade,* which differ depending on the extent of the firm's involvement in the country. The exporter must be particularly concerned with barriers affecting entering the market and profitability, including **tariffs,** which are taxes imposed on imported products, and **quotas,** which establish the absolute volume that can be imported.[6]

Some non-tariff barriers affect what businesses can be conducted overseas. For example, non-tariff barriers in the form of limited access to bids on equipment contracts have long restricted U.S. exports of telecommunications equipment to Japan because of the government-owned telecommunications monopoly in that country.[7] Other non-tariff barriers include customs documentation requirements, marks of origin, and labeling, food, and drug laws. Barriers are generally created and administered to protect domestic industries.

A fourth factor to consider is the *laws and regulations affecting the marketing mix.* Some of these include: (1) legal restrictions on product ingredients, safety features, or the language or content of product labels; (2) protection of rights to patents, brands, or trademarks;[8] (3) restrictions on content of promotional messages and access to media channels (Sweden, for example, prohibits commercials on radio and television);[9] (4) administration of pricing requirements; and (5) regulations for various transportation modes.[10]

The firm investing heavily overseas, perhaps setting up production facilities, must assess a more extensive set of political-legal factors. One factor is the *laws and regulations affecting business activities.* In the United States, regulatory agencies, such as the Occupational Health and Safety Administration, Environmental Protection Agency, and Consumer Products Safety Commission, are concerned with various areas of business activity. Other countries have similar types of regulations and regulatory agencies.

Figure 20–2 A scene in the Peking free market, where the private buying and selling of products is allowed. In countries with centrally planned economies, the ability of a marketer to price and distribute products may be limited.
©Michal Heron 1982

Figure 20–3 The style of business and business practices in this outdoor market in Togo represent cultural factors that must be understood by international marketers.
United Nations/B. Wolff

The foreign investor must also evaluate the *stability of the work force.* For example, in the 1980s the French government's efforts to modernize its industry raised the possibility of large-scale layoffs in industries such as automotives, steel, shipbuilding, and coal. Layoffs at Peugeot, a company that manufactures automobiles, divided French unions and caused fights between strikers and nonstrikers, requiring management to close one of its plants in early 1984.[11] Obviously, union dissidence and violence can wreck the best-laid production plans.

An assessment of political-legal factors must also include the foreign country's current *political relations with the trading partner.* A case in point is the United States government's limits on exports of sophisticated robots, robot control systems, and inputs for robot production to Eastern European nations and the Soviet Union. In addition to the direct impact on U.S. manufacturers, this policy also affects companies in allied Western countries. For example, the Swedish firm Asea feels the impact of U.S. controls since the United States supplies essential chips and microprocessors that go into its no-frills robot developed for export to Eastern Europe.[12]

Cultural factors. Engaging in international marketing demands a careful understanding of all **cultural factors** and practices. Regardless of the degree of involvement, the American marketers' cultural adeptness can determine success or failure in interactions with the local work force and the firm's customers, suppliers, distributors, competitors, investors, and regulatory agencies. An understanding of the first factor, the *style of business within the market,* must include (1) how decisions are made within organizations; (2) the meaning of time in negotiations and production schedules; (3) cultural practices regarding silent language such as accepted gestures and appropriate physical distance; and (4) culturally unique business practices. For example, in Hong Kong and China the commonly accepted practice is to hire a *fung shui* man to arrange office layouts, relocate offices, schedule official acts, and even to break runs of bad luck. This practice stems from the *fung shui* concept "that people should live and work in harmonious surroundings."[15] The following vignette illustrates the power of this practice in the Hong Kong market:

> It isn't any surprise that Chinese people often believe in fung shui, an ancient custom with roots deep in nature-worship, taoism and yin and yang. What is unusual is that foreigners in this bustling trading city often find their lives, too, are touched by the powerful superstition.
>
> Six years ago, Chase Manhattan Bank's regional manager, who occupied a supposedly unlucky office overlooking a graveyard, was killed in an airplane crash. A few months later, Chase moved its regional headquarters here to a new building. Chase officials say local staff concern about fung shui was one of several reasons for the relocation. Fung shui men may be called for any reason, but the commonest reasons are office relocations and runs of bad luck.

Another business practice that affects all forms of international marketing and demands careful analysis well before the entry decision is the cultural *attitude toward bribes and questionable payments*. The 1977 U.S. Foreign Corrupt Practices Act bans payments to foreign government officials and political parties, which makes doing business difficult in markets where these are accepted business practices. While the ideal trading environment bases competition on price, quality, and trade and financing terms, in reality some countries adhere to cultural traditions that make bribes and questionable payments (questionable as defined by U.S. law) necessary to doing business. Such traditions may eliminate these countries as sites of business.

A wide variety of cultural factors affect the marketing mix in foreign countries, including the obvious ones such as *languages and dialects spoken, literacy rates, race and nationalities, and geographic divisions* within the foreign market. Less obvious ones are the role of institutions, social organization of the family, and attitudes of individuals within targeted segments. The nature of *institutions, religious groups, the educational system, the role of mass media, and the family* charts the culture's evolution from traditional to modern. A focus on the family yields vital information on which members influence buying decisions or actually make the purchases. With background knowledge on the family, the international marketer can more effectively evaluate attitudes held by targeted consumer segments. To assess these attitudes, answers to these key questions are critical:

1. What are attitudes about the role of women in the society?
2. What attitudes toward technology and innovative ideas are challenging old ways and demanding change?
3. What are attitudes about the place of youth in the society?
4. What attitudes prevail regarding personal achievement and materialistic rewards for such achievement?
5. What attitudes are held about the work ethic?

The recent introduction of banks for women in Saudi Arabia illustrates the interrelationships of institutions, the family, and individual attitudes, and how these interrelationships influence cultural acceptance of new products or services. Introduced in 1980 by the Al Rajhi Company for Currency Exchange, banks for women conform with the Islamic religion's restrictions on the mingling of women and men in public places. Although the Islamic code and Saudi Arabian constitution permit women to inherit property and retain their dowries as personal property, traditional family structure still prevents most wealthy Saudi women from accepting this new service. The banks admit to minimal profits, attributing their lack of success to the reluctance of Saudi women to break with the tradition of having husbands handle their finances.

Demographic factors. Changing demographics complicate international marketing and require constant tracking. The **demographic factors** that are monitored pertain to both industrial and consumer markets. The factors focusing on industries include:

1. *The number and size of organizations* within the market
2. *The nature of ownership* (government, private, or a combination of both)
3. *Growth rates* (measured in terms of profits or asset liability ratios)
4. *Geographic location of organizations* within the target market
5. *Size and quality of the work force* within a particular industry, including quality and quantity of labor, and technical, marketing, and management skills

By tracking demographic data in relation to these factors, the international marketer can evaluate the profitability of entering the market and the costs of adaptations in the marketing mix to fit industry needs.

The marketer of consumer goods and services also must be informed on a wide array of demographic factors, some of which demand drastic reformulations of marketing strategies. *Population size, population growth rates, and the composition of households* are starting points for analyzing consumer demographics. In chapter 7, we saw how demographic changes, such as the growing number of working women, affect marketing strategies in the United States. While the United States remains the leader in the number of women employed, countries like Japan are experiencing the early stages of this trend.[16] Smaller households and the steady approach of many of the world's industrialized nations toward zero population growth (ZPG) signal future changes in household composition overseas. In contrast, third world markets with high population growth rates require yet another response from marketing strategists. Trends in the distribution and growth rates of the population by age groups are tracked, as they affect the formation of new households, household size, and the population's general composition. For example, in industrialized nations the 65-years-and-older age group ranks as a significant market segment in size and buying power. In contrast, third world markets are characterized by the youthfulness of their population. All of these factors influence the types of products that can be sold in the market.

A final population factor is the *geographic distribution and density of the population* within the market, especially:

1. The size of the urban compared with the rural population
2. The average population density comparing urban with rural areas
3. Migration rates of the market's population between urban and rural areas

This factor affects distribution and promotion strategies, as it influences the ability of the marketer to reach the targeted customers.

Trade agreements. Table 20–1 indicates the major international and regional **trade agreements.** Among the most significant developments in trade agreements from the U.S. marketer's perspective are the **General Agreement on Tariffs and Trade (GATT)** and the **European Economic Community (EEC).** The 88 GATT members and 30 associates represent the highly industrialized Western nations, including Japan, as well as some 90 less-developed nations and a handful of centrally planned economies. The GATT's major purpose is to serve as a forum for liberalizing world trade and for reducing tariff and non-tariff barriers.[17]

The EEC represents the strongest regional group to date. Its strength stems from several factors. The EEC is the largest market of U.S. products—in 1982 its ten members imported almost $50 billion worth of U.S. goods, representing approximately 22 percent of total U.S. exports. With a population of 270 million, the EEC counts 40 million more people in roughly one-sixth the land mass than the United States. At $2.4 trillion the EEC's 1982 gross national product ranked second to the U.S. total of $3.1 trillion. However, the strength of the EEC has not yet extended to its agricultural system. The community's agricultural subsidies have resulted in expensive domestic food prices and overproduction, with the latter subsidized for export sales. Weaker members like France resist reforms in agricultural subsidies demanded by West Germany, the Netherlands, and Britain. This resistance was highly visible in early 1984 when French farmers rioted in protest against the EEC's executive commission's decision to freeze prices in order to reduce overproduction.

There are three general types of trade agreements: free trade areas, customs unions, and common markets.

Free Trade Area. The basic principle of a **free trade area** is free movement of goods among members; in effect this means there are no tariffs or quotas on goods flowing between member nations. The European Free Trade Area (EFTA) is the best example of this type of trade agreement, although restrictions have been lifted on industrial goods only. Agricultural goods are still protected by each nation's restrictions.

TABLE 20–1 Selected Trade Agreements

Name	Date Formed	Membership	Purpose
General Agreement on Tariffs and Trade (GATT)	1948	88 contracting; 30 associates; 1 provisional	Trade liberalization
United Nations Conference on Trade and Development (UNCTAD)	1964	162 countries	Economic development of less-developed countries
Council for Mutual Economic Assistance (CMEA)	1949	Bulgaria, Czechoslovakia, Hungary, German Democratic Republic, Mongolia, Poland, Romania, USSR, Cuba, North Vietnam	Trade facilitation among centrally planned economies
Organization for Economic Cooperation and Development (OECD)	1961	17 European members, U.S., Canada, Japan, Australia, Iceland, New Zealand, Turkey	Trade facilitation and development of industrialized nations
Andean Common Market (ANCOM)	1967	Bolivia, Colombia, Ecuador, Peru, Venezuela	Economic integration
Association of Southeast Asian Nations (ASEAN)	1967	Indonesia, Malaysia, Philippines, Singapore, Thailand	Preferential trading area
Central American Common Market (CACM)	1960	Costa Rica, El Salvador, Guatemala, Honduras, Nicaragua	Regional cooperation
Caribbean Common Market (CARICOM)	1973	Antigua, Barbados, Domenica, Grenada, Guyana, Jamaica, Montserrat, St. Lucia, St. Christopher, St. Vincent, Trinidad, Tobago	Regional cooperation
European Economic Community (EEC)	1958	Belgium, France, West Germany, Italy, Luxembourg, The Netherlands, Denmark, Ireland, United Kingdom, Greece	Partial customs union
European Free Trade Area (EFTA)	1960	Austria, Norway, Portugal, Sweden, Switzerland, Iceland, Finland	Free trade area limited to industrial goods
Latin American Integration Association (LAIA)	1980	Argentina, Bolivia, Brazil, Chile, Colombia, Ecuador, Mexico, Paraguay, Peru, Uruguay, Venezuela	Regional cooperation

Customs Union. A more complicated type of trade agreement, a **customs union,** also has no tariffs on trade among members. It does assess a uniform tariff on trade with nonmembers. Typically designated a common market, the EEC is closer to a customs union.

Common Market or Economic Union. The most advanced type of trade agreement, a **common market** unifies all member nations' laws and regulations related to trade. The principles of free trade among members and a common external tariff on nonmember trade are also applied.

Ways to Enter International Markets

Having made the decision to go abroad and having analyzed the markets, the firm chooses an **entry mode** or a combination of entry modes. The entry modes are shown in figure 20–4 and discussed in the following sections. Each successive entry mode represents a greater amount of involvement and commitment on the part of the firm.

Exporting

Exporting represents the least commitment on the part of the firm entering a foreign market. Export sales by the 50 leading U.S. manufacturers, ranked annually by *Fortune* magazine, totaled $59 billion in 1982. Since 1980, the top five rankings have been dominated by aircraft and automotive manufacturers.[18]

The form of exporting can be directly under the firm's control or indirect and outside the firm's control. **Direct exporting** includes setting up an export department within the firm or having the firm's sales force sell directly to foreign customers or marketing intermediaries. **Indirect exporting** includes dealing through export management companies of foreign agents, merchants, or distributors.

One of the newest and most significant forms of exporting is the **export trading company (ETC),** which can be both direct and indirect.[19] The Export Trading Company Act of 1982 allows firms to set up trading houses to market their own and others firms' exports. Large trading companies like Motors Trading (General Motors), General Electric Trading Company, or Sears World Trade Corporation offer exporters established marketing networks, international trade expertise, and economies of scale.

K mart Trading Services (KTS) has joined the ranks of merchandisers setting up export trading companies, but with a novel philosophy. Instead of the standard approach, KTS has only a skeletal staff, but it has access to K mart's substantial international buying network of ten overseas offices that are staffed by 400 employees. KTS also intends to target its sales to the rapidly expanding middle class in third world markets, relying on a match between K mart's demonstrated success in mass merchandising and third world customers' needs. While exports are an insignificant share of K mart's $16.8 billion 1982 sales volume, the U.S. merchandiser considers that its expertise and position as a buyer worldwide will increase its chances of success as an international trader.

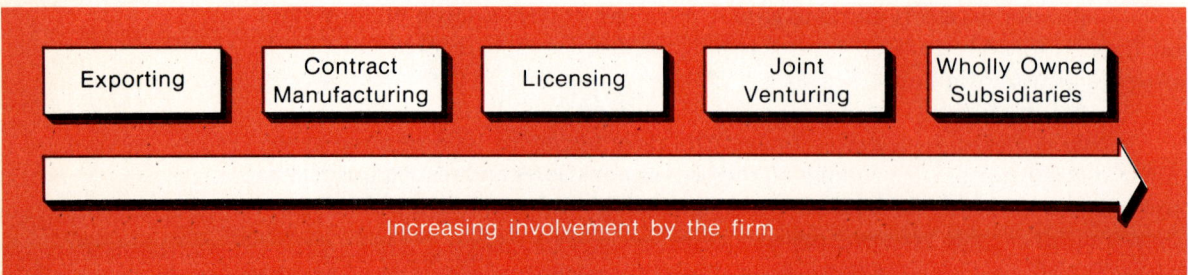

Figure 20–4 Entry modes into international markets

Chapter 20 / International Marketing

Contract Manufacturing

Contract manufacturing is an entry mode in which a U.S. firm contracts with a foreign firm to manufacture parts or finished products or to assemble parts into finished products. Typically the contracting firm supplies complete product specifications to the foreign firm, sets production volume, and guarantees purchase. Lower labor costs abroad are the major incentive for using this entry mode. This advantage is clearly illustrated in the Coleco Industries' production of Cabbage Patch dolls. Coleco contracted three Hong Kong companies to assemble 210,000 dolls per week during the 1983 Christmas season. The dolls were transported from Hong Kong to the United States in three jumbo jets chartered by Coleco. The Hong Kong company, Kader Industrial Company, assembled the major share of the dolls, molding the plastic heads and implanting and styling hair. Kader Industrial itself farmed out most of the labor-intensive production—stitching, stuffing, and dressmaking—to its wholly owned factory in China's Shenzhen, a special economic zone bordering Hong Kong. The bulk of the production was thus located in China, where labor costs are roughly half that of Hong Kong. This example illustrates how manufacturing and assembly facilities are physically located to the best advantage of each partner.[20]

Licensing

Licensing is similar to contract manufacturing, as the foreign licensee receives specifications for producing products locally, but the licensor generally receives a set fee or royalty rather than finished products. Licensing may offer the foreign firm access to brands, trademarks, trade secrets, or patents associated with products manufactured.[21] The specifications for manufacturing may be in the form of blueprints, formulas, comprehensive manufacturing instructions, or other approaches for transferring process technology. The licensor may provide technical services to guarantee quality control, and also may offer access to marketing, distribution, and management techniques.

Representing an export of technology rather than goods (as in exporting) or capital, licensing is an attractive mode in markets where political and economic uncertainties make a greater involvement risky. Licensing also is an effective mode for testing the future viability of more active involvement with a foreign partner. Due to advantages of low risk and low investment, licensing is a particularly attractive mode for small and medium-sized firms.

Franchising. Franchising is a form of licensing with special attractions for U.S. enterprises in developing international marketing opportunities. It differs from licensing principally in the depth and scope of quality controls placed on all phases of the franchisee's operation, as we saw in chapter 17. Franchisers anticipated saturated home markets in the mid-1980s, and deliberately expanded overseas to high income industrial markets in the 1970s. For example, out of all U.S. international franchises, 35 percent are in Canada; U.S.-based franchisors control roughly one-third of Canada's 350 franchises, which in turn operate more than 20,000 outlets. The franchise concept is expanding rapidly beyond its traditional businesses (such as service stations, restaurants, and real-estate brokers) to include less traditional

Figure 20–5 A Dairy Queen franchise in Tokyo.

formats, such as travel agencies, used car dealers, the video industry, and professional and health improvement services.²²

Joint Ventures

In a **joint venture,** an investing firm owns 25 to 75 percent of a foreign firm, allowing the investing firm to affect management decisions of the foreign firm. In 1983–1984, joint ventures between two foreign partners established production arrangements in the highly competitive automobile industry. These arrangements frequently involved antitrust considerations. The major controversy surrounding the proposed General Motors Corporation joint venture with Toyota Motor Corporation provides an example. The controversy revolved around the question of whether the world's largest and third-largest automobile makers could team up without directly or indirectly violating antitrust law related to price fixing and the exchange of trade secrets or future business plans. Both Chrysler Corporation and Ford Motor Company threatened suits if the government's antitrust arm, the Federal Trade Commission (FTC), approved the joint venture proposal. Joint ventures are subject to FTC scrutiny in both domestic and foreign markets, especially when the two partners are giant multinationals.

Wholly Owned Subsidiaries

When an investing firm owns enough of a foreign firm to exercise complete control, it has a **wholly owned subsidiary.** Compared to joint ventures, the main advantages of a wholly owned subsidiary include authority over management policy and the distribution of earnings and easier integration of its subsidiary operations worldwide. An example of the advantage derived from such integration is Ford Motor Company's decision to invest $400–$500 million in an automobile plant in Mexico to manufacture a small car designed by Japan's Toyo Kogyo Company. Ford owns 25 percent of Toyo Kogyo, the producer of Mazdas, and Ford even markets two Mazda models under Ford model names in Australia and Asia. The new Mexican plant will be wholly owned by Ford, and the automobiles will be sold predominantly in the United States. Eventual penetration of the Mexican market—the fourth largest market for automobiles worldwide after the United States, Canada, and Western Europe—is a probable long-term strategy. Ford's investment supports the Mexican government's policy of encouraging foreign investment in production facilities in order to generate hard currency through export sales, while low costs of Mexican labor decidedly favor Ford's decision.

The disadvantages of wholly owned subsidiaries involve the large capital investment and the risk of ownership, particularly in light of possible adverse policies by foreign governments. Such policies can range from takeovers by the foreign governments of total production assets to price controls that would substantially diminish returns on investments. For example, automobile multinationals were forced to reevaluate their Mexican operations after the government's September 1983 decree that they must shut down certain plants and make major investments in new facilities. The intent of this policy was to set up facilities capable of producing competitively priced automobiles for export, which would generate hard currency for the debt-pressed Mexican economy. Multinationals who decided to stay in Mexico included General Motors, Chrysler, Volkswagenwerk AG, Nissan, and Renault. Ford's older production facilities in Mexico were also affected.

Focus 20–2 provides an example of how a British company entered the United States.

The International Marketing Mix

The decision has been made to go abroad; the market has been analyzed; the mode of entry has been chosen. The next step is to develop a marketing mix for the product that will work in an international market. A number of decisions must be made concerning the international marketing mix; many of them are the same as the decisions to be made in creating a domestic marketing mix. We will not discuss these here, but we will examine the major decisions that pertain to international marketing.

It must be noted that there is no single international marketing mix. Rather, decisions about the marketing mix are made for each market, based on marketing research and the analysis of each market.

Product Decisions

Standardize-differentiate dilemma. One of the major product decisions is whether to standardize or differentiate the product. A **standardized product** is one that is basically the same in both the domestic and all international markets. A **differentiated product** is one that has been adapted to suit the different needs of the various markets. The economies-of-scale argument has traditionally supported standardization, as a company reduces costs by producing larger amounts

Chapter 20 / International Marketing

20–2 Focus on Marketing Strategy
HOW BEECHAM ENTERED THE UNITED STATES

The British company Beecham Group PLC is one firm that is looking to the U.S. market for expansion opportunities. Beecham executives recognize that the U.S. consumer market is perhaps the most potentially profitable. Additionally, many of the company's products have already saturated their home market. Beecham's pharmaceuticals division is made up of a line of primarily mature products, and sales growth for this division is below Beecham's goals because the company has not introduced a strong new pharmaceutical product in several years.

To improve sales growth in a wide range of business areas by entering the United States, Beecham has two strategies. The first is to acquire American firms that Beecham believes have strong growth possibilities. In 1982, the company bought J. B. Williams Company, makers of such standard American products as Geritol, Sominex, and Aqua Velva. Beecham has increased advertising efforts for these products, while making radical changes in the Williams staff in order to increase the company's revenues. Another new acquisition for Beecham is Jovan Inc., makers of fragrances. A third acquisition was the Calgon line of bath products. Although the line was not profitable at that time, Beecham has added a moisturizing bath foam among other improvements, and the line is now turning a profit. After acquiring DAP, a caulking product, Beecham is adding a line of glues.

Beecham's second strategy is to introduce British products to the American market. The company has been successful in making Aqua-Fresh gel strong in Britain and a serious challenge in the U.S. toothpaste market. Beecham marketed the toothpaste as a breath freshener and placque remover and gained 12 percent of the $700 million toothpaste market.

Beecham is also moving the American brands it acquires into foreign markets. The company recently purchased the Diane Von Furstenberg line of fragrances and will be marketing them in Europe and the Middle East.

The British company's main obstacle in the U.S. market will be the many other companies with similar products that are much more firmly established in the American market. Companies like Colgate-Palmolive and Procter & Gamble will be tough competition for a newcomer. Beecham, however, is counting on success in the U.S. market due to its marketing strategies and strong distribution channels.

Source: "Beecham: A Household Name in Britain Is Aiming at American Kitchens and Bathrooms," *Business Week*, January 30, 1984, pp. 86–87.

of the same product. Differentiation is supported by the marketing concept in that it accommodates the differences in each market, such as income distribution and the country's stage of economic development. Income and development affect consumer needs, wants, and tastes. These factors also influence the technology available and industrial users' selection of labor- versus capital-intensive production.

Another factor supporting differentiation is that foreign laws and regulations often require product adaptations to fit the needs of their consumer and industry publics as well as to protect the competitiveness of domestic industry.

Product life cycle. The concepts behind the product life cycle can influence international marketing decisions in three ways. As we saw in chapter 19, one of the strategies available to U.S. firms is to move into overseas markets. The U.S. multinational Merck & Company, for example, decided to market its new ethical drugs first in the fast-growing Japanese market. Merck expects a faster return on sales in Japan, where there is less competition and the market in cardiovascular and antibiotic products has not yet reached saturation.

The rush to develop new products has also created a climate of cooperation and the establishment of joint ventures among multinationals rather than a strictly "go it alone" internal approach to product development, as we have seen in the telecommunications and automobile industries.

In order to spread the high costs of research and development over a longer period of time by extending the product life cycle, American companies often look to marketing opportunities overseas. In low income markets there may be opportunities to offer products of earlier technological generations, such as manual typewriters, or to target an industrial rather than a consumer market segment to extend the product life cycle of some products.

Delivered performance. The concept of **delivered performance** relates to quality of both product performance and service support, which are especially critical in high technology product lines. International marketers must be able to provide both in all of their markets in order to satisfy consumers. Wang Laboratories learned the interdependence of these factors the hard way. The popularity of Wang's word processors and minicomputers in Western Europe brought a 61 percent spurt in European sales reported for 1980 and 42 percent in 1981. Wang's European subsidiaries lagged in providing customer services and support, however, and also had to break delivery promises for hardware and software when production failed to meet demand. Wang headquarters soon saw that growth in sales demands equal growth in customer services and support.[24]

Promotion Decisions

Standardize-differentiate dilemma. When creating the promotional campaign, international marketers face another dilemma of standardization versus differentiation. The analysis of the foreign market and the firm's position within the market guides the decision. While all environmental factors discussed earlier can directly or indirectly shape the promotion strategy, several factors stand out.

First, government regulations may (1) preclude advertising through certain media channels, such as television; (2) limit the number of minutes per day that television networks can broadcast advertisements, as in Great Britain and the Netherlands; or (3) strictly control the content and style of such advertising messages, such as Britain's constraints on children's products and medicines. Second, the market's communication system may limit media options, reduce the quality of message delivery, or require dependence on support services such as advertising agencies outside the market. Generally the sophistication of the communication system is highly related to the level of economic development. A third issue relates to the culture; the language, general level of education, literacy rates, and social organization all present special requirements for promotional adaptations.

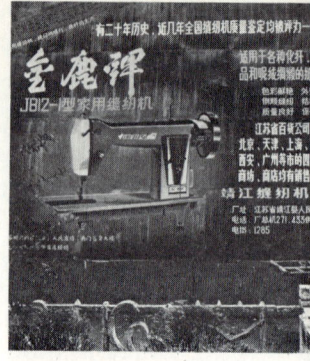

Figure 20–6 A billboard in Soochow, China. Promotional strategy may be determined by the availability of media and the general nature of the communication system in a market.
©Michal Heron 1982

Criteria for developing the promotional mix. After resolving the issue of whether to standardize or differentiate the promotional approach, the international marketing manager evaluates the promotional opportunities and methods available in the market. As the effectiveness of the various promotional tools in reaching the target segment naturally changes across and within countries, marketers consider and make decisions about the following questions:

1. What segments of the market can be reached by the tool?
2. Is the timing of message delivery appropriate to targeted market segments?
3. Are the costs of the tool justifiable in terms of its ability to reach this market?
4. What is the reliability of message delivery?
5. What is the quality of message reproduction?
6. Does the tool offer any possibilities for consumer feedback?
7. Given the expected reach, costs, quality, and other factors peculiar to the foreign market, does the tool selected adequately support promotion objectives or must other tools be added to the promotion mix?
8. Which tools does this company have the resources to use?
9. Which tool is best suited to our product?

The answers lead to the selection of the promotional tool or tools. Foreign countries with many highly differentiated market segments may require the use of multiple tools for effective market coverage.

Another promotional challenge emerges when the foreign government is the targeted customer. In Middle Eastern markets, for example, the critical step is selecting an effective agent to serve as a necessary marketing intermediary between the firm and the government agency. The character of promotion also must be reoriented when the foreign government is a centrally planned or non-market economy. While there is vast diversity among countries within Eastern Europe, the Soviet Union, and the People's Republic of China, the U.S. firm must deal with foreign trade organizations in each. These organizations generally demand thoroughly documented superiority over competing products in price and product quality and financing terms that often require a personal selling effort by top-level management. Although these lengthy demands may go against Western notions about use of time and resources, the vast size of these markets calls for accommodations by U.S. firms, particularly as the saturation of traditional domestic markets forces firms to look for overseas customers.

Selection of an appropriate pricing method depends on many factors already mentioned concerning the firm and its markets, including:

Pricing Decisions

1. The amount of foreign debt carried by a country and steps the government is taking to pay off the debt
2. The current exchange rate and trends in the exchange rate
3. Competition
4. Technological advances
5. Quotas and other trade barriers established by the government

Throughout this decade, pricing in industrialized countries will also be complicated by the aging of industries such as steel, automotives, and consumer electronics. U.S. producers exporting these products will face consistent price competition from rapidly industrializing countries with modern and efficient factories and low costs. The reactions of U.S. producers to price threats from foreign manufacturers have often led to charges before the International Trade Commission that the foreign manufacturers are "dumping" low-priced goods in this country.[25] While U.S. producers may react by seeking relief from the government, costly industrial modernization is the best avenue for the long-term resolution of this pricing dilemma.[26]

This summary of issues in the trade environment places the various pricing approaches in a realistic context. The three approaches discussed in the following sections must be evaluated against the constraints within the firm, the foreign market, and current international trade realities.

Conventional pricing methods. Three conventional pricing methods—cost-oriented, demand-oriented, and competition-oriented pricing—are also used in international marketing. Cost-oriented pricing may be used effectively to cover the often heavy market entry cost of tariffs and non-tariff barriers and taxes, and the general costs of conducting business. The other pricing methods are appropriate when used to meet specific pricing objectives the firm has in relation to the market.

Barter and countertrade. Various forms of barter and countertrade represent less traditional, although certainly time-honored pricing approaches. These approaches were described in focus 20–1. Barter and countertrade provide certain pricing advantages, including:

1. Reducing the impact of foreign governments' regulations that protect domestic industries
2. Limiting the problem of fluctuating currency values
3. Lessening risk exposure by trading products rather than unstable currencies
4. Avoiding currency exchange controls

5. Allowing purchases by countries with nonconvertible currencies
6. Guaranteeing payment from Eastern bloc and developing markets experiencing debt crises
7. Minimizing, to some extent, taxes and customs duties, although future legal regulation may preempt current advantages

Leasing. The final pricing approach, **leasing,** can provide lessees in foreign markets equipment and other expensive product items at low costs. This approach was used by multinational giants like IBM during the 1970s. Since leasing fees were often low to encourage the purchase of the leased products upon the lease's expiration, it was the foreign lessee that frequently benefited. Instead of purchasing leased equipment upon the lease's expiration, the lessee frequently turned to another supplier with more technically advanced products, leaving the original lessor without adequate returns on sizable investments in product development and manufacturing.

Physical Distribution Decisions

The costs and complexities involved in distributing and transporting goods and services internationally raise special challenges to physical distribution. Specialized intermediaries like **freight forwarders** may expedite distribution from the United States to the overseas market, where a foreign distributor may then assume the marketing responsibilities. Transportation is complicated by dependence on mixed transportation modes, each with its own rate bases and regulatory restrictions. This section will highlight trends in international physical distribution to demonstrate the importance of this marketing mix element to successful international marketing.

Distribution structure in foreign markets. A series of questions can be asked about distribution structure in foreign markets to facilitate decision making on the most profitable distribution strategy. These questions can be applied to wholesalers and retailers of consumer goods or to the wholesaler-direct channel for industrial goods. Answers will guide decisions on a pushing or pulling strategy and whether the distribution policy should be intensive, selective, or exclusive. The questions are:

1. Is the size of the channel adequate to achieve coverage of the target market, or are multiple channels required for desired market coverage?
2. Are the quality and scope of services offered by the channel adequate to support the product within the market? Is there warehousing space for necessary inventory of products and spare parts? Delivery service to channel or industrial user? And so on.
3. If the coverage and services of existing channels are inadequate and transaction costs are high, should the firm establish its own distribution channel?

Figure 20–7 In Tokyo's Ueno section, a familiar Coca-Cola truck distributes its products.

©Michal Heron 1982

4. Are there distinctive factors within the foreign market affecting channel structure to which the international marketer must accommodate? These may include laws and regulations such as resale price maintenance, culturally unique patronage patterns among consumer segments or industrial users, and so on.
5. What are the costs of channel operation in terms of volume of sales per transaction, costs of sales personnel per transaction, and overhead?

Answers to these questions also indicate the distribution system's stage of development, which is closely linked to the country's stage of economic development. For example, a surprising number of difficulties confront Chinese consumers in purchasing bok choy, a basic food staple. These include limited and primitive storage facilities, causing temporary abundance of the product followed by scarcity, inadequate long-distance surface transport stemming both from poor road conditions and unavailability of vehicles, and narrow assortments available generally to consumers.[27] These factors complicate rational physical distribution planning and add costs that may preclude market entry for certain product items at the outset.

Transportation. Computer technology offers the promise that the complexities of physical distribution will become more manageable in this decade. Mixed transportation modes are virtually essential in moving goods from the home market to the foreign market and to the final consumer. High freight costs must be weighed against time schedules and reliability of delivery. For products or components where speed of delivery is critical, selection of the transportation mode will be motivated by timing rather than expense. The manager of physical distribution must also calculate insurance rates, storage and handling costs, including the feasibility of containerization, and customs duties. For firms new to exporting, the freight forwarder may be an especially attractive alternative to handling physical distribution. The freight forwarder offers one-stop service and handles documentation, insurance, storage, and shipping to meet the exporter's requirements.

There are several types of agreements for international transportation. For example, the exporter may decide to cover all risks, responsibilities, and costs of moving products to the foreign buyer. This approach is commonly described as "Franco Delivered" or **delivered duty paid.** In another agreement, the foreign buyer may agree to assume all costs and risks, taking title to the goods at the production site or at a distribution point designated by the seller. These terms are commonly known as **ex-factory** or "as is, where is." Three additional types of agreements reflect more equal sharing of physical distribution responsibilities between seller and buyer: (1) **free alongside ship (FAS),** with the seller's responsibilities ending when goods are on the loading dock; (2) **freight on board (FOB),** with the seller's responsibilities terminated when the goods have been loaded onto the transport vessel; and (3) **cost-insurance-freight (CIF),** with the seller responsible for all logistics' costs and risks, including insurance, transportation, and mechanics, up to a foreign destination acceptable to the buyer.

Summary

International marketing spans researching, planning, and implementing all entry strategies—from exporting to culturally similar and physically close markets like Canada and marketing out of a wholly-owned subsidiary in a culturally exotic, poor, and distant market like Bangladesh. Factors that affect international marketing include saturated home markets and international competition. A trade surplus means more exports than imports; a trade deficit is more imports than exports.

Collecting information through marketing research is essential to identify the most attractive markets, to isolate the best segments within markets, and to gain an understanding of consumers' needs. Marketing research must begin with a creative definition of the research problem, including creative identifications of markets and customers. The researcher should be flexible in selecting marketing research techniques and matching them to data limitations. Data collection should not focus only on the foreign market.

The economic and financial factors within a country that affect the ability of a country to do business in it include the amount of foreign debt carried, the income distribution within potential markets, the amount of foreign investment already in the market, and the natural resource base.

Political-legal factors affecting a company's ability to do business in a foreign market include the role of the government, stability of the government, barriers to international trade (including tariffs, or taxes on imported products), laws and regulations affecting the marketing mix and business activities, the stability of the work force, and political relations between the trading partners.

Engaging in international marketing demands a careful understanding, including the style of business within the market, the attitude toward bribes and questionable payments, languages and dialects spoken, literacy rates, race and nationalities, geographic divisions, institutions, religious groups, the educational system, and the role of mass media and the family.

Demographic factors of the country also affect a company's ability to do business there.

Important trade agreements affecting international marketing include the European Economic Community (EEC). The three types of trade agreements include a free trade area, or free movement of goods among members; a customs union, or no tariffs among members but a uniform tariff on trade with nonmembers; and a common market or economic union, or union of all member nations' laws and regulations related to trade.

Direct exporting includes setting up an export department within the firm or having the firm's sales force sell directly to foreign customers. Indirect exporting includes dealing through export management companies of foreign agents, merchants, or distributors. The Export Trading Company Act allows firms to set up trading houses to market their own and other firms' exports. Contract manufacturing occurs when a U.S. firm contracts a foreign firm to manufacture, finish, or assemble parts. Licensing occurs when a foreign company is contracted to produce products to a U.S. firm's specifications. Franchising is a form of licensing with more limited quality control. In a joint venture, an investing firm owns 25 to 75 percent of a foreign firm. A wholly owned subsidiary is one in which the investing firm owns enough of the foreign firm to exercise complete control.

A standardized product is one that is basically the same in both domestic and foreign markets, while a differentiated product is one that has been adapted to suit the needs of the various markets. In order to spread the costs of research and development over a longer period of time by extending the product life cycle, American companies often look to marketing opportunities overseas. The concept of delivered performance relates to the quality of both product and service support. After resolving the issue of whether to standardize or differentiate the promotional approach, the international marketing manager evaluates the promotional opportunities.

Pricing decisions depend on factors in the international environment such as foreign debts, currency rates, competition, technical advances, and quotas. Cost-oriented, demand-oriented, and competition-oriented pricing methods are also used in international pricing. Barter and countertrade offer less traditional pricing approaches. Leasing can provide leasees in foreign markets with expensive products at low costs.

Freight forwarders may expedite distribution from the United States to the overseas market, where the foreign distributor then assumes marketing responsibilities. Types of agreements for international transportation include delivered duty paid, ex-factory, free alongside ship (FAS), freight on board (FOB), and cost-insurance-freight (CIF).

Questions for Discussion

1. What are the special problems involved in international marketing that are different from those of domestic marketing?
2. Differentiate between the free trade area and the common market?
3. Compare the conditions where direct and indirect exporting are most likely.
4. What explains the increasing importance of contract manufacturing in international marketing?
5. "Licensing and joint venture are two approaches to achieving the same end in international marketing." Comment.
6. When does licensing become especially attractive to companies interested in entering a foreign market?
7. What are the advantages and disadvantages of employing wholly owned subsidiaries in international markets.
8. Compare the attractiveness of barter and leasing to U.S. multinational companies.
9. "Standardization is equally attractive for both product and promotional decisions in international marketing." Comment.

References

1. James Kelly, "East Meets Reagan," *Time*, April 30, 1984, pp. 24–25; Pico Iyer, "Capitalism in the Making," *Time*, April 30, 1984, pp. 26–35.
2. "Debts Mount in Small Industrial Nations," *Wall Street Journal*, September 22, 1983, p. 34.
3. Vern Terpstra, "Critical Mass and International Marketing Strategy," *Journal of the Academy of Marketing Science*, Summer 1983, pp. 269–82.
4. "Quick Remedies for Deficit Aren't Seen by Trade Official in Report to Congress," *Wall Street Journal*, February 1, 1984, p. 8.
5. The three sources used include *Clements' Encyclopedia of World Governments*, Vol. 5 (Dallas: Division of Political Research, 1982) and the Fall 1983 Supplement; *Greenwood Historical Encyclopedia of the World's Political Parties* (Westport, Conn.: Greenwood Press, 1983); *The Europa Yearbook*, Vol. 1 (London: Europa Publications, 1983).
6. "Failure of Latest Farm Talks Leaves One Chance for Success Before Reagan Visit," *International Trade Reporter's U.S. Export Weekly*, July–September 1983, p. 87.
7. "AT&T Unit to Sell Data System to Japan for about $70 Million," *Wall Street Journal*, October 6, 1983, p. 47.
8. "No Bottle Trademark," *The Times*, December 20, 1983, p. 18c, shows the legal problems that the Coca-Cola Company confronted in Great Britain when they attempted to register their bottle as a trademark.
9. J. J. Boddewyn, "Advertising Taxation Is Here to Stay—and Fight," *International Journal of Advertising*, October–December 1983, p. 291.
10. Trade Data Reports, *The Exporter, A Monthly Management Review of Export Operations, Markets, Training and World Trade*, November 1983, p. 7.
11. "Peugeot Tells Poissy Workers to Stay Home," *Wall Street Journal*, January 6, 1984, p. 24.
12. "Russian Robot Makers Can't Put It All Together," *Business Week*, May 30, 1983, p. 49.

13. "U.S. Tilts Toward Iraq to Thwart Iran," *Wall Street Journal,* January 6, 1984, p. 24.
14. "A Soft-Drink War Bubbles Up in Korea: 7-Up Versus Chilsung," *Wall Street Journal,* December 15, 1983, p. 38.
15. "Some Chinese Simply Won't Make a Move Without Fung Shui," *Wall Street Journal,* December 19, pp. 1, 20.
16. "Changes Discussed in Japanese Consumers, Distribution, Regulation," *Marketing News,* October 1, 1982, p. 10.
17. Jeffrey J. Schott, "The GATT Ministerial: A Postmortem," *Challenge,* May–June 1983, p. 41.
18. See *The Fortune Directory of the Largest U.S. Industrial Exporters,* August 1980–1983.
19. "Which Way for U.S. Trading Companies," *Dun's Business Month,* March 1983, pp. 56–60.
20. "Cabbage Patch Dolls, Believe It or Not, Begin as Bok Choy Wah-Wahs in China," *Wall Street Journal,* December 8, 1983, p. 34.
21. Bethlehem Steel Corporation, a major steel and coal producer in the United States, markets its expertise to countries around the world through its wholly-owned subsidiary, Bethlehem International Engineering Corporation (BIEC). This subsidiary was set up to offer Bethlehem's technology and engineering experience to foreign countries by negotiating licenses for the sale of its patents and processes, which in turn enable foreign licensees to purchase machinery and receive assistance in coal and iron ore, mining, operating, and engineering. See "Bethlehem Sells Its Coal Expertise," *Coal Age,* September 1983, pp. 96–97.
22. See Walter S. Good, "Few Obstacles Thwart Canadian Franchising Growth," *Marketing News,* February 17, 1984, p. 11.
23. "British Car Maker's Tie to Honda Shows Why Auto Linkups Increase," *Wall Street Journal,* December 12, 1983, pp. 1, 23.
24. "Where Wang Wants Slower Growth," *Business Week,* May 30, 1983, pp. 45–46.
25. "South Korean Color-TV Manufacturers Say U.S. Dumping Ruling Is a 'Tragedy,'" *Wall Street Journal,* February 28, 1984, p. 36.
26. "Kohl to Warn Reagan on Protectionism, East-West Relations During U.S. Trip," *Wall Street Journal,* February 29, 1984, p. 32.
27. "Old Chinese Adage: No Hungry Winters if Lots of Cabbage," *Wall Street Journal,* December 6, 1983, pp. 1, 16.

OBJECTIVES

1. To identify the unique characteristics of services.

2. To discuss the special problems involved in marketing services.

3. To identify the unique characteristics of nonprofit marketing.

4. To discuss the special problems involved in nonprofit marketing.

5. To explain how such unique characteristics seem to specifically shape the marketing programs of service and nonprofit institutions.

21

Services and Nonprofit Marketing

Americans spend approximately $1 billion a day on health care. A growing number of health-care providers, including nonprofit hospitals, for-profit hospitals, and free-standing emergency centers, are competing for a share of this market by offering a wide range of services and options for consumers to choose. Some for-profit hospital companies and nonprofit hospitals are establishing outpatient surgery centers, alcohol and drug-abuse clinics, psychiatric centers, and home health-care services. To meet the needs of the increasing number of elderly patients, some are operating long-term care facilities or nursing or retirement homes. Some services, such as burn centers, intensive-care centers for premature babies, or birthing centers, fill needs of special patients. Once patients have entered the hospitals, they find more amenities, such as good food, pleasant rooms, and attentive care.

The approximately 1,000 free-standing emergency centers throughout the country provide an alternative to hospital emergency rooms. The typical center is located in a heavily travelled area, such as a popular shopping center, is open seven days a week and 18 hours a day, and tries to see and treat patients in less than 30 minutes. The cost of treatment is far less than at hospitals. The centers appeal to consumers' needs for quick medical treatment at a reasonable price.[1]

Health-care providers market their service—medicine—in some of the same ways that other businesses market blue jeans, automobiles, and soft drinks. Yet, in some very important ways, the marketing of a service such as medicine is different from the marketing of a tangible good. Nonprofit hospitals face marketing problems not encountered in businesses. Understanding how service and nonprofit marketing differ from the marketing of a tangible good is a necessary step in selecting appropriate marketing strategies. In this chapter, we will discuss services marketing and nonprofit marketing, differentiate them from the marketing of tangible and business products, and suggest ways that the differences can be handled.

The Marketing of Services

Our nation's economy has been called a service economy. In 1980, more than two-thirds of all people employed in the United States were working in a service capacity, and 66 percent of our gross national product was accounted for by services. Today, about 47¢ out of every dollar that consumers spend in America pays for services.[2] Demographic and lifestyle changes in the United States—including increasing prosperity, the growth of dual career families, and more leisure time—have led Americans to become heavy consumers of all types of services.

What Is a Service?

Services are not objects: They are products in the form of performances, deeds, or acts.[3] No physical product is transferred. Services are performed by businesses (such as banks and for-profit hospitals), by individuals (such as baby-sitters and housecleaners), or by nonprofit organizations (such as nonprofit hospitals or Planned Parenthood). They may be performed for consumers and their property or for other businesses. Services may be financial (performed by banks or brokerage houses), related to health care (provided by clinics, doctors, or dentists), professional (performed by lawyers, public relations firms, or architects), personal (such as dry cleaning or hairstyling), and business-related (such as word processing, equipment maintenance, or advertising). Figure 21–1 presents seven ways to classify products, along with additional examples for each classification. While these services vary among themselves in some ways, they all have several key characteristics in common.

Figure 21–1 Seven ways to classify services

---

1. **Who or What Is the Object of the Service?**
    a. Services to the person of the consumer
        (1) Primarily mental (theater, education)
        (2) Primarily physical (medical, haircut)
    b. Services to the customer's property
        (1) Tangible items (dry cleaning, gardening)
        (2) Intangible assets (banking, stockbroking)
2. **Discrete versus Continuous Customer-Provider Relationships**
    a. The customer has a formalized, ongoing relationship with the service provided (telephone subscription, bank account).
    b. Each transaction between the customer and a provider is a discrete event (use of a pay telephone, purchase of a postal money order).
3. **Role of Physical Goods and Facilities in Services Delivery**
    a. Customer literally consumes a nondurable good in a value-added environment (restaurant, bar).
    b. Customer acquires the right to use (rent) a durable good or physical facility for a defined period of time (hotel room, rental car).
    c. Customer consciously evaluates various physical goods and facilities that are employed in delivering the core service (transportation services, medical care).
    d. Customer normally takes physical facilities in the service environment for granted unless they materially interfere with the service delivery (sports event, adult education, postal service).

(continued)

4. **Role and Extent of Personal Service**
   a. Personally delivered service is the central component in the service package (music lessons, emotional therapy).
   b. Personal service is one of several elements in the service package but dominates the others in its importance for most consumers (legal services, health care).
   c. Personal service is one of several elements in the service package but is of secondary importance for most consumers (inexpensive restaurant, service station).
   d. There is minimal or no personal component in the service of this criterion (movie theater, subway, laundromat).

5. **Breadth of Service Package**
   a. A consumption experience is typically limited to delivery of a single service (haircut, subway trip).
   b. A consumption experience typically involves receipt of a package of several services (airline trip, motel stay).

6. **Timing and Duration of Benefits**
   a. Benefits received primarily during service delivery (theater, hotel).
   b. Benefits received primarily during a short period of time following service delivery (haircut, laundromat).
   c. Benefits received during a medium period of time following service delivery (income tax preparation, pest control).
   d. Benefits received during a long-term period following service delivery (college education, major landscaping).

7. **Nature of Customer-Provider Interaction**
   a. Customer's personal presence is required throughout service delivery (haircut, subway trip, surgery).
   b. Customer's physical presence is usually required only to initiate and/or terminate the service transaction (auto repair, laundromat, postal service).
   c. Customer can initiate and terminate service transactions at a distance (by mail or telecommunications).

Source: Christopher H. Lovelock, "Towards a Classification of Services," in *Theoretical Developments in Marketing*, ed. Charles Lamb and Patrick Dunne (Chicago: American Marketing Association, 1980), pp. 72–76. Used with permission.

Key Characteristics of Services

The marketing principles discussed in this book can be applied most effectively to services when the characteristics that make services different from tangible goods are understood. Services differ from tangible goods in four ways: intangibility, inseparability of production and consumption, heterogeneity, and perishability.[4] (See fig. 21–2.) The following discussion applies generally to all services, although there may be individual exceptions.

Services are intangible. The first major difference between goods and services is that services are *intangible*. Since they are actions, rather than objects, they cannot be seen, felt, tasted, or touched before they are purchased the way goods

Chapter 21 / Services and Nonprofit Marketing

can. Because they are not objects, services can rarely be packaged, inventoried, or transported.

The production and consumption of services are inseparable. Second, most services are produced and consumed at the same time, a characteristic called *inseparability of production and consumption.* Whereas goods are first produced, sold, and then consumed, services are sold, produced, and consumed at the same time.[5] Since the consumer must be present during the production of many services (for example, haircuts and airplane trips), the buyer comes into direct contact with the "factory." Inseparability also means that the producer and the seller are very often the same person.

Services are heterogeneous. Third, the performance of services is highly variable, a characteristic called *heterogeneity.* The quality of a service can vary from producer to producer, from day to day, and from customer to customer. Heterogeneity in service output is a particular problem for labor-intensive services because individuals providing the services (such as doctors, chefs, or hairdressers) are subject to different moods and pressures that can affect their performance. Less labor-intensive services, such as hotel lodging or an airplane trip, are easier to standardize.

Services are perishable. Finally, *perishability* means that services cannot be saved.[6] Motel rooms not occupied, airline seats not purchased, and telephone line capacity not used cannot be reclaimed and sold another day.

As we will see in the following sections, these four characteristics of services require adaptations by marketers to the traditional marketing mix. These characterisitics pose difficult problems for services marketers and often require special services marketing solutions, for strategies developed from experience in tangible goods marketing are often insufficient.

- **Intangibility.** Services cannot be sensed before they are purchased.
- **Inseparability of production and consumption.** Services are produced and consumed at the same time.
- **Heterogeneity.** The performance and quality of services are highly variable.
- **Perishability.** Services cannot be saved and sold another day.

Figure 21–2 The four key characteristics of services

Special Problems and Strategies in the Services Marketing Mix

Product problems. Perhaps the most troublesome problem relating to the service product is that supply and demand for it are not coordinated. With tangible goods, such as automobiles, a firm can save its excess supply in inventory and sell these items later in times when demand rises. Services, however, cannot be stored in an inventory. If a resort hotel does not fill its rooms during the slow season, the revenue it would have received is lost forever. The hotel cannot save the unused rooms for the peak season when demand exceeds supply.

A second problem is that service firms have no legal way to protect their new ideas and processes. With tangible goods, new inventions can be patented and protected for 17 years. On the other hand, service innovations—which involve ideas and processes—cannot be documented and, thus, cannot be patented. The only legal protection for service innovations is registration of brand names. As a result, a new service idea and process can be copied easily by competitors. Federal Express faced this problem when it introduced overnight mail delivery. Within months, many service firms had introduced services to compete with the company's idea.

Quality is a third problem related to the products of service firms. With tangible goods, manufacturing standards can be set to ensure that each item fits the quality level demanded by management. With services, quality control is quite difficult to achieve because quality depends on so many things that management cannot supervise. Management cannot always control the willingness and ability of personnel to satisfy the needs of consumers. All bank tellers or flight attendants, for example, are not equally friendly and helpful. Management cannot control, and often cannot anticipate, periods of very high demand that can result in less careful attention to consumer needs. A harried waitress during busy lunch hours may bring you the wrong order or forget to tell the cook the proper way to prepare your food. Because of this variability, the service marketer cannot know for sure that quality is consistent.

A final problem associated with a service product is that consumers participate in the production process and therefore affect the transaction. The service customer voices his or her need, consumes the service, and may provide feedback during or immediately after consumption. Consider how much your doctor's diagnosis depends on your description of symptoms, or how your haircut varies with your ability to tell the stylist what you want. Similarly, the service received by one customer can be dramatically influenced by the presence or absence of other customers. The presence of other customers may, for example, cause a higher noise level in a restaurant or a long wait in a bank; the absence of other customers (or of appropriate customers) may lessen enjoyment in a bar or dance hall.

Coping with special product problems. As we saw earlier, service businesses frequently find it difficult to coordinate supply and demand. Sometimes too much demand exists (for example, for a popular restaurant on a Saturday night) and sometimes too little demand exists (for example, for an income tax service in the summer). Companies can use a number of special strategies to align supply and demand. Figure 21-3 lists some of the strategies commonly used by service businesses to bring demand in line with supply.

Figure 21–3
Strategies useful in coping with fluctuating demand in service businesses

Strategies for Periods of High Demand

Hire extra full-time employees
Hire extra part-time employees
Use differential scheduling of existing employees during peak times
Have employees work overtime
Subcontract work to others
Let work fall behind
Take care of regular customers and allow others to wait
Turn away business
Cross-train employees to perform other tasks
Educate customers to use service during nonpeak times
Offer incentives to customers using service during nonpeak times

Strategies for Periods of Low Demand

Lay off employees
Use differential scheduling of existing employees during slow times
Use employees to perform nonvital tasks during slow times
Offer price reductions
Increase advertising
Try to increase business by calling on customers
Seek subcontract work during slow times
Offer incentives to use resources during slow periods

Source: Valarie A. Zeithaml, A. Parasuraman, and Leonard L. Berry, "Problems and Strategies in Services Marketing," *Journal of Marketing*, Winter 1985. Used with permission of the American Marketing Association.

Because services cannot be protected by patents, companies with original ideas must protect their ideas as much as they can by registering their trademarks or brand names and marketing their ideas quickly to capture as much consumer loyalty as possible. Check-a-Child, a short-term baby-sitting service, was able to protect its new idea with its unique name; although competitors can copy its idea, none can create a name as descriptive of the service. A strong organizational image also helps to protect a service's unique features. Delta Airlines, which advertises and promotes its services heavily, has created a strong image of good service that many consumers associate only with Delta.

To cope with quality control problems, a service provider can try to "industrialize service" by substituting packaged services for individualized services.[7] For example, a travel agency could offer a set of prepackaged vacation tours for the most frequently visited areas rather than prepare a unique tour for each customer. To ensure uniform treatment by employees, the Red Lobster restaurant prepares scripts for its servers and hostesses and carefully trains them to follow the scripts in a pleasant manner. While many services create a constant level of quality through use of these strategies, they may risk becoming too impersonal or alienating their work forces. Perhaps for these reasons some service businesses prefer to take advantage of the heterogeneity and customize the service to meet better the precise desires of individual consumers.

Managing customers themselves involves recognizing that customers who misuse a service may interfere with the smooth running of the whole service business, delay service personnel, and irritate other customers who are seeking service at the same time.[8] Customers may need to be given instructions on how to behave properly while consuming the service. Sometimes this is done through signs: "Please wait for the next teller," "Thank you for clearing your table," or "Shoes and shirts required."

Pricing problems. The intangibility of services sometimes causes problems in pricing. Cost-based pricing, frequently used with tangible goods (and described in chapter 12), is often hard to apply to services. Fixed and operating costs associated with services are very difficult to determine, especially when several services are being produced at the same time by the same organization. In a bank, for example, management would find it difficult to assign specific costs separately to checking accounts, savings accounts, and money market accounts since the same employees handle all three types of accounts simultaneously.

Information about the prices of services is often less available to consumers than information about the prices of tangible goods. With most tangible goods, retail stores carry a vast array of different and competing products, offering the consumer an opportunity to compare prices easily. On the other hand, many service outlets offer only one service (haircuts, medical checkups, fast food), so the consumer must visit several different providers to get competing price information. Comparative pricing information about professional services—from doctors, lawyers, and dentists, for example—is especially difficult to obtain, as industry guidelines used to prohibit advertising for these services. While advertising is now permitted, many professionals have not yet widely accepted the practice.

Coping with special pricing problems. Service companies may use a number of different methods to price their services. If a company wants to use cost-based pricing, cost accounting may be used to trace internal costs directly to specific services.[9] Some companies simply observe what their competitors are charging and price accordingly. Other service companies price their products based on the value to consumers, thereby charging different prices at different times or to different groups of customers. Resort hotels, telephone companies, for-profit hospitals, and airlines charge different rates depending on the value of the service at a given time.

Resort hotels charge more during peak season than off-season, telephone companies charge higher rates between 9 A.M. and 5 P.M. than in the evenings, and for-profit hospitals charge full price for rooms during the week and less on weekends. Movie theaters give discounts to children or senior citizens, recognizing that they are more willing to purchase when the price is less than the regular price. Airlines have special standby rates to fill seats that were not sold at the regular rates.

Promotional problems. Because they are intangible, services cannot always be readily displayed or communicated. With tangible goods, consumers often decide to buy when they browse through a retail store and see the goods on display. With intangible services, the producer has nothing to stock on the shelves. Complex goods can be demonstrated, but complex services can only be described. Deciding what to feature in a print advertisement or a television commercial for a service can also be difficult; the service itself cannot always be visualized.

Because of the heterogeneity of services, large firms with many outlets may run the risk of not being able to live up to promises about quality. Consistent performance is very difficult to guarantee. Holiday Inn's "no surprises" advertising campaign was designed to ensure consistent quality but was difficult to live up to in all of its hundreds of outlets.

In many cases, advertising may have little effect on consumers because the services advertised are high-risk purchases. While consumers have no problem buying a brand of chewing gum or a detergent based on an advertisement, they may want more assurance when trusting their clothes to a dry cleaner or their hair to a stylist. Even riskier are purchases of the services of a doctor or lawyer. While these professionals are now permitted by their national associations to advertise, consumers resist this advertising because they are not used to advertising in the professional services and because the purchases are very important to them. In these cases, consumers may use the price of the service, rather than the promotion, to judge the quality of the service.

Another problem with promotion is that small, independent service businesses cannot always afford it. Small retail stores are able to obtain advertising allowances from the national manufacturers of the tangible goods they carry, but this type of promotion, called "cooperative advertising," is less available to service firms.

A final, and important, promotion difference between services and tangible goods is the overwhelming importance of the salesperson. In many services, the salesperson—the dentist, the bartender, the teller, the hairstylist, the doctor—*is* the service. Some customers choose the service establishment because of the salesperson. Attracting and maintaining good service personnel often becomes a problem in service businesses.

Coping with special promotional problems. Service marketers can overcome some of the difficulties associated with service intangibility by using the tangibles associated with the service—for example, office decor and equipment—to promote the service. A potential customer can get an idea about the types of haircuts provided in a Command Performance hair salon by seeing its trendy interiors.

A bank customer will feel secure in a bank with high marble columns and dark-suited personnel. Jane Fonda has managed the tangibles in her Workout exercise salons by hiring only the most fit and athletic personnel. These tangibles can be featured in the service's advertising to provide visual clues about the service.[10] Consider the signals provided by Merrill Lynch's bull, TransAmerica's pyramidlike headquarters building, or Prudential's rock.

Encouraging positive word-of-mouth communications is especially important in services, since personal recommendations help the consumer feel more certain in making high-risk purchases.[11] Wendy's and Burger King generated word-of-mouth during the "Battle of the Burgers" when they used high-interest advertising to compare themselves to McDonald's. Advertising can also be helpful after the purchase by reassuring consumers that their choices were good ones (see fig. 21-4).

Personal selling is a very important part of the promotion in service businesses. Because salespeople are the key people in the organization, special attention should be devoted to their selection, training, motivation, and supervision.[12] Internal marketing, which involves applying marketing concepts to attract, retain, and motivate employees, is also a way to manage employees and encourage high performance.[13]

Figure 21—4
Through an honest and dependable-looking speaker and straightforward copy, Wang is reminding and reassuring consumers that a decision to purchase Wang office automation services is a good one.
Reproduced with permission of Wang Laboratories, Inc.

Laimute E. Druskis

Figure 21–5 When services cannot be transported, the producer may have to travel to the consumer.

Distribution problems. Since the consumer must be present for the production of many services, distribution is not the same as it is for tangible goods. A producer can manufacture a tangible good in a remote plant and then transport it to retail stores all over the country. Because services are intangible, they usually cannot be transported. Because they are often inseparable, the producer must be present to produce the service. The result is that short channels of distribution are common.

Coping with distribution problems. With services that cannot be transported, either the consumer must travel to the retail location (for example, to the hairstylist, health spa, or movie theater), or the producer must travel to the consumer (as with pest exterminators, housecleaners, or baby-sitters). Service companies must select convenient and accessible locations when the consumer travels to the service, since convenience is a major factor in consumer selection of services, such as dry cleaning, banking, or car repair.

In some cases, services can be transported through channels of distribution. New technology has now permitted distribution of some services through electronic media. For example, college courses can be transmitted from a university to consumers' homes or to branch sites through television. And Music Television (MTV) has electronically transported concerts and live performances to millions of homes.

The growth of franchising in service industries has overcome some of the problems associated with the distribution of services. Because many services required the presence of the producer, the organizations were small, locally owned and operated, and lacked professional management. Service franchise chains—such as Midas Muffler, Command Performance Hair Salons, and H&R Block Tax Service— overcame these problems by standardizing many elements of the service and providing professional promotion and management.[14] A successful service franchise is Supercuts, a chain of hair salons, which advertises guaranteed haircuts for a single price: $9.

Chapter 21 / Services and Nonprofit Marketing

Marketing in Service Firms

Service firms have been slower than tangible goods firms to embrace marketing concepts and use marketing techniques. One study found that service companies were less likely to have marketing activities performed by a marketing department, to have an overall sales plan, to use sales training programs, to use marketing research firms and marketing consultants, and to hire an outside advertising agency.[15] A recent study found that service firms, especially local firms selling to individual consumers, scored low on marketing activities, such as contacting customers to make sure they are satisfied, carefully choosing and training personnel, and conducting marketing research to understand customer needs.[16]

Why do service firms lag behind tangible goods firms in using marketing? Managers of small, local services often lack both funds and marketing training. Some service providers, such as doctors and hospitals, have traditionally had sufficient demand without needing to market themselves. Also, in the professional services, marketing has been viewed as unprofessional or unethical. Finally, some service industries, such as airlines, telephone companies, and utilities, used to be so highly regulated that some marketing mix variables could not be controlled by the marketer. Almost all these factors are changing in the 1980s; deregulation, the growth of franchises, and intense competition are projected to change the structure of service industries in the future. As a recent study pointed out:

> Service firms that are insufficiently marketing oriented are exceedingly vulnerable in the 1980s. . . . In yesterday's environment the non-marketing oriented service firm may well have competed against other firms that were not marketing oriented either. In today's environment, there are likely to be new competitors, perhaps from outside the community, perhaps from outside the industry. The new competition cannot be counted on to neglect marketing. . . . Marketing does matter. In the 1980s, it is an imperative.[17]

Nonprofit Marketing

Baltimore had a major problem with litter. Despite many efforts to encourage citizens to keep their city clean, the litter problem was one of the worst in the nation. Then Trashball was born. Trashball is a game invented to make litter disposal fun. It started with conversion of all the city's litter baskets into imitation basketball hoops with wire mesh bottoms and orange rims. Basketball slogans—such as "Dunk One," "Slam One," "Smash One"—were attached to the litter baskets. Advertisements featured a catchy jingle and basketball stars encouraging everyone to "play Trashball." On weekends, basketball players donated their time to travel to inner-city neighborhoods and "coach" city children in cleaning up their neighborhoods. The team collecting the most trash won tickets to professional basketball games. As playing Trashball became the norm, littering became uncool. Baltimore's litter problem was solved.

The marketing of nonprofit organizations and ideas differs from the marketing of business products, just as the marketing of services differs from the marketing of tangible goods. In this section, we discuss these differences, the problems they create, and the strategies used to adapt marketing to deal with these problems.

What Is Nonprofit Marketing?

Many different types of offerings fall into the category of **nonprofit marketing**. Organizations that operate in the public interest and do not seek financial profit, such as symphony orchestras, religious organizations, social action groups, and public universities, fall into this category. Organizations that exist to support an idea or a social cause, such as the American Heart Association, Planned Parenthood, and the United Way, also fall into this category. Political candidates and government agencies are also included. Figure 21–6 lists some of the major types of organizations that conduct nonprofit marketing and provides examples of each.

Nonprofit organizations have not always used marketing. Sometimes they have resisted selling and promotion; sometimes they have lacked the funds and expertise to carry out marketing. Not until the 1970s were the unique problems and opportunities in nonprofit marketing recognized.[18] During the 1980s, many nonprofit organizations are realizing that they need marketing to survive the intense competition facing them from competitors in the private sector, such as from private universities and for-profit hospitals, and to generate funds to carry out their activities.

Figure 21–6 Types of organizations that conduct nonprofit marketing

Chapter 21 / Services and Nonprofit Marketing

How Is Nonprofit Marketing Different?

As nonprofit marketing sells ideas, social causes, and activities in the public interest, the marketing environment is different and the marketing strategies employed must reflect the differences. In general, there are nine differences between business marketing and nonprofit marketing:[19]

1. *Nature of the products.* Most nonprofit organizations offer services and social behaviors, rather than tangible goods.
2. *Dominance of nonfinancial objectives.* Some form of social profit, rather than financial profit, is sought by the nonprofit organization.
3. *Need for resource attraction.* Nonprofit organizations usually cannot cover their costs from sales revenues and must seek contributions. They are often able to get such things as advertising time and labor free or at a reduced rate.
4. *Multiple constituencies.* Nonprofit organizations usually must deal with two sets of customers: donors to the service and receivers of the service. They must also consider the interests of many different constituencies, including third-party payment organizations, such as insurers, regulatory agencies, and former customers (college alumni, for example).
5. *Tension between mission and customer satisfaction.* The nonprofit organization's mission may be to get people to do things that may not appeal to them such as stopping smoking or donating blood.
6. *Public scrutiny.* Nonprofit organizations tend to attract more public scrutiny than do private firms.
7. *Nonmarket pressures.* Nonprofit organizations are often subject to pressure from outside organizations, such as government regulatory agencies, industry associations, and professional associations.
8. *Ability to obtain free or inexpensive support.* Nonprofit organizations can often get other organizations to contribute money or support. For example, the Advertising Council donates its time and services to social causes of national interest (see focus 21–1).
9. *Management in duplicate or triplicate.* Nonprofit organizations often have hired staffs as well as strong political or volunteer boards.

Another difficulty associated with nonprofit marketing is that the organizations frequently face pressure not to segment the market, especially when the segmentation leads to ignoring certain groups. When target segments are selected, they often consist of those consumers who are most resistant to their offerings.[20] Mothers Against Drunk Driving (MADD), for example, has as its objective fighting alcohol abuse. Its target segment consists of those people who drive while drunk, yet this segment views MADD as an extremist organization and is most resistant to its messages.

Problems and Strategies in Nonprofit Marketing

Product problems. Several distinct problems associated with the product make marketing in nonprofit organizations more complicated than in business organizations. One major problem is that nonprofit organizations tend to have less flexibility in shaping their products and have more difficulty formulating product concepts.[21] Rather than simple product concepts like "tastes great, less filling" or "double your pleasure, double your fun," nonprofit organizations are often selling a complex behavior or idea that cannot be neatly encapsulated.

There are other product problems. First, the offerings of most nonprofit organizations—services, social causes, ideas—are intangible, making them more difficult to explain and show than tangible goods. Second, the personal benefits that can be offered to potential customers are often weak or indirect. In a goods transaction, the buyer receives a tangible benefit in exchange for money. With nonprofit "purchases," the buyer often receives little or nothing to reinforce the purchase; the benefits from donating blood or contributing to a cause cannot always be demonstrated. Third, consumers often have no latent demand or interest in these nonprofit offerings. Few automobile drivers felt the need to "Drive 55"; while society as a whole benefited in fewer traffic deaths and in energy savings, most consumers saw little personal benefit associated with the reduced speed limit law.[22]

Coping with product problems. While many nonprofit organizations have difficulty formulating product concepts, marketing professionals can often be helpful in communicating effectively. The Advertising Council has taken many complex ideas and created memorable product concepts and advertising campaigns.

To cope with intangibility, nonprofit organizations often try to show something tangible. The Arthritis Foundation offers a free booklet on how to live with arthritis. To make the abstract idea of hunger a reality, the Save the Children Fund features photographs of actual children suffering from starvation.

To cope with absent or weak latent demand, the marketer can tie the nonprofit offering to a demand that does exist. Charities often sponsor large social occasions, such as balls or dinners, to raise money for their causes, thereby linking the charity with consumers' liking for social events.

When only weak personal benefits exist, the nonprofit organization can make the benefits more direct. Rather than an appeal to drive more slowly to save lives (a weak personal benefit), an appeal to drive more slowly to save gas and money (strong personal benefits) could be used. Rather than a plea to donate blood for the good of all people (a weak personal benefit), a plea to donate blood for a coworker or for later personal use (strong personal benefits) could be used. Direct benefits such as tax deductions, pictures and letters from an adopted child in another country, or even bumper stickers or buttons identifying contributors are ways to tie benefits more directly to nonprofit purchases.

Pricing problems. In many nonprofit situations, consumers are not charged a monetary price. Instead, "consuming" the offering involves other costs. These

21–1 Focus on a Marketing Practice
THE ADVERTISING COUNCIL

In November 1941, leading figures in U.S. advertising met to discuss how to improve the public's opinion of advertising. These executives were challenged at this meeting to find ways of using advertising for the public good. Two months later, after the attack on Pearl Harbor had drawn the United States into World War II, the War Advertising Council was formed to aid the government through advertising. Its first campaigns promoted the conversion from a peacetime to a wartime economy and the purchase of war bonds. Over the next few years, more than 100 home-front campaigns in areas as diverse as forest fire prevention and the promotion of victory gardens had been conducted.

After the war, the War Advertising Council became simply the Advertising Council and started working on problems of national interest. The council carries out its activities on a voluntary basis, and it conducts general-interest campaigns of service to the nation as a whole.

The way the Advertising Council works is simple. Private organizations and government agencies ask the council to conduct advertising campaigns to promote voluntary citizen action to help solve national problems, like alcoholism or child abuse, or to encourage donations to nonprofit organizations, such as the American Red Cross or the United Way. These proposals are analyzed and reviewed and then submitted to the council's board of directors, which votes on whether or not to accept the proposal as a major campaign. After a proposal's acceptance, a volunteer advertising agency, a volunteer coordinator, and a campaign manager are assigned to create, coordinate, and implement the campaign.

In this manner, thousands of public interest campaigns have been conducted, containing many of the most memorable symbols and slogans the advertising media have offered: McGruff the dog taking a bite out of crime; Smokey the bear reminding that only you can prevent forest fires; Iron Eyes Cody crying over pollution. And not millions, but billions, of dollars have been raised for the United Negro College Fund, American universities, the Red Cross, the United Way, and other organizations by campaigns promoting, not profit-making goods and services, but the idea of voluntary citizen action.

Source: "The Advertising Council: An American Phenomenon," *Advertising Age*, November 21, 1973, pp. 172, 174, 177.

nonmonetary costs can often be more costly to the consumer than monetary ones. Sometimes these costs involve time—the extra traveling time incurred in driving 55 miles per hour, or the personal time to drive to a hospital to give blood. In other situations the costs are psychological: some people fear or feel discomfort when giving blood, or are afraid of social disapproval from asking someone not to smoke in their presence. Other costs may involve inconvenience, such as going out of the way to put litter in a trash can rather than discarding it in the street.[23]

Courtesy of The Advertising Council

When monetary prices are involved, they are usually given other names, such as fees, charitable donations, or admission charges or tuition. While some nonprofit organizations are unwilling or unable to charge a monetary price, an increasing trend today is to raise fees or start charging for many nonprofit services often given free in the past. Because of rising costs and increasing competition, public colleges and universities are charging higher tuition, performing arts companies are raising their fees, and even churches are formalizing the donation processes.[24]

Coping with pricing problems. Anything the organization can do to decrease the nonmonetary costs associated with nonprofit offerings will improve the chances of purchase.[25] A bloodmobile that travels to donors' workplaces, for example, eliminates some of the time and inconvenience costs associated with giving blood. Placing trash cans in many places on city streets limits any inconvenience costs involved in trash disposal. Psychological costs can also be minimized. The use of celebrities for nonsmoking commercials helps make nonsmoking the accepted norm, thus minimizing the psychological cost of asking others not to smoke.

Promotional problems. Nonprofit organizations usually have limited promotional budgets and must justify any promotional expenditures they make. When consumers or businesses make a donation to a charity, they want the money to be spent on the cause rather than on advertising the cause. Donors and other publics may also resist the use of certain media, such as television, and certain messages, such as humor, hard-sell, or fear appeals.[26]

Nonprofit organizations are able to obtain free broadcast advertising in the form of public service announcements. When these are used, however, the messages must be noncontroversial, and the advertiser has little control over where, when, and how frequently ads are run. Because the advertiser has little control, advertising objectives are difficult to set and effectiveness is hard to evaluate.

Advertising is often less effective in nonprofit situations because "purchase" requires either very high or very low involvement on the part of the consumer.

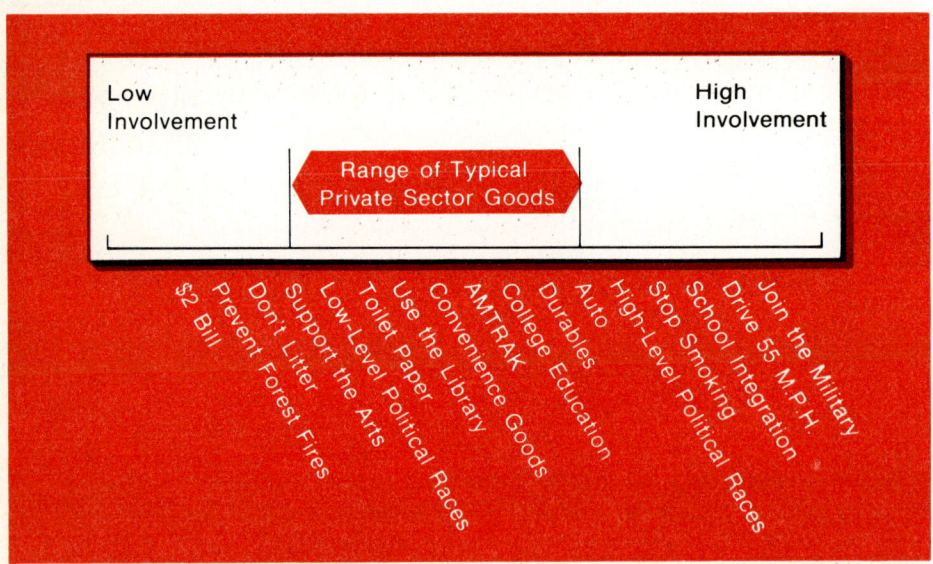

Figure 21–7
Nonprofit products on a scale from low to high involvement

Source: Michael L. Rothschild, "Marketing Communications in Nonbusiness Situations or Why It's So Hard to Sell Brotherhood Like Soap," *Journal of Marketing*, Spring 1979, p. 14. Used with permission of the American Marketing Association.

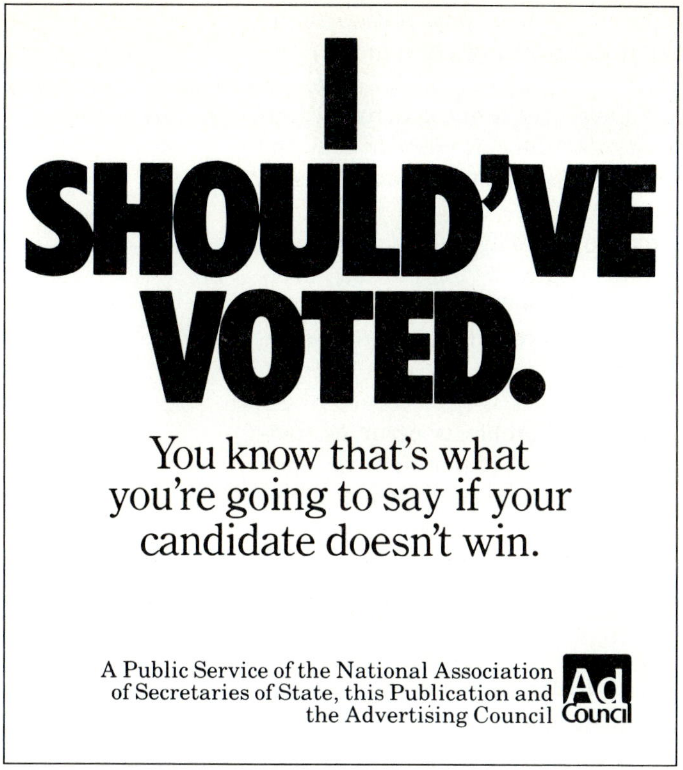

Figure 21–8 An advertisement that increases personal involvement

Courtesy of The Advertising Council

Figure 21–7 arranges some nonprofit products on a scale from low to high involvement. The higher the involvement, the greater the amount of personal commitment required on the part of the consumer. In moderate levels of involvement, marketing communications can be effective in generating a response in the consumer. However, in a low involvement case, such as "Support the Arts," interest in the offering is difficult to generate through advertising. In high involvement cases, such as "Drive 55" or "Join the Navy," the purchase requires such heavy involvement that consumers rarely can be persuaded by mass communications alone. The ability of advertising to change behavior in these cases is limited, although some nonprofit organizations use advertising campaigns to try (see fig. 21–8).[27]

Coping with promotional problems. When public service announcements are used, the marketer can maximize their effectiveness by using such strategies as creating technically good advertisements or commercials in a format that matches the media outlet's preferences, adding a local tagline, and identifying the message with a local sponsor.[28]

Marketing can exert some influence over the level of involvement experienced by consumers by strengthening personal benefits and tying the offering to a demand that already exists. The Trashball example at the beginning of this section illustrates how involvement can be increased: By making litter disposal into a game that is acceptable to the target audience, the desired behavior can be achieved. Emphasizing what will happen if the consumer doesn't make the purchase is another technique. Reducing high involvement is a more difficult problem and one that requires personal selling more than advertising. The ability of advertising to change behavior is limited in these cases.

Nonprofit firms can also use public relations and publicity to a greater extent in their promotional mix. These techniques are often less costly than media advertising and can be used effectively with a properly trained staff. Nontraditional marketing tools (such as television programs and short films) can also add to the marketer's promotion mix.[29]

Distribution problems. Two major distribution problems occur in nonprofit situations. First, since demand for the offering is often absent or weak, little incentive exists for consumers to come to the organization. Second, any channels of distribution are usually voluntary and are not under the control of the marketer. Nonprofit marketers sometimes have difficulty convincing intermediaries, such as the news media or doctors or community groups, to pass along information or support for their cause.[30]

Coping with distribution problems. Since the consumer rarely comes to the firm, the nonprofit firm must go to the consumer. Finding acceptable ways to reach the consumer is a challenge to these organizations. Some use volunteers with a network of friends and neighbors to reduce the problems associated with door-to-door canvassing. Others, such as United Way, encourage involvement by community leaders and celebrities to achieve their goals. Others send the organization to the consumer, as illustrated by the bloodmobile that travels to people's workplaces to encourage donations.

Marketing in Nonprofit Organizations

During the 1970s, managers of nonprofit organizations began to apply the principles of marketing to their services and ideas. Once considered inappropriate for nonbusiness firms, marketing has now become an integral tool for the survival of these firms in the 1980s.

Summary

Services are performances, deeds, or acts performed by businesses, individuals, or nonprofit organizations for consumers or for other businesses. Services are different from tangible goods in that they are intangible, inseparable from production and consumption, heterogeneous, and perishable.

There are some special problems involved in marketing services, including the fact that they cannot be stored or inventoried, they cannot be patented, quality control is difficult to achieve, the consumer participates in the production process and therefore affects the transaction, and the service received by one customer may be dramatically influenced by the presence or absence of others.

Companies with original ideas must protect them by trademarking their brand names and marketing their ideas quickly to capture brand loyalty. To cope with quality control problems, a service provider can substitute packaged service for individualized services. The risk of standardizing services is that they may become impersonal. Customers may be instructed as to how to behave when seeking a service.

Pricing can be a problem with services, since they are intangible. Methods of dealing with this problem include cost accounting to trace internal costs to specific services, observing competitors' prices, and pricing based on the value of the service to customers.

One source of promotion problems is the fact that the producer of a service has nothing to display. Heterogeneity presents the risk of overpromising quality. Advertising may have less impact on consumers when the service is high risk. Attracting and maintaining good service personnel often becomes a problem in service businesses.

In promotion, service marketers can emphasize the tangible aspects of the service. Well-trained personnel can function as a promotional tool.

Because most services cannot be transported, the service company must select convenient and accessible locations where the consumer travels to the service. Electronic media can transport some services, such as entertainment and information. Franchising helps to overcome some distribution problems by standardizing many elements of the service and providing professional promotion and management.

Service companies tend to use marketing techniques less than companies producing tangible goods, perhaps because they lack funds and marketing expertise, view the practice as unethical, or have been highly regulated.

Nine factors differentiate nonprofit marketing from business marketing: nature of products, dominance of nonfinancial objectives, need for resource attraction, multiple constituencies, tension between mission and customer satisfaction, public scrutiny, nonmarket pressures, ability to obtain free or inexpensive support, and management in duplicate and triplicate.

Questions for Discussion

1. What are the distinctive characteristics of a service compared with a product?
2. Explain in what way a service is promoted differently from a product.
3. Which one of the four P's (product, place, promotion, and price) is least affected by the uniqueness of a service compared with a product? Explain.
4. Why do service firms generally lag behind goods firms in using marketing?
5. How is nonprofit marketing different from marketing by business firms?

6. Identify two examples (of your own) of conflict between the nonprofit organization's mission and customer satisfaction. How would the organization resolve the conflicts?
7. In what way is service marketing similar to nonprofit marketing?
8. Identify a nonprofit institution facing a specific problem and explain how it can market itself.
9. Do you think it is ethical for nonprofit institutions to use marketing? Explain.

References

1. "The Big Business of Medicine," *Newsweek,* October 31, 1983, pp. 62–74.
2. Leonard L. Berry, G. Lynn Shostack, and Gregory D. Upah, *Emerging Perspectives on Services Marketing* (Chicago: American Marketing Association,) p. 1.
3. Leonard Berry, "Service Marketing Is Different," *Business,* May–June 1980, pp. 24–29.
4. Valarie A. Zeithaml, A. Parasuraman, and Leonard L. Berry, "Problems and Strategies in Services Marketing," *Journal of Marketing,* Winter 1985.
5. William J. Regan, "The Service Revolution," *Journal of Marketing,* July 1963, pp. 57–62.
6. Richard M. Bessom and David W. Jackson, "Service Retailing—A Strategic Marketing Approach," *Journal of Retailing,* Summer 1975, pp. 137–49.
7. Theodore Levitt, "The Industrialization of Service," *Harvard Business Review,* September–October 1976, pp. 63–74.
8. Christopher H. Lovelock, "Towards a Classification of Services," in *Theoretical Developments in Marketing,* ed. Charles Lamb and Patrick Dunne (Chicago: American Marketing Association, 1980), pp. 72–76.
9. Larry H. Beard and Valarie A. Hoyle, "Cost Accounting Proposal for an Advertising Agency," *Management Accounting,* December 1976, pp. 38–40.
10. William R. George and Leonard L. Berry, "Guidelines for Advertising Services," *Business Horizons,* 1981, pp. 52–56.
11. Duane L. Davis, Joseph P. Guiltinan, and Wesley H. Jones, "Service Characteristics, Consumer Search, and the Classification of Retail Services," *Journal of Retailing,* Fall 1979, pp. 3–21. See also Bessom and Jackson, "Service Retailing," Raymond P. Fisk, "Toward a Consumption/Evaluation Process Model for Services," and Valarie A. Zeithaml, "How Consumer Evaluation Processes Differ Between Goods and Services," in *Marketing of Services,* ed. J. H. Donnelly and W. R. George (Chicago: American Marketing Association, 1981), pp. 186–90 and 191–95.
12. David S. Davidson, "How to Succeed in a Service Industry—Turn the Organization Chart Upside Down," *Management Review,* April 1978, pp. 13–16.
13. See Leonard L. Berry, "The Employee as Customer," *Journal of Retail Banking,* March 1981, pp. 33–40. See also Christian Gronroos, "A Service-Oriented Approach to Marketing of Services," *European Journal of Marketing,* 1978, pp. 588–601.

14. Christopher Lovelock, *Services Marketing* (Englewood Cliffs, N.J.: Prentice-Hall, 1984), p. 3.
15. William R. George and Hiram C. Barksdale, "Marketing Activities in the Service Industries," *Journal of Marketing*, October 1974, p. 65.
16. A. Parasuraman, Leonard L. Berry, and Valarie A. Zeithaml, "Service Firms Need Marketing Skills," *Business Horizons*, November–December 1983, pp. 28–31.
17. Ibid., p. 31.
18. Philip Kotler, *Marketing for Nonprofit Organizations* (Englewood Cliffs, N.J.: Prentice-Hall, 1975).
19. Christopher H. Lovelock and Charles B. Weinberg, *Marketing for Public and Nonprofit Managers* (New York: John Wiley, 1984).
20. Paul N. Bloom and William D. Novelli, "Problems in Applying Conventional Marketing Wisdom to Social Marketing Programs," paper presented at the American Marketing Association Workshop originally titled "Exploring and Developing Government Marketing," Yale University, New Haven, Conn., May 3–4, 1979.
21. Kotler, *Marketing for Nonprofit Organizations;* Christopher Lovelock and Charles B. Weinberg, "Contrasting Private and Public Sector Marketing," in *1974 Combined Proceedings* (Chicago: American Marketing Association, 1974), pp. 242–47.
22. Michael L. Rothschild, "Marketing Communications in Nonbusiness Situations or Why It's So Hard to Sell Brotherhood Like Soap," *Journal of Marketing*, Spring 1979, pp. 11–20.
23. Ibid.
24. Lovelock and Weinberg, *Marketing for Public and Nonprofit Managers.*
25. Bloom and Novelli, "Problems in Applying Conventional Marketing Wisdom."
26. Franklin S. Houston and Richard E. Homans, "Public Agency Marketing: Pitfalls and Problems," *MSU Business Topics*, Summer 1977, pp. 36–40.
27. Rothschild, "Marketing Communications in Nonbusiness Situations."
28. Lovelock and Weinberg, *Marketing for Public and Nonprofit Managers.*
29. H. Mendelsohn, "Some Reasons Why Information Campaigns Can Succeed," *Public Opinion Quarterly*, Spring 1973, pp. 50–61.
30. Bloom and Novelli, "Problems in Applying Conventional Marketing Wisdom."

OBJECTIVES

1. To look ahead to the future of marketing and what it means to marketers.

2. To examine the three environmental trends—the use of computers, internationalization, and narrower segmentation—and highlight their impact on marketing decisions.

3. To discuss the future trends in the marketing mix.

4. To discuss the future trends in marketing management practices.

effectiveness measurement, 430–31
features of, 390–91
Public policy and marketing, 63–72, 77
Pulling strategy, 403, 475
Purchasing agent, 211
Pushing strategy, 475
Push money, 426

Quality as positioning method, 252–53
Quality as pricing objective, 330
Quality control for services, 610

Rack jobbers, 523
Radick, Michael D., *453*, 459
Radio, 410–11, *415*, 432
Radio Shack, 461, 464, 471, 502, 515
Ramada Inns, 324, 336, 342, 346
Rausing, Ruben, 634
Ray, Michael L., *388*, *389*, 397
Reference groups, 181–84, 198
Regan, William J., 626
Re-gentrification and buyer behavior, 193
Regional shopping centers, 515–16
Reibstein, David J., 200, 258, 295, 372, 570
Renault, 235, 593, 634
Representatives, manufacturer's, 523–24
Research, marketing
  causal, 116–17
  consumer profile study, 116
  data analysis, 130
  design of, 115–19, 135
  experience survey, 115
  exploratory, 115–16
  longitudinal study, 116
  recommendations, based on, 130
  use of secondary data, 115
Research and development (R&D), 45, 305, 312–13, 320
Research sampling, 123–26
Resources, allocation of, 43, 61, 105, 563–64
Retailer
  and cash discounts, 354
  positioning of, 252, 255
  and trade discounts, 353
Retailers, 509–12
  classified by ownership, 512–14
  classified by retailing mixes, 501–12
  classified by store location, 514–16
Retailing, 494–517, 561–62

competitive nature of, 495
definition of, 494–95
Retailing mix, 496–501, 503
Retailing-sponsored cooperative, 473
Return on investment
  and market share, 552–53
  as pricing objective, 329–30
Reynolds, R. J., Industries, Inc., 172, 551
Ricci, Claudia, *310*
Richards, Bill, 427
Rink, David R., 233
Risk analysis and strategy audit, 565–67
Risk evaluation and product development, 304–5
Risk perceived by customers, 172–73
Roberts, Mary Lou, *187*, 233
Robertson, John, 375
Robertson, Thomas S., 65, 570
Robinson, Patrick J., *210*
Robinson-Patman Act of 1936, 69, 70, 369, 371
Robotics industry, 224, 585
Rodgers, William, 569
Rogers, Everett M., *315*
Rotbart, Dean, 459
Rothschild, Michael L., *622*, 627
Rothschild, William E., 99, 106, 107
Rouse, Ewart, 75
Rudolph, Barbara, 79

Safeway Stores, 139–40, *495*, 506, 507, 512
Sales during product life cycle, 314–18
Sales force and pricing policy, 334–35
Sales force management, 449–57
Sales growth as pricing objective, 328
Salespeople
  compensation of, 452–54
  evaluation of, 454
  motivation of, 452
  recruitment of, 450–51
  training of, 452
Salesperson, roles of, 438–40, 457
Sales presentation, 444
Sales strategy, 443–46
  approach, 444
  closing, 445–46
  follow-up, 446
  handling objections, 444–45
  prospecting, 443–44
Salpukas, Agis, 349
Samples, free, 422
Samples, nonprobability, *123*, 124, 126

Samples, probability, *123*, 124–25
Sanger, David E., 372
Savitt, Ronald, *56*, 79
Schaninger, C., 200
Scheuble, Philip A., Jr., 348
Schoeffler, Sidney, 569
Schott, Jeffrey J., 603
Sears, Roebuck and Company, 75, 134, 464, 471, 495, 504, 509, 553–54, 634
Sease, Douglas R., 257
Segmentation, market, 12, 90, 236–51
  advantages of, 239–40, 256
  bases for, 242–48, 256
  benefit, 245–46, 247–48
  criteria for, 240–42, 256
  defined, 236–37, 255
Segments, market
  competition for, 249–50, 251
  ease of entry, 250–51
  growth of, 250
  receptivity of consumers, 250
  size of, 248–49
  strength of, 249
  value of, 250
Selective market coverage, 469
Selling Areas-Marketing Inc., (SAMI), 121
Selling parties, 512
Sen, Subrata K., 258
Services
  classification of, 607–8
  as components of tangible products, 291–93, 294
  distribution problems, 615
  pricing problems, 612–13
  product problems, 610–12
  promotional problems, 613–14
  in retailing mix, 500–501
Shansby, J. Gary, 258
Shapiro, Benson, P., 348, 372
Sherman Act of 1890, 66–70
Sheth, Jagdish, N., 233
Shopping centers, 515–16
Shostack, G. Lynn, 295, 626
Simison, Robert L., 257
Simmons Market Research Bureau, *121*, *122*, 409
Singh, Ravi, 570
Single-store sites, 516
Skarewitz, Norm, 295
Sloan, Pat, 372
Smith, Lee, 161
Smith, Samuel V., 25
Socio-demographic variables, 243–44
Soft-drink industry, 61, 277, 278–79, 285, 289

Software, personal computer, 461–62, 464
Sonnenfeld, Jeffrey, 373
Sony, 1, 5, 9, 10, 271, 292, 356
Specialty stores, 502–4
Speller, Donald E., 161
Spiegel Catalog, 509, 511, 634
Staelin, Richard, 161
Stanley, Richard E., *380*, 397
Stasch, Stanley F., 51
Steinberg, Bruce, *188*, 200
Steiner, Gary A., *386*, 397
Stephenson, P. Ronald, 348
Stern, L., *518*, 527
Stevens, Lawrence, 640
Storyboard, advertising, 409
Straight rebuy situation, 158, 210–11
Strang, Roger A., 397
Strategic business units, 96–101, 106, 545
Strategy, corporate, 48
Stevens, Charles W., 257
Strip shopping centers, 515
Structure, organizational, 28, 228, *229*, 232
Subsidiaries, wholly owned, 592–93
Supermarkets, 506–7
Superstores, 507
Suppliers, wholesaling services for, 518–19
Supply, law of, 338
Supply and demand for services, 610–11
Swan, John E., *220*, 233
Systems concept in physical distribution, 488

Tandy Corporation, 283–84, 351, 461, 494
Tariffs, 584
Taylor, James R., *170*
Team selling, 455, 456
Technological environment, 72–74, 78
Technology
  as new product idea source, 300–302
  and retailing, 516–17
Telecommunications industry, 53–54, 58–59, 61–63, 66, 73–74
Telemarketing, 449
Telephone survey in market testing, 307
Television
  cable, 63, 87–88, 130, 410, 543–44
  network, 91–92

Television advertising, 409–10, *415*, 432
Terpstra, Vern, 602
Testing, market, 307–8, 319
Testing, new product idea, 303–4
Texas Instruments, 351, 360, 361
Thomas, Kenneth, *215*
Thorpe, Norman, 484
Toll-free product service numbers, 291, 292
Toman, Alan, 132
Topol toothpaste, 240, 404–5
Toyota Motor Corp., 70, 253, 292, 577, 592, 634
Trade agreements, 588–89
Trade allowances, 424–25
Trademarks, 286–87
Trade policies, 66
Trade practices, unfair, 370
Trade shows, 425
Training
  as part of augmented product, 291
  of sales force, 452
Transportation in physical distribution, 480–83, 490
Truck jobbers, 523
Truth in Lending Act, 354
Tull, Donald S., 137
Tupperware, 512, 551
Tylenol, 249, 255, 280, 290, 369, 430

Unfair trade practices, 370
Uniform delivered, 356, *357*
United Airlines, 250, 328, 427
U.S. Elevator Corporation, 335, 345
U.S. Foreign Corrupt Practices Act, 586
U.S. Steel, 334, 336
United Way, 617, 620, 624
Universal product code, 128, 629
Upah, Gregory D., 626
USSR, 581, 584, 585, 596

Value and market segmentation, 250
Value and price, 21–22, 325–26
Values
  and buyer behavior, 178–79, 198
  cultural, 76, 178–79
  instrumental, 153
  terminal, 153
Variety switching, 285–86
Veblen, Thorstein, 200
Vertical integration, 271–72
Vertical marketing systems, 471–73
Volkswagen, 253, 310, 593
Volume-sensitive structure, 332
Von Hippel, Eric, 321

Waldholz, Michael, 355
Wang Laboratories, 595
Wants, customer, 9, 43
Ward, Scott, 65
Warehouses, 487
Warehouse stores, 507
Warner Amex Communications, 89, 543–44
Warranties, 291
Waterman, Robert H., Jr., 233
Webster, Frederick E., Jr., *229*, 233
Weinberg, Charles B., 627
Weiner, Steve, 527
Weinstein, Curt, 419
Weinstein, Sidney, 419
Weitz, Barton, *31*, *33*, *39*, 50, 51, 233
Wells, Ken, 306
Wendy's, 399–400, 406, 416, 495, 614
Wheeler-Lea Act of 1938, 69
Wheelwright, Steven C., 107
Wholesale Meat Act, 71
Wholesalers (*see also* Wholesaling)
  cash-and-carry, 522
  full-function, 520–22
  industrial, 520–21
  limited-function, 520–22
  mail-order, 523
  ownership of, 520–24
  types of, 519–24
Wholesaler-sponsored cooperative, 473
Wholesaling (*see also* Wholesalers), 517–25, 562
Wind, Yoram, *210*, *229*, 233, 258, 321, 569
Women in work force, 76–77, 185–86, 197
Wool Products Labeling Act, 71
Woolworth Company, 477, 504, 512
Work force, stability in international markets, 585
Wortzel, Lawrence, H., 233

Xerox Corporation, *287*, 456

Yankelovich, Skelly, and White, 195–97, 201

Zaltman, Gerald, 233
Zeithaml, Valarie, A., *611*, 626, 627
Zenith, 3, 336
Zoltners, Andris A., 372
Zone pricing, 356, *357*

22
Marketing's Future

Giant Foods, a supermarket chain headquartered in Landover, Maryland, had a dramatic demonstration of the benefits of Universal Product Code (UPC) scanning systems and computerized store operations. Executives of the 127-store chain had been aware for years that the equipment gave their business a competitive advantage. But it wasn't until the company's chief executive officer decided to change the stores' pricing strategy that people at Giant Foods understood the full weight of their competitive edge. In 1981, Giant Foods became a discount supermarket chain. Computerization and the scanning system enabled Giant Foods to take its competitors by surprise by reducing prices in the entire chain practically overnight. The pricing switch involved simply changing unit prices on store shelves and resetting prices at the scanner controller. Without an automated system, such a change in pricing would have involved switching prices on each item in each store, a process involving not only more work but one so lengthy that it would have alerted competitors to Giant's plans.

The supermarket chain's objective has been to automate every aspect of managing its stores. One tricky area for many supermarkets, including Giant, has been the stores' deli, meat, and produce departments, where food has to be weighed before it is priced. At the moment, these items are hand-keyed at the register. Giant Foods executives would like to find a way to put price codes on these items after they are weighed. The goal is to record all deliveries as they come into the store, then to use scanners at the check-out counter to gather data on which cuts of meat, for example, are selling best. Still under development is an electronic scale capable of printing UPC labels for the items it weighs.

Most other aspects of the supermarket industry are already automated, and the bene-

fits are not limited to the large chains. Owners of smaller stores often begin with personal computers to perform functions like setting up safeguards against bad checks and establishing mailing lists of their shoppers. UPC scanners are still too costly for many of the smaller stores, and the technology is advancing so quickly that a new machine today will be obsolete within a year or so. Many operators of smaller stores will wait until the technology settles before buying UPC equipment.

Hand-held microcomputers make it possible to take daily inventories of supermarket stock. As the technology develops, it is becoming more possible to link different types of in-store computer systems and storewide systems so that they can communicate with one another.

Automation is rapidly becoming standard practice in this industry. For many supermarket owners, the subject of computerization and scanning systems is a matter of education. To remain in a competitive position, supermarket operators are attending seminars and surveying available equipment, preparing to make decisions about purchasing a system. Others are already replacing outmoded equipment. In the supermarket industry, from small store to large chain, the choice is no longer whether to invest in scanning and computer equipment but which system to buy. For most supermarket operators, computerization is already a part of conducting everyday business.[1]

This chapter is my chance to pull out the crystal ball and discuss the trends I see in the field of marketing. The growing use of computers and automation, as seen in the supermarket industry, is one of those trends; changes in business practices and other trends are also described. The purpose of this chapter is to identify for you which types of jobs, industries, and business practices will be the most likely to change over the next decade.

Trends in the Marketing Environment

As you have undoubtedly seen throughout this book, the field of marketing is sensitive to developments in technology, in the economy, and in society. Particularly important to the future of marketing will be changes in business perspectives and advancements in computer technology.

One change in perspective that will have an effect on the future of marketing is the fact that recently the marketing concept has become increasingly important in business. You will recall from chapter 2 that the marketing concept is the idea that a company's primary focus for reaching its goals is meeting consumers' wants and needs. Companies are analyzing markets to determine what consumers are interested in, and they are developing appropriate marketing mixes. In the coming years, companies will continue to follow this trend toward the marketing concept.

Another trend that I expect to continue is the growth of marketing within industrial, service, and nonprofit markets. Throughout the book, we have seen that these business areas are growing rapidly. Traditionally, these areas have not used marketing techniques, but marketing is becoming increasingly important to them.

Computers

Rapid advancements in computer technology will have a major impact on marketing's future. As production costs continue to drop for computers, their availability will continue to rise. Computers are becoming more psychologically accessible as well as being more financially accessible. Many people who were once apprehensive about the new technology have gotten over their fears as they have become more accustomed to the use of computers.

People will be using computers as consumers at the same time marketers use them for analytical purposes. Banking is one area in which customers already use computers to conduct their business. With electronic banking machines, customers can now make deposits and withdrawals without the aid of a teller at any time of day or night. Soon it will be possible for customers to do their banking from home using their telephones and personal computers. (In many areas it is already possible.) A similar trend may make home shopping more widespread, making it possible for customers to order goods without even going to a store.

For marketers, the increased use of computers will provide a dramatic increase in the amount of available information, much of it concerning their customers. When consumers use computers for purchasing or conducting other business, marketers will often have a record of these activities along with consumers' names and addresses.

Each new use for computer data or advancement in the technology expands the marketing information system (MIS), making it more efficient. Data will come into the MIS on a more constant basis, and analyses will become standard procedure. What this means is that marketing will become a computer-based operation. Marketers will be able to collect and have available information on what consum-

Courtesy of AT&T Bell Laboratories.

Figure 22–1 These Florida shoppers are using a Viewtron electronic home information system terminal to examine the list of best-selling books and their prices available at a B. Dalton bookstore.

ers buy, and can use this information to plan their marketing mixes and to segment their markets more accurately.

Trends in the Market

I foresee two seemingly contradictory trends. The first is a broadening of markets through greater internationalization, or many companies' expansion through increased involvement in foreign trade. The second trend is the narrowing of markets through greater segmentation. That is, marketing efforts will focus on much smaller portions of the market, aiming at particular groups of potential buyers with very specific needs.

Internationalization. As we saw in chapter 20, international trade is growing rapidly. Because many U.S. markets have matured, some companies are moving into overseas markets in order to increase their business. Technological advancements are aiding in this trend toward expansion into foreign markets. One is better communication. Telephoning overseas has become a simple, efficient, and commonplace means of communicating overseas. Second, air transportation has

Chapter 22 / Marketing's Future

made travel between countries easier and faster, as well as making rapid shipment of goods a possibility. Improvements in packaging techniques enable companies to send perishable goods over long distances, even by ship, without worry about spoilage or contamination.

As we saw in chapter 20, international trade will increase, as will co-venturing, or the merging of companies from different countries in a joint business venture. The Renault-AMC alliance is an example. Recently, Detroit's General Motors Corporation and Japan's Toyota Motor Corporation entered such a partnership. Small, fuel-efficient cars designed by Toyota are being built in GM's California plant. One reason for this joint venture is GM's effort to meet the government's regulations on fuel economy, which the company was unable to do on its own.[2]

The government of Jamaica is currently encouraging co-venturing between its own country's businesses and foreign firms. The purpose behind these joint ventures, from the Jamaican government's viewpoint, is to introduce modern technology and agricultural methods into the country's economy.[3] Some of the firms that have united with Jamaican companies in mutually beneficial ventures are a Japanese coffee company, a British firm that harvests honey, and an Israeli company that produces fruit, vegetables, and fish.[4] UCC Blue Mountain Coffee Ltd., the Japanese firm, is able to charge more at home for the Jamaican-grown beans because they are believed to be superior to Colombian beans. The Israeli company, Jamaica Agro Products Ltd., made an agreement with the Jamaican government to use as many Jamaican workers as possible and to teach them Israeli irrigation and fertilization techniques. Meanwhile, the Israelis have gained access to better water, weather, and a more accommodating government in their Jamaican enterprise than they are accustomed to in their own country.

Co-venturing is another marketing trend that serves to expand business's markets through mutually beneficial cooperation between two or more countries.

Narrower segmentation. As you remember from chapter 9, another trend in marketing is narrower segmentation. Marketers will continue to develop products aimed at smaller portions of the market.

A company that has been very successful using narrow market segmentation is Esquire, Inc., once the publisher of *Esquire* magazine. This company dramatically increased its earnings by acquiring businesses that cater to small markets in a number of unrelated areas.[5] Wide-Lite Corporation is a lighting company that does not even attempt to compete with the major companies in the lighting industry. Instead, Esquire's Wide-Lite specializes in producing only energy-saving lighting and electronic lighting control systems. Profits have improved steadily for Wide-Lite, even at times when business has been poor for the industry as a whole. Another division, Cambridge Book Company, publishes educational materials. This division also has a narrow focus, specializing in adult educational books. Still another division publishes sheet music, focusing on instructional band music. By narrowing their focus, most of Esquire's divisions have emerged as leaders in their particular market areas.

Some catalog retailers have recently adopted market segmentation policies as well. Sears, Roebuck now publishes "specialogs," slimmer versions of its mail-order catalog designed for specific groups of Sears customers.[6] With the aid of its computer system, Sears constructs lists of customers in special interest categories. For example, a customer who charged a set of socket wrenches last month goes on the list of tool-buying customers who will receive the next Power and Hand Tool Specialog. This way, Sears reaches those customers most likely to buy tools. In the past, Sears mailed general catalogs that included virtually every item the store carries to nearly all its charge account customers, a much more costly practice. Other stores that have adopted the specialized catalog practice include Spiegel and J. C. Penney.[7] Catalogs have been designed around merchandise categories, including home furnishings, back-to-school clothes, and French lingerie. Leading in the area of mail-order retailing are several companies whose product line is already specialized, including L. L. Bean, specializing in sportswear and outdoor and camping gear; Talbots, seller of conservative clothes for women; and Brooks Brothers, makers and sellers of conservative business clothes for men and women.

Trends in the Marketing Mix

Each portion of the marketing mix—product, place, price, and promotion—is currently undergoing some degree of change. Technological advancements will be responsible for some of the major trends in the future of the marketing mix.

There will be innovations in food packaging. An example is the new type of container known as aseptic packaging. It is made of paper, foil, and plastic and keeps contents bacteria-free for up to six months without refrigeration. This method of packaging was developed in Sweden in the 1950s by Ruben Rausing, founder of Tetra Pak, a company that now has about 20 plants all over Europe, in Japan, and in Singapore.[8] Over half of Europe's milk is sold in the aseptic containers, while in the United States, this packaging method is just starting to catch on.

Product

Aseptic containers have advantages for manufacturers, distributors, retailers, and consumers. Aseptic containers are lighter than bottles or cans and are stackable so that manufacturers estimate that trucks can carry 50 percent more cases of the product at a time. Also, the trucks do not need refrigeration. Retailers also save in refrigeration costs as well as in shelf space. These savings are especially significant with respect to dairy products. About 60 percent of supermarkets' energy expenses are for refrigeration, and much of that amount is spent to keep dairy products cold. Marketers believe that this energy savings will be passed on to consumers. As the size of the average family becomes smaller, and the majority of the population grows older, the need for milk is decreasing. Consumers will benefit from a smaller package that can be stored without refrigeration until it is opened.

Ocean Spray has already begun to use aseptic packaging for its juices, and company executives are pleased with the results.⁹ Other companies that have been testing the new containers with their own products include Borden and Coca-Cola. Kraft and other food companies have been test marketing a similar package for solid foods and are generally pleased with their results.¹⁰

Place

I believe that computers will become increasingly important in the distribution process as well. Some marketers are beginning to use the computer for retailing in the same way they might use a mail-order catalog. Others are using computers within stores as selling aids.

Dayton's department store in Minneapolis uses a computerized bridal registry.¹¹ Customers can locate the names of the bride and groom and their list of desired gifts on a computer. No computer knowledge is necessary to obtain information from the registry, and the system eliminates a lot of costly clerical work for the store.

Mannington Mills, a manufacturer of vinyl flooring, rents computers to its retailers to help customers choose flooring.¹² Using the Compu-Flor system, customers answer eight questions about the size, decor, and style of the room, and their pattern and color preferences. Then the computer "suggests" several styles by their Mannington product numbers. The rest is up to the salesperson for whom this system saves a great deal of time in preliminary discussion of preferences and showing samples. Customers usually feel that the computer is an authoritative source of advice.

Financial planners at Balanced Investment Planning use computers to prepare advice concerning clients' investments.¹³ Computers are also being used in insur-

Courtesy of the Foods Division, The Coca-Cola Company

Courtesy of Ocean Spray Cranberries, Inc.

Figure 22–2 Coca-Cola's Minute Maid division and Ocean Spray have successfully introduced aseptic packaging for their juices.

Chapter 22 / Marketing's Future

Figure 22–3 Union Pacific uses a computer system to direct operations in the North Platte, Nebraska, railroad yard.

Courtesy of the Union Pacific System

ance companies to analyze clients' insurance needs and to select an appropriate policy.[14]

Subscribers to Comp-U-Card of America use home computers to shop at home. By using a special telephone number, customers have access to 30,000 products, which they can order directly from manufacturers.[15] The service offers lower prices than stores due to the fact that there is no store to maintain. Other sources are available through which consumers can scan and compare the merchandise of several stores, then order items directly from the stores. This type of system gives customers a time- and energy-saving way to comparison shop.

Computers are also playing a more critical role in the physical distribution of goods. Railroads are using computers to monitor the progress of loads of freight as they move from manufacturers' warehouses to their destinations.[16] Computerization of the system has allowed railroads to make better use of available empty cars. As a train comes into a yard, a clerk enters its identification number into the system. Other data that are already recorded include the commodity each car is carrying, its destination, and the name of the shipper. Using this system, any participating yard can locate empty cars as soon as shippers need them. In addition, the railways can keep empty cars traveling toward the most active shipping regions in anticipation of a need for them. Railway companies say that the annual improvement in the use of available cars has saved them in the millions of dollars, amounts they feel justify costly computer systems.

Price

When computerized services become more widely used, pricing will also be affected. Shopping at home via computer will give consumers equal access to virtually all alternative sellers of a particular product and eliminate the need to travel from store to store to gather price and quality information. When consumers have greater knowledge of choices, sellers will need to be more sensitive to one another's prices, as there will be little to be gained from charging more than a competitor.

Promotion

Recent developments in communication technologies—namely cable, subscription, and satellite television systems—have led to the development of *narrowcasting*, or transmitting a large number of television programs, each to a small group of people with specialized interests. As the number of television channels increases and their audiences grow, narrowcasting will have a major impact on television advertising techniques. This trend will be similar to the narrowing of market segments. Instead of attempting to reach the widest possible audience, advertisers will try to target small groups with a potentially high interest in their product. Ad time on the new stations is a great deal cheaper than on the networks and usually does not have to adhere to a strict format. These two factors will enable advertisers to run longer commercials in an audience's interest area. For example, for an audience of fashion designers, a sewing machine manufacturer could produce a how-to sewing program about the attachments available for its new machine; or for an audience of animal lovers, a pet supply manufacturer could produce a program on the training and grooming of pets featuring its own products. Narrowcasting reaches fewer people at one time, but it reaches those people advertisers most want to communicate with. The viewers all have similar traits and are relevant to the particular advertiser.

One method of advertising that could become more important in the future employs the technology of both split cable television and UPC scanners to study consumer groups' purchasing behavior. Members of a target group present an identification card to the cashier at retail outlets. Marketers then know what purchases are made by each participating person or family. With this information and split-cable techniques, advertisers can transmit different advertisements to evaluate the effectiveness of the different communications.

Trends in Marketing Management

For marketers, future developments in the field will obviously mean changes in the way they do their jobs. As a result of new retailing methods, marketers will have a great deal more information about their customers. Up to now, retailers could provide information only about the number of items sold and nothing about who

Figure 22–4 A portable computer terminal is used to assist order processing in this supermarket. A clerk is running a wand scanner over the UPC bar code to identify a product that must be ordered.

Courtesy of MSI Data Corporation

bought them. Computer-aided shopping will provide marketers with customers' names and addresses, information on which items they buy, at what price, and with what frequency. Using computers within a store will have the same result. The store that uses a computerized bridal registry, for example, can provide a record of specific items that an engaged couple has ordered. Marketers can also gather information on prices, shelf space locations, advertising budgets, and so on.

This increase in available information will enable marketers to focus more specifically on small segments of the market, a capability that, as we have seen, will become critically important. Marketers will soon have enough information to conduct regular analyses of their customers' purchasing behavior and the means to reach them directly. With larger amounts of data, marketers will rely on computers even more than they do today. Consequently, another important change in the field of marketing will be in the area of personnel.

Some businesses are already using computers not only at the management level but also to help their salespeople. We mentioned some of these companies earlier. Salespeople for two insurance companies, State Farm and Aetna Life & Casualty, use computers to reduce the paperwork involved in billing and processing claims.[17] People who sell laboratory and analytical equipment rely on an annual report of purchases in the field. Now *Industrial Research & Development*, publishers of the report, have made it available on computer.[18] Salespeople can use a desktop machine to access information on sales of a particular brand and purchases by industry and region much more quickly and efficiently than they could with the printed report.

Chapter 22 / Marketing's Future

Many marketers believe that at the management level, the field will demand those with advanced training in business and the use of computers. In the past, the kinds of people who have been successful in marketing have been those with strong verbal skills and good marketing "instincts." While these qualities will remain important, future marketers will also need to rely on quantitative skills and analytical ability.

Summary

The marketing concept, or an emphasis on consumers' wants and needs, is becoming increasingly important to marketers. Marketing will continue to grow in industrial, service, and nonprofit markets due to the fact that the packaged-goods market is mature in its marketing development.

Marketers and consumers alike will be using computers more and more in the future. Use of computers by consumers provides marketers with an increase in the available information on consumers and an expansion of the MIS.

One growing trend in the market is internationalization, or companies' expansion through participation in foreign markets. Advancements in communication and transportation make this trend possible. Many companies are becoming involved in co-venturing, or mutually beneficial business ventures based on agreement between companies from two or more nations.

Another trend that will be important to marketers in the future is narrower segmentation, or the focus on small portions of the market with special interests.

New methods of packaging will make it possible to ship more perishable products at one time, cut down on refrigeration costs, and lower prices on some food items. In the future, home shopping via computer and telephone will become a more common practice and may force sellers to be more sensitive to one another's prices. A growing trend in advertising is narrowcasting, transmitting television commercials to small groups of consumers. This method is possible because of the recent expansion in the number of available television channels.

Future marketers will need to have strong quantitative skills, analytical ability, and computer knowledge, as well as good verbal skills and marketing "instincts."

Questions for Discussion

1. What, according to the author, really explains the major impact of computers on marketing's future?
2. Illustrate with examples how computers will shape marketing activities.
3. In what way will co-venturing contribute to expanded international trade?
4. Discuss the important role of narrower segmentation in marketing's future.
5. Discuss the marketing implications of narrowcasting in promotion.
6. What factors are likely to facilitate marketing to small segments in the future?

7. If you were to be preparing yourself for marketing's future, what skills would you like to acquire? Explain.
8. Are there any other environmental trends that are important for marketing's future? Explain.

References

1. "Retail Automation Comes to the Supermarket," *Supermarket Business,* March 1983, pp. 26–31.
2. "Detroit's Feverish Maneuvering to Sell Small Cars," *Business Week,* January 9, 1984, pp. 26–27.
3. Erik Calonius, "Why Are Japanese Cultivating Coffee in Jamaican Hills?" *Wall Street Journal,* February 2, 1984, pp. 1, 24.
4. Ibid.
5. "Esquire, Inc.: Finding Profits in Fields Far Beyond Magazines," *Business Week,* February 22, 1982, pp. 78, 83.
6. John Curley, "Catalogs Are Getting Thin, Specialized," *Wall Street Journal,* September 13, 1982, p. 33.
7. Ibid.
8. Robert Ball, "Milk Wakes up the Packaging Industry," *Fortune,* August 19, 1982, pp. 79–82.
9. "Why a Paper Bottle?" *Sales & Marketing Management,* March 15, 1982, p. 80.
10. Bill Abrams and Janet Guyon, "Kraft Expands Tests on Retort Pouches," *Wall Street Journal,* February 18, 1982, p. 31.
11. "Thoroughly Modern Marriage," *Sales & Marketing Management,* July 27, 1981, p. 36.
12. Lawrence Stevens, "When Computers Do the Selling," *Inc.,* November 1982, pp. 159–62.
13. Ibid.
14. Ibid.
15. "Future Shop: Buying by Computer," *Sales & Marketing Management,* April 22, 1981, p. 49.
16. "A Bigger Load for Rail Computers," *Business Week,* February 4, 1980, pp. 89–90.
17. "Insurers Wire Their Agents into Computers," *Sales & Marketing Management,* October 11, 1982, p. 18.
18. "Easing a Salesperson's Burden," *Sales & Marketing Management,* May 18, 1981, p. 25.

CASES FOR PART V

18 Nestlé: The Infant Formula Decision

Early in 1984, executives at Nestlé, the world's largest food company, were growing tired of the accusation that the company's infant formula marketing policies were responsible for the deaths of thousands of infants. These charges had led to an international consumer boycott of all Nestlé products. Faced with mounting international pressures, Nestlé executives decided that it was time to act.

Nestlé, a Swiss corporation, is the world's principal supplier of infant formula. The company distributes its infant formula in 140 countries, although not in the United States, where U.S. companies control the infant formula market. The problem came with the marketing of infant formula in Third World countries. Critics criticized Nestlé with promoting formula as a superior and modern alternative to mother's milk and providing large quantites of free samples to people unfamiliar with its use. Boycott organizers claimed that in many Third World countries illiteracy and poor sanitary conditions, including lack of refrigeration and clean water, led to contamination of and misuse of the formula, causing dietary deficiencies, serious illness, and death. Nestlé consistently maintained that its formula was a beneficial product.

During the seven-year-long boycott, the company continued to aggressively promote sales of its infant formula in developing countries, contrary to a World Health Organization (WHO) sales code.

Nestlé, which is the world's largest food seller, has sales in 78 nations, and manufacturing plants in 55 countries. Forty percent of its revenues are from Europe and 20 percent from the United States.

Nestlé's major product is instant coffee, which it invented in 1937. By 1984, it produced more than 200 different types, which generate about 20 percent of revenues and perhaps a little more in profits. Although in 1984 there were still-growing markets, such as those in Japan and Britain, instant coffee demand in the United States was stagnant. Moreover, analysts estimated that Nestlé's market share of instant coffee sales fell from 33 percent in 1978 to 27 percent in 1982. Nestlé's second biggest product group is dairy goods, where major market consumption was also declining due to a maturing product base.

The International Nestlé Boycott Committee represented 87 labor, religious, and health organizations in ten countries. Two-thirds of them are based in the United States. About 70 American organizations had joined the boycott, including the United Auto Workers, National Education Association, National Organization for Women, and several church organizations.

Contributing to Nestlé's consideration of how to respond to the boycott was the company's profit margins, which had declined to a ten-year low of 2.8 percent in 1980, down from the 4.5 to 5 percent range of the mid-1970s. By 1982, after Nestlé divested several companies, margins were back to 4 percent. Profits reached a record $520 million in 1983.

As Nestlé managers considered what action to take, they reviewed the marketing policies that the boycott organizers found most objectionable. These policies included:

—Providing free samples of infant formula to health professionals, hospitals, and mothers
—Promoting infant formula as an alternative to breast-feeding
—Not providing formula users with warnings about the hazards of formula feeding
—Not requiring hospitals to use its products in accordance with WHO guidelines
—Giving health-care professionals gifts to encourage them to promote infant formula

Nestlé officials estimated that the costs of changing these policies would be between $15 and $20 million. Further, they had not yet been able to estimate the loss in infant formula sales or the loss of the company's market share to competitors that would result from any changes.

Sources: Based on Michael deCourcy Hinds, "Nestlé's New Formula Policy," *New York Times*, March 17, 1982, p. C10; "Nestlé Boycott Being Suspended," *New York Times,* January 27, 1984, pp. A1, A4; and Marcia Berss, "Sleep Well or Eat Well," *Forbes,* February 13, 1984, pp. 62–63.

Questions

1. Should Nestlé have marketed its infant formula in Third World countries?
2. Evaluate Nestlé's marketing practices for its infant formula.

3. Is it fair for boycott organizers to have targeted Nestlé? Why or why not?
4. What changes, if any, should Nestlé make in its marketing strategy for infant formula?
5. Should Nestlé (or any other company) be held liable for the misuse of its products? Why or why not?

19 Midway Airlines

During the summer of 1983, managers at Midway Airlines were facing a major crisis. Intense competitive pressures had led to lost customers and lower profits. Marketing executives had to find a strategy that would return the company to profitability.

Founded in 1979 at Chicago's Midway Airport, Midway Airlines experienced initial success by offering no-frills flights between a few major cities and Chicago at prices substantially lower than those of the major airlines. By late 1981, United Airlines and American Airlines had retaliated by matching Midway's low fares while offering all the traditional airline services, such as meals and beverages.

As a result, Midway's profits fell from their 1981 level of $7.6 million to only $346,000 in 1982. Even worse, the airline lost $7.8 million during the first six months of 1983. The airline was struggling for survival.

One possible survival strategy was to target the frequent business traveler (already the principal target of all major airlines). This created an enormous challenge. To wrest these travelers from the major airlines, Midway would have to add flights to match the other airlines' schedules. Yet, in 1983, Midway offered only four flights a day from New York to Chicago, compared with American's 13 and United's ten. Unfortunately, federal restrictions prevented Midway from adding flights until April 1984.

Since price wars were prevalent in the industry, Midway's low fares did not provide a competitive advantage. Further, Midway did not have programs to match the "frequent traveler, bonus ticket" programs of the major airlines. Midway also did not fly out of O'Hare Airport; while Midway Airport was closer to downtown Chicago, many more connecting flights flew out of O'Hare.

Looking for competitive alternatives, Midway conducted a consumer survey, using a "Create Your Own Airline" theme and inviting consumers to write about what they wanted in an airline. After sampling thousands of travelers, Midway found that travelers wanted roomier seating, more space for carry-on luggage, and a different meal service.

Responding to the consumer research, Midway developed a rescue plan that included refurbishing the company's aircraft, reducing the number of seats, supplying larger arm rests, and providing more luggage space. Other improvements included serving deluxe snacks instead of hot meals, buying stylish new uniforms for flight crews, and advertising heavily.

A fundamental problem with the new plan was that it would require a major fare increase. Although prices would still be 20 to 30 percent below the major airlines' regular coach fares, they would be considerably higher than Midway's existing fares.

The change would be a big gamble. The new service would be very costly in its early stages, and Midway's earnings would drop greatly for at least the first few months of the service. Particularly costly was the advertising deemed necessary to launch the new service. Alternative plans included special promotions that would give a free round trip for every five round trips flown and a business plan that would give a 15 percent discount to companies that purchased a certain quantity of tickets within a year.

Sources: Based on Harlan S. Byrne, "Midway Air Switches Low-Fare Strategy, Seeks to Lure Frequent Business Fliers," *Wall Street Journal*, December 13, 1983, p. 8; "Midway's Gamble," *Barron's*, August 29, 1983, p. 53; "An Upstart Airline Goes Upscale," *Business Week*, May 30, 1983, pp. 37–38; and Isadore Barmash, "New Tack at Midway Airlines," *New York Times*, p. D15.

Questions

1. What was the original Midway Airline strategy?
2. What are the market segments in the airline industry?
3. What are the differences between the market segments?
4. What is the role of price in airline marketing strategy?
5. What marketing strategy would you recommend to Midway?
6. How would you implement that strategy?

20 Videotex

In the near future it may become increasingly commonplace to market a broad spectrum of products and services to customers right in their homes. Videotex—computerized services that facilitate direct communication between companies offering specific kinds of information and individuals seeking that information—offers numerous potential marketing applications.

Through a computer, the user is able to select specific information of interest to him or her, which is then displayed on a video screen. The user gains time and convenience. For marketers, the service offers a means of directly reaching individuals who are specifically interested in the product or service being offered.

The consumer accesses the information or service by using the keyboard to select topics from a broad subject index page (similar to a table of contents) displayed on the screen (usually a personal computer or a specially adapted television set). Rather than waiting for a sequential presentation of all the information in a subject area, the user can choose only the information specifically desired.

The information supplied via videotex is stored in a central computer and can be continually updated. The individual terminals are linked to the central computer by telephone through a modem (a device that converts signals transmitted over telephone lines into signals that can be read by a computer). This system enables the consumer to both receive and send information to the central computer.

An alternative technology for transmitting videotex services is via a cable television network. A decoder box that sends and receives videotex signals can be built into a television set during its manufacture or can be attached to the outside of the television set and connected to the antenna terminals.

Although very few households in the United States currently have videotex, management consulting firm Booz·Allen estimated that by the mid-1990s, videotex will be in 30 million households. Moreover, it projected that videotex would provide $30 billion in annual revenues for banks, retailers, advertisers, and advertising agencies. A more conservative estimate from media consulting firm Link Resources predicted approximately 240,000 users of videotex by 1988.

The audience targeted by videotex tests consists mostly of upscale consumers ranging in age from 25 to 45 years, with an annual income of at least $40,000 and a college education. They work in professional/managerial capacities, are entertainment-oriented, and are heavy users of magazines, television, newspapers, and telephones. Videotex will focus on individuals for whom time and convenience are critical, and who are willing to pay for service.

Numerous companies in a variety of industries are spending millions of dollars to develop videotex services, most of which are aimed at the home user. The financial services industry, for example, offers important potential applications. Through electronic funds transfer, banks can reduce costs by using less paper and by facilitating bill payment and check processing. Videotex offers brokerage houses new ways to distribute financial market information to customers, and enables customers to check the status of their individual accounts.

Electronic publishing is another application for videotex. Dow Jones, for example, already delivers financial information to subscribers via videotex. Knight Ridder is marketing itself as an information company, packaging various services, such as home banking, home shopping, and news, on its system.

There also appears to be great potential in videotex for retailers. The service enables sellers to deliver detailed product information tailored to the individual information needs of customers. Through direct response, customers can then place orders using their computer terminals.

Teletext information, sometimes referred to as broadcast videotex, is an over-the-air electronic broadcast product displaying text and graphics selected by the user. The viewer presses a number on a keypad to select the "page" that he or she wishes to read. Although a number of experimental teletext services exist, three services, which have received much attention in the industry, can be used to illustrate developments in the field: CBS's EXTRAVISION, NBC's Teletext, and Time Inc.'s Video Information Service.

Originating from Los Angeles, CBS's EXTRAVISION provides 100 pages of information on news, sports, health, science, communications features, food tips, up-to-the-minute airline arrival and departure times, theater and restaurant offerings, local and national weather, business reports, and local and national advertising. The service is updated every 15 minutes.

NBC's Teletext Magazine, including full-color text and graphics, contains 75–100 pages of continuously updated information on national news, weather, and sports, as well as lifestyle features on subjects such as children's interests, personal finance, health, and travel. "Page" positions can be sold to advertisers.

A full video channel teletext service initiated by Time Inc.'s Video Information Services division in San Diego, California, and Orlando, Florida, involves a partnership with local newspapers. The newspapers provide local information content and derive their revenue from local advertisements. Delivered via satellite to cable operators, who then distribute the service to their subscribers, the service consists of approximately 5,000 pages of information and entertainment, covering a wide range of topics and available 24 hours a day, seven days a week.

Sources: Based on "The ABC's of Videotex/Teletext," *Marketing & Media Decisions*, November 1983, pp. 64–65, 112–14; "Teletext: Information Cornucopia," *Marketing & Media Decisions*, December 1983, pp. 60–63; 94–96; and "Who Wants It, for What, and Why?" *Marketing & Media Decisions*, February 1984, pp. 72–73, 168–69.

Questions

1. How dependent is videotex on market factors outside its control? What are those factors?
2. Is videotex a product or a medium? Why?
3. What are the products/services best marketed by videotex?
4. How would you market those products/services?
5. As a consumer, what information would you need before using videotex?
6. As a marketer, what information would you need before selling videotex?

APPENDIX A

Careers in Marketing

There are a wide variety of possible careers in marketing. The job descriptions that follow, based on the descriptions in the *Occupational Outlook Handbook* of the Bureau of Labor Statistics, broadly discuss types of available jobs, following the order of and complementing the text discussions.

Marketing Research

Marketing research studies provide information about the actual performance of a product in the marketplace or about consumer attitudes and perceptions. Jobs in marketing research are available in three kinds of organizations. First, there are the firms specializing in marketing research that receive commissions from large companies to supply them with research on the goods or services they produce. Second, some companies that use marketing research have in-house experts to direct their marketing research studies. Third, some advertising agencies do marketing research directly related to clients' advertising projects. All marketing research consists of the same steps: defining a problem, designing and carrying out a study to answer questions related to the problem, and analyzing and reporting the results of the study. The way in which this work is divided, however, varies.

In marketing research supplier firms, there are two complementary positions: account executive and project manager. Account executives are responsible for getting commissions for the firm, either by finding new clients or developing new projects for established clients. Based on discussions with the client about research needs, the potential budget, and time constraints, account executives prepare a bid. This includes a statement of the problem, the goals of the proposed research, a description of the research methodology and the type of analysis to be performed, a schedule, and a budget. Throughout the course of the project, account executives act as the liaison with the client (and thus receive the final credit or blame for the work). The actual execution of the study, however, is primarily the responsibility of the project manager. Account executives may work with project managers, especially by supplying input from the client, but they play a secondary role until the study is completed. Then account executives step in to do much of the interpretive part of the analysis and to formally present the results to the client in an oral presentation or a written report.

Project managers help develop the strategy for the study along with the account executive and the client, but their primary responsibility is to manage the actual execution of the study. They develop the schedule, coordinate between in-house workers and subcontractors, keep the study on schedule and under budget, and oversee the field work to ensure that it is carried out properly. Project managers also direct much of the preliminary analysis of the results. They select the applicable material, check that the quantitative analyses are performed correctly, ensure that the results are presented in the proper format, and keep the analysis relevant to the original research problem. On occasion, the project manager may even present the results to the client.

Because the account executive typically is a promotion from the position of project manager, the two positions share most educational and skill requirements. An undergraduate degree is necessary, and courses related to marketing research are helpful. An M.B.A. commands a higher salary and leads to faster promotion. Entry-level employees generally spend six to 18 months as research assistants or junior analysts, doing routine field work in research studies. They learn to conduct interviews, gather and record data, and write reports on their findings before acquiring the supervisory responsibilities that eventually lead to the project manager position. Computer, statistical, communication, management, marketing, and problem-solving skills are all important. The balance of skills shifts, however, with the move from the project manager to account executive.

In large companies that use marketing research, the project director is the key in-house position in marketing research. Sometimes project directors receive a request for information from the corporate managers who use marketing research. In other cases, they initiate the research themselves by approaching the managers and showing them how a study might prove valuable. Project directors are responsible for designing the study, including the questionnaire and the analysis to be used, but they contract out its execution. They request bids from marketing research supplier firms, select a firm to carry out the study, and then closely supervise the work of this firm. When the study is complete, project directors must interpret the quantitative results and present them to management. Because user companies cannot provide training in marketing research, project directors must have previous experience. Typically, they are hired away from marketing research supplier firms. Other large companies that have their own marketing research departments do not contract out the execution of their studies. An in-house marketing research department usually has a staff of analysts headed by a director of marketing research. The team works together to design and execute its studies, analyze the results, and make appropriate recommendations.

In advertising agencies, marketing research personnel work with a small support staff, so that they become directly responsible for almost every aspect of research studies. Clients may initiate the research work with a request for information, marketing research personnel may suggest the research to a client, or the agency may decide to do a study to provide evidence in support of an advertising proposal to a client. Marketing research personnel then develop a formal research proposal, much like the bids prepared by account executives in marketing research supplier firms. Once a proposal is accepted, they either directly oversee the execution of the study or hire subcontractors to do the field work. Marketing research personnel are unique in carrying out the entire analysis, including the purely quantitative portions, by themselves. The other marketing research positions already described rely on support staff to handle the basic computer and statistical work. Once the analysis is finished, the marketing research personnel formally present the results to the client. Because of the breadth of this position, there is a strong emphasis on candidates' credentials. Either a Ph.D., much research experience, or an M.B.A. with a research focus is generally needed, although there are some entry-level openings for B.A.s. Equally strong quantitative and communication skills are necessary. See figure A-1 for information on educational requirements and salary prospects for marketing research careers.

Product Management

Product managers are responsible for the success of a single product of a large firm. They are generalists, involved with everything that affects their product, including advertising strategy, market research, product research, budgeting, production, distribution, sales, and legal issues. Product managers have limited decision-making powers. After they develop a strategy for their product and programs to carry it out, they must secure the approval and cooperation of other departments, as we saw in chapter 2. Much of their energy is focused on persuading the various functional departments of the firm to implement these programs. This is difficult because they are competing with all the other product managers for the limited time and resources of the other departments. Thus their major role is to communicate with and coordinate the efforts of the functional departments. The position is typically short term; after two to four years the product manager either is promoted or leaves the firm.

Most persons pass through multiple assistant positions before becoming a product manager. A B.A. is essential to getting these positions, and some marketing courses are preferred. Neither an undergraduate marketing major nor an M.B.A. is

Educational Requirements

A bachelor's degree is usually sufficient for entry-level positions in marketing research. Courses in marketing, as well as other fields such as statistics, English composition, psychology, economics, and sociology, are good preparation for marketing research work. A strong background in computer science is also helpful. A graduate degree, such as a master's in business administration, is usually required for specialized positions and advancement in the marketing research field. Those with strong backgrounds in quantitative research methods, including sociologists, economists, and psychologists, can also qualify for more specialized or supervisory positions.

Earnings

- Starting annual salaries:
  - Holder of B.A. $12,000–$17,000
  - Holder of M.B.A. or other graduate degree $21,500
- Annual salaries in more advanced positions:
  - Senior analysts $27,000
  - Marketing research directors $40,000–$50,000

Job Outlook

The best opportunities will exist for those with graduate degrees in business, including marketing research, statistics, and computer science. Employment in the marketing research field is related to economic conditions. When business activity and personal incomes are on the rise, new products and services are developed and a greater amount of marketing research is needed compared to the amount needed in periods of slow economic growth. Employment of marketing research analysts is expected to increase faster than the average for all occupations during the 1980s since increasing competition in the marketplace necessitates increased information and advice from marketing research analysts.

Source: *Occupational Outlook Handbook*, 1982–83, (published biennially by the U.S. Bureau of Labor Statistics), pp. 109–10.

Figure A–1 A career in marketing research

currently required, however. Characteristics such as aggressiveness, confidence, and creativity are considered more important. Communication and organizational skills are crucial for product managers, while some analytical and problem-solving skills are also needed.

Promotion

Promotion is a difficult field to get into because of intense competition for the limited number of jobs available (see fig. A–2 for supplementary information about careers in advertising). Job hunters should not overlook the less well-known opportunities outside of advertising agencies, with sales promotion agencies, public relations agencies, specialty advertising distributors, in-house sales promotion departments in consumer goods companies, and public relations positions with companies and associations of all kinds.

Advertising agencies have four different types of marketing positions: account executive, media planner, copywriter, and art director. Account executives primarily act as the liaison between the client and the agency's creative people. They communicate the client's needs and opinions to the creative people, help develop an advertising strategy, and contribute ideas to the project. They must evaluate and criticize what is produced by the creative people, screening it before it is presented to the client. A second important part of the job is to coordinate the work of the creative, production, and media buying departments to put together a total advertising package. Account executives must present the resulting advertising campaign to the client, get the client's approval, and then monitor the creative and production departments until the work is completed on time and under budget. M.B.A.s dominate the account executive position. Prior experience is extremely important, but there are some trainee positions available in the largest agencies and there is some upward mobility from general handyman or gofer positions in the smallest

**Figure A–2
A career in advertising**

Educational Requirements

A bachelor's degree is usually the minimum requirement for any position in an advertising agency. Depending on the specific position, a major in journalism, art, business, or liberal arts can be as suitable a preparation as a major in advertising. Managerial positions often require a master's degree in business administration or advertising; experience in marketing, finance, and economics is also helpful. Copywriters must have good writing skills and are often helped by experience in journalism or college degrees in English or communications. Art directors must have experience in the graphic arts field, for which post-secondary school training is not required but strongly recommended.

Earnings

- Starting annual salaries:

Holder of B.A.	$10,000–$18,000
Holder of M.B.A. or M.A. in advertising	$18,000–$25,000

- Annual salaries of experienced workers:

Account executive with 5–10 years experience	$25,000–$40,000
Accounts supervisor	$40,000–$50,000
Accounts director	$60,000+
Art director	$30,000–$40,000
Junior copywriter	$20,000+
Senior copywriter	$40,000–$60,000
Media department head	$30,000
Media buyer	$18,600

Job Outlook

Employment growth in the advertising industry is tied to the growth of the overall economy. If the economy is healthy, there will be new products and services to be advertised and an increased number of consumers due to population growth. Layoffs, however, do not necessarily depend on the overall economy nor do they affect only inexperienced workers. Even those who have seniority can be laid off if an agency loses an important account, for example. In general, employment for advertising workers is expected to increase at the average rate for all occupations through the 1980s.

Sources: *Occupational Outlook Handbook, 1982–83* (published biennially by the U.S. Bureau of Labor Statistics), pp. 235–37; John W. Wright, *American Almanac of Jobs and Salaries* (New York: Avon, 1982), p. 508; and S. William Pattis, *Opportunities in Advertising* (Lincolnwood, Ill.: National Textbook Co., 1984), p. 50.

agencies. Communication, analytical, and creative skills are all important, as well as attention to detail and planning ability.

The copywriter and art director together are responsible for actually creating the advertisements. In a group meeting with the account executive, they learn what the client wants and what the goal of the advertising campaign is. If they have not worked on this particular product before, they gather information on the product itself, the company, and previous advertising efforts. The copywriter and art director then meet together to establish a theme for the advertisements. The copywriter supplies a written or spoken text, while the art director produces sketches illustrating the visual component of the ads. Their work must both fit the tone and mood set by the advertising strategy and communicate the theme agreed upon. In addition, the art director must oversee the in-house production staff or free-lance professionals who produce the ads in their final form. Both jobs demand creativity and the ability to give concrete form to advertising concepts. Copywriters need a B.A. and writing skills in addition, while art directors must have some experience in art (although not necessarily the ability to produce finished artwork).

The media planner calculates in which media to place the advertisements in order to reach the desired audience in the most cost-effective manner. This decision is based on the advertising strategy, the client's budget, and the availability of media time and space. The media planner then requests bids from the appropriate media and evaluates them based on cost, audience size, and audience characteristics. After the client approves the plan, the media planner negotiates the actual media buy. In agencies that have media departments, this entire process may be divided among a media planner, analyst, and buyer, under the supervision of a media director. A B.A. is necessary, and a background in marketing or some business experience is helpful. Two different skills are involved: quantitative skills in order to calculate the demographics and costs and communication skills in order to deal with media representatives.

Sales promotion is a specialized activity handled by sales promotion agencies or in-house sales promotion departments in consumer goods companies, rather than by advertising agencies. Its activities are strictly limited to developing promotional programs in order to increase sales. Free samples, coupons, contests, and refund offers are typical promotions. Sales promotion personnel have a position parallel to that of account executives in advertising agencies. They develop campaigns and then coordinate the efforts of creative and production departments to execute them. Most sales promotion personnel have experience in advertising, sales, or marketing. Because sales promotion is less creative and more of a straightforward marketing problem than advertising, creativity is less important than communication and problem-solving skills.

Public relations is becoming increasingly important, so that opportunities, responsibilities, and salaries are all on the rise. Public relations personnel may work for a variety of organizations, including advertising agencies, public relations agencies, companies, and associations. They determine what the public relations goals are for their particular organization or project, identify the occasions when public relations are called for, and organize events or programs to build the image of the organization. In order to serve successfully as a continuing link between the organization and the media, public relations personnel must develop contacts both inside the organization and in the media. They need to know what is happening in the organization before they can publicize it, and they need to know what is currently attractive to the media before they can place a story. Writing press releases and persuading the media to use them forms a large part of the job. Public relations personnel also must continually evaluate the success of their efforts in order to improve their performance. A B.A. and communication skills are necessary for the job, while experience in journalism is a definite advantage. Figure A–3 has additional information about educational requirements, salaries, and job outlook for public relations workers.

Novelty advertising is another growing field. This involves giving away with-

Figure A–3
A career in public relations

Educational Requirements
Many of those who enter the field of public relations have a background in journalism, whether it be a bachelor's degree in journalism or work experience in the news media. Numerous disciplines can be helpful preparation for a career in public relations, such as English, political science, psychology, and economics; some firms want their public relations staff to have background in areas related to the business of the firm itself. Writing for a college publication or campus radio station is also good experience for someone seeking a public relations job. A graduate degree in public relations can prepare one for an administrative or managerial position. Although salaries in nonprofit organizations are lower, such organizations are a good place for one to gain experience prior to applying for a position in a more competitive and well-paying firm or advertising agency.

Earnings
- Starting annual salaries:
    - Holder of B.A. (higher for holder of M.A.) $10,000–$13,000
    - Positions in the Federal Government:
        - Holder of B.A. $15,200
        - Holder of M.A. $18,600
- Overall median salary for the public relations profession $35,000
- Overall median salary for Federal Government positions $30,000
- Median annual salaries for top level positions:
    - Overall median $38,000
    - In a hospital (nonprofit) $30,000
    - In an agency $34,800
    - In a public relations consulting firm $50,000

Job Outlook
Employment for public relations workers is expected to increase at the average rate for all occupations during the 1980s. There is a great deal of competition for beginning jobs, and the outlook appears best for those with a strong academic background and some media experience.

Sources: *Occupational Outlook Handbook*, 1982–83 (published biennially by the U.S. Bureau of Labor Statistics), pp. 194–95; John W. Wright, *American Almanac of Jobs and Salaries* (New York: Avon, 1982), pp. 476–77; and S. William Pattis, *Opportunities in Advertising* (Lincolnwood, Ill.: National Textbook Co., 1984), p. 50.

out obligation goods that carry an advertising message. Matchbooks, pens, calendars, and T-shirts are common examples. The novelty advertising intermediary advises customers about the kinds of goods available, product quality, and costs. Because intermediaries keep up to date on what products manufacturers are offering, they can make creative suggestions to customers about what might be appropriate for their needs. Once the customer makes a choice, the novelty advertising intermediary arranges for the best possible price and quick delivery. Most people enter the field as salespeople working under an intermediary. They learn the business and then set up on their own.

Sales

Sales is perhaps the largest field in marketing, so it offers many job opportunities. People generally move directly into sales positions after some kind of training period. A B.A. is helpful but not necessary for most jobs in sales. Technical sales is an exception; both undergraduate technical degrees (for example, in engineering) and M.B.A.s are valuable. Communication skills are obviously essential, as are the organizational skills needed to efficiently manage one's time. In addition, semitechnical and technical sales demand some problem-solving, analytical skills. Sales experience can lead to a career in sales management or to careers in other branches of marketing, including marketing research and sales promotion.

As order getters, salespeople are responsible for only one or a very few products. They make one-time presentations to individual consumers, and they are paid entirely on a commission basis. Insurance and houses are examples of the commodities handled by order getters. It is an exceptionally independent position: the salesperson makes all the decisions regarding when, how, and on whom to call within a given territory. The majority of the time is spent actually making calls. This includes making an established sales presentation, handling questions, and then either closing the sale or ending the call as quickly as possible. Because salespeople have to find individual consumers directly, their hours are often irregular. In addition to making calls, salespeople have to do paperwork for all completed sales.

Distribution channel sellers deal with merchandise being sold in bulk to distribution channels for resale. For the most part, salespeople handle established accounts, so they build up a long-term relationship with the customer (often a professional buyer) during the course of regular calls. Salespeople provide a variety of services to the customer, including inventory, the stocking of shelves, and new merchandising ideas. At the same time, they try to persuade the customer to give their products a larger share of the total inventory and more and better shelf space. Salespeople also have an important communications role. They relay information about new products and special offers to the customer and carry back information about customer attitudes, competition, and customer complaints. Distribution channel sellers handle a good deal of paperwork, work long hours, and spend some time away on business trips.

There are numerous types of manufacturers' sales jobs. Some manufacturers' sales workers deal with nontechnical goods and do not require formal education to be knowledgeable about their products. On the other hand, workers in industrial and semitechnical sales, where the products sold are industrial or business supplies, such as medical supplies and radio time, often have college degrees in science or technical fields. Someone selling medical supplies, for example, might have a degree in chemistry or pharmacy. There is fierce competition among suppliers, so that salespeople must attract and retain customers by offering them more and better services. They provide information about new and existing products, try to tailor the products to the customer's situation, and make educated suggestions about how their product could solve the customer's problems. In addition, they act as a liaison with the supplier company, arranging for other services such as delivery, maintenance, and reordering. This type of sales involves a lot of preparation work and long hours.

Complex or professional sales is a unique field, because it deals with complex industrial goods that are expensive and that must be closely matched with the customer's needs in order to be valuable. In this area of sales, workers often need college degrees in specialized fields, such as engineering or computer science. For example, a computer is not necessarily an asset to a business unless it has the capabilities and software the business needs. Commercial real estate and hospital equipment are other examples of complex goods. The salesperson provides the customer with technical expertise about the product and its applications. Thus a large part of the salesperson's job involves learning about the product and keeping up with new developments. Concluding a sale is a long-term, problem-solving process, during which the salesperson learns about the customer's business and matches it with the correct product. After the sale is made, the salesperson is responsible for assuring that the customer uses the product correctly and for resolving customer problems (see fig. A–4 for information related to careers in sales).

Physical Distribution

Physical distribution is a large field offering a wide variety of work situations. It consists of everything needed to move goods from the production line to the consumer. Thus it includes warehousing, inventory planning and control, shipping and receiving, traffic, transportation, customer service, and logistics. The five types of firms that employ people in physical distribution are: manufacturing firms that must distribute their products; marketing intermediaries such as wholesalers, distributors, and retailers; public warehouses; transportation companies such as airlines, railroads, parcel services, and truck lines; and consulting firms with a physical distribution specialty. The larger the firm, the higher the educational standards and the less likely that entry-level personnel must do physical labor.

The field is changing rapidly because of a new emphasis on cost efficiency and the introduction of computer technology. Because of the new sophistication in physical distribution, there will probably be an increasing demand for skilled personnel. Among the most valuable skills will be familiarity with computers, management and communication skills, salesmanship, and mathematical modeling and

Educational Background
The majority of sales workers go through a formal training period to prepare them for their jobs. For this reason, a college degree is not always required for sales work, especially when the products are of a nontechnical nature. However, a bachelor's degree is becoming increasingly desirable for manufacturers' sales workers dealing even with nontechnical products. Education in the fields of science, engineering, and computer science is also becoming an asset to those dealing with more complex and technical products.

Earnings
- There are several different compensation plans for sales workers:
  1. Straight salary
  2. Straight commission based on the dollar amount of sales
  3. Salary plus commission
  4. Salary plus bonus
  5. Salary, commission, and bonus

Bonus payments may be determined by individual sales performance, performance of a group of sales workers, or the performance of the entire company.
- Starting annual salaries:
  - Manufacturers' sales workers — $13,900–$15,400*
  - Wholesale trade sales workers — $18,500
- Annual salaries of experienced workers:
  - Manufacturers' sales workers — $17,400–$33,500*
  - Wholesale trade sales workers — $23,000–$49,500

Job Outlook
The need for sales workers depends partly on economic conditions and consumer preferences, so employment opportunities can vary from year to year. There is a good deal of turnover in most sales jobs. The overall growth of employment opportunities in sales positions is expected to be at the average rate for all occupations during the 1980s.

---

*Total compensation will be higher because of commission and/or bonus payments.
Source: *Occupational Outlook Handbook, 1982–83* (published biennially by the U.S. Bureau of Labor Statistics), pp. 243–45, 253–54.

Figure A–4
A career in sales

---

systems design abilities. Likewise, a B.A., especially with course work in related fields, will be increasingly important for upward mobility. Summer or part-time experience in warehouses is helpful. Graduate education is not necessary, but it commands higher salaries, especially in technical areas.

The goal of distribution managers is to maximize the cost-efficient distribution of a product. They coordinate their efforts with many other departments and contribute information to decisions about packaging, materials handling, production, scheduling, inventory control, new-product development, product pricing, and promotional activities. Distribution managers have direct responsibility over the location, number, and configuration of warehouses; inventory control; equipment and systems design and operation; transportation methods, routes, and rates; and order entry and processing.

Operations personnel are responsible for the day-to-day activities of a distribution center or warehouse. They schedule labor, equipment, docks, shipping, and storage; manage staff; maintain equipment and facilities; deal with carriers and customers; and cope with emergencies as they arise. The goal is to cut costs while making sure that shipments go out on time. A second aspect of the job is planning for the future. Operations managers must decide whether to expand facilities, to lease or purchase equipment, to update equipment, or to adopt new distribution technologies to handle new products.

Distribution analysts or planners evaluate the performance of physical distribution through quantitative analyses. They address a wide variety of issues and provide administrators with information and recommendations on which to base decisions about daily operations. They track and evaluate transport costs, inventory levels, and the like on a continuing basis. They examine alternatives in systems design, for example, comparing the use of company-owned facilities with public warehouses. They evaluate the potential of new technologies for equipment, transport, and information processing. In addition, they interpret information to provide a basis for planning for the future. For example, they forecast service levels and future equipment, facilities, and personnel needs.

Traffic and transportation personnel arrange for the physical movement of the raw materials coming into a firm, the finished products leaving the firm, and the unfinished goods being transferred internally. Their goal is to maintain high levels of service while reducing costs to a minimum. Specifically, they analyze what kind of carrier should be used and then select a particular transport company after negotiations about price, scheduling, and the like. In addition, they manage company-owned transportation fleets and compare the costs of such fleets with public transport.

Inventory control personnel forecast the demand for products, initiate the appropriate production runs, and maintain an inventory sufficient to supply customers. They must coordinate with the other departments that have an interest in inventory levels and mediate between their contradictory demands. The sales department, for example, wants large inventories of all items so that customers' orders can always be filled promptly. In contrast, the finance department wants to keep the inventory as small as possible to reduce costs. The production department wants to stock large inventories of a few items, because long production runs are most efficient. Inventory control personnel may also be responsible for the stocks of raw materials and supplies on hand.

Customer service personnel are responsible for maintaining good relationships with customers. They try to prevent problems by ensuring that ordering and delivery operations run smoothly and that billing policies are equitable. They evaluate the efforts of other departments that affect customer satisfaction, including advertising effectiveness, product quality, and shipping efficiency. They keep records on reordering frequency, returned goods rates, and ordering consistency that reflect the levels of customer satisfaction. When problems and complaints do arise, customer service personnel correct them.

The work of physical distribution consultants is similar to that of other business consultants. They contact potential clients in order to get commissions, investigate physical distribution problems during an on-site visit, analyze the problems, prepare and deliver a proposal, execute the program proposed, do more analysis, and deliver further recommendations. The job involves frequent travel and requires strong problem-solving skills in addition to communication skills.

Retailing

There are two separate career paths in retailing today: merchandising and management. Summer or part-time experience in retailing, although not a necessity, does make it easier to get a job and to advance. A college degree (not necessarily with a business focus) is now essential for promotion to middle- and upper-management levels, but an M.B.A. is not a major advantage. An entry-level position is typically as some kind of trainee. Both experience in retailing and an M.B.A. are rewarded with higher starting salaries. Figure A–5 has information related to educational requirements and earnings prospects for careers in retailing.

**Figure A–5
A career in retailing**

Educational Requirements
Since prior retailing experience is helpful for getting a position in retailing, opportunities for high school graduates are available. However, a college degree (in any field, not necessarily in fields related to merchandising) is becoming an increasingly desirable qualification for those wishing to enter training programs for more advanced administrative or supervisory positions.

Earnings
- General annual salary range for buyers $19,000–$28,000
- Median annual salaries for buyers in private industry:

"Off-the-shelf" items —Group I	$14,900
Group II	$18,500
Specialized items —Group III	$22,900
Group IV	$27,777

Buyers in department stores and other mass merchandisers are generally among the most highly paid. The Group I-IV notation indicates the four categories of buyers used by the U.S. Bureau of Labor Statistics.
- Annual salaries for store managers:

Small store	$10,000
Department manager	$20,000–$35,000
Large department store head	$100,000

Job Outlook
Employment in the retail industry is expected to increase about as fast as the average for all occupations throughout the 1980s. Competition for jobs as buyers and managers is becoming stronger, since these jobs attract many college graduates.

Sources: *Occupational Outlook Handbook, 1982–83* (published biennially by the U.S. Bureau of Labor Statistics), pp. 26–28, 249–50; John W. Wright, *American Almanac of Jobs and Salaries* (New York: Avon, 1982), p. 481; and *Your Career Opportunity in Merchandising and Marketing*, Careers Series, no. 48 (Chicago: Institute for Research, 1980), p. 22.

The central position in merchandising is that of buyer. Buyers have total responsibility for generating a profit in their departments by selecting merchandise that will sell briskly and by guiding the promotion of that merchandise in the store. Buyers base their purchasing decisions on the budget assigned them, the physical capacity of the store, a knowledge of consumer preferences, and the direction in which the industry is moving. They bargain with wholesalers to receive the best possible price and delivery terms, as well as to ensure receiving the quantity and the assortment of styles and colors desired. Once the merchandise arrives in the store, buyers train the sales force in how best to promote it. They coordinate their efforts with the advertising department or agency employed by the store. Buyers must watch sales volume closely and make price changes, reorders, and order cancellations as appropriate. Communication and organizational skills are crucial in this position, as well as aggressiveness.

The store manager's responsibilities are broader, and management and merchandising skills are more important. Store managers supervise personnel in all departments and oversee the daily opening and closing of the store, the maintenance of all facilities and equipment, the display of merchandise, stock levels, cleanliness, security, customer service, and the like. They track the performance of the store and of each department, making timely decisions in order to capitalize on opportunities and minimize losses. They also talk with customers to get general feedback about the store's performance and to handle specific complaints. While store managers are entirely responsible for the store's profits, their actions are limited by the budget and the policy decisions made by central management. Their position as the liaison between the store and central headquarters is a special challenge.

APPENDIX B

Marketing Arithmetic

Arithmetic is an important aspect of marketing since numbers are a useful tool in the marketing decision process. Numbers can provide information about sales, costs, and certain ratios, or relationships between various financial components of a company's operations. These figures aid marketers in understanding the company's strengths, needs, and financial position.

In this appendix we will look at three major areas of marketing arithmetic: the operating statement and balance sheet, markups and markdowns, and financial ratios.

To illustrate the application of marketing arithmetic, we will consider the operating statement and balance sheet of prototypal Computer Manufacturing Company (CMC), a producer of computer hardware sold in the business, educational, and consumer markets.

The Operating Statement

The **operating statement** is the record of the money a company takes in and pays out during a given time period. Depending upon the company, an operating statement is issued either at the end of the year or at the end of each quarter. The statement's "bottom line" shows the company's net profit or net loss.

**Figure B–1
Simplified operating statement of Computer Manufacturing Company (CMC) for 1983 (dollars in thousands)**

Gross sales	$908,942
Sales returns and allowances	12,530
Net sales	896,412
Cost of goods sold	324,676
Gross margin	571,736
Expenses	422,654
Income from operations	149,082
Other	
Interest expense	(8,988)
Other income	1,976
Income before taxes	142,070
Taxes	
Federal	54,000
State and local	10,000
Net profit	$78,070

To arrive at that bottom line, the operating statement proceeds through a series of arithmetic steps, subtracting expenses from sales revenue to come up with a net profit. Figure B–1 depicts the operating statement for Computer Manufacturing Company.

What are gross sales and net sales? **Gross sales** is the total amount that CMC billed its customers during 1983 for computer hardware, or $908,942. (All amounts are in thousands of dollars.) As is common, some of CMC's customers returned hardware they had purchased because of damage or for other reasons. **Net sales** for 1983 is the company's sales for the year after returns and allowances have been subtracted. As shown in figure B–1, CMC's net sales totaled $896,412.

The cost of goods sold is subtracted from net sales on the operating statement to find **gross margin,** or gross profit, in this case totaling $571,736. The gross margin, then, is the difference between the amount CMC paid for the materials it used to produce the hardware and the amount it received for the hardware from its customers.

To determine its **net profit,** CMC subtracts the expenses incurred in producing the hardware and taxes from the gross margin. In this case, the net profit is $78,070.

Appendix B / Marketing Arithmetic

The Balance Sheet

While the operating statement is a financial summary of the company's activities over a given time period, a **balance sheet** is a quick picture of a company's assets and liabilities at one specific point in time. Any balance sheet reflects the equation:

$$\text{Assets} = \text{Liabilities} + \text{Stockholders' Equity}$$

Figure B–2 depicts a balance sheet for CMC on December 31, 1983.

Assets are all the items of value that CMC owns or that are owed to CMC. **Liabilities** are CMC's debts and any other claims by others on CMC's assets. **Stockholders' equity** is the assets of the business belonging to the owner. Since CMC is a public corporation, the owners are its stockholders.

The balance sheet in figure B–2, then, shows how CMC's money and other assets are invested or used and how much CMC owes to others on December 31, 1983. Let's examine it more closely.

The first category on the balance sheet is current assets, which includes CMC's cash and securities, receivables (the money owed to CMC by its customers), and the inventories of unsold goods that CMC has in stock. The total of all these items is $476,922. The property and equipment CMC owns, totaling $170,012, are added to this figure, as is the $158,210 for other assets. CMC's total assets (current assets + property and equipment + other assets) are $805,144.

CMC's current liabilities include notes payable, accounts payable (money it owes to creditors), unpaid expenses, and taxes it will owe. Current liabilities total $310,034. CMC's long-term liabilities include long-term loans it has taken out and

Figure B–2 Simplified balance sheet for Computer Manufacturing Company (CMC), December 31, 1983 (dollars in thousands)

Assets		Liabilities and Stockholders' Equity	
Current assets		Current liabilities	
Cash	$12,394	Notes payable	$70,508
Marketable securities	7,378	Accounts payable	58,632
Receivables	286,614	Other expenses	90,544
Inventory	170,536	Taxes	33,540
Total current assets	476,922	Advance payments	56,810
		Total current liabilities	310,034
Property and equipment	170,012		
		Long-term liabilities	
Other assets		Long-term borrowing	26,728
Noncurrent receivables	98,228	Deferred taxes	36,030
Other	59,982	Total long-term liabilities	62,758
Total other assets	158,210		
		Total stockholders'	
Total assets	$805,144	equity	432,352
		Total liabilities and	
		stockholders' equity	$805,144

Appendix B / Marketing Arithmetic

deferred taxes. Long-term liabilities total $62,758. CMC's total liabilities (current liabilities + long-term liabilities) are $372,792. The total liabilities added to the stockholders' equity equal $805,144, or the same amount as total assets.

As we will see in the next sections of this appendix, numbers from the operating statement and the balance sheet are used in calculations that aid marketers in decision making.

Markups and Markdowns

In order to stay in business, a marketer must make a profit. The amount of profit, referred to as the **markup,** is expressed as a percentage. The following formula shows the relationship of markup to cost and selling price.

$$\text{Cost} + \text{Markup} = \text{Selling Price}$$

Markups can be figured in one of two ways—based on cost or based on selling price. The ways work as follows.

Suppose it costs CMC $100 to produce a certain computer printer; CMC wants to mark the printer up $50 and sell it for $150. The markup percentage based on cost is the dollar markup ($50) divided by the cost of producing the printer ($100), which equals 50 percent. If the markup is based on selling price, the percentage is the dollar markup ($50) divided by the selling price ($150), or 33⅓ percent.

As an example, assume that it is CMC's policy to use the selling price in determining markup margins, that the cost to CMC of producing a certain printer is $80, and that CMC has an average markup of 64 percent. How does it calculate its selling price for the printer? It uses the formula: Selling price = cost + (margin × selling price). Adding numbers has the formula work out as follows:

$$\text{Selling Price} = \$80 + (.64 \times \text{Selling Price})$$
$$.36 \text{ Selling Price} = \$80$$
$$\text{Selling Price} = \$222.22$$

CMC then sells the printer to marketing intermediaries for $222.22.

At some point, CMC may develop a new, faster printer to replace the present printer. To decrease the inventory of the present printer in its warehouse, CMC may decide to employ a **markdown,** which is a reduction in the selling price.

Let's suppose that CMC produced 100 of the printers at $100 per printer and sold them for $150 per printer. The company sold 50 of the printers at $150 each. It then marked the printer down to $125 and sold 25 printers at the reduced price. The company's markdown percentage is figured through the formula:

$$\text{Markdown Percentage} = \text{Dollar Markdown/Total Net Sales in Dollars}$$

In the case of CMC's printers, the dollar markdown is $625 (25 printers at a reduction of $25 each), and total net sales are $10,625 for 50 printers at $150 each and 25 printers at $125 each. Putting these figures into the formula shows that CMC had a markdown percentage of 5.8 percent.

Financial Ratios

The computer manufacturer with the highest markup percentage does not necessarily enjoy the highest profit. Total profit is affected by such variables as the number of printers or terminals that can be sold at a given profit margin and operating efficiency. These factors must be carefully considered by CMC's marketers, who analyze figures from the operating statement and balance sheet to help make decisions about which components to make, how to distribute and promote them, and how to price them.

Specific relationships between various parts of the financial statements can be understood through **ratio analysis.** These ratios provide clues about the status of particular aspects of the business. There are three major areas of analysis where ratios are especially useful: the company's financial strength—that is, how much cash and other assets it currently has, as compared with its debts; investment efficiency and operating efficiency—that is, how effectively the company and its resources are being managed; and profitability.

Ratios pinpoint areas that may be problems or that may require further study. Generally ratios are satisfactory when they fall within a given range and unsatisfactory when they are out of the range in either direction.

In order for ratio analysis to be of maximum use, it is important to know the specific objective of each calculation: What is the information being sought? Marketers must also bear in mind that ratios represent past data and can provide only clues about the future.

The other limitation of financial ratios is that they ignore the time dimension. They depict only one point in time. It is therefore useful to compare various ratios for a company over time in order to discern trends. Moreover comparing a company's ratios with those of other firms in the industry can help marketers to ascertain whether the conditions indicated are found in the industry overall or whether they are specific to one company.

Figures for CMC can help illustrate the calculation and application of various financial ratios. We will now look at some of the major ratios. When each ratio is calculated, it is compared to the average ratio for companies within its industry. Ratios vary greatly from industry to industry, depending on the particular environment and conditions.

Current ratio. The current ratio is used to analyze the ability of a company to pay off its short-term debts. It is calculated by the formula:

$$\text{Current Ratio} = \text{Current Assets/Current Liabilities}$$

Using the figures from CMC's balance sheet, we see that the ratio is:

$$\text{Current Ratio} = \$476{,}922 \,/\, \$310{,}034 = 1.5$$

Quick ratio. The quick ratio is a way to determine the ability of a company to pay off its current liabilities without relying on future sales or the sales of its inventory. It is calculated by the formula:

Appendix B / Marketing Arithmetic

Quick Ratio = Current Assets − Inventory/Current Liabilities

For CMC, the quick ratio calculates as:

Quick Ratio = $476,922 − $170,536 / $310,034 = .98

Gross margin ratio. The gross margin ratio tells CMC what percentage of its sales is gross margin. Recall that gross margin is the difference between the amount CMC paid for materials used to manufacture its products and the amount it received from customers when it sold the products. The formula for this calculation is as follows:

Gross Margin Ratio = Gross Margin / Net Sales

For CMC, the gross margin ratio calculates as:

Gross Margin Ratio = $571,736 / $896,412 = .64

Thus, an average of 64 cents out of each of CMC's sales dollars is gross margin.

Net profit ratio. The net profit ratio tells CMC what percentage of sales is net profit. Recall that net profit is the profit CMC cleared after allowing for cost of goods sold, expenses, and taxes. The formula for net profit ratio is as follows:

Net Profit Ratio = Net Profit / Net Sales

For CMC, the net profit ratio calculates as:

Net Profit Ratio = $78,070 / $896,412 = .087

Thus, CMC clears 8.7 cents profit on each dollar of merchandise it sells, after paying cost of goods sold, expenses, and taxes.

Operating expense ratio. The operating expense ratio tells CMC the percentage of sales dollars required to pay expenses. The expenses include selling expenses, administrative expenses, and general expenses. The formula for operating expense percentage is as follows:

Operating Expense Ratio = Total Expenses / Net Sales

For CMC, the operating expense ratio calculates as:

Operating Expense Ratio = $422,654 / $896,412 = .47

Thus, CMC spends an average of 47 cents out of each sales dollar to pay expenses.

Stockturn rate. The stockturn rate indicates how many times a company's inventory turns over, or is sold, during a given time period, usually a year. Normally, the higher the stockturn rate, the higher the management efficiency and company's profitability.

Stockturn rate can be calculated either on the cost of goods sold or on selling price. Those two formulas for calculating stockturn rate are as follows:

Stockturn Rate = Cost of Goods Sold / Average Inventory at Cost
Stockturn Rate = Selling Price of Goods Sold / Average Selling Price of Inventory

For CMC, the stockturn rate calculated by the first formula is:

Stockturn Rate = $324,676 / $170,536 = 1.9

To find the average selling price of inventory requires another calculation. Since we determined CMC's gross margin percentage to be 64, we know that selling price is approximately 2.77 times cost. Thus, we can multiply the average inventory at cost times 2.77 and obtain the approximate average selling price. Thus, for CMC, the stockturn rate calculated by the second formula is:

Stockturn Rate = $896,412 / $472,384 = 1.9

Thus, from either means of calculating we see that CMC turned over its inventory approximately 1.9 times during 1983.

Return on investment (ROI). Return on investment measures the profit made on the resources invested in CMC in 1983, so that the profit can be compared with alternate uses of the same resources. The formula for calculating return on investment is as follows:

ROI = Net Profit / Investment

We can extract the net profit figure of $78,070 from CMC's operating statement. Accountants have various methods of calculating investment. Here we will use the average of total assets found on CMC's balance sheet for December 31, 1982 and December 31, 1983. The average is $855,222. The ROI is calculated as follows:

ROI = $78,070 / $855,222 = .092

Thus, we find that CMC has received approximately a 9.2 percent return on its investment in producing computer hardware. More often, ROI is viewed on a per project or per investment basis, rather than on total assets. For CMC, we could look at the investment in the development of one printer and the profit generated by that printer.

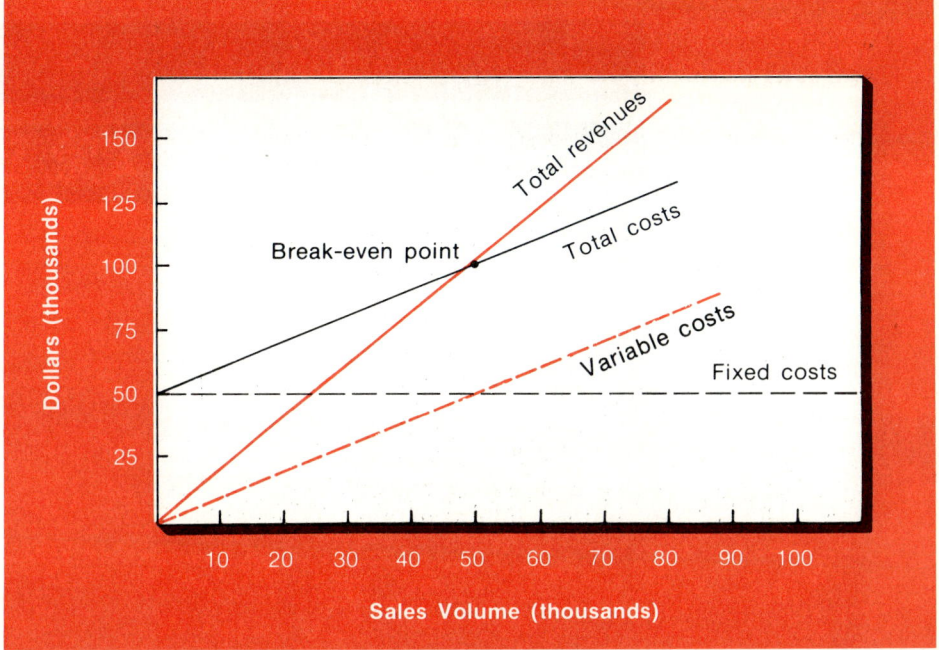

Figure B–3 The break-even point

Break-even Analysis

No matter which of the four price-setting methods is used, marketers will want to know at what point the company breaks even. How is the break-even point determined? The **break-even point** is where a firm's **total costs,** including its fixed costs and its variable costs, are equal to its **total revenues.** Total revenues are determined by multiplying the price per unit by the number of units sold.

A break-even point is shown in figure B–3. We will discuss the figure with an example. Suppose that Mr. Harris, a candy maker, has fixed costs of $50,000 per year and variable costs of $1 per box of candy. If he sells the candy for $2 a box, his unit margin is $1. The break-even point is 50,000 boxes, or $100,000 in sales. If he sells a box of candy for $1.50, the unit margin is $.50; the break-even point is 100,000 boxes, or $150,000.

This appendix has explored some of the arithmetic calculations that can be of assistance to marketers. While there are numerous other calculations that can help to clarify marketing decisions, the examples presented here provide some notion about the information that can be obtained.

GLOSSARY

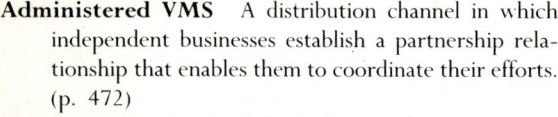

Administered VMS A distribution channel in which independent businesses establish a partnership relationship that enables them to coordinate their efforts. (p. 472)

Advertising "Any paid form of non-personal presentation and promotion of ideas, goods, or services by an identified sponsor." (pp. 17, 390)

Agents Wholesalers who represent manufacturers in a specified geographic area. (p. 464)

Antitrust legislation Government legislation that attempts to maintain competition among business firms by diffusing economic power so that market forces will be maximized. (p. 67)

Approach The salesperson's method of initial contact with the qualified prospect. (p. 444)

Attitude "A learned predisposition to respond in a consistently favorable or unfavorable manner with respect to a given object.". (p. 174)

Auction companies Brokers that bring buyers and sellers together and provide a forum for the examination of the products. (p. 524)

Automatic response buying (ARB) A buying situation that may be triggered by a type of problem recognition that is so specific that little room is left for decision making. (p. 158)

BCG matrix A technique of portfolio analysis devised by the Boston Consulting Group. (p. 555)

Bidding and negotiated pricing A pricing method in which the seller and buyer work out between themselves a price for a service or product. (p. 344)

Billboards An out-of-doors advertising medium that includes transit advertising, road signs, and printed shopping bags. (p. 411)

Bonus packs A sales promotion in which manufacturers offer the consumer more of the same product for the same price. (p. 424)

668

Brand A name, term, sign, symbol, or design, or a combination of them, intended to identify the goods or services of one seller or group of sellers and to differentiate them from competitors." (p. 279)

Brand loyalty The tendency for a customer to intentionally purchase the same product repeatedly. (p. 284)

Brand mark A symbol or design that represents the company. (p. 279)

Brand name "A word or group of words that identifies the product's seller to the customer." (p. 279)

Broker A wholesaler who attempts to bring buyers and sellers together. (p. 520)

Budget planning The process by which a company decides how to allocate resources. (p. 563)

Business definition The identification of the market a company plans to serve and the general type of product or service the company will promote to the specific market. (p. 90)

Business logistics The flow of materials and information from procurement of raw materials by the manufacturer to manufacturing/processing to the consumer. (p. 479)

Buying center The decision-making unit involved in a specific organizational buying decision. (p. 213)

Cannibalization Competition between two products manufactured by the same company compete for the same market with one product threatening to take market share away from the other. (p. 278)

Cash-and-carry wholesalers Wholesalers who do not employ an outside sales force and do not offer financing or delivery of products to customers. (p. 522)

Cash discount A pricing method involving offering a lower price to those customers who pay cash as opposed to those who use credit cards. (p. 354)

Cash rebate A pricing strategy in which the seller maintains the list price of a product but gives the buyer a partial rebate for buying a particular product at a particular time. (p. 356)

Catalog or mail-order retailing A retailing method in which consumers choose merchandise from catalogs at home and order goods by mail. (p. 509)

Catalog showrooms Retail operations at which customers select merchandise from a catalog and then go to the store to pick it up. (p. 509)

Central business districts (CBDs) Centers of retail activity located in a central or "downtown" area of a city. (p. 514)

Chain stores Two or more stores owned by one retailer. (p. 512)

Channel of distribution The series of intermediaries through which a product passes to reach the final customer. (pp. 17, 463)

Closing The point at which the customer agrees to buy the product. (p. 445)

Cluster sampling A sampling method in which each subgroup has the same characteristics as the population as a whole. (p. 125)

Clutter Several ads running close together so no single ad stands out. (p. 410)

Commission merchants Brokers used by small farmers to sell their annual harvest. (p. 524)

Commodities Products that are differentiated only by their uses and not by their suppliers. (p. 279)

Common carriers Vehicles companies hire to transport goods. (p. 483)

Communication mix The different forms of communication an organization chooses based on the communication objectives and the nature of the receiver. (p. 392)

Company mission A statement of the company's product or service, the customer needs that this item will satisfy, and the general means the company will use to meet those needs. (p. 94)

Competition-oriented pricing method A pricing method in which prices are set relative to those of the competition, based on a company's desired position or relative perceived value. (p. 334)

Competitive advantage The degree to which a company maintains an edge over its competitors. (p. 545)

Competitive environment The marketplace in which firms compete among themselves for business and resources. (p. 60)

Components Items that the company purchases to resell as part of its total product. (p. 275)

Consumer magazines Popular, nationally distributed magazines with large circulations. (p. 414)

Consumer products Products purchased by consumers for their personal use. (p. 272)

Contests A form of promotion that stimulates excitement and interest in products by offering a big prize

Glossary

for entering a contest connected with the product. (p. 422)

Contract carriers Companies that provide vehicles for physical distribution to other companies under long-term contracts. (p. 483)

Contract manufacturing A firm contracts with a foreign firm to manufacture parts or finished products or to assemble parts into finished products. (p. 591)

Contractual VMS A distribution channel in which cooperation and coordination are achieved through legal contracts. (p. 473)

Controlled experiment A causal study in which researchers design a study and manipulate variables to measure the effects of different conditions on groups of subjects. (p. 117)

Convenience goods Products that sell mainly because they are available; they usually involve little comparison shopping or effort to buy. (p. 272)

Convenience sample A nonprobability sample in which subjects are chosen on the basis of their availability. (p. 126)

Cooperative advertising The manufacturer of a product helps to fund advertising saying that the product can be purchased at a particular retail store. In turn, the retailer buys a certain volume of the manufacturer's product. (p. 424)

Corporate VMS A distribution channel in which all the parts of the channel are owned and the tasks are performed by one corporation. (p. 471)

Cost-oriented method A pricing method in which a company adds a standard margin of profit to the costs of production. (p. 330)

Countertrade Systems of exchange that use goods for payment instead of money. (p. 580)

Coupons A form of promotion in which the consumer gets a discount off the price of the product. (p. 423)

Cultural and social environments The set of factors, attitudes, and beliefs held by a society that give overall direction to behavior in economic, political, and social affairs. (p. 74)

Customary pricing Pricing according to what the customer would expect the price to be for a particular product, based on custom and tradition. (p. 358)

Customer-oriented method A pricing method in which the marketer assesses the value of a product or service to the consumer and uses that value as a ceiling in determining price. (p. 340)

Customer service The output of the physical distribution system—the effectiveness of which is commonly measured by product availability and order cycle time. (p. 488)

Customs union A trade agreement that does not impose tariffs on trade among member nations but does assess a uniform tariff on trade with nonmembers. (p. 589)

Decision-making unit (DMU) The individual or group in a household or corporation that makes the decision to buy a product. (p. 142)

Decoding The process of taking the message and putting it into familiar terms. (p. 381)

Delayed-quotation pricing Setting one final price only when items have reached the stage of finished goods. (p. 366)

Delivered performance International marketers must be able to guarantee high-quality product performance and service support (especially in high-technology lines) in order to satisfy customers. (p. 595)

Demand curve A pricing tool that shows how much of any given item customers are willing and able to buy at various prices during a given time. (p. 338)

Demand-oriented method A pricing method based on the laws of supply and demand that focuses on finding the price where, given the overall level of demand at that price, total profit will be the greatest. (p. 338)

Demographics The study of the characteristics of human populations. (p. 184)

Department stores Retail stores that typically carry a wide assortment of goods in moderate depth. (p. 504)

Depth of the product mix The number of different products in each product line. (p. 276)

Deregulation The lifting of government regulation over the activities of firms so that the environment may become more competitive. (p. 65)

Discount stores Stores that offer a broad but not very deep assortment of merchandise at a lower price. (p. 508)

Discounts Reductions in prices directed toward members of the distribution channel or toward final customers. (p. 353)

Diversification The business strategy of offering new products to new markets. (p. 547)

Door-to-door retailing A retailing method in which merchandise is sold to consumers in their homes. (p. 511)

Drop shippers Those who pass orders from customers to manufacturers who will ship directly to the customer. They do not maintain inventory or take possession of the goods. (p. 522)

Economic environment The factors that affect the ability of suppliers to provide goods and services and the ability of buyers to purchase those goods and services. (p. 56)

Elastic A condition when demand for a product changes in direct correlation to the price of the product. (p. 339)

Emergency goods Goods that are purchased because they are needed immediately. (p. 273)

Encoding The process of putting the information in the message into a form that will be understood by the receiver. (p. 380)

Equipment The machinery used to manufacture goods. (p. 274)

Escalator clauses Price increases that are automatically implemented, based on a previously stated formula. (p. 366)

Exclusive market coverage Granting exclusive rights to an intermediary to sell a particular product in a territory. (p. 469)

Experimentation In a marketing research study, the independent variable is manipulated, and changes in the dependent variable are measured in order to determine whether there is a causal relationship between variables. (p. 129)

Exporting A mode of entry that involves a company sending its merchandise to another country for sale there. (p. 590)

Extensive problem solving A buying situation in which each stage of the buyer decision process is carried out in considerable detail. (p. 159)

Facilitating functions Those functions that ease the transfer of the products from producer to customer. (p. 466)

Facilitators Intermediaries who assist but do not control or direct the flow of goods and services through the distribution channel. (p. 464)

Family branding Using one brand name to label different products made by the same company. (p. 281)

Feedback The message the receiver sends back to the source. (p. 381)

Fixed costs Overhead costs that include all expenses incurred regardless of how many products are produced. (p. 330)

Flighting An advertising pattern that calls for a product to be advertised heavily and then not at all. (p. 416)

Focus group A small number of people including a moderator who gather to discuss a marketing issue. (p. 127)

Follow-up The actions in providing all the services attached to the product and analyzing a customer's postpurchase satisfaction in order to determine whether the customer will buy again. (p. 446)

Franchise A contractual agreement between the owner of a business system (the franchiser) and another person or organization (the franchisee) that wishes to use the franchiser's business system. (p. 473)

Free trade area A trade agreement that specifies not imposing tariffs or quotas on goods flowing between member nations. (p. 588)

Freight absorption A method of geographic pricing in which the seller absorbs the costs of shipping a product. (p. 356)

Freight on board (FOB) A method of geographic pricing in which the buyer absorbs the shipping costs of a product. (p. 356)

Full-function wholesalers Merchant wholesalers who perform the full range of wholesaling functions. (p. 522)

Functional organization A system in which specific units are established within the marketing department to handle basic marketing functions. (p. 31)

Geographic pricing A system of modifying the price based on the buyer's geographic location or the distance the product has to be shipped. (p. 356)

Hierarchy of effects The progressive thoughts and opinions consumers have about a product. (p. 383)

Household A decision-making unit consisting of a group of consumers who purchase and use the products together. (p. 142)

Impulse goods Items that consumers purchase without planning to do so. (p. 273)

Incentive programs Promotions in which a manufacturer or distributor provides a bonus to a channel member who buys a certain volume of the product during a given time period. (p. 424)

Individual branding The practice of using separate brand names for each product in the product mix. (p. 283)

Individual consumers Individuals who make the decision to buy a product to satisfy a personal need. (p. 142)

Industrial products Products marketed to organizations for commercial use, or to carry out their activities. (p. 274)

Inelastic A state of demand in which the demand remains constant as prices are lowered or raised. (p. 339)

Informative message The type of messages used to create greater demand for a product in its growth stage. (p. 404)

Innovators Customers who buy a new product while it is in the introductory stage of the PLC. (p. 314)

Installations Buildings, factories, and major heavy equipment used by an organization. (p. 274)

Intensive market coverage Distributing a product in as many locations as possible. (p. 468)

Intermediaries Those people who play a role in getting a product from the producer to the consumer, such as wholesalers, retailers, agents, brokers, jobbers, and manufacturers' representatives. (p. 463)

International marketing Researching, planning, and implementing all entry strategies—from exporting to culturally similar and physically proximate markets to producing and marketing out of a wholly owned subsidiary in a culturally exotic, poor, and distant market. (p. 579)

Interview A method of data collection in which trained interviewers ask consumers questions about a product or service. (p. 128)

Introductory message The type of message used to publicize a new brand. (p. 404)

Involvement The intensity of interest with which consumers approach the marketplace. (p. 177)

Joint venture An agreement in which an investing firm owns 25 to 75 percent of a foreign firm, allowing the investing firm to affect management decisions of the foreign firm. (p. 592)

Leads Potential buyers of a product or service. (p. 443)

Learning "A relatively permanent change in behavior occurring as a result of experience." (p. 173)

Learning curve Production costs decline as output rises, partly because of the economies that come from producing a high volume of the product but more important because workers learn over time how to produce products more efficiently. (p. 338)

Licensing An agreement in which a foreign licensee receives specifications for producing products locally and the licensor usually receives a set fee or royalty. (p. 591)

Limited-function wholesalers Merchant wholesalers who provide only one or a few of the wholesaling functions. (p. 522)

Limited problem solving (LPS) A buying situation that implies previous satisfactory use of a product, with a small amount of conscious decision making. (p. 159)

Logistical functions Operations, such as storing, transporting, sorting, and breaking down bulk quantities into smaller quantities, that are needed to get a product from the producer to the customer. (p. 466)

Maintenance selling Activities that assist and keep the customers the company has. (p. 449)

Manufacturer's representative A wholesaler who acts as an intermediary between the manufacturer of a product and the potential buyer. (p. 523)

Market A situation in which there is a transfer of goods and services. (p. 8)

Marketing "The performance of business activities that direct the flow of goods and services from producer to consumer or user." (p. 8)

Marketing concept The satisfaction of customers' needs while meeting the objectives of the organization. (p. 8)

Marketing control The system of monitoring the results of the marketing plan to ensure that the plan is achieving the objectives that were set and that it is cost-effective. (pp. 19, 564)

Marketing information system A data base of relevant information that is continually and systematically collected for use in problem solving and decision making. (pp. 11, 130)

Marketing mix The appropriate combination of the following four elements: product, price, place, and promotion (the four P's). (p. 13)

Marketing orientation The company concentrates on gathering information from the market it is trying to serve and uses it to balance products, customers, and all the marketing elements to achieve profitable production and sales volume. (p. 6)

Marketing plan A plan that sets forth specifically the activities that enable the company to fulfill the strategy it has outlined, based on the business definition. (pp. 18, 562)

Marketing research "The systematic gathering, recording, and analyzing of data about problems relating to the marketing of goods and services." (pp. 11, 110)

Marketing strategy The activities of finding a competitive advantage, planning for the company's growth, analyzing the company's portfolio, and allocating the company's resources. (pp. 19, 545)

Market management A system in which each market the company serves is assigned a manager who plans and coordinates all marketing activity aimed at a particular market segment. (p. 37)

Market segment A group of consumers who can clearly be identified as having similar needs and wants. (p. 12)

Market segmentation The process of dividing consumers into groups on the basis of similar sets of needs and/or wants for marketing purposes. (pp. 12, 236)

Markup The percentage of the variable costs the company adds to the total costs of a product to determine a price. (p. 331)

Mass merchandisers Retailers who practice a strategy of low margins and high turnover. They must sell large volumes of merchandise and appeal to a mass market in order to be successful. (p. 506)

Matrix management A system in which a company uses both market managers who are accountable for the profitability of the markets *and* product managers who are responsible for the management of product lines. (p. 39)

Motives The forces that activate behavior and are aimed at fulfilling needs. (p. 166)

Needs Discrepancies between an actual and a desired state of being. (pp. 9, 166)

New-product development process A seven-step process designed to bring new products to market. The steps consist of idea generation, screening, idea testing, business analysis, product development, market testing, and commercialization. (p. 300)

Nonprofit marketing Marketing strategy for organizations that do not seek financial profit. (p. 617)

Observation A method of data collection where researchers use a human observer or a mechanism to monitor people's responses. (p. 127)

Odd/even pricing A pricing method involving setting an odd price at slightly less than an even one can suggest a substantially lower price. (p. 357)

Order getters Salespeople who identify prospects and sell the prospects products that will meet their needs. (p. 446)

Order processing A primary physical distribution function; the activities involved in transmitting a customer's order to the firm, processing it, preparing for its shipment, and finally, delivering it. (p. 486)

Order takers Salespeople who meet customers who already know what they need and take orders from them. (p. 446)

Organization A business, government, or nonprofit organization where the decision to purchase a product is institutionalized, with many formal procedures to follow. (p. 142)

Organizational structure A system that shows how a company arranges and allocates work among its employees. (p. 28)

Package A physical container and label that protects products during shipping and can serve as a storage container after the product has been purchased. (p. 289)

Penetration A pricing strategy usually used when a product or service is similar to competing products which involves setting a low initial price that does not cover the firm's costs. (p. 358)

Perception The manner in which a person selects, organizes, and interprets the stimuli to which he or she is exposed. (p. 170)

Personal selling A two-way communication between a company's salesperson and the customer; a message is tailored to a specific customer and is usually in the form of an oral presentation to that customer about the product. (pp. 17, 390)

Physical distribution The movement and storage activities required to make the firm's product available to customers. (pp. 17, 478)

Place The marketing activity involved with getting the product physically from the manufacturer to the place where consumers can buy it. (p. 13)

Point-of-purchase displays Displays presented by the retailer to appeal to the final consumer. (p. 423)

Population The total number of cases that possess some set of qualifications of interest to researchers. (p. 123)

Portfolio The collection of the business and products in which a particular company is involved. (p. 554)

Portfolio analysis An evaluation of the portfolio made to decide which businesses should be continued and which should be sold and whether the firm should make new acquisitions. (p. 554)

Position "The place a product occupies in a given market, as perceived by the relevant group of customers." (p. 252)

Positioning The activity of trying to get customers to perceive a company's product differently than they perceive what competitors are offering. (p. 252)

Price The second part of the marketing mix; the amount that is paid to purchase a product. (pp. 3, 325)

Price discrimination Offering one product at different prices to different segments of the market because different customers have different sensitivities to price. (p. 363)

Price cross-elasticity A pricing system in which the price of one product in a product line has an effect on the other products in that same line. (p. 361)

Price-fixing Illegal collusion between competitors in setting prices. (p. 369)

Price incentives Sales promotions used to stimulate demand for a product by offering a member of the distribution channel money off the price of a product. (p. 422)

Price leadership A pricing practice in which large companies set the price for their industries while smaller companies adopt identical prices. (p. 336)

Price sensitivity A change in sales that results from raising the price of a product. (p. 327)

Primary data Information gathered specifically for the purpose of addressing the present problem. (p. 123)

Probability sample A sample in which members are selected by an objective process. (p. 124)

Product Any idea, service, or tangible good that a consumer can acquire through a monetary transaction or an exchange. (p. 271)

Product life cycle (PLC) The pattern of a product's existence, consisting of four stages: introduction, growth, maturity, and decline. (p. 313)

Product line Several slightly varied but closely related products that a company groups under one brand name. (p. 275)

Product mix The total group of products one company sells. (p. 275)

Product management A system in which each product category is assigned a manager who plans and coordinates all marketing activity for that product. (p. 32)

Profit margin The money a company makes after subtracting the fixed costs and the variable costs from the sales. (p. 330)

Promotion The marketing activity involved with communicating a message to the consumer about a product a firm is offering. (p. 13)

Publicity A form of communication not directly sponsored by the company and not directly geared toward stimulating sales. (pp. 17, 390)

Purchasing agent An individual who is responsible for buying products for an organization. (p. 211)

Quantity discount A reduction in price offered for purchasing a large volume of a product. (p. 353)

Quotas Barriers that establish the absolute volume of products that can be imported into a country. (p. 584)

Rack jobber A wholesaler who sets up and maintains racks of merchandise in a retail store. (p. 523)
Raw materials Items that are reformulated to go into the product. (p. 274)
Reference group "That group whose presumed perspectives or values are being used by an individual as the basis for his or her current behavior." (p. 181)
Regional shopping center The largest type of shopping center, containing up to eight large department or discount stores and up to 250 specialty stores; often serves a wide area. (p. 515)
Retailing The activities that involve the sale of goods and services to the final consumer. (pp. 17, 494)
Retailing mix The combination of decisions a retailer makes in formulating marketing strategy. (p. 494)
Return on investment (ROI) A long-term pricing objective that involves comparing the use of money to make a profit on a product versus investing that money elsewhere. (p. 329)

Sales presentation The message and method of delivery of the message the salesperson presents to the qualified prospect. (p. 444)
Sales promotion "Those activities, other than personal selling, advertising, and publicity, that stimulate consumer purchasing and dealer effectiveness." (pp. 17, 390)
Sample A relatively few representative members of the larger population from which researchers draw conclusions about the group as a whole. (p. 123)
Sampling The process of selecting individual members from the population to make up a representative group. (p. 123)
Secondary data Information that has been gathered for a purpose other than the one at hand. (p. 115)
Selective market coverage Attempting to distribute a product only through those retailers that meet a producer's criteria as to image, location, or market segment served. (p. 469)
Services Products in the form of performances, deeds, or acts. (p. 607)

Shopping centers Groups of stores located on a piece of property that is controlled by an owner. Shopping centers can be neighborhood, community, and regional. (p. 515)
Skimming A pricing strategy usually used when a product or service is unlike any other in the marketplace that involves setting an initial high price. (p. 358)
Specialty goods Goods that consumers are willing to go out of their way to buy because they prefer the qualities of one brand over another. (p. 274)
Specialty stores Retailers who concentrate on sales of one merchandise line. (p. 502)
Staple goods Frequently purchased products. (p. 273)
Strategic business units (SBUs) Free-standing units within an organization, with their own customers, customer needs, and technologies. (p. 96)
Strategy audit A tool that helps companies review their marketing plan and chart an altered course in response to these various trends. (p. 565)
Supermarkets Mass merchandisers who sell mainly food and grocery items. (p. 506)
Supplies Products that are used less directly in the manufacturing process, such as items that are used to maintain manufacturing equipment or items that keep records of productivity. (p. 275)

Tariffs Taxes imposed on imported products. (p. 584)
Technological environment Inventions, developments, and advances that affect the marketing environment. (p. 72)
Territory A specific geographic area in which there are a certain number of customers or potential customers that a salesperson calls on. (p. 455)
Total costs A company's fixed costs plus its variable costs. (p. 667)
Total revenues A company's income determines by multiplying the price per unit by the number of units sold. (p. 667)
Trade agreements Pacts made between countries that set up agreed-upon guidelines that participating countries must follow. (p. 588)
Trademark A legally protected portion of a brand that distinguishes it from other brands and also protects a product from being copied and sold by other companies. (p. 286)
Traditional channel Each member of this channel of

distribution is independent of the other and tries to maximize its own position in relation to the others. (p. 471)

Transactional functions Actions, such as buying, selling, and risk taking, that directly influence the transactions among manufacturers, intermediaries, and customers. (p. 465)

Unfair trade practices Illegal pricing actions taken by wholesalers and retailers to sell products below cost or with a very low markup to attract customers with the intention of destroying competition. (p. 370)

Variable costs Expenses that increase directly with each additional unit of a product that is produced. (p. 331)

Vertical marketing system (VMS) A distribution channel that is centrally managed as a total system. (p. 471)

Volume-sensitive A cost-oriented pricing structure where discounts are given to large orders. (p. 332)

Wagon or truck jobbers Self-employed merchants that operate out of their own trucks. (p. 523)

Wants Goods or services that consumers desire. (p. 9)

Warehouse The place where inventory is stored. (p. 487)

Wholesaler "A firm which buys and resells merchandise to retailers and other merchants and/or to industrial, institutional, and commercial users but which does not sell in significant amounts to ultimate consumers." (pp. 17, 517)

Wholly owned subsidiary An agreement in which an investing firm owns enough of a foreign firm to exercise complete control over management policies and distribution of earnings. (p. 592)

Width of the product mix The number of different product lines in the product mix. (p. 276)

Word-of-mouth Communication in which a receiver passes along information and attitudes to others. (p. 382)

INDEX

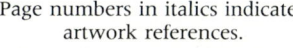

Page numbers in italics indicate artwork references.

Aaker, David A., 258, 381
Abell, Derek F., 96–98, 106, 107
Abrams, Bill, *282*, 257, 569, 640
Advertising, 22, 42–43, 401–19:
   corporate image, 225–26
   expenditures, 401, 409, 411, 413, 415
   and mass media, 180–81, 198, 225
   media scheduling, 415–16
   media selection, 406–8
   message, 404–6
   objectives, 401–3
   and price, 367
   and product, 227, 401–19
   and specific media
      out-of-doors, 411–12
      print media, 412–15
      radio, 410–11
      television, 88–89, 91–92, 180–81, 409–10
Advertising, cooperative, 424

Advertising Council, 618, 619, 620–21, *623*
Affective attitudes, 175
Agents, manufacturer's, 523–24
Airline industry, 61, 65, 102, 208–9, 250, 328, 337, 364, 426–27, 562
Albion, Mark S., 373
Allstate Insurance, 134, 553–54
Alsop, Ronald, 372
Alternatives, evaluation by buyer, 153–54
American Broadcasting Company (ABC), 87, 89, 91–92, 96
American Cyanamid, 437–38, 439
American Express, 292, 428–29, 543–44, 554
American Hospital Supply Corporation, 449
American Marketing Association, 8, 11, 25, 110, 137, 279, 295, 401, 458, 527
American Motors Corporation, 235, 236, 633
American Telephone and Telegraph, 3, 53, 58–59, 63, 66, 70, 89, 242, 416, 550
Ames, B. Charles, 51, 233
Anderson, Erin, *31, 33, 39,* 50, 51
Anheuser-Busch, 255, 365
Ansoff, Igor, 569
Antitrust legislation, 67–70, 78
Appel, Valerie, *419*
Apple Computer, Inc., 269–71, 272, 274, 275–76, 277, 278, *279,* 280, 286, 293, 361
Aseptic packaging, 634–35
Aspirational groups, 182
Assael, Henry, 161, *179,* 200, 233
Association of American Railroads, 484–85
Atari, 351, 429
Atlantic Richfield Company (ARCO), 354
Attitudes and buyer behavior, 174–76, 198
Audit Bureau of Circulation, 413
Automatic buying response, 158
Automobile industry, 176–77. 235–36, 237–39, 244, 253, 291,

677

Automobile industry *(continued)* 336, 356, 357–58
Automobile tire industry, 310–12

Baldwin, William, *521*
Ball, Robert, 258, 640
Banking industry, 9, 10, 15, 16, 293, 631
Barksdale, Hiram C., 627
Barmash, Isadore, 527
Barriers to market entry, 105, 560–61
Barter, 597–98
Bauer, Raymond A., 201
Bausch & Lomb, 163–64
Bauschard, Suzanne, 282
Beard, Larry H., 626
Beatrice Foods, 276, 402
Beer market 4, 168, 169–71, 182, 242, 254–55, 365
Bellenger, Danny, N. 161
Benefit segmentation, 245–46
Bernhardt, Kenneth L., 161
Berning, Carol Kohn, 161
Bernstein, Peter, 107
Berry, Leonard L., *611*, 626, 627
Bessom, Richard M., 626
Best, Roger J., 168, 200
Bidding, competitive, 223, 227, 344, 347
Blackwell, Roger D., 161, *190*, 295
Blattberg, Robert C., 258
Bloom, Paul N., 627
Bloomingdale's, 3, 252, 255, 474, 504, 510
Boddewyn, J. J., 603
Boeing Company, 208–9, 552
Bonoma, Thomas V., *212, 214*
Booz, Allen & Hamilton, 309, 321
Borden Inc., 387, 635
Boston Consulting Group Matrix, 555–56
Bouvier, Leon F., 200
Boyd, Harper W., 233
Brand, trademark of, 286–87
Brand loyalty, 284–86
Branding, 279–87, 294
　family vs. individual, 281–84
　importance of, 280–81
Braniff, 61, 65
Bristol-Myers, 272, 290
Brock, William, 582
Brokers, wholesale, 423–24
Brown, F. E., 348
Brown, S. A., *56*
Bruce, Grady D., 200
Budgeting and marketing strategy, 563–64, 568

Buell, Victor, 50
Buesing, Thomas, 258
Burger King, 399–400, 402, 406, 407, 416, 614
Business analysis in new-product development, 304–5, 319
Business definition, 10, 86ff.
　in lodging industry, 93
　and strategy audit, 565–67
　in television industry, 91–92
　in university MBA program, 92–93
Buyer behavior
　and age, 184
　and attitudes, 174–76, 198
　as base for segmentation, 244
　and demographic factors, 184–93, 198
　and economic factors, 179–80
　and educational level, 189
　and ethnic group, 191–92
　and gender, 185–86
　household, 193–97, 198
　and income, 186–89
　and learning, 173–74, 198
　and lifestyle, 169–70, 198
　and mass media, 180–81, 198
　and motives, 166–67, 198
　and occupation, 180–90
　organizational, 202ff.
　and perception, 170–73
　and personality, 167–70, 198
　and place of residence, 192–93
　and reference groups, 181–84, 198
　and self-concept, 168
　and social class, 190–91
　and values, 178–79, 198
Buyer decision process, 144–56, 160
Buyers, roles of, 143–44, 159
Buying center, organizational, 213–17, 229–30, 232
Buying situations, 155, 156–59, 160, 231–32
　automatic response buying, 158
　extensive problem solving, 159
　limited problem solving, 159
　organizational, 158, 210–11
Buzzell, Robert D., 569

Caldwell, William M., IV, 65
Calonius, L. Erik, *503*, 640
Campbell Soup Company, 91, 139, 254, 278, 288, 289, 297–98, 300, 411, 472, 546
Cannibalization, 278–79, 283
Carey, Susan, 527
Carley, William M., 209

Carlson, Eugene, 257
Carriers, 483
Carter, Hawley Hale, *504*
Cash discount, 354
Cash rebates, 328, 356
Catalog (mail-order) retailing, 509–10
CBS Cable, 87–89
Celler-Kefauver Act of 1950, 69
Central business districts, 514–15
Chain stores, 512–13
Chakravarty, Subrata N., 348
Chesebrough-Pond's, 558–59, 560
Chessie Systems Railroads, 286–87
Child Protection and Toy Safety Act, 71
China, People's Republic of, 577–79, 581, 585, 596, 599
Chrysler Corporation, 149, 151, 581, 592, 593
Churchill, Gilbert A., 137
Civil Aeronautics Board, 64, 483
Clayton Act of 1914, 68, 70
Clewett, Richard M., 51
Coca-Cola Company, 61, 277, 278–79, 285, 286, 328
Cocanougher, A. Benton, 200
Coffee market, 99–100, 277
Cognitive attitudes, 175
Communication, informal, 227
Communications network, organizational, 211–13
Competition
　and antitrust legislation, 67–70
　and demand forecasting, 103
　and deregulation, 65–66
　effect of brand loyalty, 284
　identification of, 90–92, 98–100
　and marketing environment, 60–63, 77
　during product life cycle, 314–18
　and segmentation, 240
Competitors
　positioning by, 255
　pricing in response to, 364–65
Computers
　home, 100, 173, 351–52
　in inventory management, 486
　personal, 204, 231, 269–72, 277, 351–52, 360, 361, 365
　and retailing, 516–17
Conative attitudes, 175
Coney, Kenneth A., 168–200
Conflict-resolving strategies, organizational, 232
Consumer behavior, 162ff.
Consumer Credit Protection Act, 71
Consumer Product Safety Act, 71

Consumer protection legislation, 70–72
Cookware, 113–14
Cooper, L. R., *187*
Coors Brewing Company, 4, 242
Cron, William L., 348
Cross-elasticity, 340, 361–62
Crowther, John F., 372
Cunningham, Isabella C. M., 201
Curley, John, 640
Customer-oriented price strategy, 340–43, 346, 347
Customers, wholesaling services for, 518

D'Amato, Nancy, 295
Data, primary, 123
　methods of collecting, 126–30
　samples, 123–26
Data, secondary, 115, 119–23
Datsun, 253, 411
Davidson, David S., 627
Davis, Cary B., 200
Davis, Duane L., 626
Day, Cecil B., 324
Day, Diana L., 569
Days Inns, 324–25, 332, 333, 336, 339, 342, 346
Dean, Joel, 372
Decision maker, role of, 143
Decision making, multiattribute model, 153–54
Decision-making units, 142–43, 159
Delayed-quotation pricing, 366
Della Bitta, Albert J., 200
Delta Airlines, 483, 611
Demand, and production capacity, 365–66
Demand, consumer, and new product ideas, 300–2
Demand, effect of advertising on, 402
Demand forecasting, 10, 11, 43, 101–4, 106
Demand-oriented price strategy, 388–40, 347
Deregulation, 64–65, 484
Digital Equipment Company, 5, 455
Discounts, 353–56, 370
Discount stores, 508–9
Dissonance, cognitive, 156
Distribution
　and marketing mix, 17
　during product life cycle, 314–18
　and product line, 278
Distribution channels
　conflict in, 475–76
　decisions about, *99*, 155

intermediaries in, 464–67
　management of, 473–76
　power in, 474–75
　structure of, 476–77
　traditional, 469–71, 490
　vertical marketing systems, 471–73
Distribution, physical, 478–89, 490
　cost trade-offs, 489
　functions of, 478–88
　systems concept, 488
　total cost concept, 489
Diversification, 547, 550
Doan, Michael, 258, 581
Dobson, Ricardo de P., 200
Door-to-door retailing, 511–12
Dow Chemical, 345, 520
Drop shippers, 522–23
Dunn, M. M., *56*
Duncan, Delbert J. 79

Eastman Kodak Company, 1, 38, 375–77, 378–79, 382, 390, 391, 393
Economic environment, 56–60
El-Ansary, A., *518*, 527
Elasticity of demand, 388–40
Electronic marketing, 448–49
Electronics industry, 143
Electronic transportation, 482
Energy Policy and Conservation Act, 71
Engle, James F., 161, *190*, 257, 295
Englemayer, Paul, 288
English, Mary McCabe, *282*
Entry into market, barriers to, 560–61
Entry modes for international markets, 590–93
Environmental factors, 54ff.
　and buyer behavior, 179–80
　controllable vs. uncontrollable, 55–56
　internal vs. external, 55–56
Error in research design, 118
Escalator clauses, 366
Evaluation, postpurchase, 155–56
Exclusive market coverage, 469
Experience curve, 360, 552–53
Experimentation to collect data, *126*, 129–30
Exploratory research, 115–16
Exporting, 590

Facilitating functions of intermediaries, 466–67
Fads, *317*, 318
Fair Credit Reporting Act, 71

Fair Debt Collection Act, 71
Family
　dual-income, 187
　households, 193–95
　life cycle, *194*, 195
　lifestyles, 195–97
　roles, 197, 586–87
Family Dollar Stores, Inc., 493–94, 495, 499, 500, 509
Farris, Charles I., *210*
Farris, Paul W., 373, 570
Fashions, *317*, 318
Feder, Barnaby J., 396
Federal Communications Commission, 66
Federal Express, 227, 247, 610
Federal Food, Drug, and Cosmetic Act, 71
Federal Trade Commission, 70, 592
Financial services industry, 543–44
Fishbein, Martin, 161
Fishyback transportation, 482
Fisk, Raymond P., 626
Flammable Fabrics Act, 71
Fleishmann's, 387
Flexibility and media selection, 407
Flexible pricing, 345
Focus groups, *126*, 127, 141
Food and Drug Administration, 72, 144–45, 289
Ford Motor Company, 4, 237, 336, 345, 403, 592–93
Foremost-McKesson, 517, 518
Franchises, 473, 591–92
Frazier, Gary L., 348
Free alongside ship (FAS), 600
Free trade area, 588
Freight absorption, 356, *357*
Freight forwarders, 598
Freight on board (FOB), 356, *357*, 600
Frito-Lay, Inc., 297–98, 300, 301, 302, 303–4, 304–5, 309
Functional organization, 31–32

Gabor, Andre, 348
Galligan, Mary, 24
Galling, Walter, 258
Gallo, E. & J., Winery, 552, 560
Gatekeeper, role of, 143–44
Gatignon, Hubert, 372
General Electric Business Screen, 557–58
General Electric Company, 99, 139, 208–9, 282–82, 292, 402, 559–60
General Foods, 157, 297–98, 401
General Mills, 36–37, 195–97

General Motors Corporation, 4, 70, 235–36, 292, 332, 336, 345, 486, 581, 633
Generic products, 282
George, William R., 626, 627
Giant Foods, 506, 629–30,
Gillette, 283, 327–28, 356, 360, 423, 547, 559
Goldstucker, Jac L., 161
Good, Walter S., 603
Good Housekeeping, 407, 408, 413
Government, role of in international markets, 584
Goyder, D. G., *69*
Grainger, W. W., Inc., 521
Grand Union Company, *506*, 507
Gray, David A., 50, 51
Great A&P Tea Co., Inc., 495, 506, 512
Group members
  cohesiveness and influence, 182–83
  similarity of and influence, 183
  visibility of consumption among, 182
Growth, strategies for, 547–50, 551, 568
Gruen, John, 107
Guiltinan, Joseph P., 373, 626
Guyon, Janet, 320, 640,

Haley, Russell I., *245*, 257
Halston, 498, 499, 510
Hambrick, Donald, 569
Harris, Louis, and Associates, 201
Hart Schaffner & Marx, 248, *504*
Hatch, Robert W., 36
Hawkins, Del I., 137, 168, 200
Hayes, Linda Snyder, 348
Hayes, Thomas C., *222, 276*
Health-care market, 605–6
Heany, Donald F., 569
Henderson, Bruce D., 98, 106, 107, 570
Hernandez, Sigfredo, 233
Hewlett-Packard, 345, 360
Hierarchy of effects, 383–89
Hirschman, Elizabeth, 201
Hise, Richard T., 51
Hlavacek, James D., 233
Holiday Inns, Inc., 324–25, 335–36, 346, 578, 613
Hollander, Stanley, 79
Hollie, Pamela G., 295, 320, 569
Holusha, John, 257
Homans, Richard E., 627
Horney, Karen, 167
Houston, Franklin S., 627
Hoyle, Valarie A., 626

Hughes, G. David, 79
Hume, Scott, 397
Hyatt Hotels Corporation, 324, 335–36, 342–43

Iacocca, Lee, 149
Ideas, new product, 300–304, 319
Inflation and pricing policy, 366, 371
Influencer, role of, 142
Information search
  in buyer decision process, 148–52
  in organizational buying process, 225–27
Information sources
  for buyers, 148–49
  for marketing researchers, 119–30
  for organizational buyers, 225–27
Ingene, Charles A., 372
Initiator, role of, 142
Innovators, 314, *315*
Intensive market coverage, 468–69
Intermediaries in distribution channel
  facilitating functions, 466–67
  logistical functions, 466
  transactional functions, 465–66
  types of, 464, 489–90
Intermodal transportation, 482–83, 484–85
International Business Machines (IBM), 5, 54, 63, 270, 274, 277, 292, 314, 336, 351–52, 361, 365, 428, 429, 456, 461, 471, 474, 553, 598, 461
International marketing, 576ff.
  environment, 579–80
  legal factors, 584–85
  and marketing mix, 593–600
  political factors, 584–85
International Telephone and Telegraph (ITT), 1, 5, 9, 10, 11, 15, 16, 17, 19
Interstate Commerce Commission, 64, 483, 484
Interviews to collect data, *126, 128*–29
Introduction stage of products, 314, 363
Inventory management, 483–86, 490

Jackson, Barbara P., 348
Jacoby, Jacob, 161
Japan, 208, 584, 587, 595
Jervey, Gay, 396
Jewel Cos., Inc., 506, 282
Johnson & Johnson, 184, 249–50, 284, 317, 549

Johnston, Wesley J., *212*, 233
Jones, Wesley H., 626
Journal of the American Marketing Association, 413
Jovan, Inc., 114, 126, 130, 594
Juhan, Jerry, 310

K mart, 244, 252, 255, 462, 475, 477, 494, 498, 509, 515, 516
Kassarjian, H., 200
Katz, Daniel, 200
Kaufman, Carol, 233
Kefauver-Harris Drug Amendments, 71
Kelly, James, 602
Kelly, Patrick, 51
Kiechel, Walter, III, 569
Kinnear, Thomas C., *170*
Kirshbaum, L. J., *187*
Kizer, G. E., 233
Kleinfield, N. R., 157, 295
Kneale, Dennis, 258, *301*, 456
Kollat, David T., 295
Korvette, E. J., stores, 495, 509
Koshetz, Charles, 75
Kotler, Philip, 25, 569, 570, 627
Kraar, Louis, *393*
Kraft (foods), 551, 635
Krugman, Herbert E., 397

Larson, Erik, 257
Lavidge, Robert J., *386*, 397
Lawrence, Paul R., 373
Learning curve, 360
Leasing in foreign markets, 598
Lehner, Urban C., 257
Leonard, Barry, 251–52
Lever Brothers, 277, 421, 560
Levi Strauss & Company, 32, 50, 75, 248, 548, 549
Levitt, Theodore, 25, 233, 295, 626
Levy, Michael, 372
Licensing, 591
Life Savers, 286, 289–90
Lifestyle and consumer behavior, 169–70
Limited, The, 495, 499, 502, 504
Liquid Filtration Systems, 205–6, 208, 211, 216, 220–21
Little, Arthur D., Inc., 99–101, 106, 107
Location, 498–99, 514–16
Longitudinal study, 116
Louden, David L., 200
Lovelock, Christopher H., 200, 608, 626, 627
Luck, David J., 50

Machalara, Daniel, 295
Mackenzie, George F., *29, 30*
MacMillan, Ian, 569
Magazines, consumer, 414–15
Magazines, trade, 413–15
Magazine advertising, 413–15
Magnin, I., 474, 504, 505
Magnuson-Moss Warranty/FTC Improvement Act, 71
Maher, Philip, 581
Mail surveys to collect data, *126,* 129
Maintenance selling, 449
Malls, shopping, 515–16
Market
   changing components in, 103, 106
   targeting of, 4–5, 10–12, 90–94, 96–100, 101–4, 342, 409, 497, 498
Market coverage and distribution channel, 468–69, 490
Market management, 38–39
Market share, 105
   as pricing objective, *326,* 327–28, 334, 346, 365
   strategies for increasing, 552–53
Marketing
   and analysis of competition, 5
   aspects of, 2–9
   and company's objectives, 5
   and consumer needs, 3
   criticisms of, 19–22
   defined, 8–9
   and price, 21–22
   and product quality, 21
   and public policy, 63–72
Marketing concept
   defined, 8
   historical development, 6–7
Marketing control, 19, 105, 564–67, 568
Marketing department
   communication within company, 43, 44, 45–47, 49
   communication with customers, 41–44, 49
   communication with distributors, 44, 49
   growth of, 29–31
   role of, 41–47
Marketing department organization, 31–41
   functional organization, 31–32, 49
   market management, 37–39, 49
   matrix management, 37–39, 49
   product management, 32–37, 49
Marketing environment, 9, 47, *48,* 52ff., 228, *229*
   of organization 206–9

Marketing information system, 11, 130–35, 136, 631–32
Marketing mix, 13–17, 48, 60–61
   international, 593–600
   and the marketing plan, 562–63
   and segmentation, 241
Marketing orientation, 29–31, 45–46
Marketing research, 108ff.
   criteria for using, 113–14
   process, 111, 114–30
Marketing strategy, 18–19, 48, 75, 98, 105, 355, 393, 454, 503, 510, 542ff.
   and budgeting, 563–64
   establishing a competitive advantage, 545–47
   factors in creating, 550–63, 568
   and growth matrix, 547–50
   and marketing control, 564–67
   and portfolio analysis, 554–58
   and product life cycle, 318–19
Markets, identifying international, 580–89
Markup, 331–32
Marshall, Stuart, 312
Marth, Del, 295
Martin, Warren S., 233
Mary Kay Cosmetics, 450, 451, 452, 454, 477, 511
Maslow, Abraham, 8–9
Mass merchandisers, 506–12
Matthias, Rebecca, 301
McCann, John M. 198, 200, 570
McCosh, Andrew M., 349
McDaniel, Carl, 50, 51
McDonald's restaurants, 75, 399–400, 402, 403, 405, 406, 407, 416, 473, 516, 614
McGrath, Anne, 348
McGuire, William J., 199
McLuhan, Marshall, 180–81, 198, 200
McNeil Pharmaceutical, 249, 255, 280, 290, 369, 430
Media scheduling, 415–16, 432
Media selection criteria, 406–8
Media, mass, 149, 155, 198
Mendelsohn, H., 627
Menzies, Hugh D., 458
Merchandise in retailing mix, 499
Merrill Lynch, Pierce, Fenner and Smith, 478–79, 480, 614
Message, advertising, 404–6
Miaoulis, George, 295
Michelob, 255, 318
Miller, Jeffrey, 233
Miller Brewing Company, 4, 168, 255, 365, 422
Mintz, Steven, 427

Mirro, 113–14, 125, 126, 130
Missionary salespeople, 448
Mitsubishi, 5, 9, 10
Modified rebuy situation, 158, 210–11
Monroe, Kent B., 372
Montgomery Ward, 509
Moriarty, Rowland T., 258
Morin, Stephen P., 151
Morris, Betsy, 125, 320
Morrison, Ann M., 36–37, 321
Morton, Michael S., 349
Moschis, George P., 200
Motivation of sales force, 452
Multiple channels of distribution, 475–76
Mutter, John, 65
Myers, John G., *381,* 397

Nabisco, Inc., 297–98, 309, 314, 560
Narver, John C., 79
National Purchase Diary, 121–22, 145–25
Neale, A. D., *69*
Needs, customer, 9, 20–21, 43
   identification of, 90, 91–94, 96–100
   satisfaction by products, 271–72
   and segmentation, 239
   and strategy audit, 565–67
Needs of organizational customers, 157, 223–24
Negotiated pricing, 344, 347
Neighborhood shopping centers, 515
Neiman, Janet, 137
Newman, Joseph W., 161
Newspaper advertising, 413
New task buying situation, 158, 210
Nielsen, A. C., Company, 89, 121, 127, 356, 409
Nieman-Marcus, 244, 504
Nonprofit marketing, 616–24, 625
Novelli, William D., 627
Nulty, Peter, 295

Objectives
   of company, 5, 94–96, 106, 545, 564
   of organizational buyers, 224
Ocean Spray, 36, 130, 634–35
Odd/even pricing, 358
Off-price retail stores, 509, 510
Opinion leaders, 149, 150–51
Order getters, 446
Order processing, 486–87, 490
Order takers, 446–47
Organization as buyer, 142, 202ff.
Organizational buyers, 217–21

Organizational buying behavior
　buying situations, 158, 210–11
　and communications network, 211–12
　influences on, 205–21, 228, *229*, 231
　and marketing environment, 206–9, 228, 231
　a model of, 228–31
　and nature of organization, 209–13
　power bases in organization, 213–14
　and technology, 206–7
Organizational buying process
　evaluation of alternative suppliers, 223, 227–28
　identification of needs, 223–24
　identification of suppliers, 223, 225–27
Organizational structure, 28, 228, *229*, 232
Out-of-doors media, 411–12, *415*, 432
Oxenfeld, Alfred R., 372

Packaging, product, 289–90, 294, 487
Panel discussion
　in market testing, 307
　in product development testing, 303
Paranka, Stephen, 349
Parasuraman, A., *611*, 626, 627
Pearce, John A., III, 107
Penetration, as media selection criterion, 407
Penney, J. C., *495*, 498, 499, 504, 509, 510
People Express Airline, 102, 328, 546
PepsiCo, 4, 277, 278, 285, 547, 578
Perception process, 383
Perceptions, consumer, 170–73
Perceptions, organizational buyer, 219–21
Personality and consumer behavior, 167–70, 198
Personal selling, 436ff.
　communication, 440–42
　goals of, 442, 457
　and product life cycle, 392
Personnel in retailing mix, 501
Pessemier, Edgar A., 295, 321
Peters, Thomas J., 233
Pharmaceutical industry, 103, 145–46, 148, 151–52, 155, 246–47, 249, 250, 290, 594

Physical attributes in retailing mix, 501
Piggyback transportation, 482, 484–85
Planning profile of strategy audit, 565–57
Point-of-purchase displays, 423
Polaroid Corporation, 1, 203–4, 278, 291, 375
Porter, Michael E., 569
Portfolio analysis, 105, 554–58
Positioning, product, 13, 252–55, 256
Power, base of, in organization, 213–14, 232
Power in distribution channel, 474–75, 490
Prestige pricing, 358
Price
　definition of, 325–26
　and marketing mix, 15–16, 232ff.
　methods of setting, 330–46
　　bidding, 344–46, 347
　　competition-oriented, 334–37, 346, 347
　　cost-oriented, 330–34, *335*, 346–47
　　customer-oriented, 340–43, 346, 347
　　demand-oriented, 338–40, 347
　as positioning method, 252–53
　in retail stores, 499–512
　and value, 21–22, 325–26
Price cross-elasticity, 361–62
Price discrimination, 363–64
Price elasticity, 338
Price-fixing, 369–70
Price sensitivity, 327, 333–34, 421
Pricing
　and advertising, 367
　delayed quotation, 366
　distribution, 367
　geographic, 356, *357*, 370
　legal issues in, 369–70
　penetration policy, 358–60, 370
　prestige, 358
　product line, 360–62
　psychological, 357–58, 370
　skimming policy, 358–60, 370
Pricing objectives, 326–30, 346
　market share, *326*, 327–28, 334, 346
　and product quality, *326*, 330
　profit, *326*, 327, 330
　profit maximization, *326*, 327, 338
　return on investment, *326*, 329–30
　sales growth, *326*, 328
Print media, 412–15, 432
Procter & Gamble, 27–28, 32, 34,

35, 44, 50, 61, 92, 277, 283, 292, 300, 318, 401, 421, 559, 560, 594
Product
　class, 255, 314
　differentiated, 334, 339, 547, 593–94
　and distribution channel, 476–77
　standardized, 593–94
Product development
　reasons for, 299–300
　steps in process, 300–13
Product life cycle
　and new products, 548
　and pricing, 327–30, 362–64
　and product line, 278
　stages of, 313–19
　variations in, 317–18, 320
Product line
　modifications and extensions of, 277–79
　pricing, 360–62
Product management, 32–37
Product mix, 275–76, 293
Product quality and price, 171–72
Production orientation, 6, 29–30
Products
　augmented, 271–72
　consumer, 272–74, 293
　farm, 275
　industrial, *273*, 274–75, 293
　and marketing mix, 14–15
　and price, 367–68
　and segmentation, 239–40
　strategies for introduction, 558–60
Profit as pricing objective, *326*, 327
Profit Impact of Marketing Strategies, (PIMS), 553
Profit maximizing as pricing objective, *326*, 327, 338, 344
Promotion, sales
　consumer, 390, 422–24, 426–27, 432–33
　effectiveness measurement, 427–28
　features of, 390
　and marketing mix, 16–17
　objectives, 420–28
　and product life cycle, 314–18, 394
　trade, 390, 424–26, 433
Promotional mix
　in international markets, 595–96
　for retailing mix, 499
Prospecting, 443–44, 457
Prototype in product testing, 303
Psychographics, 169, 244, 247
Psychological pricing, 357–58, 370
Publicity, 428–31, 433